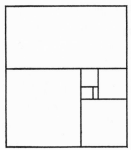

AESTHETICS AND PROBLEMS OF EDUCATION

EDITED BY RALPH A. SMITH

UNIVERSITY OF ILLINOIS PRESS
URBANA, CHICAGO, LONDON
1971

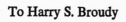
To Harry S. Broudy

GENERAL SERIES PREFACE

Readings in the Philosophy of Education is a series of books that reprints significant articles, excerpts from books, and monographs that deal philosophically with problems in education.

The distinctive feature of this series—for there are numerous books of readings—is that the selection of materials and their organization are based to a large extent on the results of a three-year project supported by the U.S. Office of Education and the University of Illinios. A team of philosophers of education with consultants from both philosophy of education and general philosophy scanned and appraised thousands of items. Their final selection was presented in a report entitled *Philosophy of Education: An Organization of Topics and Selected Sources* (Urbana: University of Illinois Press, 1967) and a Supplement prepared by Christiana M. Smith and H. S. Broudy and issued in 1969 by the University of Illinois Press.

Unfortunately, not all college libraries are equally well stocked with the items listed in the report, and even with adequate resources, getting the appropriate materials to the student is sometimes a formidable task for the instructor.

Accordingly, several members of the original team that worked on the project agreed to help bring out this series. The series is made up of two groups. One group devotes a separate volume to each of the following problem areas in education: the nature, aims, and policies of education, edited by Adrian Dupuis; curriculum, edited by Martin Levit; teaching and learning, edited by Donald Vandenberg. The second group is made up of a number of volumes each of which brings together significant materials from one or more of the philosophical disciplines as they bear on all the problem areas of education: epistemology and metaphysics, edited by Donald Vandenberg; value theory, edited by Philip G. Smith; philosophy of science, edited by

Martin Levit; and aesthetics—the present volume—edited by Ralph A. Smith.

Because they are problem-oriented, the volumes of the first group, used as a set, are appropriate to the initial course in the philosophy of education whether offered to undergraduates or at the master's level. Individually or in various combinations they can also be useful in courses of administration, methods, principles, curriculum, and related fields.

The volumes in the second group—stressing as they do materials from a special division of philosophical study—are suited to specialized and advanced courses. Some instructors may wish to use both types of treatment in their courses.

Ralph A. Smith, the editor of the present volume, is the author of a number of important anthologies on aesthetic education and as editor and founder of *The Journal of Aesthetic Education* has been a key figure in the development of the field.

HARRY S. BROUDY
General Series Editor

PREFACE

About This Volume

The majority of writers in this volume use materials from the field of philosophical aesthetics to clarify and understand the basic problem area of aesthetic education. Selections are subsumed under the major headings used in the original project report, *Philosophy of Education: An Organization of Topics and Sources,* i.e., The Aims of Aesthetic Education, Curriculum Design and Validation in Aesthetic Education, and Teaching-Learning in Aesthetic Education. There are no writings listed under Organization and Policy, as this category contained few entries in either the original report or 1969 Supplement. I have substituted for this section a new one entitled Historic Ideas of Aesthetic Education which contains essays on the aesthetic ideas of Plato, Friedrich Schiller, Herbert Read, and John Dewey, and an essay by Susanne Langer. This section has been placed at the beginning of the volume to provide a context for the selections to follow.

In organizing articles I have generally accepted the placement of items by workers of the original project staff, thinking it advisable in only a few cases to shift an item from one category to another. Since the project reports contain far more references than could be produced, material readily available elsewhere has not been included. This partly explains why systematic articles *about* Plato, Schiller, Read, and Dewey are used rather than original sources themselves. However, it is also difficult to extract concise statements of these writers' views on aesthetic education, and this is a second reason for including these critical essays. Further, since it was assumed that this volume would be used in both beginning and advanced courses in aesthetic education, and as supplementary reading in other courses, items of varying length and complexity were selected, although the reader will encounter no highly technical analyses.

The articles in this volume testify to the growth of the literature in the field of aesthetic education over the past two decades, a portion of it stimulated by the appearance of the quarterly *Journal of Aesthetic Education.** Still, space limitations prevented inclusion of more articles on each of the arts, and omission of anything on architecture, theater, and dance is regrettable. The same reason also accounts for the absence of literature devoted specifically to the topics of the humanities and creativity (William Arrowsmith's "Film as Educator" being the sole exception). If there is sufficient interest, perhaps a future volume in this series can be devoted to the above omissions.

The Meaning of "Aesthetics"

Finally, a few words about the meaning of the term *aesthetics*. It is helpful to distinguish three types of aesthetics: *scientific, analytic,* and *synoptic* or speculative. Scientific aesthetics encompasses a large variety of empirical studies and is best exemplified today in psychological inquiries, although scientific aesthetics also includes sociological and anthropological investigations. Typically, psychological aesthetics asks what happens when persons experience works of art or aesthetic objects in a large variety of experimentally controlled situations, with the nature of aesthetic preferences or judgments currently a popular research topic. Owing to the nature of this series there are no items of psychological aesthetics reprinted in this volume. The selection "What Is Art For?" by Rudolf Arnheim, an eminent psychological aesthetician, might seem an exception, but a reading reveals that his discussion is philosophical in nature. Neither is D. W. Wheeler's summary of recent curriculum theory in aesthetic education a strictly psychological account.

Analytic and synoptic aesthetics on the other hand are both philosophical in character. When philosophical aesthetics takes the form of a close scrutiny of the ways in which critical concepts such as *intention* and *expression* function in aesthetic theories or in ordinary talk about art, when there is an effort to construct

---

* Published by the University of Illinois Press at Urbana-Champaign. Publication as a subscription quarterly began in January 1968 with Vol. II after two complimentary trial issues (Vol. I, 1 & 2, 1966). There were no 1967 issues.

or reconstruct the logic of such critical concepts, or still further when the aim is simply to understand better the rational grounds for any statement made in the aesthetic domain, it is analytic aesthetics that is being done. Synoptic aesthetics, or what may also be called speculative or programmatic aesthetics, is more encompassing and comprehensive than either of the foregoing kinds. Typically, it utilizes insights from all types of aesthetic inquiry (and from other disciplines as well) to frame a conception of the roles of art and aesthetic experience in the good life.

Although relatively pure specimens of different types of aesthetics are easy to identify, they may in certain instances overlap and perhaps more than occasionally get confused. The bent of a particular author in this volume should be apparent, so I will say nothing more about the style and methods of the various selections.

Acknowledgments

I am grateful to the writers and their publishers for permission to reprint the material contained herein. I am also indebted to William P. McLure, Director of the University of Illinois Bureau of Educational Research, and J. Myron Atkin, Dean of the College of Education, for kindly making time and assistance available to assemble the volume. Mrs. Maxine Buehler, Mrs. Barbara Lacour, and Mrs. Susan Inskeep provided competent editorial and typing assistance and, as in other publishing ventures, it has been a pleasure to work with the courteous and professional staff of the University of Illinois Press.

I am happy to dedicate the volume to Harry S. Broudy, with whom systematic, persuasive philosophy of aesthetic education begins in the modern era.

R. A. S.

CONTENTS

SECTION ONE

HISTORIC IDEAS OF AESTHETIC EDUCATION

INTRODUCTION

Many writers have remarked that Western philosophy begins with a quarrel about the relative merits of poetry and philosophy to serve as guides to the good life. Today, when the physical and social sciences are firmly enthroned as the preeminent disciplines of social worth, and when the arts and humanities are understood to perform functions different from those of the sciences and philosophy, it requires a special effort of the historical imagination to understand why Plato used his full critical powers to banish certain kinds of art from the education of the young. Why, Eric A. Havelock asks, should Plato take what seems to us such a puzzling view of the arts? Why "like a Greek St. Paul warring against the powers of darkness" should he inveigh against the poetic aesthetic experience? It is only when we interpret *The Republic* as an indictment of Greek traditions, especially of its conceptions of education, and not primarily as a political treatise, that we can put Plato's attack on art in proper perspective. And in Greek education poetry and poets enjoyed a popularity and status that is perhaps comparable only to the entertainment media and broadcasters of our own time.

In Plato's view the imitations of poetry were twice removed from reality and thus issued from an inferior epistemology. Accordingly, their place had to be superseded by the superior insights of philosophy, the true guide to knowledge of the Real. The idea of *mimesis* figures prominently in Plato's critique, and Professor Havelock's analysis of the different meanings the term has in Plato's philosophy helps to gain perspective on one of the key concepts in the philosophy of art and aesthetic education.

Behind every text, as Albert William Levi [1] has insightfully demonstrated, there is not only a man and a family and a social

---

[1] *Humanism and Politics* (Bloomington: Indiana University Press, 1969). See Ch. 5 for an interesting discussion of Schiller.

milieu but also distinctive historical experience. If Plato's vigorous reaction to the existing state of Greek culture and educational philosophy is not sufficient proof of this, the writings of Friedrich Schiller should remove all doubt. Disillusioned with the unfolding events of the French Revolution, yet firmly convinced of the gradual and inevitable evolution of the idea of political freedom, Schiller turned to an analysis of the role of art in human life and culture. Aesthetic education, he came to believe, especially as it encourages contemplation of art's immortal examples, affords the development of the play impulse which ultimately unifies conflicting sensuous and formal impulses—a harmonization that was a necessary prelude, Schiller believed, to the synthesis of conflicting beliefs in the larger social and cultural crisis. Walter Grossmann explains the meaning of play in Schiller's writing and shows how his idea of aesthetic education is closely tied to his notion of cultural evolution.

If the existing state of Greek culture was back of Plato's concern, and the disastrous events of the French Revolution behind Schiller's, the dehumanizing consequences of the Industrial Revolution, especially its divisive and fragmenting effects on human sensibility, provided the animus for Herbert Read's thought. Following Schiller in spirit if not in details of pedagogic prescription, Read helped to popularize the slogan "education through art"—the title of his major book on education. Michael J. Parsons explains how Read's discourses on education, though dependent on insights from a variety of fields, including psychology, psychoanalysis, art history, and anthropology, almost always reveal their origins in a definition of art as the discovery of form. When used most carefully by Read, art in this sense "refers not to particular works but to the activity of mind that produced them, and this activity is distinguished, not by the medium or media with which it works, but by its place in the total economy of mind." Parsons elucidates the shifting meaning of art in Read's writing and further explains how education through art bears on intellectual and moral education. If *mimesis* is the key concept in Plato's aesthetics, and *play* in Schiller's, *intuition, form,* and *integration* loom large in Read's educational aesthetics. Through the intuition of form—which in certain respects is also an expression of emotion—and as a result of consequent insights and personal integration, persons may ultimately clarify the self and educate their emotions. Beyond the general truths which this view of education implies for educational practices, Parsons also indicates the value of Read's career as a humane protest against the tendencies toward alienation inherent in technological development.

The disrupting effects of social change that concerned Schiller and Read, a distaste for existing philosophic dualisms, plus the placement of a high value on the unity of experience prompted John Dewey in his classic study of aesthetics to redefine art *as* experience, a form of experience having the qualities of completeness, coherence, and consummatory satisfaction. In doing so, however, Dewey created a number of distinctions which, while they have proved fruitful for the stimulation of further philosophizing in both aesthetics and education, are not free of ambiguity and may in fact be at odds with the general thrust of his thought. This possibility is explored in C. M. Smith's essay. Even though, she points out, Dewey was reluctant to distinguish sharply between the entities and activities of the mind, Dewey did seem to shift back and forth between (*a*) his more "popular" conception of art as highly unified experience which under certain conditions may be characteristic not only of distinctively aesthetic but also of industrial, political, and economic enterprise, and (*b*) a "narrower and more specialized" sense of art as the aesthetic experience of works of fine art in which the temporal unity of aesthetic experiences is subordinated to the immediate intuition of quality. In addition to the analysis of the problem to which these different definitions of art give rise, she further examines the relations between meaning and knowledge in Dewey's aesthetics, and she asks, in conclusion, whether Dewey's aesthetics does after all provide an adequate theoretical base for a philosophy of aesthetic education. To the list of key concepts or ideas thus far discussed in this section, Dewey adds the trinity *experience, immediacy,* and *pervasive quality.*

Finally, in her persuasive and influential writings Susanne Langer sets forth an interpretation of art that construes it as both signaling cultural advance with its capacity to create new styles of feeling, and as a stabilizing force in culture by virtue of the important artistic education it provides. Above all, art creates perceptible forms expressive of human feeling. The forms of feeling, Langer thinks, are congruent with the vital forms of human sentience to which the discursive structure of language is denied access. Only through works of art, she believes, can the life of feeling be formulated and expressed for our conception. That is, art objectifies feeling so that we can contemplate and understand it. Because it contributes to self-knowledge and provides insight into all phases of life and mind, art has cognitive value. Key notions in Langer's theory are *feeling, form,* and *expression.* Her special use of *symbol* should also be noted. Insofar as there are "enemies" to be subdued, they are inadequate understanding of the proper nature and function of art and, as in Plato, bad art that corrupts feeling, "a large factor in the irrationalism which dictators and demagogues exploit."

The historic ideas of aesthetic education included in this section do not exhaust the number of writers who have influenced educational thinking. Aristotle is conspiciously absent, but the relevant portions of his writings have been widely reprinted and so are not reproduced here. Further, it should be apparent that the writings in this section bear on all the problem areas of aesthetic education; they are all more or less explicitly relevant to the problems of aims, curriculum, and teaching-learning. Still, it seemed advisable to group them together in an introductory section to provide perspective on the volume's topic.

PLATO ON POETRY

Eric A. Havelock

It sometimes happens in the history of the written word that an important work of literature acquires a title which does not accurately reflect the contents. A part of the work has become identified with the whole, or the meaning of a label has shifted in translation. But if the label has a popular and recognizable ring, it can come to exercise a kind of thought control over those who take the book in their hands. They form an expectation which accords with the title but is belied by much of the substance of what the author has to say. They cling to a preconception of his intentions, insensibly allowing their minds to mold the content of what they read into the required shape.

These remarks apply with full force to that treatise of Plato's styled the *Republic*. Were it not for the title, it might be read for what it is, rather than as an essay in utopian political theory. It is a fact that only about a third of the work concerns itself with statecraft as such. The text deals at length and often with a great variety of matters which bear on the human condition, but these are matters which would certainly have no place in a modern treatise on politics.

Nowhere does this become more evident to the reader than when he takes up the tenth and last book. An author possessing Plato's skill in composition is not likely to blunt the edge of what he is saying by allowing his thoughts to stray away from it at the end. Yet this terminal portion of the *Republic* opens with an examination of the nature not of politics but of poetry. Placing the poet in the same company with the painter, it argues that the artist produces a version of experience which is twice removed from reality; his work is at best frivolous and at worst dangerous both to science and to morality; the major Greek

Reprinted by permission of the author and publishers from pp. 3–15, 20–31 of Eric A. Havelock, *Preface to Plato* (Cambridge, Mass.: Harvard University Press), Copyright 1963, by the President and Fellows of Harvard College.

poets from Homer to Euripides must be excluded from the educational system of Greece. And this extraordinary thesis is pursued with passion. The whole assault occupies the first half of the book. It is clear at once that a title like the *Republic* cannot prepare us for the appearance in this place of such frontal attack upon the core of Greek literature. If the argument conforms to a plan, and if the assault, coming where it does, constitutes an essential part of that plan, then the purpose of the whole treatise cannot be understood within the limits of what we call political theory.

Plato's Argument

To the overall structure of the work we shall return a little later. Let us for a moment consider further the tone and temper of Plato's attack. He opens by characterizing the effect of poetry as "a crippling of the mind." It is a kind of disease, for which one has to acquire an antidote. The antidote must consist of a knowledge "of what things really are." In short, poetry is a species of mental poison, and is the enemy of truth. This is surely a shocker to the sensibilities of any modern reader and his incredulity is not lessened by the peroration with which, a good many pages later, Plato winds up his argument: "Crucial indeed is the struggle, more crucial than we think—the choice that makes us good or bad—to keep faithful to righteousness and virtue in the face of temptation, be it of fame or money or power, or of poetry—yes, even of poetry." If he thus exhorts us to fight the good fight against poetry, like a Greek Saint Paul warring against the powers of darkness, we can conclude either that he has lost all sense of proportion, or that his target cannot be poetry in our sense, but something more fundamental in the Greek experience, and more powerful.

There has been natural reluctance to take what he says at face value. Plato's admirers, normally devoted to his lightest word, when they reach a context like the present start looking around for an escape hatch, and they find one which they think he has provided for them. Just before this peroration, has he not said that poetry may offer a defense of herself if she can? Has he not confessed to her overpowering charms? Does he not admit reluctance to expel her, and does this not mean that in effect he recants? He does indeed so confess, but to think that his confession amounts to a recantation profoundly mistakes his intention. Indeed, the terms in which he makes the concession to poetry, to plead her case if she chooses, are themselves damning. For he treats her in effect as a kind of prostitute, or as a Delilah who may seduce Plato's Samson if he lets her, and so rob him of his strength. She can charm and coax and wheedle and enthral, but these are precisely the powers that are so fatal. If we listen, we dare to do so only as we counter her spell with one of our own. We must repeat over and over to ourselves the line of reasoning we have previously followed. We must keep on our guard: "We have our city of the soul to protect against her."

The mood of this passage uncovers the heart of the difficulty. Plato's target seems to be precisely the poetic experience as such. It is an experience we would characterize as aesthetic. To him it is a kind of psychic poison. You must always have your antidote ready. He seems to want to destroy poetry as poetry, to exclude her as a vehicle of communication. He is not just attacking bad poetry or extravagant poetry. This is made even clearer during the course of the argument he builds against her. Thus the poet, he says, contrives to color his statements by the use of words and phrases and to embellish it by exploiting the resources of meter, rhythm, and harmony. These are like cosmetics applied as an outward appearance which conceals the poverty of statement behind them. Just as the graphic artist employs illusionism to deceive us, so the acoustic effects employed by the poet confuse our intelligence. That is, Plato attacks the very form and substance of the poetized statement, its images, its rhythm, its choice of poetic language. Nor is he any less hostile to the range of experience which the poet thus makes available to us. He can admittedly represent a thousand situations and portray a thousand emotions. This variety is just the trouble. By his portrayal he can unlock a corresponding fund of sympathetic response in us and evoke a wide range of our emotions. All of which is dangerous, none of it acceptable. In short, Plato's target in the poet is precisely those qualities we applaud in him: his range, his catholicity, his command of the human emotional register, his intensity and sincerity, and his power to say things that only he can say and reveal things in ourselves that only he can reveal. Yet to Plato all this is a kind of disease, and we have to ask why.

His objections are taken in the context of the standards he is setting for education. But this does not help us one bit to solve what seems at least a paradox in his thought, and perhaps, if judged by our values, an absurdity. For him, poetry as an educational discipline poses a moral danger, and also an intellectual one. It confuses a man's values and renders him characterless, and it robs him of any insight into the truth. Its aesthetic qualities are mere frivolities and provide unworthy examples for our imitation. Thus argues the philosopher. But we surely, in estimating the possible role of poetry in education, would turn these judgments upside down. Poetry can be morally uplifting and inspire us to the ideal; it can enlarge our moral sympathies; and it is aesthetically truthful in the sense that it often penetrates to a reality as to a mystery which is denied to prosaic intellects. It could do none of these things in our eyes without the language and the images and the rhythm which are its peculiar possession, and the more of this kind of language you can put into a humane educational system the better.

Small wonder, as we have said, that Plato's interpreters have been reluctant to take him at face value. The temptation in fact to do otherwise is overwhelming. Was not the master a great poet himself, commanding a style which if it chose could abandon abstract argument in order to appeal to all the resources of the imagination either by vivid portraiture or by symbolic myth? Could a writer of such sensitive prose have really been indifferent, nay hostile, to the rhythmic arrangement and the verbal imagery which are the secrets of the poetic style? No, he must have been ironic or temporarily petulant. He cannot, surely, have meant what he said. The attack on poetry can and must be explained away, cut down to size, rendered innocuous enough to fit our conception of what Platonism stands for.

So runs subconsciously the argument, and like all such it reflects the modern prejudice which finds it necessary from time to

time to save Plato from the consequences of what he may be
saying in order to fit his philosophy into a world agreeable to
modern taste. This may be called the method of reduction—a
type of interpretation that can be applied also to certain facets
of his politics, psychology, and ethics—and it consists in pruning his tall trees till they are fit to be transplanted into a trim
garden of our own making.

The pruning process has been applied quite liberally to that
section of the *Republic* which we are looking at now. Several
types of instrument have been used for the purpose, and applied
to different parts of the argument. On the overall issue, Plato is
accommodated to modern taste by arguing that the program of
the *Republic* is utopian and that the exclusion of poetry applies
only to an ideal condition not realizable in the recognizable
future or in earthly societies. One might reply that even in that
case why should the Muse of all people be selected for exclusion
from Utopia? But in fact this kind of evasion of Plato's argument depends as we have said upon the assumption that the
Republic (so-called) is all about politics. Is that not the label
on the bottle? Yes, it is, but we must recognize that the contents of the bottle when tasted in this instance report a strong
flavor of educational but not of political theory. The reforms
which are proposed are considered to be urgent in the present
and are not utopian. Poetry is not charged with a political offense but an intellectual one, and accordingly the constitution
which has to be protected against her influence is twice defined
as "the polity within the soul."

The critics have sought another instrument of evasion by
supposing that the more extreme parts of Plato's polemic are
directed against a passing fashion in literary criticism which had
been fostered by the Sophists. They, it is argued, had sought to
use the poets artificially as a source of instruction in all useful
subjects, and had pushed these claims to absurdity. This explanation will not work. Plato to be sure speaks of the "champions"
of poetry but without identifying them as professionals. They
seem rather to be the more vocal representatives of common
opinion. He also speaks of these claims as though Homer himself were pushing them; that is, as though public opinion shared

this exaggerated opinion of Homer. As for the Sophists, it is not usually remarked, as it ought to be, that Plato's argument here counts them not as his enemies but as his allies in the educational battle he is waging against the poets. This may not conform to the critics' usual preconception of where to place the Sophists in relation to Plato, but for the moment at least Plato has placed them in a context which prohibits the belief that in attacking poetry he is attacking their view of poetry.

Defensive criticism has yet another weapon in its armory: this is to argue that Plato's target, at least in part of what he says, is not to be identified with poetry as such but is to be confined to drama and even to certain forms of the drama which followed a current fashion of extreme realism. The text however simply cannot stand dismemberment in this fashion, as though Plato at one point focused on Homer, Hesiod, and drama, and at another point on drama alone. It is true that tragedy is in the forefront of his mind, simply because, we suggest, it is contemporary. But the striking thing is his constant refusal to draw a formal distinction between epic and tragedy as different genres, or between Homer and Hesiod on the one hand (for Hesiod is also mentioned) and the tragic poets on the other. At one point he even uses language which suggests that "tragedy," that is drama, is a term by which to define all poetry, applying equally to "epic and iambic." It makes no difference, he seems to imply, whether we mean Homer or Aeschylus. He defines the subject matter of the target he is attacking as: "Human action, whether this action be autonomous, or the result of external compulsion, and also including what men think or feel about their actions; that is, how they interpret their effect in terms of weal or woe to themselves, and their corresponding joys and sorrows." This definition applies as vividly to the *Iliad* as to any stage play. Indeed, Plato goes on to illustrate what he means by citing the poet's description of a father's grief at the loss of his son. This plainly is a reminiscence of an instance cited earlier in the *Republic,* where Plato is thinking of Priam's collapse at the loss of Hector.

Scholars would not have been tempted to confine Plato's target in these contexts to the drama, were it not for the fact that the philosopher does seem to be occupied to a rather extraordinary extent with the emotional reaction of an audience to a public performance. . . . It does indeed supply one of the clues to the whole puzzle of what Plato is talking about. In our modern experience the only artistic situation which can provoke such public response as he describes would be the performance of a stage play. So we are tempted to conclude that Plato has his eye exclusively on the stage, forgetting that in Greek practice epic recital equally constituted a performance, and that the rhapsodist apparently exploited a relationship to his audience analogous to that of an actor.

These attempts to lessen the impact of Plato's assault do so by trying to disperse it over a variety of targets. They are well-meaning, but they misconceive the whole spirit and tenor of the argument. It forms a unity; it is launched, as we shall notice in a later analysis, first against the poetized statement as such and second against the poetic experience as such, and it is conducted with intense earnestness. Plato speaks passionately in the tones of a man who feels he is taking on a most formidable opponent who can muster the total forces of tradition and contemporary opinion against him. He pleads, he argues, he denounces, he cajoles. He is a David confronting some Goliath. And he speaks as though he had no choice but to fight the battle to a finish.

There is some mystery here, some historical puzzle. It cannot be solved by pretending it does not exist, that is, by pretending that Plato cannot mean what he says. It is obvious that the poetry he is talking about is not the kind of thing we identify today as poetry. Or more properly that his poetry and our poetry may have a great deal in common, but that what must have changed is the environment in which poetry is practiced. Somehow, Plato is talking about an overall cultural condition which no longer exists. What are the clues to this mystery which has so altered our common values that poetry is now esteemed as one of the most inspiring and profitable sources for the cultivation of mind and heart?

Before seeking an answer to this problem it will be necessary to enlarge it. Plato's polemics against poetry are not confined to the first half of the last book. Indeed he reminds us as much in his preface to the book which recalls that poetry "so far as mimetic" had already been refused acceptance. The reference is to an analysis of the *lexis* or verbal mechanisms of poetry which had been offered in the third book of the *Republic* and which itself followed a previous attack upon poetry's content (*logoi*). This attack had begun before the end of Book Two, when Plato proposed a policy of stern and sweeping censorship of the Greek poets, both past and present. What guidance, he asks himself and his readers, can traditional poetry give us in morality? His answer is: very little; that is, if we take the stories told of the gods, heroes, and ordinary men at all seriously. They are full of murder and incest, cruelty and treachery; of passions uncontrolled; of weakness, cowardice, and malice. Repetition of such material can only lead to imitation by unformed and tender minds. Censorship is the sole resort. Plato's position is not very different, in short, from those who have advocated a similar editing of the Old Testament for younger readers, except that, the condition of Greek mythology being what it was, his proposals had to be more drastic.

So far, the philosopher's objectives are understandable, whether or not we think they are mistaken. But he then turns from the content of the stories told by the poets to consider the way that they are told. The problem of substance is succeeded by the problem of style, and it is at this point that the sympathetic reader begins to feel mystified. Plato proposes a useful if rather simple classification of poetry under three heads: either it reports what is happening through the mouth of the poet, or it dramatizes what is happening by letting the characters speak in their own person, or it does both. Homer is here again in the forefront of the philosopher's mind; he is an exponent of the mixed style, whereas tragedy is wholly devoted to the dramatic. . . . For the present it suffices to observe that Plato obviously is hostile to the dramatic style as such. To be sure, as it turns out, he will tolerate it; that is, he will tolerate the poetry of dramatized situation and speech provided the characters thus presented are ethically superior. But by the time he recalls this context at the beginning of the tenth book he has forgotten he was even as tolerant as that. Through most of what he says in Book Three there persists a strong undercurrent of suspicion and dislike for the dramatic empathy as such. A purely descriptive style he seems to think is always preferable, and he suggests that if Homer were paraphrased to produce a purely descriptive effect, what he is saying would reduce itself to insignificance. We cannot, that is, evade the feeling that even in this discussion, so much less drastic in its proposals than that of Book Ten, Plato is revealing a fundamental hostility to the poetic experience per se and to the imaginative act which constitutes such a large part of that experience. And this should be puzzling.

Poetry in the Republic

An approach to a solution of the puzzle must begin by first taking the *Republic* as a whole and getting it into perspective, in order to ask: What is the overall role which poetry plays in this treatise? Is it confined to the passages so far reviewed, which give analytic attention to what the poet says? No, it is not. The formal thesis which is to be demonstrated and defended in the body of the *Republic* is proposed for discussion at the opening of Book Two. "Socrates" is challenged to isolate the principle of morality in the abstract, and as it may exist as a moral imperative in the soul of man. It is to be defined and defended for its own sake; its rewards or penalties are to be treated as incidental, and it is to be demonstrated that this pure type of morality is the happiest human condition. This challenge dominates the plan of the entire work, and while it is formally answered by the end of Book Nine it continues as the moving cause of the argument of Book Ten.

Why is the challenge so crucial? Surely because it marks an innovation. Such a pure morality has never before been envisaged. What Greece has hitherto enjoyed (says Adeimantus in a passage of great force and sincerity) is a tradition of a half-morality, a sort of twilight zone, at best a compromise, at worst a cynical conspiracy, according to which the younger generation is continually indoctrinated in the view that what is vital is not so much morality as social prestige and material reward which may flow from a moral reputation whether or not this is deserved. Or else (and this is not inconsistent) the young are insensibly warned that virtue is the ideal, of course, but it is difficult and often unrewarding. For the most part a lack of principle proves more profitable. Do not the gods so often reward the unrighteous? And immoral conduct in any case can be expiated quite easily by religious rites. The overall result is that the Greek adolescent is continually conditioned to an attitude which at bottom is cynical. It is more important to keep up appearances than to practice the reality. Decorum and decent behavior are not obviously violated, but the inner principle of morality is.

This is an indictment of the Greek tradition and the Greek educational system. The chief authorities cited in support of this type of twilight morality are the poets. Homer and Hesiod are named and quoted, as well as others. It would thus appear that the *Republic* sets itself a problem which is not philosophical in the specialized sense of that term, but rather social and cultural. It questions the Greek tradition as such and the foundations on which it has been built. Crucial to this tradition is the condition and quality of Greek education. That process, whatever it is, by which the mind and attitude of the young are formed lies at the heart of Plato's problem. And at the heart of this process in turn somehow lies the presence of the poets. They are central to the problem. They emerge even here at the beginning of the treatise as "the enemy," and that is how they are made to play out their role in Book Ten.

Once the *Republic* is viewed as an attack on the existing educational apparatus of Greece, the logic of its total organization becomes clear. And once it is appreciated that the poets are central to the educational apparatus, the successive critiques of poetry fall into place. That part of the argument which deals directly with political theory occupies only about a third of the nine books, and when it interposes itself, it is to provide successive excuses for progressive discussions of educational theory. The political framework may be utopian; the educational proposals certainly are not. Thus in Book Two, the problem having been proposed, a problem which concerns the construction of justice in the soul of the individual, the device is used of describing first a political society in the large, which shall then correspond to the individual in the small. The evolution of this society is pursued to the point where a "guardian class" emerges as the key class in the state. Whereupon the argument promptly turns to consider their education, and we get in effect a program of revised elementary and secondary education for existing Greek practice. This concluded, the argument reverts briefly to politics, in order to describe the three-class state and its virtues in precise detail. Then comes the psychology of the individual soul, a theory obviously devised to conform to Plato's educational objectives. Some more political, social, and economic theory then follows—the equality of the sexes, the communization of the family, and the role of limited war—until the paradox is proposed that the only safe and suitable recipient of political power is the philosopher. This is a novelty. Native philosophers are to say the least a minority group, and their character is defined in explicit contrast to that of the theatergoer, the audience at dramatic performances, and the like. Once more, by implication, the poets emerge as the enemy. Then, after a picture of the present ambiguous status of the philosopher in existing societies, according to which he is now a fool and now a criminal, we are confronted with the problem of his proper education, and are introduced to the secret of the fount of true knowledge upon which his intellectual integrity is built. And then in the seventh book, the most important book in the *Republic,* there follows the elaborate curriculum which is to train him for his task. It ascends through mathematics to dialectic, and it is to be made available to the age group between twenty and thirty-five, and it is to be obtained only on a competitive basis, which at successive stages weeds out the lesser abilities. This concluded, the argument through Book Eight reverts to political theory. The degeneration of societies and of individuals from the ideal is presented in four successive stages before, in Book Nine, Plato returns to his original question. Absolute morality as opposed to current morality has now been defined; it is the condition of the true philosopher. Is it also the happiest condition for men? And after answering yes, Plato in the tenth book turns back to a piece of unfinished business. He had defined the new curriculum of the Academy, but he had not explained the total absence therein of poetry. Its exclusion has now become logical and inevitable for its genius is wholly incompatible with the epistemology which lies behind the new program. So the poets, revealed briefly in Book Five as the enemies of the philosophers, are now in Book Ten fully exposed and expelled from the discipline that must reign over the philosophic stage of instruction.

From this perspective, the educational argument of the *Republic* moves through two main stages: the primary and secondary curriculum, called *mousike,* and the university curriculum of Book Seven. For each of these, a political excuse is furnished, by the introduction of the guardians in Book Two, and of the philosopher kings in Book Five. At the first level, the traditional poetic curriculum is to be retained but purged, and purged according to principles which seem to us a little curious; at the second level it is to be unceremoniously thrown out.

This is a great and a splendid argument, a major document in the history of European culture. It marks the introduction of the university system into the West. But it proposes for the modern mind several problems which are historical. Why in the first place, in the existing educational system of Greece, is poetry treated as so absolutely central? It appears, if we are to follow Plato, to enjoy a total monopoly. Why in the second place does Plato propose such curious reforms in the field of poetic style? Why is dramatization so significant, and why does he think it is so dangerous? And third, why does he feel it is essential to throw poetry out of the university curriculum altogether? Which is exactly the place where modern taste and practice find it possible in humane studies to exploit the full possibilities of the poetic experience. Why does Plato feel so committed to a passionate warfare upon the poetic experience as such? The answers to these questions may not be irrelevant to a history of the Greek mind.

Mimesis

We have spoken of the undercurrent of Plato's hostility to the poetic experience as such—a phenomenon so disconcerting to the Platonist, who may feel that at this point in his thinking the master has let him down. Plato's critique of poetry and the poetic situation is in fact complicated, and it is impossible to understand it unless we are prepared to come to terms with that most baffling of all words in his philosophic vocabulary, the Greek word *mimesis.* In the *Republic* Plato applies it in the first instance as a stylistic classification defining the dramatic as opposed to descriptive composition. But as he goes on he seems to enlarge it to cover several other phenomena. As these are comprehended, some of the clues to the character of the Greek cultural situation begin to emerge.

The word is introduced as he turns in Book Three from the kind of tale narrated by the poet to the problem of the poet's "technique of verbal communication." This cumbrous phrase may be adequate to translate the overtones of the Greek word *lexis,* which, as is made clear when Plato proceeds, covers the entire verbal apparatus, rhythmic and imagistic, at the poet's disposal. The critique which now follows, on careful inspection, divides into three parts. Plato begins by examining the case of the poet per se, his style of composition and the effects he may achieve. In the middle of his argument he switches to consider problems connected with the psychology of the "guardians," that is, of his citizen soldiers, problems which he regards as related, but which certainly pertain to a different class in the community, for citizen soldiers cannot be said by any stretch of the imagination to be poets. Later still, he turns back again to the problem of poetic composition and style, and the poet rather than the guardian once more occupies the field of vision. Let us survey first what is said in the two passages on the poets and their poetry.

Plato begins by arguing in effect that in all verbal communication there is a fundamental distinction between the descriptive method and that of dramatization. Homer is still the prototype of both. His poems divide into the speeches which are exchanged, as between actors, and the statements which intervene, spoken by the poet in person. The former are examples of *mimesis,* of dramatic "imitation" or "impersonation"; the latter are examples of "simple rehearsal" or as we might say, straight narrative in the third person. Epic is thus in toto an example of the mixed mode of composition, whereas drama exemplifies only mimetic composition. Plato's words make it clear that he is not interested in the distinction between epic and tragedy as genres, which we find familiar, but in basic types of verbal communication. Drama according to his classification is comprehended under epic, as is narrative. He hints as much when, in answer to the suggestion of Adeimantus that he is preparing to exclude drama from his ideal state, he replies: "Perhaps; but perhaps also my target is bigger. I don't yet know. We have to proceed whither the logic of our argument carries us": a hint which looks forward to the more fundamental critique of Book Ten, and warns us that the formal distinction between epic and drama is not in itself relevant to his philosophic purpose.

So far, we conclude, the term *mimesis* has been usefully and rather precisely applied to define a method of composition. But there is slipped in, during the course of this part of the argument, a very curious statement: "When the poet speaks a speech in the person of another, he makes his verbal medium (*lexis*) resemble the speaker"—and then Plato continues: "Any poet who makes himself resemble another in voice or gesture is imitating him" (and hence practicing *mimesis*). Now, this on the face of it is a nonsequitur. The missing link which has slipped out between these two statements would run as follows: "Any poet who makes his verbal medium resemble the speaker is making himself resemble the speaker." Now this, if applied to the creative act of composition on the part of the poet, is patently untrue. The poet applies his conscious skill to choosing words temporarily appropriate to Agamemnon. So far from "imitating" Agamemnon in his own character, he must keep his own artistic integrity detached, for in a moment the same skill is to be employed to put appropriate words in the mouth of Achilles. But Plato's supposition would be approximately true if it were applied not to the creation of a poem but to an actor or reciter who recites it. He in a measure does have to "identify" with the original supplied to him by the creative artist. He has to throw himself into the part precisely because he is not creating it but reproducing it, and this reproduction is for the benefit of an audience whose interest and attention he must engage. He can refuse to "imitate," and get only a luke-warm response.

The first puzzle concerning *mimesis* as the word is used by Plato has now already appeared. Why use it to describe both an act of composition which constitutes an act of creation, and a performance by an actor who is a mouthpiece or a reciter? Is this a loose and confusing use of the word, or is Plato expressing faithfulness to a cultural situation which is alien to our own?

When in the last third of his argument Plato returns to the poet's case, the ambiguity between the situation of the creative artist and that of the actor or performer is maintained. It is im-possible to be sure which of them in any given sentence is more prominently before the philosopher's eye. Considered as an "orator," our Platonic poet will prefer a style with a minimum of *mimesis* and a maximum of description. His indulgence in extreme forms of *mimesis,* extending even to the growls and squeals of animals, will be in direct proportion to his inferiority as a poet. And then Plato adds a comment which is in part a stylistic analysis and in part a philosophic judgment: "The dramatic-mimetic mode involves all-various shapes of changes." It is polymorphous and, we might say, exhibits the character-istics of a rich and unpredictable flux of experience. The de-scriptive mode cuts this tendency down to a minimum. Are we then to admit the performance of that kind of versatile poet whose skill can enable him to be any kind of person and to represent any and everything? Emphatically no. Clearly, then, the situation of the creative artist and of the performer of a work of art still overlap each other in Plato's mind.

But this peroration raises still another problem which we have touched on in the previous chapter. Why is the philosopher so profoundly hostile to the range and versatility which drama-tization makes possible? It has been argued that his target is merely the extreme and uncouth realism of some contempo-raries. But philosophic objection is taken to variety and range in principle, and will apply to good drama as well as bad. How comes it that a poetic virtue (in our eyes) which enlarges both range of meaning in the product and emotional sympathy in the audience is converted by Plato precisely into a vice?

In the intervening section of his argument Plato suddenly turns from the poets and performers to consider the young guardians of his state, and he applies the mimetic situation to their case. "Are they to be mimetic?" he asks. Now they presumably are not going to be either poets or actors, but citizen soldiers, and in that case, how can the problem of *mimesis,* if it be a matter of artistic style and method, affect them at all? The clue lies in the "occupations," "pursuits," "procedures," or "practices" (all of these are possible translations of the single Greek word *epitedeumata*) which are admittedly central to the life of these young men. They have as adults to become "craftsmen of freedom" for the state. But they also have to learn this trade, and they learn by practice and by performance, in fact by an education in which they are trained to "imitate" previous models of behavior. Hence *mimesis* now becomes a term applied to the situation of a student apprentice, who absorbs lessons, and repeats and hence "imitates" what he is told to master. The point is made all the clearer when Plato recalls that earlier social and educational principle which required division of labor and specialization. The young guardians pose a problem of training. Their assigned task will not be narrowly technical but one which requires character and ethical judgment. These he says are precisely the result of a training which employs constant "imitation" carried out "from boyhood." Clearly therefore the context of the argument has shifted from the artistic situation to the educational one. But this only complicates still further the mystery of the ambivalence of *mimesis.* Why should Plato, not content with applying the same word both to the creation and to the performance of the poem, also apply it to the learning act achieved by a pupil? Why in fact are the situations of artist, of actor, and of pupil confused? Nor does this exhaust the ambiguities of the word. For as he warms to his theme of the pupil-guardian and how his moral condition depends on the correct kind of "imitations," the pupil seems to turn into a grown man who for some reason is continually engaged in reciting or performing poetry himself which may involve him in unfortunate types of imitation. He had better, says Plato, be on his guard to censor his own performance. In short, not only is the poetic situation confused with the educational, but the educational is then confused with the recreational, if that is the correct word by which to describe the mood of adult recitation.

It is therefore not much wonder if scholars and critics have had difficulty in deciding precisely what Plato does mean by *mimesis*. And before we leave Book Three, there is still one more complication we have to notice. The word as introduced was used to define only one *eidos* or species of composition, namely the dramatic, to which was opposed both the "simple" style of direct narration and the "mixed" style which employs the two together. To this meaning it adheres through most of the argument on style. But before the end is reached, Adeimantus without objection from Socrates can speak of that "imitation of a virtuous model which is simple." Is this a slip, or are we to infer that imitation is a term which is also applicable to nondramatic types of poetry? And so to all poetry qua poetry?

This is precisely the turn given to the word as the argument of Book Ten unfolds itself. True, the poetry to be banned is at first qualified as "poetry in so far as it is mimetic," but this qualification then appears to be dropped. Plato as he says himself has now sharpened his vision of what poetry really is. He has transcended the critique of Book Three, which confined itself to drama as its target. Now, not only the dramatist, but Homer and Hesiod come into question. Nor is the issue any longer confined to protecting the moral character. The danger is one of crippling the intellect. And why this? The answer, he replies, will require a complete and exhaustive definition of what *mimesis* really amounts to. This answer depends on whether we accept the Platonic doctrine, established in the intervening books, that absolute knowledge, or true science if we so choose to call it, is of the Forms and of the Forms alone, and that applied science or skilled technique depends on copying the Forms in artifacts. The painter and the poet achieve neither. Poetry is not so much non-functional as anti-functional. It totally lacks the precise knowledge that a craftsman for ex-

ample can apply to his trade, still less can it employ the precise
aims and goals which guide the skilled educator in his training
of the intellect. For this training depends on the skill of calculation and measurement; the illusions of sensible experience are
critically corrected by the controlling reason. Poetry per contra
indulges in constant illusionism, confusion, and irrationality.
This is what *mimesis* ultimately is, a shadow-show of phantoms,
like those images seen in the darkness on the wall of the cave.

We have summarized the decisive part of this argument. . . .
But it is now obvious that *mimesis* has become the word par
excellence for the overall linguistic medium of the poet and his
peculiar power through the use of this medium (meter and
imagery are included in the attack) to render an account of
reality. For Plato, reality is rational, scientific, and logical, or
it is nothing. The poetic medium, so far from disclosing the
true relations of things or the true definitions of the moral
virtues, forms a kind of refracting screen which disguises and
distorts reality and at the same time distracts us and plays
tricks with us by appealing to the shallowest of our sensibilities.

So *mimesis* is now the total act of poetic representation, and
no longer simply the dramatic style. On what grounds could
Plato apply the same word first in the narrower sense and then
in the broader? And how, we repeat, can we explain in this
broader sense the fundamental philosophic hostility to the
poetic experience as such?

As he dissects the poetic account, so he also seeks to define
that part of our consciousness to which it is designed to appeal,
and to which the poetic language and rhythm are addressed.
This is the area of the non-rational, of the pathological emotions, the unbridled and fluctuating sentiments with which we
feel but never think. When indulged in this way they can weaken
and destroy that rational faculty in which alone lies hope of
personal salvation and also scientific assurance. *Mimesis* has
just been applied to the content of the poetized statement. But
as he considers the appeal of this kind of statement to our
consciousness, he is drawn back into portraying the pathology
of the audience at a performance of poetry, and *mimesis* re-
sumes one of those meanings it had assumed in Book Three.

It now is the name of the active personal identification by which the audience sympathizes with the performance. It is the name of our submission to the spell. It describes no longer the artist's imperfect vision, whatever that may be, but the identification of the audience with that vision.

For this meaning of *mimesis,* Book Three, we repeat, had prepared us, and if Plato had used the word only or mainly in this sense we would have less difficulty in understanding the usage. "Imitation," regarded as a form of impersonation, is an understandable conception. Though we might argue that the good actor may re-create his part anew, in general his performance is readily viewed as an act of imitation. We raise our eyebrows, or should, at the further application of the word to the involvement of the audience in a performance. Plato's descriptions in this context have a ring of mob psychology about them. They do not sound too much like the mood and attitude in which modern theatergoers attend a play, still less like the kind of attention a pupil gives to his lesson. We in fact have to notice here a hint of a curious emotionalism on the part of the Greeks which is alien to our experience. It is all part of the larger puzzle still unresolved.

But nothing is quite so hard to digest, if modern values and sensibilities are taken into account, as that picture of *mimesis* which Plato gives when he applies the word to the very content of the poetic communication, the genius of the poetized experience. Why on earth, we wish to ask, should he attempt to judge poetry as though it were science or philosophy or mathematics or technology? Why demand that the poet "know," in the sense that the carpenter knows about a bed? Surely this is to degrade the standards of poetic creation by submitting them to criteria which are unworthy or at least improper and irrelevant. Need the poet be an expert in the matter that he sings of? Such a presupposition does not make sense.

This however is precisely the supposition that Plato in Book Ten adopts without question, and it brings us to confront our last and most crucial problem in the search for clues as to what all this means. We saw in our review of the treatise as a whole that, as educational theory is central to the plan of the *Re-*

public, so also poetry is central in the educational theory. It occupied this position so its seems in contemporary society, and it was a position held apparently not on the grounds that we would offer, namely poetry's inspirational and imaginative effects, but on the ground that it provided a massive repository of useful knowledge, a sort of encyclopedia of ethics, politics, history, and technology which the effective citizen was required to learn as the core of his educational equipment. Poetry represented not something we call by that name, but an indoctrination which today would be comprised in a shelf of text books and works of reference.

Plato in the tenth book is quite explicit: "Our next task is a critical examination of tragedy and Homer the prototype thereof. We are told in certain quarters that these poets possess the know-how of all techniques and all human affairs pertaining to vice and virtue, not to mention divine matters." These claims in Plato's eyes are impossible to maintain. Let us however, he says, ignore for the moment the claim to technical competence and come instead "to those major matters of supreme value on which Homer undertakes to speak, warfare, military leadership, politics and administration, and the education of men." Thus phrased, the claim becomes Homer's own. That is, Plato is reporting the traditional estimate placed upon his poetry, and that estimate crystallized itself in the conception of Homer as the Hellenic educational manual par excellence. He proceeds to expose it as false and asks rhetorically "if he had really been able to educate men and make them better . . . then who have been his pupils and his protégés?" The Sophists have their following, which at least proves their educational effectiveness. But where are Homer's followers, or Hesiod's?

The question sounds too much like an *argumentum ad hominem*. Plato at any rate turns from rhetoric back to dialectic, and proceeds to demonstrate at length the complete gulf between the truth, as understood by reason, and the illusions effected by poetry. And then, as he begins to approach the terminus of his polemic, he cites once more that conception of Homer which he finds so impossible: "When you encounter encomiasts of Homer who say that this poet has educated Hellas for the purpose of administration of human affairs and of education therein; that he is the correct authority to be taken up and learnt, since this poet can guide the conduct of man's entire life. . . ."—in the face of this claim one can only reply gently—"You may be as good a man as is possible under the circumstances . . ." (that is, as a product of Homeric education); but nevertheless, Homer as we have him is not admissible. Yet how hard it is to do this, exclaims Plato. Don't we all feel Homer's spell? But still our feeling for him, though traditional and deep, is a love that we have to renounce, so dangerous it is:

"Our *eros* for this kind of poetry is bred in us by the educational nurture characteristic of the better polities." But it is perilous, and we shall say over to ourselves our rational antidote to it, "taking great care less we fall back again into this immature passion which the many still feel."

It is clear from these statements that the poets in general and Homer in particular were not only considered as the source of instruction in ethics and administrative skills but also enjoyed a sort of institutional status in Greek society. This status received, as it were, state support, because they supplied a training which the social and political mechanism relied on for its efficient working.

All this forces us to realize that Plato assumes among his contemporaries a view of the poet and his poetry which is wholly unfamiliar to our way of thinking. We assume that the poet is an artist and his products are works of art. Plato seems at one point to think so too, when he compares the poet to the visual artist, the painter. But he does not make this comparison on aesthetic grounds. In fact, it is not too much to say that the notion of the aesthetic as a system of values which might apply to literature and to artistic composition never once enters the argument. Plato writes as though he had never heard of aesthetics, or even of art. Instead he insists on discussing the poets as though their job was to supply metrical encyclopedias. The poet is a source on the one hand of essential information and on the other of essential moral training. Historically speaking, his claims even extend to giving technical instruction. It is as though Plato expected poetry to perform all those functions which we relegate on the one hand to religious instruction or moral training and on the other to classroom texts, to histories and handbooks, to encyclopedias and reference manuals. This is a way of looking at poetry which in effect refuses to discuss it as poetry in our sense at all. It refuses to allow that it may be an art with its own rules rather than a source of information and a system of indoctrination.

This is to us an astonishing assumption, but once accepted, it provides the logical excuse for Plato to apply to poetry that philosophic critique which he does by placing poetry in relation to the Theory of Forms. The Theory is epistemological; it seeks to define the character of that knowledge which we would call universal, exact, and final. Mathematical science will in this instance suffice as an example. Applied science is not alien to this theoretic kind of knowledge. On the contrary it applies it by using the unique and exact Forms as models which are copied in existing material products. Beds in the plural are the carpenter's copies of the unique Form of bed. But the poet simply talks about a bed in his poetry without knowing anything about it or attempting to make it. This kind of argument is perhaps fair to Homer if Homer is really pretending to be a manual on the manufacture of beds and the like. For if so it is a bad manual, says Plato. It is not composed by that kind of man who technically understands beds or ships or horses or anything else. On the contrary what he is doing is simply painting word portraits of what beds look like in a thousand different confusing situations, and he is effective only in the illusions he is able to create by verbal and rhythmic images, not in exact procedures for manufacture.

This is the *"mimesis* at second remove" to which Plato consigns the poet in the more fundamental part of his critique in Book Ten. This use of *mimesis* essentially indicates that the poetic statement is mummery; it is illusionism, as opposed to the carpenter's mechanical exactitude and faithfulness, and the term is applied to the entire basic content of the poetized statement as such and not just to drama.

Such is the last and final metamorphosis of *mimesis* at Plato's hands. It is truly a protean word. But behind the puzzle of its application in the sense of total poetic illusionism is that second puzzle which gives rise to the first. This is, we repeat, to us the astonishing presumption that poetry was conceived and intended to be a kind of social encyclopedia. If it was so designed, it was obviously by Plato's day doing a very poor job. It could not carry out this task according to the standards which Plato required in the Academy. The hallmark of his own curriculum is conveyed in the Greek term *episteme* for which our word science is one possible equivalent. The graduate of the Platonic academy has passed through a rigorous training in mathematics and logic which has equipped him to define the aims of human life in scientific terms and to carry them out in a society which has been reorganized upon scientific lines. The poet as a possible claimant to fulfill this role thus becomes an easy target; we feel too easy. He should never have been placed in such an inappropriate position in the first place. Plato should never have done this to him. But he does do it, and we have to ask why.

SCHILLER'S AESTHETIC EDUCATION

Walter Grossmann

. . . To delineate a concept that is definitely rooted in the Greek world of Paideia is hazardous. Yet it is appropriate to ask what "aesthetic education" meant to one who used the term so boldly and who made his own aesthetic achievement a means of advancing his educational ideals. All such questioning implies a conviction that the work under consideration will also speak to us today and enrich and widen our own aesthetic education.

That Schiller's work has not slipped beyond the horizon of interest can be demonstrated by a few quotations from works dealing with vital contemporary problems.

Franz Leopold Neumann writes that "Schiller's analysis of modern man reaches far beyond his own time and is still valid; it might well be that only today we can become fully conscious of the truth of Schiller's *Letters on Aesthetic Education.*" [1] Heinrich Popitz, reflecting on the alienated man, states that "Schiller's answer to the problem of political emancipation transcends the limitations set by the conditions of his times. The humanist has given (in the Aesthetic Education) an answer which remains of fundamental significance: all social action is dependent on respect for man and cannot endanger the physical existence of any human being." [2] And Herbert Marcuse in his philosophical inquiry into Freud finds that "Schiller's letters on the *Aesthetic Education of Man* aim at a remaking of civilization by virtue of the liberating force of the aesthetic function: it is envisaged as containing the possibility

From the *Journal of Aesthetic Education,* vol. 2, no. 1 (January 1968): 34–41. An earlier revision of this article was first printed in *The Germanic Review,* vol. 34, no. 1 (February 1959): 39–49. Reprinted by permission of *The Germanic Review* and the author.

[1] Franz Leopold Neumann, *Angst und Politik,* in *Recht und Staat in Geschichte und Gegenwart,* 173 and 174 (Tübingen, 1954), p. 10.

[2] Heinrich Popitz, *Der entfremdete Mensch, Philosophische Forschungen,* N.F., vol. 2 (Basel, 1953), p. 36.

of a new reality principle." [3] Eduard Spranger well defined the
significance of the term "aesthetic education" in the thought of
Schiller's time: "Aesthetic education is a concept current in
German literature of the Enlightenment. It means education
towards art as well as education by art, the latter offering advice
and moral improvement." [4] In the *Aesthetic Education* [5] Schiller has gone beyond this educational concept of art and has
made art an integral part of his idea of the evolution of mankind.

Schiller did not base his *Aesthetic Education* on general
principles or set out to develop an idea. He sought an answer
to what he considered the most vexing problem of his generation: why the legitimate struggle of the French people for
human rights and political freedom did not lead to a reign of
freedom and humanity, but instead to violence and terror. His
terse formulation "the moral possibility was wanting, and the
favorable moment found an apathetic generation" (35, V)
throws the responsibility on the agents. For Schiller, then, the
problem of general political evolution became at once that of
man's education. In the context of the philosophical speculation of his time, an answer had to be found to the question of
how the human being can emerge from the state of nature and
enter the state of reason. The expression "state of nature" is
used here to describe a state built upon hazard, necessity, and
force rather than upon reason—a viewpoint quite the converse
of Rousseau's more widely accepted glorification of a form of
life previous to the bondage of society. The challenge is to
transform this state of nature (*Naturstand*) into a state founded
upon reason. The very capacity to undertake such a task makes
of the animal a human being, "remodeling the work of need into
a work of his free choice, and elevating physical into moral

[3] Herbert Marcuse, *Eros and Civilization* (Boston, 1955), p. 180.
[4] Eduard Spranger, "Schiller's Geistesart," *Abh.d. Preussischen Akade-
mie der Wissenschaften,* Jahrgang 1941, Phil.-Histor. Klasse, p. 42.
[5] Under this abbreviated title all references are made to *On the
Aesthetic Education of Man in a Series of Letters* (New Haven, 1954)
(*Über die ästhetische Erziehung des Menschen, in einer Reihe von
Briefen,* 1793–94). All subsequent references in the text will be to this
edition. The Roman numeral will refer to the letter that is quoted.

necessity" (28, III). The state of necessity is in Schiller's eyes
bare of any moral authority. Therefore, any attempt, such as
the French Revolution, to eliminate it is legitimate. Although
the state of reason lifts the individual out of the state of nature,
it does not necessarily change him into a moral agent. That is
why the French Revolution was a failure. The remainder of the
Aesthetic Education treats this crucial problem—what was the
vital factor which was lacking in France?—how can the evolutionary program be attained? [6] Great as Schiller's disillusion-
ment over the recent experience is, he does not become pes-
simistic, but indicates the moral path for the idealist: "Those
who do not venture out beyond actuality will never capture
Truth" (60, X).[7]

The ideas of human development and the destiny of man
appear as early as Schiller's lecture *Was heisst und zu welchem
Ende studiert man Universalgeschichte?* The idea of a long
and slow evolution also belongs to this work, written before
Schiller's change of attitude toward the French Revolution. But
the problem of the transition from one state to another has
never before been much in the center of Schiller's interest. His
lifelong concern with the study of human nature, his studies
of the Kantian *Critique of Practical Reason,* and his personal
acquaintance in these years with Fichte inspire him to attack
the anthropological side of this question. His own creative
crisis and the beginning friendship with Goethe push him
toward a reappraisal of his own aesthetic values and philosophy.

A suitable starting point for such an undertaking appeared
to Schiller to be a critique of Kant's ethical rigorism. He assumed that his own view of man was identical with Kant's, yet
that different conclusions had to be drawn from the same

[6] In view of these later trends in Schiller's thinking a letter written on
October 15, 1792, to Körner is of interest. "Undoubtedly you know
Mirabeau's pamphlet *Sur l'Education.* . . . It speaks well for the book
and its author that he was anxious, even amidst the birthpangs of the
French constitution, to perpetuate it eternally through a purposeful edu-
cational system." Schiller, *Briefe* (Stuttgart, 1892), III, 221.

[7] In the last year of his life, Schiller wrote to his friend Wilhelm von
Humboldt: "In the end we both are idealists, and we would be ashamed
to have it said that circumstances shaped our personalities, and that we
did not shape destiny." *Ibid.,* VII, 226.

anthropological concept. Martin Werner has pointed out recently the basic differences between Schiller's and Kant's view of man and thereby demonstrated that Schiller's argumentation against Kant is founded on a philosophical misunderstanding.[8] Whether Schiller's equation of his and Kant's views is objectively incorrect is not a question of serious moment in this paper, because it is on this assumption that Schiller's ideas unfold.

To Schiller (and, as he believed, to Kant), man appears as a sensuous-rational creature. Three possibilities result from this interpretation of man: the first is that reason may suppress the demands of man's sensuous nature; the second is that his impulses may subjugate his free intellectual faculties; the third is that the impulses of physical nature may harmonize with the demands of his free reason. Kant, according to Schiller, denies the third possibility, deciding exclusively in favor of the primacy of reason. Schiller, however, advocates the value and importance of the third possibility. Such an idealistic belief does not imply an unrealistic view of human nature. Schiller summarized his experience as a young medical student in his thesis *Über den Zusammenhang der tierischen Natur des Menschen mit seiner geistigen* (1780), a study showing psychosomatic insight. The dramas of his youth are filled with keen and critical observations on character, family relations, and the fabric of his society. The year he published the *Aesthetic Education* he wrote to Goethe: "Philosophy always seems ridiculous whenever it wants to enlarge knowledge by itself and to give laws to the world without acknowledging its dependency on experience."[9]

The questions of evolution with which the *Aesthetic Education* is concerned are the following: how can the dualistic individual achieve a harmonious ideal self or, in universal terms, how can mankind grow into a state of moral freedom? Schiller's aim is to establish an equilibrium between the sensuous drives and the rational and moral imperative. Yet, in addition to the

---

Cf. Martin Werner, *Der protestantische Weg des Glaubens* (Bern, 1955), I, 611–21.

Schiller, *Briefe,* IV, 294–96.

conflict he sees between these drives, he recognizes that a time element is involved: "The sense-impulse comes into operation earlier than the rational, because sensation precedes consciousness, and in this priority of the sense-impulse we find the key to the whole history of human freedom" (97, XX). The solution of the conflict toward which Schiller is striving hinges on his interpretation of man's various faculties. Schiller assigns to reason the task of finding and establishing the laws for an ideal community. He does not endow reason with any dictatorial or magical powers to achieve its goals. These can only be realized "through courageous will and lively feelings" (48, VIII). Glancing at the world around him Schiller adds that the mirages of falsehood and superstition have been dispelled by reason, and the failure of the good community to emerge is not to be blamed on any weakness of reason but on some resistance in man's soul to truth due to a lack of courage of the heart to dare to know. Only in the education of man's feelings, therefore, lies hope that reason ultimately will prevail. But as reason, according to Schiller, cannot act immediately upon feelings—"man cannot pass directly from sensation to thought" (98, XX)—a new power has to be introduced, a power which creates a balance between the rational and sensuous forces and brings about an intermediary stage. In assigning to art the power to educate mankind lies Schiller's original contribution. Art has the capacity to act upon man's feelings immediately. Schiller introduced into man's cultural evolution a stage for which he found his own term: "If we call the condition of sensuous determination the physical, and that of rational determination the logical and moral, we must call this condition of real and active determinancy the *aesthetic*" (99, XX). This middle stage in Schiller's novel triadic structure is next to be examined.

What Schiller understands as aesthetic condition comes out most clearly in a rather negative definition of its origins, which opens a cleavage between utilitarian civilization and disinterested culture. "When therefore we discover traces of a disinterested free appreciation of pure appearance, we can infer . . . the real beginnings . . . of humanity. But traces of this sort are actually to be found already in the earliest crude attempts which man makes to embellish his existence—makes even at the risk of imparing it thereby in regard to its sensuous contents" (132, XXVII).

For Schiller the earliest disinterested activity of man is the first step toward cultural evolution. The fact that such an activity is not determined by physical necessity makes it free. Schiller detects the first signs of such a human activity in play and coins the term "play-impulse" (*Spieltrieb*) to describe the particular impulse toward this activity.[10]

In earlier passages of the letters Schiller made the statement that, beyond man's fundamental impulses (*Grundtribe*), sensuous and moral (the two fundamental impulses), a "third . . . is quite inconceivable" (67, XIII). By introducing the "play-impulse" Schiller has contradicted himself, or at least failed to make clear his distinction between fundamental impulses and any other impulse. The moral impulse defined as an impulse powerless to act upon the will, while at the same time able to suppress the senses, is sheer nonsense. Schiller does, however, recognize a historical sequence in the fields of action of the impulses. He has given priority to the sense impulse over the moral impulse and has also recognized the necessity of an intermediate stage. If we consider how small our knowledge of the genesis of drives is and how careful Freud, the great modern theorist on the subject, is in suggesting solutions, we are compelled to admire the sensitive efforts of Schiller. With his recognition of the importance of renouncing the satisfaction of physical wants for the sake of cultural evolution and his introduction of a hierarchy of impulses, he has anticipated the direction of modern views on cultural evolution.[11]

Play is to Schiller the first phase of the aesthetic stage. It is an activity freed from necessity and expressive of an abundance or superfluity of undertermined energies. It is exercised and enjoyed

[10] "Allow me to call it provisionally the play-impulse, until I have justified the term" (64). Jacob and Wilhelm Grimm, *Deutsches Wörterbuch* (Leipzig, 1856), 1. Abt., 2422, acknowledge Schiller's originality in this word formation.

[11] The idea of periodicity of drives can well be related to the genetic sublimation theory as discussed in Freud's *Civilization and Its Discontents,* p. vii.

for its own sake. Schiller observes that such action and expression not determined by necessity can be found even in the animal world. "The animal *works* when deprivation is the mainspring of its activity, and it plays when . . . superabundant life is its own stimulus to activity" (133, XXVI). Schiller certainly would not speak about the "culture" of primitive man or animals, but in play-activity he finds the presupposition of the rise of culture in general, and aesthetic culture (its first stage) in particular. J. Huizinga devotes his last comprehensive work, *Homo Ludens,* to a study of the place of the play-element in culture. It is surprising that Huizinga does not see the close relationship between his views and those of Schiller. It is even more surprising in view of the fact that in *Homo Ludens* Huizinga refers to the *Aesthetic Education* as "a theory designed to explain the origin of plastic art in terms of innate 'play-instinct' (*Spieltried*)." [12] Thus he regards Schiller's work as important only for its contribution to the psychological origins of art. But there is a further fundamental agreement between the eighteenth-century philosopher-poet and the twentieth-century cultural historian. Schiller's major contention concerning play is that it involves freedom from necessity and therefore lifts man above his physical stage. Huizinga's general definition of play reads thus: "A stepping out of common reality into a higher order." [13] He summarizes his introductory remarks thus: "First and foremost, then, all play is a voluntary activity. Play to order is no longer play: it can at best be but a forcible imitation of it. By this quality of freedom alone, play marks itself off from the course of the natural process. . . . It may be objected that this freedom does not exist for the animal and the child; they must play, because their instinct drives them to it and because it serves to develop their bodily faculties and their powers of selection. . . . Child and animal play because they enjoy playing, and therein precisely lies their freedom." [14] Schiller has given the play-drive a formative role in the evolutionary process and a definite place in it. Huizinga faces the

[12] Johan Huizinga, *Homo Ludens: A Study of the Play-Element in Culture* (London, 1949), p. 168.
[13] *Ibid.,* p. 13.
[14] *Ibid.,* p. 7.

same issue and attempts a careful analysis: "When speaking of the play-element in culture we do not mean . . . that civilization has arisen out of play by some evolutionary process, in the sense that something which was originally play passed into something which was no longer play and could henceforth be called culture. The view we take . . . is that culture arises in the form of play, that it is played from the very beginning. . . . In the twin union of play and culture, play is primary." [15] One might challenge Huizinga's correctness in disavowing the role which the evolutionary process plays in his theory, but for us his importance lies in the conformity of his idea with Schiller's in its main point, to wit, that play is a pioneer of culture. Schiller's conception of the fate of play in a progressing evolution will be discussed presently.

Play is then the outgrowth of superabundance. The delight of the senses lifts man out of the circle of physical determinism. At this point, Schiller tries to find the borderline between play and art. His formulations are not too successful. His assertion that play is guided by a free association of ideas while art obeys a law is weak. The weakness lies, however, in the definition of play rather than in the definition of art. Schiller illustrates his thought by the following example: "While the Trojan host with shrill cries storms like a flight of cranes across the battlefield, the Greek army approaches quietly, with noble tread. In the Trojans we only see the arrogance of blind strength, in the Greek the triumph of form and the simple majesty of law" (136, XXVII). The "shrill cries" of the Trojans as well as the "noble tread" of the Greeks are free actions instigated by the play-drive. The Greeks' mode of action belongs to a later stage of cultural education than the Trojans'. Schiller introduces a distinction between physical play, which would apply to the Trojans, and aesthetic play, which describes the Greek movements. With this recognition of the actual education of drives Schiller comes even closer to the modern concept of sublimation than with the previously mentioned concept of the hierarchy of drive-expressions. The difference between the Trojan and Greek expressions of the same drive lies in the fact that the one is a show of free emotions, while the other is a show of free emo-

[15] *Ibid.,* p. 46.

tions obeying a law of reason. In the sphere of aesthetic play, law can assert itself. Huizinga might well be quoted here again: "If . . . play cannot be directly referred to the categories of truth or goodness, can it be included perhaps in the realm of the aesthetic?" [16] Schiller shared this point of view when he considered play a step toward the achievement of aesthetic culture in an irreversible evolution tending toward the moral stage of mankind, the realm of the true and the good. The comparison of the Trojans and the Greeks leads to a definition of the aesthetic phase in which physical impulses and the demands of reason find their harmonious expression. "To watch over these two impulses, and to secure for each its boundaries, is the task of culture, which therefore owes justice equally to both, and has to uphold not only the rational impulse against the sensuous, but also the latter against the former" (68/69, XIII). The real work of art presents this harmony in its accomplished form, or, to use Schiller's term, "living shape" (*in der lebenden Gestalt*) (76, XV). The idea of *lebende Gestalt* is by no means confined to works of art, but is extended to the human personality and to human society. The work of art is a free creation, not the determined response to physical need. It presents matter subdued by form; it also appeals to our senses and educates our emotions. The aesthetic state has overcome the physical state of necessity. Physical desires, emotions, and feelings have undergone an education which sets them in harmony with the eternal law. Carried away by the splendor of this concept, Schiller writes enthusiastically in the final, twenty-seventh letter: "the dynamic state can only make society possible by curbing Nature through Nature; the ethical State can only make it . . . necessary by subjecting the individual to the general will; the aesthetic State alone can make it actual, because it carries out the will of the whole" (137–138, XXVII).

The question arises immediately: does this statement reverse the previously established order of the three stages, the physical, the aesthetic, and the moral? There is probably no direct answer to the question. The *Aesthetic Education* has as its

[16] *Ibid.*, p. 7.

theme exactly what its title promises. The description of the moral stage is not promised, nor is it given. Let us admit that the statement leaves a philosophical problem open and even implies a contradiction in Schiller's idea of evolution. More important than the reconciliation of such contradictory thoughts, however, is the prevention of a misinterpretation of Schiller's concept of the aesthetic state. The claim of the superiority of aesthetic values over morals had become a favorite one with the budding generation of romanticists. Schiller's *lebende Gestalt* never meant moral law sacrificed to misconceived beauty. Well aware of romantic fallacies, he made the meaning of harmony between senses and the moral law clear once more in an essay published in the *Horen* in the same year as the *Aesthetic Education*. In *Uber die notwendigen Grenzen beim Gerbrauch schöner Formen,* Schiller writes: "Abuse of the notion of beauty, as well as the pretentious efforts of the imagination to claim for itself the legislative where it only possesses the executive power, have been so detrimental both in life and in science that it is of the utmost importance to define correctly the proper limits of the use of beautiful forms." [17] This thought is elaborated in a later passage in the same essay. "But the pretensions of taste, when they directly influence the will, are a matter for more serious concern; for it is one thing when an immoderate interest in beauty hinders the extension of our knowledge and quite another thing when it vitiates character and causes us to neglect our duty." [18] The aesthetic state involves no glorification of aestheticism at the expense of moral power. Aesthetic education prepares man to be a human being, embracing life in its fullness without overstepping the measure set up by the imperative of reason. It is an education necessary in order to make man a

[17] Friedrich Schiller, *Sämtliche Werke,* Sämtliche Werke, Säkular-Ausgabe (Stuttgart), XII, 121.

[18] *Ibid.,* XII, 143. Irving Babbitt in his reckoning with romanticism also directs his attack against Schiller, ". . . by encouraging the notion that it is possible to escape from neoclassical didacticism only by eliminating masculine purpose from art, he opens the way for the worst perversions of the aesthete, above all for the divorce of art from ethical reality." (Irving Babbitt, *Rousseau and Romanticism* [Boston, 1919], p. 43.) Babbitt pushed Schiller into a camp in which the romanticists and neoromanticists would be all too glad to have him.

free individual who has assimilated the demands of this imperative in such a way that they have become his second nature.
In this stage he is neither a slave of his physical desires nor of
his reason. A harmonious society cannot be achieved until its
members have attained aesthetic culture. In the French Revolution Schiller recognizes an attempt to establish such a society
by men who had not yet reached the stage of aesthetic culture.
The result of such attempts, and all similar attempts, Schiller
has described in a passage of the seventh letter which reads
like prophecy:

> The gift of liberal principles becomes a piece of treachery
> to the whole, when it is associated with a still effervescing
> power and reinforces an already overweening nature; the law
> of conformity becomes tyranny towards the individual when it
> is combined with an already prevailing weakness and physical
> limitation, and so extinguishes the last glimmering sparks of
> spontaneity and individuality.
> The character of the time must first, therefore, recover from
> its deep degradation; in one place it must cast off the blind
> force of Nature, and in another return to her simplicity, truth
> and fulness—a task for more than a single century. Mean-
> while, I readily admit, many attempts may succeed in detail,
> but no improvement in the whole will thereby be achieved,
> and contradiction of behavior will always demonstrate against
> unity of maxims. In other quarters of the globe humanity may
> be respected in the Negro, while in Europe it is dishonoured
> in the thinker. The old principles will remain, but they will
> wear the dress of the century, and philosophy will lend its
> name to an oppression which was formerly authorized by
> the Church. Terrified by the freedom which always declares
> its hostility to their first attempts, men will in one place throw
> themselves into the arms of a comfortable servitude, and in
> another, driven to despair by a pedantic tutelage, they will
> break out into the wild libertinism of the natural State.
> Usurpation will plead the weakness of human nature, insurrec-
> tion its dignity, until at length the great sovereign of all
> human affairs, blind Force, steps in to decide the sham con-
> flict of principles like a common prize-fight (46–47, VII).

Although the concept of cultural evolution is an idea, Schiller
developed it in relation to his empirical understanding of human
nature and historical evolution. As to the dating of the stages,
he has himself provided the answer. Referring to the physical

and the aesthetic stage he writes: "I recall once more that both these periods, though they are indeed necessarily to be distinguished from each other in idea, are in experience more or less intermingled. We are also not to think that there has ever been a time when Man has been situated only in the physical state, or a time when he has shaken himself completely free from it" (n. 119, XXV). The question whether the aesthetic state can ever become a reality concludes the *Aesthetic Education.* "As a need, it exists in every finely tuned soul: as an achievement we might perhaps find it, like the pure Church, or the Pure Republic, only in a few select circles. . . ." Schiller in his own time thought he had found it in a circle around himself, in Goethe, Wilhelm and Caroline von Humboldt, Caroline and Lotte von Lengefeld, individuals who were *lebende Gestalten.* His cultural evolution is, however, not an evolution reserved for an elite, even if at a particular moment only an elite approaches its ideals. It is important to stress this point, especially in view of Schiller's opposition to the French Revolution. In one of the letters to his benefactor, the Danish prince, which form the first draft of the *Aesthetic Education,* Schiller wrote these sentences, which contain the core of his social thinking even after his turning away from the revolution. "The task of education and enlightenment has to start with the improvement of a nation's physical conditions. The mind must first be freed from the yoke of necessity before it can be guided towards freedom. . . . Man is very little as long as he only lives in a warm home and has enough to eat, but he has to live in a warm home and he has to eat enough if his moral imperative shall have a chance to elevate him." In the *Aesthetic Education* the same thought is expressed in mellower fashion. "The greater part of humanity is too much harassed and fatigued by the struggle with want, to rally itself for a new and sterner struggle with error" (49, VIII).

Although most of us, though not all of us (in a global sense far too few), live in the warm home, Schiller was correct that the warm home is not enough to assure the development of moral and aesthetic education. Aesthetic education, as postulated by Schiller, might meet its greatest challenge in the affluent society of the mass media age. . . .

HERBERT READ ON EDUCATION

Michael J. Parsons

What does Herbert Read say about theory of education, and what are we to think of what he says? He has been influential in education in a number of ways. He has, for instance, been partly responsible for our interest in the aesthetic value of children's paintings and for our increased reluctance to force adult or realistic styles of art on children. To this, and to many other points, he has lent his prestige as a critic and a historian of art and, what is more interesting from the point of view of this analysis, he has also claimed to support them with a theory. It is this theory that I shall be concerned with here.

The exposition and defense of the theory comprise the major parts of his books on education. Though he offers many kinds of empirical evidence on its behalf (for example, evidence from psychology, psychoanalysis, the history of art, anthropology), it is apparent that it is centrally a theory in philosophical aesthetics. Aesthetics, it may be said, is always the starting point of any serious discussion, whether of society, psychology, politics, or education; and the heart of aesthetics, in his view, is the attempt to discover the "nature" of art. To understand his views on education, therefore, one has to understand what he thinks art is.

This is not the place, however, for a detailed discussion or exposition of Read's aesthetics as such. My intention is rather to discuss the educational relevance of his theory of the "nature" of art, and to confine exposition of that theory to what is required for this purpose. Similarly, what comment or criticism is offered will be concerned with its adequacy as an educational theory and not as an aesthetic one. This undertaking seems worthwhile because Read himself eschews system and is not always clear on the relationship of his theory to particular recommendations. I doubt whether anyone has read *Education*

From the *Journal of Aesthetic Education,* vol. 3, no. 4 (October 1969): 27–45. Reprinted by permission of the *Journal* and the author.

through Art for the first time without being confused by its suggestive diversity and lack of obvious structure. It is important, then, to try to estimate wherein its chief contribution to education as theory lies.

Fortunately, it is the general structure and not the detail of Read's aesthetics that is important as theory for education. Moreover, the broad outline of his theory of art is not original (as he would be the first to acknowledge), but is a part of the major modern tradition in aesthetics. To say this is not to deny Read originality or distinctiveness at many points; it is only to say that the central idea in his aesthetics—what art "is"—is similar to that of well-known figures in modern aesthetics, figures that Read constantly invokes. This tradition is indicated well enough for my purpose by Susanne Langer, who describes her own work as a part of

> a philosophy of art on which many aestheticians have already labored, the theory of expressive form. Despite all blind leads, shortcomings, or mistakes that they may see in each other's doctrines, I believe that Bell, Fry, Bergson, Baensch, Collingwood, Cassirer, and I (not to forget such literary critics as Barfield and Day Lewis, and others too whom I have not named and perhaps not even read) have been and are, really, engaged on one philosophical project.[1]

The close comparison of Read with different writers in this list would undoubtedly show some differences of emphasis and detail; so would the comparison of different statements of Read himself. My point is, however, that these differences are not of great importance for answering the question with which I start. The interest and originality of Read for the theory of education lies in the fact that, having these views of the nature of art, he is convinced of their significance for the conduct of education generally and has, one might say, famously written to persuade us also. The unoriginality of his aesthetics in its general aspects is in a sense a preliminary point in favor of his educational writings, since it means that they rest on views which, though not universally accepted, are at least not idiosyncratic.

[1] *Feeling and Form* (New York: Charles Scribner's Sons, 1953), p. 410.

II

I shall begin by trying to say what I think the educational significance of Read's aesthetics is not. What I say may challenge a
few conceptions in the field, though I shall say here no more
than Read has said himself.

First, there are no curricular "implications" to it. That is to
say, Read's general ideas are not such that one can easily derive
from them specific recommendations for the curriculum of the
schools. Rather his ideas are more properly regarded as ruling
out, or devaluing, certain kinds of study. This point is discussed
below.

It might be objected that surely one of the things he advocates is more emphasis in the schools on the visual arts. Now it
is true that he does advocate this at times; but my point is that
his advocacy is not connected logically with the argument that
rests on his aesthetic theory, an argument that may be summarized by the slogan "education through art." [2] This is an impor-

---

[2] For instance, Read discusses the role of visual imagery in thinking and in the development of thinking in connection with his discussion of the eidetic image in *Education through Art*. (Ch. 3, see esp.
pp. 49–60.) This is a topic on which much empirical research has been
done, and what he wishes to say is not, in itself, very controversial. He
wishes to say that the visual imagination is not only an ornament of
thought but in some situations may be an autonomous mode of thought
with its own advantages and disadvantages. In particular, it has advantages where the situation calls for a high degree of originality or inventiveness. This is a message not unfamiliar to art educators today. It is
found, for instance, in Rudolf Arnheim, "Visual Thinking"; in Gyorgy
Kepes, ed., *The Education of Vision* (New York: Braziller, 1965); and
in V. Lowenfeld and W. L. Brittain, *Creative and Mental Growth,* 4th
ed. (New York: Macmillan, 1964), Ch. 1. Evidently it is of considerable
importance to inquire into the relative value of the various media for
the conduct of kinds of thought in different kinds of situation. But it is
confusing not to emphasize that the distinction between visual and other
imagery is quite different from the distinction between reflective and
intuitive modes of thought. It is the latter which is important to Read's
conception of the nature of art. Another argument for a greater stress
on the visual arts in our schools today, which is often associated with
the above argument, is based on the claim that the visual image plays a
larger part in social communication than it did formerly, through the
spread of photography, film, television, and magazines. This forms a
minor theme in Read's writing—see, e.g., *The Grass Roots of Art* (New

tant distinction to make, partly because Read himself does not always clearly observe it. He does, however, often say that in talking about the visual arts in education he intends the generalization to be made to the other arts. For example:

> In all our discussions of the place of art in education, there is admittedly a tendency to confine our observations to pictorial art. . . . Let me therefore make it perfectly clear to you that anything I have to say about the art of children, and its importance in education, applies to all the arts.[3]

Moreover, this assertion, that what he has to say applies "to all the arts," leaves open what is to count as one of the arts. One might think, as *Education through Art*[4] leads one to believe, that he intends to include all the traditional arts, widely construed, under this head, and consequently to suggest that work in the traditional media should be emphasized at the expense of other kinds of work usually found in the school curriculum. Elsewhere he states what I think is his more permanent and consistent opinion:

> Our aim is not two or more extra periods. We demand nothing less than the whole 35 into which the child's week is now arbitrarily divided. We demand, that is to say, a method of education that is formally and fundamentally aesthetic, and in which knowledge and manual ability, discipline and reverence, are but so many easy and inevitable by-products of a natural childish industry. . . .

> . . . .

> . . . the integral education which I conceive is relatively indifferent to the fate of individual subjects, since its underlying assumption is that the purpose of education is to develop generic qualities of insight and sensibility, which qualities are fundamental even in mathematics and geography.[5]

York: Meridian Books, 1964), p. 109—but has been elaborated by others, e.g., Gyorgy Kepes, in the introduction to the volume cited above.

[3] *The Grass Roots of Art,* p. 109.

[4] 3rd ed. (London: Faber and Faber, 1958). Hereafter referred to as ETA.

[5] *Ibid.,* pp. 220–21.

From this it appears that art is not one or some of the "subjects" in the common curriculum, but is something more like a method whereby any "subject" may be taught. No change in curriculum structure itself is required therefore; mathematics and geography may be retained, but should be taught through a method that is "formally and fundamentally aesthetic." Consequently Read's message is of interest to all educators, and not only to the teachers of the visual arts.

The reason for thinking this is Read's more permanent opinion is that "art," when he is using it most carefully, does not have reference to any particular media. It refers not to particular works but to the activity of mind that produced them; and this activity is distinguished, not by the medium or media with which it works, but by its place in the total economy of mind.

The most general account of this activity is that it is the discrimination of form in things: what Croce called "intuition." To discriminate form in things is to become aware of what they are for the first time; it is to notice what qualities they have. In a strict sense, it is to see (or hear) properly.[6] Perception itself is therefore a basic form of the activity of art, an idea that pervades Read's writings. For example:

> The most neglected factor in education is the autonomous mental activity that is constantly at work transforming the multiplicity of visual impressions into apprehensible unities, forms that intuitively reflect our feelings. Every such act of visual cognition is itself an elementary artistic form. . . .[7]

This activity of apprehending forms is evidently an intellectual affair, in a broad sense, though it is not reflective or self-conscious. That is to say, it cannot be produced at will by deliberation, nor can it proceed according to previously formulated rules; yet it has to do with cognition. Most of what we think of as perception is in fact only recognition; we do not apprehend the form afresh but are reminded of a form that we previously apprehended. Instead of investigating the object before us and responding in terms of its actual qualities, we impose upon it the

[6] *Icon and Idea* (New York: Schocken Books, 1965), pp. 17–18.
[7] *The Redemption of the Robot* (New York: Trident Press, 1966), p. 170.

form it reminds us of and respond in those terms. It may be that verbal formulations are the most common forms that are imposed in this way on reality; in principle, however, any kind of form will suffice. But the cognition, as opposed to the recognition, of qualities, which is the basic form of art, is an achievement that is not to be taken for granted. It requires effort, and the most fundamental form of that effort is attention.

What in this is most immediately relevant is the implication that the activity of art is not limited to any particular medium. Nevertheless, it is clear that it requires a medium of some kind. It must deal with forms that can be apprehended in terms of the senses; one cannot discriminate qualities that are not the qualities of a medium.[8] But the notion of a medium is wide enough to include as possible candidates for art reports of scientific research, batting strokes at cricket, the gestures of peasants, and algebraic symbols. Moreover, it does not necessarily refer to physical reality. An object imagined in the mind is as much dependent on a medium as is an object actually seen or created in a physical sense; it is an affair of colors and lines, or of words, or of tones and rhythms, and so on, as is the perception of "real" objects. It follows that an imagined object may be as much a case of art as one that has been "externalized." Read is not consistent on this latter point,[9] but it is clear that he wants to count the observation of one's own daydreams and spontaneous fantasies as art and as a paradigm of the best "method of education." [10]

I conclude, therefore, that Read does not mean to be recommending curricular changes when he advocates "education through art." He does not always make this perfectly clear himself because he uses the word "art" somewhat ambiguously, with the sense, in addition to that just outlined, both of the "pictorial arts" and of "all the arts" as traditionally conceived. He moves uneasily between these three senses of the word, as, for example, in the transition from the end of the sixth chapter of ETA, where "art" (evidently in the widest sense) is the answer to the

[8] *Ibid.*, pp. 153–54.
[9] *Art and Society* (New York: Pantheon, 1945), p. 112.
[10] *Education through Art,* pp. 191–92.

"mass psychosis" represented by twentieth-century society, to the beginning of the seventh chapter, where he discusses some problems in the teaching of the pictorial arts. Nevertheless, my conclusion is supported by various explicit assertions in Read's writings; for example, the following passage directly asserts the connection between the aesthetic theory and the attitude to the curriculum already illustrated:

> . . . those activities which we denote by such words as "imagi-native," "creative," "originating," "aesthetic," do not represent a subject with definite limits which can be treated like any other subject and allotted its two or five or seven periods in a competitive time-table, but are rather an aspect of mental development which is all-embracing—which is, indeed, no aspect but a *mode* of mental development. The imaginative does not stand over against the logical, the originating against the didactic, the artistic against the utilitarian, as a claimant to which a concession must be more or less unwillingly made; the two processes are in absolute opposition, and though the end we desire may be called a synthesis, our contention is that the basis of all intellectual and moral strength lies in the adequate integration of the perceptive senses and the external world, of the personal and the organic. . . .
>
> It follows that from our point of view the wrangle over the time-table is as unnecessary as it is unseemly.[11]

Read refers here to the "absolute opposition" of the discursive and nondiscursive. I do not think this is meant to deny the corollary of what has been said, that the reflective activities of the mind depend (in some sense) on the nonreflective activity of art; this is indeed one of Read's more frequent assertions. It refers rather to the autonomy of the nonreflective, and to the danger that forms already articulated may interfere with the apprehension of new forms. Recognition prejudices perception, and it is the insistence on the school's failure to allow for this that is Read's most characteristic note.

There is one possible and general kind of exception to this conclusion, which Read himself does not explicitly discuss. It derives from the fact that, in Read's view, to discriminate form is also to express emotion, where "expressing an emotion" is

[11] *Ibid.,* p. 220.

virtually equivalent to becoming aware of the character of an emotion. For to discriminate the form of something is to discover what significance it has for one, and that is to discover the character of the emotion, or "feeling," it gives rise to. The first way of talking about it is to talk about the "objective aspect" of art, the latter, about the "subjective aspect." [12] The general reason why the activity of art has this dual aspect is that an emotion is necessarily something that is directed toward an object, and in normal circumstances varies with the object. Thus, in a passage already quoted, Read mentions "forms that intuitively reflect our feelings." This notion of art as "expressing emotions" is common to the aesthetic tradition to which Read belongs, and is so pervasive in his work that its presence may perhaps be excused further substantiation here.

The point of Read's expression theory of art is that it leads directly to the notion of art as a means for exploring the self,[13] and to the consequent claim that one of the purposes of education is to assist the child in clarifying his emotions and discovering his self. In Read's work this is associated with psychoanalytic interpretations of art, though this does not seem to be necessary. In either case it seems to me that if we take this seriously, then we may find that some media, notably the "traditional" media, are better than others for this purpose. Some, it may be found, are not well suited in this respect. Read urges us to treat mathematics as art in school; but mathematics, conceived as a medium for the exploration of emotion, may have a very restricted range. It seems at first sight to be limited to the expression of those emotions attendant upon the discovery and use of mathematical relationships. No doubt those emotions are important and in some people may be very strong, but it seems hard to deny that they play a small part in the emotional range of most people. The consequence seems to be that mathematics as an art medium should not play a large part in the curriculum. This, however, is a speculative inference, since Read himself does not discuss it.

I have said that to advocate "education through art" in Read's

12 *Ibid.*, p. 28.
13 *Icon and Idea*, Ch. 5.

sense is not to recommend specific changes in the school curriculum. Is it then to recommend a way, or a method, of teaching or, more generally to talk about the "manner" rather than
the "content" of education?

If we mean anything specific by "method," then I think the
answer is once again no. We will not find in Read's theory any
grounds for preferring one particular procedure in teaching,
nor any suggestion that there are certain steps or stages necessary for good method. He explicitly disclaims knowing which
methods are most effective in any kind of teaching.[14] This is
partly the modesty of the nonprofessional;[15] but he also believes
that in principle good teaching methods cannot be prescribed in
advance:

> It is easier to describe the methods which have bad results
> than those which have good results, for the former are definite
> and decisive, the latter infinitely subtle and uncertain. The bad
> results are always produced by a method which is too con-
> scious and deliberate, by a discipline which is imposed from
> without, which is the command of a drill-sergeant. The good
> results are produced apparently by no method at all, or by a
> system of hints and suggestions. . . .[16]

It need hardly be said that it would be a mistake to conclude
that, because there are many times when the teacher is required
to do nothing overt or obvious, he is unnecessary; it is simply
that the particular ways in which, or the points at which, the
teacher is useful cannot be determined in advance.

Read believes that definiteness in teaching method is unattainable because method in that sense is possible only when
the outcome can be foreseen. Means can be calculated where
the end is known; and the greater the detail in which the end
is known, the more specific one can be in fashioning the means.
But the end of teaching is the stimulation of art and the particular form that it will take is unknown. This is necessarily so for,
according to Read, art is unreflective or "spontaneous." It is

---

[14] This is not to say that Read does not do this on other grounds;
see J. S. Keel, "Sir Herbert Read on the Teaching of Art," *School Arts*,
vol. 63 (December 1963): 19–21.

[15] *Education through Art*, p. 13.

[16] *Grass Roots of Art*, pp. 107–8.

not the product of calculation or reflection. The attempt to calculate or predict the end interferes with the activity in question, since that activity consists in giving shape to what is yet unknown. That is to say, reflection must work with forms that have already been articulated, with words, for example, whose meanings are very largely determined in advance of their use; but art does not. To employ a discursive language in this way is to impose shapes on what one is dealing with, with the assumption that one already knows its character. In different terms, reflection is the product of consciousness, which is why it can be produced at will. But consciousness is the product of art, for until some of the features of things have been discriminated one cannot be conscious of them. And consciousness is always consciousness of something. What one is not conscious of, one cannot reflect upon. This is why the discursive use of symbols—reflective thinking—is said to be dependent on art; it is also said to be in "opposition" to art because the reflective mind can interfere at will with the spontaneous activity by directing attention in predetermined directions. Habitually done, this is the death of art. It is also detrimental to the mind as a whole because it cuts off the supply of images relevant to reality for the reflective intellect to work with. And this is what the teacher does to the child when she starts out with a formulation of what is to be learned and insists on the child making a similar formulation. The discipline which is required to keep the classroom experience from being chaotic, and which is supplied "from without" the child's experience by the teacher with such a method, should arise from the activity itself; that is, from being attentive to the qualities of the materials being used.

What Read has to say about method is therefore largely negative. The teacher must avoid being too rigid or domineering. She must not change what the child is doing so much as discover what he is trying to do and then offer to help to improve it. In any case, she should avoid the traditional emphasis on rote learning and formal definitions. "Education through art," then, is not unlike some current slogans about "learning through discovery." "Discovery" is no less slippery a concept than "art"; and it is clear that such slogans can have little to say about teaching method, except negatively. For neither discovery nor art is a method or a way of teaching or learning; rather, they are achievements. One may discover something in any one of a number of ways, or merely by luck. To insist on "learning through discovery," therefore, is only to protest against some ways of teaching which are not likely to produce discovery. The same is true of "education through art," and what is most likely to prejudice the achievement of art in school is the teacher's assurance that the proper outcome of the lesson has already been decided.

"Education through art" is similar to "learning through discovery," too, in that it protests the same kind of teaching method. This is evidently because "art" in Read's sense means something not unlike "discovery," though it is a much more inclusive term. They both refer to the achievement of insight, though "art" refers to more than is usually meant by this. This confirms the suggestion that it would be a mistake to look for a method of art in any way parallel to the "method of science" that Dewey proposed as a model for educational method.[17] The method of science is concerned with the verification of insight and not with its initial achievement. It is the business of the reflective intellect and is therefore susceptible to system and method. But it depends upon insight for the supply of hypotheses that it tests; it cannot itself supply them. And the creative processes of scientists are similar to those of painters and of children—for they are all a part of "art." This is especially true of the more original and important scientists.[18]

III

So far, I have argued against looking to Read's theory of art for specific recommendations regarding the practice of education. This is far from arguing that his work has no value; it is only to begin to say what that value is.

The value of Read's theoretical work, in general terms, may

[17] As has been done, for instance, by David Ecker in "The Artistic Process as Qualitative Problem-Solving," *Journal of Aesthetics and Art Criticism,* vol. 21, no. 40 (Spring 1963): 283–90.

[18] *Education through Art,* p. 53.

be said to be largely the value of continuing protest. His whole career may be seen as a protest against certain powerful tendencies in modern society and education, tendencies that stifle spontaneity, freedom, and art. What he sees himself protesting against varies not in character but in extent. At its most expansive, it is very broad; he has never lost the revolutionary sense that characterized his generation:

> . . . the secret of our collective ills is to be traced to the suppression of spontaneous creative ability in the individual. The lack of spontaneity, in education and in social organization, is due to that disintegration of the personality which has been the fatal result of economic, industrial, and cultural developments since the Renaissance.[19]

Against these developments, he urges three main points. The first and most important is that art is a proper object of the school's concern in its own right. The second and third are that it is also instrumental not only in the achievement of the discursive forms of knowledge but also in the achievement of true morality. I shall consider these claims briefly in turn.

The claim that art is intrinsically valuable and that therefore the school should foster it has often been made, though less often acted on. His theory of art, as I have interpreted it, puts this plea in a slightly different light. For the argument is not that the school should attempt to educate the emotions as well as the intellect, or that the practice of art has a role in the maintenance of mental health, or that, in general, there is something of value in addition to the intellectual with which the school should be concerned. It is rather that art is valuable because intellectual activity is valuable; that because the school has to do with the latter, it should have to do with the former. It is an extension of the scope of the notion of the "intellectual," which is achieved by the definition of art as the discovery of form. For Read this is doubtless the most important reason why the school should be concerned with art, though it may not be the most politic on which to dwell.

To emphasize that the activity of art is a condition of acquiring an understanding of discursively formulated knowledge, such

[19] *Ibid.,* p. 201.

as the schools have always concentrated on, is to emphasize that in many cases it is equivalent to what we would normally call "insight." For to acquire a new concept involves two logically different steps: learning the word for the new concept and discriminating the kinds of things which are to be counted as cases of the concept. The more important and difficult of these is clearly the latter step of deciding what is to count as a case covered by the concept. This requires the activity which Read calls "art." For example, imagine drawing a triangle on a board and saying to a child: "This is a triangle." (I choose an example from geometry partly to emphasize an earlier point: that "art" is not restricted to the visual arts or to the traditional media.) To understand the word "triangle" the child must discriminate the drawing from whatever other marks and scratches may be on the board; and, contemplating the drawing, he must discriminate its triangularity from its color, its size, and so on. Such a discrimination is done visually, not verbally, that is, using line as the medium, not words. If the discrimination is not made, then learning the word "triangle," Read would say, is useless, and perhaps worse than useless. It is at best an exercise of memory, an external handling of symbols. This is what Read thinks the schools have typically encouraged; they have attempted to hand over the discursive forms of knowledge without the necessary prior engagement in the activity of art. This is done by the method of being told something and then trying to remember it.[20]

It might be objected that the case of discriminating a triangle, while it might fit the definition of art as "intuition," does not apparently fit that of art as "the expression of emotion." Such an objection would neglect the fact that the two definitions are alternative descriptions of the same activity. In this case the form discriminated for the first time by the child expresses for him his feeling for triangularity, where "feeling" is the emotion directed toward the triangle. Such an emotion is ineffable in other

[20] For a well-known paper that asserts the same point of view in relation to the teaching of mathematics, see Gertrude Hendrix, "Learning by Discovery," *The Mathematics Teacher,* vol. 54, no. 5 (May 1961): 290–99.

terms; it may perhaps be said to be an anticipation of the meaning that is yet to be developed into conceptual knowledge, and it is perhaps felt simply as a sense that the form discriminated is important. We may doubt that in this case there is an emotion to be "expressed" only because the form "triangle" has for most of us long been formulated and articulated in discursive terms. Our perception of it is therefore always a case of recognition and not art. But in the case of a scientist or mathematician working on the frontiers of his subject, the aspect of expression as opposed to that of intuition becomes more noticeable; there is a more obvious dependence on felt significance, less on the guidance of knowledge already formulated by someone else. These are the cases where the activity of art is most obvious, and which, in Read's judgment, are most analogous to the situation of the child.

Of course, this is a very general interpretation of what Read is saying, and it is not all clear how it is to be interpreted in practice. One way of putting the difference is to say that we have been discussing the logical, or perhaps the epistemological, priority of art to the higher cognitive functions; but the practical question is whether or not art must also be temporally prior. It is clear that logical priority does not necessarily imply temporal priority. It may well be that one learns discursively about the triangle before one has really understood what a triangle is and that the discursive knowledge about it is valueless until one understands what a triangle is. But it may also be that knowing about triangles promotes the understanding of what a triangle is, that the use of the word prompts attention to the form. It may also be that the two occur simultaneously: that as soon as something is pointed out to one, one understands the distinction being made, though one may not have been able to make the distinction without having it verbalized by another. Indeed, one might be tempted to say that this is just what we mean by "instruction": the attempt to bring about the discriminative activity of the learner by passing on the discursive forms of knowledge. And it might be held that it is a good thing for the instructor to speak at times a little beyond the immediate grasp of his students, to leave them puzzling with articulated symbols they do not fully understand; that is, deliberately to put the discursive stage temporally before the nondiscursive on which it logically depends. Read does not discuss this question directly, nor does he distinguish the two orders of priority, with the result that one cannot be certain how he intends to be interpreted in practice on the matter of instruction. But his discussions of the role of the teacher do seem to preclude any systematic instruction in this sense. The passage already quoted points in this direction; and the familiar roles in which the teacher is cast, of midwife, friend, and fellow-artist,[21] concur. The reasonable conclusion is that in Read's opinion any attempt to pass on the discursive forms of knowledge which does not provoke an immediate response in the child is to be deplored. Unless the child can understand at once, though the activity of art, the meaning of the symbol used, to insist that he remember or try to understand it is useless. Perhaps it is also harmful because it may prejudice the child's present opportunities of meaningful discrimination.

Read's point in connection with morality is similar and can be stated very briefly. Just as knowledge does not lie in the mere possession of discursive symbols, but in their understanding, so morality does not lie in the mere performance of certain acts. These are the outward forms, and morality requires an understanding of their character as moral acts. Such an understanding is both an awareness of the characteristics that make the act moral and the feeling that accompanies such an awareness. If one is to understand that an act one is doing is morally good, then one must *feel* that it is morally good; else it is all mere obedience or hypocrisy:

> The sense of right and wrong is a subjective sense; if I do not *feel* what is right and what is wrong, I cannot act rightly and wrongly, except under compulsion. To *know* a code of right and wrong is to know someone else's conception of right and wrong.[22]

It follows in just the same way that requiring the remembering of a set of rules and exacting obedience to them has little to do with moral education. Preaching would be the activity that is

[21] *Education through Art,* Chs. 8 and 9.
[22] *Anarchy and Order* (London: Faber and Faber, 1954), p. 123.

parallel with instruction in the previous discussion; and it seems to Read to be our typical method:

> The only method of moral education developed in the modern world is education by precept. These are the laws, these are the commandments, this is done and that is not done by the best people: obey, conform, go and do likewise.[23]

It may well be said that, if this interpretation of Read's general point is right, his protest goes too far in the opposite direction. To make the point about the necessity of the activity of art in school, it does not seem necessary to preclude all instruction (in the sense of "instruction" just indicated). And to insist on the image of the child as an artist or a creative scientist is not sufficient, though it may be salutary.

The point might be made by pointing to the common-sense distinction between the answer to a problem in mathematics which satisfies the child's sense of fittingness, and the one which is right. Granted that before any solution can be understood by the child he must discriminate and pay attention to the logical character of certain relationships dictated by the problem. Such an intuition necessarily sees itself as plausible; or more accurately, the intuition arises at a level which excludes consideration of validity and invalidity.[24] The intuition must be had before the question of correctness can arise. This is a necessary condition of doing any mathematics at all. But what Read apparently fails to take into account is the fact that certain relations may appear logical to the child, and therefore certain arguments valid, which do not guarantee that validity. To leave the matter there is to assume that whatever is plausible is right. We know very well that apparent validity is quite compatible with actual invalidity, where that actuality is determined by the discipline of mathematics. Indeed, a large part of the history of mathematics consists in the progressive demonstration of uncertainty on points previously considered certain. The generalizations and rules currently accepted as the structure of mathe-

[23] *The Grass Roots of Art*, p. 114.
[24] Cf. B. Croce, *Aesthetic as Science of Expression and General Linguistic*, trans. Douglas Ainslie (New York: Noonday Press, 1955), pp. 3–4.

matics by mathematicians represent a public accumulation of the results of the intuitions of centuries. It is well to take the child's intuitions seriously, but one doesn't have to believe that certain answers or generalizations are right in any absolute sense to agree that they may be better (in a mathematical sense) than others the child devises. It is not a matter of indifference whether the child comes to understand and share what is held by mathematicians to be good math, for it is the best so far devised. If the child could construct for himself alternative systems of equal validity, then perhaps it would not matter; but he cannot.

There is, therefore, for practical purposes, a right answer or answers to the kind of questions with which the school must deal, as well as a number of wrong answers. When a child finds a wrong answer satisfactory, it is because in the formulation of the problem he has made inappropriate distinctions or irrelevant connections, demonstrated ultimately by the kinds of tests used in the appropriate discipline. It is the teacher's function to bring the child to see this inappropriateness or irrelevance wherever possible. But this is often possible only through deliberate instruction, and may require periods during which the child relies on the teacher's authority and not on his aesthetic sense of what is fitting. For it is important that the child learn to check his insight against the rules, and to understand the difference between an answer that pleases him and a correct one. He must be prepared at times to have faith in the rules when his own insight will not support them, and to acknowledge that his own sense of fittingness does not guarantee truth. Otherwise he will become intolerantly dogmatic. So there may even be cases where instruction must begin by disrupting the learner's present sense of fittingness in order to build a more complex harmony. Many a child, for instance, begins by finding it obvious that deficit financing at the government level is wrong, or that certain social rights and privileges belong to members of one race but not of another. It may require the intervention of a considerable body of theory to bring him to see otherwise. Even where such intervention is unsuccessful, it is desirable that he understand the kinds of tests and forms of argument that are considered relevant by others.

It is true that, in the case of the mathematician or scientist working on the frontier of his subject, personal insight must be relied on beyond, and sometimes even in spite of, the rules. This is, after all, the origin of the rules. But the question is whether the identification of the learner with the research scientist (or the artist) is appropriate in this respect. For the judgment of the mathematician or scientist is one which has learned to be tentative and self-searching. It is, moreover, as scientific judgment, subject to the judgment of all other qualified scientists and relevant procedures of verification. This is not necessarily a good model for the child in school who has not absorbed the tradition of the subject. To use it is to underestimate the difficulty of absorbing that tradition and of achieving the disciplined judgment in question. Such a model presupposes the possession and use of systematic knowledge which a child cannot be expected to have and the acquisition of which is unlikely without deliberate instruction.

The same point could be made in connection with Read's conception of morality. What he stresses is the fact—for I take it to be a fact—that no action is morally good unless the actor performs it because he has intuited its fittingness in the circumstances. What he fails to allow for is the possibility that the child's intuition may omit some elements of the situation which are morally relevant or include some which are morally irrelevant. It is true that we do not agree in matters of morality as much as we do in those of science, but Read would not want to claim that morality is only a matter of opinion, any more than he would claim that what is logically valid is only a matter of opinion. When objective facts have moral relevance, that relevance is the same for everyone. Our very concept of morality implies that moral rules are both prescriptive and universal. For the child to be moral, therefore, he must bring his own actions under a rule which he recognizes as applying equally to all.[25] Without this the child is not a moral agent, and his intuitions of fittingness are not sufficient to make him so. It follows

[25] See R. M. Hare, "Adolescents into Adults," in T. H. Hollins, ed., *Aims in Education* (Manchester: Manchester University Press, 1964), pp. 47–70.

that he must come to see his own intuitions as fallible and capable of correction. A part of the teacher's task is to make this correction possible.

To generalize this objection, it may be said that Read neglects and perhaps depreciates the public character of knowledge and morality and the importance of methods of verification and rules in its achievement. One might offer at least three reasons for this, two of which have already been mentioned. The first is that, when he is talking theoretically, he is concerned with essences, or definitions. He is concerned to say what education is, or, as it is more usually put, what the "aim" of education is, exactly as he wants to say what art is. His answer is therefore a statement of ultimate unities and not of proximate differences. It is not a practical answer, not likely to be of much use in answering the questions of practice that teachers may want to ask.

The second reason is that he writes in reaction to a situation in which, as he saw it, education was construed as not much more than bringing children to obey rules, just as art was conceived as wholly a reflective enterprise. The heat of his reaction may have led him to overemphasize his point: the importance of the missing element of insight and creativity.

A third factor is what seems an excessive optimism in the sufficiency of the uninstructed individual. In school we are to do away with, not guidance, but systematic instruction in the elaborate, verbalized structures of the various arts and sciences and of morality. But these cannot be produced anew by any child; they are interpersonal achievements which have been built over centuries; they constitute the fabric of our civilization, and no individual can assimilate more than portions or add more than fragments. Though they must be embodied in individuals, they are neither innate nor created by any one person. The tentative and inquiring spirit of both science and morality, for instance, is not native to the human mind; it is a product of institutions and dependent on education. There was a time, perhaps, in favored spots on the earth, when that spirit could be taken for granted in most people because it was assimilated unconsciously in the process of living in society. But, if so, that time has passed. The institutional character of civilization has become more apparent now than ever before. There is ever more and more to be learned deliberately, and we are more aware of the cases where the processes of unplanned assimilation have not been successful. It may be that Read's optimism is due to the carrying over of this assumption from an earlier time to one where it is no longer appropriate. He overestimates, it seems, the level which the uninstructed can reach through interaction with nature and society and the ease and inevitability with which this learning may be achieved.

To illustrate the consequences of this optimism, I point to the passage in ETA where he claims to be summarizing Plato on education and quotes the passage from the *Republic:*

> Our young men, dwelling, as it were, in a healthful region, may drink in good from every quarter, whence any emanations from noble works strike upon their eye or ear, like a gale wafting health from salubrious lands, and win them imperceptibly from their earliest childhood into resemblance, love, and harmony with the true beauty of reason.[26]

Both Plato and Read stress the importance of the arts in the formation of attitudes. But what guarantee do we have that such attitudes will be rational and desirable? To ensure this, Plato proposed the censorship of the philosopher-kings, and modern democracies acknowledge the formal principles of justice, morality, and the objective verification of knowledge. Read however has only his faith that each man will of his own accord come to formulate these principles organically: an optimism for which we might think history offers little encouragement.

IV

To make these criticisms is not necessarily to depreciate Read's work or to be hostile to his point. Rather, it is to take him seriously and to suppose that he has something of value to say. He seems to have suffered by being accepted uncritically by some of those within art education and by being dismissed equally uncritically by some of those outside it. Criticism is necessary if one is to see the value of his work. Moreover, if

[26] *Education through Art,* p. 64.

the negative aspects of the criticism take as long to say as do the positive, that does not mean that they are as important. It may be only that they are more complex.

Read's work, then, is valuable in the first place because it is a statement of general truths. The most important of these general truths is summed up in the first two sentences of Whitehead's well-known essay on the aims of education: "Culture is activity of thought, and receptivity to beauty and humane feeling. Scraps of information have nothing to do with it." [27]

To insist on this is in some circumstances to make a protest, and I have said that this is the best way to view Read's work. It is beside the point to object that such a protest is negatively put, for that is the nature of protest. It is true that constructive statements of equal scope and truth may be preferred, but we do not have so many statements of general truths that we can afford to be cavalier with them. Protest is the stuff that classics are made of, at least in education. This is not to say that I would want to claim that ETA, or any other of Read's books on education, has the stature to be called a classic. It is not that they are too extreme—witness the *Republic* and *Émile*—but I think none of them is clear or consistent enough.

Furthermore, Read's protest is by no means an eccentric one. Just as (according to my interpretation) his insistence on the image of the learner as an artist does not have an anti-intellectual purpose, so it is not made from outside the gates of society. Though he attacks our developing life style and denounces a widespread "dissociation of consciousness," [28] he writes from within a major tradition of our civilization. He calls attention to the image of the artist in education because we appear to ignore it, although we have long been aware of its appropriateness. Similarly he thinks we are in danger of overlooking the fact that moral acts must be freely chosen. Only this aspect makes sense of that other part of the logic of our concept of morality which I have said Read neglects: that moral acts must be seen as falling under rules which are prescriptive

[27] *The Aims of Education* (New York: New American Library, 1949), p. 13.
[28] *Education through Art,* p. 197.

and universal. These two together constitute the essence of rational morality, again as we have long known. Read is not, therefore, seeking to depreciate morality but to defend it against an immoral society. One might say the same kind of thing about the publicly verified knowledge of the sciences. He does not expect children to have less science because of his proposed emphasis on the aesthetic. Rather, he thinks they will have more because they will better comprehend abstract formulations, having formulated their equivalents themselves.

It is perhaps a familiar message in our time that education implies understanding as well as the simple possession of verbal formulas or external skills. The distinction rests on what seems to be a general fact about people, that they may be unaware of some part of their environment through inattention and can say and do things without being aware of their significance. That is to say, attention is not an automatic reflex but an achievement. It is something that requires effort and in which failure is quite possible. If awareness were automatic, if it did not require effort and could not fail, then the dependence of the discursive symbols on the nondiscursive and the reflective levels of mind on the intuitive, would be only a logical truth. Insisting on the distinction would be of little practical importance. But as it is, it is a psychological truth, though one so general that it is easily overlooked. We should be grateful for the energy with which Herbert Read protests our overlooking it.

THE AESTHETICS OF JOHN DEWEY AND AESTHETIC EDUCATION

C. M. Smith

The cohesiveness between John Dewey's educational prescriptions and his general philosophy—his views on liberalism, democracy, intelligence, science, individualism, etc.—has been noted frequently enough. What will be attempted here is an investigation into the question whether a similarly close connection can be presumed to exist between Dewey's aesthetics as elaborated in *Art as Experience* [1] and the kind of recommendations for aesthetic education that would be consistent with his broad educational objectives. To put it differently: the aim is to see whether the main thrusts of Dewey's thinking on art coincide with his major philosophical concerns and, if not, to indicate possible consequences of discrepancies found for the theory and practice of schooling in the arts. The project calls for an effort to gain some understanding of certain key points in Dewey's aesthetic theory, and it is to this end that the greater portion of the present discussion will be directed.

Art in Experience

There is at least one respect in which Dewey quite obviously intended his aesthetics to be of a piece with his general philosophy: his emphasis on experience. For Dewey the main task of aesthetics was to restore continuity between art and "the everyday events, doings, and sufferings that are universally recognized to constitute experience." [2] "Philosophy of art," he said, "is sterilized unless it makes us aware of the function of art in relation to other modes of experience, and unless it indicates

From *Educational Theory,* vol. 21, no. 2 (Spring 1971): 131–45. Reprinted by permission of *Educational Theory* and the author.

[1] John Dewey, *Art as Experience* (New York: Capricorn Books, G. P. Putnam's Sons, 1958; first published 1934).

[2] *Ibid.,* p. 3.

why this function is so inadequately realized, and unless it suggests the conditions under which the office would be successfully performed." [3] As it develops, Dewey actually accomplished more than he set out to do, at least if one takes seriously—as many have—one of the main emphases in his thinking on art. For instead of merely reconnecting art to everyday living, he allowed it to be absorbed by experience. This, at any rate, seems to be the import of his saying that "art is a quality that permeates experience," [4] and "art is a strain in experience rather than an entity in itself." [5] Several ramifications of this assertion might be elucidated by following Dewey's methodological recommendation to go "back to experience of the common or mill run of things to discover the esthetic quality such experience possesses." [6]

But here Dewey is not to be taken at his word, for the experience he bids us examine is not at all "common run." Rather, it is to be *an* experience and as such must meet a variety of quite stringent requirements. Granted, then, that art can be found only in *an* experience, what is it? The most liberal interpretation would be to say that the aesthetic is whatever allows experience to qualify as *an* experience, but this still leaves a number of possibilities, and it is not clear whether the whole range of them would amount to a specification of necessary and sufficient conditions. It may seem picayune to demand rigor where Dewey perhaps did not wish to speak with great precision. However, if it is thought that art is an element or strain in experience rather than an independent entity and if, as educators have been quick to point out, important pedagogical considerations would derive from this view, it should be helpful to be able to isolate just what it is that is aesthetic about *an* experience. The candidates for "the aesthetic" may be roughly categorized under two rubrics: structural or formal properties of the experience itself, and qualities of the subjective reaction of the individual having the experience (though

[3] *Ibid.,* p. 12.
[4] *Ibid.,* p. 326.
[5] *Ibid.,* p. 330.
[6] *Ibid.,* p. 11.

Dewey probably would not have countenanced such a "separation").

To begin with formal properties: "An experience," explains Dewey, "has pattern and structure." [7] This apparently is what Dorothy Walsh has singled out as definitive of the aesthetic, for she says: "In discussing the nature of *an* experience, Dewey is intent on emphasizing the fact that *an* experience may be said to have 'aesthetic quality.' Certainly when and if an experience has a marked formal pattern of inception, development, and consummation, the claim that it has aesthetic quality is plausible enough." [8] Also on the formal side would be the relationship between the objective components in *an* experience, specifically, the intimate interconnection of means and ends. Dewey states, "all the cases in which means and ends are external to one another are non-esthetic. This externality may even be regarded as a definition of the non-esthetic." [9] Conversely, then, one of Dewey's several definitions of the aesthetic would be the integration of means and ends in *an* experience.

The means-ends continuum seems to have a subjective or emotional counterpart in the fact that in *an* experience no conscious awareness exists of the discrete phases the individual passes through while living the experience. *An* experience is "not just doing and undergoing in alternation, but consists of them in relationship." [10] It may not be far wrong to say that the aesthetic in experience is constituted by a feeling of unity or unification.

However, elsewhere in Dewey's writing on art it becomes evident that this emotional or intuitive unity is brought about not so much by the seamless flow of doing and undergoing as by the presence of "pervasive quality." The importance Dewey attached to this notion cannot be escaped, and more will have to be said about it further on. D. C. Mathur has taken pervasive quality to be the "key concept and guiding thread of

[7] *Ibid.*, p. 44.
[8] Dorothy Walsh, *Literature and Knowledge* (Middletown, Conn.: Wesleyan University Press, 1969), p. 84.
[9] Dewey, p. 198.
[10] *Ibid.*, p. 44.

Dewey's theory of art." [11] But like so many others, it is a very vague idea, for pervasive quality is sometimes described as that which causes attention to move in a unified direction instead of wandering; [12] yet it is also something that pervades every part of the whole as well as being the quality which uniquely identifies the experience as a whole. At still other times Dewey seems to have thought of it as a general feeling tone or emotional background against which experience plays itself out. Whatever its nature, there is some justification for saying that "pervasive quality *is* aesthetic quality." [13]

But is it? For still another interpretation is possible according to which the aesthetic is not so much a unifying presence throughout experience but a feeling of consummation that concludes the experience. Mathur, for instance, decided that "the final phase of the 'moving' experience is what Dewey calls its 'consummatory phase' and, as such, is aesthetic in nature." [14] Dewey has described this feeling of relieved tension as the "closure of a circuit of energy." [15]

The point of it all is this. Since Dewey's definition of art as a quality or strain or element in experience is the more popular one, there is some virtue in showing that what is popular is not necessarily simple and clear-cut. Any educator subscribing to the notion that aesthetic education will take care of itself as long as the student has experiences containing the requisite aesthetic element (or elements) might still be in a quandary concerning the conditions that would need to be satisfied. Whether any educator would be well advised to take his cue from this particular emphasis in Dewey's aesthetics is a question to be discussed yet.

[11] D. C. Mathur, "A Note on the Concept of 'Consummatory Experience' in Dewey's Aesthetics," *The Journal of Philosophy,* vol. 63, no. 9 (April 28, 1966): 225.

[12] Dewey, p. 192.

[13] Richard J. Bernstein, *John Dewey* (New York: Washington Square Press, 1966), p. 96.

[14] Mathur, p. 226.

[15] Dewey, p. 41.

Aesthetic Experience

In addition to what will hereafter be referred to as his "popular version," Dewey also elaborated a narrower and more specialized view on aesthetic experience which he resorted to on the many occasions when he spoke of art not as a quality in *an* experience, but more in terms of "the arts" in the generally accepted sense. D. W. Gotshalk believes that Dewey was perhaps not sufficiently aware that he did have two quite distinct conceptions of aesthetic experience. "He moves in and out of them noiselessly," Gotshalk says, "as if they were the same, now emphasizing one, now the other. . . . Dewey seems torn between the recognition that fine art is different and an egalitarian horror of anything different, and he adjusts his sights to one view or the other, and gives changed meaning to the concept of the aesthetic according to the situation or context in which he is operating." [16] It will be one of the objectives of the remaining pages to support the contention that, had Dewey recognized how far he had moved toward positing a discontinuity between art and everyday events in his separate versions of "aesthetic experience," he might also have realized the subversive consequences (subversive, that is, of some of the emphases usually associated with his educational thought) of the special way in which he characterized that difference.

It is now time to adjust one's sights to the identifying marks of what Dewey called predominantly or distinctively aesthetic experience, which in its pure form is experience involving works of fine art. This is how he defines it: "In a distinctively esthetic experience, characteristics that are subdued in other experiences are dominant; those which are subordinate are controlling— namely, the characteristics in virtue of which the experience is an integrated complete experience on its own account"; [17] and "the factors that determine anything which can be called *an* experi-

---

[16] D. W. Gotshalk, "On Dewey's Aesthetics," *The Journal of Aesthetics and Art Criticism,* vol. 23, no. 1 (Fall 1964): 131–38; reprinted in Ralph A. Smith, ed., *Aesthetics and Criticism in Art Education* (Chicago: Rand McNally, 1966), p. 142.

[17] Dewey, p. 55.

ence are lifted high above the threshold of perception and are made manifest for their own sake." [18] It was pointed out previously that the factors which cause any experience to be an integrated experience are "the aesthetic"; this is now dominant, controlling, and enjoyed for its own sake. Because of the ambiguities surrounding "the aesthetic" in experience, it is somewhat difficult to know just what is being lifted above the threshold of perception; but this is a minor point. What deserves special attention is that in distinctively aesthetic experience, as it highlights what is aesthetic in *an* experience, the emphasis is on *qualities*. And this opens up a topic—the qualitative—which cannot be treated here with anything approximating the philosophical sophistication it demands. But neither can it be sidestepped, for Dewey is emphatic that "the material of the fine arts consists of qualities; that of experience having intellectual conclusions are signs and symbols having no intrinsic quality of their own." [19]

One of the most important distinctions between ordinary and dominantly aesthetic experience, then, is in the "material" used by each, that of distinctively aesthetic experience being qualities. It sounds convincing, because one normally thinks of art as being properly attended to in terms of its sensuous, formal, expressive, etc., qualities. Yet this is not necessarily what Dewey had in mind, although in his more relaxed moments he does speak of works of art as "having" such and such qualities. Generally, though, he wanted qualities to be understood as belonging to a context rather than "residing" in the mind or in external objects. This would allow qualities to cut across one of the dualisms he despised, viz., the separation between the mental and the physical. As properties of situations, qualities would not be exhausted by sense qualities or primary or secondary qualities; they could also make their appearance in the guise of tertiary or pervasive qualities.[20] In all these forms, one would assume, qualities could come to constitute the material of dominantly aesthetic experience. Important is that one is led back once more to the concept of pervasive quality.

[18] *Ibid.,* p. 57.
[19] *Ibid.,* p. 38.
[20] Bernstein, pp. 94–95.

It is by virtue of being "pervasive" that quality can exercise control over experience, and whenever the development of an experience is found to be controlled through reference to quality, that experience is dominantly aesthetic in nature.[21] An explanation of this somewhat foreign notion might be that in distinctively aesthetic experience the qualitative tone determines what elements may or may not be incorporated into that experience; and as anything incongruent with pervasive quality is rejected, it could be said that quality guides and directs that experience. This also makes sense out of Dewey's saying that in dominantly aesthetic experience characteristics which are ordinarily subdued are controlling. For intellectual experience, while it does of course operate against an emotional background, keeps the qualitative subordinated and is controlled by *its* materials, i.e., the import of signs and symbols. Futhermore, it is now seen why Dewey can maintain that in distinctively aesthetic experience aesthetic quality may become manifest for its own sake. If the qualitative aspect of experience exercises a control that excludes everything extraneous, then certainly quality may penetrate to the foreground of awareness and be consciously enjoyed.

To assert that specifically aesthetic experiences are instituted for the purpose of enjoying qualities leads to still another distinction between them and ordinary experiences. This is the matter of interest or result. Experiences "are dominantly intellectual or practical, rather than *distinctively* esthetic, because of the interest and purpose that initiate and control them. In an intellectual experience, the conclusion has value on its own account. It can be extracted as a formula or as a 'truth,' and can be used in its independent entirety as factor and guide in other inquiries. In a work of art there is no such single self-sufficient deposit." [22] What Dewey has recognized here is a peculiarity of experiences with art sometimes referred to as "self-enclosedness" or "disinterestedness"; namely, the fact that such experiences are sought for no ulterior reasons and that nothing further is expected to come of them. But this perfectly

21 Dewey, p. 50.
22 *Ibid.*, p. 55.

respectable phenomenon must raise some misgivings when a general good-making feature of experience—as understood by Dewey—is called to mind. And this is precisely the fact that experience, to be valuable, *should* leave a "deposit," something that can provide a starting point for or material in new experiences, something enabling the individual to move onward and outward. Measured against this standard, would not distinctively aesthetic experience mark a point of stasis, disruption, discontinuity? Would not education designed to lead to such experience violate Dewey's stipulation that education should be growth for further growth? In other words, do not Dewey's specifications for predominantly aesthetic experiences render these experiences somehow incomplete or inferior, according to the criteria for good experiences that hold elsewhere in his philosophy?

This negative judgment might be avoided if a case could be made that what Dewey calls "distinctively aesthetic experience" is not merely experience with a special emphasis, though still subject to the canons applicable to good and complete experiences in general, but that it is a special *kind* of experience with unique characteristics and benefits. It is now suggested that arguments in favor of such a view could be derived from the preceding discussion. That is to say, Dewey's "dominantly aesthetic experience" might be shown to be sufficiently different in significant ways—in material (qualities); in interest or purpose (enjoyment of qualities for their own sake); in control (by pervasive quality); and in outcome (none beyond the consummation of the experience)—to be called a separate sort of experience, *aesthetic experience.* (The phrase will be used in this sense throughout the remaining pages.) As such, aesthetic experiences would be distinct from intellectual or practical experiences that may attain to the status of *an* experience when they feature elements or qualities which Dewey has chosen to call "the aesthetic."

It would now appear that what had been called the "popular version" of Deweyan aesthetics does not go far enough educationally. (It will be argued later that it also contributes to some gross misunderstandings). For if there is such a thing as an aesthetic experience which is sufficiently different from and more subtle and complex than "the aesthetic" in *an* experience, then providing consummatory experiences in schooling cannot be all there is to aesthetic education. In what sense it would be deficient as art education should become clear once Dewey's vision of the special office of the fine arts is recognized.

The Work of Art

An evaluation of Dewey's assumptions about the purpose and function of art presupposes some clarification of his conception of the work of art; this will be attempted presently. Yet to say that discussion now shifts from aesthetic experience to the work of art proper would be misleading in a fundamental sense, because for Dewey these are not strictly separate entities. As Monroe C. Beardsley puts it, Dewey was "haunted by the spectre of separations and oppositions," and this to such an extent that he often deplored "even distinctions that have been carefully won by long thought, and have proved helpful to many." [23] Whether Dewey's attempt to obliterate the distinction between the work of art and aesthetic experience supports Beardsley's contention remains to be seen.

And it is a difficult issue, because as so often in his writings, Dewey uses the phrase "work of art" in both the ordinary and his own special senses, hence misinterpretations are bound to occur. Generally, though, there is little doubt that for Dewey the work of art is not what issues from the hands of the artist; that is only the "art object." This object is but one ingredient in an experience which he describes as follows: ". . . the uniquely distinguishing feature of esthetic experience is exactly the fact that no . . . distinction of self and object exists in it, since it is esthetic in the degree in which organism and environment coöperate to institute an experience in which the two are so fully integrated that each disappears." [24] This experience is *the* "work of art," [25] because "a work or art no matter how old

[23] Monroe C. Beardsley, *Aesthetics from Classical Greece to the Present* (New York: Macmillan, 1966), p. 337.
[24] Dewey, p. 249.
[25] In the remainder of this essay, the phrase "work of art" will be enclosed in quotation marks whenever it is used in this special sense.

and classic is actually, not just potentially, a work of art only
when it lives in some individualized experience." [26] Perhaps
Dewey merely wishes to point out that works of art which,
after all, have been framed for aesthetic perception rather than
for consumption or cogitation, have to be experienced actively
to fulfill whatever function they may have. But what he really
seems to be getting at is that the art object has to be experienced
in a *special manner:* "For to perceive, a beholder must *create*
his own experience. And his creation must include relations
comparable to those which the original producer underwent." [27]

This last statement will be shown to contain a tension which
in itself is one of the difficulties with Dewey's aesthetics.
Furthermore, it will be argued that attempts to resolve it in
either of two possible directions will lead to additional problems, especially for the educator. The opposition is between
the exhortation that the experience be the percipient's own
creation and the insistence that it also be somehow analogous
to the experience of the artist. Now "comparable relations" is
probably vague enough to coexist with "create," but elsewhere
Dewey also asserts that "we lay hold of the full import of a
work of art only as we go through in our own vital processes
the processes the artist went through in producing the work." [28]
This is specific enough to require reduplication of the artist's
pulse rate and heartburn, insofar as they were caused by his
creative travail. In any case, one way of interpreting Dewey is

[26] Dewey, p. 108. It must be admitted that doubts can be raised
concerning how far Dewey actually meant to go toward identifying
the work of art with aesthetic experience, for on p. 326 he says: "Art
is a quality that permeates experience; it is not *save by a figure of
speech,* the experience itself"—(my italics). However, he also insists
that "As a piece of parchment, of marble, of canvas, it remains . . .
self-identical throughout the ages. But as a work of art, it is recreated
every time it is esthetically experienced" (p. 108). And even more
emphatically: "The *product* of art—temple, painting, statue, poem—
is not the *work* of art. The work takes place when a human being
cooperates with the product so that the outcome is an experience that
is enjoyed because of its liberating and ordered properties" (p. 214).
It is this latter interpretation of "work of art" which is basic to Gotshalk's critique whose general thrust informs much of the present
argument.

[27] *Ibid.,* p. 54.

[28] *Ibid.,* p. 325.

that the beholder is urged to re-create imaginatively the original artistic process. But this imposes a task which some aestheticians [29] have thought to be as impracticable as it is irrelevant to the apprehension of aesthetic value. It is impossible because the finished product rarely contains clues unambiguous enough to permit a retracing of the creative process. And it is a fairly irrelevant undertaking because a work of art is always more than a record of its inception and development; how it was brought into being does not indicate a great deal about how it should be evaluated. Enough has been said to suggest that attempts to resolve the aforementioned tension by stressing *re*-creation, that is, by assimilating aesthetic to artistic experience, are likely to send art appreciation and the teaching of art off in an unpromising direction.

However, many educators are wont to emphasize "creativity" even in aesthetic experience, and they seem to have a spokesman in Dewey when he says that the beholder "must *create* his own experience." The question is, how is this to be understood? Surely Dewey could not have meant to make the utterly trivial assertion that the percipient's experience must be *his own;* it could not be anybody else's. The emphasis therefore seems to lie on *creating* the experience. This, of course, contradicts the notion that the beholder *re*-creates the artist's experience, for no one should be urged to be original while paying close attention to what another person has done or intended to do. One must therefore assume that the beholder is given a free hand with the work of art and is encouraged to manipulate the elements of his experience toward a novel outcome, the "work of art." That the "work of art" is thus created anew by each percipient in his interaction with the art object seems also to have been D. W. Gotshalk's understanding of Dewey. Gotshalk points out that on this view there can be, strictly speaking, no *one* work of art; it will be something fundamentally different for each beholder, and a multitude of "works of art"

[29] A well-known argument against the idea that what the artist intended and went through is of importance to appreciation and criticism is found in William K. Wimsatt, Jr., and Monroe Beardsley, "The Intentional Fallacy," Ch. 1 in Wimsatt, *The Verbal Icon* (Lexington: University of Kentucky Press, 1954).

will result from the experiences different persons have with the same art work. However, this leads to an outcome that should have been uncongenial to Dewey. For each beholder of a particular work "will be sealed off in his own private aesthetic world, and discussion, communication, sharing, cooperation, and all the other fine things Dewey wished to emphasize as essential to high-grade human experience, will break down here, since on this level a common basis in a common *work of art* on which they might rest is non-existent." [30] High-grade educational experiences with art would, of course, be similarly called into question.

Perhaps the problem can be traced to certain misconceptions about the nature of art objects which Dewey may have entertained. One concerns the importance of the public character and objective features of art works. While Dewey was of course correct in pointing out that aesthetic experience should require active engagement on the part of the percipient, he failed to realize that this is not incompatible with Gotshalk's assumption that an art object "becomes actually what it is as a work of art only when we appreciate it properly, and that proper appreciation is not remaking the work of art but apprehending what it actually is as made." [31] It could be that Dewey was led to underestimate the status of the work of art "as made" by his general theory of experience. For him an object is always external and unformed prior to being experienced; it acquires meaning, becomes an object of knowledge, only as the individual interacts with it during the experiential process. Now it is possible that, despite his obvious sensitivity to art, Dewey classed art objects with external objects, that is, things to be subjected to transformation. But there is reason to doubt that works of art are rightly thought of as unformed external things in quite this sense, for they already represent unique transformations of antecedently existing material. Moreover, they may be embodiments of meaning and should be respected as such rather than being reworked capriciously or "creatively." An implied educational requirement would be that students be

[30] Gotshalk, p. 144.
[31] *Ibid.*, p. 145.

induced to play close attention to works of art as made and be taught the skills and procedures requisite to doing this properly.

In short, it is suggested that Dewey, through his commitment to the preeminence of experience as the creative transformation of the externally given, elevated the percipient's experience to "the work of art." Consequently, he may have tended to leave the public status and objective character of works of art in some doubt. "As a result," says Gotshalk, "he makes the crucial difference between the physical and the artistic to lie in the seclusive and esoteric and private experiences of individual percipients. This is idealism come home to roost with a vengeance." [32] But when aesthetic experience, and hence the "work of art," are thought of as being excessively private, subjective, and unsharable, they also become *uneducative* in a Deweyan sense. Somewhat similar conclusions will be among the outcomes of a closer inspection of another of Dewey's focal concerns, one which had been present tacitly in much that went before. This is the concern with *immediacy,* a topic which will also provide the appropriate context for indicating—and questioning—Dewey's ideas about the function of art in the lives of men and society.

Immediacy: Value, Meaning, Communication

The quest for immediacy has been called one of the main motifs of nineteenth-century thought.[33] It was evident, for instance, as a thread running through much of Charles S. Peirce's philosophy in the form of "firstness" or "suchness," and Dewey extended this preoccupation into the present century. Immediacies are final, indivisible; they are intuited, felt, or "had"; in short, they are qualities. It is indispensable to an understanding of Dewey's philosophy to keep in mind that qualities are directly or immediately experienced but never directly *known*. In fact, Dewey's distinction between "knowing" and "having" can hardly be overemphasized. The objective to be pursued now is to bring the knowledge/immediacy dichotomy into relationship

[32] *Ibid.,* p. 146.
[33] Bernstein, p. 89.

with the claim Dewey wants to make for the function of art and with his contention that "it cannot be asserted too strongly that what is not immediate is not esthetic." [34]

The first move is a step backwards to what had been called the "popular version" of Deweyan aesthetic experience. Since what is not immediate cannot be aesthetic, "the aesthetic" in *an* experience must be felt, had. Earlier it was shown that in Dewey's view the consummatory phase of experience was one of the loci of the aesthetic; it deserves another look. This consummatory phase does not merely terminate experience. As a problem is solved, continuity restored, and an apprehension of the interpenetration of means and ends (unity) achieved, a positive emotional reaction occurs. Consummation, in other words, is experienced as a good, a value. This is another significant feature of Dewey's thought: values too are immediate, had (as distinct, of course, from the methodic, mediated, deliberate *value inquiry* aimed at testing alternative goods and creating conditions that make the enjoyment of value experiences possible). Now when Dewey maintained that anything to be aesthetic must be immediate, he naturally did not mean to say that everything which is immediate is therefore aesthetic. Hence there is no theoretical constraint for holding that values, being felt or had, are always aesthetic sorts of goods. Yet there are two reasons for suggesting that, although "immediacy" could be considered as merely subsuming concepts such as the aesthetic in general, the qualitative, pervasive quality, aesthetic unity, consummation, aesthetic value, etc., the relationships among these concepts are too unclear to guard against simple equations between "the aesthetic," "immediacy," and "value." One is that Dewey himself does not seem to have been overly careful to map the distinctions between these terms. The other reason is that on at least one occasion Dewey apparently did identify value with art or the aesthetic. This, at any rate, seems to be the most sensible reading of his celebrated statement: "Art, the mode of activity that is charged with meanings capable of immediately enjoyed possession, is the complete culmination of nature, and [that] science is prop-

[34] Dewey, p. 119.

erly a handmaiden that conducts natural events to this happy issue." [35] "Art" in this context is perhaps best understood as not merely the "fine arts," but as prototypical value experience in general, i.e., that for the sake of which all theoretical, scientific, and practical endeavors are ultimately undertaken: things immediately had and enjoyed, things such as consummations, values, and—it now appears—*meanings*.

But before exploring the consequences of including meaning among the things immediately enjoyed, it might be instructive to pause and see what the confusion of concepts hinted at above has done to certain views of education in the arts and of education in general. Accepting the notion that the aesthetic is an element in experience (but generally ignoring Dewey's strict requirements for *an* experience), that it is a value or good, and that it is immediate in the sense of being other-than-knowledge, many educators have been led to identify "the aesthetic" with "the non-cognitive." Hence the non-cognitive has come to acquire both the honorific status of being aesthetic and a presumption of being valuable. Thus provided with an aura of respectability, the non-cognitive has been further extended in at least three educationally interesting ways. First of all, it has been linked to "the qualitative," a concept itself closely connected with immediacy and, through a conversion of dubious validity, with the aesthetic. And great hopes have been held out for the educational benefits of allowing free rein to qualitative thinking, problem-solving, etc. [36] Second, the non-cognitive

[35] *Ibid.*, p. 26. Dewey is here quoting from his *Experience and Nature* (Chicago: The Open Court Publishing Company, 1925), p. 358. A similar interpretation of "art" as paradigmatic value experience may be derived from Dewey's statements in *Art as Experience:* "In art the forces that are congenial, that sustain not this or that special aim but the processes of enjoyed experience itself, are set free. That release gives them ideal quality"; and ". . . art operates by selecting those potencies in things by which an experience—any experience—has significance and value" (p. 185).

[36] Among thoughtful delineations of this view are: David W. Ecker, "The Artistic Process as Qualitative Problem Solving," *The Journal of Aesthetics and Art Criticism,* vol. 21, no. 3 (Spring 1963); Nathaniel L. Champlin, "John Dewey: Beyond the Centennial," *Educational Leadership,* vol. 18, no. 1 (October 1960); and Francis T. Villemain, "Democracy, Education, and Art," *Educational Theory,* vol. 14 (January 1964).

has been interpreted as "the affective." Consequently, whatever is affective in experience or in an educational situation comes to be seen as aesthetic and thereby as valuable, which in turn has led to the notion that it is at least as important to encourage the student to emote as it is to make him think. Third, the non-cognitive is frequently equated with the "non-verbal." From this it is concluded that some of the educationally most valuable experiences are of such a kind that it would be vain to try to "verbalize" them; and, by only a slight further extension, "the aesthetic" becomes whatever cannot be made sense of otherwise. Art education, when taught as a separate subject, is claimed to train students' affective responses by involving them in qualitative operations. But it is particularly suitable for "the non-verbal child"; for, though he may never learn his "three r's," his education is still doing him a great deal of good (other-than-knowledge = the aesthetic = something valuable and desirable) and no further trouble need be taken about him. All this by way of proposing that an unwise emphasis on certain unclear aspects of Dewey's aesthetics, in conjunction with the "popular version," can easily lead down the path of least cognitive strain to the kind of anti-intellectualism and educational irresponsibility that would have appalled Dewey.

A return to the subject of meaning in aesthetics focuses discussion once again upon aesthetic experience in the narrower sense recommended previously. It is now seen that capacity to provide immediately enjoyed meanings is still another feature which sets aesthetic experiences off from ordinary ones. Dewey believed that unmediated or intuited meaningfulness is exemplified by the work of art. Words and symbols, he says, represent objects and actions in the sense of standing for them, just as a signboard points to its referent. But meanings belong to words and signboards only by convention, not intrinsically. In art, by contrast, meanings "present themselves directly as possessions of objects which are experienced. Here there is no need for a code or convention of interpretation; the meaning is as inherent in immediate experience as that of a flower garden." [37] It is through its ability to embody meanings im-

[37] Dewey, *Art as Experience*, p. 83.

mediately that art can perform the functions Dewey would assign to it. "Men associate in many ways. But the only form of
association that is truly human . . . is the participation in
meanings and goods that is effected by communication. The expressions that constitute art are communication in its pure and
undefiled form." [38] And again: "In the end, works of art are
the only media of complete and unhindered communication
between man and man that can occur in a world full of gulfs
and walls that limit community of experience." [39]

These specifications for the purposes of art are indeed com-
mendable. Still, the matter cannot be allowed to rest here. The
question is not whether works of art do have or communicate
meanings—this is a perennial issue in aesthetics which certainly cannot be settled within the present context. Rather,
the problem is whether this position is compatible with some of
the main principles of Dewey's aesthetics and some of the chief
emphases of his general and educational philosophy.

An initial doubt concerning art's ability to provide for unhindered and complete communication can be raised simply
by recalling the uncertain status in Dewey's thought of the work
of art as a public object. If the "work of art" is what each
percipient freely creates during his interaction with the art
object, it should follow that the resultant meaning of the work
is whatever it means to that person at that particular time. It
is not easy to imagine how anything this ineffable and irre-
trievable could contribute to community of experience and a
sharing of meanings.

However, the more interesting question is how well Dewey's
conviction that the arts are the only media of pure and undefiled communication can maintain itself in the face of his un-

[38] *Ibid.*, p. 244.

[39] *Ibid.*, p. 105. One may wonder how this could be reconciled with
the assertion that "scientific method is the only authentic means at our
command for getting at the significance of our everyday experiences in
the world in which we live" (Dewey, *Experience and Education* [New
York: Macmillan, 1956], pp. 111–12). If works of art are the best
instruments for the communication of meaning, it should also be
possible to say of them that they provide a way of getting at the significance of everyday experience. But what would this do to the primacy
of scientific method?

relenting differentiation between knowledge (associated with intelligence, mediation, inquiry, scientific or experimental method, instrumentality, etc.) and the aesthetic (associated with immediacy, the qualitative, felt value, intrinsic meanings, etc.).

It might be helpful to inquire first just what Dewey could have meant by saying that in art "meaning is as inherent in immediate experience as that of a flower garden." How can a flower garden have meaning? A particular garden may mean a great deal to a particular person because of the memories and images it evokes. But this is meaning by association; it is neither immediate nor intrinsic. One could also say that a flower garden means something like "man creating beauty in the environment." Yet this type of meaning is arrived at via a cognitive process: the garden is recognized as an artifact and then classified among those transformations of the environment which can be said to manifest a concern for beauty. And there is nothing unmediated about this, either. There may be no sense at all in which a flower garden can be thought of as possessing meaning, and Dewey may simply have chosen a poor example. A flower garden, like most natural and man-made objects and like many works of art, can certainly be enjoyed aesthetically in terms of its design, color, and other sensuous and formal properties without being expected to have or express meaning. Therefore, a first modification of Dewey's sweeping claim for art's benefits might be to propose that communication of meanings is not a legitimate function of *all* works of art.

This is not to deny that many works of art, the great masterpieces among them, are frequently conceded to have, express, or convey messages, import, meanings, etc. Dewey says this meaning is immediately enjoyed and hence would not be knowledge; he also contends that there is to be participation, sharing, communication. How can this be? The difficulty is not easily enunciated in an age so hospitable to talk about "meaningful experiences." But supposing that all beholders of a particular work of art came to agree that it was "meaningful," perhaps even very much so, what are they sharing? What has been communicated? It is now suggested that "is meaningful" can also translate into "has *a* meaning," "means *something*," and that this is a more apt conception of "meaning" in art. A work of art is not really characterized by a free-floating, generalized meaningfulness. It does not just mean; one usually feels that it has the capacity to enrich awareness in a more or less definite way (though one would not expect to find an *exact* verbal equivalent of that meaning). Furthermore, since Dewey insists that the meanings which come through in experiences with works of art are capable of being held in common, he should also have wanted to admit that persons who share in being affected in certain ways by certain art objects would wish to converse about the enlightenment they have received, to communicate and compare their ideas. All of which adds up to a first question: if it can be asserted that art brings about fairly specific forms of enlightenment which, moreover, must at least convey an impression of intersubjectivity to arouse expectations of communication and sharing of experiences, how reasonable is it to deny art status as some *form of knowing?*

The same question may be approached via a somewhat different route by asking how sensible it is to insist that meaning in art is immediate, i.e., unmediated and noncognitive. Many philosophers of art would agree with Dewey's view that immediacy is what contrasts the aesthetic most strikingly with ordinary experience and hence is a feature to be retained at all theoretical cost. But there is another way of thinking, sometimes identified as "semiotic aesthetics," of which a vastly simplified version follows. According to this position meaning is not an attribute of a work of art in the way its colors, shapes, textures, etc., are. What a work of art expresses or means somehow (just how is another puzzle in aesthetics) emerges from the totality of its properties and is such that any major change in the work's qualities would also produce a change in meaning. It is because meaning or expressiveness is so closely dependent upon the work's perceptual features that it has come to be thought of as intrinsic, as a possession of the work; there is, in other words, no consciousness of having gone "behind" the work to what it stands for. And it is of course true that, since each work of art is individual and signifies whatever it does mean or express through the unique constellation of its qualities, it is most unlike a character in a rule-governed symbolic system such as discursive language, as was duly noted by Dewey. Nonetheless, as the work of art is other than that which it refers to, expresses, or exemplifies metaphorically, there is enough conceptual distance in the aesthetic situation to satisfy the logical requirements of symbolization, though it is symbolization of a peculiar kind.[40] But a symbolic process is a cognitive process. Consequently, the apprehension of meaning in art is thought of more appropriately as being mediated, cognitive—the result of an attempt to make sense of a datum in the environment—than as being of the nature of an immediate, emotional, or reflex-like response to a stimulus.

Since, as mentioned before, the debate concerning immediately embodied versus mediated meaning (or no meaning at all) in the arts is very much alive, it would be arbitrary to insist that Dewey *ought* to have taken a stand on the cognitive, mediated side of the issue. However, there is some justification for holding that this would indeed have given him a more cohesive aesthetic, and it is found in his allegation that works of art are the *most complete* form of communication. "To communicate" is what is sometimes called a success verb, for it makes sense to say that a person is communicating only when his message is being received and comprehended. Successful and complete communication, then, would seem to involve a sender, a message, a medium, and a recipient of the message who comes to understand its import. It is suggested that this fairly extended chain of relations is explained more plausibly in terms of stages in a process than in terms of a series of unrelated flashes of immediate awareness. Furthermore, if communication is not complete until understanding has been accomplished, there ought to be some method for ensuring success and criteria for determining it. But "method" and "criteria" are concepts commonly associated with deliberate, mediated activities. The point here is not to argue that methods or procedures

---

[40] A recent work on the symbolic processes in art is Nelson Goodman's *Languages of Art: An Approach to a Theory of Symbols* (Indianapolis: Bobbs-Merrill, 1968).

of verification similar to those in the sciences should or could apply to the arts—that there is or should be a way of determining unequivocally what a work of art means and a procedure for making sure everyone "gets" that meaning. Rather, the intention has been to suggest that Dewey's strong emphasis on complete communication through art is somehow at odds with his equally strong emphasis on the immediacy of the aesthetic.

To summarize the arguments in connection with immediacy: If art *is to perform* the communication function Dewey has assigned to it, it is difficult to see how it can be said to do so successfully without some *form of mediation* being involved. And if art *does in fact operate* in the manner described by Dewey, i.e., if it allows persons truly to share in meanings, then it is difficult to see why this may not be considered as a *form of knowing*. Briefly, Dewey's wise and generous view of the role of the arts in the life of the individual and society echoes the general tone of his educational and philosophical concerns but seems to be undermined by his separation of art from knowing.

In conclusion, there are two areas in which the foregoing explorations might have some significance for aesthetic education. First is the practical conduct of art teaching. It was found that on the popularly accepted view of Dewey's aesthetics, art is dissolved into experience in general, thus no special subject of instruction seems to remain. In Dewey's more specialized version of the aesthetic, the work of art as a public object disappears in an experience so private and esoteric that it is hard to estimate just what pedagogical measures could be of much help.

Second, there is the matter of a workable philosophical foundation for aesthetic education. If the preceding pages have succeeded in making any point at all, it should have been to discourage attempts at constructing a theoretical base for teaching in the arts upon Dewey's thought. For it would be exceedingly difficult to make such a foundation consistent with three equally "Deweyan" aspects: (1) the major emphases in his social and educational thought, specifically (*a*) intelligence and its instrumental nature, (*b*) growth and the continuity of experience, and (*c*) the acquisition of shared meanings through deliberate and intelligent social interaction; (2) some of the theoretical presuppositions of his aesthetics, specifically (*a*) the claim that the aesthetic is not a form of knowing, (*b*) the essentially discontinuous, self-enclosed nature of aesthetic experience, and (*c*) the private, subjective character of the "work of art" and its meaning; (3) many of the insightful things Dewey has written about the arts which have not received attention here and which are not necessarily in harmony with either (1) or (2), above.

THE CULTURAL IMPORTANCE OF THE ARTS

Susanne Langer

Every culture develops some kind of art as surely as it develops language. Some primitive cultures have no real mythology or religion, but all have some art—dance, song, design (sometimes only on tools or on the human body). Dance, above all, seems to be the oldest elaborated art.

The ancient ubiquitous character of art contrasts sharply with the prevalent idea that art is a luxury product of civilization, a cultural frill, a piece of social veneer.

It fits better with the conviction held by most artists, that art is the epitome of human life, the truest record of insight and feeling, and that the strongest military or economic society without art is poor in comparison with the most primitive tribe of savage painters, dancers, or idol-carvers. Wherever a society has really achieved culture (in the ethnological sense, not the popular sense of "social form") it has begotten art, not late in its career, but at the very inception of it.

Art is, indeed, the spearhead of human development, social and individual. The vulgarization of art is the surest symptom of ethnic decline. The growth of a new art or even a great and radically new style always bespeaks a young and vigorous mind, whether collective or single

What sort of thing is art, that it should play such a leading role in human development? It is not an intellectual pursuit, but is necessary to intellectual life; it is not religion, but grows up with religion, serves it, and in large measure determines it.

We cannot enter here on a long discussion of what has been claimed as the essence of art, the true nature of art, or its defining functions; in a single lecture dealing with one aspect of art, namely its cultural influence, I can only give you by way

From M. F. Andrews, ed., *Aesthetic Form and Education* (Syracuse, 1958), pp. 1–18. Repinted by permission of Syracuse University Press and the author.

of preamble my own definition of art, with categorical brevity. This does not mean that I set up this definition in a categorical spirit, but only that we have no time to debate it, so you are asked to accept it as an assumption underlying these reflections.

"Art" in the sense here intended—that is, the generic term subsuming painting, sculpture, architecture, music, dance, literature, drama, and film—may be defined as the practice of creating perceptible forms expressive of human feeling. I say "perceptible" rather than "sensuous" forms because some works of art are given to imagination rather than to the outward senses. A novel, for instance, usually is read silently with the eye, but is not made for vision, as a painting is; and though sound plays a vital part in poetry, words even in poetry are not essentially sonorous structures like music. Dance requires to be seen, but its appeal is to deeper centers of sensation. The difference between dance and mobile sculpture makes this immediately apparent. But all works of art are purely perceptible forms that seem to embody some sort of feeling.

"Feeling" as I am using it here covers much more than it does in the technical vocabulary of psychology, where it denotes only pleasure and pain, or even in the shifting limits of ordinary discourse, where it sometimes means sensation (as when one says a paralyzed limb has no feeling in it), sometimes sensibility (as we speak of hurting someone's feelings), sometimes emotion (e.g., as a situation is said to harrow your feelings, or to evoke tender feeling), or a directed emotional attitude (we say we feel strongly *about* something), or even our general mental or physical condition, feeling well or ill, blue, or a bit above ourselves. As I use the word, in defining art as the creation of perceptible forms expressive of human feeling, it takes in all those meanings; it applies to everything that may be felt.

Another word in the definition that might be questioned is "creation." I think it is justified, not pretentious, as perhaps it sounds; but that issue is slightly beside the point here, so let us shelve it. If anyone prefers to speak of the "making" or "construction" of expressive forms, that will do here just as well.

What does have to be understood is the meaning of "form,"

and more particularly "expressive form"; for that involves the very nature of art and therefore the question of its cultural importance.

The word "form" has several current uses; most of them have some relation to the sense in which I am using it here, though a few such as "a form to be filled in for tax purposes" or "a mere matter of form" are fairly remote, being quite specialized. Since we are speaking of art, it might be good to point out that the meaning of stylistic pattern—"the sonata form," "the sonnet form"—is not the one I am assuming here.

I am using the word in a simpler sense, which it has when you say, on a foggy night, that you see dimly moving forms in the mist; one of them emerges clearly and is the form of a man. The trees are gigantic forms; the rills of rain trace sinuous forms on the window pane. The rills are not fixed things; they are forms of motion. When you watch gnats weaving in the air, or flocks of birds wheeling overhead, you see dynamic forms— forms made by motion.

It is in this sense of an apparition given to our perception that a work of art is a form. It may be a permanent form like a building or a vase or a picture, or a transient, dynamic form like a melody or a dance, or even a form given to imagination, like the passage of purely imaginary, apparent events that constitutes a literary work. But it is always a perceptible, self-identical whole; like a natural being, it has a character of organic unity, self-sufficiency, individual reality. And it is thus, as an appearance, that a work of art is good or bad or perhaps only rather poor; as an appearance, not as a comment on things beyond it in the world, nor as a reminder of them.

This, then, is what I mean by "form"; but what is meant by calling such forms "expressive of human feeling"? How do apparitions "express" anything—feeling or anything else? First of all, let us ask just what is meant here by "express"; what sort of "expression" we are talking about.

The word "expression" has two principal meanings: in one sense it means self-expression—giving vent to our feelings. In this sense it refers to a symptom of what we feel. Self-expression is a spontaneous reaction to an actual, present situation, an event, the company we are in, things people say, or what the weather does to us; it bespeaks the physical and mental state we are in and the emotions that stir us.

In another sense, however, "expression" means the presentation of an idea, usually by the proper and apt use of words. But a device for presenting an idea is what we call a symbol, not a symptom. Thus a word is a symbol, and so is a meaningful combination of words.

A sentence, which is a special combination of words, expresses the idea of some state of affairs, real or imagined. Sentences are complicated symbols. Language will formulate new ideas as well as communicate old ones, so that all people know a lot of things that they have merely heard or read about. Symbolic expression, therefore, extends our knowledge beyond the scope of our actual experience.

If an idea is clearly conveyed by means of symbols, we say it is well expressed. A person may work for a long time to give his statement the best possible form, to find the exact words for what he means to say, and to carry his account or his argument most directly from one point to another. But a discourse so worked out is certainly not a spontaneous reaction. Giving expression to an idea is obviously a different thing from giving expression to feelings. You do not say of a man in a rage that his anger is well expressed. The symptoms just are what they are, there is no critical standard for symptoms. If, on the other hand, the angry man tries to tell you what he is fuming about, he will have to collect himself, curtail his emotional expression, and find words to express his ideas. For to tell a story coherently involves "expression" in quite a different sense: this sort of expression is not "self-expression," but may be called "conceptual expression."

Language, of course, is our prime instrument of conceptual expression. The things we can say are in effect the things we can think. Words are the terms of our thinking as well as the terms in which we present our thoughts, because they present the objects of thought to the thinker himself. Before language communicates ideas, it gives them form, makes them clear, and in fact makes them what they are. Whatever has a name is an object for thought. Without words, sense experience is only a flow of impressions, as subjective as our feelings; words make it objective, and carve it up into *things* and *facts* that we can note, remember, and think about. Language gives outward experience its form and makes it definite and clear.

There is, however, an important part of reality that is quite inaccessible to the formative influence of language: that is the realm of so-called inner experience, the life of feeling and emotion. The reason why language is so powerless here is not, as many people suppose, that feeling and emotion are irrational; on the contrary, they seem irrational because language does not help to make them conceivable, and most people cannot conceive anything without the logical scaffolding of words. The unfitness of language to convey subjective experience is a somewhat technical subject, easier for logicians to understand than for artists; but the gist of it is that the form of language does not reflect the natural form of feeling, so we cannot shape any extensive concepts of feeling with the help of ordinary, discursive language. Therefore the words whereby we refer to feeling only name very general kinds of inner experience—excitement, calm, joy, sorrow, love, hate, etc. But there is no language to describe just how one joy differs, sometimes radically, from another. The real nature of feeling is something language as such —as discursive symbolism—cannot render.

For this reason, the phenomena of feeling and emotion are usually treated by philosophers as irrational. The only pattern discursive thought can find in them is the pattern of outward events that occasion them. There are different degrees of fear, but they are thought of as so many degrees of the same simple feeling.

But human feeling is a fabric, not a vague mass. It has an intricate dynamic pattern, possible combinations, and new emergent phenomena. It is a pattern of organically interdependent and interdetermined tensions and resolutions, a pattern of almost infinitely complex activation and cadence. To it belongs the whole gamut of our sensibility, the sense of straining thought, all mental attitude and motor set. Those are the deeper reaches that underlie the surface waves of our emotion and make human life a life of feeling instead of an unconscious metabolic existence interrupted by feelings.

It is, I think, this dynamic pattern that finds its formal expression in the arts. The expressiveness of art is like that of a symbol, not that of an emotional symptom; it is as a formulation of feeling for our conception that a work of art is properly said to be expressive. It may serve somebody's need of self-expression besides; but that is not what makes it good or bad art. In a special sense one may call a work of art a symbol of feeling, for, like a symbol, it formulates our ideas of inward experience, as discourse formulates our ideas of things and facts in the outside world. A work of art differs from a genuine symbol—that is, a symbol in the full and usual sense—in that it does not point beyond itself to something else. Its relation to feeling is a rather special one that we cannot undertake to analyze here; in effect, the feeling it expresses appears to be directly given with it—as the sense of a true metaphor, or the value of a religious myth—and is not separable from its expression. We speak of the feeling *of,* or the feeling *in,* a work of art, not the feeling it means. And we speak truly; a work of art presents something like a direct vision of vitality, emotion, subjective reality.

The primary function of art is to objectify feeling so we can contemplate and understand it. It is the formulation of so-called inward experience, the "inner life," that is impossible to achieve by discursive thought, because its forms are incommensurable with the forms of language and all its derivatives (e.g., mathematics, symbolic logic). Art objectifies the sentience and desire, self-consciousness and world-consciousness, emotions and moods that are generally regarded as irrational because words cannot give us clear ideas of them. But the premise tacitly assumed in such a judgment—namely, that anything language cannot express is formless and irrational—seems to me to be an error. I believe the life of feeling is not irrational; its logical forms are merely very different from the structures of discourse. But they are so much like the dynamic forms of art that art is their natural symbol. Through plastic works, music, fiction, dance, or dramatic forms we can conceive what vitality and emotion feel like.

This brings us, at last, to the question of the cultural importance of the arts. Why is art so apt to be the vanguard of cultural advance, as it was in Egypt, in Greece, in Christian Europe (think of Gregorian music and Gothic architecture), in Renaissance Italy—not to speculate about ancient cavemen, whose art is all that we know of them? One thinks of culture as economic increase, social organization, the gradual ascendancy of rational thinking and scientific control of nature over superstitious imagination and magical practices. But art is not practical; it is neither philosophy nor science; it is not religion, morality, nor even social comment (as many drama critics take comedy to be). What does it contribute to culture that could be of major importance?

It merely presents forms—sometimes intangible forms—to imagination. Its direct appeal is to that faculty, or function, that Lord Bacon considered the chief stumbling block in the way of reason, that enlightened writers like Stuart Chase never tire of condemning as the source of all nonsense and bizarre erroneous beliefs. And so it is; but it is also the source of all insight and true beliefs. Imagination is probably the oldest mental trait that is typically human—older than discursive reason; it is probably the common source of dream, reason, religion, and all true general observation. It is this primitive human power—imagination—that engenders the arts and is in turn directly affected by their products.

Somewhere at the animalian starting line of human evolution lie the beginnings of that supreme instrument of the mind—language. We think of it as a device for communication among the members of a society. But communication is only one, and perhaps not even the first, of its functions. The first thing it does is to break up what William James called the "blooming, buzzing confusion" of sense perception into units and groups, events and chains of events—things and relations, causes and effects. All these patterns are imposed on our experience by language. We think, as we speak, in terms of objects and their relations.

But the process of breaking up our sense experience in this way, making reality conceivable, memorable, sometimes even predictable, is a process of imagination. Primitive conception is imagination. Language and imagination grow up together in a reciprocal tutelage.

What discursive symbolism—language in its literal use—does for our awareness of things about us and our own relation to them, the arts do for our awareness of subjective reality, feeling, and emotion; they give form to inward experiences and thus make them conceivable. The only way we can really envisage vital movement, the stirring and growth and passage of emotion, and ultimately the whole direct sense of human life, is in artistic terms. A musical person thinks of emotions musically. They cannot be discursively talked about above a very general level. But they may nonetheless be known—objectively set forth, publicly known—and there is nothing necessarily confused or formless about emotions.

As soon as the natural forms of subjective experience are abstracted to the point of symbolic presentation, we can use those forms to imagine feeling and understand its nature. Self-knowledge, insight into all phases of life and mind, springs from artistic imagination. That is the cognitive value of the arts.

But their influence on human life goes deeper than the intellectual level. As language actually gives form to our sense-experience, grouping our impressions around those things which have names and fitting sensations to the qualities that have adjectival names, and so on, the arts we live with—our picture books and stories and the music we hear—actually form our emotive experience. Every generation has its styles of feeling. One age shudders and blushes and faints, another swaggers, still another is godlike in a universal indifference. These styles in actual emotion are not insincere. They are largely unconscious —determined by many social causes, but *shaped* by artists, usually popular artists of the screen, the jukebox, the shop window, and the picture magazine. (That, rather than incitement to crime, is my objection to the comics.) Irwin Edman remarks in one of his books that our emotions are largely Shakespeare's poetry.

This influence of art on life gives us an indication why a period of efflorescence in the arts is apt to lead a cultural advance: it formulates a new way of feeling, and that is the beginning of a cultural age. It suggests another matter for reflection, too: that a wide neglect of artistic education is a neglect in the education of feeling. Most people are so imbued with the idea that feeling is a formless total organic excitement in men as in animals that the idea of educating feeling, developing its scope and quality, seems odd to them, if not absurd. It is really, I think, at the very heart of personal education.

There is one other function of the arts that benefits not so much the advance of culture as its stabilization; an influence on individual lives. This function is the converse and complement of the objectification of feeling, the driving force of creation in art: it is the education of vision that we receive in seeing, hearing, reading works of art—the development of the artist's eye that assimilates ordinary sights (or sounds, motions, or events) to inward vision and lends expressiveness and emotional import to the world. Wherever art takes a motif from actuality—a flowering branch, a bit of landscape, a historic event or a personal memory, any model or theme from life—it transforms it into a piece of imagination and imbues its image with artistic vitality. The result is an impregnation of ordinary reality with the significance of created form. This is the subjectification of nature that makes reality itself a symbol of life and feeling.

The arts objectify subjective reality and subjectify outward experience of nature. Art education is the education of feeling, and a society that neglects it gives itself up to formless emotion. Bad art is corruption of feeling. This is a large factor in the irrationalism which dictators and demagogues exploit.

FURTHER READING

Beardsley, Monroe C. *Aesthetics: Problems in the Philosophy of Criticism.* New York: Harcourt, Brace & World, Inc., 1958. A major work in philosophical aesthetics.

————. *Aesthetics from Classical Greece to the Present.* New York: Macmillan, 1966. Now the standard history of the field. Excellent for discussions of Plato and Aristotle.

Coleman, Francis J., ed. *Contemporary Studies in Aesthetics.* New York: McGraw-Hill, 1968. Analytical studies in aesthetics.

Dworkin, Martin S. "Aesthetics and Education," *Journal of Aesthetic Education,* vol. 2, no. 1 (January 1968): 21–29. Also printed as the general editor's foreword in the Earl of Listowell, *Modern Aesthetics: An Historical Introduction.* New York: Teachers College Press, 1967, pp. ix–xvii. The latter concentrates on Italian, German, and French writers not readily available in English.

Eisner, Elliot W., and David W. Ecker, eds. *Readings in Art Education.* Waltham, Mass.: Blaisdell, 1966, Ch. 2 passim.

Hospers, John, ed. *Introductory Readings in Aesthetics.* New York: The Free Press, 1969. Prepared with the student rather than the philosopher in mind.

Jarrett, James R. *The Quest for Beauty.* Englewood Cliffs, N.J.: Prentice-Hall, 1957. An introductory text in aesthetics.

Osborne, Harold. *Aesthetics and Art Theory: An Historical Introduction.* New York: E. P. Dutton, 1968. A study in the history of ideas that examines aesthetic ideas in the work of artists, practical men, and theorists.

————. *The Art of Appreciation.* New York: Oxford University Press, 1970. Written with the practical aim of encouraging development of aesthetic percipience.

Schwadron, Abraham. *Aesthetics: Dimensions for Music Education.* Washington, D.C.: Music Educators National Conference, 1967.

Smith, Ralph A., ed. *Aesthetics and Criticism in Art Education: Problems in Defining, Explaining, and Evaluating Art.* Chicago: Rand-McNally, 1966.

————. *Aesthetic Concepts and Education.* Urbana: University of Illinois Press, 1970. Philosophical essays on aesthetic experience, feeling, tacit knowing, medium, intention, creativity, style, metaphor, etc.

Sparshott, Francis E. *The Structure of Aesthetics.* Toronto: University of Toronto Press, 1963. A major work in philosophical aesthetics.

Stolnitz, Jerome. *Aesthetics and Philosophy of Art Criticism.* Boston: Houghton Mifflin, 1960. An introductory text.

THE AIMS OF AESTHETIC EDUCATION

INTRODUCTION

The writings in this section may be appraised by deciding how successfully they perform the duties of a theory of educational aesthetics, to use Harry S. Broudy's expression, or, in D. W. Gotshalk's terms, the extent to which they satisfy the requirements of a domain interpretation of aesthetic education. The first two selections by Broudy and Gotshalk may thus be understood as attempts to map the basic aims and problem areas of aesthetic education.

Dividing his essay into discussions of the relevant classes of problems to be solved, Broudy, in an essay that marks the beginning of renewed systematic concern with educational aesthetics in philosophy of education, sets forth his ideas regarding the nature of aesthetic experience, the peripheral status of aesthetic education in the schools, the problem of justifying aesthetic education, and the problem of standards. For Broudy, a case for aesthetic education rests on showing what aesthetic experience can do for an individual in his quest for the good life. For the student this ultimately implies "the ability to derive pleasure from the contemplation of a wide variety of objects that can or do express in intuitale form the meaning of the more complex and subtle modes of experience; and, by such contemplation, help to produce the kind of life that finds its expression in the so-called 'good' works of art."

For D. W. Gotshalk fulfilling the requirements of a domain interpretation of aesthetic education implies (*a*) the characterization of the differentiating aim structure of aesthetic education, (*b*) the portrayal of what is involved in realizing this aim structure, and (*c*) the indication of the outcomes consistent with (*a*) and (*b*). Accordingly, he interprets the aim of aesthetic education as "the development of sensitivity to aesthetic values"— a type of sensitivity that raises intrinsic perception to a major activity valuable in its own right. Gotshalk properly points out that aesthetic education is a lifetime pursuit and that the schools' task is merely to seek general directions. In particular he thinks the aims of aesthetic education can be realized by carefully probing outstanding works of art in their depth, width, and height. The intent is not necessarily to celebrate masterpieces but to awaken and refine aesthetic response.

In the next essay R. A. and C. M. Smith concentrate on the justification question and conclude, after an explanation of Monroe Beardsley's distinction between intrinsic and inherent value, that aesthetic education may be justified on three levels: what it contributes to aesthetic enjoyment, the special kind of awareness aesthetic experience provides, and the special form of knowledge works of art afford. This latter level is doubtless the most difficult to support, but if it can be defended, the authors maintain, it is the best argument the educator has to help advance aesthetic studies in the schools. When interpreted in appropriate detail, the grounds on which aesthetic education can be justified become aims and outcomes of aesthetic instruction.

In a comprehensive essay E. F. Kaelin explains the relations between philosophical aesthetics and aesthetic education as a subdomain of educational theory and of both of these to the actual conduct of teaching-learning. Kaelin's peculiar contribution to educational aesthetics derives from his studies in phenomenology, a type of philosophical inquiry not familiar to most American students. For Kaelin, the task of aesthetic educators is to provide guidance in the art of making aesthetic judgments which, when properly understood, result not only in intensified and clarified experiences that are intrinsically satisfying to individuals having them, but also in a variety of social benefits.

The special kind of knowledge that is believed to accrue through the experience of art is analyzed by L. A. Reid, who argues that "aesthetic experience is a kind of knowledge *sui generis,* knowledge of meaning wholly embodied in the aesthetic object. . . ." Reid thinks his notion of "embodied meaning" is an improvement over Susanne Langer's idea of "symbolic form."

A noncognitive view of art's function, in contrast to Reid's cognitive view, is set forth in David W. Ecker's account of qualitative intelligence, a concept advanced by a group of educational philosophers who over the past two decades have been attempting to extend certain ideas expressed in Dewey's later philosophical works. As in Reid, the central task is to explain the special functioning of the properties of works of art. For Ecker this involves an explanation of a work of art as a qualitative symbol. Such symbols are created by artists who exercise qualitative problem-solving capacities.

Iredell Jenkins indicates the ways in which aesthetic education may be said to contribute to moral refinement. Taking the aesthetic to be one of three coordinate ways of exploring the world (the other two being the cognitive and the affective), he explains what we discover in works of art and the diverse ways in which we do it. In particular men are disposed to be influenced by things which they experience with heightened concern and interest, and the vividness with which good art highlights actuality inevitably colors a person's attitudes and conduct. Thus good art has important educative values while pseudo-art is anti-educative. Further, just as society deems it important to control the ill effects of pseudo-science and pseudo-technology, so also, Jenkins thinks, it should be concerned about the possible harmful consequences of pseudo-art. The outcomes of aesthetic education for Jenkins have both a facilitating and an inhibitive character. In connection with the former, aesthetic education permits access to the rich content of art, while with regard to the latter it functions to control aesthetic disvalue.

Exemplifying the foregoing thesis that response to art affects our interpretation of life, Maxine Greene and James L. Jarrett emphasize human understanding and personal or self-knowledge as important aims of literature education. By imaginatively identifying with the characters and situations in fiction we gain insight into others and ourselves. Greene in particular thinks the literary experience conveys a sense of what it is like to be alive at a certain moment in time, an experience that can help students to confront their inner voices and ultimately to shed conventional modes of being. This view is shared by Jarrett, who emphasizes that it is the special (dramatic) ways authors select and shape their situations which is responsible for inducing responses that go beyond those of the casual onlooker in ordinary life.

Rudolf Arnheim endorses the purpose of art posited by others in this section insofar as he believes art can provide insight into our common humanity. He concludes, after a critical review of prevalent psychological theories of art, that not only literature but also abstract art can accomplish this end. In the formal properties of abstract art we experience "the behavior of basic patterns of forces characteristic of what happens inside and outside all of us."

Finally, F. E. Sparshott brings together the large number of objectives that can be stated for aesthetic education and discusses possible conflicts among them. While recent theorizing in philosophical aesthetics has tended to emphasize the distinctiveness of each of the arts rather than their common properties, Sparshott believes that this is merely current philosophic fashion and that the arts may be grouped together for educational purposes by virtue of the fact that they pose common problems for teaching and learning. In the study of all the arts, habits of perceptual attention must be changed and refined, appreciation as well as understanding must be developed (which implies the cultivation of both analytic and synoptic powers), and in all the arts similar problems of learner resistance and personality must be dealt with. In general, Sparshott concludes, "doubts about aesthetic education based on the supposed lack of unity of the arts seem to have less substance than the less notorious diversities of aim. . . ."

SOME DUTIES OF A THEORY OF
EDUCATIONAL AESTHETICS

Harry S. Broudy

The choice of this topic was prompted by the cavalier attitude of some educational philosophers toward the aesthetic modes of experience; an attitude not unlike that entertained by busy, high-minded husbands toward their wives—an attitude of inconspicuous appreciation that is not allowed to interefere with the zeal to defy, defend, or denounce communism, build democracy, fight for causes, and improve the social order. Now, important as all these indubitably are, I submit that a philosophy of education does not discharge its obligation in the aesthetic area with a few fine phrases about "appreciation." What follows is an outline of the requirements of an educational aesthetic theory that does try to fulfill such an obligation.

A theory of aesthetics is no intellectual lady of leisure, but a theory of educational aesthetics is a positive drudge. Not only does it have to be conversant with the difficulties peculiar to aesthetics proper, but it is also beset by the special problems that swarm whenever one generation tries to influence the taste of another.

Types of Relevant Problems

Three classes of tasks would seem to be relevant to a well-developed theory of educational aesthetics. First, it has the duty of defining aesthetic experience in such a way that its relations to, and distinctions from, other modes of experience become articulate. Such logical dissection is properly the province of aesthetics itself, but the educational philosopher must at least decide, and rationally if possible, which type of aesthetic theory he shall espouse or reject.

In the second place, the theory has to say something intelli-

From *Educational Theory*, vol. 1, no. 3 (November 1951): 190–98. Reprinted by permission of *Educational Theory* and the author.

gent about such questions as: Why does popular taste vary so much from the taste of the "highbrows"? Are there any grounds for asserting that one art object is better than another? What are these grounds? These and allied questions are, perhaps, not purely educational ones, but neither are they purely aesthetic. They lead us into philosophical labyrinths, and even if it were true that we come out of them no wiser than we went in, the journey is unavoidable.

This cluster of questions impinges also on what has been called the sociology of aesthetics, because obviously tastes and standards have something to do with a culture. And the moment it is asked how people get their taste or their lack of it, the searchlight swings to education. But sooner or later it also swings to aesthetics, philosophy in general, psychology, sociology, anthropology, and, indeed, to every discipline that is not wholly trivial. For what discipline, pray tell, does not have its finger in the cultural pie?

A third group of problems are more distinctively educational. For example: How shall we account for the peripheral place of aesthetics in our educational scheme? Why do twelve years of propaganda on behalf of the "finer" things in music, art, literature, and drama produce so little change in the Hooper ratings, sales of periodicals, books, the box office receipts of movies, plays? Why is it that so many of our secondary school graduates become or remain illiterate in most of the aesthetic languages? Why is it that the stereotyped speech, dress, song style, art, triumphs so inexorably in the taste of so many of our people? By judicious subdivision, this list can be lengthened, but it may serve as a sample of the sort of problems which a well-developed theory of educational aesthetics cannot dodge. It goes without saying that our theory must do all this accounting for, and explaining of, with an economy of means and simplicity of method that put contending theories to logical and methodological rout.

This paper, at the discretion of the author, is not required to present such a well-developed theory of educational aesthetics. It need not, therefore, practice what it preaches. There is, however, an obligation to *illustrate* how such a theory would operate.

The Problem of the Nature of Aesthetic Experience

As a sample of the first kind of problem, let us probe a bit into the nature of the aesthetic experience. There is a substantial, although perhaps not universal, agreement that the aesthetic experience is not to be identified with the intellectual processes of relating propositions to each other, or to the discovering of hitherto unknown relations among phenomena. Nor is it to be identified with the practical experience of seeking means to ends. Certainly, it is not primarily an economic activity, nor a religious one.

Having said this much, have we also said that the aesthetic experience is unrelated to the true, the good, and the holy? There is no time to argue this matter now. For myself, it seems more congenial to assume with Plato that the true, good, and beautiful are coordinate revelations of a metaphysical unity, so that if we find beauty that is evil and falsehood that is good, our knowledge of reality is still incomplete. Consider these quotations:

> *Fritz Glarner:* I'm trying to bring about a purer, closer understanding between form and space, which are equivalents.
> *Jimmy Ernst:* He must crystallize his expression to bare essentials.
> *William Keinbosch:* I try to get at the inner reality by careful observation of outer reality.
> *Stuart Davis:* He seeks the most direct way of expressing direct perception of an object, perceiving the reality of that object in terms of the painting of it.
> *Willem de Kooning:* Painting isn't just the visual thing that reaches your retina—it's what is behind it and in it.
> *Robert Motherwell:* My painting takes on this particular abstract quality because this way I can express my search for a direct mystical experience.

These six quotations sound like excerpts from treatises on metaphysics—and not very recent metaphysics at that—yet they are excerpts from statements by six abstractionists in defense of their art made as late as January 21, 1951, in the *New York Times Magazine,* and I venture to guess that Plato would have found them congenial to his own views on art.

What then is the aesthetic experience? I tend to agree with Ducasse in the use of the term *aesthetic activity* to cover (*a*) the creating of works of aesthetic art, (*b*) aesthetic contemplation, and (*c*) aesthetic appreciation.

To create a work of aesthetic art is simply to use skill to produce objects intended for aesthetic contemplation. Aesthetic contemplation, in turn, is

> . . . a combination of attention with a certain interest: To contemplate aesthetically an object one attends to is to be at the moment interested in, and as it were to listen for, the particular sensations, feelings, moods, emotions, sentiments, or other directly intuitable qualities, which the object exhibits or expresses.[1]

Aesthetic appreciation, according to Ducasse, "whether analytical or ingenuous, is valuation of an object in terms of the pleasure or displeasure it give us in the mere contemplation." [2]

For education, the three phases of aesthetic activity need to be clearly distinguished. Aesthetic contemplation, as Ducasse defines it, requires no special pedagogical effort, and neither do aesthetic creation or appreciation, for we are all indulging in these spontaneously every time we *note* the appearance of anything, or whenever we sweep a floor, or express a liking or dislike for the appearance of anything. If formal education has any business in this area, then it is somehow to modify or direct the doing of what comes naturally.

In the second place, education for creating works of aesthetic art is not the same as education for aesthetic contemplation or appreciation. Because these three phases of aesthetic activity are *relatively* independent variables, it pays to be clear as to the degree of facility or competence we propose to achieve in each area.

I would suggest that with respect to aesthetic *creativity,* the educational goal is the ability to objectify in sensuous form the emotional significance of experience *to the artist's own satisfaction.* If another can contemplate it aesthetically and derive plea-

[1] C. J. Ducasse, "Aesthetics and the Aesthetic Activities," *The Journal of Aesthetics and Art Criticism,* vol. 5, no. 4 (1947): 166.
[2] *Ibid.,* p. 167.

sure from so doing, i.e., if there is a successful communication, that is all to the good—but the latter is not essential. Creative art whose purpose is self-expression *only* need not be *good* by any *universal* standard.

With respect to aesthetic contemplation, the goal is reciprocally two-fold: the ability to derive pleasure from the contemplation of a wide variety of objects that can or do express in intuitable form the meaning of the more complex and subtle modes of experience; and, by such contemplation, help to produce the kind of life that finds its expression in the so-called "good" works of art.

Aesthetic appreciation can mean anything from the history of art to the study of the sex habits of artists. Educationally, *study about* art objects is instrumental to creativity and contemplation. Courses in art appreciation are depreciated at the moment, but they can and often do serve as the gateway to genuine aesthetic experience. Indeed, some art products are opaque until analysis of an admittedly nonaesthetic nature makes the aesthetic communication possible; e.g., the beauties of Greek poetry to one who has no knowledge of Greek, the theory of nonrepresentational art to people who know no other kinds, or the idioms and pronunciations of Chaucerian English to most Englishmen.

The Problem of the Peripheral Status of Aesthetic Education

Even casual reflection on the universality and indispensability of aesthetic activity in all its phases would lead us to expect that it would enjoy high priority in any educational scheme. When, therefore, a culture so rich and complex as ours still regards aesthetic education as a desirable nonessential, explanations are in order.

A well-developed theory should (1) show that this peripheral status of aesthetic education is a fact, (2) account for apparent exceptions to the generalization, such as the thriving state of commercial art, and the centrality of aesthetic activity in the kindergarten and nursery school, (3) account for the discrepancy between the almost incessant aesthetic activity of all human beings in their daily living and their malaise in the presence of highbrow art, and (4) trace the historic circumstances that presumably produced the situation under discussion.

That aesthetic education is still a second-rate citizen in the educational republic is witnessed by its expendability in times of economic distress. Adequate disposal of the apparent exceptions I cannot undertake here, although I believe it can be done; the question of highbrow and otherbrow art is taken up a little later. The historic considerations I shall have to dismiss with the following suggestions:

1. Biological life can go on without cultivated aesthetic activity. It is not essential to life, however indispensable it may be to the good life. The universal hunger for aesthetic experience can be satisfied by natural objects and spontaneous creations that do not need formal instruction. Folk art is an example.

2. The religious views of the founders of this country, or at least some of them, made it inevitable that the aesthetic experience would be regarded as frivolous; even the religious life itself was pretty well purged of aesthetically satisfying elements. It is not so long ago that a career in the arts was viewed as a certain road not only to poverty but to damnation as well.

3. Our history as a pioneering people who had to conquer a continent before they could enjoy it put a premium on an activistic, pragmatic, technological attitude that was bound to brand the aesthetic experience as a slightly effeminate irrelevance.

4. Finally, our inability to complete the conquest of the material environment, or more accurately, the difficulty of knowing when the conquest is properly over, helps to keep the aesthetic aspect of life in its status of a deferred *desideratum*.

The Problems of Justifying Aesthetic Education

If the theory we are constructing has been successful in proving that aesthetic education is being neglected, and if it has been plausible in its explanation of this neglect, it now faces the further problem of justifying any attempts to alter the situation. Now, to justify what has already been defined as either self-justifying or nonaesthetic is no mean trick, and I leave this dialectical opportunity with no little regret.

A number of possible justifying arguments come to mind: We can point out the generic unity of all creative activity and argue that there can be transfer among its diverse modes. Thus invention, scientific thinking, and aesthetic creation do have in common a facility for the rearranging of previously experienced elements into new configurations. When Sandburg says that "the fog comes on little cat feet," and a child calls eraser scraps "mistake dust," and a painter shows the four sides of a barn at once, and a writer speaks of something as being as "relentless as a taximeter," and a man converts a runner into a wheel, and a Newton sees the analogy between apples and planets, there is manifest an activity of mind that seems to be of the same weave despite the differences of coloration.

It may very well be that our indifferent success with creativity in the nonaesthetic modes may be related to our neglect of its cultivation in the aesthetic modes. Thus the flexibility we need to think scientifically, or to make new and better mousetraps, is not furthered by permitting early congealment in our modes of speech, dress, music, etc.

Another line of argument may be called psychoanalytic or mental hygienic. It is simply the old observation that aesthetic expression or activity is the most traditional and most successful form of sublimation the race has yet found. We can, with great plausibility, insist that our adolescents in secondary education are driven into less desirable detours by the itches of this period precisely because of their aesthetic inadequacies.

Another argument may be called the humanistic one. It says that the scope and quality of human experience are enriched through the vicarious experience afforded by the art products of the race.

Any or all of these arguments are good as far as I am concerned, because I believe them to be true, but there is one that should not be omitted. It is, briefly, that unaided by formal education, aesthetic experience is likely to be restricted to the easy, the obvious, the ordinary, the superficial, the stereotyped. If anyone is disposed to reply, "So what?" I confess that I would not know how to answer, except to *promise* that life will be more satisfying if matters are otherwise arranged.

Why Tastes Remain "Low"

Now would be the time to proceed with a bill of particulars designed to produce the good life via aesthetic education. There remain, however, a number of facts that at face value do not make sense. The problem is to find a hypothesis that will remedy this. The facts are these:

1. The creative spontaneity of young children manifested so freely in all media of aesthetic activity—song, dance, drawing, drama—somehow seems to peter out by the time of adolescence.

2. This drying up of artistic originality is accompanied by a shrinking of aesthetic literacy, so that most adolescents are lucky if they can express themselves to their own or anyone else's satisfaction even in one medium—and, of course, some can't manage even one.

3. The third fact to be explained would be the scant success of formal public education in effecting any widespread genuine fondness for the "finer" flowers of art, literature, drama, and music.

To account for these and kindred facts, I would suggest the hypothesis that aesthetic activity for most people is arrested at the intellectual and emotional level of adolescence, and that this arrest is caused by such factors—among others—as the lag of techniques behind the need for expression and the pressure of socially unavoidable stereotypes. Now, if this hypothesis is correct, it ought to follow that popular art should be adolescent in theme and in the demands it makes on the individual's intellectual and emotional development in general, and on his artistic equipment in particular.

Educators have been rightly impressed with the artistic originality and facility of children, and some of them have elevated this fact into an educational principle, viz., to prolong this aesthetic fluency as long as possible by refraining from imposing any requirement other than the satisfaction of the creator. And there is nothing wrong with the principle so long as the creator is satisfied. But with age, the distinction between fantasy and reality becomes clearer, and the colorful conglomerations that expressed very adequately for the five-year-old the meaning of a rainy day may not be satisfactory to the twelve-year-old. I would hazard a guess that for every individual in every aesthetic medium there comes a critical time when either techniques have to be cultivated consciously to keep pace with his expressive needs or the medium is abandoned.

Such cultivation is not generally undertaken, because it is likely to be difficult and because there is an easier alternative, viz., to utilize means of expression that do not require such cultivation. Pranks, athletics, slang, fads are easily available substitutes in the social milieu. Indeed, peer age approval is jeopardized unless such alternatives are utilized. On the contemplative side, the adolescent finds his nascent adulthood and the vicissitudes and joys thereof adequately expressed for him in the various media of popular art.

It is not surprising that popular art is so admirably suited to adolescents. Popular art in all its forms tends to hover around the problems of adolescence, viz., either of getting along in it, or getting out of it, or getting back to it. Contrasts are sharp and obvious; the ending is happy; and, above all, the symbolism conforms to the pervailing stereotype. The hero and heroine, success and failure, sorrow and elation, must follow well-known patterns and plots.

The form must be equally accessible. Rhythm is emphatic and clear, the melodic line uncomplicated. In the graphic fields, the delineation is unambiguous; color patterns are fairly striking, albeit conventional. That some adolescents are often highbrow about popular art, e.g., swing, bebop, etc., is only an apparent paradox. It shows what the aesthetic potentialities of an adolescent really are; he can make extraordinarily fine discriminations when he is moved to exert himself. But even here, the number of adepts is small compared to the mass of bobby-sox swooners and middle-aged escapists for whom the obvious holds no terrors.

It is understandable why the so-called classics or highbrow arts are, by and large, not popular—the occasional success of a Shakespearian play, symphonic selection, or abstract painting to the contrary notwithstanding, for, to be sure, anyone who can bring out the features of so-called classics that adolescents (regardless of chronological age) can apprehend, and which they can recognize as expressive of their yearnings, will evoke satisfaction.

This locates the distinction between highbrow and popular art in the complexity and subtlety of the expression, or in the complexity and subtlety of the theme, or both. Some of Verdi's operas are simple enough in theme but not in expression. Tolstoy's expression in *War and Peace* is not too bad, but the theme is bewildering. Proust, I would suggest, is easy neither in form nor substance. I dare say that we are all highbrows in the fields of our greatest competence, i.e., where we can make the finer discriminations, and the brow descends proportionately in other fields. Classics are highbrow in this sense of the word, for they are couched in a language that presupposes a high order of symbolic facility. Leaving modern poetry aside for the moment, what about this passage in *Lear* quoted by Randall Jarrell in the *Partisan Review* (January-February 1951)?

> Never any.
> It please the king his master, very late,
> To strike at me, upon his misconstruction,
> When he, conjunct, and flattering in his displeasure,
> Tripped me behind: being down, insulted, railed,
> And put upon him such a deal of man,
> That worthied him, got praises of the king
> For him attempting who was self-subdued,
> And in the fleshment of this dread exploit
> Drew on me here again.

Jarrell quite rightly insists that poetry—the better sort—is always obscure. The obscurity is not always, or even for the most part, arbitrary. As experience gets more complex, the artistic products or objects that express its emotional significance are likely to require a more complex symbolism. If the artist sees reality in a new light or in a new form, its expression will be at first obscure, strange, and difficult, and will make great demands on the symbolic and imaginative powers of the observer.

Popular art, then, is suitable to an immature symbolic facility and to relatively undeveloped powers of aesthetic discrimination. But there is, perhaps, an even more fundamental reason for the popularity of popular art. It is that it reduces life itself to rather simple denominators. There is a sense in which popular art is the most abstract of all, for it fastens on such a view of life as we have, or are likely to have, only during our adolescent years. Like great art, popular art deals with the generic themes of love, victory, defeat, comedy and tragedy, home and wandering, but whereas great art treats these as seen through the eyes of maturity, popular art re-creates them every month as seen through the eyes of the adolescent. Compare, for example, what love means to a sixteen-year-old girl, who flits from one awkward swain to another, to what love means to a woman who has nursed a husband through a critical illness, or who has learned to love a rather pompous ass just because she has realized why he is pompous and an ass. To such a woman, the ice cream soda music of a musical comedy may be inadequate to express love. She may now need a Shakespeare or a Wagner or even a Dostoevsky—if only she can understand their language. If not, she may repair to the soap opera which confuses a recital of domestic woes with tragedy.

The Problem of Standards

We are now close to the embarrassing question of what is good art, and whether one aesthetic experience is better than another, and if so, on what grounds. Now the doctrine of *de gustibus non est disputandum* is a comfortable one for educators, because it reduces aesthetic education to the providing of opportunities for aesthetic experience. Unfortunately, we cannot avail ourselves of it. For even if we were to agree that standards of aesthetic preference will mature or somehow emerge automatically, the teacher approves the resultant standard, disapproves, or stays neutral. If she approves or disapproves actively, she is using a standard of her own; if she stays neutral—and genuinely so—she might as well not be in the classroom at all, or perhaps the pupils might as well not be, because if neutral variety is the goal, the selection in any classroom is seriously limited in both neutrality and variety. So, either there are standards or there is no such thing as aesthetic education.

Standards are bad only if they are imposed on oneself and pupils without rational justification. Can a theory of educational aesthetics exhibit standards that a teacher can justify to herself, the pupil, and the public?

In education standards have to be stated with a high degree of objectivity. This may not be impossible, provided the standards are not themselves purely aesthetic. I would suggest, therefore, that educationally we try to define "better" in terms of what we want an aesthetic experience to *do* for an individual in achieving the good life.

Without even trying to explore the subtleties of theory in this matter, it seems to me that education can have standards if it argues something like this: An aesthetic object is "good" for the individual if it is an aesthetic success, i.e., objectifies for the maker an emotionally significant aspect of experience; or it is good *objectively* if it expresses a significant mode of experience for any observer who is equipped to receive it. To say that one aesthetic object is objectively "better" than another means that the experience of objectifies is more discriminating, more inclusive, more pervasive—in brief, more mature. If symphonic music is "better" than "bebop," then it is on grounds such as these.

If you ask me to state what is more discriminating, more mature, etc., then I shall be forced to appeal to your experience in such matters. I submit that to a high degree these criteria are empirically verifiable, i.e., they need not beg the question by saying that famous works of art are objectifications of the most mature experience.

We are saying, in effect, that while there is no predicting what aesthetic object will actually give a particular individual pleasure or pain or indifference, there is a ladder or hierarchy of emotional experience in terms of maturity, subtlety, and complexity, and there are corresponding variations in art products. When level of need and level of expression match, we have a genuinely satisfying aesthetic experience—and outside of school that's the end of it. However, the educational conscience is bothered by these questions: Is the experience of the person as mature, subtle, etc., as his potentialities warrant? Or is his development prematurely arrested?

With respect to aesthetic education, this kind of standard makes the goal or aim of such education two-fold. On one hand, it aims at an emotional and intellectual maturity that will render stereotyped, immature, obvious art products aesthetically inadequate. On the other hand, it undertakes to provide the symbolic skills required by more mature forms of expression and impression. But inasmuch as education ranges from the very early childhood years to those of very late adolescence, the proportion will vary at each level of education. One can hypothesize that, in the elementary years, the chief emphasis will be on opportunities for expression; that, in the early adolescent years, the problem of acquiring techniques may be paramount to ward off the imminent aesthetic inarticulateness; and that, in higher education, the exploration of highly mature forms of art might take precedence over other phases.

It is the reciprocal character of impression and expression which presupposes an aesthetic literacy that young people are sometimes reluctant to achieve. Hence, there comes a time in education—in aesthetic education too, if you please—when the educator must insist on the kind of literacy that will make intellectual and emotional maturity through vicarious experience possible at a later date. This meant that plays, poems, pictures, and music that do reveal facets of experience not yet lived through by the pupils may be presented to adolescents for their "maturational values" even though they are not aesthetically enjoyed at the time. Whether they are famous or not doesn't matter, provided the teacher can justify their maturational values. But of equal importance is aesthetic literacy in many media, and even more important than that is the attitude that the total burden of aesthetic communication is not wholly on the artist.

It is difficult to see how aesthetic literacy and competence is any less, or any more, valuable than the kinds our schools now do make primary; and it is equally difficult to defend the notion of the aesthetic as a desirable nonessential. We shall know that this attitude has changed when the requirements for promotion at various steps on the educational ladder specifically demand proof of such literacy. This state of affairs, however, requires a long process of self-clarification anent the aesthetic mode of experience in life and education. Such clarification, it seems to me, it is the business of the educational philosopher to provide in a theory of educational aesthetics.

AESTHETIC EDUCATION AS A DOMAIN

D. W. Gotshalk

. . . aesthetic education may be discussed in many ways. In this essay, I would like to discuss it as a domain, and to ask specifically what is required to interpret it properly as a domain. "Domain" means any area of human activity having an established and distinctive purpose structure.[1] Physics, transportation, journalism, law, pathology are among countless illustrations of domains. Each includes many human activities along fairly well-established lines, and each has a purpose and a different purpose. Law is not physics, nor does it aim to be physics; similarly transportation and journalism and the others, despite connections and some common attributes. Domains often exist inside domains or as subdomains. A culture may be defined as a system of domains with their subdomains included. In discussing aesthetic education as a domain, I shall understand it as a subdomain of education and as an integral part of culture. What then are the requisites for properly interpreting this segment of human activity in the domain manner?

I

Unquestionably the leading feature of a domain is its purpose structure. This structure differentiates a domain since it embodies the characteristic directions of its activities. The aims of a lawyer are many; so are those of a transport worker. But a lawyer in handling a case in court is not moving cargo from place to place. Nor is a journalist at his desk, nor a physicist in his laboratory, except incidental to other business. In their characteristic jobs, agents such as these have very different aims, and these aims differentiate their activities. The first requirement of interpreting a domain as individuated or set off from

From the *Journal of Aesthetic Education,* vol. 2, no. 1 (January 1968): 43–50. Reprinted by permission of the *Journal* and the author.

[1] *Patterns of Good and Evil* (Urbana: University of Illinois Press, 1963), Ch. 6.

other domains therefore would seem to be to discern its differentiating aim or purpose structure.

As a subdomain of education, one might propose that aesthetic education be described as that educational activity directed primarily to the development of sensitivity to aesthetic values. Other educational activities (teaching mathematics, demonstrating laboratory techniques) might develop this sensitivity incidentally. But aesthetic education is that one among all such endeavors that aims primarily and preeminently at this kind of development. Such might be a proposed characterization of the distinctive purpose structure of aesthetic education as a domain. But if it were, it would really be only a beginning. One would need to spell out at once the meaning of the key terms of the proposal, "sensitivity" and "aesthetic values" particularly. Elsewhere I have suggested that aesthetic experience and the values in aesthetic experience can be adequately described in terms of intrinsic perception or perception (Greek *aisthesis*) raised to a major activity valuable in its own right, and I have given an analysis of intrinsic perception highlighting the psychological powers and background value inclinations that enter into its operation.[2] On this view, aesthetic education would be primarily education in intrinsic perception, and the more precise and complete description of the distinctive purpose structure of the area would be in terms of the powers and background and all else involved in this kind of perception.

Specification in detail of the differentiating aim structure of aesthetic education, then, would be the first step required in its domain interpretation. The next step I think would be to describe what is involved in the proper actualization of this structure. What kind of realization would be required of the person to be educated? What kind of objects would best serve this realization?

II

In connection with the first question—the kind of realization required of the person being educated—it seems hardly necessary

[2] *Art and the Social Order* (New York: Dover, 1962), Ch. 1.

to say that aesthetic education, as all others, is a lifetime pursuit. Moreover, most people are flawed aesthetically in some respects. They respond weakly to certain colors or to certain subtleties of human motivation. Even the most expert and devoted aestheticians are not always paragons of responsiveness. In a domain interpretation, therefore, an answer to this first question might better be stated in terms of directions to be sought than goals to be reached. The most general direction to be sought, of course, is increase of aesthetic sensitivity in the person being educated. The more specific directions I think would be increase of aesthetic sensitivity in width, height, and depth.

To increase aesthetic-depth sensitivity in the person being educated increases awareness of the value layers of an aesthetic field. Some say that sensitivity to aesthetic values means fine discrimination of lines, colors, shapes, tones, textures, odors, and flavors. Certainly this is a part of what is meant. But at the performance of a narrative ballet, to catch the colors and rhythms and also the dramatic relations of the dancers and to hold these relations vividly within the framework of attention, is also to grasp what the aesthetic object is offering. Interpersonal relations, which are so rich in imaginative literature, are as real for discernment and for enjoyment of intrinsic quality as line and color and rhythm. In any case, here is a problem of aesthetic realization that would have to be considered. How deep are the layers of value in aesthetic fields? What kind of grasp in the person being educated does realization of this depth entail?

Height and width raise parallel questions. The aesthetic surface, the lines and colors and sounds and other sensory features just mentioned, often greatly delight those with remarkable aesthetic sensitivity. Indeed, pleasant objects generally do, and for all people at some time and some people all the time, these are the objects par excellence of aesthetic attention. But is this the width of the aesthetic field? Or does this field include other objects, the grotesque, the sinister, the ugly, and the unpleasant generally? And if it does, what kind of experience in the person does a value realization of this variety as aesthetic entail? These questions state some major problems of width.

As to height, the problem here would not be with the diversities of the field (width) nor the subleties (depth) but with the concentration of values at any one point, a high or low concentration. An aesthetic surface may have no depth, but in its surface it may have a richer realization of aesthetic possibilities than an item with depth. Compare a finely woven rug with a hollow melodrama. The practical problem of height would be to know the aesthetic possibilities of an item and to discern the degree of fulfillment of these possibilities in the actual item, a high or low degree. A domain interpretation of the field would note that this knowledge and discernment would be needed in this connection, and would indicate ways for a person to acquire such knowledge and discernment as he can.

III

Turning to the second question about objects serving best the domain end, objects, as aesthetic instruments, vary considerably. Natural objects, and objects in practical and social life, frequently have charm, and at times deserve sustained attention. But works of fine art have some advantages. Not only are they intended for aesthetic attention ordinarily, and accessible at more times and places that are free from the distractions of practical and social life. Usually their chief superiority is that at their best, and in so many other cases, they contain a far greater concentration of aesthetic values. They possess intrinsically so much in so little, while natural objects and practical utilities, with notable exceptions, ordinarily have more diffuse or diluted aesthetic offerings.

In any case, works of fine art are certainly among the prima facie instruments available for aesthetic education, and part of a domain interpretation of this field would be to describe their use for this purpose.

This description might take several forms. The historical is likely to be favored. But there are other ways. One is to present works of fine art as having four dimensions: materials, form, expression, functions. A work of fine art is an array of material: sounds, colors, lines, shapes, bodily movements, words, or several such materials. It is a form or complex system of relations integrating these materials. A work of fine art is an expression conveying many things, from abstract qualities such as zest, verve, eagerness, melancholy to concrete characters and scenes such as Innocent X and Guernica. A work of fine art is a unit with a function, an entity performing or shaped to perform a certain task: to satisfy its creator, to be aesthetically exciting, to make money, to pass the time. Finally, each of these four dimensions can have not only its own intrinsic interest but can contribute to the aesthetic value and interest of the other three. The granite of a statue, for example, can contribute a certain solidity and strength to the noble figure being expressed in the statue, whereas another material such as soap or porcelain would not. And this instrumental relation of material to expression illustrates a relation that can be found between any two dimensions of a work of fine art.[3] According to this four-dimensional conception, then, statues, poems, paintings, musical compositions, and the others, can house as many as sixteen single or multiple aesthetic values or disvalues: the four internal to the four dimensions, at least one to each; and the twelve between the four dimensions, three from each.

Such a conception suggests a very comprehensive way of displaying the values in works of fine art for aesthetic attention, and using it for this purpose in an episode of aesthetic education, it would illustrate the kind of clarification of the object field that a domain interpretation might appropriately contribute.

IV

Concerning works of art as object instruments, at least one further question would deserve special consideration in a domain interpretation. This is the question of selection and emphasis.

Works of fine art have been produced in countries all over the world. Even for an aesthetic education of lifetime span some selection obviously is needed. What principle should be

[3] *Ibid.*, Part II, pp. 87–169.

used? Should one select a relatively few works from every country and every century? Or should one concentrate on a great number from a very few times and places? In using works of fine art as instruments a great opportunity also exists to show how the various fine arts are related, the broad unity of the art domain. The four-dimensional conception, for example, suggests strong lines of unity. But even here the question is how to develop this best. Should one select a few dozen very diverse major works from our own Western tradition: paintings from Giotto to Matisse, statues from the early Greeks to Brancusi, musical compositions from Montiverdi to Schoenberg, buildings from the Parthenon to the Guggenheim Museum, dramas from Aeschylus to Sartre, poems from Sappho to Eliot, novels from Fielding to Hemingway? Would such a diversified selection of Western works from the diverse arts still be entirely competent to indicate such broad interrelations as exist among the arts? Or would it be advisable to step outside the Western tradition?

Some people oppose a controlled education in the fine arts, where the educator maps out the field and procedures. They think the chief duty of the educator is to expose the learner to works of art and let him acquire his education from this exposure. Is this emphasis desirable? Lately many have opposed it, and for good reasons, since there is so much in so many works of fine art—the poetry of Dante, the painting of Watteau, the music of Bach, the sculpture of Michelangelo—that is not visible to the blank mind and at the same time can be made evident and exciting by a searching, probing mind irradiating a masterpiece. Still, the question remains whether the *ex cathedra* approach gets the best results. What surely is wanted everywhere in aesthetic education is growth of the sensitivity of the learner. The aim is not to celebrate masterpieces, to promulgate art doctrine, to teach art history, but to awaken and enlarge the aesthetic response of individuals. Any emphasis achieving this result should certainly be most welcome, and all such emphases should remain experimental and tentative, and student response rather than sacred tradition clearly should be the deciding factor.

V

A domain interpretation of aesthetic education, then, would describe its differentiating aim, and the subjective realizations and objective instrumentations involved in the actualization of this aim. Means and ends, delineated in appropriate detail, would be its first major topics. But a domain has a human setting. It exists in relation to other domains and as part of a culture. To complete a portrait of aesthetic education as a domain, therefore, it would be necessary to view it in its human setting and to describe its place in the system of domains called culture.

At least three questions seem pertinent and important in this connection. What does aesthetic education, in pursuing its own differentiating aim, contribute to cultural life? What ends besides its differentiating aim can it serve? What activities in a culture can it be combined with, consistent with its differentiating purpose? The specific answers to these questions naturally will be determined by one's specific interpretation of the differentiating aim structure and the factors in its actualization. Let me suggest the general line which such specific answers might take.

What does aesthetic education in pursuing its own end contribute to cultural life? An answer to this question might begin with a redescription of the psychological powers and value inclinations nurtured by aesthetic education. Then one might indicate the role of these powers and inclinations in shaping character and personality, individual behavior, and group conduct.[4] Or one might note that by developing certain standards of taste in its own domain, aesthetic education can have considerable influence in other domains where its devotees operate: in artistic creation, in civic enterprises such as the beautification of surroundings, in private enjoyment.

The second question concerning the other ends of aesthetic education would introduce more explicitly the topic of other domains. Many domains have purposes in common. This is

---

[4] *Ibid.,* Ch. 9.

why they are often confused, and domains deeply distinct are sometimes proclaimed to be identical. Besides enhancement of our aesthetic responses, aesthetic education can give us historical information, insight into human nature, entertainment, therapy, understanding of artistic foibles, some or all of these values, and many more. Achieving such ends does not make aesthetic education identical with history, psychology, or any other domain, but it does raise important questions. One of these is the relation of these achievements to the distinctive aim of the domain. Do they flow internally from the pursuit of the domain's distinctive purpose? Or are they, some or all, only externally connected with its major aim? [5]

This question has a bearing on the third question above listed about the combination of aesthetic education with other cultural pursuits. How much does overlap in ends affect such combining? Aesthetic education has a certain job to do. But even with some overlap in end achievement, a job does not necessarily combine easily with another. No doubt aesthetic education can be combined very effectively with most other forms of education, and not merely with education in the humanities, but also in the sciences, indeed in most fields where reflection on an area of attention is central to the education. But even here the combinations would have to be selected and scheduled. To interpose paramount aesthetic concerns in the midst of a crucial scientific experiment might not be to the advantage of aesthetic education or scientific understanding. Other activities in a culture present similar difficulties in more aggravated form: war, riot, social and physical turbulence. The relation of aesthetic education to these activities would raise some very interesting problems.

VI

To clarify its differentiating aim structure, to portray what is involved in actualizing this structure, and to indicate the cultural contributions and combinations consistent with the aim structure and its actualization: these might be said to be the

[5] *Ibid.*, Ch. 10.

requirements of a domain interpretation of aesthetic education. The integrating of aesthetic education with its cultural surroundings would be designed to exhibit its widest and most general value possibilities. The clarification of the internal components of aesthetic education—its differentiating aim and its actualizing agencies—would be designed to point up its more special and unique value possibilities.

In this way, a domain interpretation of aesthetic education, combining internal clarification with cultural perspective, would enable us to see the exact size and shape of this important area of human activity.

JUSTIFYING AESTHETIC EDUCATION

R. A. and C. M. Smith

A defensible policy proposal for the inclusion of aesthetic education in the curriculum should supply satisfactory answers to two basic sets of questions. (1) What is the function of aesthetic education in the life of the individual and society? Is it distinctive and significant? (2) Is it necessary that the content and procedures distinctive of aesthetic education be acquired through formal schooling? Is it possible in other words to demonstrate or argue that the skills, concepts, attitudes, and dispositions involved cannot be acquired through the informal processes of acculturation?

Many subjects taught in schools today have little difficulty qualifying on the first count. It is superfluous to plead the need for teaching English, mathematics, and the sciences. The issues are not nearly so simple, however, in the case of aesthetic education which, as here characterized, amounts to instruction in ways of understanding works of art. What do both the individual and society stand to gain? What is the study of works of art good for? Since schooling is a practical enterprise dependent on various sources for financial support to sustain and advance its activities, such questions, however much one would like to avoid them, cannot be burked.

To ask for a positive function of art locates analysis in the most problematic territory of aesthetic inquiry; the question stubbornly defines attempts at mapping and precise understanding. Few aestheticians [1] are prepared to say that art is

From the *Journal of Aesthetic Education,* vol. 4, no. 2 (April 1970): 37–51. Reprinted by permission of the *Journal* and the authors.

[1] "Aestheticians" here refers primarily to philosophers of art who teach courses called "philosophy of art" or "aesthetics" in (usually) colleges of liberal arts and sciences. Occasionally there is confusion regarding (*a*) *aesthetics,* a philosophic discipline or field of study, (*b*) *aestheticians,* (*c*) *aesthetic experience,* which is the structural form of experience or perceptual focus of awareness under certain conditions, and (*d*) *aesthetic education,* which, as indicated herein, implies a conception of education that uses concepts, principles, and procedures from

trivial, but precisely wherein its importance lies is a matter of considerable debate. In view of this situation the best strategy seems to be to make a selection from various aesthetic theories which appear to be sensible and advantageous from the point of view of justifying a program of aesthetic education.[2]

To begin, it is often held that to inquire after art's function is a futile if not illegitimate pursuit, as it is the glory and singular distinction of art to have no function at all. Art has intrinsic value, which implies that beauty needs no excuse for being. Because versions of this viewpoint are quite common, it will be instructive to ask in what sense, if any, art can be said to have intrinsic value, where "intrinsic" means the exclusion of function, means, or instrumentality.

An intrinsic good is one that is generally wanted for its own sake; nothing is desired beyond it.[3] However, it is doubtful whether intrinsic value as the terminal point of desire can belong to physical objects or things. What is desired is not the object as such but the pleasure or satisfaction of possessing, using, or experiencing it. Intrinsic value is thus confined to experiences or states of mind and not to objects. And works of art are no exception. Upon close examination works of art are found to be valued or wanted *ex*trinsically. That is to say, works of art are instrumental to or a cause of a type of experience which may be called aesthetic enjoyment, satisfaction, pleasure, or some other denotation approximately synonymous. Again, then, it is aesthetic *experience* which is sought as an end in itself; it is aesthetic experience that has intrinsic value.

Now it is not too difficult to understand the origin of the notion that works of art have no function and are to be enjoyed primarily for their intrinsic value. They are after all among the

aesthetics which are helpful in developing the capacity to have refined and enlightened aesthetic experiences of works of arts.

[2] Such choosing and selecting invites the charge of eclecticism. However, it is not the desire to be eclectic but rather the nature of the subject matter that dictates the multiple grounds of justification presented here. Efforts that attempt to encompass the varieties of art and aesthetic experience within a single purpose or function tend to be too exclusive.

[3] Cf. Monroe C. Beardsley, "Intrinsic Value," *Philosophy and Phenomenological Research,* vol. 26, no. 1 (September 1965): 1–17.

most self-sufficient and valuable objects men know of. That is, works of art are not consumed, they are generally not useful in the struggle for survival, and even their economic value is not commensurate with their worth qua works of art (rarity, antiquity, and the vagaries of the art market often being more determinant). Perhaps the reason for ascribing intrinsic value to the art object lies in the confusion of *intrinsic* with *inherent* value, and it will be profitable to explore this distinction.

Monroe C. Beardsley has pointed out that a work of art has *inherent* value when its potential to lead to a desired experience is correlated, at least roughly, with its artistic value, such that the more highly the work of art is rated according to strictly aesthetic criteria, the greater the effect it is capable of producing.[4] Inherent value can be further differentiated from a work's incidental effects which do not seem to be correlated with artistic merit. (Muzak that soothes discontented bureaucrats is an instance.) It is important, then, to keep in mind this distinction between intrinsic and inherent value.

Yet is a case for aesthetic education made merely by insisting that time should be set aside in the curriculum for instruction and practice in intrinsically enjoyable aesthetic experiences to which works of art are instrumental? Only unabashed hedonists are likely to be convinced. For to assert that art can be enjoyed intrinsically is not tantamount to saying that it is *valuable* in the sense of being *worthy* of being enjoyed. People seek enjoyment of many things for their own sakes. But is a thing desirable, meaning justifiably desired, merely because many persons, even most, report that they like it, that they find it intrinsically enjoyable? What one wants to know, then, is whether aesthetic enjoyment is intrinsically *valuable,* worthy of being desired. The question has now shifted from what is art good for to what is aesthetic experience good for, apart, that is, from the pleasure that accrues to the person.

It may be that no affirmative answer to this question is possible. "Intrinsic desirability" pulls in two directions: the adjective "intrinsic" tells us to pay no attention to anything but

[4] Beardsley, "The Aesthetic Problem of Justification," *Journal of Aesthetic Education,* vol. 1, no. 2 (Spring 1966): 29–39.

the thing called desirable, while the noun "desirability" tells us to look farther afield. For to call a thing "desirable" suggests that alternatives have been considered and the desirable thing selected on account of its implications and consequences.[5] If this view is correct, there may be no way to resolve the dilemma. The difficulty, however, may perhaps be mitigated by weakening the conditions that establish either desirability or intrinsic character.

It might be possible to maintain, for instance, that aesthetic enjoyment is valuable, worthy of being chosen, but disavow the intrinsic value of the experience. The state of being pleased by works of art would then be considered as *instrumental* to still some further good. Such arguments are not uncommon. Aesthetic experience, while not always so called, has been thought desirable because it contributes to personal integration and maturity, because it fosters a kind of general creativity which can be transferred to different sorts of endeavors, because it shapes the emotions or helps render emotional reactions appropriate to their contexts, etc. Some of these claims have been closely argued, are not necessarily unreasonable, and should not be arbitrarily dismissed. On the other hand there are considerations which caution against their uncritical acceptance. First, it is possible that purported psychological adjustments are not correlated with a work's artistic value but are among its incidental effects. If so, then is art the most desirable and effective means of achieving such outcomes? There is little concrete proof, if any, that aesthetic enjoyment has instrumental value as here defined. Furthermore, there are several common-sense observations which would appear to refute such contentions. Artists, for instance, are not necessarily models of well-integrated personalities, nor are critics, even after a lifetime exposure to art's persuasive, emotion-shaping potentiality. Hence it might be concluded that the above interpretations of the purported effects of art do not yield an adequate justification for aesthetic experience and aesthetic education.

But then, how do we establish that aesthetic experience is intrinsically valuable and desirable? Popular acclamation is not

[5] Beardsley, "Intrinsic Value," pp. 13–14.

to be discounted altogether, for if enough people say something is worth having there is prima facie plausibility that it is in fact worth having. But what counts even more is the testimony of persons with impressive credentials in the world of art. It is obvious that sustained interest in art is one of the permanent characteristics of the human race and that works of art constitute a priceless heritage of mankind. A common way to condemn a period is to say it didn't cultivate or achieve excellence in the arts. The conservators of this heritage, moreover, have been primarily our critics, historians, and connoisseurs. Whatever the biases of particular periods or the judgments of designated aesthetic conservators, they have been and will continue to be a major court of appeal regarding aesthetic worth. In brief, the case for the intrinsic desirability of aesthetic experience, as in all other domains, is made by appealing to the judgments of professionals.

But even if a professional court of appeal is accepted as a way of deciding what is valuable, has a *specific* benefit thereby been assigned to art? Perhaps it is time to rephrase the question from "What is art good for?" to "What can art do that nothing else can?"

Since the position to be adopted here is that aesthetic enjoyment can be intelligibly characterized as qualitatively different and distinct from other types of pleasure, the search for art's unique function or functions is led back to the art object proper, or, more specifically, to those of its properties which are rightly characterized as aesthetic because they give rise to aesthetic enjoyment. However, the circularity of defining aesthetic qualities in terms of aesthetic enjoyment is immediately evident, and this has been said to be a mark of weakness in several aesthetic theories. It will suffice here to supply one example (Beardsley's) of how to avert circular argument.

1. *Aesthetic enjoyment* is (by definition) the kind of enjoyment we obtain from the apprehension of a qualitatively diverse segment of the phenomenal field, in so far as the discriminable parts are unified into something of a whole that has a character (that is, regional qualities) of its own.

2. *Aesthetic value* is (by definition) the capacity to provide, under suitable conditions, aesthetic enjoyment.

3. *Positive critical criteria* are (by definition) properties
that are grounds of aesthetic value.

From propositions 2 and 3 it follows that:

4. Positive critical criteria are (analytically) properties that
help or enable an object to provide aesthetic enjoyment.

And from propositions 1 and 4 it follows that those features
of an object that are mentioned in the very definition of aesthetic enjoyment—unity, complexity, and intensity—will necessarily be positive critical criteria. . . .

There is no circularity, then, in defining aesthetic value in
terms of aesthetic enjoyment, and defining aesthetic enjoyment in terms of the properties enjoyed.[6]

What could rightly be claimed for aesthetic education up to
this point may be summarized as follows: Aesthetic education
may be legitimately established as a distinct area of instruction
because its principal objects of study, works of art, have the
function of affording a kind of enjoyment which (*a*) is qualitatively unique in the sense that only works of art, or more precisely those of their inherent properties designated as aesthetic
on the basis of critical criteria, can provide it in high degrees
or magnitudes; (*b*) is an intrinsic enjoyment which is actively
pursued for its own sake; (*c*) may well be an intrinsic value,
in the sense of being an experience which is justifiably desired,
if the testimony of connoisseurs and critics is given weight. But
it may still be asked whether enough has yet been said to satisfy
the curriculum designer who is obliged to render a satisfactory
explanation for spending the taxpayer's dollars on one type of
course rather than on another. Is aesthetic enjoyment enough?
Or are there reasons other than the prizings of professionals
which can justify art as a valuable enterprise?

The matter is perhaps best approached by expanding on one
peculiarity of works of art: the self-sufficiency, self-enclosedness, and inherent nature of their value potentialities and of the
experiences in which they are realized. These characteristics,
among others, are important to notions about art frequently
grouped under the label of "play" theories of art.

[6] In "The Discrimination of Aesthetic Enjoyment," *British Journal
of Aesthetics,* vol. 3, no. 4 (October 1963): 296–97. Beardsley shows
that several prominent aesthetic theories are based on circular reasoning.
See also Morris Weitz, "The Role of Theory in Aesthetics," *Journal of
Aesthetics and Art Criticism,* vol. 25, no. 1 (September 1956): 27–35.

Because art has no utility in the normal sense, these theories hold that its creation and contemplation are the result of an excess of energy, a form of play in which man can be completely free and hence fully human. All other aspects of life suffer from subordination to two crushing demands. One is the need to appease the appetites and assure survival in the service of which man's creativeness and energy are pitted against a resisting material environment and exhaust themselves in the struggle with the physical world. The other is the set of demands issued by moral laws to which action must remain responsible. In the artistic imagination, however, it is said these limiting conditions are suspended. Man is able to manipulate at will and in a free, joyous display of energy the most tractable aspects of reality: perceptual appearances, colors, shapes, contours, and sounds—things which do not defy him in the ways recalcitrant matter does. And he is also outside the jurisdiction of moral imperatives as his work needs to justify itself only by aesthetic standards and cannot be "right" or "wrong" ethically. (A judgment that a work is "harmful" does not reflect an evaluation of its strictly aesthetic properties.) Briefly, then, the leading ideas of play theories emphasize the moral freedom of art versus the moral responsibilities of ordinary life, contemplation versus appetite, excess energy versus toil and fatigue, and appearances versus reality.[7] Those who subscribe to this kind of thought then go on to say that art adds a most desirable dimension to human existence: a realm in which man can function with complete freedom and efficacy.

Such a view of the function of art could serve well for purposes of education justification except for at least two serious liabilities. One is the connotations of the term "play." Although "play" is given a positive association with freedom and self-sufficiency, the stigma of "mere" play in the sense of trivial activity is difficult to erase. Second, theories of this nature tend to be encumbered with heavy metaphysical commitments and presuppositions.

Nonetheless, the art-as-play argument yields a notion that

[7] F. E. Sparshott, *The Structure of Aesthetics* (Toronto: University of Toronto Press, 1963), p. 207.

can prove fruitful educationally. It is the contention that art affords freedom from everyday concerns (without being mere escape), i.e., that the making and contemplation of art occur in a different modality of experience. This argument is grounded in the fact that art is a matter of perceptual qualities, of sensuous appearances as opposed to substance (what a thing is made of) and utility (what it is good for). One should add, "appearance for its own sake," not as a symptom or portent of something else.

It is in this attention to perceptual qualities that another value can be realized which is often lost sight of in the onrush of ordinary experiences: the uniqueness and pecularities of objects. It has been asserted that persons cannot find their way in the world if they rely merely on general ideas and standardized procedures. This may be an overstatement, for people do in fact get along quite nicely by generalizing, classifying, perceiving things as instances of classes rather than as unique entities, etc. But it is only when absorbed in the perceptual presence of a thing, writes Iredell Jenkins, that "we are making the personal acquaintance of some feature of the environment that before was only an entry on a filing card. In these moments we are brought back to the concrete body of the world, and our experience of particular things becomes rich and intense." [8]

Briefly, if it can be judged worthwhile that persons be made cognizant of the perceptual richness and peculiarities of things, then yet another function may be posited for the aesthetic: it "reveals" something, it augments man's consciousness of his world. Something is experienced in the act of aesthetic beholding which is unattainable through normal goal-directed transactions with the environment.

It should be noted that a shift of language has occurred in the preceding paragraph from "work of art" to "the aesthetic" in a wider sense. "Aesthetic" here implies a distinctive response or perceptual focus variously called disinterested contemplation, aesthetic beholding, or aesthetic experiencing. A case

[8] Iredell Jenkins, *Art and the Human Enterprise* (Cambridge: Harvard University Press, 1958), p. 232.

could be made that if the schools find ways of teaching pupils to regard things aesthetically, i.e., in their uniqueness and peculiarity, they would be performing a genuine service. But where does this leave works of art which, as assumed herein, should be the preeminent objects of study in aesthetic education? This leads to the next consideration.

Works of art may be characterized as perceptual entities designed for aesthetic contemplation; in a sense they "demand" to be experienced aesthetically.[9] As such, then, they may be said to afford enriched or more intense forms of aesthetic experience. But whether works of art can engender in beholders a more generalized predisposition to regard the world aesthetically is an empirical question. Furthermore, if this disposition to savor the particularity of things were the prime value to be actualized through aesthetic education—and one should not retreat from the claim that it could be at least one of the desirable outcomes—then works of art would be only instruments in the fostering of this disposition.

Educators might feel that this is still too restricted a function to assign to works of art. The question thus becomes: Is there anything beyond freedom from everyday concerns, beyond the intrinsic enjoyment of individuality and particularity, the sensuous richness, the unity, diversity, and intensity of perceptual wholes that accrues in aesthetic experience? Can art enrich awareness in still more fundamental ways?

These questions have pushed discussion to the point of making some kind of cognitive or knowledge claim for works of art, and this is an issue on which philosophers of art are perhaps most sharply divided. One reason for this is that the standards for an affirmative answer to the question of whether art is knowledge, or whether something can be "known" through art, are today prohibitively high.[10] Still, the argument here is

[9] This does not imply that works of art have always been, are now, or will be designed *only* for aesthetic contemplation. Nonetheless, as Harold Osborne has pointed out, even works having religious or magical functions exhibit aesthetic properties which are redundant to their utilitarian functions (*Aesthetics and Art Theory* [New York: E. P. Dutton, 1968], p. 11).

[10] Beardsley, "The Aesthetic Problem of Justification," p. 30. Beardsley stops short of making a cognitive claim for art.

that aesthetic education is most convincingly supported by the contention that it is one of the functions of art to provide a kind of insight which is eminently worth having but which cannot be derived from the study of any other subject.

There has been no dearth of speculation about what can be known through art: the radiance of divine truth, the ideal, the absolute, archetypal images or racial memories, and the like. Prominent among theories which hold that something becomes known in aesthetic experience is that of Susanne Langer. A very abbreviated treatment of some aspects of Langer's philosophy is attempted here, not with a view to urging its adoption as a definitive statement, but because she presents a particularly interesting and well-developed theory.

The theory turns on an interpretation of the image-making propensities of the human mind and the vital function of mental images: ". . . we apprehend everything which comes to us as impact from the world by imposing some image on it that stresses its salient features and shapes it for recognition and memory." [11] Now images are important not only because they help us order the raw sense data received from the external world; they also appear to perform a similar office with regard to *all* passages of sentience. Life processes set up tensions and resolutions within the organism, some of which rise to what Langer calls the "psychical phase"; they are felt. However, they are not felt merely in some dim, vague fashion but are, in fact, apprehended. And to be apprehended, feelings have to be structured for recognition, for it is the peculiarity of human sensibility to record itself in images and to do so according to certain principles of representation. One could say, then, that just as imagination abstracts the semblances of external objects, so it also imposes form on the felt tensions of the life processes.

Imagination presumably operates in all individuals, but it is the artist who is capable of projecting these images of feeling into visible or audible form. Consequently, "the work of art is not a 'copy' of a physical object at all, but the plastic 'realization' of a mental image. Therefore the laws of imagination, which describe the forming and elaboration of imagery, are re-

[11] Susanne K. Langer, *Mind: An Essay on Human Feeling,* vol. I (Baltimore: Johns Hopkins Press, 1967), p. 59.

flected in the laws of plastic expression whereby the art symbol takes its perceptible form.[12] The work of art, according to Langer, is an objectification of feeling. She also refers to it as a "symbol," and as such it is capable of symbolizing, representing, or standing for a particular feeling. Now the work of art is able to function as a symbol in this sense because it shares its *logical form* with the mental image of feeling. And this morphological identity between the feeling and its artistic representation, in turn, is possible because the artist, in deploying the perceptual materials with which he works, is constrained to follow the laws of representation according to which the primitive, spontaneous mental image had been fashioned. It can thus be said that the work of art "presents a form which is subtly but entirely congruent with forms of mentality and vital experience, which we recognize intuitively as something very much like feeling; and this abstract likeness to feeling teaches one . . . what feeling is like." [13]

Two points of Langer's theory are especially noteworthy. First of all, the intuitive recognition of feeling in a work of art does not mean *having* that feeling. The essence of sadness, for instance, is apprehended not at times when persons are sad, but when they are presented with an artistic image of it. Second, when Langer calls the work of art a symbol, she does not say that art is a symbolic system similar to discursive language. The structure of discursive language is atomistic, and elements are manipulated in a single projection according to the logical rules of grammar. Art, however, does not build up meanings by accretion; its elements are not interchangeable. Each work, as she emphasizes repeatedly, is unique, self-sufficient, untranslatable, and indivisible. The vital emotional experience it symbolizes is of the kind for which verbal discourse is peculiarly unsuited.[14] Art, in other words, affords nondiscursive knowledge.

Since it is the purpose of the present discussion to discover in what sense a cognitive claim for art could be made defensible, one might want to conclude with Langer that it is the function

[12] *Ibid.*, p. 95.
[13] *Ibid.*, p. 67.
[14] *Ibid.*, p. 103.

of art to articluate the individual's own life of feeling for him, to make him conscious of its elements and its intricate and subtle fabric. The social importance of art would then rest on its capacity to reveal "the fact that the basic forms of feeling are common to most people at least within a culture, and often far beyond it, since a great many works do seem expressive and important to almost everyone who judges them by artistic standards." [15]

A note of caution must be entered, however, for the attempt to base an educationally useful knowledge claim solely upon Langer's philosophy of art would ignore some of the objections that can be raised against her approach. As has been indicated, Langer asserts that art has meaning and that this meaning is a matter of its relation to feeling, i.e., that one attains to a knowledge of feeling because its form finds an analogue in a work of art. And such knowledge would go well beyond what one commonly designates as "emotions," for Langer has enormously extended the inner life of feeling to include all passages of sentience, even the "feeling of rational thought." [16] But she has also made the meaning of art hypothetical; it rests, according to John Casey, on dubious metaphysical grounds. Casey asks:

> How do we *know* that works of art stand in a relation of logical analogy to forms of feeling? Have we any way of becoming acquainted with these "forms" apart from their artistic (or religious or mythical) expression, so that we can compare them with the works in which they are said to be instantiated, and so decide whether they have been satisfactorily realized? Clearly we cannot; the essence of these forms is that they are ineffable. They cannot be described since for anything to *be* a description it must have a form in common with what it describes. To attempt to describe a form would be a category mistake.[17]

In other words, Langer has claimed that we know something through art, but she has not satisfactorily explained how we know that we know. However, even if the connection between

[15] *Ibid.,* p. 64.
[16] *Ibid.,* p. 104.
[17] John Casey, *The Language of Criticism* (London: Methuen & Co., 1966), p. 67.

the work of art and the life of feeling of which it provides knowledge were as close as Langer tries to make it, it would still not be a logical connection.

This particular difficulty appears to be avoided in Nelson Goodman's attempt to account for the logical connections that *can* be supposed to obtain in art,[18] and the aesthetic educator might profit from looking at it as one of the alternatives to Langer. Goodman's major theme is that aesthetic experience *is* cognitive experience distinguished by the dominance of certain symbolic characteristics and judged by standards of cognitive efficacy.[19] He clearly makes a cognitive claim for art and proceeds to show *how* cognitive functioning in art is to be explained. He accomplishes this through an examination of the logical relationships that prevail in those modes of symbolization dominant in the arts, and he concludes that the aesthetic is distinguished by the preponderance of four "symptoms": syntactic density, semantic density, repleteness, and exemplificationality.

But while, according to Goodman, the aesthetic is subsumed under—or is a special case of—symbolic functioning and hence cognition, it also develops that those logical relationships distinctive of the aesthetic call for more than sound logical equipment to be apprehended; they demand sensitivity and the active cooperation of the emotions. In Goodman's view, the emotions become "a means of discerning what properties a work has and expresses." [20] One is reminded that "the cognitive, while contrasted with both the practical and the passive, does not exclude the sensory or the emotive, that what we know through art is felt in our bones and nerves and muscles as well as grasped by our minds, that all the sensitivity and responsiveness of the organism participates in the invention and interpretation of symbols." [21]

It may thus be seen that while Langer has been said to have

[18] Nelson Goodman, *Languages of Art: An Approach to a Theory of Symbols* (Indianapolis: Bobbs-Merrill, 1968). See also the essay review of this work, "Symbolic Systems, Cognitive Efficacy, and Aesthetic Education," which appeared in vol. 3, no. 4 (October 1969) of this *Journal,* pp. 123–36.

[19] *Ibid.,* p. 262.

[20] *Ibid.,* p. 248.

[21] *Ibid.,* p. 259.

extended the inner life of feeling, Goodman may be said to have
extended the inner life of cognition. Langer, starting from a
dubious connection between art and feeling, arrived at a cognitive claim for art—nondiscursive knowledge. Goodman, starting with a cognitive claim for art through the subsumption of
the aesthetic under cognitive and symbolic functioning in general, arrived at what to some may seem a somewhat dubious
organismic and overly subjective definition of the cognitive.
However, each position emphasizes the point that "art is both
rational *and* of an essentially emotional nature—and hence significant for human beings." [22] And this is really all the educator
needs to feel justified in saying that art is not merely subjective,
a matter of feeling and enjoyment, but that it involves a unique
kind of knowing which is worthy of being provided for through
formal schooling.

And once it is admitted that something can be known through
art, there should be little objection to suggesting that prominent
among things apprehended in works of art are metaphorical
images of and feelings or emotions attendant upon human ideals, norms, and life styles, for these are matters for which the
more conventional forms of expression are singularly inadequate. It would be difficult, for instance, to formulate a completely satisfactory verbal definition of such concepts as "nobility" or "dignity." Yet instances of these ideals are immediately
recognized in individuals possessing the requisite qualities and in
works of art expressing or instantiating them, whether one accepts Langer's notion of congruence of logical form, Goodman's
metaphorical exemplification, or any other explanation.

Now even though art may be said to communicate nondiscursively in the manner suggested above, it should not be conceived merely as an adjunct, a supplement to discursive language
that rounds out meanings where words fail. Art's effectiveness
reaches beyond a neutral, noncommittal display of meanings
and values. For if it is the case that aesthetic beholding is an
enjoyable occupation, that men delight in experiencing things in
their perceptual uniqueness, sensuous richness, and unified formal structure, then it also makes sense to argue that, while being
thus pleasurably engaged, persons may be seduced into contem-

[22] Casey, *The Language of Criticism,* p. 62.

plating and possibly assenting to the human import and ideals which works of art express.[23] It is the function of art, then, to make values vivid and persuasive as no other medium can.

The arguments offered in defense of assigning an educationally meaningful function to art may now be summarized under three headings:

1. *Aesthetic enjoyment.* Works of art function instrumentally toward the provision of satisfactions which are intrinsically desired. Furthermore, the preferences of cultural conservators (critics, historians, connoisseurs, and other professionally qualified persons) indicate that art offers worthwhile, desirable opportunities for being pleasurably engaged. The possibility of incidental values, such as therapeutic uses of aesthetic enjoyment, was not ruled out, but neither was it admitted as a major argument for aesthetic education. It was further contended that aesthetic pleasure is qualitatively distinct because it is grounded in objective properties of works of art.

2. *Aesthetic experience.* Aesthetic pleasure accrues within a distinctive kind of experience. The self-enclosed, self-sufficient nature of this experience was noted and taken to mean the property of being unrelated for the most part to considerations of utility, associated trains of thought, or abstract speculations. This feature of aesthetic experience permits its interpretation as a kind of important play which, in turn, has sometimes been associated with a realm of ideal human freedom and creative power. On a more modest plane, the self-sufficient character of aesthetic experience is said to be the condition for becoming aware of the particularity and perceptual richness of things.

3. *Aesthetic knowledge.* It was then suggested that through the enjoyable contemplation of the perceptual properties of certain works of art, something may be added to awareness which, though definitely nondiscursive, has nonetheless been claimed by many to be some kind of knowledge. It was further proposed that the cognitive claim could be elaborated to mean that art can afford a grasp of ideals, norms, or notions of human perfection.

[23] Cf. Harry S. Broudy, "The Role of the Humanities in the Curriculum," *Journal of Aesthetic Education*, vol. 1, no. 2 (Autumn 1966): 24.

But there are further problems. Even if general concurrence with such a high estimation of the function of art could be secured, there still remains the requirement to show that aesthetic experience demands the intervention of formal schooling. The need for explicit instruction in matters aesthetic is of course frequently denied, and for a variety of reasons.

Very briefly, one argument against requiring aesthetic education is that people like art anyway. This assertion is bolstered by impressive statistics of steadily increasing concert and museum attendance and record-buying. Second, it is often claimed that aesthetic preferences are matters of personal taste about which there can be no rational disputes—*de gustibus non est disputandem.* That is, people tend to be rendered confident in their likings because of the fairly widespread belief that there are no objective standards in matters of taste. Third, because the arts are apprehended perceptually, it is thought that no special training should be necessary. One need only look, listen, feel, and read.

Now, with regard to the first argument, the numerical increase in cultural activity is apparently correlated with the growth of the college-educated segment of the population.[24] This, in turn, can mean one of two things, neither of which would invalidate a plea for aesthetic education in the public schools. It may be said that for most students the years of college include some form of art education or appreciation which molds their aesthetic preferences. Or it may mean that college-educated persons are more likely to become members of an urban or suburban social class which prizes cultural experiences for their social rather than for their aesthetic values. The second and third sets of reservations concerning the need to have formal aesthetic education in the public schools cannot be set out here but have been dealt with elsewhere in the context of a discussion of aesthetic criticism.[25]

Up to this juncture, curricular justification of aesthetic educa-

[24] William J. Baumel and William G. Bowen, *Performing Arts: The Economic Dilemma* (New York: Twentieth Century Fund, 1966). See also the editorial of the January 1969 issue of this *Journal.*

[25] See "Aesthetic Criticism: The Method of Aesthetic Education," *Studies in Art Education,* vol. 9, no. 3 (May 1968): 13–32.

tion has rested upon what may be termed its *facilitating* or fostering aspects. The attempt has been to indicate that art may have important functions and that art cannot become fully efficacious in the lives of individuals and society without formal instruction. Another rather powerful class of arguments frequently advanced in behalf of some sort of arts program is based on the presumed *inhibiting* potential of such instruction. Aesthetic education is needed, it is said, to counteract the pernicious influence of certain works of popular art or the mass media. The question is how and to what extent the theoretical framework presented here permits incorporation of this line of thought.

It will be remembered that some misgivings were expressed regarding the alleged therapeutic values of art. If it is doubtful that good art can engender desirable personal traits, would it be fair to assert that the excess of violence, for instance, found in "bad" art (especially in much of the mass media) predisposes viewers to antagonistic behavior? Unambiguous evidence of such harmful effects may one day become available, but it is not really needed to shore up a justification for aesthetic education.

To indicate why this is so requires some enlargement of the concepts of "good" as opposed to "bad" art. Both terms when used in an aesthetic context refer to aesthetic qualities, not to content or the morality of the message. In simplest terms, a "bad" work of art is one that does not come off; it falls short as judged by aesthetic critical criteria. However, a bad work of art is often intended by its creator to satisfy high standards; it fails due to the artist's ineptness. Popular artists, by contrast, often do not subscribe to high standards to begin with; they compromise in order to sell and entertain. Hence it is perhaps more appropriate to call such production "pseudo-art" rather than "bad" art. And what, one might ask, is so bad about pseudo-art that we need to marshall the forces of aesthetic education against it? Nothing except that it shortchanges the percipient. Perceptually, it relies on the immediate sensuous appeal of a few striking elements while neglecting to explore the possible varieties and subtleties of relations and properties. It falls short in meaning or import because whatever pseudo-art expresses or conveys tends to be shallow and trite. In sum, pseudo-art attracts, it tempts aesthetic contemplation, but offers meager and shoddy rewards.

The inhibiting function of aesthetic education vis-à-vis popular art is simply this: aesthetic education offers as alternatives examples of better, richer, more worthwhile forms of experience, in the hope that persons will come genuinely to prefer what they have come to know as being better. As Iredell Jenkins says: "It is the chief function of art to overcome [the] tragic consequences of man's voracious but untutored aesthetic taste. The tendencies that pseudo-art merely confirms, real art trains and transforms." [26]

[26] Jenkins, *Art and the Human Enterprise,* p. 243.

AESTHETIC EDUCATION: A ROLE FOR AESTHETICS PROPER

E. F. Kaelin

. . . . Is there ground for assuming that aesthetic education rightfully constitutes a division of the society of professional educationists? And if so, can its program best be developed by encouraging men working in the several disciplines to form a cooperative, interdisciplinary concern? Or can a newer single discipline be created to handle its problems? The first step to be taken in this attempt is the clear delineation of the aims and resources of our public educational institutions: here, with particular reference to the aesthetic.

Current practice is of some help in laying out the division of labor. Aesthetics is an established philosophical discipline concerned with the description and evaluation of aesthetic experiences. Whether this is done by constructing a general theory whose purpose is to explain our everyday aesthetic preferences and judgments or by clarification of the language used to express preferences and judgments, the field of inquiry is adequately, if not clearly, delineated as one in which some kind of reason is given for our aesthetic judgments. And the discipline may be considered as meta-theoretical insofar as it stipulates the conditions under which some of these reasons may be considered "good," i.e., well-founded.

If it be admitted, then, that a primary use of language is the expression of aesthetic judgments, and such judgments are taken on experiences of a certain specifiable kind, aesthetics as a philosophical discipline will concern itself both with a description of these experiences and the evaluation of reasons given for the judgments made upon them. In a word, aesthetics as a normative science must clearly distinguish between the aesthetic and the nonaesthetic (descriptive analysis) and between the

From the *Journal of Aesthetic Education,* vol. 2, no. 2 (April 1968): 51–66. Reprinted by permission of the *Journal* and the author.

aesthetic and the unaesthetic (normative prescription). That the latter depends upon the former should be obvious: any disagreement in judgment must be reduced, if at all, by an examination of the conditions under which a given object is experienced. The question here is not "Do you like x—and why?" but rather "What, precisely, is it that you like?" Only upon finding an answer to this question is the more crucial question possible: "Is your reason for liking this object aesthetically relevant?" Not any old preference will do. He who would become a specialist in aesthetic education must familiarize himself with the methods and results of philosophical aesthetics, dedicated to finding answers to just such questions as these.

The second established discipline is education itself, the realm of "educationists," whose task is the instruction of teaching methods, the design of educational curricula, and a justification, philosophical or otherwise, for the dispersal of public funds in carrying out specific programs of public instruction. It is at this level of professional interest that questions of the following sort can, and should, be asked: "Why teach art, rather than mathematics, science, or the communications skills? If art is to be thought of as a necessary element of the child's curriculum, at what age should his instruction begin? To what lengths should it be pushed? Are our methods to be based upon a model of scientific communication? Or is teaching more like an art than a science? Educational questions have a way of proliferating almost to infinity. What makes a good teacher? How can we assure ourselves that our educational training produces good teachers?

Answers to these questions must be found by research. But what kind of research? If Dewey is right—that philosophy, properly conceived, is already a general theory of education—then our research must be philosophical, in the best, most comprehensive sense of this term. But no way of doing philosophy is proper which ignores the results of sciences which have established the facts of a problematic situation, and none is proper which imports its standard of evaluation from a realm of experience external to the one standing in judgment. Thus, if teaching is a science, it must be judged by scientific standards even if the subject being taught is art; and if an art, it must be judged by the best artistic standards, even if the subject being taught is a science.

In the following I shall argue that aesthetic education is a proper subdivision of educational theory in general; that its theory is conceivable in terms of an "aesthetics proper" (in which the value of aesthetic experiences to individuals is continuous with that accruing to a society which encourages such experiences); that a single method—phenomenology—may be applied to show this continuity; that the value of aesthetic experiences to individuals and to society constitutes a sufficient justification for instruction in the arts; and, finally, that the same method used to establish the foregoing may be developed into a general educational research tool.

II

Consider the first two of the aforementioned theses. Professors of both philosophy and education have been known to be guilty of assuming that knowledge of the general implies that of a specific skill. Thus, if philosophy is a general technique for the analysis of linguistic puzzles, he who is skilled in resolving such puzzles (either by semantical clarification or logical derivation), without further training in the specific subject matter of his discipline, may go to work on the language of scientists, art critics, moral agents, or what have you, with equal facility. Teach a prospective teacher the psychology of learning (and what, pray tell, about that of teaching?) and he should be able to teach anything at all. Armed with this marvelous tool, the coach may double as instructor of art appreciation; and, when the need arises, he may even fill in for the ailing teacher of the physical sciences.

Those of us, on the other hand, who have been trained primarily in a subject matter discipline have been just as guilty of assuming that knowledge of the discipline suffices for our qualification as teachers. The day comes, however, when we are dismissed for being something less than an inspiring teacher, and we are faced with the shortcomings of our own assumption;

a knowledge of motivation and of the basic teaching skills are both necessary tools for the competent performance of our professional tasks.

Perhaps it was the philosophers' awareness that a knowledge of the rules for semantical and logical analysis is prerequisite to an efficient performance in the philosophy of science, history, art, and conduct that led to the current philosophical preoccupation with linguistic expertise. But by no stretch of the logical imagination can a necessary condition be raised to the status of sufficiency. All our logical technicians need to do to perceive the limitations of their practice is to engage in a conversation with scientists, historians, artists, and ordinary human beings faced with the problem of moral decision. Tools alone do not make a teacher or a philosopher.

But the possession of both, the tools and a knowledge of the phenomena of a first-order human activity may succeed in the tasks for which each alone has been observed to fail. Not motivation in general, but motivation in, through, and toward a specific subject discipline is the mark of a successful teacher; not logic as the clarification of meanings in general, but logic as clarifying the meanings within a particular frame of reference defines the practice of the philosopher who would leave his mark on the institutions of society. Educationists who are looking for a workable philosophy of education have already indicated their interest in achieving, not expertise, but a competent degree of expertness in education.

If specialists in aesthetic education are to succeed where "generalists" have failed, they must ground their theory and research in a thoroughgoing understanding of the facts of aesthetics, where once again philosophy may be of some consequence, if only to guarantee that aesthetics is properly conceived.

We move, in a step, to the second of our theses. Whether, in old-fashioned terms, aesthetics is considered the science of beauty or of beautiful objects or, in more recent terms, it is thought of as "the science of expression considered as a general theory of linguistics," the practitioners of the discipline have a choice: to narrow the field to a limited set of objects or judgments, or to broaden it to include the full range of consequences such objects and judgments have on the lives of individuals and their society.

As the science of the beautiful, aesthetics concerned itself with the appreciation of natural objects or artifacts expressive of an ideal beauty. Plato so conceived it. But Plato was a complete philosopher. He likewise observed that poets produced objects that tended to arouse the passions of the populace, and so proposed a law restricting the freedom of the makers of rhymes whose products produced social disharmony.[1] Thus, at the very beginnings of aesthetics considered as a philosophical discipline, two observations were clear: (1) if we observe the practice of artists, we find that they pursue a value other than the representation of an ideal beauty, and (2) the consequences of this pursuit may be such as to warrant some measure of social control.

Modern fascistic and contemporary communistic states have faced the same problem. They could maintain their notion of an ideal society and incorporate the works and activity of creative artists within it only by limiting creativity—by stipulating what goal is to be pursued by the working artist.

Contemporary Soviet society is one of the few which has succeeded in professionalizing its artists, but not without some loss in the potential value of truly creative expression. For the Soviets, socialist realism is useful, as is nationalistic music; the rest is "decadent Westernism," "empty formalism," or "reactionary bourgeois expressionism." And there are many artists in our own country who fear federal subsidization of the arts for similar reasons. The federal arts projects of our own government during the 1930's sponsored art which was as socially realistic as anything produced in Russia; and if these schemes did allow artists to meet some of their economic obligations, the price of this socialization of the artists was allowing the payer of the fiddler to call the tune. The free artists of both countries have preferred to remain underground.

It is not being argued that an "aesthetics proper" is to be developed which would enable the administrators of a given society to adjudicate the disputes arising around the conflict of

[1] *Republic,* Book X.

values in society. That is still the task of sound philosophical thinking. What is being urged is that aesthetics proper concern itself with making clear the claims of artists that they can contribute to society what only they can, only under the conditions of freedom. If an aesthetic idea is a discovery by an artist manipulating the materials of his craft, then for there to be any such ideas, the artist must be allowed the freedom to experiment. He will have succeeded in communicating with his fellows if others are capable of rediscovering the idea as it has been embodied in his work.

Aesthetics proper, then, may be thought of as the discipline concerning itself with artistic communication—with the description of creativity, of works of art, and of artistic appreciation. The consummation of this activity, submitted to the discipline of material embodiment, allows for the institutionalization of a basic human impulse: that which impels toward excellence in creative expression; and this may or may not have anything to do with our love of or preference for beautiful things. And all this is only to say that aesthetics proper is a philosophy of art, where art is considered an institution of the general society. Lest this last term create a fear of creeping sociologism, it should be noted that "society" means here only the nexus of communicating individuals interacting via institutional means.

If such a discipline can be developed, it would be obvious how the two senses of the word "culture" tend to flow back into one. In the anthropological sense, "culture" is nothing more than the fixation of basic human activities which in the first instance were appreciated as works or expressions of "fine" culture. If we approve of an anthropologist's studying the artifacts of a lost civilization in an effort to determine the culture of its people, the reason is supplied by the fact that art has always been an institution of society, sometimes free and sometimes controlled, but always serving to unite people into a single appreciative audience. Art by its very nature serves to produce community.

To perform his task, and to justify the expenditure of public funds therefore, the aesthetic educationist must study the intricacies of these socio-artistic relationships. Otherwise he is likely to continue to appear before the authorities, hat in hand, mouthing such platitudes as "After all, it is good to have some cultured people around." But the questions may always be asked, "Is it? How do you know? And what makes you think you can produce a cultured person?"

III

The confusion of traditional aesthetics is as pronounced in its supposed results as in its methods. The Plato of the *Symposium* spoke of a single, all-encompassing science of the beautiful, to be based ultimately upon an intuition of beauty itself. But in the other writings of Plato one can find descriptions of art objects as imitations, as pleasing form, and even as expression insofar as they are capable of evoking strong states of passion or of soothing the soul wracked by disquieting humors. His method was simple: ordinary description of single events, and dialectical reasoning for the determination of an essence. Through centuries of speculation by artists, critics, and philosophers, aesthetic interest in the single event slipped out of the picture in favor of essential descriptions: "the aesthetic object" and "the aesthetic experience" replaced our everyday concern with aesthetic objects and aesthetic experiences. When we return to this concern we find that not all objects of art represent something, that anything one can think of has some kind of form, and that all human experience is accompanied by some kind of emotional state: anaesthesis is unconsciousness.

Careful philosophers drew the necessary conclusions. Imitation is neither necessary nor sufficient for the success or failure of a work of art; and although form is necessary, it is not sufficient to differentiate an aesthetic from a nonaesthetic awareness. Expression, when carefully analyzed, may qualify as both necessary and sufficient for a complete description of a work of art, provided that the expressiveness of the work is considered in the total context of the experience it affords. As long, that is, as the expressiveness is felt by some subject, whether the artist or his audience, a context of experience is established which enables a reflective individual to determine the reason or reasons for his aesthetic judgment.

Today two methods of aesthetic analysis dominate the philosophical scene. The first is the "good reasons" school, employing
the logic of ordinary language to judgments of aesthetic worth;
the second is phenomenological, likewise employing ordinary
language, but merely to describe the structures of aesthetic experiences. Although the one is interested primarily in "aesthetic
concepts," and the other in "aesthetic categories," the claim to
success made for each must be measured in terms of "referen-
tial" or empirical adequacy.[2] After all, if I cite as a reason for
my aesthetic judgment the presence of something which is not
to be found within the structures of experience, no one will be
convinced of the goodness of my reason. It seems obvious, then,
that some kind of awareness of the expressiveness of aesthetic
contexts in general is a prerequisite—not for having aesthetic
experiences, but for knowing what to look for as reasons for
approval in a specific case. The concepts or categories may be
as general as you please; their application must always be
specific and testable within the given context of experience upon
which the judgment is made.

In what follows, the context of experience will be considered
as a locus of interaction between the object being judged and
the critical judge. It opens with the percipient's contact with
the work and comes to closure in his critical appraisal of its
intrinsic worth.

The first condition necessary for having experiences of the
kind being referred to is—for the want of a better term—called
"openness." Heidegger refers to existential openness (*Erschlos-
senheit*) as a constitutive state of human existence (*Dasein*),
divisible into three "equiprimordial" moments: affectivity, understanding, and expression (*Rede*).[3] To treat openness as if it
were a constitutive state of the being of humans is to claim, at
least, that everyone is capable of verifying his existence; and to
call them "equiprimordial" is to state, at least, that no temporal
precedence may be attributed to the one or the other. We may
feel, then come to an understanding of the object of our feeling,

[2] See David W. Ecker, "Justifying Aesthetic Judgments," *Art Education*, vol. 20, no. 5 (May 1967).

[3] Martin Heidegger, *Sein und Zeit* (Tübingen: Max Niemeyer, 1957),
pp. 134–66.

and finally express what we have understood; or the expression and understanding may be simultaneous, both being defined by the modification of a subject living in the midst of an individually significant "world."

For roughly forty years now, the philosophical world has feigned to misunderstand what the German has said. But artists have not, nor have perceptive psychoanalysts. They know that an individual subject is capable of living in a unique universe, that this universe is expressible, and that what is expressed is capable of being understood by him who cares enough to respond with his own openness. I have elsewhere explained the usefulness of Heidegger's *existentialia* as pedagogical tools for instruction in the creative aspect of aesthetic communication.[4] Here I shall limit my discourse to the manner in which aesthetic experiences come to closure.

To do so, it is necessary only to show what categories of human experience are relevant to an interpretation of a specific aesthetic context; or, what is the same thing, to show the limits of relevance to aesthetic responses. We know, for example, that any human subject may react in any direction and with any intensity to any stimulus, and may compound the difficulty by reacting to his own prior reactions. The question is always: What kind of response is relevant to the given object? The answer to this question is formulable in terms of categories which describe a "context of significance."

In order to insure relevance from the outset, we may start with effectuating "the phenomenological *epoché,*" i.e., attend only to the object as it conditions our present experience. Husserl referred to this practice as "putting the world into brackets"; [5] more accurately, for the purposes of understanding the metaphor, one should say "outside the brackets" which enclose our present state of consciousness as it is directed to its object. Ordinary language calls this bracketing an attitude: it is one in which we consider the experience of the object for what it is, rather than as a sign of an occurrent phenomenon of nature.

---

[4] See my "The Existential Ground for Aesthetic Education," *Studies in Art Education,* vol. 8, no. 1 (Autumn 1966): 3–12.

[5] See his *Ideas,* tr. W. R. Boyce Gibson (New York: Collier, 1962).

That is another attitude, one we call "scientific" or "natural," in which our responses are interpreted in terms of natural or physical laws. To bracket out the significance of the world would, of course, be ruinous for any project having as its aim the understanding of natural laws. It is not ruinous, however, and indeed may be the only practicable means available to the person who would come to an understanding of the data of an immediate experience. And only in those can intrinsic values be found.

Let us begin, then, by placing brackets around an immediate consciousness and its object; we have an intuition, or direct awareness of quality, and analysis may begin. In the next step, any workable set of aesthetic concepts may be applied: matter and form, subject and treatment, or local and regional properties. The test of their success is their ability to make our perception clearer. If they fail, we reject them; just as we reject them if, semantically considered, they fail to point out unique referents within the context of experience. I prefer "surface" and "depth."

Both are experiential terms; both are analytical and not to be thought of as affording a rule for creating or appreciating works of art. They merely state what might be found in a given work of art, and both are not always found in every work of art. If a work is nonobjective, there is no depth, as I shall define it; and if it were possible to experience the relations between ideas and images of objects without tying such an experience to physical or sensuous counters or marks, there could be surfaceless expressions as well. A response to mathematical or logical relations would be a case in point.

According to D. W. Prall, whose work is still the best available on the subject, an aesthetic surface is the felt quality of any organized sensuous field.[6] For example, the structures of music exist in sound (and silences); of architecture, in masses (and empty space); of nonobjective painting, in space made visual by line and color. Indeed, ultrapurists look for nothing but these medial values and their moodal accompaniment.

But some surfaces thicken. And on this point Prall's explana-

[6] *Aesthetic Judgment* (New York: Crowell, 1929), Chs. 3–5.

tory apparatus breaks down. It seems completely arbitrary to insist that a shape has value only as creating a space within a painting if indeed that space is recognizable as a bull or a horse. When we respond to a shape as a representation of bull or horse, our experience deepens: more of the world is now includable within our brackets. If we look more closely, we can identify other objects: a broken warrior, frozen in rigor mortis, his severed arm still clutching a broken sword; a mother in agony over the death of her child; a woman falling through the shattered timbers of a burning building; a flickering light; a wounded dove, its peace gone astray; a lamp-bearer rubbernecking into the carnage, with one arm grotesquely projecting into the center of the piece and the other gripping protectively at her exposed breasts; etc. Let the mind play over these images and an idea grips the understanding: the wages of war, as it is currently conducted, are death and destruction. This is no game fought between man on horse and irritated bull on a blistering Spanish afternoon. The attack occurred at night, as the light's last flicker attests. Man, woman, child, and horse are all dead or dying, suffering, or fleeing along with the dove of peace. The bull almost impassively contemplates the scene. Salvation, when things come to such a pass, must be found in his persistence and courage. The virtue of the brave bull is to resist to the end the torments of his persecutors. So interpreted, our experience of *Guernica* deepens and comes to closure in a single act of expressive response in which we perceive the fittingness of this surface—all broken planes and jagged edges in the stark contrast of black and white—to represent this depth, the equally stark contrast of the living and the dead, the flickering of the light repetitive of the condition of those flitting in between.

If the theory is correct, depth paintings always pose the problem of relevant interpretation. Whose interpretation is acceptable? The one which gives maximal significance to all the counters within the experiential context. An idea not traceable to images, an image not controlled by the organization of the surface, is irrelevant. In another place,[7] I have constructed

---

[7] "Method and Methodology in Literary Criticism," *School Review,* vol. 72, no. 3 (Autumn 1964): 289–308.

the following list of postulates for the interpretation of an art-work's significance:

(1) Aesthetic expressions are context-bound; i.e., no one discriminable element within the context has a significance considered absolutely, or outside of relation to other elements.

(2) The context is constructed by the network of relations set up between the counters of a given medium: surface to surface, depth to depth, and overall surface to overall depth.

(3) The significance of the total context (not its signification, which no work of art has, considered as a whole, although it is in part composed of significations) is the felt expressiveness of the funding counters; i.e., the experience of the relations between surface counters and (where apposite) between these and any depth counters out of which the total context was constructed.

Other aestheticians have referred to such constructs as "the object of criticism." [8] "Object of appreciation" would do just as well. Such things come to exist only in the experience of persons who have opened themselves to the expressiveness of a sensuous surface and allowed their understandings and imaginations to be guided by controlled responses set up thereon. This is not to claim that an actual aesthetic experience begins with an awareness of the surface and then proceeds to closure in an idea, nor that there is only one interpretation of the given work; but only that the system of postulates devised to interpret the meaning of aesthetic categories affords a method of critical procedure, according to which any image or idea which is not traceable to the organization of some sensuous surface is patently irrelevant. What we put *into* the brackets is a system of relevant counters. We begin with an experience, and end, if the work is good, with a clarified and intensified experience. If, on the other hand, our second experience (the post-analytic) is more confused and less intense, our judgment can only be that the work is not good.

[8] Stephen C. Pepper, *Basis of Criticism in the Arts* (Cambridge: Harvard University Press, 1949), pp. 169–71.

IV

If the value of an aesthetic object is the experience it affords, the value of adopting a given method for instruction in artistic appreciation should be the guarantee of relevance in response. A work of art is not an invitation to respond in any way whatsoever. It is, however, a call to the sharing of human values as these are expressed within the artistic context. And the test that such communication is authentic can be constructed only if the viewer is led to adopt the same criteria of judgment as the sincere artist who is constantly checking on the clarity of his own expression. Aesthetic judgment is central to the development of the institution we seek to describe, and training in aesthetic judgment is necessary for a greater participation by the several members of the social body in the effectiveness of this institution. If this can be achieved, finally, the social worth of both creation and appreciation may be taken as established.

We began by bracketing out irrelevancies, the better to comprehend the significance of aesthetic experiences and their intrinsic worth to the members of society capable of enjoying them. As a result, everything extrinsic is declared irrelevant: all didacticism, all moralism, all propaganda falls without the enclosing grasp of our brackets. And if this is the case, the value of art is not in the truths it may propagate. But this is only to say that the function of art is not to teach, preach, or incite to political action. Viewed in this light, the institutionalization of art around one of these extrinsic or ancillary functions is readily seen as a misunderstanding, and the professionalization of artists within such a social structure as a violation of artistic freedom. No wonder, then, that creative artists stubbornly refuse the blandishments of federal governments, whether Soviet or American. What remains to be constructed is a social system in which aesthetic freedom to experiment and to create, the autonomy of aesthetic objects, and the responses of informed audiences are regulated by the sole relevant aesthetic criterion: the aesthetic judgment of perceptive individuals. And this is what no society has yet succeeded in doing on a massive scale. It cannot be done, moreover, unless aesthetic judgment becomes a universal requirement for graduation from institutions of public instruction.

The sooner this training is begun, the better; it can be started in the child's first drawing class. Waiting for a class in aesthetics, which is usually not taught until the upper classes of college, is a waste of human resources. For this reason, it seems to make greater sense to instruct the teachers of our public schools in the art of making aesthetic judgments, and to allow them to pass on this technique to their pupils and students. Such is the task of the profession of aesthetic education.

But the case is not completely established. We have as yet to make clear the values of aesthetic education to the students and to society considered as a whole.

First, for the students. The successful artist, submitting his imagination to the discipline of the materials of a given art medium, learns skills no other endeavor can afford: to make a sensuous construct of immediate significance to himself. We call it a work of art. Aided by the properly trained teacher, other students are brought to an understanding of this significance, and thus to have their own imaginations or understandings controlled by the perceptual structures of the student-artist's construct. For verbally handicapped children this may be the only way to permit communication and hence participation in the greater social scheme. Does the value of aesthetic education stop here?

Obviously not. But to make this clear we must now widen the scope of our restricting brackets. No truly human activity can remain thus restricted for too long. Having aesthetic experiences and making aesthetic judgments, however autonomously we consider the objects of such experiences and judgments, make a difference in the personalities of those having or making them; and the ability to make aesthetic judgments can have tremendous social consequences. Here once again training in aesthetic judgment contributes what no other academic discipline can do so well.

It will be recalled that one of the rules for the determination of aesthetic significance prohibited assigning an absolute value to any single counter in the aesthetic object. Any idea discriminable within the context has only that value assignable to it as is perceivable from the manner of its portrayal in context. The habit of judging images or ideas so expressed, and of determining their significance within the ranges of feeling actually felt, produces a type of personality no society can afford to be without. We can place the value of an expression on an image or idea considered out of context; but if we do, we are producing a scientific or a religious personality. We can place values on ideas and images for their use in propagandizing one political program; but if we do, we are producing a political fanatic. Who needs them? Certainly a truly open society does not.

Disciplined judgment may be admitted as a corrective to bigotry and fanaticism, but in what sense does the scientific endeavor stand in need of the kind of restriction, or correction, we find desirable? This case is not as easy as the others.

It seems obvious at the outset that contextual judgments are necessary for the correct development of science itself. The significance of a successful hypothesis is its workability, i.e., its explanatory and predictive power. One must consult the context of available data and the existing state of knowledge merely to come to a workable hypothesis, and there must be a further return to the data of experience to test whether or not it actually works as supposed. Surely nothing could be more careful or disciplined. So much is certain.

The question becomes more complicated, however, when we realize that not even the scientific impulse is immune from fanaticization. This happens every time scientific discoveries are applied toward the construction of needless gadgets, whether simple infernal machines or monstrous institutions. The crash program to construct the atomic bomb was a perfect case in point—applied science at its best. Unfortunately, there are no clearly definable scientific principles for guiding the decisions to use the bombs; that's a moral or aesthetic question. To make such a decision one must be able to imagine the quality of a life in the world once the bombs have been dropped—the aesthetic, and then to weigh this quality against that projected upon the world if they are not to be dropped—the moral.

Moreover, since technocracy is the trend of today's warring ideologies, the problem becomes much broader than a simple decision to use or not to use a bomb. The social sciences, from which one might seek some guidance for solving this kind of social problem, are themselves contributing to the dangers of the fanaticized scientific consciousness. With only a little more progress in genetics, we could be only a step away from *Brave New World,* the prototype of contemporary horror tales. But that novel, like the others (*On the Beach, 1984,* and *Fahrenheit 451*), gives ample testimony that an aesthetic consciousness has its role in determining human motives.

Science, then, needs fulfillment and can find it only in the further development of moral and aesthetic consciousness. Science for science's sake, without application to the problems of men, is as empty a catchword as art for art's sake. Both activities are meaningful to the degree that they enrich the lives of men. This they can do only by remaining true to their intrinsic purposes: science to uncover the truth, and art to present the quality of a lived experience in a perceptual context.

In widening our brackets to include the effects of having aesthetic experiences on individuals and societies, we arrive thus at an hypothesis which may be empirically verified by using the techniques of the social sciences. Take two groups, one for control, and measure the differences for having the one submitted to the discipline of aesthetic judgment. It would be surprising indeed if the aestheticized group did not respond differently from another randomly selected from the overall population. If one were adequately trained to the experience of quality and the process of applying an aesthetic criterion to the problems of its judgment, and the results were significantly positive, we should have made the case for institutionalizing the aesthetic impulse. Aesthetic education would then be a necessary part in the instruction of every child in a democratic community, and not something "nice" to be allowed if the other, more pressing, conditions of life permit. Art is not a leisure-time activity, but a necessary condition for the goodness of life.

V

One thesis remains. Can phenomenology, or a revised form thereof, be applied as the method of educational inquiry? The answer would seem to be affirmative if a model for educational practice could be erected that is consistent with that constructed for aesthetic communication above. Research has already begun.

Suspecting that the explanatory model of science has been defective for the prediction of desirable educational results, professors Ecker and Eisner [9] indicate two sources of difficulty: first of all, current research, statistical in character, is concerned with groups or classes of individuals, not with the specific manner in which a given individual reacts to his own classification or to his specific situation; and, of course, the teacher, too, though he may think that his procedures are rationally constructed upon scientifically observable phenomena, faces the same necessity of individual decision. Thus Ecker and Eisner write:

> Findings from statistical research must be treated with the utmost care in making teaching decisions designed to affect particular cases. The usefulness of such findings is realized only if artfully transformed. This kind of transformation is difficult because some of the actions the teacher employs in the teaching act may be only tenuously influenced by the findings he may want to use in the classroom. That is, his own behavior as a teacher may not be controlled, in the main, by a rational consciousness logically guiding his day-to-day, personal interactions with students.[10]

And they go on to speculate:

> . . . it may not be too far-fetched to entertain the thought that some of the preconscious aspects of teacher behavior may be among the most artful and beneficial of the teaching act.[11]

Here we find the beginnings of a new approach. Teaching itself may be considered an art, and not in the merely technical sense

---

[9] *Readings in Art Education* (Waltham, Mass.: Blaisdell, 1966), pp. 14–19.
[10] *Ibid.*, pp. 15–16.
[11] *Ibid.*, p. 16.

of the word. A teacher manages a complex system of qualities. What he does at any given moment must depend upon what he sees developing between the students and himself. His aim is always increased communication, i.e., participation in the social process.

If the second of the limitations Ecker and Eisner have found for the use of a totally scientific method in teaching—the ethical question of which value the teaching and learning is to be thought of as accomplishing—is understood to be solved by the decision to learn and teach art rather than good citizenship or what have you, then the total picture becomes somewhat clearer. The teacher in his classroom is an artist communicating the value of his subject discipline—in this special case, art—through the medium of class interaction.[12] If our model worked once before, it may well work once again. All we have to do is to learn to put brackets around the autonomously significant context. They would include ourselves as observant educational researchers and a successful teacher manipulating the counters of his medium. To be sure this will give us no rules for producing successful teaching, just as aesthetics gives us no rules for the production or appreciation of art works; but it should go far toward enabling us to create the educational categories needed to control further observations.

Do we dare construct these educational (aesthetic) categories? If we do, and if we succeed, our criteria of judgment on specific cases will always be found in the interpretation of a given context, since each context found to be significant bears within its own structure the criterion of its significance. This is perhaps the ninth criterion to be added to the list suggested by professors Eisner and Ecker;[13] or, on the other hand, the only one needed to replace the other eight.

[12] My "The Existential Ground for Aesthetic Education."
[13] Eisner and Ecker, *Readings in Art Education,* p. 24.

KNOWLEDGE AND AESTHETIC EDUCATION

Louis Arnaud Reid

The development of aesthetic sensibility through the arts or through the appreciation of natural forms is, in many schools in England at least, a neglected aspect of liberal education in the later years of school life. Aesthetic education—the very expression is loaded—is perhaps a nice "refinement" to be added to the sterner processes of knowledge-getting, and it tends to be pushed aside as the demands of technological civilization increase. Aesthetic sensibility programs no computers and butters no bread. Not only this, it is not even (or so it is thought) "knowledge." Pure science is not only a basis for the usefulness of technology—it is desirable in itself as increasing our understanding of the structures of nature. So do geography and history increase our knowledge of the world of nature or of the interplay between human decisions and events. But the enjoyment of a symphony or a poem or a sculpture, a painting or a dance—this is "enjoyment" perhaps, but it does not (it is held) increase knowledge. Again, to play music, write verse, paint, sculpt, or dance—these are perhaps "expressions," but not knowledge. So popular and even educated opinion seems to assume.

I think this widely accepted assumption is quite wrong. It is of course obvious that the aesthetic experience of art or nature is not at all knowledge of the same kind as, say, scientific knowledge or historical knowledge. Science and history attempt to discover facts of different kinds, discounting as far as possible the influence of idiosyncratic, personal factors, striving for an objectivity in which personal feelings are not involved. Aesthetic experience involves personal feeling and could not (I think) be aesthetic without some of it: it is value knowledge rather than knowledge of independent fact. Yet subjective involvement does not entail that the experience is only subjective, only "feeling." Mature aesthetic experience of a Rembrandt portrait or of a

From the *Journal of Aesthetic Education*, vol. 2, no. 3 (July 1968): 41–49. Reprinted by permission of the *Journal* and the author.

Bach fugue involves, surely, knowing of a highly discriminative kind, a kind which requires much education. Moreover, if we think of the history of culture, aesthetic knowledge through all the arts—dance, drama, music, literature, painting, sculpture, and the rest—is one of its most important aspects. If this is true, any "liberal" education which leaves out the dimension of the aesthetic or makes it an optional extra has seriously lost its sense of proportion.

In the following paper I shall be thinking of the aesthetic aspect of the arts only. ("The arts" are much wider than "the aesthetic"—although in another sense the aesthetic is much wider than the arts.) I shall argue that aesthetic experience is a kind of knowledge sui generis, knowledge of meaning wholly embodied in the aesthetic object and in this way different from all other knowledge.

I say "meaning embodied" as distinct from "meaning expressed." The word "expression" is sometimes used to mean what I call "embodiment." I formerly sometimes used it in this way myself (e.g., in my *A Study in Aesthetics*). Very often it is not. When we talk of art as "expressing something," we may ask, *what* is it that is expressed? A piece of music, for example, or a dance, or a poem may be said to express a certain mood or a certain idea. There is no harm in this language up to a point; it partially describes something which is the case. But although art can be expressive in various senses, I think "expression" is not the right word to indicate the *central* concept of the aesthetic, partly because it tends to direct our attention to something other than the perceived work of art itself—the ideas which the poem expresses or the mood behind the music or the dance. Although the use of the word "expression" can be carefully guarded (e.g., as in Susanne Langer's most sophisticated writings) so that it does not attract our attention to something other than the work of art itself, the word embodiment as emphasizing the inseparability of form and content seems to me a much safer word to use.

If it is used in aesthetics, it must be understood to have a technical meaning, a sense in which the very form of the symbol is in a sense part of its meaning. (I shall return to this.) "Embodiment" *can* also be used in an ordinary nontechnical sense, as when we say an idea is embodied in a formula or memorandum. But here the formula or memorandum consists of symbols, the particular perceived forms of which are unimportant so long as they convey the meaning. Or if I say, "The book is on the table," the words express or embody the meaning in an ordinary sense. There is nothing aesthetic about that; it can be said in any language. The symbol here is mostly a necessary instrument to the meaning. Form aesthetically embodying meaning, on the other hand, is not merely instrumental to the grasp of aesthetic meaning: attentive perception of the form is an essential part of the apprehension of the meaning.

A. E. Housman has a piece about the feelings of a condemned man waiting for the striking of the clock which will be the sign for his execution. The poem is about this, the poem "expresses" and expresses (one conjectures) the feelings of the poet who wrote it. When we read aloud, intelligently, and with full emphasis, the words of the poem, the total meaning of what we know there can only be known as it is embodied in the poem.

> He stood, and heard the steeple
> Sprinkle the quarters on the morning town.
> One, two, three, four, to market-place and people
> It tossed them down.
>
> Strapped, noosed, nighing his hour,
> He stood and counted them and cursed his luck;
> And then the clock collected in the tower
> Its strength, and struck.
> —A. E. Housman, *Eight O'clock*

I do not claim that there is anything new to the critic or the aesthetician in this idea of embodiment. What I would maintain is that it is seldom taken with serious consistency and that many of the important problems of the relation between art and life are misconceived because this central fact of the aesthetic is forgotten.

I have briefly contrasted meaning as expressed in the symbols of ordinary language with meaning embodied. There was implied in this a suggestion that the symbol of aesthetic embodiment, if properly called "symbol" at all, must be a very special kind of symbol. This must now be developed.

Is the work of art in *any* sense clearly a symbol? In some ways it seems to be, and in others not. Perhaps the term "work of art" is ambiguous, and is being used in at least two different senses.

The term "work of art" is indeed in a very obvious sense ambiguous. It can mean (*a*) the physical objects that hang on walls or are otherwise displayed in galleries, and which may be looked at in various unaesthetic ways—e.g., by the servitor in the gallery as so much weight to be lifted about, or by some meticulous scientist who wants for some reason to measure areas of color or formulate geometrical patterns in pictures or sculptures. *Mutatis mutandis,* the same could be said of other kinds of art. Although such a use of "art" is quite common and understandable, it is also clearly inadequate. "Works of art" are not just physical objects to be observed or shifted about casually; they are also (*b*) consciously made artifacts to be enjoyed aesthetically. In this sense, everything under heading (*a*) might be described not so much as art, but as the physical conditions—perceived or otherwise—for the existence of "art" in any full sense.

These conditions for the full existence of art might be called "symbolic" conditions—though as actually described under heading (*a*) they are not even that: the supposed servitor or scientist does not think of them as symbols but as perceived material objects. They *could,* however, be counted as "symbols." Let us call, for short, by the name "perceptua" what is presented to our senses when ordinary words and sentences are used, or when we look at pictures or listen to pieces of music. In the case of meaningful words and sentences the perceptua are, clearly, taken as symbolic. In the case of pictures or pieces of music, it may be argued that the perceptua again have to be taken as symbols. Although pictures and music *can,* as we have said, be taken as just occupying so much space or filling the air, they can also be taken as aesthetically meaningful, and therefore, it might be argued, symbolic. I say "might be argued" because, since the perceptua are (aesthetically) meaningful, they would appear to be "symbols." One usually assumes that, where there is meaning, there are perceptua which mean, and these are what we call "symbols." But although it is quite clear that the perceptua involved in the use of ordinary meaningful words and sentences are "symbols," and it looks as though exactly the same reasoning should be applied to the perceptua of art, the perceptua of art have a relation to their aesthetic meaning which is so different from the relation of the perceptua (heard or written words and sentences) of ordinary language to *their* meaning, that the word "symbol"—which seems entirely appropriate in the latter case—cannot be assumed without argument to apply to the perceptua of art in the same or even in an analogous way. There is a difficult question and a problem which can be suppressed by the too-easy use of the word "symbol" as applied to art perceptua.

The plausible case *for* a distinction between perceptua and aesthetic meaning may seem obvious. Patterns of paint or sound are in one sense quite distinguishable from their aesthetic meaning and can be pointed to; meaning is *not* just patterns of paint or sound. As a piece of analysis, this seems self-evident. It is a piece of analysis, however, and when we think of "art" in sense (*b*) above, the opposite and apparently contradictory fact emerges. This is the inseparability of "aesthetic surface" and "meaning." In *aesthetic* experience of art (as distinct from a philosophical analysis) there seems to be no distinction between perceived patterns of paint or sound and their meaning. We do not, aesthetically, see or hear (1) patterns of paint or sound, *and* (2) say or think or suppose or know that they "mean" so and so. This is why Langer (at times) prefers "expressive form" rather than "art symbol." I prefer it too (at times), but I prefer to say that we apprehend patterns of paint or sound, not as "meaning something" or "expressing something," but as *meaningful:* in other words there is a unique thing, *embodied meaning*. This is quite different from the relations of words and sentences to *their* meanings. The words and sentences refer to things or concepts or propositions which are their meanings and —although one cannot apprehend clearly concepts or propositions without some words and sentences—words and sentences have a meaning which is distinct from them. It must be so, because (as we said) the same meaning can be stated in different languages, written in different-looking alphabets (English, Russian, Greek, etc.). In art, there is no such distinct meaning: aesthetic meaning is so bound up (as ordinary verbal meaning is not) with the particular individual shape, form, color, etc., of the perceptua that it cannot be stated adequately in any other way. *This* exact meaning can be said in no other "language." The meaning of the perceptua of art is certainly not separate from them and, in aesthetic experience, often not even distinguishable. It is this which makes the use of the word "symbol" very questionable as applied to art.

Is it a contradiction of the very idea of symbol to say that the form of the aesthetic perceptuum, the form of the aesthetic "symbol," aesthetically perceived, is *part* of aesthetic meaning? In a way it is: in another way, perhaps, it is defensible. Certainly, if we were to say of ordinary symbols—words, sentences, mathematical formulae—that their perceived shape or form was "part" of their meaning, we should certainly be wrong, because here the particular symbols used are not only distinct, but *separate* from their meanings. The words, the sentences, the formulae, are one thing: symbols, noises, marks. The concepts and propositions which they mean are another. They are clearly separate, because, as we know, there can (on the one hand) be many sets of symbol perceptua for one single conceptual and propositional meaning: and on the other hand, the perceptuum is separate from the conceptual or propositional meaning because it is a different sort of thing from it. But of the *aesthetic* symbol these things are not true. Philosophically or conceptually speaking, the aesthetic perceptuum can, and for logical purposes must, be distinguished from *what* it means, its meaning. In one sense it is the patterns of shape, sound, etc. (the perceptua, in one sense the "symbols") which *have* meaning, distinguishable from them. "In one sense":—that is the sense in which the aesthetic symbol is a species of the genus "symbol," sharing the nature of all symbols. Yet, although this common distinction between symbol and meaning must be sustained in the case of the aesthetic symbol, and has just been applied to it, it leaves out the "something more" which is an essential characteristic of the aesthetic symbol, and so fails to differentiate it.

I said that "philosophically or conceptually speaking" the "aesthetic perceptuum," the "symbol," must be distinguished from *what* it means. This is a necessary and proper carry-over from general language about symbols. But it is inaccurate and misleading language too. For if it is strictly the *aesthetic* symbol, the perceptuum *aesthetically* apprehended, which is meant, there is *no* distinction (in aesthetic experience) between the aesthetic perceptuum and its aesthetic meaning, and certainly no separation. It is this kind of thing which is hinted at when we say that the aesthetically perceived pattern is, or is "part" of, its meaning. At least it is not a downright mistake (as we saw that it is a mistake if applied to ordinary symbols, which are not only distinct from but separate from their meanings). But it is language full of difficulty and obscurity. Why?

If we talk in aesthetics about the aesthetic symbol and aesthetic meaning, we are talking a meta-language which is continuous with talk about symbols in general. In this general language, as has been made clear, "symbol" and "meaning" are distinct, and correlative. If we are applying this language to aesthetics, we can distinguish between the form or "shape" of the perceptuum as perceived aesthetically (the "symbol") and its aesthetic meaning. In this kind of language it would be nonsense to say things like "the symbol means itself," or, "the symbol is part of its own meaning." It is nonsense because a symbol cannot mean "itself" (the symbol) or part of itself.

But we can also talk another kind of language—perhaps it might be called a "first-order" language—a language which attempts to describe what actually happens in aesthetic experience itself. Aesthetic experience has to be known at first hand if we are to attempt to begin to understand it, for it is a unique kind of experience. Supposing we have had such experience, we find, when we begin to try to describe it, that we are forced into the language of metaphor and analogy, a language which can suggest and point but which requires what may be called the "aesthetic leap" to be fully understood. Suppose, then, that we are trying to talk this language. We should not, I think, use at all *naturally* the language of "symbol" and "meaning" as distinguishable ideas, for this language belongs to a more general philosophy of symbolism. We should talk naturally not of "perceptua-symbols" meaning things but (as I suggested) of the forms of a picture or sculpture or dance or piece of music as "just full of meaning" or "meaning*ful*." We should be talking of embodiment, or meaning embodied.

The knowing of art is the knowing of embodied meaning. But the question arises, How do we know that we are knowing? We seem to know the aesthetic meaning of the work immediately, but this seeming to know is a kind of claim which has to be justified in some way. Feeling that we know is no guarantee of genuine knowledge. Learning to know meaning in art takes time and education, and if we talk in this way there must be criteria of successful learning and education.

These are enormous, involved, and very important questions which I regret I cannot enter upon here. I can only make the following brief observations dogmatically and without argument.[1] (1) Knowing aesthetically is not, *in itself,* "knowing about" but intuition of an aesthetic gestalt, for which there is no substitute. (2) But "knowing about"—about materials, structures, techniques, schools, idioms, fashions, social background, motivation, and history of art—is most necessary for the intelligent understanding of the arts. Such knowledge must be personally assimilated, must not remain as gobbets of information, as inert ideas. If assimilated it can transform seeing, hearing, and aesthetic understanding. (3) Critical talk about the arts, whether read or heard, or, even better, critical conversations between people who are not only sensitive and knowledgeable but genuinely anxious to progress by listening to and learning from one another—this is one of the best ways of illuminating and enriching the understanding of an art or a work of art. It can be applied to school, to discussion between teacher and pupils, where the pupils are encouraged to be honest and open in the expression of their judgments, guided tactfully (and

[1] Some references to these questions are made in two papers of mine: "On Talking about the Arts," *Philosophy,* vol. 41, no. 158 (October 1966); and "The Arts, Knowledge, and Education," *British Journal of Educational Studies,* vol. 15, no. 2 (June 1967). It is much more extensively dealt with in *Meaning in the Arts* (New York: Humanities Press, 1970).

never snubbed) by the teacher towards more discriminating perception. And, needless to say, the interplay between "appreciating" and "doing" art is a basic way of coming to understand it. (4) There is no final "proof" that aesthetic understanding has been attained and, of course, no formula which can be substituted for sensitive experience. An aesthetic judgment must always be a personal one. But this does not entail pure subjectivism, for we *can* communicate with one another about works of art, can analyze and discuss (with the kind of reasonableness which is appropriate to art) the art objects before us. Although there will always be some disagreements, especially about contemporary art, there is no insuperable obstacle to progress of understanding—so long as the points of disagreement are analytically clear. Out of disagreement, reasonably conducted, can develop a more mature understanding and appreciation. Indeed, it is just in this way that through time some consensus of opinion about the work of the Masters has been built up. One test of the understanding of the work of an artist is how we talk together about him.

The knowing and understanding of aesthetic meaning, then, is nourished and enriched from many sources, but in the end all this must be gathered into the intuition of a gestalt of transformed *embodied* meaning. The immediacy of this insight gives to aesthetic education an aim and character quite different from other parts of the curriculum. In other subjects—mathematics, science, history—we learn through symbols, linguistic or otherwise, which express concepts and propositions which in turn express abstracted characteristics of what we may loosely call the "world." We learn about the world in terms of language whose forms are mediate between ourselves and concepts and propositions and known by (relatively) disembodied intellect. But art knowledge of embodied meaning has a directness paralleled by nothing else (except, possibly, by our face-to-face knowledge of other persons). It is not, in itself, a "knowing that" but a knowledge by acquaintance in which the whole person participates. In the embodiment symbol, the perceived world is no longer a set of cues for further thought or action; its form is contemplated with rapt attention. We are confronted with embodied meaning in the form of the symbol itself in a way which does not happen in other academic studies. Aesthetic experience is a total form of living experience, a participating life which is too often absent from school learning. It gives knowledge of a unique kind which can be had in no other way. This is one basic reason why it should be accepted as a "must" in every liberal education. . . .

THE DEVELOPMENT OF QUALITATIVE INTELLIGENCE

David W. Ecker

. . . .

One of the traditional aims of education has been to develop, unfold, or release human intelligence. In this historic view, intelligence is generally conceived as consisting of the rational or reasoning powers of man. The conception of intelligence, which is equated with cognitive activity, is usually joined with the idea that reasoning at its best is a means by which man can get to know reality, the nature of the good, higher truths, or God. This "absolute knowledge," valued as the most worthy of human goals or ends, is to be achieved by dialectical, deductive or a priori methods of discursive thought. But whatever spiritual values are obtained by this kind of thought are more than offset by the notorious failure of these dialectical methods to solve the insistent and demanding problems of men—the problems of survival in the face of the vicissitudes of nature, as well as the problems of associative living. In striking contrast are the enormous successes of the empirical method and procedures of modern science in solving many of the problems of this world, among them the control of disease, maintenance of a food supply and adequate shelter—even the problem of national defense, where the most abstract of the physical sciences have practical bearings on human affairs. Thus scientific knowledge is instrumental; it is valued as a *means* rather than as an ultimate end. If an "ultimate" *end* be sought, perhaps a plausible candidate would be human intelligence itself. The success of science has persuaded some contemporary educators that the method of science is the method of intelligence. Indeed, Dewey argues that the method of science originates from the practical affair of living; it is the method of experience made explicit and more re-

From *Studies in Art Education*, vol. 5, no. 1 (Fall 1963): 77–80. Reprinted by permission of *Studies in Art Education* and the author.

fined for the purpose of gaining more control over the means and ends of experience.

What is to be noted about the alternative values placed upon intelligence in the history of education is that formal schooling has traditionally directed human intelligence toward the "oughts" and the "ultimate" goods of life—sometimes, as of yore, to the rewards of a "life hereafter"—typically separating these ends from the practical, daily means of existence. The first is spiritual; the second is corporeal. The rejection of this dualism which sets ends apart from means stems from the practice and conclusions of science. A scientific alternative to dualism holds that goals are obtainable only as we have hypotheses that direct us to perform those operations which conceivably secure the ends sought. Thus means and ends are not to be taken as dichotomous, but as functionally related items to be identified in inquiry. *Intelligence, as here conceived, is the procedure of ordering means to ends; it involves purpose and control.* Intelligence is always an affair of experience; it is a dynamic process which arises from past experience; it acts significantly to modify the context of present experience; and it is assessed in terms of its consequences in future experience. It is, then, a reconstructive, creative activity whereby present materials (alternative means) are selected and rejected on the basis of whether they will secure anticipated futures (selected ends).

The question arises as to how, or in what sense, the past and future can be available in a given present. What is the material mediated? The answer given by some investigators is that the materials of intelligence, or purposeful thought, are *symbols*. That is, the past and possible futures are *represented* in the present. Materials in the present signify either events already taken place or imagined future events.

If intelligence can be fairly described as the relating of means to ends, is it also fair to hold, as traditionalists often do, that intelligence is exhausted by and limited to rationality, to the manipulating of linguistic symbols—words or numbers? It would seem that such human activities as sports, games, hunting, the fine arts, and warfare contain examples of both purposes and controls which *do not* primarily involve linguistic materials.

Yet materials *are* manipulated; means *are* related to anticipated ends. For example, a spear fisherman assembles his diving gear —a mask, compressed-air gun, flippers, aqua-lung (he rejects a rod, reel, and net)—as appropriate means for his anticipated ends: his quarry, a deep sea bass (not seaweed, coral, or plankton). Other means employed are the techniques of submerging, swimming, and breathing, while stealth and attentiveness characterize his actions. Were he able to speak as he acts, he could probably describe his intentions, doubts, fears, and choices among possible maneuvers. Yet while he may think the words "bass," "undertow," "riptide," "shark," "danger," when the referents for these words are not present, he may also think or "picture" the nonpresent referents themselves. This is prima facie evidence in support of the claim that means-ends orderings that are not linguistic are present in experience. Apparently, purposive behavior or activity is not limited to overt linguistic behavior, or even to unspoken verbal thoughts, but includes imaginative, pictorial, or other orderables. "Planning-seeking-spearing fish" behavior, since it is not random, but a case where means and ends are selected and rejected, is also a mode of intelligence.

A host of problems now present themselves. If logic is the normative science which yields controls or regulations for valid reasoning—the kind of thought which consists in the manipulation of propositions—then what is it that acts to regulate or control such nonverbal, purposive behavior as I've described? If there are other than the controls for knowing, are they symbolic? If there is more to intelligence than knowing, what is the significance of this idea for art educators? Can the controls over *artistic* means-ends orderings be located?

I think they can and have been located.[1] There is abundant

[1] One may find in John Dewey's essay, "Qualitative Thought," perhaps the earliest original source of ideas in the English language relevant to the task of building a methodological conception of artistic control; i.e., its means-ends and method. The range of ideas in this document focuses on his central theme that ". . . the immediate existence of quality, and of dominant and pervasive quality, is the background, the point of departure, and the regulative principle of all thinking." Further, he states, "Construction that is artistic is as much a case of genuine thought as that expressed in scientific and philosophical mat-

evidence in art history that artists do order lines, textures, volumes, and colors as qualitative *means* to achieve their qualitative *ends*—objects that we call examples of impressionist, constructivist, and international styles of painting, sculpture, and architecture, respectively. We can pin these labels on art because critics have provided us with these theoretical symbols, each of which refers to a pervasive quality characterizing a series of art works. However, the critic's naming activity comes *after* the creation of what is named; e.g., the label "cubism" appeared on the scene subsequent to the appearance of the quality pervading the paintings of Picasso, Braque, and Gris in the first decade of this century. I am suggesting here that the availability of labels for styles—or titles for individual works—is not a necessary condition for one's being able to locate the artist's nontheoretical control; the controlling quality is already empirically available. Further, I am claiming that the pervasive quality acts as a *qualitative criterion* by which the artist selects, rejects, and relates qualitative means, from among available qualities, to achieve his qualitative end-in-view. His criterion and his method are as one.

ters, and so is all genuine aesthetic appreciation of art, since the latter must in some way, to be vital, retrace the course of the creative process." (*Philosophy and Civilization* [New York: Minton, Balch & Company, 1931], p. 116.)

Dewey's suggestions and methodological analyses of controlled production in the arts, found scattered throughout his writings, have since been so revised and critically extended as to have yielded certain fundamental changes in the Deweyan formulation of the philosophy of experimentalism. This work was initiated by F. T. Villemain in "The Qualitative Character of Intelligence," and continued by N. L. Champlin in "Controls in Qualitative Thought" (both unpublished dissertations, Columbia University, 1952). See also their article, "Frontiers for an Experimentalist Philosophy of Education," *The Antioch Review,* vol. 19 (1959): 345–59. Of further interest is "John Dewey Centennial: A Special Section," coedited by Villemain and Champlin, *Saturday Review,* November 21, 1959, pp. 16–26. This manifesto draws the broad implications of the notion of qualitative intelligence for American education, as does Villemain's article, "Democracy, Education and Art," *Educational Theory,* vol. 13, no. 4 (Fall 1963). For a technical and analytical statement, see Villemain's "Methodological Inquiry into Aesthetic Subject Matter" (*Proceedings of the Seventeenth Annual Meeting of the Philosophy of Education Society,* Detroit, Michigan, March 26–29, 1961, pp. 151–67).

Now, qualities to be considered as *symbols* must be shown to act in a representing or mediating capacity. At the same time, they must be distinguished from cognitive or "theoretical" representation and mediation. In support of the idea of "qualitative symbol," we may profitably consider the possible intention behind this amusing and paradoxical statement: "If everything we perceived were white, there would be no white." "White" as a term, here, would be meaningless; since it apparently refers to everything, it thereby refers to nothing. We see that a quality is distinguishable only as there is a relationship or contrast noted, say, a white figure on a blue ground. However, to *distinguish* a color is not necessarily to *name* it. In fact, we do not have enough color words in the English language to name even a small part of the colors artists have created, discriminated, and ordered in their work. The labels on paint tubes do not assist in the artist's qualitative task. So I think we have a qualitative symbol when a quality represents the relationship which would present it, the relation which established it as a distinguishable characteristic in the world. This triadic relation generates quality as symbol. While a theoretical symbol represents anything *other than* itself, a qualitative symbol represents a system of relations in which itself is included, i.e., the qualitative symbol presents itself and represents the relation of contrast. Hence artistic ordering may be properly viewed as an example of *qualitative intelligence.*[2]

To generalize these findings, in both linguistic and qualitative ordering, the distinctive feature of human conduct is its symbolic structure; the ends-in-view, objectives, or intended futures are represented in present conduct through the office of symbols, which are in some sense an outgrowth of past experience. Our task is not only to describe the controls actually at work in art,

[2] Qualitative intelligence understood as qualitative symbolic mediation is, of course, derived from the above sources and has provided the specific motivation and direction for the writer's own work in "Toward a Methodological Conception of Problem and Control in Art Education" (unpublished dissertation, Wayne State University, 1962), and other papers; e.g., "The Artistic Process as Qualitative Problem Solving" (*The Journal of Aesthetics and Art Criticism,* vol. 21 [Spring 1963]: 283–90).

but also to propose reconstructions of those controls which are to be used for the purpose of future orderings. Moreover, it is essential to realize that qualitative ordering is not confined to painting, sculpture, and drawing activities. It is going on in the classroom, on the playground, and in life, but does so, for the most part, unattended. That is, qualitative orderings have not received systematic attention from educators, schoolmen, or art teachers; this mode of intelligence has been neglected in educational theory and generally ignored in practice. It is because education is essentially a *moral* undertaking that the kind of reconstructive activity I have proposed is so vital—one in which art teachers should be engaged. The consequences to be expected of this kind of inquiry are general formulations as prescriptions for directing qualitative intelligence. It is precisely this kind of inquiry that has been so lacking in the central doctrines of art education. . . .

AESTHETIC EDUCATION AND MORAL REFINEMENT

Iredell Jenkins

The chief impediment to attaining a balanced view of the inter-relationship of art, morals, and education is the predisposition —largely unconscious but for that reason only the more disruptive—to interpret each of these elements in too restricted a manner. In the context of this issue, we tend to treat morality as though it were concerned only with sex and physical violence: we regard education as a strictly formal process carried on in schools, and we think of art exclusively in terms of the masterpieces that we encounter in museums, concert halls, libraries, and the great monuments of the past. Under this intellectual dispensation, aesthetic education is equated with art appreciation, and the moral significance of art is reduced to fruitless arguments about the definition of obscenity and limits of censorship. So if this problem is to receive the kind of consideration that its importance demands, the necessary first step is the cultivation of a broader and more realistic attitude toward its component elements.

I shall start, then, by stating as briefly as possible the manner in which I think the terms "art," "morality," and "education" must be conceived if we are to do justice to them separately and to understand their mutual involvement. These preliminary statements can be only rough, provisional stipulations rather than definitions; but they are necessary to initiate the discussion, and the whole of the ensuing argument will in effect be an elucidation of them.

With this qualification, "morals" shall refer to the entire complex of habits, attitudes, and purposes in terms of which we grasp and interpret the world and plot our courses through it. These habits are of various sorts. Without seeking to be exhaustive or systematic, we can easily identify habits of percep-

From the *Journal of Aesthetic Education,* vol. 2, no. 3 (July 1968): 21–39. Reprinted by permission of the *Journal* and the author.

tion, feeling, thought, judgment (or evaluation), and intention. These habits—with the attitudes and purposes that they engender and that cluster around them—determine to a great extent the ways in which we see things and situations, the meanings we attach to them, the values we set upon them, and the behavior we adopt to deal with them. Much of this concrete furniture of morality consists of what modern psychology has taught us to call "stereotypes," "prejudices" and "preconceptions," "preferences," "goals" or "ends in view," and "established behavioral patterns." Despite the shift of vocabulary, this account corresponds quite closely to the doctrine that Aristotle wove around the concept of "moral virtue." For both, our morality summarizes the expectations and aspirations with which we face the world and conduct our lives.

By "education"—which in this context of course means moral education—I refer to the whole variegated set of processes through which these habits, attitudes, and modes of interpretation are acquired. This acquisition occurs in various ways: by example and precept, by instinct and indoctrination, by persuasion and the pleasure principle, by gradual accretion and traumatic encounter. Much of this process of moral habituation or education is formalized and made explicit through such institutions as the family, the church, schools, and the community, which make a systematic effort to establish certain approved patterns of feeling and behavior, standards of conduct, ideals, and goals. But a great deal of it occurs in a haphazard manner, depending upon the specific influence that the environment exerts, the achievements that it encourages, the lessons it teaches, and the concrete things and situations that it presents as desirable. Moral education is at least as much imitation as inculcation; the former is almost certainly more effective, for here we select and adopt what appeals to us, while in the latter we are at the best passive and disinterested recipients.

The term "art" presents greater difficulties, and it will require more time and a closer effort to settle its meaning in even a preliminary and provisional manner. There is certainly abundant disagreement and debate concerning the specific habits, attitudes, and purposes that men should be encouraged to acquire;

and the same is true concerning the exact procedures that are useful and proper in fostering this acquisition. That is, the issue is often joined regarding both the contents that morality should embody and the techniques that education should employ. But at least there would be, I think, wide acceptance of the broad character and function that I have ascribed to these two above. With respect to art, it seems quite impossible to reach any level of discussion, however basic and general, that can afford a similar agreement. When we ask that simple question, "What is art?" seeking merely to identify the primitive source from which it springs and the pervasive features that it exhibits, we already find little but acrimonious dispute. The briefest glance at the table of contents of any anthology of aesthetic writings will make this clear: theorists disagree vehemently concerning even the fundamental categories in which art is to be described and explained. In the course of these disputes, three concepts have emerged as leading candidates for the role of the first principle, or basic category, of aesthetic theory: these are the notions of *imitation, expression,* and *form.* Each of these doctrines has served as a theme on which numerous variations have been played, and there have been attempts to develop theories in the borderland between these concepts, such as abstract expressionism, surrealism, and cubism. But the categories of imitation, expression, and form have maintained their primacy, and the adherents of each have been too intent on spreading their sectarian gospels to make any serious attempt at reconciliation and synthesis. Whatever the situation may be among the churches, the ecumenical spirit has not made much progress among aesthetic schools, each of which, it seems, would rather be dead than Red.

In truth, the relationship among these doctrines is one of complementarity rather than contradiction. They represent different perspectives and approaches to the aesthetic field; and any one of them, in isolation from the others, is a distortion and absurdity. Certainly no one would want to maintain that art is a "mere" imitation, in the sense of a copy or replication—like a plaster cast or a stenographic report, to cite the familiar instances—of an already existent reality. But no more would we want to maintain that art is a "sheer" expression and revelation of the artist's personality; we would not then take art as seriously as we do, especially when we bear in mind the flaws and aberrations that are such frequent accompaniments of the artistic temperament. And if art were indeed "pure" form, which had being but no meaning, then nine-tenths of what has been written by historians and critics of art—not to mention the responses of the wider audience and the intentions of artists themselves—would be absolute nonsense.

But even though these doctrines are alternative routes to a common truth rather than divergent paths to different destinations, it is still necessary to choose among them as conceptional apparatuses. Faced with this option, I prefer to take my stand on the category of imitation. The reason for this choice is that the concept of imitation asserts an intimate and essential relationship between art and reality: here I am using the term "reality" in a large, loose, and nonprofessional sense to include anything whatsoever that we encounter in experience. In brief, the doctrine of imitation, unlike the doctrines of expression and form, establishes an immediate and inalienable connection between the work of art and the work of the world. This in turn enables it to do greater justice to the felt quality of aesthetic experience, to the concerns and the behavior of artists as they create, and to the character of works of art. And certainly if art is to have any moral significance—apart from that of constituting a distinct and unique region of value of its own—its meanings must be rooted in the same world where we lead our lives as moral beings.

Immediately a critical question arises: "What is art an imitation of?" The classical answer to this question, first stated by Plato in the *Symposium* (as one of his several and conflicting theories of art) and most fully developed by Schopenhauer in Book III of the *World as Will and Idea,* was straightforward and unembarrassed: art imitates and discloses the world of forms or ideas, the realm of being as distinct from that of becoming. This aesthetic doctrine persists, long after its metaphysical theory has been rejected, in the familiar notions that art reveals the essence of things, or the ideal that underlies the actual, or the region of values rather than facts, or the inner meanings that hide in the heart of things. But these proposals are empty subterfuges, lacking the courage of their convictions and trying to hide their intellectual bankruptcy behind a pretentious verbal facade. When the modern temper becomes fully self-conscious, it altogether rejects the classical dualistic metaphysic of being and becoming, asserting instead that "nature" is all inclusive, self-sufficient, and self-explanatory. This view can be epitomized in two propositions. First, actuality exhausts reality. Second, science exhausts actuality. Together these assert that the scientific account of things is adequate and complete. So there is nothing left for art to imitate. Art can claim no distinctive realm to which it alone has access; and any account that art gives of the actual—of the space-time world that is our whole environment—must by stipulation be inferior to that given by science. As the contemporary mind commits itself to these seductive half-truths, the category of imitation fades away like the Cheshire cat, to be replaced by those of expression and form. The result of this is to segregate art in a realm of its own, isolating it from the affairs of the world and the concerns of life and depriving it of all moral significance. Where art speaks only of itself, it cannot have any meaning for the larger contexts of existence. If this situation is to be repaired by restoring the concept of imitation to a central role in aesthetic theory, we must find a satisfactory answer to the question of what it is that art imitates. That is, we must identify the subject matter of art— that to which it refers and regarding which it affords clarification—in a manner that will at once save the significance of art and be acceptable to contemporary modes of thought.

II

There are two general ways to solve the problem of artistic subject matter. One is to identify some region or type of reality— some mode of being or some specific elements—to which art has either an exclusive or a privileged access. This is the classical solution of Plato and Schopenhauer, embodied in the theory of forms; and it is the solution of those who hold that art discovers and reveals essences, or ideals, or values, or surface qualities.

The other approach is to identify *not* some specific subject matter, but rather a specific and distinctive way of dealing with any subject matter whatsoever. I shall adopt this latter solution. This is to say that the reach of art is universal and all embracing. Anything at all of which we become aware can and does arouse an aesthetic interest and receive artistic treatment. Art knows no boundaries or limitations, but demands the right and asserts the need to deal with everything that we encounter in experience.

I think that this claim is both empirically obvious and theoretically sound. The most casual examination of artworks reveals that their subject matter coincides with the reach of human awareness and concern. This subject matter includes physical objects recognized as units, parts of these, their surface qualities, their structure, the moods that seem to haunt them, the threats and promises they hold. It includes the emotions, attitudes, passions, and aspirations of men, as well as the situations and problems that men face, the motives these bring into play, the alternatives they offer, the purposes they generate, and the outcomes in which they issue. It includes the conditions and institutions with which society confronts man, and the values he pursues through these. And it includes, of course, the perceptual qualities and the formal structures that together compose the texture of our sense experience. It is quite impossible to name any subject matter—anything at all that man discriminates in consciousness and in which he becomes interested—that has not been treated artistically and embodied in works of art. It is the world in its entirety that is grist for the artist's mill. With the adoption of this position, a critical question arises.

What is the distinctive character of the aesthetic way of regarding things, and what is the unique enlightenment that art brings to experience? My answer to this question rests upon the thesis that art is one of three coordinate ways of exploring the world and improving our acquaintance with it. I have elsewhere argued this position in detail,[1] and I must here content myself

[1] *Art and the Human Enterprise* (Cambridge: Harvard University Press, 1958); "The Human Function of Art," *Philosophical Quarterly,* vol. 4 (1954): 128–46.

with stating it quite baldly. The fundamental point upon which this account rests is the recognition that experience is always composed of three strands, or moments. To be aware of anything at all and to hold it in consciousness is, as it were, to see it simultaneously from three perspectives, and so to regard it as having a threefold character and as playing a triple role. We experience this thing, in the first place, as being just the actual concrete thing that it is, asserting its own unique characteristics and standing quite alone. We experience it, in the second place, as existing in a world of other things, related to these in a multitude of ways, and occupying a definite position within a systematic context. We experience it, in the third place, as impinging upon ourselves and our lives, as fraught with various meanings for us, as demanding that we treat it in various ways to explore its promise and avert its threat.

These moments of experience—or dimensions of consciousness—I shall identify respectively as the *aesthetic,* the *cognitive,* and the *affective* components of experience. With respect to them, I would at once insist upon two points. First, these moments are present throughout consciousness: every experienced occasion has its aesthetic, cognitive, and affective aspects. Second, these moments are of coordinate value and significance; no one of them has priority of any sort over the others. In a very great deal of experience, these elements do not separate out, and we do not become aware of them as distinct. Rather, things are given to us in experience as fully three-dimensional and as a synthesis of these moments. But there are a sufficient number of experienced occasions when one of these perspectives becomes dominant and subordinates the others, though these are always present. Then our awareness and concern are concentrated on one aspect of things, experience takes on a distinctive coloring, and we push our acquaintance with things in a specific direction. If the aesthetic component dominates, our attention is centered on the *particularity* of things; it is their assertion of their individual existence and character that holds our interest, so we are led to regard things from their own point of view and to explore them on their own terms. When the cognitive component is dominant, our attention centers on the *connectedness* of things; it is the similarities and regularities that run among them that hold our interest, so we are led to regard things as items in an abstract schema and to explore the patterns of order and connection that bind them together. When the affective component dominates, our attention centers on the *import* of things; it is their immediate impact upon us and their availability to our uses that fills our concern, so we are led to regard things from the perspective of ourselves and to explore the possibilities and the threats that they offer us and the ways in which these can be manipulated so as to serve our own purposes.

It is in these terms that I would explain the aesthetic life, from the most transient and spontaneous encounters with particularity to the most carefully contrived and highly sophisticated works of art in which particularity is finally clarified and embodied. The aesthetic process begins with those simple occasions when we are momentarily fascinated by something we encounter; and this may be anything at all—the play of light and shadow on a wall, a face seen in a crowd, an emotion we undergo, a human situation that is brought home to us, a pattern of sensuous elements, social conditions and their impact upon the people who live under them, a future goal that appears to us as desirable, a landscape glimpsed from a speeding car. This primitive aesthetic apprehension of the particularity of things, though present in all experience, is usually so tentative and fleeting, and is so closely fused with awareness of their connectedness and import, that it passes unnoticed; these strands do not appear separately, but coalesce to compose what we call "a thing." Experience becomes fully aesthetic when our attention focuses sharply on the particularity of the thing before us. We then become aware of this thing as existing uniquely and in its own right. Awareness of its connectedness and import fades to the penumbra of experience; we rescue the thing from the generalities, the stereotypes, the preconceptions and prejudices, the habits of perception, thought, and action under which it is usually cataloged and disguised; and we attend to what the thing tells us of itself rather than what our categories and purposes ascribe to it.

This apprehension of particularity sometimes occurs suddenly and spontaneously, without apparent effort on our part or artificial assistance from others. These are those happy occasions when some feature of the natural or human world is given to us with a freshness and clarity it does not ordinarily have, so that we "see" it in a new light and with enhanced acuteness and intentness. But far more usually, as we are brought face to face with particularity, we realize that this does not adequately reveal itself on first acquaintance. It hints at more than it discloses; it is obscure, ambiguous, and fleeting; we sense meanings that we cannot fully clarify and retain, so this acquaintance must be more closely cultivated. But this effort is beyond the ordinary run of men: most of us have neither the innate capacity nor the acquired training to bring the particularity of things into a sharp and stable focus. If particularity is to be made available to us, it must be discerned by men of a special talent and discipline and then embodied in a form that brings it within our reach. These men are artists, and their search and outcome are what we know as art.

The case here is in no wise different from that which holds in the cognitive and affective dimensions of the life of the mind. The generality of men do not claim for themselves, nor expect of their fellows, that they can trace and explicate the connectedness of things or measure and manipulate their import. We assign these undertakings to those whom we call scientists—more broadly, theorists—and technologists. The task of the scientist is to discover the patterns of order and connection that run through the world: he *explains* things as *facts*—that is, as elements in a systematic schema. The task of the technologist— the moralist, the preacher, the engineer, the doctor, the lawyer —is to intervene in the course of events and direct it toward favorable outcomes: he *controls* things as *values,* that is, as vehicles of man's needs and purposes. The task of the artist is to articulate the precise structure and the rich texture of experienced objects and situations and events: he *presents* things as *entities,* that is, as unique beings that are fully concrete and determinate in their own right.

A word of qualification and caution is necessary here, to

guard against a semi-mystical worship of art as a revelation of the ultimate and absolute nature of things. Our grasp of things as entities, like our grasp of them as facts and values, is a blend of what we find in them and what we bring to them. What the artist presents to us is no unglossed version of reality: an entity is not a noumenon. It is, rather, a product of the artist's acumen, sensitivity, and persistence: in short, it embodies *his* vision of the world. This is the truth of expressionism. Furthermore, the work of art in which this vision is embodied is not a replication of what the artist has already achieved in some inspired and instantaneous insight or intuition. Rather it is a highly refined and compressed distillation of the artist's repeated encounters with particularity, and it is carefully contrived to confront us with this particularity in a definite way and to elicit from us a tightly controlled encounter with it. That is, the work of art is skillfully composed to hold our attention within itself and to define the course of our experience. This is the truth of formalism. But this painfully achieved and carefully wrought work— this formalized expression—does embody and convey to us an entity; this entity is the outcome of the artist's effort to remove things from the shadow cast by our preconceptions and prejudices, our categories and purposes, and to see them in their own characters. So what the work of art presents to us is a refined version of the particularity of the actual thing or occasion that precipitated the artist's venture. That is, it returns us to the body of the world and the flux of experience with an insight that has been clarified and disciplined by the artist's vision. This is the truth of imitation.

III

If the preceding interpretation is sound, then the moral significance of art and the importance of a proper aesthetic education can be readily established. So I will now proceed to draw these lessons of the position I have defined. In order to render the argument explicit, I shall trace its course briefly and almost schematically.

It is a central thesis of my doctrine that art speaks to us of the natural and human world of ordinary experience. However esoteric art may become, the source from which it issues and the material upon which it draws are public. The empirical evidence to support this theoretical claim is abundant and obvious. We frequently do refer the content that we derive from works of art to the "real" objects and events that compose the world (this is of course most apparent in representational art; but it is also largely true in abstract or nonobjective art, though here the subject matter is more subtle, the content more tentative, and the reference more ambiguous). Artists speak of their work as intended to sharpen our powers of apprehension, and to afford us a clearer vision of the things and situations that we encounter and of our entanglement with them. We speak of works of art as somehow revealing the essential character and structure of things, and so as rewarding attention with a closer grasp of reality. In short, we continually effect a transfer of meaning from art to life.

This is what must be meant when it is said, as it commonly is, that art embodies universal meanings and references. And there is nothing whatsoever paradoxical or mysterious about this. As I have argued above, art is concerned with the particularity of things, which it presents as unique, concrete, and determinate. But art inevitably speaks of things familiar: of objects and scenes in nature; of man's emotions and dreams, purposes and aspirations, hopes and fears, and doubts; of human relations and social conditions and the conflicts these generate—in brief, of the whole range and milieu of existence. This is the *subject matter* of art.

It is what the artist says about these things when he presents them as entities that is unexpected, challenging, and revealing. This specific illumination of what is generally familiar is the *content* of art. This content can be given only in and through the work of art itself: it exists only as embodied, and it cannot be translated or paraphrased. But we certainly can and do identify the subject matter to which this content refers. And we equally can and do ascribe to this subject matter what we have gleaned from art. That is, we realize that the content the artist reveals to us can be discerned as a real character of things themselves. In articulating his own unique encounters and experiences with things, the artist clarifies our own equally unique, but not so clearly realized, encounters and experiences. We will never sense or feel, undergo or express, just what the artist did, but what we discover in his work will be assimilated into the body of our experience, and so will influence what we experience in the future. Art has a universal relevance because it enhances the sensitivity that we bring to our encounters with things and occasions which, though themselves unique, are similar to those presented to us in works of art.

Because of this carry-over from art to life—from content to subject matter—art plays a large role in shaping our view of the character of the actual things and occasions that we encounter and deal with. It is generally held—quite independently of what specific aesthetic theory one espouses—that art has the power of arousing an intense reponse in its beholders, of fastening attention closely upon itself, and of tightly controlling the experience that it elicits. And men are inevitably influenced by the character and quality of those things to which they attend with heightened interest and concern. This is equally true of the "fictional" world of art as it is of the "real" world of nature: it is quite unreasonable to think that the experience of art takes place in a psychic vacuum, having no impact and leaving no trace on memory and imagination, perception and emotion and thought. Quite to the contrary, what we gather about the "artificial" things that art presents is transferred and ascribed to the "real" things of the world. We certainly distinguish these realms, but we do not segregate them. Rather, our experience is stocked from both, and moves easily back and forth between them. Hamlet is both a unique person and an epitome of man when he is torn by doubt and vacillation. When we speak of someone as "a Hamlet" or "a Don Quixote," "a Casper Milquetoast" or "a Walter Mitty," our opinion of him is fashioned at least as much by art as by direct acquaintance. Art is thus a major contributor to our catalogs of familiarity. It does a great deal to define the terms in which we approach, interpret, and deal with the world, from the simplest perceptual operations to the most complex moral judgments. How and what we see and hear; our settled views of different types, classes, and races of men; our opinions of social customs and institutions; the expectations and purposes with which we face the future; what we think to be desirable, valuable, right, and permissible—all of this comes to us quite largely through artistic presentation.

If this argument is to have its full force, two important and often ignored points must be borne in mind. In the first place, I think that art occupies a far larger place and plays a far more significant role in our lives than we usually recognize. We seriously underestimate the influence of art because we tend to view it in very esoteric and restricted terms. We think of art as being only what we find in museums, libraries, theaters, and concert halls; we suffer seriously from what John Dewey never tired of denouncing as an obsession with "fine art." Admittedly, the generality of men do not spend large amounts of time in these places. From this we conclude that most men have little or no aesthetic susceptibility and are untouched by the influence of art.

This is a gross error. In fact, man has a voracious aesthetic appetite. Men desperately want—in the double sense of both needing and desiring—to be aroused to a vivid and stimulating awareness of the things around them. They have an intense interest in and curiosity about the objects, people, and events that make up the furniture of the world: they are eager to have these presented with a sharp and compelling focus, so that they can engross themselves in them. We can see this impulse at work equally in the infant, the child, the youth, and the adult. All of these, in their various ways, are fascinated by the particularity of things, and are eager to escape the generalities and routines that govern so much of life and to be brought into intimate touch with things. When contemporary men turn to the cinema or music hall, to illustrated magazines or the television set, the true romance or the soap opera, they are voicing the same demand as their remote ancestors when they gathered to sing and dance, to listen to stories, or to gaze at pictures on the walls of caves, or as their more sophisticated brothers when they go to the museum, the theater, or the concert hall. In all of these cases, men are seeking to render more vivid, and so at once to celebrate and commemorate, the ordinary occasions of life.

This brings me directly to my second point, which is that this aesthetic appetite is both urgent and undiscriminating. Like most other human drives and capacities, this one requires careful training and an educated acquaintance with works of art if it is to reach a high development and fulfillment. Until it has been properly cultivated, man's aesthetic taste is apt to be led astray by art that is shallow, trivial, or even deceptive. Here it is necessary to make a distinction between good art and bad art, or what I prefer to call pseudo-art. Heretofore I have been talking about good art, which embodies a sensitive and sincere insight into particularity. Pseudo-art is work that embodies no intention or effort to see and feel things more finely, that contains no fresh insights, and does nothing to sharpen our experience of particular things. Instead of contributing to our vision, such work feeds upon our hopes and fears, flatters our preconceptions and prejudices, and smothers our discernment under banalities. Pseudo-art fills our awareness with a make-believe world from which failure is eliminated, and in which effort is unnecessary because the good always conquers and all our wishes come true. This distinction between art and pseudo-art is admittedly difficult to define precisely in theory and even more difficult to draw exactly in practice. But it is nonetheless always important and usually obvious. The appeal of pseudo-art is great, for it offers us easy escape to a world that knows only ease, pleasure, and vicarious success. Much of so-called popular art falls under this indictment, filled as it is with sentimentality, banality, inspirationalism, edification, and the happy ending.

Just here a most important fact must be recognized. For a very wide audience, it is largely pseudo-art that actually serves the artistic function. That is, it is pseudo-art to which many people attend and respond the most readily, and from which their sense of the actualities of life and the world is stocked. When we look at this matter realistically and functionally, and from the point of view of education and morality, we see that we must modify our earlier definition of art. Now we must say that art is whatever *pretends* to present particularity, and *is accepted* as doing so.

It is this fact, which I take to be ineluctable, that makes the quality of art and of aesthetic education so important. Unless we take the twin steps of making good art accessible to men and cultivating their appreciation of it, then they are going to prove susceptible to pseudo-art. The situation in the aesthetic domain of life is no different from that in its cognitive and affective domains. The generality of men rely upon the scientist to explain the connectedness of things, and upon the technologist to control their import. Since we accept the opinions and advice of those whom we regard as "experts," and since our powers of independent judgment are limited, we are largely at their mercy. So we can be deceived by pseudo-science and misled by pseudo-technology. Similarly, we can be deluded by pseudo-art.

We accept the challenge of this situation very seriously in the cognitive and affective domains. We take elaborate precautions, through academic training, professional associations, rigorous criticism and testing of ideas, and other means, to assure that those who speak authoritatively as scientists will be fit for the role they assume. We take similar steps in the case of our technologists: our engineers, lawyers, doctors, manufacturers. And here we add the heavy weight of government supervision and regulation. Furthermore, we pay a good deal of attention to the scientific and technological education of the lay audience; that is, we try to familiarize men with accepted doctrines and sound procedures, to warn them against imposters and quacks, and to provide them with rough criteria for distinguishing substance from shadow.

We do very little, if any, of this in the aesthetic domain. Here, despite a good deal of lip service at the altar of fine art, we seem content to leave men at the mercy of whatever clamors for their attention and appeals to their untutored taste. As regards art, relativism reigns, permissiveness is the watchword, and one is expected to know only what he likes. I think the reason for this deplorable state of affairs is simple and obvious: although we honor art and surround it with ceremonious deference, we do not really respect it. We somehow feel that art is grand and noble, but we have no clear sense of its role in the direction of our lives or its contribution to our well-being. Since we cannot identify the function and purpose of art, we cannot feel it as really significant, and so we do not take it with deep seriousness.

I would hope that the preceding account has sharpened this vagueness, repaired this uncertainty, and given explicit justification to the adoration we have felt for art but have been unable to explain. If my argument is sound, art, by defining our sense of the particularity of actual things and occasions, exercises a crucial influence on the terms in which we confront the world and order our lives. That is, art plays a critical role in man's moral education, in the sense in which I have defined those terms. And if this is once recognized, it should be compellingly clear that society must acknowledge in the aesthetic domain the same two fundamental obligations that it accepts in the cognitive and affective domains: to assure that good art is available and that men are cultivated to appreciate it.

IV

In closing, it is necessary to anticipate two objections that are sure to be urged against this position, and to correct a common misunderstanding. The objections focus on the first of the points made just above: that we must be concerned for the quailty of art because of its moral significance. The misunderstanding has to do with the second of these points, and clouds our conception of aesthetic education. I shall deal with these matters only briefly, and in that order.

It is first objected that the view here presented degrades art by reducing it to a subservient status and making it the mere hand-maid of morality. This, it is held, would deprive the artist of his freedom, subject him to control by alien and ignorant authorities, and force him to serve purposes that are not his own as an artist. Further, it would mean that works of art are judged against standards that are altogether extraneous and irrelevant to artistic merit. Finally, it would make of art a purely didactic and hortatory device. In sum, art would become a branch of propaganda.

If the fears and charges expressed by this objection were well founded, they would indeed be lethal, for this would constitute a travesty and betrayal of art. But the objection itself is misconceived and distorted. The effective answer to it is based on the distinction between final and instrumental, or intrinsic and extrinsic, values. A work of art itself, as an artifact, is merely a physical object having certain properties and characteristics. It is not a value itself—either intrinsic or extrinsic—but is a vehicle of value. It embodies values that the artist has discovered and wrought from his experience, and it conveys analogous values through the aesthetic experiences that it elicits. But what of these experiences themselves? What mode of value do they have? I would maintain that aesthetic experience has a dual character and status, and hence a dual value. In the first place, it is just this experienced occasion, a moment of delight and fascination, suffused by awareness of the art work before it. As such, it has final or intrinsic value. But that is not the end of the matter. For, in the second place, this aesthetic experience is absorbed into the body of experience, and there deposits the meaning that it has gleaned from the art work. In other words, every aesthetic experience has a history composed of two moments, which I shall identify as *discovery* and *assimilation*. In the first, we encounter the art work on its own terms, discover its content, and are absorbed and delighted by it. In the second, we absorb this content into our catalogs of familiarity, refer it to the subject matter from which the artist derived it, and so enrich our acquaintance with this region of life and the world.

Artists, critics, aestheticians, and aesthetes have been so entranced by the first of these moments that they have made it the exclusive locus of artistic and aesthetic value and have denied the reality and significance of the second moment. Moralists have been so impressed by the impact and power of the second of these moments that they have made it the locus of value, and have neglected and minimized the claims of the first. Both of these views are understandable, but neither is defensible. For I think it is obvious that these moments are equally real and important. Each of them does undoubtedly occur. And each of them carries its unique load of value. Art affords us moments of unparalleled zest and delight, when our whole being is gladdened and exhilarated: this is the intrinsic value of art. But art also affords us insight into the particularity of actual things and occasions; or, if it is pseudo-art, it deludes us regarding these. This is the extrinsic value of art. To insist upon the second is not to deny or denigrate the first. Quite to the contrary, the extrinsic values of art are dependent upon its intrinsic values. The ultimate criteria of art must be purely aesthetic: good art cannot be immoral. But no more can pseudo-art be moral. To urge that we have an obligation to make good art available and accessible, and to contain the inroads of pseudo-art, is not to undermine the integrity of the artist. It is, rather, to remind ourselves that this integrity must be promoted and its outcome made public.

The second objection springs directly out of the first. It protests that this emphasis on the extrinsic value of art both entails and justifies censorship. The answer to this depends on what one means by censorship. If this is taken to imply the creation of an official body which will approve or ban art works solely on the basis of their extrinsic value—that is, by reference to their subject matter and the manner in which this is treated—then the objection is groundless. For the view here presented does not advocate, much less require, this kind of treatment of art. Quite otherwise, it insists that the determination of the sort of work that is to be encouraged, and the appreciation of which is to be cultivated, is a matter to be settled on purely aesthetic grounds. Good art, by definition, sharpens and deepens our insight into the actual character of things and occasions, and so must be true. If art frequently confronts us with what is ugly, brutal, tawdry, senseless, and tragic, that is because these are real aspects of life and the world, and it is best for us to acknowledge them, not gloss over them. The only legitimate concern here is to distinguish between good art and pseudo-art, and then to encourage (not impose) the former and discourage (not forbid) the latter.

If "censorship" means the exercise of judgment, discrimination, and selectivity, then I think the objection must be granted but its validity denied. For these are activities in which we engage, and the outcomes of which we apply, in all regions of life that we take with real seriousness. Anyone who is at all an advocate of an open society, and who wants to do more than perpetuate an established order, recognizes that change is a prerequisite of life and that freedom of expression is a precondition of intelligent and fruitful change. The mind must be free to inquire, to explore, and to exploit all of the multifarious possibilities that experience lays open to. But it is also recognized that the methods and processes of change must somehow be controlled. And this entails that the outcome of this free ranging of mind, and the modes of action that it suggests and supports, must be anticipated and evaluated before we allow them free access to the public and free play in practice.

Discrimination and selectivity are of the very essence of life. And the effort to refine their exercise is at the heart of civilization. We do this in a highly systematic and organized manner, and without qualm as to its justification, in many fields of endeavor. In science and technology, in medicine and manufacturing, in law and politics, and even in such intimate areas of life as morality and religion, we insist that the ideas, products, practices, and purposes that are proposed supply some credentials before we adopt them or even permit them to plead their cause to the general public. The famous "free market of thought" of Mr. Justice Holmes has never been more than a fiction.

This exercise of discrimination and selectivity is admittedly both delicate and dangerous. It is difficult to define with any exactness the criteria to be applied, and equally difficult to decide what persons are to be vested with authority and what procedures they ought to use. Selectivity continually threatens to degenerate toward suppression; but, on the other hand, freedom threatens to degenerate toward license. But we cannot evade this problem no matter what its difficulty. The effort to deal with it practically is certainly as old as society, and its theoretical consideration is at least as old as Plato. If artists, critics, and devotees expect art to be granted immunity from this exercise of selectivity, then they are baying at the moon. Such inviolability is inherently unreasonable; it has never been afforded any other group engaged in a serious endeavor, and it surely will not be accorded to art. I think that artistic activity has been as unhindered as it hitherto has in this country largely because it was not regarded as particularly important. But this situation is changing rapidly. Artists are insisting upon their social significance, and their claim is being recognized. This being so, society is sure to pay closer and more critical attention to the activities and output of artists. This is the price of importance, and it may be a very heavy one.

Under these conditions, it behooves the artistic community to accept the responsibility of exercising discrimination and selectivity in its own house. If it does not do this, then an extraneous censorship is sure to be imposed, which will at once touch off movements toward the two extremes of suppression and license. One aspect of this self-discipline should certainly be directed toward exposing pseudo-art and minimizing its appeal. But what is more needed is a positive effort in two directions: first, to encourage the creation of good art that will speak to the concerns and capacities of men; second, to cultivate the sensitivity and taste of men so they can enjoy good art and escape the lure of pseudo-art.

This second point brings me to the misunderstanding that I mentioned at the beginning of this section. Put briefly, this consists in a widespread tendency to confuse aesthetic education with art appreciation. We act as though instinctive capacity and spontaneous development combine to equip men to appreciate even quite sophisticated works of art if these are introduced with a minimum amount of "interpretation" and "background material." But there is no sufficient reason to believe this; and there are very good reasons, both empirical and theoretical, to believe the contrary.

Good art is not notoriously simple, straightforward, and easily grasped. To the casual eye, its meanings often appear obscure and ambiguous, its structure tortured and devious. It is only when we have made the work of art our own that its lucidity and coherence come to the fore. This achievement requires patience and discipline. And while biographical, historical, stylistic, and iconographic initiation are essential to this aesthetic preparation, it is neither the most important nor, especially, the most elemental factor. This role belongs rather to the training and cultivation of our inherent powers of sensation, feeling, and expression. To really grasp a work of art is primarily to relive it after the manner of the artist in making it. No work of art can ever be more than a synopsis and syllabus of the experience it embodies and serves to evoke. It is up to us to recreate the full text. We certainly do this under the careful guidance of the art work. But we can follow this guidance only if our faculties are prepared for the journey. Our visual, auditory, tactual, and kinesthetic senses must be acute and practiced; we must have a working familiarity with the medium of the art; we must be taught to attend closely to the actual things that the world presents and the lived occasions in which these issue.

Yet it is exactly this indispensable basic training that we most often neglect. After all, our untutored use of our senses is usually adequate to our needs; we can express ourselves well enough in speech and writing to be understood; we can discriminate textures and forms; our sense of rhythm is adequate to enable us to sing and dance; we can recognize our emotions and give the responses they require. All of this being the case, we assume that we are ready to appreciate the most compactly and finely structured works of art. Our conspicuous failure to bring most college students to an appreciation of literature— which comes to them in a medium with which they have been familiar since childhood—should have shaken this belief. If so, the lesson has not yet sufficiently penetrated our practice. We do not expect anyone to move at once from the familiar pronouncements of common sense to a comprehension of relativity, evolution, Mendelian genetics, the principle of the separation of powers, or the doctrine of the Trinity. Yet we seem to expect, or assume, the exact analogue of this in art. We try to take people from mudpies to Henry Moore, from the childhood colorbook to Titian or Kandinsky, from musical chairs to Beethoven, from kindergarten verse to John Donne and T. S. Eliot; and we try to affect this passage with a bridge built only of factual, technical, and theoretical information.

This is to misconstrue the nature of appreciation, and to treat it as though it were exclusively an intellectual act carried on at arms' length, with the audience and the work of art meeting on a neutral ground of ideas. But in fact, appreciation is primarily participation. It cannot be learned but must be done. And this doing requires that our sensory, emotional, and expressive powers be properly nurtured and cultivated. In the last analysis, and in its most fundamental terms, *art is performance*. In the aesthetic life, whether as creators or appreciators, we are above all performing: we are effecting a transformation of experienced meanings to a higher level of clarity and stability. So our access to art is measured by our ability as performers— our ability to enter fully, and not only intellectually, into the artist's undertaking. It is only in this way that men can be brought to a vivid and rewarding appreciation of good art. And if this achievement is not made possible for them, then they will surely seek satisfaction in pseudo-art, in which they can participate with no trouble or training, since it merely repeats their own most obvious and superficial fantasies. If we are not sensitive and alert to these full demands of aesthetic education, both artistic creation and appreciation will deteriorate, and moral refinement must suffer accordingly.

LITERATURE AND HUMAN UNDERSTANDING

Maxine Greene

What is the function of imaginative literature in the lives of men? What do we take "human understanding" to mean? If we enable young people to engage with awareness and appreciation in the illusioned worlds created by literary artists, will they emerge with heightened knowledge about the world in which they live? Will they be better equipped to make enlightened value judgments? Will they have learned more about themselves as human beings—more about the human condition at this particular moment of time?

When contemplating such questions, one is at first inclined to see in literary art a kind of countervailing force at a time when "whirl" is apparently king, when life seems to affect thousands of people as if it were a perpetual Happening. By this is meant an inchoate, directionless experience, and affair of simultaneities, lacking beginnings, middles, and ends. It is the kind of experience which purportedly surrounds and involves those concerned but which demands of them an attitude of detachment, the attitude described as "cool." Can imaginative literature be viewed as an anti-Happening, a resource of form and purposiveness? Can it be treated as a kind of window on a domain of meaning which has somehow been lost from view?

Answering such questions affirmatively, one may be brought to a stop if the first works of art that come to mind are contemporary ones. "Literary art," after all, must be in some sense encompassing; and there are clearly numerous modern works which major critics, at least, consider to be art. Among these are certain well-known novels: Thomas Pynchon's *V*, for example, with its passive antihero named Benny Profane, his "Whole Sick Crew of Friends," and the mannequin named Shock who is a veritable emblem of Benny's inanimate self; Kurt Vonnegut's *Cat's Cradle,* with its account of the religion called

From the *Journal of Aesthetic Education*, vol. 2, no. 4 (October 1968): 11–22. Reprinted by permission of the *Journal* and the author.

Bokonism, built on the premise that "all the true things I am about to tell you are lies." There is as well, William Burroughs's *Naked Lunch,* full of creatures in process of continual transformation or decomposition, characters motivated mainly by dread of the antihuman, demoralization, depersonalized controls. Even with these few works in mind, can one begin by presenting literature as a resource or a window? Are not many exemplary works explicitly concerned with rendering disorder, fragmentation, the sense of shattered forms?

There are those who might insist that novels like the three mentioned ought not be taken to exemplify literary art. The *Iliad* is art, such skeptics would say, with its heroic seekers after *arêté* or excellence, its speakers of words and doers of deeds. Greek tragedies are art, with their capacity to purge and exalt through presentations of the forms of human action. *Hamlet, Macbeth,* and *King Lear* are works of art, with their multiple dimensions of meaning, their exemplary characters, the magnitude of what they reveal. So is *Paradise Lost* a work of art, with its memorable antihero and the "fortunate fall" to which his rebellion leads. It is not only that such works have been treated as masterpieces by many generations of men. People conceive them to be prototypes because they seem to raise their sights so high, to expand their vision so remarkably. Also (and this seems equally important) they display images of greatness, of human grandeur and valor. It matters not if the heroes of the great works are flawed and fallible. A murderous, consciously sinning Macbeth is more acceptable than an ordinary, decent Benny Profane, at least within the fictional realm of art.

Is this not because the very word "art" still summons up for many individuals images of order and wholeness, of something larger and more luminous than life? The *agon* of a Macbeth is experienced as an offense against the moral order; his crimes are felt as threats against the balance of nature. Because this is so, readers are made sharply aware of the significance of equilibrium and the necessity for its restoration. There is nothing "out there" for Benny Profane to challenge or offend. Murder would not put out the son at his moment of historic time. Incest would not cause a plague to break out in his city. Knowing this, when readers encounter contemporary works they may feel their vision flattened, devoid of the dimensions assumed to be essential when experiencing "literary art."

Such readers may be willing to acknowledge that the mighty have fallen and that the stature of man has diminished; but many *need* to believe that, in this perilous and faithless time, works of art retain their capacity to disclose man in his "true" pride and potency—and, by doing so, to make us understand what has been too long obscured. They may point to Goethe's Faust, Melville's Captain Ahab, Stendhal's Julien Sorel, Hawthorne's Hester Prynne, Flaubert's Emma Bovary, Tolstoy's Anna Karenina, Dostoyevsky's Karamazovs, Joyce's Leopold Bloom. Ambivalent, flawed though such characters may be— damned though some of them surely are—they seem to possess a quality of indestructibility, a dignity potent enough to reconfirm an ebbing faith in man. What is Yossarian compared with these—Yossarian of Heller's *Catch-22,* that account of army life proliferating into a bureaucratic nightmare, refusing all identity? What is the frightened suburbanite named Stern in Bruce Jay Friedman's novel, or Alan Harrington's "secret swinger" who disintegrates so totally, or Gabriel in Roth's *Letting Go,* the young man who is so ashamed of his secure circumstances and so proud of his own shame? What kind of understanding can works like these provide? The tendency frequently is, when confronting the significance of literary experiences for human understanding, to set such works aside.

When one does this, however, one may be dodging the crucial issues posed by literary art in general and taking "understanding" to mean some imaginative or intuitive grasp of something fundamental which is "out there" in the universe, something which normally eludes both theoretical scientist and earthbound ordinary man. The prose and poetry which permit readers to summon up images of wholeness and grandeur appear to sustain such a view of "understanding." The works which evoke broken, wasteland images, emptiness, and formlessness cannot sustain such a view; and the predilection is, too frequently, to exclude them from the category of art.

If some viable relationship between the functions of imaginative literature and the growth of understanding is to be defined, it may be necessary to widen the categories in use to include all works which, according to appropriate aesthetic criteria, may be judged to be works of art. Among the criteria which might be considered appropriate are the complexity, density, intensity, and unity of any given literary work. Conceived as a structure of linguistic meanings, the work might also be evaluated in terms of the levels of meaning which are discernible, and in terms of the dimensions in which thematic materials are interwoven with and related to plot and imagery. It would be relevant to note how the feelings evoked by certain words are balanced and harmonized with other feelings, attitudes, interests—yes, and cognitive meanings. The degree of ordering might be taken into account: the ways in which the diverse component elements are amalgamated and ordered into a polyphonic whole. The content of *Antigone,* or *Catcher in the Rye,* or *Faust* (or that which each one succeeds in expressing) is an emergent from the interactions of form, arrangement, and technique. Content cannot, therefore, be abstracted or paraphrased without fundamental distortion. It follows that no work of art can be judged to be art for its content alone; nor can content alone be treated when literature's contribution to the growth of understanding is explored.

The notion that the understanding (if any) to be gained is of some ideal dimension of reality does not appear to be tenable. Neither does the notion that literature adds to our factual knowledge, our understanding of what *is*. Given what is now taken to be "knowing" in scientific and many philosophic circles, a work of art is most likely to be conceived as a particular artist's formed symbolic rendering of his own subjectively experienced world. "Art" cannot be absolutely defined, but aesthetic creation is generally taken to be a mode of transmuting some of the stuff of human experience into symbolic and expressive form. Literature is a mode, then, of imaginatively transmuting such stuff into language which is shaped and structured until it takes on symbolic and expressive form. A reader encounters—when he involves himself with a poem or a novel—a patterning of sounds, a play of images, a structure of intricately organized meanings with the power to address his senses, feelings, and intelligence at one and the same time. They may enable him to become conscious of a kind of message which cannot be paraphrased, which does not even exist except at the moment when the reader is actively engaged with the work. It need not be "true" in any empirical sense, although—within the frame of fictionality—it may be wholly believable. It need not be translatable in any way at all. But it is a message, nonetheless, about the human condition. It is an expressive rendering of what it is to be alive at a particular moment of time.

Each work of art, moreover, possesses its own autonomy—communicates its own unduplicatable message. It is not contingent upon something being reflected or referred to in the culture or the universe beyond. Once created, it exists objectively in the world: an essence, wholly realized and complete. When a reader involves himself with it, permits his imagination to work so that he can enact what happens in it, the poem or the story becomes an event for him. He need not stand away from it, asking: "What does it say? What does it mean?" He need not try to look through it, as if it were transparent, to something outside the work. If he knows enough to attend to the book, to engage himself with the language in its permutations, to involve himself with created characters and their relationships, with the clashes and resolutions in the space that is the work, he will find himself shaping his own experience in the course of his reading. He will be enabled to build—out of what has been evoked in him—an imaginary, fictive world which is a semblance of the illusioned world that is the book. For this to happen, however, the reader must remember that an imaginary work is opaque. Unlike a newspaper article or a historical essay, its function is not to refer to events or ideas outside. The reader who knows how to pay heed to language, form, technique, and the play of symbols will find meanings emerging only as he discovers and recreates within himself the form of the literary work.

The literary artist, then, cannot be considered to be a camera or a recorder—or, as Balzac said he was, a "secretary to society." Even so, the artist might well say, as Joseph Conrad once did: "I want to make you see." His intention to enable the reader to "see" may be embodied (almost visibly) in the work he has made. To see what? Certainly not the absolute, the really real. Not the Leviathan, nor the heavens, nor the pit. To see, rather, the resemblances, conjunctions, illuminations revealed by metaphor; to see human beings, created human creatures, separated out from the flow of everydayness, given a particularity, a presentness within the domain of art; to see the shapes and details of the perceived world as evoked by the protean work of language; but, most of all, to see inside the self, the consciousness.

A work of art, when attended to for its qualities, for what it *does,* can release a reader into his own subjectivity, his own inner world. In fact, it must release him if the work is to be encountered as art. Released this way, jolted, perhaps shocked into self-confrontation, the reader will find himself breaking with comfortable, habitual ways of seeing and thinking. He will break with stereotypes and mechanical routines, at least for a time. Under the guidance of the work of art, he will find himself forming some aspect of his consciousness as never before.

Suppose he is reading Conrad's "The Secret Sharer," which he can only engage with by means of his own experiences of being young and alone and held suddenly responsible. Framing what he sees, looking from a certain distance, he will respond to the words he reads by recalling, perhaps, feelings of isolation, of uncertainty, now given sensuous embodiment in images of a windless tropical sea, an empty deck in the warm night, the silvery shape of a man in the water who hangs on to a ladder and whispers in the silences. The reader, in some manner, will be envisaging his feelings, contemplating them, even as—before long—he engages with the young captain and his difficult choosing in defiance of the laws of land and sea. Objectifying, as it were, distancing his own experience, forming the materials of his own consciousness in a new way, with new significances, the reader will be to some degree remade. If learning is, in one dimension, to reconstruct experience, it may be said that the reader has "learned," even though what he has learned cannot be stated discursively, cannot be translated into fact nor assimilated in some fund of knowledge. He has been enabled to *see* what he may never have seen in quite that fashion before.

Is it not the case, some might ask, that an encounter with a great, time-tested masterpiece will almost inevitably make a reader see more? It is probably true that the works which have survived through the centuries are uniquely rich and multivalent, and that they possess the power to move, delight, and perhaps exalt diverse kinds of persons in diverse ways. But it does not necessarily follow that modern readers will have a richer or a more enlightening experience with them than with other, somewhat less complex works of art. All depends on the availability of the meanings and, perhaps, on the relevance of the surfaces to the perceived world of the reader concerned.

People in different periods of history have responded variously to the works of Shakespeare, for instance. It is well known that, in the eighteenth century, the playwright seemed to offer nothing at all. It is likely, too, that those who read *The Divine Comedy* in the sixteenth century (since they tended to be an elite, trained in literary study) were capable of responding at least on the four levels proposed by Dante. The credal component, the beliefs creating one of the poem's levels of significance, was available as it is not today. Certain modern readers may respond more intensely to the purely aesthetic qualities of the work; but, as T. S. Eliot and others have made clear, *The Divine Comedy* we experience today is simply not the one experienced three centuries ago.

What sort of vision, what sort of "understanding" can literature make possible today? There are clues to be found in some of the presentations of contemporary art. An artist, living in a culture at a particular historic moment, may be taken to be a peculiarly sensitive historical being responding to a forever receding present, forming his feelings about the world as he experiences it in that fluid present, giving them objective embodiment in works of literary art. There is a sense in which he lives in the same world as the one inhabited by his fellow artists; there is another sense in which he is articulating an awareness of or feeling about the world obscurely experienced by contemporaries who have no way of expressing what they encounter and inwardly know. If this is so, there are clues to be found in modern artists' works, difficult as they often are, which may be more readily accessible than those to be discerned in works rendering an older world. If nothing else, a moment or two spent with contemporary artists may offer insights into the constructs or fictions by means of which life is confronted in the present moment. To know these fictions is to know something about the ways in which human beings typically confront the experience of being alive in the modern world. Insights of this sort may well help clarify what imaginative literature today may move men to understand.

Why use the term "fictions," when everyone knows dependable truths of many sorts are made available by the sciences? One reason for using the term relates to the way scientific truths are now expressed. As George Steiner (in *Language and Silence*) has most recently reminded us, the events in the social and physical worlds in which men make their lives today are described by scientists in increasingly abstract notations, formulae which can neither be translated into words nor transmuted into the visual forms traditionally depended upon to give people pictures of the real. In Steiner's view, it is as if the universe has been overtaken by a kind of silence, in the sense that what is called "reality" has become unnameable, unspeakable. Albert Camus, when he described the experience of the absurd, was saying something similar. One encounters absurdity, he said, when one hurls one's most deeply felt questions at the universe —questions about the meaning of life, the purpose of suffering, the density of man—and receives no answer. One becomes abruptly conscious of muteness, utter silence; and this is the consciousness of the absurd. Only the human being can experience it and confront the disparity between his desire for answers and the fulfillments available to him. Only the human being can respond by inventing his own orders (or his own fictions) where none are provided, by seeking out his own visual forms.

This seems to be what the artist is doing today. He, of all men, may be most intensely aware of the discrepancies between expectation and actuality, between what the human being aspires toward and what he can perceive and conceive. Or, like Roquentin in Jean-Paul Sartre's *Nausea,* the artist may be expressing some of what it is like to live in a world where something shapeless and viscous, called "reality," is forever at odds with the paradigms of traditional form. The paradigms, after all, are unforgettable. No artist begins de novo when he begins seeking ways to give his feelings or experiences form. The imaginative writer begins—and continues—within an existing tradition. Like the painters described by Ernst Gombrich in *Art as Illusion,* the writer is incapable of contemplating the world with an "innocent eye." His perceptions are conditioned by the ways in which previous writers have rendered human existence. A great writer will play with his medium, experiment with techniques, develop—on the basis of what others have done before him— his own modes of perceiving and presenting what he perceives.

He may adapt existing conventions to his own needs; he may break with tradition, as did James Joyce, as Robbe-Grillet says he is doing today. But if it were not, for instance, for Dostoyevsky's creation of an "underground man," opposing his rebellious subjectivity to the laws of science and the regulations of industry, later artists might never have perceived the computerized world in opposition to their private selves. If Joyce had not explored techniques for rendering the stream of consciousness, if Marcel Proust had not presented what it might be like to plunge through the fluid stuff of memory into time past, later artists would not have seen life as a field of transient sensations, nor rendered time as duration; and, surely, those who read might well see their own existence through different eyes. Now that they have participated in Joyce's and Proust's visions, there is no going back again.

The point is that, in the history of each art form, and in human history as well, there is an awareness of certain conventional ways of seeing and shaping experience. These conventions give rise to paradigms, which are standard or traditional ways of making sense of reality. There are multiple challenges to the paradigms, as certain artists perpetuate them, others deviate and defy, and still others, finding them irrelevant to what they personally experience (as William Blake found the Newtonian scheme irrelevant) break through the restraints of inherited forms. Techniques change; styles change and generate further changes. But men remain haunted by the old paradigms, the traditional fictions: by linear patterns begining in conflict and ending in resolution, by the ancient forms of human action, by what Frank Kermode calls (in a book of the same name) "the sense of an ending," by a world of phases, patterns, sequences—by a domain of dependable form.

If there are analogies between the messages being communicated by literary artists today, they center on the feeling of what it is to be alive (and to write about it) at a moment when the old paradigms no longer hold. What contemporary writers may be expressing is in some measure indicative of what their mute fellow citizens would express, if they were gifted enough to give their own experiences expressive form.

Like the one presented in Donald Barthelme's *Snow White,* the world as encountered today is frequently a provisional one, lacking hierarchies and completions. Literary artists seem to understand that what men feel and think they know have become somehow problematic. This is partially because they are mediated not only by conscious experience but by all sorts of hidden forces, unconscious desires (now recognized as such), fantasies. Recognizing this, recognizing the insufficiencies and contingencies of language itself, how can anyone today be absolutely sure?

The images and events presented by literary art frequently affect readers today as if they have been strained through the half-lit, inner realm which is so familiar to every modern man. It is not hard to recognize the nightmare underworld in Selby's *Last Exit to Brooklyn,* appalling though it may appear, nor the Gothic inner world in Flannery O'Connor's stories, nor the violent acting out in Evan Hunter's *Diary of a Rapist* and Norman Mailer's *American Dream.* Few readers are startled (although they may be shaken) by the imagery in Sylvia Plath's searing poems: "Dying," she wrote (as an example), "is an art like everything else, I do it exceptionally well." Nor are readers surprised by the characters in Harold Pinter's plays, those cold, desperate people who speak such a familiar language, with so many repetitions, misinterpretations, and tautologies that it becomes at length sinister and absurd. Audiences somehow come to recognize, through Pinter's work, that lies are told because people have lost control of words and are misled by speech.

Their world, too often, is Steiner's silent, secretive world, ruled by nameless powers; and beyond it hangs the old world of paradigms and tradition—the world in which people spoke with clarity, self-assurance, and elegance, in the conviction that their words reflected the logic of the cosmos.

Contemporary writers are inevitably sensitive to the decline of logic in the public domain, to the flattening of values and the erosion of moral agreements, to the absence of acknowledged grounds for claims of "good" and "right." Relativism and moral sterility are presented in work after work. An example is John Barth's *End of the Road,* which begins with an implicit question having to do with how a man can commit himself to stable norms and at once remain free to experience life. The story tells of Jacob Horner, who lives in a "weatherless" realm, without a clear sense of identity, and who makes a futile effort to take responsibility for someone else and thus to identify himself as a person. But the initial question is never answered, perhaps because it cannot be. Barth, like his contemporaries, exists in an era when men continually talk of experiencing themselves as unpredictable, two-faced creatures, capable of fantastic invention and organization—capable, too, as Steiner reminds us, of reading Goethe or Rilke the night before locking innocent people in a gas chamber.

How can this be surprising, at a time when Strangelove-like chance can cheat even computerized controls? Is it any wonder that the computerized society preoccupies modern writers and frequently moves them to extremes in their efforts to express legitimate feeling, to say what is authentic and "true"? In a domain of impinging stereotypes, commercials, abstract formulations, where language is used as deceptively by government officials as it is by advertisers, how can the artist whose medium is words ever be *sure?*

Grotesque and wasteland fictions, nonetheless, are not the only ones we see. Nor are they the only relevant ones, as Saul Bellow has been saying, and Bernard Malamud, and several others. Bellow's work, particularly *Herzog,* may even constitute an indication of the mergence of new modes of ordering, newly forged images of man. Moses Herzog, seeking connection with his fellowmen, trying to make sense of things, insists that there is something better than "mass man"; he struggles to reject the "dreariness" of the alienated age. In Malamud's *The Fixer,* Yakov Bov recognizes that he has "stepped into history" and, through terrible suffering, creates himself as heroic man. Recalling these books, contemplating such affirmations as those which occasionally appear in works ranging from Ralph Ellison's *Invisible Man* to William Styron's *Confessions of Nat Turner,* we are made aware of the diverse modes of ordering experience by means of language. No patterning, no fiction can be identical with the traditional paradigms nor wholly satisfy the desire for encompassing meaningfulness; but, as we become conscious of possibility where the shaping of orders is concerned, we become freer to make sense of things in the face of the void.

This making sense is, finally, a mode of understanding. Perhaps it is the mode of understanding to be expected from encounters with all literary art—contemporary art and those works which are rendered contemporary by incorporation into a modern consciousness. Informed encounters, then, with literature perceived as art cannot be expected to add to the store of verifiable knowledge; nor can they be expected to redeem those who experience them, to make readers better, wiser, more humane. They may, however, enable individuals to break through the conventional mental and emotional sets which stifle inquiry and hinder growth. Releasing imaginative activity, they may stimulate self-reflectiveness and, with it, self-creation. They may, by communicating an awareness of the momentousness of being human and responsible, arouse those who try to form their own experience, to pursue meaning—in fact, to learn.

And then, perhaps, those who take the risk of engaging with works of art may become somewhat like people who have had the experience of crawling out of destroyed buildings after a bombing. They may become like Will, in Walker Percy's *The Last Gentleman,* who finds (having been liberated to see): "Everything looked strange. He could see things afresh." Or they may become like the narrator in *Invisible Man,* waiting at the last to emerge: "In going underground, I whipped it all except the mind, the *mind*. And the mind that has conceived a plan of living must never lose sight of the chaos against which that pattern was conceived."

It may be the perception of "chaos," of the disparity between what is experienced and what is sought, that moves men to try to understand. Trying, we also may conceive new plans of living of our own, new forms, new modes of ordering our lives as we live and are enabled to see. This active, synthesizing understanding may be what is made possible—uniquely possible—by experiences with literary art. Is there any capacity more deeply human, more essential for survival in the world?

COMING TO KNOW PERSONS, INCLUDING ONESELF

James L. Jarrett

The listing of the aims of education is an activity with a long and partly honorable history, ranging at least from Plato's *Republic* right down to what must be a sizable number of faculty curriculum committees now meeting and discovering anew that they must first of all address themselves to desired goals in order to justify their requirements and electives. Sometimes the goals have been found to be numerous and specific, sometimes few and broad: The Educational Policies Commission in *The Purposes of Education in American Democracy,* published in 1938, discovered some forty-three such purposes, whereas the same Commission in 1961 uncovered *The Central Purpose of American Education.* To be sure, R. S. Peters has asked "Must an Educator Have an Aim?" and has seemed to answer that he need not; but what he means is that listing aims is a pretty empty rhetorical exercise unless something is said about procedures, and that indeed more can be learned about real aims from examining actual or proposed procedures than from the abstract formulation of aims themselves, an idea which very much warrants a fresh statement, for all of the lifetime of effort that John Dewey devoted to its espousal.

I am interested in an aim which might be given a familiar rhetorical expression: "Know thyself!" or, "Improve your knowledge of human persons!" although it might be more acceptable to educators in some such form as, "The educated person has an understanding of his own self and of other selves," and would thus take its place alongside such celebrated purposes as "Health Knowledge. The educated person understands the basic facts concerning health and disease" and "Democracy in the Home. The educated person maintains democratic family relationships." But, interestingly, personal knowledge and self-

Reprinted from *The Monist,* vol. 52, no. 1 (1968), La Salle, Illinois, with the permission of the author and publisher.

knowledge are not among the forty-three aims—nor do they belong to the seven cardinal objectives of an earlier commission, and of course they are not *the* central purpose of American education, although possibly rationality, which *is,* may be thought large enough to cover knowledge of selves among much else. Indeed, I confess to some surprise that personal knowledge and self-knowledge, at least in my somewhat cursory survey of educational aims and objectives and purposes, get pretty much ignored, although some might well argue that they are implicit in those aims which speak of "wisdom" or in such a statement as that of Maritain's that the aim of education "is to guide man in the evolving dynamism through which he shapes himself as a human person. . . ."[1] In any case, I feel confident that there is sufficient rhetorical power in such a command as "Know thyself" that if someone said to almost any aim-formulating committee, "See here, we havn't said anything about self-knowledge; don't you agree that that should be in?" he would probably encounter little opposition.

However, he might draw an objection should there be someone in the crowd who is trying to think of curricular and instructional procedures appropriate to each of the professed aims. Perhaps it would go like this: "You see, we have said something about understanding numbers and numerical relationships, and about government and politics, and about health and physical dexterity, and we know pretty well the sorts of courses that would conduce to these and other sorts of knowledge and skill, but what the devil do you do about something as vague as 'Self-knowledge'? Can you really teach that? Are we going to start a new course called 'Self-Knowledge 1-A' or something like that?" A rebuttal, of course, might begin by pointing out that it is by no means necessary to have a one-to-one relationship between aims and courses; some aims are implicit in several courses. For instance, one hopefully learns to speak and read his

[1] Jacques Maritain, "Man's Nature and the Aims of His Education," *Education at the Crossroads* (New Haven: Yale University Press, 1943), reprinted in William K. Frankena, ed., *Philosophy of Education* (New York: Macmillan, 1965), pp. 38–39. Comenius, especially in the early half of *The Great Didactic,* is one who takes self-knowledge as an important educational aim.

native language in courses other than that which very specifically and continually organizes itself around this aim; and what of "critical thinking," a popular educational objective—is it not cultivated in a variety of contexts, often somewhat indirectly? Still, it may be that "self-knowledge" is in a somewhat less fortunate condition than the commoner aims: perhaps it really is being neglected in the schools. Without here deploring this possible neglect and rallying the forces for the adoption of this old/new imperative, I should like to try to say something about what meaning can be given such an aim by showing how the study of literature may conduce toward its realization. I believe there are other studies too which might be and sometimes are useful in this way, but here I shall confine myself to literature.

Surely it is no uncommon claim for works of literature that they may assist in self-knowledge. Here, for instance, is the closing sentence of a review . . . in the *Times Literary Supplement,* with Vladimir Nabokov's novel *Despair* under consideration: "Certainly, in this fascinating novel, he takes a heartless Olympian glee in the fact that, if a work of art *is* a mirror, then what it chiefly shows the eager, trusting reader, is himself." [2]

To be sure, this is put more hypothetically than usual, but it is likely to stir reminders of flatter assertions. But what is it to be shown oneself, as in a mirror? What is it to be assisted to self-knowledge? What is this self that one may presumably be more or less ignorant, more or less knowledgeable, about?

We speak not only of knowing facts, knowing propositions, knowing truths, and knowing how, but of knowing him and her and—oneself. To claim to know oneself seems to involve such subordinate claims as being able to predict how one will behave in a variety of circumstances, being able to specify one's principal interests, preferences, and aversions, being able to overcome the biases associated with "subjectivism," and even to take important advantage of one's unrivaled access to the inside of one's own mind.

Now, a fair amount of literature affords us the illusion at least

---

[2] "Looking Glass Death," *Times Literary Supplement,* July 28, 1966, p. 655.

of getting acquainted with certain fictional characters in a fashion somewhat similar to that in which we are acquainted with ourselves. That is, we are privileged in our access to their thoughts, feelings, desires, and aversions, becoming acquainted with these, so to speak, from the inside, somewhat as we do our own. Not wholly, of course, for we still depend upon symbolization to tell us about these mental states, but, largely through the process known as identification, we in some measure learn these feelings as if they were our own—by feeling them.

If this coming to be acquainted with a fictional character is somewhat like the process of feeling plus reflection through which we extend our acquaintance with ourselves, there is also some resemblance between the ways in which we respond to fictional characters and to real-life persons whom we meet. In the one case and the other, we respond to the other person dramatically, dialectically—as contrasted, for instance, with knowing him as a fixed and isolated and inert object. We not only mark down his features and characteristics, but we like or dislike him, respect him or hold him in disrespect, fear him or feel comfortable with him, and even modify these attitudes according to how he feels or would feel about us.

It is a commonplace of critical praise that an author has made the reader feel that he knows this or that character *personally,* not only in being privy to some of his secrets as in real life one could be with hardly more than a very few persons, but also in the sense of knowing the character as a whole person, this in contrast to the severe selectivity dictated by the relevant interests of a lawyer, a social case worker, or another professional who might have occasion to know quite a lot about certain other persons. However, this does not constitute a claim that the reader is likely to have a truly comprehensive knowledge of a fictional character. For instance, if a novel or a play is adapted for filming, there will always remain considerable leeway in casting, and the part of the audience that has read the book beforehand will, perhaps, be somewhat surprised at how the actor looks and behaves, simply because they have added certain features to the author's account. There seems to be a temptation to exaggerate the extent of one's acquaintanceship with a favorite character because of the intensity of that acquaintanceship in selected respects.

One cannot burke the fact, however keen the "knowing" is, that what one knows in such cases is a *fictional* character, and this presents some difficulties. For instance, two students may differ in the extent to which they are acquainted with Sancho Panza, but even of him who may be said to know Sancho extremely well—*what* does he know beyond the assignment of characteristics by Cervantes to his character? To the extent that Sancho is a type, one's acquaintance with him may be said to be less personal and more abstract, as the sociologist might say, "One sort of person often encountered in such and such a society is. . . ." To the extent that one's acquaintance is personal, the character seems not to admit of generalizations; that is, he is unique, and then no matter how profound one's knowledge be of Sancho it is nothing but a knowledge of Sancho. Bergson belived that herein lies an essential difference between comedy and tragedy: characters are funny insofar as they are rigid: our laughter is a corrective.[3]

Yet surely Bergson is wrong in saying that we never speak of "a Hamlet" or "Oedipus." He is not less wrong if he is suggesting that Falstaff or Sancho Panza is any less individualized than the protagonists of tragedy or pathos. In short, this distinction, though ingenious, is unhelpful, for the memorable character seems always both unique and richly suggestive. To know the character as unique is to have a kind of, or at least an analogue of, "personal knowledge." To know him as representative is to be able to generalize from him to some larger group, not excluding that very large group, human beings. Oedipus is unrepeatable; yet he is said to symbolize the common fate of the human male. Falstaff is a bar-fly, a hanger-on, a toady, but such a one as never was on sea or land.

John Stuart Mill tried to make out a case for a distinction between poetry and prose fiction as corresponding to two kinds of truth: "The truth of poetry is to paint the human soul truly: the truth of fiction is to give a true picture of life. The two

[3] Henri Bergson, *Laughter,* trans. C. Brereton and F. Rothwell (London: Macmillan), passim.

kinds of knowledge are different, and come by different ways, —come mostly to different persons." [4] There is perhaps something in this, but surely not very much, for though we may think of the novel as in general more concerned to describe societies and less concerned to be introspective than poetry, the exceptions are so numerous as greatly to weaken the generalization. However, Mill's passage has value in pointing to the worth of concerns and achievements of literary artists: to help us know ourselves and to know others.

No good end is served in making of personal knowledge something mysterious, not to say occult; at the same time, one needn't feel bound to behavioristic models or other molar schemes which declare vast stretches of human experience inscrutable, ineffable, and therefore—at it were—illegal; that is, beyond the reach of the laws of logic and science, and hence insusceptible of knowing. Again, "knowing" *can* be defined in such a way, but then one immediately is set groping for another word which will name the "cognizing" done by the novelist and by the novel reader when the aesthetic instruments of the prose fictionalist are employed upon human beings and their relationships.

It is time to look at a few examples. The protagonist of *Lord Jim* is diagnosed by an authoritative character within the novel as a "romantic." It is a concept which the novelist provides his reader to toy with, a category into which a complex personage may be, at least provisionally, fitted. Still, by itself, the process of categorizing is aesthetically sterile. We need to see the man acting, behaving, reacting in a variety of circumstances, tests—all of them—of the precise nature of his character. He is shown to fail, to suffer unduly from his failure because of a loss of face in his own eyes. Perhaps he has idealized himself and cannot accept behavior antithetical to the dictates of that ideal. In any case, there ensues a series of attempts at regeneration, each finally failing, until success at last seems gained, only to have circumstance go against one who has by

[4] John Stuart Mill, "Thoughts on Poetry and Its Varieties," reprinted in Albert William Levi, ed., *The Six Great Humanistic Essays of John Stuart Mill* (New York: Washington Square Press, 1963), p. 6.

then won the romantic title of Lord Jim and won too the intense love of a beautiful girl. Still, the last threat proves to be a yet more exalted occasion on which to exhibit his true ideality: his death is, for him, his transfiguration, his redemption, a redemption, one feels, that could be realized only in death, indeed only in such a violent death.

Deliberately, the story has been recast here in abstract terms, though in full realization that this does violence to the full aesthetic impact which the novel has, in order to sketch the cognitive content of the work, short of any capsule morals or theses. If alongside this account there was strung a series of "and thens," that is, a recounting of the story, as nearly as could be, in terms just of what happened, we would have in these *two* accounts not items to be added together to equal the novel as Conrad wrote it by any means, but at least outlines sufficiently different and complementary to give one some grasp of what is there to be attended to. Now, one *comes to know* Jim, know him as a complicated man, a driven man, a man possessed of a destiny, a man of great power and of a fatal weakness— and so on. If then one claims that from this case of coming to know a fictional individual, one has also come to know something of traits found more commonly in persons who do not altogether fit in the "type," no doubt to some extent including ourselves, it will be only in part fair to demand to know *what* has come to be known, if that *what* expects stout, propositional answers. All the same, one knows that it is possible to be possessed of the illusion of knowledge, so some accounting of what is claimed to be learnable from the novel seems called for.

In describing literature as to a large extent "subjective," some think that it is thereby assigned to a realm (1) completely available to the subject and (2) completely inaccessible to any other subject. This is wrong on both counts. We are all of us frequently wrong about our own subjective life. This is clearly illustrated by the not uncommon admission: "I thought I was in love." Or by the question, asked (let us say) seriously, "Do you think I'm a jealous (grouchy, quick-tempered, forgiving) person?" This latter kind of question not only betokens the possibility of inadequate or mistaken self-knowledge, but also of adequate and correct knowledge of one person's inner being by another.

"Personal knowledge" as the term here is employed has as its object (though the very word "object" has often been assimilated to detached, impersonal knowing, I-it knowing, rather than I-thou) the self (one's own or another) as existing, and not merely as essential. But so to say compounds the paradox: Antigone, Hamlet, Leopold Bloom do not exist, and yet it is as if they do, and their individuality is therefore never to be sacrificed to type or generalizations, however much they might suggest and even symbolize universals.

However, uniqueness is only part of what is required. Although every self is just what it is, selves differ radically in interestingness and memorableness. The literary artist tries to create characters who will not only seem "real" but be memorable. Whereas the person who is trying to describe a friend feels bound to select traits which truly belong to the one under scrutiny—he may "project," but this will amount to that much error—the novelist's projections are as legitimate as any selection he makes from live models. One of the things one has to learn about reading literature is to attend to the details as probably significant in having been selected for mention. If in real life a companion is while talking playing with a letter opener, chances are we pay it little mind; in a story or a play, we would almost certainly register this fact as significant: combined with other mannerisms such behavior enables us to "know" the character. The configuration of traits *is* the character, and one of the things we sometimes commend in the "skillful and perceptive portrayer of character" is the economy of his selection: by the mention of only a handful of qualities, he has seemed to put us in the presence of a person both distinctive and credible. It may be a very flat character, say a serving maid who responds to both praise and scolding with "I do my best, mum," and yet this little refrain may be used so tellingly that we feel there really is little else to the person than what has been thus revealed. Or the character may be subtle, profound, possessed of deep feelings, played upon by dark, unconscious forces; though this portrayal will doubtless take more time and space, its economy may be even more impressive, our conclusion being that the character has infinite, inexhaustible resources.

Just as, without any doubt whatsoever, the painter may through his paintings train the eye of the beholder, not just to see more of his own paintings, or someone else's paintings, but apples, boulevards, clouds, a foot, rain on the ocean, and the coyness that may lurk in an old woman's eye; so may the writer of fiction train us to be more observant of human traits and of configurations of traits. At his best he is a disrupter of our stock responses ("How considerate the child is to give his brother the first bite!" "A lie is a lie." "He who hesitates is lost."), replacing them with somewhat surprised recognitions. Though reality will never be that neat, and though we be on our own (alas!), still we may now do better.

Since the artist must turn inward for at least some of what he observes and records, his successes in observation and expression betoken some success in self-knowledge. Jung has said, "Anyone who has insight into his own action, and has thus found access to the unconscious, involuntarily exercises an influence on his environment." [5] Why "involuntarily"? Very possibly the artist, who surely is one example of this sort of agent, *wants* to influence his environment. Yet never mind that: he does. Speaking of "modern art"—presumably abstract painting —Jung says:

> Though seeming to deal with aesthetic problems, it is really performing a work of psychological education on the public by breaking down and destroying their previous aesthetic views of what is beautiful in form and meaningful in content. The pleasingness of the artistic product is replaced by chill abstractions of the most subjective nature which brusquely slam the door on the naive and romantic delight in the senses and their obligatory love for the object. This tells us, in plain and universal language, that prophetic spirit of art has turned away from the old object relationship and toward the—for the time being—dark chaos of subjectivisms.[6]

[5] C. G. Jung, *The Undiscovered Self,* trans. R. F. C. Hull (New York: New American Library, 1957), p. 121.
[6] *Ibid.,* pp. 121–22.

There are at least two things to notice here: (1) Jung's recognition that art plays different roles in different times, and of course as among different artists in any time, not always directing the eyes of the beholder to the inner things, but sometimes doing so, and powerfully; (2) Jung's assertion that the artist may be a psychological educator. Thus the "traits" before under discussion are by no means always those that are open and overt: the artist, perhaps by direct accounts of feelings, perhaps by the exhibiting of T. S. Eliot's "objective correlatives," reveals to us what is below the surface, first in the fictional character, but then, through our confirmatory experience, now that our attention is newly directed—I speak, of course of the successful case—of somewhat similar states of affairs in real persons, including ourselves.

It seems a safe enough generalization that most of us shy away from much probing below the surface of our consciousness, unless a crisis of some sort befalls us, something which calls for a regrouping of our psychic forces. Crises may then be the typical occasions of raids into what is in more serene times off-limits. Fiction may be said to have as one of its functions the inducing of vicarious crises, dramatic occasions in which we participate not just as casual onlookers, but as partially identified undergoers—to borrow a phrase from social science methodology, as participant observers. It is hard to say this precisely, because the situation cannot be wholly assimilated to any other kind of experience: the "detachment" and "repose" of the aesthetic attitude is part of it, but so is the imaginative involvement in the feelings and thoughts and actions of the characters. Since "It is just a story"—the classic adult reminder to the child not to get carried away by an exciting tale—we protect ourselves from a vast personal upheaval. Still, because we can thus share and see the personal relevance of the fix into which the protagonist has fallen, we are with him driven into ourselves for a reassessment.

This is quite a lot, but not yet the whole of the tale-teller's contribution to our self-knowledge. He also—at least such is often the case, especially with the works we come to prize—is our Virgilian guide in this underworld journey, pointing to features of that landscape which would go unobserved or misunderstood without his help.

A poem of Gerard Manley Hopkins may afford us an interesting case to analyze.

"Spring and Fall: To a Young Child"

Márgarét, are you gríeving
Over Goldengrove unleaving?
Leáves, liké the things of man, you
With your fresh thoughts care for, can you?
Áh! ás the heart grows older
It will come to such sights colder
By and by, nor spare a sigh
Though worlds of wanwood leafmeal lie;
And yet you wíll weep and know why.
Now no matter, child, the name:
Sórrow's spríngs áre the same.
Nor mouth had, no nor mind, expressed
What heart heard of, ghost guessed:
It ís the blight man was born for,
It is Margaret you mourn for.

Taking our cue from the poem's opening, let us this time suppose that the poet asks questions rather than makes assertions. Not, however, questions like the poem's first one, which must be rhetorical; but questions like: Is it not the case that as humans grow older they lose some of their sensitivity to nature, turning their emotions elsewhere? Is there, then, some single source of sorrow, finally ineffable, which accounts for the tears of both child and adult? If so, is it the spring and fall, the rise and decline, the steady progress toward death of man, that is the underlying cause of our sorrow, early and late?

The question form needs justifying, especially since this particular poem appears to contain some rather flat assertions: "Sorrow's springs are the same," and others. My justification lies in the poetic, the artistic context of the assertions. This whole context says: art, make-believe, contrivance, aesthetic effect, beauty, contemplative mood. A poem is "something to think about." ("Think" of course here including "feel" and a wide range of mental acts.) Its form gives it a tentativeness, a suggestiveness, a lightness, and a deftness that is wanting in theological discourse, in psychology, in physics—a point which Philip Wheelwright has effectively made. However, it is not miles away from *some* philosophy, which too may have or be meant to have or be best read as having more the air of airing notions to tease out thought than of plunking down dogmas.

Supposing then that we read poetry as if entertaining some questions, the questions I am here concerned with are the kind addressed to each reader as having a store of experience on which to draw for his answer. He may, after so drawing, say, "Yes, it is rather (quite a lot, somewhat, a little, only a very little, not at all) like that." If there is also implicit in this answer the remark, "I hadn't quite thought to put just that question before," then we have, I think, an example of how a work of literature may afford some direction toward our own introspective search for enlightenment.

Socrates complained that everywhere he met men who knew the techniques of their job, but had failed to inquire into the deeper principles, the ultimate justifications for acting as they did, as professionals, as citizens, as friends and lovers, as artists. Wisdom and virtue, he taught, come neither from nature nor nurture; that is, neither from inheritance, directly, nor yet from being specifically taught. Still, some men become wise and others do not, presumably from having been helped to "remember" what they once knew. As he is represented speaking to Meno: "And if the truth about reality is always in our soul, the soul must be immortal, and one must take courage and try to discover—that is, to recollect, what one doesn't happen to know, or more correctly, remember, at the moment." Then he almost immediately adds: "I should not like to take my oath on the whole story, but one thing I am ready to fight for as long as I can, in word and act—that is, that we shall be better, braver, and more active men if we believe we are in right to look for what we don't know we can never discover." [7] I take Socrates here to mean that whether or not there is literal truth in his story about a previous life—it is the sort of thing he is forever relating a myth about—there is certainly some sense in which we are latently wise, having the truth within ourselves, but requiring

7 Plato, "Meno," trans. W. K. C. Guthrie., 86b–c.

mining and smelting for the pure ore to come to hand. John Wisdom has said rightly that the philosopher tells people what they already know—and yet occasionally surprises and even enlightens them in the process.[8]

So too with the poet; good literature is full of "shocks of recognition." Exceedingly common is the claim that though a certain poem or story has not really taught us anything new, it has put something we already sort of knew in a particularly striking and impressive way, indeed in a way we hadn't ever quite thought of before. Oftentimes it is something about unique selves.

In James Joyce's short story, "Araby," we read of a young boy developing a strong attraction for a neighbor girl, whom he secretly watches from a window and follows at a distance down the street.

> At last she spoke to me. When she addressed the first words to me I was so confused that I did not know what to answer. She asked me was I going to *Araby*. I forgot whether I answered yes or no. It would be a splendid bazaar, she said she would love to go.
> "And why can't you?" I asked.
> While she spoke she turned a silver bracelet round and round her wrist. She could not go, she said, because there would be a retreat that week in her convent. Her brother and two other boys were fighting for their caps and I was alone at the railings. She held one of the spokes, bowing her head toward me. The light from the lamp opposite our door caught the white curve of her neck, lit up her hair that rested there and, falling, lit up the hand upon the railing. It fell over one side of her dress and caught the white border of a petticoat, just visible as she stood at ease.
> "It's well for you," she said.
> "If I go," I said, "I will bring you something."

The boy is promised the treat, but when the day comes, his uncle is late in getting home, and by the time the boy gets to the bazaar it is closing down. He wanders futilely around the stalls; but no one seems inclined to wait on him, the shop attendants being busy with gossip, and he leaves in utter frustra-

[8] John Wisdom, "The Logic of God," *Paradox and Discovery* (Oxford: Basil Blackwell, 1965).

tion, facing now the prospect of a disappointment before his inamorata. But Joyce's word is not "disappointment," and the girl is not mentioned. Here is how the story ends:

> Then I turned away slowly and walked down the middle of the bazaar. I allowed the two pennies to fall against the six-pence in my pocket. I heard a voice call from one end of the gallery that the light was out. The upper part of the hall was now completely dark.
>
> Gazing up into the darkness I saw myself as a creature driven and derided by vanity; and my eyes burned with anguish and anger.

I suspect most readers are keenly moved by this story, though at first they may be puzzled as to why, the incident itself being so "slight" and all. On reflection one becomes aware of some of the things the artist has done to express and to evoke the precise feelings here relevant. In the most economical way he has presented to us the intensity of the attraction which this shy, sensitive boy feels toward the girl. He is captured and played with, turned round and round like her silver bracelet, by a girl who lives in a shine of light. He wants to go to the bazaar because she commended it; he can think of no way of pleasing her except by bringing her something. But at the bazaar he is blocked by his own indecisiveness and by the preoccupation of the shopgirls, chattering and laughing with two young gentlemen. The lights go out on this already dismal scene, and he is alone to reflect upon—himself, his vanity, his anguish, his anger: the words are not too strong though they are perhaps more nearly the words of the adult remembering than of the boy speaking to himself at the time, to name his feelings. And for us as readers they name what is implicit in the scene, what exists vicariously in us, though we too had not known the names of the feelings until they were supplied.

This story is in one way very particularized, very local. It could happen, in detail, only in Ireland. Chances are great that we've not known anything in our own experience *very* much like that. And yet . . . the universal features are no less evident. Universal? Doubtless that is claiming too much out of ethnocentrism, but at least very common in our society.

One of the things we are highly likely to think is, yes, that's how it would be—almost, that's how it was. Now, this is not just a jog to memory. Indeed to the extent that we regard this scene as a set of variables to be replaced by our *own* particular, somewhat similar experiences, we are not reading well—or the writer is not writing well. Yet we do less particularly call up the feelings, now *his* feelings but somehow filled out with our own. And we see them and feel them better for the shape given them by the writer.

Or, finally, take a story in which we do not, at least to a very considerable extent, "identify" with a character, but instead keep our distance, usually either because we are amused by or critical of the persons displayed. Ring Lardner's "Some Like It Hot" would be a good example of the first, and would warrant analysis in this regard; however, let us look at the other kind, and take for our case in point V. S. Pritchett's strong story, "Sense of Humour." The sense designated in the title is, we soon learn, the outstanding characteristic of the girl of the story, who manages a small commercial hotel in a town in the English midlands. The quality of her humor is clearly brought out in her being reduced to hearty laughter in learning that the father of the commercial salesman she is flirting with is an undertaker. " 'Don't mind me,' he said, 'I'm Irish.' 'Oh, I see,' I said. 'That's it, is it? Got a sense of humour.' "

The narrator, the salesman, learns that he is, in courting the girl, shutting out her former suitor, a garage mechanic, who dumbly and ineffectually protests in the only way he can conceive, by continually following, usually on his motorcycle, the lovers. Finally, the rejected suitor is killed on the road, and the girl, apparently grief stricken, now accepts the salesman as a physical lover. Their triumph is celebrated by a macabre journey in the family hearse; returning the mechanic's corpse to its native town; the lovers in front acknowledge with pride the salutes of the townspeople, while they are still "followed" by the defeated man pushed to the limit of his passivity, as they rise to near incredible heights of cynicism.

In the hearse:

> I looked at her and she looked at me and she smiled but still did not say very much, but the smiles kept coming to both of us. The light-railway bridge at Dootheby took me by

surprise and I thought the coffin gave a jump as we took it.
"Colin's still watching us," I nearly said.
There were tears in her eyes.
"What was the matter with Colin?" I said, "Nice chap, I thought. Why didn't you marry him?"
"Yes," she said. "He was a nice boy. But he'd no sense of humour."

I used the words "near incredible," and we do perhaps resist this severe a damnation, especially of persons we are seeing so intimately. The first person narration, as always, initially invited an identification, but this was soon rendered impossible by the callousness of the central character, and by the end, our rejection has mounted to contempt, but *that* is to say that it does not give way to incredulity. No, we end by saying, "Yes, there are such people. God help us." Still, this is not to say that the process is simply one of recognition ("Oh, you mean old Elmer Grasseeds") or of classification ("He is simply a case of the cynical, callous salesman type.") Yes, we may have known persons somewhat similar, and we no doubt do some classifying, but the great contribution the author makes to our sensibility is the choice of *situations* that dramatically and starkly reveal what in real life we seldom have a chance to see so distinctly. The blend of sentimentalism and insensitiveness of the final sentences is the pure essence:

> I was proud of her. I was proud of Colin, and I was proud of myself. And after what had happened, I mean on the last two nights, it was like a wedding. And although we knew it was for Colin, it was for us too, because Colin was with both of us. It was like this all the way.
> "Look at that man there. Why doesn't he raise his hat? People ought to show respect for the dead," she said.

Some may object: that rejection, that distancing of the distasteful characters, was it not perhaps a little glib? Is it all that simple: that these are nasty people, not unlike some we have known, and now perhaps seen a little more clearly? May this too not contribute to our self-knowledge, even possibly as much as the contemplation of the nature of characters with whom we identify?

I want to accept the rebuke and make amendment. Here,

perhaps, the Jungian notion of "the shadow" may help. That is, each person has certain inferiorities in his total self of which he may be almost wholly unaware, and furthermore which he may well resist coming to recognize and acknowledge. Still and all, it is said, he responds to images of this aspect of the self, having a strong antipathy, for instance, to a character in a dream.

Now sometimes in literature we suspect that two or more characters are not so much separate persons as aspects of a single self. A perfect example is Faust and Mephistopheles—not only in Goethe, but perhaps in all versions of the story. The diabolic one is nasty, unscrupulous, sly, constantly menacing, and of course powerful, though not all-powerful. The several Karamazov brothers have often been interpreted as constituting a single self, with the half-brother Smerdyakov—again inferior, sniveling, insidious—as the shadow figure. Perhaps Sancho Panza could be so interpreted too, but here the matter is exceedingly complex. In such cases, to the extent that there is identification with the protagonist, there may be also another kind of identification, perhaps usually less conscious, with the shadow character.

However, with characters like that of the "I" in the V. S. Pritchett story or of Jason in Faulkner's *The Sound and the Fury* or of the title character in Kingsley Amis's *One Fat Englishman* or of Iago in *Othello,* possibly the strength of our feeling against the unpleasant one is drawn from our recognition (with lesser or greater consciousness) of him as an embodiment of our own inferiorities.

Yet here is a source of further self-knowledge, for on anybody's accounting (I put it so in order not to identify this part of the analysis at all closely with Jung) knowing oneself entails knowing whatever about oneself is inferior, negative, ugly, evil, as well as that one more happily salutes. Indeed, given the resistance that typically accompanies any attempt to know this shadow, the work of literature may be an especially useful means of affording access to a striking embodiment of some of these features.

I have tried to indicate, briefly, some of the meaning that may be attached to the claim that works of literature may be sources of, or at least conducive to, an increase of knowledge about persons, including oneself. The poet and the writer of fiction has been shown helping the sensitive reader ask, and even in some measure answer, such questions as, "Who is Sylvia?" "Who is Finnegan?" "Who is Godot?" and also "Who am I?" Seeing literature in such a way may very well be suggestive of a number of decisions on the part of teachers and school administrators. For instance, insofar as this end is to be stressed, some works may better warrant selection for class or individual reading than others. Some ways of teaching, some ideas about what to pay attention to, may also be suggested. If, finally, literature, taught in certain ways, may indeed help students become better acquainted with themselves, then at least it becomes possible to give new consideration to this as a legitimate aim of education, not now as merely a rhetorical flourish, but as the kind of end which is given substance by its attachment to specifiable means.

WHAT IS ART FOR?

Rudolf Arnheim

"What is art for?" is a fairly new question. To be sure, discussions about the nature of art go far back in recorded history. We find them in Plato in the West, and in Confucius in the East. These men, however, were concerned with problems such as: Is art good or bad? What kinds of painting or music are good, and which are bad? Who is suited to produce the proper kind of art? But the question of what art is for was hardly raised. Everybody seemed to think he knew that.

If, however, one had raised the question at any time until about a hundred years ago, one would have been told—and I shall limit myself here to the visual arts—that art serves to make the gods present and visible, to show the power and splendor of kings or other princes, to show and preserve the sight of important or beautiful things or events or persons, to transmit strong feelings from one person to another, or, finally, to decorate the human environment.

None of these answers is likely to satisfy many of us these days, and this for several reasons. First of all, there has arisen the notion that the subject matter in art is unimportant. This view we must consider unfortunate even though we recognize that it served therapeutic purposes in its day. Influential critics maintained that if a person looking at a painting asks, "What does this represent?" he demonstrates that he has no understanding of art. He does not know that what counts are the colors and shapes in themselves and that the aesthetic experience consists, as Roger Fry put it, in the "contemplation of formal relations" (7). This attitude, fundamentally different from what had been taken for granted in all other cultures we know of, led eventually and logically to the complete abolition of subject matter—that is, to what is known as abstract art. Naturally, the neglect or outright removal of subject matter

From *The Record—Teachers College,* vol. 66, no. 1 (October 1964): 46–53. Reprinted by permission of *The Record* and the author.

called into question all the traditional assumptions about the nature of visual art because they were essentially based on subject matter. If subject matter is not supposed to count, we must ask again: What is art for?

Toward Life's Enhancement

Our dissatisfaction with the traditional answers also derives from what might be called the psychological sophistication of our time. We have come more and more to be explicit about the presence of deeper psychological motives behind practical purposes visible at the surface. To illustrate: If we ask why a man takes a wife, the surface answer will be that he needs a sexual partner and somebody to run the house and to produce and raise the children. The psychology-minded will reply that what really counts is the enrichment of experience resulting from the union of man and woman, the harmony of mutual understanding, the sense of security, or the sense of personal fulfillment. The psychologist will react similarly when asked why men work. He will point out that we work not in order to "make a living" but in order to "live," and he will proceed to elaborate on what he means by that. Of course, mankind has always been aware of these deeper psychological and spiritual reasons, but they rarely needed to be spelled out. They were hidden behind the practicalities of survival, comfort, government, or religion.

And so it was with art. Roger Fry once began an essay on aesthetics with the following statement by a painter, whom he identified as "an eminent authority": "The art of painting is the art of imitating solid objects upon a flat surface by means of pigments" (7). Fry referred to this statement, a garbled quotation from an article written by Maurice Denis in 1890, as a definition and called it "delightfully simple." But even he asked immediately: Is that all? What Denis had actually written was the following admonition: "It must be remembered that any painting—before being a war horse, a nude woman, or some anecdote—is essentially a flat surface covered with colors arranged in a certain order" (9). It was a warning against the neglect of formal aspects but susceptible to being exploited as a credo of formalism. On the whole, the theorists of our century have spoken more tangibly on what art is *not* than on what it *is*. Thus Benedetto Croce tells us clearly that art is not a physical fact, that it serves no practical purpose, that it cannot be judged as to its ethical value, and that it does not convey any conceptual knowledge. Positively, Croce affirms that art is "intuition," leaving us almost totally in the dark, however, as to what that means and what it is for (4).

This was fifty years ago. In the meantime things have gone further. Nowadays when you discuss the purpose of art in public, you can count on an angry young man getting up and saying, "What makes you think that art has a purpose? Art merely *is*. Painting and sculpture exist the way stars and animals and trees exist. What is man good for? Why does he exist? The question was answered in the Book of Genesis, but not many of us still believe in the answer—perhaps because we no longer believe in the question."

The angry young man is not alone. I have heard artists and philosophers talk the same way. Let me try to counter this challenge with the weapons of the psychologist. As a psychologist I always have to keep in mind one particular difference between living organisms and inorganic things: everything living is the product of evolution. Everything a human being or an animal or a plant is or does or strives for serves the purpose of survival; in other words, it is purposive with regard to the enhancement of life. This holds true for the human mind. Everything about the human mind, including its very existence, and everything produced by the human mind must be reducible to the enhancement of life.

This formula is so simple that it obviously calls for qualification, especially concerning the destructive tendencies in man; it also calls for a more precise definition of what is meant by "life" once we go beyond purely biological needs. Nevertheless, I shall neither qualify nor define but simply say that I can see various ways of describing the purpose of art and that I shall limit myself to the discussion of one approach which yields two answers. One of these answers is fashionable; the other, to my mind, is the more important one by far.

Freud and the Wish

Through pictorial images, man is capable of creating a world which resembles the world of reality in essential ways and which he is able to manipulate at will. Since the pictorial world resembles what we call, somewhat unphilosophically, the real world, it can serve two purposes: it can represent and interpret the real world, and it can also replace it, i.e., serve as a substitute for it. Because this fictitious world can be manipulated at will, it can be shaped in such a way as to serve our wishes best. This latter property of the pictorial world has supplied the fashionable answer to the question: What is art for? It is the answer supplied by Sigmund Freud half a century ago.

To Freud, more than to any other man, we are indebted for the strict application of the principle that all human activity is purposive. Perhaps in the long run, this will turn out to have been his greatest accomplishment. Freud reasoned that we live in a disappointing world, one which frustrates some of our most powerful needs. One way of handling these frustrations is to escape to another world, made by ourselves to our own specifications, and to fulfill in that artificial environment the wishes that plague us in the real and so largely uncontrollable one. Freud called this solution of the problem of life neurotic, and he did so for good reasons. Neurosis is indeed best described as a way of avoiding the challenges of life. And we can certainly speak of evasion if somebody resorts to a world of images in order to enjoy the illusion that his desires are being satisfied (5).

In a classic short paper, *"Der Dichter und das Phantasieren,"* translated under the title, "The Relation of the Poet to Day-Dreaming," Freud compared, in 1908, the artist to the dreamer (6). Both, he said, conjure up a world in which their wishes are fulfilled. Surely, here is an answer to the question: What is art for? At least, the Freudian theory points to certain aspects of artistic imagery, which we shall be all the more willing to acknowledge when we remember that Freud wishes his theory to be applied "not to those writers who are most highly esteemed by the critics. We will choose," he said, "the less pretentious writers of romances, novels, and stories, who are read all the same by the widest circles of men and women."

Freud, for his purposes, was at liberty to pick any kind of imagery he chose. Perhaps he was even obliged to use the products of imagination preferred by most people. We, however, do not have that freedom because we are concerned with the nature of art and must, therefore, speak of art at its purest. For our purposes, the theory must fit art where it is most itself. Even on that plane, to be sure, we realize, for example, how many works of painting and sculpture in Western civilization have praised the beauty of the female body. We also remember that the artists who produced these images were males. This impressive phenomenon surely illustrates Freud's suggestion, although it proves by no means that we are dealing with compensations for sexual frustration. These works are just as likely to be one aspect of sexual fulfillment, in which bodily consummation is topped with the pictorial celebration of womanhood.

Images as Reality

There are, however, other, more basic objections to the Freudian theory of artistic motivation. I will mention two. Are we ready to accept Freud's assumption that a person who dwells in a world of images is operating outside of reality? Is the world of physical existence, the world of bodily action and material consummation, the only real world, whereas the products of the spirit are mere reflections of that reality? What a curious assumption this is, considering that the capacity to detach himself from the entanglement with the immediately given situation and to reflect upon that situation is a most distinctive characteristic of man, and considering further that image-making is the most striking manifestation of that detachment (8).

In order to make an image, a person must place himself outside the situation he is depicting. To do this does not necessarily mean to evade the situation. On the contrary, image-making is an extraordinarily direct way of facing life. Man faces life not by what body does to body, but by what the mind does through the body. For example, courage is entirely an accomplishment of the mind, not of the body. In fact, vehement physical activity is a favorite way of avoiding the challenges of life. One can bury one's head in action as the ostrich buries his in the sand. On the other hand, a true image-maker meets reality in the contemplation of its appearance, thereby displaying a concentrated courage not found in many men of action. It is said that when Dante Alighieri walked in the street, the women turned around and whispered, "This is the man who has been in hell!" And in hell he had been indeed, although his body never left the surface of the earth.

Picasso, in conceiving and developing his mural *Guernica,* had to penetrate the nature and the meaning of the civil war in Spain with pitiless directness, with the concentration of a solitary man, undistracted by physical action—as he might not have been, had he been among the fighters on the battlefield. Or, if I may use a mythological symbol, it was by looking into a mirror—the polished shield of Athena, who was the goddess of wisdom and the arts—that Perseus was able to kill the monstrous Medusa without being turned into stone by the ghastly sight.

Thus, the look into the mirror, the concern with reflections, is by no means necessarily an escape from reality. Image-making *can* be an escape if it is misused by neurotics; but then, neurotics will misuse anything.

A further comment should be made on Freud's theory of artistic motivation. What he says about art as wish-fulfillment reminds us of what is known in the aesthetic realm as the embodiment of an ideal. Many styles of art, especially the classical ones, aim at the presentation of perfection. We only need to remember classical Greek sculpture, or the gods and pharaohs of Egypt, or the pictures of wise men or saints in China or in the European Middle Ages. Or we may think once more of the many beautiful women populating painting from Botticelli to Renoir. Here indeed we seem to find impressive confirmation of Freud's contention, contradicted though it is, on the other hand, by the many instances in which the painter, and sometimes the sculptor, depict the ugly, the dreadful, the deformed, or the merely ordinary.

Artistic Validity

But is wish-fulfillment, as the psychoanalyst intends it, in fact identical with the quest for the ideal? I believe it was Picasso who once jokingly referred to the plight of a painter who likes blonde women but finds that only dark-haired ones will fit his pictures. Good artists are constantly on guard against the trap of falling for what is likeable and attractive to them personally. To be sure, often the initial conception of a work of art is inspired by private experience and by private preference. However, so powerful are the demands of the artistic task that these private elements drop out unless they can stand the test of artistic validity.

What is this test of validity? Freud, an uncannily keen observer who often saw beyond what his theories could explain, discusses not only the similarity of artist and daydreamer, but also the differences between them. The artist, he says, can rid his fantasies of their repulsively private character. But why should private fantasies be repulsive to others? We know the psychoanalytic answer to that question. But I am not sure that private fantasies are rejected because they reveal the objectionable ambitions and sexual yearnings of the daydreamer.

What we object to, it seems to me, is that such fantasies serve so nakedly the personal interests of their creator. They tend to distort reality rather than to illuminate it. We react to them the way we do to the conversation of a person whose every thought is generated by his own wishes. We feel exploited without being able to profit from the exploitation. We are presented with private wish-fulfillment rather than the embodiment of an ideal.

What then is an ideal? It is an image of what man should strive to be. It is not essentially concerned with what one would *like* to be but with what one understands one *ought* to be. The statues of the Greek athletes were not born from wishdreams. They were normative statements on what a Greek citizen should be like. As such, they confronted the beholder with a demand and a challenge, and only secondarily with a source of satisfaction. They made a man look upon his own potentialities—that is, upon his duties.

We conclude that a work of art, whether it represents the perfect or the imperfect, is not determined by what the artist likes but by what, in the artist's view, the work requires in order to be objectively valid. When Cézanne spoke, as he did insistently, of *réalisation,* he did not refer to the expression of personal wishes but to the image of what the world in front of his eyes looked like. The yardstick constantly applied by the artist is in the question: Is this true?

The demand for truth does not have to be put forward by the artist. It arises more effectively from the work itself. It is implicit in the decisions the artist makes when he searches for what is needed, rejects what does not look right, and accepts what fits. Elements motivated by nothing better than personal preference or resentment drop like an empty cocoon or are transformed into a vital part of the emerging creature.

The initial impulse for the work may have been that of a Peeping Tom or the pleasure of self-indulgence. But if all goes well, the work soon takes over and imposes its own demands in a process that may be called automatic purification. Perhaps this is the true meaning of "sublimation." If so, sublimation is not the replacement of a striving unacceptable to society with a related one that *is* acceptable, but the transformation of egocentric needs into the requirements of a life situation—a transformation brought about by the demands of that life situation itself. Needless to say, we are pointing here to one of the most valuable ethical and educational aspects of artistic activity.

Art's Normal View

By giving you my reactions to Freud's theory of artistic motivation I have implicitly suggested a very different answer to the question: What is art for? I will now deal with art as an interpretation of life. In this approach to our problem, I have been greatly influenced and encouraged by the writings of the late Ananda K. Coomaraswamy (3). If I were asked which one piece of writing should be read by every student of art—be he an artist, a theorist, or an educator—I would recommend the essays of this Indian scholar. They are likely to irritate, but our complacency needs this most wholesome irritant.

Coomaraswamy speaks of the "normal view" of art, which, as he convincingly shows, has been held in substantially the same way in all mature cultures. From this view, however, we have deviated in recent centuries. The deviation manifests itself in our misinterpretation of the word "aesthetic." We tend to define "aesthetic" as what delights the senses. Alexander Gottlieb Baumgarten, who introduced the term into our usage in 1735, used the term "aesthetic" in its original Greek meaning of what pertains to sensory perception (2). Art, he held, is cognition by means of the senses. The rationalistic barrenness of such a definition should not prevent us from recognizing that this view of art has essentially prevailed through the ages.

To be sure, art is delectable, but so is anything that serves any need at all. To define art as what is delectable is not only to say nothing about it but also to degrade it. Suppose now we reformulate the rationalistic definition somewhat and assert that art makes us experience what it means to be a human being and to live in this world. Here also a number of objections arise.

We are likely to be told that if art is described as an instrument of cognition, it is reduced to a purely intellectual procedure. This, we are told, does not do justice to the richness of artistic experience. The definition is also accused of charging perceptual imagery with a task it is incapable of fulfilling. Both of these objections derive from the artificial separation of perception and thought. We have been trained to think that the sense of vision does nothing better than provide the raw material of knowledge, whereas only the intellect can make sense out of perceptual data.

Our very language, however, repudiates such a view. When we say, "This makes sense!" we are saying, literally: "This produces a sensory experience." It becomes visible to the eyes. There is no reference to an intellectual operation, if by "intellectual" we mean the handling of disembodied distillates of experience. I cannot demonstrate here the nature of "visual thinking" but can only assert that we are becoming increasingly aware of its importance. I would be willing to say that true productive thinking in any field of knowledge, be it science, engineering, political strategy, or art, takes place in the realm of the senses. Conversely, artistic creation and the receptive experience of works of art are eminently successful ways of *thinking* about our existence (1).

Perceptual Generalities

All thinking requires generalizations; it requires concepts. And if the question is asked whether there can be perceptual concepts, the answer is yes. Here again I must limit myself to undocumented assertions. Suffice it to say that when a person looks at an object, he perceives it not only as a unique, individual thing, but first and foremost and quite inevitably as a *kind* of thing. Perceiving is tantamount to the perceiving of generalities. Even when we see a portrait, we are not simply struck by something irreducibly unique, but by a particular combination of general traits; otherwise no kind of sympathy with or understanding of the person portrayed would be possible. It is these perceived generalities that make visual thinking possible. They are also the basis of art.

Such facts of psychology, furthermore, supply an answer to those new partisans of art-for-art's-sake who maintain that a painting or piece of sculpture has no meaning but merely exists. From what we have said about perception, it follows that whenever somebody fashions an object, be it for artistic purposes or not, he produces willy-nilly not only a specific thing but a *kind* of thing, which, for that reason, "makes sense." There is only one way of preventing an object from being significant beyond its own individual existence—by giving it a disorganized and inexpressive appearance. In that case, the object cannot be "read" by the eye and therefore has no meaning other than that of its own particular being.

In conclusion, our reasoning shall be applied briefly to what is known as abstract art. If art is intended to give us the experience of what it means to be a human being in this world, then paintings and sculpture that do not show us the things surrounding us may seem to fall short of their purpose. Abstract art is said not to represent nature. In some important ways this is certainly true. But is it true in all ways? Here we must remember that even traditional representational art portrays not so much the things of nature as the nature of things. Coomaraswamy asserts that, according to what he calls the normal view, "art is an imitation of the nature of things, not of their appearances." This is expressed in such statements as, "Art imitates nature in her manner of operation."

What is meant here is not easily understood so long as we look at realistic works of art. But realism is the exception rather than the rule in the world history of art. Most styles of art clearly deviate from the appearance of things, doing so in a wide variety of ways. Medieval Japanese painting is unrealistic in one way, ancient Mexican sculpture in another. What is the purpose of these differing shapes? We may say that all of them, each in its own way, attempt to make us experience through forms and colors the behavior of basic patterns of forces characteristic of what happens inside and outside of all of us. Those patterns of forces may impress us most directly in the sweep of a Japanese lady's gown or the famous ocean wave by Hokusai—or, just as directly although quite differently, in the heavy volumes of the symmetrical Mexican clay figures. But once we look out for them, we find that they act with the same strength in the shapes of Leonardo's men and women or in the light cast upon earthly shadow in Rembrandt's paintings. And it is these visible forces that express most directly the meaning of the work of art.

Statements of Reality

Once such patterns of forces have been discovered to be the carriers of expression in traditional art, we realize that they are not dependent upon the representation of objects. The Japanese wave may vanish, but its sweep may remain. To be sure, we give up a powerful means of expression when we abandon the so-called subject matter in painting and sculpture, and there are reasons to believe that in the long run we shall not wish to put up with the loss. But there is also a gain in the purity of form and the directness of expression which has often been compared, somewhat loosely, with the pure sounds of music. Be this as it may, abstract art surely resembles all other art in that it, too, makes statements about reality and that in these statements reside its meaning and its justification.

This is as far as I shall carry our considerations. My answer to the question: What is art for? is incomplete; but so is any answer to any question. To pretend that one has answered or has been answered completely may be gratifying; but it is not helpful.

References

1. Arnheim, R. "What Do the Eyes Contribute?" *Audio-Visual Communications Review,* vol. 10 (1962): 10–21.
2. Baumgarten, A. G. *Reflections on Poetry.* Berkeley: University of California Press, 1954.
3. Coomaraswamy, A. K. *Christian and Oriental Philosophy of Art.* New York: Dover, 1956.
4. Croce, B. *Breviario di estetica.* Bari: Laterza, 1933.
5. Freud, S. *A General Introduction to Psychoanalysis.* Garden City, 1943.
6. ———. "The Relation of the Poet to Day-Dreaming," in *On Creativity and the Unconscious.* New York: Harper Torchbooks, 1958.
7. Fry, R. *Vision and Design.* Harmondsworth, England: Pelican, 1920.
8. Jonas, H. "Homo Pictor and the Differentia of Man," *Social Research,* vol. 29 (1962): 201–20.
9. Rewald, J. *Post-Impressionism from Van Gogh to Gauguin.* New York: Museum of Modern Art, 1956.

THE UNITY OF AESTHETIC EDUCATION

F. E. Sparshott

Distinctions drawn by theorists often fail to coincide with those recognized by practical men. That is not surprising. If a distinction has practical significance it is unlikely that practice will leave it for theory to discover, and if practical distinctions were theoretically adequate there would be nothing for science to discover. One therefore supposes that the idea of aesthetic education, whatever its theoretical difficulties, has practical application. Presumably the activities grouped together under that head really do go together. Traditions and conveniences of curriculum organization, grant-operating practices of foundations and governments, likely coincidences in the talent and training of teachers, public expectations, identity of accommodation and equipment required—such factors as these doubtless make aesthetic education seem a natural unity. And in practice what seems to be so really is so. Nonetheless, to a philosophical aesthetician whose orientation is purely theoretical, the idea of aesthetic education seems fraught with potential confusion, and journals and research projects devoted to "aesthetic education" may combine aims of whose divergence their sponsors do not always seem conscious. In what follows I indicate some such divergences that seem theoretically possible. I do not claim that policies recognizing them would prove better than policies that ignore them. I merely suggest that to draw explicit attention to the diversity may make it easier for practitioners to decide whether it should be ignored or not.

Can the arts be brought under the general category of the aesthetic? So to bring them is to treat them on a par with natural objects that merely serve as occasions of agreeable experiences, admiring contemplation, or whatever. But this is to miss at least part of their point, since every work of art is made by a man for his fellow men. If education in the arts is to be

From the *Journal of Aesthetic Education,* vol. 2, no. 2 (April 1968): 9–21. Reprinted by permission of the *Journal* and the author.

included in aesthetic education, we must introduce two major distinctions. Because works of art are made and not found, an education in the arts may include an initiation into the domain of practice as well as a refinement of sensibility; and because they are made by men for men, and thus enter into the stream of human intercommunication, they must be understood as well as enjoyed, so that the function of interpretation must be added to that of simple presentation. And on the basis of this twofold distinction we may discriminate at least twelve different practical objectives that one may set oneself within the general area of aesthetic education.

First, and perhaps traditionally most often, one may set out to enhance the subject's appreciation of any work of art with which he may be confronted—the traditional objective of courses in art appreciation and music appreciation. But, second, one may set out to make him more sensitive to beauty in general, in nature as well as in art: that is, to make him more responsive to certain acknowledged values in the visual and auditory domains. And there may be a great difference between appreciating what somebody has done and simply responding sensitively to presented patterns. Then, third, one may aim to increase responsiveness not to beauty but to the perceptible environment in general—an aim which John Cage has notably set himself.[1] There is a very great difference, on the face of it, between producing a beauty-lover and producing a generally noticing sort of person; and just as the predominance of the first of our objectives has led to the comparative neglect of the second, the prestige of the first two together has often led to the complete obliteration of this third, which some might hold to be more important than either.

With the general cultivation of perceptual awareness we begin the transition from an affective to a cognitive emphasis, which predominates in our fourth objective, brought to public awareness but scarcely yet acclimatized in educational procedure by Marshall McLuhan: to make people media-conscious.[2] Whether

[1] John Cage, *Silence* (Cambridge: M.I.T. Press, 1966), p. 10.
[2] Cf. H. A. Innis, *Empire and Communications* (Oxford: Clarendon Press, 1950). Innis's research is the source of McLuhan's fundamental ideas.

or not one accepts McLuhan's opinions one must admit the importance of the study he recommends: the study of the ways in which information reaches us from our total environment, which is neither nature nor art but a cultural sensorium of whose mechanisms and operations we tend to be, but need not be, unaware.

Reverting from the environmental to the particular but remaining within the cognitive, we may propose a fifth objective: to make people more knowledgeable about the arts. This is often thought of as a lazy man's way of pursuing our first objective and teaching art appreciation, in that the easiest thing to learn and teach is memorizable data; but it seems to me a reasonable goal in its own right. The arts do have their own history, which is a large part of the history of mankind, and those enclaves of Western civilization (as of other civilizations) which retain the ideal of the cultivated man include a knowledge of the history and natural history of the arts, as of other history, as an important part of that ideal. Men should know what men have done and thus what men can do.

As a sixth objective we may list what might seem only a variant of the fifth: to impart a critical vocabulary. It is reasonable to suppose that a man who cannot articulate his responses can scarcely respond, and a person armed with a critical terminology will at least not find himself at a loss when confronted with works of art; and, not being at a loss, he will lack what may well be the principal occasion for hostility to art. Critical vocabulary has its complexities: part of it is classificatory and descriptive and pertains to the practices of particular arts; part of it is formal and analytic and tends to relate to the specifically aesthetic aspects of works of art. And of this latter vocabulary, though part at least is specific to particular arts or related arts, part is common to all the arts. The implications of teaching the different parts of this vocabulary, or of differentially emphasizing the parts, are profoundly different. Some of those interested in the arts are historically oriented and others are formally oriented; some react differentially to different arts and some are generally "arty." To impart one sort of vocabulary to a subject is to encourage him to become one of these types of person rather than another. This we may call the "say and see" method of teaching.

A second possible variant of the fifth objective is the seventh: to acquaint the subject with the world's great masterpieces. The difference between doing this and imparting a general knowledge of art history may seem almost over-subtle but can be of great importance. In the latter case one is imparting a knowledge of one of the branches of human endeavor, a branch to which many have contributed and in which one may oneself reasonably participate. But an education in masterpieces approaches the arts from below, as manifestations of a capacity beyond any reasonable hope of emulation.

An eighth objective that aesthetic education may set itself is to improve the subject's discrimination between good and bad art. One may teach appreciation simply in order to equip the subject to get from any work whatever may be in it to be got, without suggesting that an overall attitude of acceptance or rejection to any work is even appropriate. And that was the import of our first objective as we formulated it. But one may equally well think that the first thing to teach is discrimination, on the ground that a commercially oriented society surrounds its citizens with vast quantities of bad art, the appreciation of which merely unfits one for finer things. Both practices are familiar, and the objectives and life philosophies they represent are polar opposites. One may be called democratic, the other elitist. The difference between them is closely analogous to that between a sympathetic and a moralistic attitude to human frailties.

The ninth objective is almost the converse of the eighth, and is perhaps less commonly pursued in the lower echelons of the pedagogic profession, though it is much advocated in certain circles. Its purpose is to open the subject's mind to new and unfamiliar styles of art, and to inculcate a habit of such openness. Those who propose this objective do so on the grounds that the cultural pressures of society at large will insure that people become adequately adept in handling whatever familiar repertoire of forms their society may wield, and that what is necessary as a conscious educational undertaking is rather to make sure that the mind does not remain confined within these existing conventions. Styles change so fast today that actual new styles cannot wait for the ordinary processes of cultural osmosis but need conscious championing, and in the process of such advocacy one may instill a generalized receptivity to styles yet unknown. One may feel like retorting that in recent decades the avant garde has moved suspiciously close to Madison Avenue and that novelty and fashion in the arts have even too ready a hearing; but this really applies only to certain self-consciously sophisticated circles, and remains quite untrue of most people, who remain either hostile to whatever looks strange or, if receptive, merely unintelligently docile like sheep in a blizzard. As regards the relation of such teaching of openness to the indoctrination in existing styles, one may indeed wish to demur from the suggestion that the latter may be left to social pressures. Rather, we seem to be faced with the same situation here as in most other fields, that the earlier stages of education impart current doctrines and handy skills, whose validity is undermined by later stages in which general principles and methods are acquired, a process of reversal scandalous to idealists in all ages but probably not only unavoidable but salutary. However, it remains true that the objectives are distinct.

The objectives thus far considered have related to the enjoyment and understanding of an environment or of artifacts taken as given. But since works of art must be made before they can be enjoyed, an aesthetic education might reasonably include such making. Here one may include three objectives. The first, and the tenth overall, has some affinity with the ninth: one may seek to make the subject more creative, or at least to encourage him not to become less creative than he already is. Creativity, the ability to perceive the unexpected and act on it in unforeseen ways, is the active counterpart to that openness to unfamiliar styles which we have just discussed.

Creativity can be manifested in making works of art, but it need not be, for the production of art has an important technical aspect which notoriously need not involve any sort of originality. We may therefore recognize as an independent eleventh objective the instilling of the practice of artistic production in one or more fields. Such practice has its own value, as recreation or as therapy, quite independently of any aesthetic value that its products may have.

Finally, as our twelfth and last objective, one may seek not to instill the actual practice of the arts but to impart skills that may or may not be used. One may make it one's educational aim not to influence a person's choices but to equip him to carry out effectively whatever choices he may make. One does not teach children arithmetic in the hope that they will become calculators, but in case they may need to calculate. Similarly, one may teach children how to read music, or how to draw, not in the hope that they will become artists, but so that they will have the necessary competence should they ever wish to make use of it.

The objectives now listed differ from one another so widely that one might reasonably wish to pursue some without caring to pursue others, or even while actively inhibiting the pursuit of others. They require different instructional procedures, and what contributes to one may not contribute to all the rest, though doubtless there will be a lot of overspill. For example, anyone who has learned to play trombone can play trombone if he wants to, but he will not necessarily want to, nor will his skill necessarily make him more creative, more receptive to new art forms, more sensitive to any aspects of his environment, more sophisticated about media, or better able to tell good music from bad. But presumably, in acquiring his skill, he will have become knowledgeable about at least some sorts of music and familiar with the rudiments of the vocabulary of music criticism. It would clearly be unwise to depend on such random overspill and chance freedom from contamination; it is safer to assume that more than one objective will be attained only if more than one is sought, and actively to guard against any side effects one wants to avoid. However, as things are, if I am right in my guess that the objectives of aesthetic education are not in practice discriminated with any system or clarity, it must be presumed that most teachers and institutions do more or less deliberately direct their efforts at covering some vaguely delineated set of these objectives—or, at least, pursue practices likely to encompass them; for most of us know teachers who have no clearer objective than, first, to effect some improvement in the general cultural condition of their charges, and, second, to get them through whatever tests of accomplishment the local system may prescribe.

Some recent philosophers of education have argued that it is in fact better for educators not to be too clear about their objectives; in most people, the sense of what would constitute an improvement and the personal tact for dealing with face-to-face relations are more reliable than any theoretical guidance they are capable of formulating for themselves or learning from others.[3] To the extent that this is true, any criticism of aesthetic educational practices on the score of theoretical unclarity would be foolish. But without prejudging the merits of this issue one may insist that the mistrust of theory can be carried too far. No doubt in actual teaching situations abstract considerations may often be a hindrance, but teaching situations arise only in accordance with plans, however rudimentary, and planning can only proceed on some notion of what general sorts of ends are worth pursuing and what sorts of means are likely to attain them, even if one also takes into account the extent to which one likes or dislikes whatever one happens to be doing already. Practical muddle, however desirable, must at some point be vitiated by theoretical analysis.

The coexistence of our twelve objectives in an undifferentiated mishmash might be thought at best advantageous and at worst innocuous, on the grounds that at least the means to some of the objectives will be the means to others, so that there will be a beneficent fall-out, and that one can pursue any of the objectives without prejudice to any of the others. At the worst, one's sins will be sins of omission. But although the first point seems sound, the second may not be, as has been suggested in the very exposition of the objectives themselves. To make this point clear, I enumerate some possible conflicts among them.

The first and fifth objectives may conflict, especially in the stress of the classroom situation: although theoretically the more a person knows about the arts the better he should be able to appreciate them, it is notorious that the associations of the con-

[3] R. S. Peters, *Ethics and Education* (London: Allen and Unwin, 1966) may be taken in this sense.

fining and oppressive context in which academic knowledge is acquired may inhibit its life-enhancing use outside the school. In fact there is nowadays a tendency to regard good books (for example) as proper objects of classroom study and not as objects for private delectation, and "It wasn't on my course" is put forward quite seriously as a reason for not having read some masterpiece of world literature.

The first and eighth objectives may conflict, since to teach discrimination can inhibit the enjoyment of what is judged bad, and to teach appreciation is to teach how to appreciate what is to be found even in the worst works.

The second and third objectives may conflict, because to instill a sense of beauty may distract attention from the actual qualities of any appearances not thus singled out; conversely, to instill a habit of perceptual discrimination may undermine the practice of distinguishing the beautiful from the ugly. A beauty that really is in the eye of the beholder need have no antonymous ugliness.

The second and sixth objectives may conflict, for although someone who wields a critical vocabulary should be able to understand what he enjoys and hence enjoy it even better, it is also possible that possession of such verbal weapons may lead one to ignore whatever they cannot be exercised on; there is a danger of losing the faculty of delighting in sunsets and wildflowers, because there is nothing to say about them. Conversely, there is the risk that even in relation to what can be criticized one may be too busy displaying one's expertise to enjoy its object.

The third and seventh objectives may conflict, because an emphasis on extreme cases and strong experiences may render one dissatisfied with the everyday. Conversely, those who believe in teaching us to use our senses are often opposed to the very idea of "elitist" art.[4]

The fourth and seventh objectives may conflict because, as McLuhan's own teaching shows, to think of the medium as the

[4] See, for example, Barry Lord, "Centennial Prizes 'Well Deserved,' " *Arts/canada*, no. 111/112 (August/September 1967): "No matter how high the 'quality' of the 37 works inside the gallery, the visitor *knows* that he can get a better perspective on the present and future state of the arts by taking a walk down Yonge Street. . . ."

message distracts one's attention from the messages that are not the medium but are what users of the medium use it for. Conversely, to focus on selected artifacts is necessarily to distract attention from the pervasive character of information as a process, from the fact that a medium is a medium.

The fifth and seventh objectives may conflict, because knowing about something can become a substitute for acquainting oneself with it directly. Children escorted round a gallery by a loquacious guide and later asked to write a composition on what they have seen may indeed be shown what to look for and encouraged to look at it closely, but they may also be led to substitute listening for looking and to treat art as an occasion for verbalization.

The fifth and ninth objectives may conflict, because the more one knows about the arts the less inclined one may be to think that one has an infinite amount more to learn. If one learned about art at school, whatever one did not learn about at school is not art. Conversely, people who want to keep minds open to novelty are often hostile to connoisseurship and art history, which, they say, distract attention from the spiritual adventure which is the life of art to the dissection of the outworn husks whence that life has fled.

The fifth and tenth objectives may conflict, because to clutter the mind with knowledge about what has been done may render it less able to think of new things to do, just as a child is linguistically creative only until he has learned to speak "properly." Conversely, art teachers who emphasize "creativity" may make their subjects not only ignorant but impatient of established techniques.

The sixth and ninth objectives may conflict, because people with a ready-made vocabulary will want to use it, and will be hostile to whatever resists its application. Conversely, those who would keep minds open to new styles often do so by urging their subjects to develop trustworthy reactions and not try to analyze, since analysis must necessarily be carried through in terms of what existed before, and the new work is precisely what did not exist before.

The sixth and tenth objectives may conflict, because a person with a critical vocabulary may try to produce things to which his vocabulary will apply, thus converting his tools of analysis into formulae for the fabrication of art-like objects; conversely, making a person creative may encourage him to imagine "what it would be like to do that" in place of determining with the aid of analytic discourse what precisely has been done.

The seventh and ninth objectives may conflict, because one may come to judge other works by the closeness of their superficial resemblance to established masterpieces. More insidiously, one may expect new works to come up to the standard of excellence that those masterpieces represent, an expectation that can only lead to dissatisfaction with virtually all contemporary work. Much deploring of contemporary art does in fact reflect this preposterous double standard, by which the average of one epoch is contrasted with the supreme achievement of another.

We may interject here a note on a difficulty (closely connected with the conflict last mentioned) inherent in the pursuit of the seventh objective itself. Unless one happens to be working in one of a very few metropolitan centers, and most of the time even then, one has to rely on reproductions: slides of paintings and buildings, recordings of music. A recording is likely to be more "perfect" than any live performance the student will hear —not only because the performers are more skillful but because alien sounds are excluded, any errors are removed by tape-snipping, and electronic tinkering will produce a balance impossible to achieve in the concert hall—but for these very reasons what results is not a performance at all but a simulacrum that distorts some aspects of the music it mimics and quite omits others. And though the reproduced paintings will be of higher quality than any actual canvases likely to be available, they are of course not paintings but artifacts of another kind that resemble real paintings in some aspects only. As for sculpture and architecture, the extent to which the artful photograph has imposed its alien standards on those arts has become something of a scandal. The love of art instilled through reproductions is a love of surrogates, a false taste whose refinement may unfit its owner for the real world. The museum without walls is a house of dreams.

The seventh and tenth objectives may conflict, because the very power of the masterworks of the past may swamp the subject's individuality. Conversely, creative people may become hostile to masterpieces just because they pose this threat.

The seventh and eleventh objectives may conflict because anyone who is continually confronted with standards to which he cannot hope to conform is likely to stop competing. Conversely, the practicing artificer is unlikely to be uniformly responsive to the great works of the past, but will more likely judge them by whether they offer anything he can use for his own work. Artists are seldom catholic in their tastes.

The eighth and ninth objectives may conflict, because people in the habit of discriminating are likely to discriminate before they have the necessary understanding of the case in hand. Conversely, those who are always ready to be surprised by art may extend their mental hospitality to what their judgment would have led them to dismiss as worthless, on the grounds that "you never know!" Critics may shrink from exposing work that seems to them obviously fraudulent or meretricious, for fear of aligning themselves with those earlier critics who condemned Beethoven or Cézanne.[5]

The eighth and tenth objectives may conflict, because a man who is not prepared to make mistakes will make nothing, and a man who worries about whether his work is any good will be unable to concentrate on the task in hand. Conversely, creative persons are likely to abstain from value judgments, partly from fear of sharpening a weapon that may be turned against themselves, partly because they value creativity itself too highly to worry whether what gets created was worth creating.

Finally, the tenth and twelfth objectives may conflict, because techniques tend to go with traditions. A person who has been systematically taught to develop his creativity may also have been taught to despise accepted ways of doing things, and hence have been discouraged from acquiring relevant kinds of com-

[5] Thus the author of a letter in the *Listener* for November 23, 1967, thinks it sufficient reply to an article deploring Schoenberg's influence on contemporary music merely to quote two nineteenth-century attacks on Beethoven. Apparently by disparaging an artist's work one proves him a genius.

petence. Conversely, one can only acquire a technique by doing things with it, and the things one does while learning will usually be things the like of which have been done before. Moreover, in an examination system one is likely to be tested for a mechanical competence divorced from relation to any aesthetic aims, as when one writes baroque pastiche for a doctorate in music, and this cultivation of pointless virtuosity may damage one's creative faculty.

The above list of possible conflicts, long as it is, is not exhaustive. I have not tested all sixty-six possible combinations for potential conflict, and have left out some obvious ones which merely duplicated principles already exemplified. On the other hand, not all the conflicts named are necessary, and some may not be actual. Some, though often alleged to exist, may be figments of popular mythology, or may just happen to give rise to tensions in abnormally constituted individuals. Others may be gratuitous, arising from bad teaching. It is even possible that the tactful pursuit of any of our named objectives is compatible with the tactful pursuit of any other. One hopes indeed that it is so, but from the policy point of view not too much can be made of it. Whatever is taught will often be taught by bad teachers or by good teachers on off days. A policy that will do harm unless administered by first-rate people is simply a bad policy.

The possible diversity of aims covered by the general notion of aesthetic education is even greater than I have as yet made it out to be. I have assumed without argument that the concepts used in defining the various objectives mentioned are themselves free from relevant complexities. But this may not be the case. For example, the phenomena vaguely referred to as "creativity" may include a number of different propensities which have little in common from the psychological point of view and which might be cultivated differentially; it might even be that to cultivate some of them would inhibit others. Whether this is in fact so or not is for the psychologists to say. Considerable research has been done in the area, but I am not aware of any that is directly relevant.[6]

[6] See, for example, Sidney J. Parnes and Harold F. Harding, eds., *Source Book for Creative Thinking* (New York: Scribners, 1962).

Another example of an untested assumption in our discussion is the use of the concepts of "the arts," "art," and "work of art," which assumes that the various sorts of activity and product thus designated have enough in common that it makes pedagogical as well as administrative sense to set up a program in "the arts." But this assumption is questionable. It is, indeed, a commonplace of writing in aesthetics in the last twenty years that the supposed unity of the arts is adventitious, arising out of certain historical accidents mostly in the seventeenth century.[7] This being so, it is clear that this assumption at least was one we had no right to make.

In what ways are painting and music-making similar or functionally interrelated? It is notoriously not the case that good painters are usually accomplished musicians, or even lovers or critics of music. Nor is anything that one does to teach a person to make or enjoy music calculated to help him to enjoy or produce paintings. The equipment used is different, and the qualifications that one needs to teach music do not qualify one to teach painting. One suspects that their joint presence under the aesthetic umbrella is due precisely to the administrative and financial pressures or ambitions mentioned at the beginning of this paper. Painting and music tend to occupy analogous slots in a curriculum, to have similar academic status, to be funded from the same sources, and to be objects of the same attitudes on the part of school principals and their governing bodies. These suspicions may be deepened by the reflection that every theorist who speaks of the fine arts as a group having a real functional unity includes literary arts within the group. But how often do programs for aesthetic education include literature in their scope? Literature belongs in a different niche, along with language skills, and so is relegated to a different area of practical concern.

The argument from the diversity of technique and talent, however, is not conclusive. Setting aside the loss of literature as an unfortunate practical necessity, perhaps to be mitigated by establishing separate programs in "creative writing," one may de-

[7] Cf. F. E. Sparshott, *The Structure of Aesthetics* (Toronto: University of Toronto Press, 1963), pp. 104–8.

fend a measure of pedagogical affinity for the different arts by saying that they all proceed, at a sufficiently abstract level, from common principles. The stock reply to this claim is that the level on which this is true is so abstract as to be of merely theoretical significance. Such terms as "balance" and "rhythm" can indeed be meaningfully applied to works of more than one art, but such use depends on tricky and sophistical analogies and represents a sort of cleverness that only hinders a true understanding of works of any one art.[8] It is true such values as beauty, creativity, and originality are common to all arts, but this fact is only of mild interest to the theorist of axiology or philosophical anthropology and can find no practical application in any actual program of instruction. These replies, however, though not incorrect, are insufficient to undermine the unity of the arts. Grouping the arts together for educational purposes is justified, however many respects there may be in which they differ, provided that there are some common problems which they all pose for teaching and learning. And it does seem that the tasks of teachers of appreciation in all the arts must have at least this much in common, that they must instill in their charges habits of perceptual attention; that they must evoke appreciation as well as understanding; and that accordingly they are likely to encounter similar resistances and personality problems. Even the community of principle may turn out to be of practical significance, insofar as in the description and evaluation of works of any art one may need to distinguish and then to synthesize formal, expressive, and social aspects. Finally, the allegation that the unity of the arts is a recent and to some extent an arbitrary dogma has less force than its proponents seem to suppose. A social fact is no less real for its origins being accidental, and a belief in the unity of the arts will obviously tend actually to unify them. And the very fact that artistic institutions as at present constituted do have a certain solidarity poses a common set of political problems for teachers and organizers of teaching

[8] It appears that the common practice of using words appropriate to one art to describe works of another art is itself a product of the critical doctrine of the unity of the arts. Cf. Susanne K. Langer, *Mind: An Essay on Human Feeling* (Baltimore: Johns Hopkins Press, 1967), p. 189ff.

in all the arts. The practical basis of these doubts about the unity of the arts is no doubt the fear that teachers and theorists will overstress the common aspects at the expense of the unique aspects of the various arts, with a resulting vapidity and excessive generality. And this danger, which the associations of the phrase "aesthetic education" themselves suggest, may be very real. But on the whole, for all the publicity they have received, doubts about aesthetic education based on the supposed lack of unity of the arts seem to have less substance than the less notorious diversities of aim that have occupied most of our attention.

FURTHER READING

Arnstine, Donald. *Philosophy of Education: Learning and Schooling.* New York: Harper and Row, 1967. Chs. 6 and 7.

Broudy, Harry S. "The Structure of Knowledge in the Arts," in Stanley Elam, ed., *Education and the Structure of Knowledge.* Chicago: Rand McNally, 1964, pp. 75–120; reprinted in R. A. Smith, ed., *Aesthetics and Criticism in Art Education.* Chicago: Rand McNally, 1966.

Crawford, Donald. "Philosophical Aesthetics and Aesthetic Education," *Journal of Aesthetic Education,* vol. 2, no. 2 (April 1968): 37–49.

Knapton, James, and Bertrand Evans. *Teaching a Literature-Centered English Program.* New York: Random House, 1967. Chs. 1, 2.

Dewey, John. "Affective Thought in Logic and Painting," in *Art and Education* (1929). 2nd ed. Baltimore: Barnes Foundation, 1947, pp. 95–104.

Greene, Maxine. "Real Toads and Imaginary Gardens," *The Record—Teachers College,* vol. 66, no. 5 (February 1965): 416–24; reprinted in Adrian Dupuis, ed., *Nature, Aims, and Policy.* Readings in the Philosophy of Education Series. Urbana: University of Illinois Press, 1970, pp. 296–308.

Lansing, Kenneth. *Art, Artists, and Art Education.* New York: McGraw-Hill, 1969.

Leonhard, Charles. "Human Potential and Aesthetic Experience," *Music Educators Journal,* vol. 54, no. 8 (April 1968): 39–41, 109–11.

Reid, L. A. *Meaning in the Arts.* New York: Humanities Press, 1969, Chs. 15, 16 passim.

Reimer, Bennett. *A Philosophy of Music Education.* Englewood Cliffs, N.J.: Prentice-Hall, 1970, Ch. 6 passim.

Smith, R. A. "Aesthetic Foundations," in Dwight Allen and Eli Seifman, eds., *The Teacher's Handbook.* Chicago: Scott, Foresman, 1971.

White, J. P. "Creativity and Education: A Philosophical Analysis," *British Journal of Educational Studies,* vol. 16, no. 2 (June 1968): 123–37; reprinted in Jane R. Martin, ed., *Readings in the Philosophy of Education: A Study of Curriculum.* Boston: Allyn and Bacon, 1970, pp. 122–37.

CURRICULUM DESIGN AND VALIDATION IN AESTHETIC EDUCATION

INTRODUCTION

The decade of the 1960's provided educators with a number of curriculum proposals that include aesthetic education as a component of instruction. The most important of these are presented in this section.

In Philip Phenix's *Realms of Meaning* the third realm is the realm of aesthetic meaning. It is the *particularity* of aesthetic meaning, claims Phenix, that distinguishes it from the more general symbolic meanings found in other fields, e.g., in mathematics and the empirical sciences. Phenix thinks it does not really matter whether we call the apprehension of aesthetic meaning "knowledge" or "understanding"; what is important is that we acknowledge the distinctive nature of aesthetic meaning. Since the fine arts are particularly suitable for the study of aesthetic meanings, providing pure and unambiguous exemplars, they, along with the basic concepts of aesthetics, constitute principal pedagogical materials. The parts of Phenix's book reprinted here consist of a general explanation of aesthetic meaning and an illustration of the ways in which aesthetic meanings are manifested in music and literature.

The next two selections reflect renewed interest in value education in both the United States and England. The selection by Harry S. Broudy emphasizes the development of a disposition for enlightened cherishing as an important outcome of value education—an outcome that includes both appreciation, an educated taste that combines likings and reasons, and a strategy for making choices in situations in which many likings and reasons vie for position. While a number of different value subjects could conceivably engender enlightened cherishing, the arts are selected as the principal curriculum vehicle for achieving this outcome. This choice stems from the belief that a person's value system is shaped primarily by identifying with models. Although the most powerful source of such models in our own time is found in the mass media of entertainment, the models of the media are unsuitable for education because of their tendency to depict life as superficial and stereotyped. Still, since introjection of a model seems to be the way value schemata are shaped, Broudy suggests that it might be advisable for the schools to adopt a similar mechanism, substituting, however, the more serious exemplars of the aesthetic heritage for the stereotyped images of the mass media. Substantive and procedural aspects of an exemplar approach to aesthetic education are articulated in light of this conception of value education.

For R. F. Dearden directions for value education derive on the one hand from what comprises a person's welfare, on which he says there is some consensus, and on the other from the importance to persons and society of the values of personal autonomy and rational choice. The achievement of these latter goals presupposes an understanding of the basic elements of choice, and an awareness of these elements is best achieved, Dearden thinks, by teaching basic forms of understanding. The particular system of interrelated concepts and organizing principles and the validation procedures for determining correctness or adequacy in a given domain of understanding, claims Dearden, are what distinguish one basic form of understanding from another. For purposes of contrast, all of the forms of understanding discussed by Dearden are reprinted.

D. K. Wheeler provides a helpful summary of recent curriculum schemata either directly or indirectly relevant to aesthetic education. He first reviews the concepts of developmental task and behavioral objective characteristic of recent psychological orientations to curriculum building and research and then compares and contrasts the contributions made by philosophers of education, conveniently juxtaposing the substantive curriculum components of Phenix, Tykociner, and Broudy. Wheeler's own ideas regarding curriculum process stress the differences between goals and objectives and the need to be clear about such things as inital behavior, intended as opposed to actual outcomes, and process versus product.

The curriculum model described by Stanley S. Madeja and Harry T. Kelly provides an illustration of how the government-supported regional educational laboratory, a new phenomenon in education, thinks about curriculum in general and about one of its specific subdomains, aesthetic education, in particular. After indicating some of the problems that attend curriculum planning in a democratic society, the authors explain the grounds on which the disciplines were assigned strategic significance: ". . . intellectual discourse is relatively unaffected by ethnic background, geographical location, community values, etc." The authors stress that the purpose of the model they present is to help curriculum developers construct materials for aesthetic education, and that it is not intended to provide a system of instruction for a school.

The next three selections provide samples of curriculum thinking in the areas of literature, music, and visual art. Alan C. Purves discusses the pedagogical problem of sequence and concludes that curriculum building in literature does justice to the complexities of the field by focusing on what a sensitive reader does when he reads a work of literature. Central to the reading of literature, Purves claims, is the aesthetic ability to comprehend metaphor. In short, "if the humanities are courses in perception and response rather than in a body of lore . . . then the structure and sequence of those courses will deal in the modes of perception and expression relevant to the arts they encompass."

Perhaps the most interesting features of Bennett Reimer's effort to fashion a curriculum for general music education at the junior high school level is a heavy theoretical reliance on the aesthetics of Susanne Langer, an emphasis on listening to masterpieces as opposed to performance and self-expressive activities, and the finding that young minds, from the inner city to the wealthy suburb, can perceive and enjoy music often thought remote from their immediate needs and interests. In this connection, Reimer's article might be instructively read with Donald Arnstine's in this section.

Elliot W. Eisner presents a curriculum model that attempts to synthesize both traditional and contemporary conceptions of art education. Accordingly, the domains of the art curriculum identified are the productive, the critical, and the historical. After a brief account of changing conceptions in the field, Eisner explains the manner in which content (concepts and principles) was specified and how objectives (instrumental and expressive) were interpreted for each curriculum domain. Additional characteristics of Eisner's curriculum have to do with a rationale for teachers, motivation activities, supportive instrumental devices, and evaluation instruments and procedures. It is doubtless true, as Eisner concludes, that curriculum building goes to the heart of the formal educational enterprise revealing as nothing else the uses and limitations of theory.

Finally, Donald Arnstine thinks that art courses as currently organized are not likely to contribute much to aesthetic education since they convey the erroneous impression that art study is basically different from other types of learning. The organization of courses around the arts, Arnstine believes, is predicated on misconceptions about the nature of works of art and the locus of aesthetic quality. Arnstine analyzes these misconceptions and concludes that while courses in the study and appreciation of art may after all further the aims of aesthetic education, important changes in approach should be made, particularly as regards use of contemporary and popular art and the objects of everyday life. From a realization that aesthetic quality does not reside exclusively in works of art, Arnstine widens the brackets of aesthetic education to include the artistically organized presentation of any field of study whatsoever, a move that implies a transformation of the conventional role of the art teacher. In Arnstine's interpretation of aesthetic education "all studies are initiated and carried forward by what is of immediate appeal and in which sensitivity to artistic presentations themselves is maintained and developed, because what is presented is perceptibly significant to the world in which students live." Such a view, while not shared by other writers in this section, is not inconsistent with the ideas of Herbert Read (see Section One) or those of Kenneth Conklin (see Section Four).

THE AESTHETIC REALM OF MEANING

Philip H. Phenix

Just as the empirical meanings in the sciences are essentially different in kind from the conventional meanings in the symbolic realm, so the aesthetic meanings in the arts differ in kind both from symbolic and from empirical meanings. The chief feature distinguishing aesthetic meanings from symbolic and empirical meanings is the *particularity* of the former. Symbolic meanings are *general* in the sense that the conventional forms are devised to serve as bearers of meaning in an indefinite number of instances. Symbol systems are formal types in which the structural pattern alone matters and not the particular concrete instance of utilization. Similarly, science is general in the sense that the particular data of observation are not the goal of inquiry, but only the raw material for generalization and theory formation. Knowledge in language is primarily of general patterns of expression, which may be used in a great variety of particular contexts. Knowledge in science is ideally of general laws and theories, connected with observable particulars by way of prediction and verification.

In the aesthetic realm, on the other hand, the object of knowledge is the singular particular form. The primary concern is not with types of things—not with kinds and classes of things—but with unique individual objects. Essentially, every aesthetic object is incomparable. To classify it is to engage in an activity which is empirical, or perhaps philosophical, rather than properly aesthetic.

One may raise the question whether aesthetic meanings really deserve the name of knowledge at all. This is a matter on which opinions differ. Some prefer to limit the term "knowledge" to the strictly discursive and cognitive fields (i.e., mathematics and empirical science). Others prefer a wider reference, comprising meanings in the other realms, including the aesthetic. The question is not of much importance. What is important is that by whatever name they are called, the distinctive meanings in each of the realms be acknowledged and understood. If the narrower interpretation of the term "knowledge" is preferred, a broader concept such as "understanding" may be used for the arts and the other nonempirical fields.

Aristotle made a useful distinction between the *theoretical* or *speculative intellect* belonging to mathematics, science, and philosophy and the *practical intellect* [1] belonging to art and morals. The spheres of practical intellect may further be divided into the activity of *making,* which belongs to the arts, and the activity of *doing,* which belongs to morality. The understanding of art, therefore, is of making particular things and of particular things made. In other words, meanings in the arts refer to particular *works,* i.e., individual things which have been brought into being as a consequence of work.

Aesthetic meanings are gained by *acquaintance* and not by *description,* as in the case of empirical meanings. Each work of art contains its own meaning and speaks for itself. Its significance cannot be embodied in separable symbolic patterns, as in the sciences. Knowledge in science is *about* kinds of things in certain of their aspects. Understanding in the arts is *of* particular things in their wholeness. Scientific knowledge is *mediated* by general symbolic forms. Aesthetic understanding is *immediate,* referring directly to the objects perceived. Empirical knowledge is mediated by general *concepts.* Aesthetic understanding is attained in direct *perception.* The content of scientific knowledge is expressed in *propositions,* statements that may be called true, false, or probable, or as holding within certain limiting conditions. Aesthetic understanding is not contained in propositions, but in particular presented objects. While aesthetic objects may contain propositions as in the case of poetry and drama, these propositions merely contribute to the content of

---

[1] Here "practical" is used in a broad sense, to refer to any active transformation of things, not merely to "utility" in the ordinary sense. Thus, "practical" as here used includes the activity of the "fine" artist as well as the craftsman.

the work of art, and their truth or falsity is not the measure of the aesthetic meaning of the work.

Moreover, descriptive propositions may be used to give information about a work of art, such as its origins and effects, the processes used in making it, and the designer's intention. Such information does not in itself yield aesthetic understanding. It may, however, call attention to perceptual features in the work which would not otherwise be noticed and in this fashion become relevant to the aesthetic meaning. . . .

The language of science is discursive, aiming at precise literal descriptions organized according to the principles of ordinary logic and reaching perfection in the formulas of mathematics. The language of art, on the other hand, is nondiscursive, symbolical, and metaphorical, and is organized according to the different logic of presented forms. Furthermore, the language of science is more readily separable from the expressions in which it is employed than is the language of art, where expressive materials and expressive content are virtually inseparable. Thus it is possible to have well-developed autonomous disciplines of mathematics and ordinary grammar, but not of the languages of music and painting.

For a philosophy of meaning, the realy crucial distinction is between empirical and aesthetic meanings and not between knowledge of natural things and of things made. For, on the one hand, the sciences regularly deal with things made, and, on the other hand, one may have aesthetic understanding of natural objects. Man-made products (i.e., works of art, in the broad sense) are properly studied in physics, chemistry, and the social sciences (especially anthropology). Also, the natural world of stars, plants, and people is an endless resource for aesthetic delight. The essential distinction in type of meaning is between the descriptive, generalizing approach to things in the empirical realm and the immediate attentive perception of individual objects in the aesthetic realm—in either case regardless of whether the things described or perceived are man-made or natural objects.

The fields of science and art are therefore by no means mutually exclusive. One may find deep aesthetic meaning in things which are studied scientifically; for example, in interesting crystal formations or in the ritual patterns of a primitive tribe. The theoretical structures of science may be themselves aesthetically admirable. Likewise, things which have been made to yield aesthetic delight, such as buildings or the sounds of a symphony, can be analyzed empirically, and the activities of the creative artist can be subjected to scientific scrutiny. The empirical and aesthetic realms are thus not divided by the nature of the objects treated or by ostensible subject matter, but by the kinds of understanding gained—the difference being between the general-descriptive and the individual-perceptive modes.

Aesthetic meanings are herein treated in connection with a study of the arts because it is through the arts that aesthetic understanding is most directly and deliberately cultivated. Of particular significance in this regard are the *fine arts,* traditionally comprising these seven: music, poetry, painting, sculpture, architecture, dance, and drama, which have been commonly regarded as the main source of the aesthetic heritage of mankind. Actually, of course, nature provides far more extensive resources for aesthetic experience, and the many artifacts constructed for other than aesthetic purposes (in the "practical" arts and crafts) exercise a much more pervasive influence on the aesthetic consciousness of mankind than do the fine arts. Nevertheless, the fine arts are particularly suitable for the study of meanings and for the special attention of educators because they provide the basis for the analysis of distinctive varieties of aesthetic signification in the most pure and unambiguous forms and because they are an excellent foundation for the explicit pursuit of aesthetic meanings through education. The fine arts are to the aesthetic cultivation of mankind what the pure sciences are to the general development of empirical competences.

Music

Following this preliminary general orientation to the aesthetic domain, we shall now proceed to consider several major varieties of aesthetic meaning within the fine arts, beginning with the field of music.

The subject matter of music consists of individual *musical compositions*. A "musical composition" is a patterned sequence of sounds which has a beginning and an ending and is deliberately created for an aesthetic purpose—that is, to be listened to for its own intrinsic interest and not for any ulterior utilitarian ends. The meaning of each musical composition belongs to that composition alone and is not derived from its membership in any collection of such compositions.

Music is similar to language, in that both consist of patterned sound sequences. The essential difference is that the sounds of music are not formed into conceptual symbols which communicate discursive meanings. Musical sounds directly impart their own qualitative meanings; they do not stand for ideas, as do the elements of intelligible speech.

Because music is made up of sounds, any given musical work is ephemeral; it is gone as soon as the last note has been sounded. In order to make re-creation of the work possible, a composition may be recorded by means of some sound-reproducing device, and it may be put into written form using certain conventional notations. The written score can then be read by performers, who render the composition with more or less fidelity to the composer's original intention for the benefit of other listeners. While composing, performing, and listening are substantially different activities, calling into play quite different skills, all three embody the same kinds of musical meanings. Using the medium of sound, the composer fashions the forms of musical meaning by the power of his creative imagination. The performer reconstructs those meanings, employing sound-producing instruments appropriate to the composition. The listener responds to these meanings in the corresponding patterns of his own feeling states. The perceptual content is similar to all three; only the initiatives and the modes of active participation are different.

A musical work is a pattern of sounds and silences. The sounds may include irregular and complex vibrations called "noise" (such as produced by percussion instruments), "vocables," that is, the sounds of speech (in songs), and "tones," which consist of regular and relatively simple vibrations. Each tone is characterized by "pitch" (measured by its fundamental frequency of vibration), "tone color" (depending on the distribution of subsidiary frequencies, or harmonic vibrations), "loudness" (measured by the amplitude of vibration), and "duration."

The pitches used in music may vary over the entire range of audible frequencies, just as in speech an indefinite variety of phonetic elements is possible. Ordinarily, however, just as only certain phonemes are used as the sound basis for a given language, so in music certain distinguishable tones are selected as the basis for composition within a given musical tradition. For example, most European and American music of the last few hundred years has been based upon some selection of tones from the *chromatic scale* (the successive notes on a piano).

Although musical scales are arbitrary conventions, they are not ordinarily adopted without a rational basis. The *diatonic scale,* for example, consists of a succession of *octaves,* each of which contains seven distinct tones and follows the same pattern of whole and half steps (depending upon the mode, e.g., major and minor), the frequency of vibration doubling in the ascent from one octave to the next. The chromatic scale results from inserting half steps of the diatonic scale, yielding twelve tones to the octave. A *whole tone scale,* with six distinct tones, results from using only whole steps in passing through the octave.

Most music in the Western world has been so constructed that in any given section of the composition one particular tone (the *key* or *tonic* of the scale) serves as a kind of basis of orientation or reference for all the other tones. Different compositions may be written in different keys, and modulations from one key to another may be made within a composition. It is also possible to construct *atonal* music without any such reference tones. In music of this type some principle other than tonality is adopted to lend coherence to the work. Non-Western music is generally constructed on a different basis from that of the West and therefore sounds odd to those accustomed to ordinary Western tonality.

Actual musical tones seldom consist of a single frequency of vibration. The *fundamental* vibration is nearly always accompanied by *harmonic* vibrations whose frequencies stand in simple numerical ratios to the fundamental. The relative amplitudes of these constituents of the tone are responsible for its *color* or *timbre,* and these amplitude patterns are consequences of the structure of the instrument used for producing the sound. Musical understanding includes familiarity with the many kinds and shades of tone color and with the varieties of musical instruments employed (including the human voice). These instruments range from simple pipes, membranes, and strings, through more complex systems of the same, controlled by keys and valves, to the newer electronic instruments based on the oscillations of electrical circuits.

Music comes into being when tones are organized into significant patterns, and the understanding of music results chiefly from sympathetic attention to these patterns. The most fundamental musical patterns have to do with *rhythm,* that is, the time relationships of tones. *Meter* is the pattern of regularly recurring accents, indicated by the *time signature* (e.g., 4/4, 5/4, 6/8, signifying four or five quarter-note beats or six eighth-note beats per measure). *Tempo* is the number of beats per minute, indicating the speed of the music. Rhythm goes beyond meter and tempo, and properly refers to the entire temporal organization of tones into phrases and the larger musical forms produced by the patterned combination of phrases.

The meaning of music is most intimately connected with the rhythmic sense, which in turn is directly related to the fundamental human experience of *time.* Time is measured by movement, rooted in the human organism in the regular pulses of the heart and in the periodicities of breathing, with its recurrent cycles of cumulation, tension, and release. The meaning of music is not simply a matter of intellectual comprehension. It is also an act of organic response in which the vital rhythms upon which life depends are brought into relation to the sound patterns of the music. Roger Sessions sums up this idea as follows: "Music is significant for us as human beings principally because it embodies movement of a specifically human type that goes to the roots of our being and takes shape in the inner gestures which embody our deepest and most intimate responses." [2]

An organized succession of tones constitutes a *melody,*

[2] *The Musical Experience* (Princeton, N.J.: Princeton University Press, 1950), p. 19. Reprinted by permission of the publisher.

which is also referred to as a *voice part,* whether or not it is actually sung. A composer working out a melody, an instrumentalist attempting to play it, or a listener seeking to understand it, may profit greatly by voicing the melodic line because in so doing his whole being is caught up in that rhythmic flow of sound which is the soul of music.

The basic unit of melody is the melodic *motif,* an elemental tonal pattern that is capable of expansion and development into larger sequential structures. Motifs are stated, contrasted, and restated in hierarchies of rhythmic patterns comprising *phrases* (some complete, others incomplete, leading on to further resolutions), *periods,* and a great variety of more complex *melodic* forms, such as stanzaic, binary, ternary, song, rondo, dance, etc. These melodic constructions are analogous to the patterns of discourse built up in prose and poetry using words, phrases, clauses, sentences, and paragraphs as parts of literary compositions.

Combined tones formed by sounding two or more tones simultaneously constitute *chords.* Different combinations of tones produce quite different effects, with varying degrees of *consonance* and *dissonance,* depending on the simplicity or complexity of the ratio in which the respective tonal frequencies stand. Chord patterns are an important part of musical structure. They are closely connected with tonality because the tones from which chords are constructed are selected from the scales in which the music is composed. Chords are also connected with rhythm, some being "chords of movement," because of their dissonance and the sense of incompleteness produced by them, others being "chords of repose," because of their consonance and the resulting sense of finality.

The weaving together of different sound patterns yields musical *texture.* Melodies accompanied by chords constitute *harmonic texture,* while melodies combined with other melodies comprise *contrapuntal* or *polyphonic texture.* Music which is only a single melody is called "monophonic," and music which has one melody with chords is called "homophonic."

In general, the sounding together of tones is called "harmony," whether as combined melodies or as chords. Harmony lends depth and richness to musical expression that is not possible using only single notes in temporal sequence. Melody and harmony together permit the construction of a two-dimensional manifold of sound in which the horizontal melodic lines are associated with vertical harmonic distributions, and the whole is visually represented by the form of the two-dimensional musical score.

Just as complex melodies are built up from melodic motifs by expansion, repetition, and contrast, so melodies and chords may be combined into successively larger musical patterns. The larger forms have been classified into such traditional categories as minuet, scherzo, rondo, theme and variations, passacaglia, fugue, and sonata, each with its characteristic structure. For example, the form of the first movement of the classical sonata consists of three main parts: exposition (usually repeated), development, and recapitulation, the exposition using two or more closely related keys with two or more contrasting themes, which are further elaborated in the development and finally restated in a single key in the recapitulation. An introduction may precede the exposition and a coda may be added as a final summing up. A complete musical composition may consist of a combination of several of these larger forms. Thus, a classical sonata, string quartet, concerto, or symphony usually consists of three or four movements, of which the first is in the sonata (or "first movement") form.

While the analysis and classification of musical forms is important to the musicologist, such theoretical knowledge does not in itself constitute musical understanding, which also requires direct sympathetic awareness. Preoccupation with theory sometimes interferes with the comprehension proper to music by diverting attention from the hearing of the work itself to ideas about the work. Nevertheless, musical meaning is communicated by the sound patterns which the theorist discerns and names, and anyone who seeks musical understanding or hopes to teach it needs a knowledge of the structure of sound that is the source of musical delight to the practiced listener. The value in the conceptual study of musical forms is in the direction of attention to aesthetic possibilities hitherto unnoticed or otherwise only imperfectly sensed.

The ultimate object of aesthetic attention in music is not the several forms and qualities disclosed by analysis, but the musical composition as a whole. Hence, if a piece of music is to qualify as a composition worthy of aesthetic interest, it must have a certain organic unity among its parts. It may not be simply an aggregate of separate elements, no matter how interesting each element may be in itself. The principle of unity in variety is central in all aesthetic endeavors. The source of significance in all of the arts—and indeed also of aesthetic delight in natural objects—is in the weaving of contrasting parts into a single complex whole.

The meanings of a musical composition rest principally on its *musical ideas,* a term referring to those tonal or rhythmic patterns that provide the points of departure for the composition or of an episode or aspect of the composition. A "musical idea" may be a motif, which becomes the basis for larger melodic development, or a chord from which further harmonic elaborations grow. It may also be a rhythmic figure worked out in a variety of interesting modifications and contrasts. Musical ideas are the source of organic quality in the composition in that they lend it its distinctive character as a unique whole and embody its charracteristic internal directions of growth. They are the formal factors binding the elements of the composition into a whole so as to impart a sense of life and motion.

Enrichment of experience through music depends upon openness to the boundless variety of possible musical ideas. A person's musical understanding is unnecessarily impoverished if he limits himself to certain traditional, conventional, and habitual musical patterns as being the only ones he considers authentic or admirable. Anyone who wishes to enlarge and deepen his aesthetic insight must practice receptivity to unfamiliar musical forms (including the initially strange forms of non-Western music), listening to them hospitably and without preconceptions, until such inherent power to delight as they possess makes itself felt. Each work should be invited to speak its own message and to stand on its own merits alone, for it is in the perception of the singular work of art, and not in the conceptual classes to which the abstractive intellect may assign it, that its aesthetic meaning consists.

Musical understanding in the final analysis is consummated in love. As earlier pointed out, although a knowledge of music theory, including an ability to analyze patterns of rhythm, melody, harmony, and tone color—the basic elements of all music—may be helpful, such rational competence does not in itself disclose aesthetic meanings. Such meanings derive from the cultivation of self-forgetful delight in the direct contemplation of the patterns of musical statement, contrast, accent, progression, repetition, and variation that critical analysis describes. . . .

Literature

Of all the arts probably the most widely influential in the communication of meaning are the arts of literature. Since language is a highly developed means of expression for purposes of general communication, the literary artist has the advantage of employing a commonly accepted and widely understood medium. In contrast, music, and visual arts, and even the arts of movement, make use of symbolic forms not so generally understood.

On the other hand, the use of language as the medium in the arts of literature also creates special difficulties for literary understanding. Though the same vocabulary and grammar apply to literature as to other kinds of meaning, as in science, personal relations, and ethics, the uses of language in the several realms are not of the same logical types. Hence literary meanings may more readily be confused with meanings in other fields than can meanings in such fields as music, painting, and the dance, in which the medium is not language. It is easy, for example, to read a poem incorrectly as though it were a statement of fact, while one could hardly do the same for a sonata. However, the possible confusion in the uses of language in the language arts does parallel the confusion in the visual arts between aesthetic presentation and literal visual representation.

A major problem in the study of literature is to distinguish the various functions of language. Language used for aesthetic purposes conveys different meanings from language used for nonaesthetic purposes. Unless these distinctions are carefully made, literature cannot be rightly interpreted and its intended meanings will be missed or distorted.

. . . The literary use of language is *nondiscursive*. Even though the same vocabulary and syntax are used in literature as in ordinary discourse, the connotation of the verbal symbols is different. In literature, language is deliberately exploited for its *expressive* effect rather than to indicate, denote, or describe things for practical purposes. In everyday discourse language is a tool of social adjustment—an effective means of organizing human energies for dealing with the natural and human environment. Literary language, by contrast, is used to stimulate *contemplation*. The literary work is to be enjoyed for its own sake and not for any extrinsic ends. Its language is intended as itself a source of aesthetic delight and not as a means to any other end, whether practical (as in everyday affairs and in the technical fields) or theoretical (as in the pure sciences).

A central concept in the art of literature (as, indeed, in every art) is *imagination*. Literary language is used imaginatively rather than literally. A work of literature is not meant as a series of literal propositions, but as a construction designed to stimulate the imagination of the reader. The term "imagination" does not necessarily imply the use of language to evoke mental images, though this effect may occur. The term is intended to refer more broadly to the use of language to create new forms of experience—"worlds of the imagination"—which are not meant to represent ordinary actuality, but to effect a transformation of everyday experience. Literary language, regardless of the particular forms of composition in which it is used, is essentially *fictional*. It is not designed to convey literal truth, but to present significant invented objects for imaginative contemplation.

As in the other arts, works of literature are *ideal abstractions*. No matter how "realistic" a work may appear, it is an idealization in the sense that certain aspects of experience are abstracted from concrete actuality for special emphasis. Each work is deliberately designed for certain aesthetic effects and never merely to recapitulate the haphazard, contingent quality of concrete actuality.

The subject matter of literary study is primarily the *individual work*—whether poem, novel, play, or essay. Each such work is a unique whole, with its own proper beginning, middle, and end. Literary understanding, from the aesthetic point of view, consists in the perception of the work in its singularity, as a particular complex organization of verbal symbols communicating ideational, emotional, and sensuous meanings pertaining to that one work alone. The aesthetic function of literature is to provide individual objects for serious non-acquisitive contemplation.

The effects of literature, of course, usually extend beyond the aesthetic realm. For example, a great deal of empirical knowledge may be acquired in reading novels or seeing plays. In fact, literature is one of the best sources of insight into personality and culture. Fiction is sometimes a more valuable source of information about the natural world than even the literal factual descriptions of science. Literature may also be used for a variety of practical purposes, such as emotional therapy, moral instruction, and ideological persuasion. Though all these functions may be performed by literature, they are incidental to the unique literary function of providing objects of aesthetic interest. All the other purposes can be served by other means: factual information by empirical descriptions, catharsis of emotion by psychotherapy, character training by moral education, and shaping of commitments by political, philosophical, and religious instruction. Only literature itself can provide the distinctive aesthetic values communicated by the particular patterns of language comprising individual literary works.

A preliminary phase of literary scholarship consists in establishing as clearly as possible the content and circumstances of composition of the works to be read. The determination of content is the task of *textual criticism*. In the writing down and subsequent reproduction and transmission of a piece of literature many opportunities for error and uncertainty may arise. In the work of textual editing of manuscripts and printed materials the scholar uses all available evidence to produce a text that is as close as possible to the intention of the author. In the case of old, obscure, or widely dispersed writings the text may be difficult to establish and the results only moderately probable. In other cases the text may be virtually certain.

The study of the circumstances of composition (sometimes referred to as *higher criticism*) may provide further information of value in understanding a literary work. Included here are such matters as date, authorship, authenticity, place, occasion, and historical context. The evidence used to ascertain these factors may be both *external* (drawn from outside the work itself) and *internal* (gained from an analysis of the language, style, allusions, and explicit statements in the work).

Textual and higher criticism are highly developed forms of literary scholarship, depending upon a variety of special disciplines, including archaeology, paleography, bibliography, and linguistics, as well as upon knowledge of such more general fields as history, science, and philosophy. Nevertheless, it is clear that the meanings resulting from such critical scholarship are empirical and not aesthetic. Hence, the student of literature who knows only how to edit a text and how to determine such facts about it as chronology, authorship, and purpose is only on the threshold of literary understanding. In themselves these investigations do not yield distinctive literary knowledge, but only information that may be useful later in gaining such knowledge.

Once the text and the circumstances of composition are established as well as possible, the next step is to investigate the meaning of the work. René Wellek and Austin Warren, in their incisive *Theory of Literature,*[1] distinguish two kinds of approaches to the study of literature: the *extrinsic* and the *intrinsic*. According to the extrinsic approach, a piece of literature is to be interpreted in relation to the biographical, psychological, social, economic, political, and ideological factors presumed to have influenced it. Contrariwise, under the intrinsic approach the starting point for literary scholarship is the structure of the literature itself rather than the external factors.

From the standpoint of a critical philosophy of meaning, the

[1] Harcourt, Brace & World, New York, 1942. The analysis in the present chapter draws heavily upon Wellek and Warren's book.

intrinsic approach is clearly the more essential because it pre-supposes the distinctness and relative autonomy of literary understanding in the aesthetic mode. However, this judgment does not exclude the study of extrinsic factors, provided they are shown to be relevant to the intrinsic significance of the work itself, as the following discussion of some of the main types of extrinsic factors will indicate.

A literary work cannot rightly be interpreted simply as a fragment in the *biography* of the author. Art is not simply a means of self-expression. It is not merely symptomatic of the artist's personal feelings. It is, rather, the objectification of a communicable inner life. When a novel, poem, or play does make use of materials from the author's life, these materials are transformed for literary purposes. The value of the literature is entirely independent of how nearly its content corresponds to the biographical facts. Thus, while biographical knowledge may help to explain allusions in an author's works, the chronology of his writings, and the relationship of the work to the works of other writers or to the events of the time, these factors are not in themselves aesthetically significant. They are aesthetically relevant only as they disclose perceptual qualities in the work itself that might otherwise go unnoticed.

Similarly, the *psychology* of literary composition tells nothing about the aesthetic meaning of literature. The fact that an author composed his work for neurotic reasons or that his work reflected certain personality characteristics may provide interesting psychological data, but no basis at all for aesthetic judgment. Nor is the psychological truth of a novelist's or dramatist's characterizations of any inherent artistic value. Psychological information can contribute to aesthetic under-standing only if it permits the discrimination of qualities and relationships that might otherwise be perceived less clearly. For example, certain aspects of the structure of *Hamlet* may well be illuminated by Ernest Jones's psychoanalytic interpretation of the play, and Kafka's novels may likewise remain aesthetically obscure without the insight into them provided by depth psychology.

Sometimes literature is unintelligible apart from the *social, economic,* and *political* situations which it reflects. To the extent that this is the case, the proper literary meaning of a work depends upon understanding these extrinsic factors. Yet it is an error to evaluate any work as literature on the basis of its contribution to any social goals (as, for example, the Marxists do). Being "true to life" may or may not advance artistic worth. All that social factors do is to provide materials for the creation of literary values; they do not themselves determine those values.

In like manner, while a study of the history of *ideas* may yield valuable information for the interpretation of literature, works of literary art are not intended as philosophic treatises and are misjudged if so regarded. Like all the other extrinsic factors, intellectual movements and philosophic reflections can be utilized by authors in the construction of literature for aesthetic purposes. It is only in relation to these purposes that such factors may be considered relevant.

Finally, it is not even justifiable to explain literature by reference to the *other arts.* For example, literature is sometimes linked with music or painting as exemplifying a certain spirit (e.g., romantic or baroque). Each art evolves in its own way, in accordance with its own tempo and internal structures. Despite the common characteristics of the aesthetic mode, each field within the arts is relatively independent of the others in its historical career, and none can be interpreted in terms of the others. Thus, nonliterary aesthetic factors are also extrinsic to the art of literature and belong to literary interpretation only where they contribute to the aesthetic significance of particular literary compositions.

The central fact is that the objects of knowledge, in the art of literature, are particular verbal patterns designed to serve specific literary purposes. The significance of each work inheres in its own structure. The import of the work itself does not refer to the subjective experience or intention of the author nor to the sum of the readers' reactions. The meaning of the work is a system of intersubjective values, that is, of perceptual abstractions that the work has the power to evoke in all who read it attentively and sympathetically.

In certain respects the intrinsic structure of literature is similar to that of music. In both cases *sound* is an integral part of the aesthetic effect. While the sound of music is nearly always physically audible, the sound of literature may be either audible (as in recitations and in drama) or, more commonly, heard only with the "mind's ear." In both music and literature sound contributes to aesthetic effect both by the inherent qualities of the sound elements and by the relations between these elements. The study of inherent sound qualities as they contribute to aesthetic effect in literature comprises the topic of *euphony*. Much of the delight of literature consists in the immediate sensuous appeal of the words used.

The relation between the sounds expresses the sense of time, which is fundamental in literature as well as in music and the arts of movement, and indeed in all the arts. The key concept for the relational element of sound is *rhythm*. Rhythm is so important because it is deeply rooted in nature, with its alternations of day and night, of seasons, and of growth and decline. Human life is experienced as a cyclic alternation of work and rest, conflict and reconciliation, contrast and resolution. Language itself exhibits rhythm in the patterning of words, phrases, clauses, sentences, and larger complexes. Literature differs from ordinary language in exploiting much more fully the rhythmic possibilities of language, by greater regularity in the stress distributions and by a variety of other phonetic and syntactical devices, including *rhyme* and *alliteration*. Rhythm is sometimes thought to apply only or mainly to poetry. Actually it is an essential feature of all types of literary art, whether prose or poetry.

Rhythm is a general term referring to the varied patterns that give a work of art organic quality. Much more limited and specific is *meter,* which refers to the patterns of rhythm in poetry. The study of poetic meter is *prosody*. The classical graphic model of metrical analysis uses as units *feet* with two or three syllables each, either short (unaccented) or long (accented), such as iamb (ᴜ–), trochee (–ᴜ), anapaest (ᴜᴜ–), dactyl (–ᴜᴜ), and spondee (– –). Other systems use musical notation, acoustical methods, or formalistic treatment of the patterns (Gestalt) of whole sentences. Whatever the method used, the goal of metrical analysis is to illuminate the sound and time relationships in the poetry in order that the maximum aesthetic effect of the work as a whole may be enjoyed.

Beyond the rhythmic and metrical factors, in which literature has much in common with music, literature also makes use of the rich semantic resources of language. In fact, it is on this resource of meaning that the special quality of literature as an art depends. As already pointed out, the literary use of language differs from its practical and scientific uses in not being tied to literal reference. The art of literature depends upon the possibility of using language *figuratively,* i.e., nonliterally and nondiscursively.

Figurative usage is of several kinds. Literary *images* are particular perceptions (presentations) which also stand for something inner and ideal (representations). Images may be connected with visual, auditory, olfactory, kinesthetic, thermal, or any other type of sensation. *Symbols* likewise are objects that refer to something other than themselves and that are also for contemplation in their own right. They differ from images chiefly in that they are less occasional and more recurrent. Thus, images to which certain meanings are regularly attached may become symbols. A third basic literary concept, which overlaps both image and symbol, is that of *metaphor*. Here a sensuous image that means one thing is used to refer to something else that bears an inner likeness and to which attention is drawn by the nonliteral reference. Inherent in metaphor (as indeed in all figurative use of language) is a principal of *analogy*—an intuition of qualitative likeness between different things—and of *double vision* in which two distinct but related things are held in creative tension in the imagination.

The imaginative quality of literary expression is further exemplified in the use of *myth*. In literary theory this term does not refer, as it does in common parlance, to a false or fantastic story, but rather it refers to the narrative presentation of archetypal, eternal, ideal, or eschatological meanings, in terms of events in the sensible space-time world. Myths are an expression of important social meanings through concrete images. They convey a picture of the shared convictions of a community of the faithful, whether or not the community is regarded as religious in the traditional sense. Thus, one can speak of the "myth of progress" or the "myth of the master race," as well as the Jewish myth of creation or the Christian myth of the Second Coming of Christ.

In the complete literary work the various patterns of sound and of imagery, symbol, metaphor, and myth are organized into a single expressive whole. The resulting works are of various kinds. Modern literary theory usually divides them into *fiction* (including novel, short story, and epic), *drama* (prose or verse), and *poetry*. Such genre distinctions may be made on the basis of outer form (metrical and structural patterns) and of inner form (purpose, attitude, and tone). They are somewhat arbitrary, and are today considered fluid and descriptive rather than (as formerly) rigid and prescriptive. Since the meaning of the individual work, in the organization of its elements into an expressive whole, is the objective of literary understanding, classifications by genre, analyses of style, ordering by periods, and other such activities of technical literary scholarship are useful (like extrinsic criticism) only as they help the reader to discover the values inherent in individual works and not if they take the place of aesthetic perception of the works themselves.

In all the arts, including literature, the aesthetic excellence of the work is a consequence of skillful *composition,* in which contrasting elements are brought together into a whole which conveys a powerful "illusion of reality." While the goal of literature is not an accurate representation of life, such as literal descriptions can provide, the artist does aim to present a convincing portrayal of human existence. In narrative fiction, for example, the meaning is expressed by a *plot* (a series of episodes organized with appropriate scale and pace to tell a compelling tale), by *characterization* (in which, using a variety of methods, the persons whose destinies are interwoven in the plot are vividly presented), and by *setting* (the environment in which the plot occurs and through which the characters express themselves). Other forms of literature use a great variety of other methods of composition to achieve the desired literary effects.

In summary, literature is the art in which language is the

medium of aesthetic expression. The subject matter of literary study is the individual literary work, which is a figurative particular presentation of significant intersubjective abstractions. To understand literature it must be studied intrinsically to discover the unique patterns of sound, rhythm, meter, and semantic figuration as they are used in the creation of singular unitary compositions. Extrinsic factors may also add valuable insights, but only as they are employed to illuminate the inherent structure of each work itself.

THE AESTHETIC FORM OF UNDERSTANDING

R. F. Dearden

Values and the Curriculum

. . . .

Our society presents not just one monolithic world view, but many, often competing, views as to what is valuable in human life. And in respect of this plurality of values a common, public school, which in practice the great majority of children are legally compelled to attend, ought not to be in any way partisan as between these varied ideals of life, even if some of them have the backing of powerfully entrenched interests. There are other educational agencies which will present partisan views to those who choose to listen to them. With what values, then, can the school be concerned in its educational function? Out of what is it to construct its curriculum? There are, it would seem, two valid and, in part, overlapping answers to these questions.

First, in spite of the modern pluralism on values, there remains a substantial content to the notion of a person's good on which there is rightly a consensus of opinion, and from which some indications for procedure and content can be gained. These considerations are, in part at least, hinted at in Plowden's remarks on the features of the society into which children will grow up. They include: (i) being economically viable, which points to the "basic skills," and to mathematics, science and language; (ii) living with others in a justly ordered form of social life, which points to social science and moral education; (iii) engaging in worthwhile leisure activities, which points to a rich range of extracurricular provision, such as field games, clubs, and societies, both religious and secular; (iv) enjoying physical and mental health, which points to physical education and to an informed sensitivity in teacher–pupil relationships and classroom arrangements; (v) appreciating the value of

From *The Philosophy of Primary Education* (New York, 1968), pp. 59–78. Reprinted by permission of Humanities Press and the author.

the forms of personal relationship involved in love, family life, and friendship, which perhaps indicates such things as sex education, "domestic science," and moral education once again.

The second answer is less obvious but extremely fruitful. . . . If the school is not to prejudge the choice of the values by which one is to live, this does not mean that it has no role at all in relation to that choice, for rational choice is itself rich in its presuppositions. First, and most importantly, it presupposes that one will indeed choose, and not just be told what to believe and do. To presuppose that is already to take for granted the value of personal autonomy. . . . This . . . has many implications for the procedures of teaching.

But the exercise of rational choice also presupposes, as the other aspect of a personal autonomy based on reason, a well-grounded understanding of one's situation in the world. This leads on to the fundamental question: What forms of understanding are basic constitutive elements in rational choice? The answer to this would seem to be as follows: mathematical, scientific, historical, aesthetic, and ethical. But before tracing further the possible curricular implications of those basic elements in rational choice, four points demand careful clarification: (i) What is meant here by a "form of understanding"? (ii) What is the principle upon which the various forms are distinguished? (iii) In what sense are they "basic" elements in choice? (iv) How do they relate to the emotions?

Forms of understanding. First of all, a distinction must be made between having an understanding of something and just possessing some information about it, though the one necessarily involves the other, of course. A fairly widespread view of knowledge, especially in the elementary school tradition, is of it as an assemblage of isolated facts memorized in more or less the same verbal form in which they were learned. This might appropriately be called the "rucksack" view of knowledge, for the two relevant features of a rucksack are that it is loosely attached behind and that it can be more or less full. The rucksack view of knowledge, then, equates it with useful information, and since only its usefulness is what makes it worth having, the grounds for regarding it as true are really not very important.

It is sufficient if one has it on good authority, such as that of a teacher. All of this fits in very well with the general authoritarian ethos of the elementary tradition.

When the 1931 Report implicitly devalued "knowledge to be acquired and facts to be stored," it was surely with such a rucksack view of knowledge in mind, as it has been with the many child-centered theorists since who have scornfully referred to "subjects," and to the artificialities of setting up "watertight compartments" between them. Of course, it is not asserted that knowledge has *no* value, which would involve an immediate and obvious paradox since this is itself something claimed to be known, but rather knowledge is implied to be no great thing by comparison with the joys of self-directed activity. Acquiring knowledge is therefore depreciatingly referred to as a process of "topping up pots," "plastering on facts," and "verbalism," and its result is said to be one-sided people whose poor virtues can be revealed only in quiz programs and examinations.

Furthermore, self-directed children can always get information when they want it because, first, they have good attitudes toward knowledge, even though they do not actually possess it, and second, they have learned how to learn, and have only to deploy this universal information-getting skill as the need arises to become as well placed as the next person. This skill roughly comprises a knowledge of the usefulness of reference books and of their classification, together with a certain facility in scanning indexes and tables of contents.

Neither the informational view of knowledge nor the child-centered reaction against it, however, begins to approach the kind of understanding intended in this book. Some would not even accord the title of "knowledge" to such an assemblage of facts. Professor Scheffler, for example, writes that "knowledge requires something more than the receipt and acceptance of true information. It requires that the student earn the right to his assurance of the truth of the information in question. New *information,* in short, can be intelligently conveyed by statements; new *knowledge* cannot." [1]

[1] Israel Scheffler, "Philosophical Models of Teaching," in *The Concept of Education,* ed. R. S. Peters (London: Routledge & Kegan Paul, 1967), p. 106.

Yet the confusion between the two things that Scheffler is carefully distinguishing occurs just because both *are* referred to as "knowledge" in ordinary usage, and having something on good authority, such as that of a teacher, is regarded as giving the right to an assurance of truth. Admittedly, there must come a break with authority at some point: the teachers get it from the lecturers, the lecturers get it from their books, the books draw on the journals, and the journals, at least, were written by people who actually did some first-hand finding out. But of the investigators the children would know nothing, and would not need to in order properly to be said to "know" what they had been taught.

If, however, we regard Scheffler as not just reporting to us about ordinary usage, but as recommending to us how knowledge should be regarded compatibly with placing a high value on personal autonomy, then his recommendation is very acceptable. If we value personal autonomy, then it is indeed fitting that a person should not simply think what others authoritatively tell him to think. He should either find out for himself, or at least be educated sufficiently to regard authorities as provisional only, and to form some estimate of the reasonableness of what he is told. For told he must be about many things.

Neither the rucksack view of knowledge as a loosely attached load of information, nor the gratifyingly simple idea that it is sufficient to have good attitudes and a universally applicable information-getting skill, meets the requirement of finding out for oneself, or at least forming a reasonable estimate of what one is told. The rucksack view emphasizes and encourages dependence on authority, while the "good attitudes" view has a naïvely oversimple notion of how much can be learned simply by opening one's eyes or reading the words in a book. Understanding, in our sense, involves mental structures, ways of experiencing, which are progressively acquired only over a period and through the teaching of one who himself has such an understanding.

There are two elements constitutive of such structures: (*a*) systems of interconnected concepts and organizing principles, and (*b*) validation procedures for determining the truth, rightness, or adequacy of the various ideas entertained. As soon as one inquires further into such an understanding, it turns out not to be a single, monolithic whole, but to involve quite distinct and nonarbitrary forms. Knowledge, in this sense, is not a seamless robe, but rather a coat of many colors. Far from being "divorced from life," it slowly transforms our very notions of ourselves, of "life" and of "the world."

. . . [T]wo examples will . . . serve to illustrate the point at the primary school level. In the elementary school tradition, "arithmetic" was regarded as a set of "number bonds" to be memorized, and a set of computational procedures in which to be drilled. One learned one's tables and how to "do" long multiplication: "first, put down a nought, then. . . ." Nature study, to take a second example, consisted largely of learning the names of the parts, and facts about the lives, of various plants and animals talked of or read about.

In terms of structures of understanding, however, one would think rather in terms of number concepts and the basic laws of arithmetic, with procedures learned and practiced within the context of coming to grasp such concepts and principles. The hope of this would be a greater degree of mastery shown both in better retention and in much wider transfer and application. And instead of a mainly classificatory and typically second-hand study of nature, there would be actual observation and an introduction of experiment. Plants would be grown, variables tested, and measurements taken. Again, such an approach involves at least beginning to grasp concepts and principles which are far from being restricted to the actual cases observed.

The division of forms. The second point for clarification concerned the principle upon which the various forms of understanding are distinguished. Knowledge can, of course, be categorized in a great variety of ways,[2] but our own categorization follows Hirst's[3] in being based on distinct kinds of meaning and validation procedures, or alternatively, the sorts of concepts

[2] P. H. Phenix, "The Architectonics of Knowledge," in *Education and the Structure of Knowledge,* ed. S. Elam (Chicago: Rand McNally, 1964), Ch. 2.

[3] P. Hirst, "Liberal Education and the Nature of Knowledge," in *Philosophical Analysis and Education,* ed. R. D. Archambault (London: Routledge & Kegan Paul, 1965).

involved and the kinds of reason-giving appropriate. By "reason" here is not meant the causal explanation of why someone comes to hold a particular belief, but the justificatory considerations which can logically be given for holding the belief. Each of the forms of understanding thus distinguished has its own way of answering the two questions "What do you mean?" and "How do you know?" And each has its own kind of "critical thinking," and its own ways of being creative.

What actual forms of understanding men have evolved answering to this description can be determined only by an examination of the knowledge that we do now have, and not in any high-handed a priori way. Five such forms were mentioned above, with the primary school in mind, and we shall now proceed to a discussion of each of them. Nothing more than a brief delineation can be attempted here, but even a more elaborate attempt to state fully what each of them involves would necessarily leave out the unstatable, "tacit" understanding of those who, from long experience, have come to know their way about in each of these forms of understanding.[4] One final caution: we are *not* at this stage concerned with how or in what order to introduce primary school children to these forms of understanding, but *only* with showing the distinctive nature of each of them.

(*a*) *Mathematics*. Mathematics has its own distinctive concepts, such as number, square root, prime, fraction, integral, and function, though some of these *words* may have other uses elsewhere, of course. It also has its own validation procedure, namely a step-by-step demonstration of the necessity of what is to be established. Often there are many procedures to choose from. To demonstrate that $23 \times 12 = 276$, one might begin $23 \times 12 = (23 \times 2) \times 6$, or $= 23 \times (10 + 2)$, and so on, depending on such considerations as economy and elegance.

The validation procedures of mathematics are never empirical, never based on observation of the world or on experiment, but are demonstrations internal to the system specified by the appropriate set of axioms and definitions. If $6 + 4 = 10$, this is not because experience has shown it to be so, though exceptions might yet be found to occur. If six things and four things resulted in twelve things, that would not falsify the numerical equation $6 + 4 = 10$. It would only show that we *must* have made a mistake. Perhaps the groups of things were not counted correctly, or some things were counted twice, or the things were unstable. It is therefore highly misleading as to the nature of mathematics to regard it as an "environmental study," as does *Primary Education in Scotland*.[5] This, however, does not imply that the *learning* of mathematics must begin with its logically most primitive elements.

In order to get application to the world, the non-empirical systems of mathematics require all sorts of auxiliary conventions to be adopted and assumptions to be made. Suppose it is asked whether there are more things in classroom A than in classroom B. Even this simple enough application of number concepts requires a convention as to what is to count as a "thing": separate pieces of furniture? bodies? specks of chalk? molecules? Again, in the application of geometry to the world, conventions have to be adopted as to what in the real world will be taken to represent a "point" (a pencil dot?), or a "line" (the edge of a ruler?), or a "plane" (a desk top?). If there is to be measurement, there must not only be an appropriate concept of the dimension of measurement, whether length, time-lapse, angle, weight, volume, speed, or area, but a convention must be adopted as to what will count as a convenient unit of that dimension.

Assumptions also have to be made, fortunately usually quite safely, about the stability of the world throughout the period of our application of some mathematics to it. If things constantly divided or coalesced, like raindrops on a window, or if shapes bent and twisted all the time, the application of mathematics in such cases would become difficult or impossible. Indeed, the actual proclivity of the world to show such instabilities is something that has deliberately to be compensated for at the levels of accuracy at which a draftsman may work, both in respect of his paper and his slide rule. Neither keeps quite still.[6]

(*b*) *Science*. The sciences, like the systems of mathematics, have their own interconnected concepts, though again words used to mark them may have other uses elsewhere. Such concepts include atom, magnetic field, cell, neuron, reflex, sublimation, trade cycle, extended family, anomie and reinforcement. The validation procedure for a scientific hypothesis, put highly schematically, is to deduce what consequences one would expect upon such a hypothesis, and then to observe whether things are so. Instruments may be used to assist this observation, and experiment to control it.

If things are indeed so, that does not strictly "prove" the hypothesis, for such an observation might also be the consequence of some *other* hypothesis. But if things turn out not to be so, then this does disprove some at least among the assumptions being made. With highly abstract theories, the step from theory to observation may be long and elaborate, even involving different classes of scientific worker, but there must be some point at which the theory stands or falls by actual observations.

Much of scientific reasoning is, of course, mathematical in form, but this does not mean that science is just a kind of mathematics. It only uses mathematics. Suppose I wish to predict the actual velocity of a falling stone after a given time. I may start from the equation $s = ut + 16t^2$, then differentiate to get $ds/dt = u + 32t$, and finally substitute given values for the variables, so finding that, starting from rest, the stone will be moving at 96 ft/sec after 3 seconds. But now there are two independent questions to ask: (i) Is the mathematics correct? (ii) Is what these inferences lead one to expect actually confirmed by observation? If the expectation is not confirmed, then no matter how impeccable the mathematics, the originally assumed law is false, or else its application in this case involves some false assumption. Observation, not mathematical accuracy, is the test of truth in science.

    [6] D. Gasking, "Mathematics and the World," in *Logic and Language,* 2nd ser., ed. A. G. N. Flew (Oxford: Blackwell, 1953).

Scientific discovery does not typically begin with observation, however. If one tried to begin with observations, which observations should be made? Should one just take a notebook, look around, and make notes? Should a psychologist just put some rats in a maze and then watch to "see what happens"? What would be relevant? What would be worth observing? There is a popular view that scientific discovery is an accident that might happen to anybody. Did not Newton just chance to be in the orchard when the apple fell? Perhaps he did, but if so the point is that it was Newton who chanced to be there, and he was not just any observer but one who was preoccupied with certain problems, moreover problems perceptible only to people initiated into a certain tradition of inquiry. As Bruner remarks, "discovery, like surprise, favors the well prepared mind." [7]

Science is not the progeny of a thoroughly promiscuous union between sense and the world, but is the outcome of an evolving tradition of inquiry. As such inquiry develops, the testing of a theory may well become no simple matter, since observational testing itself embodies theories, for example optical, physiological, and psychological theories, but such difficulties largely lie beyond the primary stage of schooling. Even at that stage, however, the most elementary testing of one's expectations may go awry. "Brass" may turn out to be magnetic (brass-coated steel drawing pins), or steel may turn out not to be an electrical conductor (because it is painted).

(c) *History.* In turning from mathematics and science, the paradigm examples of standard validation procedures and therefore of "objectivity," to history, art, and ethics, the delineation of what is involved is much less clear-cut. It is therefore very tempting to be depreciative of these kinds of understanding, to accuse them of not providing "hard facts," of having no "laws" and hence, by implication, of being veritable carnivals of "subjectivity." But why should everything be judged by the

[7] J. S. Bruner, "The Act of Discovery," in *Readings in the Psychology of Cognition,* eds. R. C. Anderson and D. P. Ausubel (New York: Holt, Rinehart and Winston, 1965), p. 607.

standards appropriate to mathematics and science? It would be apposite here to recall Aristotle's caution when he said, in the first book of his *Nichomachean Ethics,* that it is a mark of an educated man that in every subject he looks for only so much precision as its nature permits.

History is not just the study of the past, for geology, paleontology, and the prehistory of man are also concerned with the past. History, roughly, is an attempt to construct, on the basis of such evidences as survive, a narrative of particular human actions and activities. It is not a species of imperfect sociology concerned with forming general laws about certain kinds of occurrences, such as revolutions, so much as with the happenings involved in some particular occurrence, such as the French Revolution.[8]

Since it is the actions and activities of men that are being described, the assumption is made that men do, for the most part, act rationally, if not always reasonably, so that the ordinary concepts of human motivation rather than specially constructed theoretical concepts give much of the meaning to the narrative. For example, when a historian of art tells us that in much of northern Europe in the sixteenth century painters increasingly turned to the painting of portraits, as did Holbein, and when he explains this change as an effect of the Reformation, with its puritanical hostility to images as idolatry, then we readily begin to understand the motivation at work. Painters who had derived much of their income from painting altarpieces and devotional pictures were now forced to seek a livelihood elsewhere, as in something unobjectionable like painting portraits of the well-to-do.[9] We do not need a special *new* set of concepts to understand this; familiar ones will do quite well. But "sixteenth century," "Reformation," and even "puritanical" may be regarded as distinctively historical concepts here.

Again, the validation procedures for historical narrative cannot easily be set out for all to see, and still less to apply. We

8 W. Dray, *Laws and Explanation in History* (London: Oxford University Press, 1957), Ch. 2.

9 E. H. Gombrich, *The Story of Art,* 11th ed. (London: Phaidon, 1966), Ch. 18.

might be tempted into a comparison with observation in science by pointing to such "hard facts" as monumental inscriptions, coins, documents, buildings, utensils, books, weapons, and so on. But the "hardness" attaches only to what we have *now;* to see what these things *were* calls for interpretation, both as to their significance and their authenticity. "The facts" have actually to be established; they are not just given for all to see.[10]

The establishment of "the facts" is a process inseparable from the construction of the narrative. "The historian validates evidence, constructs factual material and develops his interpretation, all at the same time, checking each aspect by reference to the others."[11] Doubtless in the construction of such a narrative there are endless opportunities for bias and prejudice to operate, and doubtless they do operate, but the activity of being a historian is not a solitary one. His labor can be judged and criticized by his fellow historians, and his theses qualified, modified, or even shown to be quite implausible. Such assurance of objectivity as is possible resides as much in this public assessment and criticism as in the scruples of the individual, as Karl Popper has so often stressed in connection with science.[12]

(*d*) *The arts.* The aesthetic is not, of course, confined to the arts. We may be aesthetically aware of natural objects, such as the sea and the sky, and aesthetic considerations enter, though as properly subordinate to other considerations, into mathematics, science, history, and every kind of practical activity, whether it involves the production of new or the arrangement of existing objects. Nor is the aesthetic confined to the beautiful, unless we so extend the meaning of that vague word until it does no work at all. A tragedy such as King Lear, or Rembrandt's portrait of himself as an old man, may powerfully impress us in many ways, but beauty does not seem to be one of them.

[10] W. Walsh, *An Introduction to the Philosophy of History* (London: Hutchinson, 1951), Ch. 1.

[11] L. R. Perry, "Objective and Practical History," in *Proceedings of the Philosophy of Education Society,* Annual Conference, 1966, p. 42.

[12] K. R. Popper, *The Open Society and Its Enemies,* 4th ed. (London: Routledge & Kegan Paul, 1962), vol. 2, Ch. 23.

To confine our discussion to the arts, however, we can see clearly enough how the two features of concept and validation procedure enter into aesthetic understanding and judgment. The arts may, like history, use quite familiar words, such as rhythm, harmony, expression, and balance, though giving them new senses or new ranges of application. New concepts may be evolved appropriate to composition and style, such as sonata form, coda, foreshortening, flying buttress, baroque, arabesque, and atonality. New kinds of aesthetic object and new methods of production may be conceived, such as the concerto, the novel, the sonnet, fresco, and etching. The arts, then, involve both familiar concepts in new applications, and quite new concepts arising in the development of different traditions and their criticism.

The validation procedures of aesthetic judgment present considerable difficulty to anyone seeking to state them, partly because there is no obvious sense in which the work of art is an attempt to approximate to something already "given." There appears to be no reality about which the work of art is an attempt to state the truth, as in science and history. In mathematics, once the definitions and axioms are laid down, the rest of the system, as yet untraced, is already by implication "given." In science and history, there is an attempt to find laws and furnish narratives which in some sense "correspond" to what actually occurs or has occurred; otherwise they would be fictions and fantasies adrift from reality.

But a work of art is not already implied, waiting only to be traced, or "there," waiting to be discovered. It is the artist's creation and, in a sense, its own world. Again, it would be very odd to respond to a painting or a piece of music by saying that one did not believe it. Even the most "representational" of art, such as trompe l'oeil or the "theater of fact," cannot simply imitate without ceasing to be art. Art, even representational art, involves selection and rejection, rearrangement, accentuation, enhancement, and omission.[13] Add to this the disputed nature of many aesthetic judgments, and we may conclude that one

[13] J. Stolnitz, *Aesthetics and Philosophy of Art Criticism* (Boston: Houghton Mifflin, 1960), Ch. 5.

man's opinion is as good as another's. We may see the picture or hear the music and find nothing at all to interest us in it, wondering if aesthetic judgment is not some kind of conceit, or social game. For how could an object be "there" if we cannot see or hear it?

Nevertheless, there is better and worse judgment, just as there is better and worse art. What the judgment is about we are not likely to appreciate without an appropriate understanding and gaining of familiarity. A good critic does not make us reminisce, or chat about the artist's wife, or convey to us his private and idiosyncratic associations with the work. He so describes the work that we come to see what the aesthetic object is, and agree to or dissent from his judgments about it. He picks out the first and second subjects, points to modulations, draws our attention to qualities of melody and harmony. He explains the setting of a "representational" work, for instance the religious story depicted, draws attention to movement and countermovement, the careful distribution of figures, the effect of certain highlights, how the expression has been caught and the face modeled by the use of light and shade, and how perfect balance has been achieved without seeming to follow a rule. Yet he cannot provide us with any set of simple rules for this process of criticism, because a feature which is entirely fitting in one work would be painfully dissonant or unbalancing in another. But by degrees he can lead us to a greater understanding and appreciation, and begin to develop in us some capacity for critical judgment and discrimination.

(e) *Ethics.* A common enough view of ethics, and one which is, perhaps, the result of a post-Victorian reaction against authority, is that it is a rather niggling set of injunctions to do with sex, charity, and self-denial. But this is far from being the truth. Ethics is concerned with all human values, and with the rules, principles, standards, and ideals which give them expression. In relation to action and choice, therefore, ethics must be conceded primacy over each of the forms of understanding we have so far considered. This is not to say that ethical considerations ought to bend or twist the findings of science or history, or that art should be subordinated to a political requirement that it exhibit "social realism," but it is to say that the attribution of value to the *activity* of being a scientist, historian, artist, or follower of the arts is an ethical matter.

Even aestheticism, the subordination of everything to aesthetic appraisals, is itself an ethical choice. It is to say that art ought to be regarded as the highest value in human life, and that cannot *itself* be an aesthetic judgment. The necessary primacy of the ethical in relation to action and choice shows itself more clearly, however, when values conflict, as they do when scientific research requires experiments on people, when history is rewritten to glorify a party or dictator, or when works of art lead to crime. For in such cases we are forced into greater self-consciousness about the valuations to be placed on various human activities, valuations which had, perhaps, lain concealed from ourselves until the conflict arose.

Because of this primacy, ethical evaluation is one of the areas which always offers a temptation to the authoritarian to legislate for others how they ought to live, and to visit them with punishments and inconveniences if they do not comply. But of any authority we can always ask, though it may sometimes be imprudent to do so, why we ought to do what he says we ought to do. This is to ask for reasons, for statements of what makes it right, or sensible, or wise, so to act, which raises the whole problem of the validation of ethical judgments.

Asking for reasons also implicitly asserts one's autonomy, as a person to whom good reasons have to be given in order to gain compliance. Furthermore, such reasons will be reasons for anyone, other things being equal, so that the would-be authoritarian must submit himself to the same ruling which he prescribes for others. Reason, equality, and personal autonomy are therefore very intimately connected concepts. To ask for reasons is to assert one's autonomy, and to submit to reason is to place oneself equally with others under its sway. But independence of authority in no way precludes one, of course, from choosing to avail oneself of the advice, experience, and judgment of others, and doubtless we are often wise to do so.

A convenient distinction within the ethical can be drawn

between social morality and individual ideal.[14] By "social morality" here is meant the system of interpersonal regulation in terms of which certain important kinds of restraint are demanded and certain actions required. So important are these, in fact, that we often embody them in laws in order to give them precision, to emphasize their importance, and to provide a remedy in case of their disregard. The general concepts involved in this sphere are those of right, wrong, duty, and obligation, though there are many more specific concepts which mark out what is to be approved or disapproved in some concrete connection.

The validation of the rules of social morality is ultimately in terms of such fundamental formal principles as fairness or justice, and the consideration of people's interests or good.[15] Conceptions of people's interests are, of course, variable. They vary with the beliefs and local circumstances of a society, and with the particular roles in which we may be acting. One has duties as a father, as a friend, as a teacher, as a citizen, as well as more general duties not attaching to any particular social role. Some of these latter may briefly be mentioned.

Two formal principles of social morality have already been mentioned, but there are many general rules safeguarding basic interests we share. Such rules concern control over various kinds of inclinations, such as aggressiveness, greed, sexuality, and intolerance of differences. These prohibit killing, injury, cruelty, and the subtler kinds of hurtfulness, such as rudeness, spite, and causing embarrassment; they safeguard property; they constitute roles, such as those of courtship and marriage, for the expression of sexuality; they restrict intrusion upon and interference with others.

Other rules concern not so much control over inclinations as the recognition of positive obligations to others. These include obligations towards one's children, truth-telling, promise-keeping, cooperation in joint enterprises, and rendering assistance

[14] P. F. Strawson, "Social Morality and Individual Ideal," in *Christian Ethics and Contemporary Philosophy,* ed. I. T. Ramsey (London: S.C.M. Press, 1966), Ch. 15.

[15] R. S. Peters, *Ethics and Education* (London: Allen and Unwin, 1966), Pt. 2.

to others in need. Though none of these basic rules is absolute, in that one may always be overridden by another on a particular occasion, they are together basic conditions of social life. They may be largely taken for granted in a well-ordered state of affairs, though when they are absent, life, as Hobbes said, is "solitary, poor, nasty, brutish and short."

But basic interests do not comprise the whole of ethical life and, granted an underpinning of basic moral rules such as those just mentioned, there is room for considerable variation in individual ideals. Concepts more characteristic at this level are those of good, bad, worthwhile, desirable, satisfaction, happiness, and health. Political liberty, social justice, and education are key enabling conditions for appreciating the possibilities of choice at this level. We may value, above all, family life and friendship, or the pursuit of the arts, or scholarship, or the membership of some church, or social work, or being close to nature, or being in certain company, or inventing, or risk and adventure, or some combination of these and many other valued activities. Social science, literature, and history reveal to us further possibilities.

Validation here involves the negative condition of compatibility with basic morality, but beyond that, coming to see for ourselves and appreciating the descriptions under which various ways of living are to be praised, admired, and perhaps chosen to be followed. Such choice is not, of course, something made in five minutes, but is rather a matter of a steady growth in understanding and gaining in conviction of the rightness, for oneself at least, of some particular way of living, some fundamentally worthwhile ideal of life.

(*f*) *Religion.* It might be argued that religion merits a place in the curriculum on precisely the same grounds as do the forms of understanding already discussed; for religion, it might be said, is surely an important element in understanding our situation in the world. It has its interconnected concepts, such as God, grace, sin, heaven, immortal life, damnation, and, more recently, "ultimate ground of all our being." Again, it has what look like distinctive validation procedures in religious experience, in historical revelation through Christ and the prophets, and in the "proofs" of natural theology. Obviously justice to these claims cannot possibly be done in a page or two, but at least a gesture is possible toward some of the issues that it raises.[16]

Religion, of course, is not just a matter of religious doctrines. It involves moral injunctions, rituals of worship, and institutions. Thus by combining creed, code, cult, and church it presents not just one possible activity among others, but a whole way of life. Nevertheless, there is good reason for taking the credal basis of doctrine as central. It has already been pointed out in an earlier section that prayer and worship presuppose belief in God, and "belief in" presupposes "belief that," which in turn raises questions of *truth*. Religion is about God, moreover a God who is not just the correlate of our attitudes and aspirations, but who is "there" whether we believe Him to be so or not. Furthermore, how can the members of a church regard themselves as offering worship to the *same* object unless there is some set of intelligible and true beliefs to furnish a criterion of sameness here?

Questions of belief and truth can, of course, be evaded. One can say that here is a mystery which places God beyond our comprehension. One can welcome paradox and be undismayed by any contradictions that may be uncovered. One can follow Kierkegaard in speaking the language of "commitment" and of "leaps of faith." The effect of this is to put religion beyond the reach of rational scrutiny, but by the same token no one is given any reason to follow in making the same commitments and leaps. Moreover, there are questions to do with the relations between belief and will here which, when raised, seem to indicate that such commitments involve a loss of integrity and a lapse into what Sartre calls "bad faith." One cannot *make* one's beliefs about God be true simply by energetic affirmations, or by a settled will to believe.

[16] For some recent discussions, see A. G. N. Flew and A. C. MacIntyre, eds., *New Essays in Philosophical Theology* (London: S.C.M. Press, 1955); B. Mitchell, ed., *Faith and Logic* (London: Allen and Unwin, 1957): F. Ferre, *Language, Logic and God* (New York: Harper and Row, 1962); and N. Smart, *Philosophers and Religious Truth* (London: S.C.M. Press, 1964).

The reason why questions of belief and truth are evaded or bypassed by some is easy to see. Grave difficulties are involved in trying to answer them. Religious experience and historical revelation already presuppose, rather than establish, belief in God. No experience could by itself establish the existence of its supposed object, and secular history establishes only that certain people said that they had certain beliefs and experiences: it cannot validate those beliefs and experiences in religious terms. Nor do the traditional proofs stand in much better case since Kant's criticisms of them and later refinements of those criticisms. The ontological argument falsely supposes that the existential application of a concept can be determined without going outside a system of definitions. The cosmological argument at most shows that a first cause is conceivable, but from then on is the same as the ontological argument. As for the teleological argument, why should it be conceded that there is *design* in the world, or just *one* designer, or that the designer is *God?*

Further difficulties are raised by God's goodness and justice. In relation to His goodness, there is the classic objection of the evil in the world that is suffered by innocent people. Either God cannot stop it, in which case He is not omnipotent; or He will not stop it, in which case He is not good. In relation to His justice there are problems to do with human freedom and responsibility which go back to Pelagius. Either I am not able to choose the good by myself, in which case how can I justly be held responsible and punished for a wrong choice; or I am able to choose, in which case my freedom limits God's omnipotence and my nature cannot be so sinful as to need God's redeeming grace.

There are other objections which, though not in logic strictly relevant to the truth or falsity of religious claims, nevertheless seriously affect our estimates of the likelihood that certain claims would, on further inquiry, turn out to be true. These "weakeners," rather than objections, include the following: post-Freudian explanations of religious belief in terms of wishes for security; the post-Darwinian removal of religious discourse from the field of factual claims about human origins; sociological observations on the ways in which religious institutions become vested interests and are even consciously used in the ways that Plato recommended; comparative studies showing that there are many different religions, all firmly holding their contrary doctrines to be true and often having their own stock of confirming miracles, etc. These facts, as was said, are not strictly relevant to any particular truth claim, but they are very relevant to our estimates of the individuals who make the claims.

Prior to questions of truth or falsity, however, are questions of intelligibility. What does it *mean* to say that one "believes in God"? Images may give the appearance of meaningfulness, but once religious notions are stripped of their anthropomorphic imagery, what is left as the object of belief? Yet stripped of such imagery they must be, for God is transcendent and to worship images is idolatry. Nor are matters helped if pictures are replaced by concepts, such as love, will, power, father, and creation, for such concepts get their meaning from their *human* use, and cannot literally apply to God. They can be no more than heavily qualified analogies, but the admission of this may be judged to result in what Flew has called "death by a thousand qualifications." [17] And why should God not be tall, fat, sulky, or impatient, only in a "different but analogous sense," of course? Again, how is God, who is eternal, perfect, and therefore *lacking* in nothing, to be related to a world which is changing in time and with which God is not satisfied? As a final strain on our credulity, how are we to conceive of our survival after death? In what sense could a disembodied soul be a *person,* capable of self-reference and of individuation from other souls?

Of course, no one of these is a decisive objection. In response to any of them further distinctions of sense can be made, arguments distinguished, analogies drawn, and possibilities held to be open. Powerful sentiments incline us to go on trying to say something intelligible and to establish its truth. We may in a certain mood be struck, as was Wittgenstein, by the *amazing* fact that there is a world at all. We may feel a debt of gratitude for being alive which searches for some object to whom to

[17] Flew and MacIntyre, *New Essays in Philosophical Theology,* p. 97.

express it. We may want some way of articulating our awe in the face of the world and of life, some way of focusing our highest aspirations and of reassuring ourselves in the face of our inevitable death. We may even want to be comforted to such an extent that we willfully silence honest doubt, and make animated attacks on anyone who disturbs us in our self-deception. Our quandary, as A. C. MacIntyre suggests, would seem to be that we cannot accept Christian theology, while at the same time it provides the only vocabulary we have in terms of which to raise certain fundamental questions about human life.[18]

Thus nothing is ever finally settled here. Sensitive and intelligent people can be found on both sides. And because the claims of religion can finally be neither substantiated nor dismissed, while on the other hand *if* they are true they must be of the highest importance, we cannot presume to settle the matter on behalf of others, whatever we may decide in our own case. For these reasons it was argued earlier that children in the schools should certainly learn *about* religion, for instance in literature and history lessons, and later in lessons specifically devoted to the *discussion* of religious questions, but that it would be unjustifiable to indoctrinate or deliberately attempt to initiate, as is done by many at present. No doubt this is an uneasy compromise, but it does have regard to how things are. . . .

[18] A. C. MacIntyre, *Secularization and Moral Change* (London: Oxford University Press, 1967), p. 69.

ENLIGHTENED PREFERENCE AND JUSTIFICATION

The most noticeable characteristic of our value experience . . . is that it contains two components that are only loosely related. One may be called the attitudinal component, the other the theoretical or justifying component. The first tells what one likes; the second tries to give reasons for liking it.

The attitudinal component is being formed from the first day of life, with the result that the origin of many of our likes and dislikes is a mystery to ourselves, our parents, and even to our psychoanalyst. By the time the youngster enters school, he is already equipped with a repertory of preferences, often without knowing how he came by them and whether they are beneficial or harmful. But this much he does know: his likes and dislikes are not turned off and on at will or at mother's or teacher's request. Even when strong arguments are presented to persuade him that his dislike of tomatoes or Fiji Islanders, for example, has no basis in fact, that he would like them if he tried, even when he agrees that he ought to like them, his viscera and emotions continue on their customary course.

This age-old war between heart and head has it pedagogical counterpart in the circumstance that two distinct types of learning are involved in value education. Tastes and dispositions are, in the first instance, products of conditioning that takes place in the home, in the streets, and, to a lesser extent, in the school. It must be remembered that the pupil spends only a few hours a day in school, and that the school does not have the machinery to reinforce systematically anything save scholastic achievement and a respect for the mores of the school community. The school can, at best, modify the tastes already formed. The

From Harry S. Broudy, B. Othanel Smith, and Joe. R. Burnett, *Democracy and Excellence in American Secondary Education* (Chicago, 1964). Reprinted by permission of Rand McNally & Co. and the authors.

young pupil's existing preferences and attitudes do not sample the totality of value possibilities very well, either with respect to depth or range. In every value domain—social, recreational, civic, moral, intellectual, aesthetic, and religious—there are levels of preference. In his informal environment, the pupil has probably not encountered the level of preference exhibited by value experts. Just as one expects the school to bring the expert's thought to bear upon the pupil's inexpert knowledge, so it is reasonable for the school to bring the expert's values to bear upon the pupil's rudimentary taste.

This leads to the second phase of value education, namely, justification of taste or attitude. Although it is not the purpose of the common school to turn out specialists in the arts or philosophy, the significant criterion for evaluating the effectiveness of value education is a change of preference in the direction of connoisseurship. Connoisseurship, in turn, means not only liking something, but also liking it because it has certain qualities prescribed by some theory as being essential to admirable objects. The curriculum problem, therefore, is to find works of art or literature or philosophy which can serve as invitations to like and admire, on the one hand, and as exemplifications of the theories in terms of which they have come to be regarded as deserving of esteem, on the other.

One can say that the interpretive frame for valuing and evaluating is constituted by a set of likings and aversions, together with a set of concepts (criteria) of what likings are approved or disapproved by some reference group. The ordinary man's likings and aversions, at any given moment, are shaped by his own experiences of pleasure and pain and by the approval rules of his normal reference group. Adherence to these rules insures that the desire to be approved and esteemed is fulfilled. For this purpose, the ordinary man needs no formal tuition in taste. The milieu in which he lives and works channels his tastes efficiently. His speech, dress, household decorations, as well as his life heroes and heroines, without his even being aware of it, fall into the stereotypes of his reference group. The price of comfortable membership in his family circle and in his work group is acquiescence to the stereotype, but it is a price men are quite happy to pay.

The problem of formal value education arises only when the school wishes the tastes of the public to be shaped by the tastes of a special reference group called experts or connoisseurs. We then say to the ordinary man, "Shape your likings so that they will coincide with the likings of the experts." To follow this advice, the ordinary man not only has to recondition his preferences, he must also change his criteria of what makes an action or an object worthy of his admiration.

The problem of value schooling is to reshape the already formed preferences or likings of the pupils by changing their value reference groups. In a way, this is not very different from what the school tries to do in the cognitive area, for there, too, schooling extends and refines common sense and knowledge by resorting to the thought of the expert. In another sense, the task is more complicated, because (1) changes in attitudes are harder to bring about than changes in belief; (2) there is less consensus on criteria for evaluation than for truth; (3) we know less about teaching for appreciation than teaching for understanding.

In both cognition and evaluation, so far as schooling is concerned, the pupil has to *do* some knowing and liking and judging as the experts do it, and he has to become aware of the operations involved in doing these things properly. The curriculum has to provide means and materials for both types of experience. It also has to decide how to organize these materials for instruction.

Perhaps something further should be said at this point about an apparent gliding over the problem of choosing which standards the school is to encourage or, indeed, if it is to encourage any. To some readers, the decision to use the connoisseur as the standard of value will smack of dogmatic traditionalism. Disagreement among experts in the arts is notorious. Which experts is the school to choose?

Theoretically, it is interesting and important to ask whether there are or can be objective value standards, standards of right and wrong, good and evil, the beautiful and the ugly. Educationally, however, especially at the secondary level, there is only one solution to this problem: to rely on the experts in these fields as the school relies on experts in other fields. The school does not determine what is "good" chemistry, and it does not determine what is "good" literature or art. "Good" means what men who have devoted their professional lives to the study of these domains have agreed is good. Truth here is not simply consensus, but rather the consensus of the body of persons qualified to have expert opinions.

Where these experts do not agree, the school can only proceed on the principle that the major alternatives deserve to be presented as the best guidance available. Expert disagreement does not license the ignorant or change the nature of expertness. On the contrary, this kind of disagreement is the best incitement to inquiry into grounds of disagreement, an important first step to becoming an expert on one's own account. There is enough agreement among the experts as to what the significant examples of the fine arts and the humanities are to supply more than enough material for any secondary school curriculum. And although, admittedly, the agreement about the more remote past is perhaps greater than about current works, the more recent past has also been studied with sufficient care to permit choices that are not arbitrary and whimsical. Certainly, there is enough agreement not to warrant a fearful withdrawal from the art, literature, and philosophical thought of the recent past.

Who are the value experts? Presumably, those men and women who have experienced and reflected upon what gives the highest satisfaction in each value domain. It is to the great artists, writers, philosophers, and saints that we look for wisdom. Because the pupil cannot replicate the expert's life directly, the school has recourse to the reports of value experts, the connoisseurs of life. These reports, in the form of works of art, systems of philosophy, and religions, present the pupil with an array of possibilities far richer and far more subtle than he could ever imagine. But connoisseurship is also required to comprehend and appreciate these reports.

These great works represent the aspirations of the race. They are value affirmations that integrated and vividly expressed the character of the successive epochs in our history. Their influence reaches into the present. One may loosely call these value exemplars "classics," not only because they have been admired and preferred by generations of experts, but also because they furnish the experts with the criteria for judging them "excellent." The Parthenon is not artistically superb because it conforms to certain rules; on the contrary, some of the rules for good art were derived from the Parthenon. Classics in any field are not only highly satisfactory objects on their own account, but the source of norms of "proper" satisfaction as well. Therein lies their pedagogical value, for in learning to appreciate them, the pupil not only likes what the connoisseur likes, but he is at the same time exposed to the source of the criteria that the connoisseur has used to justify the liking.

Learnings for Appreciation and Choice

Value education has two outcomes. One is appreciation—an enlightened taste that combines likings and reasons. The other is a strategy for making choices in situations in which many likings and many reasons jockey for position. A curriculum should make provision for instruction leading to both of these outcomes.

The appreciative act, combining cherishing and appraising, is always directed toward an individual object or action. We appreciate this picture or that poem. We are pleased by this person's character or repelled by that act of cruelty. Appreciation is not identical with choosing or deciding, because we can appreciate without taking the kind of action that forces us to choose. A woman may appreciate more than one man at the same time, but legally she can marry only one; hence, if she marries she has to choose. One does not have to choose between Beethoven and Mozart unless one is forced to make a judgment about their comparative merits or to exclude one rather than another from a concert program. The appreciative act is particular and unidimensional. Choice, however, may mean acting upon alternative and often conflicting strands of appreciation. It can be unidimensional, as when one chooses to buy one painting rather than another, but often it is multidimensional, as when one is asked to make decisions that involve preferences in painting, music, literature, poetry, and morals.

In such complex situations, not only is one referring to and using well-established likings and attitudes, he is also called upon to establish priorities among them and to make cognitive judgments as to causes and probable consequences. Thus, an attitude toward taxation involves attitudes toward the Republican and Democratic parties, toward their respective economic theories, their theories as to the ultimate worth of the person in the social order, notions of social justice, and dozens of other "appreciations" relevant to the situation.

It seems unrealistic to expect training in the appreciation of literature to help one weigh alternatives in problems of taxation, even though some literary judgments might be relative to the decision. Appreciations in the various value areas are related to social problem-solving in the same way that knowledge of each of the basic sciences is related to the developmental studies.

In an important sense, molar (complex) social problem-solving integrates all the other types of learning discussed. For this reason, educational theorists have advocated this type of problem-solving as *the* design for the curriculum. There is no doubt that this integrative experience must be introduced somewhere in school. If the writers reject it as the only way to organize material for instruction, it is because, as is pointed out below, learning to integrate knowledge and feeling does not of itself provide the diverse appreciations and knowledges to be integrated. Educational theorists have always sought the alchemist's stone in the form of a single type of instruction that would achieve learnings in the symbolic skills, basic concepts, appreciations, and judgment. Thus far, no such stone has lived up to its promise, and until one does, we have to regard learnings for appreciation and learnings for choice as two different strands of the curriculum. . . .

Aesthetic Exemplars as Materials for Value Instruction

Appreciations, having to do with likings for individual objects or activities, direct us to the various types of value experience: economic, health, social, civic, recreational, intellectual, moral, aesthetic, and religious. In each field, one can shape preferences and provide justification for them. Each area has its own scholars and experts, its own traditions and disciplines. One way to design the curriculum is to provide instruction in these disciplines: in the fine arts, ethics, aesthetics, literature, and religion.[1]

Can we introduce the formal study of ethics, aesthetics, theology into the high school? Can we add them to literature and the fine arts as fields for systematic study? Is there room in an already crowded program of studies for them?

There is another problem. If literature or the fine arts are to be taught, should they be taught only for *aesthetic* appreciation, that is, for their artistic merit, or should they also be taught as lessons in morality, religion, and social justice? Or are they to be taught *primarily* as means to instruction in the extra-aesthetic values? The argument has been advanced that works of literature (*Grapes of Wrath*) or drama (*Death of a Salesman*) could be used to interest young people in social issues and problems of social conflict.

In summary, should materials be selected for each type of value in which we wish to improve the taste and judgment of the pupil, or is there one type of material that can perform this service for all the value areas?

The disadvantage of the separate-subject approach is that the student can be exposed to the *concepts* for evaluation without necessarily having the direct kind of experience that the experts regard as "good." This could be the case even in courses *about* literature and the fine arts. This is why Aristotle thought ethics an inappropriate study for the young, whose experience with moral predicaments was meager. Vicarious experience can extend and enrich direct experience but cannot be substituted for it. Further, the nonspecialist evaluates "molar" rather than "atomic" situations, that is, complex, holistic problems rather than separate economic, moral, or aesthetic ones. Only the specialist abstracts from the total situation to make judgments in one value dimension.

---

[1] Theoretically, any value area can be represented in the curriculum, and the writers' reasons for not organizing their curriculum in this way have already been presented in previous chapters.

If, on the other hand, one type of material is used, which shall it be: aesthetic, intellectual, moral, religious? To answer this question, it may help to ask how people shape their value schemata insofar as they are not simply imposed on them. The writers suggest that they do so primarily by introjecting or identifying with a model. This model can be a particular person or a person who represents a style of life, for example, the military leader, the industrial tycoon, the surgeon, or the artist. One forms a self-concept based on such a model and thereafter tries to behave consistently with this concept. To teach values, accordingly, is to shape the pupil's value model.

Where do we get our models? From the family, school, and many other sources, but among the most powerful sources in modern society are the mass media of entertainment. Popular fiction, music, drama, poetry, and painting present value models in the persons of their heroes and heroines, and, unwittingly, their villains as well. Because these life styles are stereotyped, they are easily understood, and because they are repeated so often, they act as conditioning agents. They invite imitations, while the culture is providing strong reinforcement for such imitation. They influence national value commitments by affecting the aesthetic experience of the populace.

Contrary to common impression, the ordinary citizen uses his aesthetic faculties in a wide range of circumstances; he does not restrict them to concerts and visits to museums. For example, the appearance of objects is an important determinant of attention in general. It is an important factor in the price of such objects of ordinary use as refrigerators, automobiles, clothing, and so on. Furthermore, one expects all important activities to be underscored by some sort of aesthetic form. Weddings and funerals have to be carried on amid appropriate sounds, costumes, and gestures. Banquets must have speakers, religions their rituals, special occasions their celebrations. The arts are called upon to render experience more impressive by making it more dramatic and vivid than it otherwise would be.

Not less important is the degree to which common experience relies on appearance for clues to the nature and behavior of objects and people. A certain conformation of landscape betokens serenity or loneliness. A certain type of face warns us against undesirable character traits associated with it, more often than not mistakenly. Science reduces our dependence on appearances as clues to the nature of things, but it will be a long time before we can dispense with them, even in the most sophisticated forms of experience.

Men use models furnished directly or indirectly by the arts to evaluate and even to understand their experience. Oscar Wilde long ago, and many writers in more recent years, noted that we are more likely to test reality by the images the arts have created for us than to test images by reality. Newspapers, magazines, movies, and television, as well as the serious arts, are forever exhibiting models of life, of what we are supposed to find and admire in the world: the way a sunset should blaze, the way a fashionable woman should dress, the way the American man should react to his wife's complaints and to Russian threats. Slogans, trademarks, pictures, and fiction all create shapes and images that trigger certain expectations and emotions.

Ideals, personality traits, life styles, and value schemata acquire their social power by hypnotizing the public with their charm, a charm that operates through aesthetically grasped images. Popular arts are used in entertainment and advertising to amuse or persuade the customer. The serious artist also portrays his impressions of the world and life, and he, like the advertising man, also wants to charm his public. But whereas the advertiser and propagandist use the work of art as a means to their own and often nonaesthetic ends, the serious artist is committed to expressing what he sees, hears, and feels by creating objects that have high aesthetic and artistic quality—that are aesthetically authentic. The nonaesthetic or extra-aesthetic results are for him incidental, although to the society in which he lives the priorities may be reversed. The school, however, has to insist on both art for art's sake and art for goodness's sake, that is, for social significance.

If this is the social-psychological mechanism for value training, it may be advisable for the school to make use of a similar mechanism. In other words, the school also can present life styles as they appear in the arts, but not in the popular arts. Displayed in literature, drama, painting, and music, life models acquire an attractiveness that engages the emotions as well as the intellect. They are invitations to feel and cherish as well as to understand.

To follow this strategy, one can approach value education through what are called value exemplars, as they are encountered in notable instances of literature and the fine arts. Appreciative learning can be regarded as a type of aesthetic learning, a learning of how to perceive and appraise aesthetic objects, natural and contrived. It means that one looks to the arts, literature, and drama for models rather than to history and philosophy, or, better, one looks to such historical and philosophical ideas as have received high artistic expression.

Let us be clear on this point. To study all value exemplars via their artistic expressions is not a substitute for the study of ethics, aesthetics, and religion. However, given the limitations of time and the fact that attitudinal as well as cognitive components are essential to appreciative learning, the choice of the aesthetic vehicle for value education seems justified.

If works of art are to bear this heavy curricular burden, they have to be *great* works of art as well as *good* ones. A good work of art has met the criteria of artistic quality with respect to form, technique, and aesthetic interest. A great work of art has to have "significant form" and must express an important aspect of life. Usually it covers a wide range of values and portrays them with a clarity and intensity not found in everyday experience. Moreover, each art form has its own distinctive objects and canons of appraisal. To learn to appreciate a painting is not automatically to learn to appreciate poetry. Hence, the samples have to be chosen so that the major arts are represented.

The Teaching of Exemplars

Can we point to some systematic way of teaching exemplars? Or are we reduced to exposing pupils to a wide variety of them and hoping for some mystical alchemy to do the rest? Are we to give pupils a watered-down studio training in one of the arts and hope that this will permeate taste and judgment in other value areas? Or shall we rely upon survey courses? For our purpose, it will be sufficient if a plausible case can be made out for the first alternative, namely, that some systematic way of teaching exemplars is possible.

In appreciation, the use made of schooling is predominantly associative, but one has to be extremely careful about the type of association that occurs. A work of art in any medium is an illusion. Literally speaking, a painting is a pattern of shapes and colors, but it is a work of art if one is led to see the shapes and colors as having lifelike qualities: tension, resolution, opposition, force, cheerfulness, sadness, loneliness, anger—any and every shade of feeling whether there are names for them or not—operating in a space and time of their own. The ability to see and hear life as color or sound patterns requires imagination, or, in other words, it requires a way with images.

However, no work of art can serve as a metaphor to him who does not bring the other half of the metaphor to it. There has to be a store of images that are already analogous to the forms of life and feeling for the work of art to be seen or heard properly. Keeping in mind that the work of art should not make us think *of* this or that but rather that it must look or sound *like* this or that, it is clear that we must learn the images of the culture and perhaps of the race in order to appreciate serious works of art.

The word "snake," for example, elicits somewhat different associations than "serpent," but it is difficult, one would guess, for anyone in our culture to respond to either word without complex imagery and feeling tone. However, it is hard to believe that a man thoroughly steeped in mythology and poetry would respond with an association complex comparable to that of a schoolboy or an adult whose schooling ended in the sixth grade. Part of the task of value education is to provide materials for imaginative construction based on cues and symbols presented by perception in general and art works in particular. In turn, experience with a work of art enriches the store of images.

Appreciative learnings are used replicatively only insofar as the attitudinal component is aroused in the value situation. When judgments about works of art are parroted as learned, they are used replicatively, albeit precisely in the way they ought not to be used. Value learnings are used applicatively only by the expert or the specialist, such as the scholar or connoisseur. As with other learnings, the citizen, for the most part, uses value learnings interpretively, that is, to reflect upon his likings and the criteria for judging them. To construct his evaluational map he uses the exemplars as anchor points for judgment.

Levels of Appreciative Learnings

There are four levels of aesthetic judgment on which the critical response can be made:

1. The vividness and intensity of the sensuous elements in the work of art: the affective quality of the sounds, colors, gestures, and so on;

2. The formal qualities of the object, its design or composition;

3. The technical merits of the object, the skill with which the work is carried out;

4. The expressive significance of the object, its import or message or meaning as aesthetically expressed.

These four levels also mark off the domains of appreciation instruction. The first three are primarily unidimensional, but the fourth need not and perhaps cannot be. The first three are topics in the study of painting, music, poetry, literature, and drama. In each medium, one has to learn how to use the appropriate senses with discrimination, how to discern and judge its adequacy, and how to relate design to artistic styles and types. Finally, enough training in performance is needed so that one can get the feel of the appropriate techniques. How much of the latter is required by the educated layman for appreciation is still a matter of controversy, but it seems clear that it is not so little as is now required in customary courses on appreciation, and probably far less than is prescribed for professional training of artists.

The case is different with the appreciation of the significance or import of the book or art work being studied. The import always goes beyond the work of art, even though it must be perceptually present in the work of art. What ideal, what conception of this or that aspect of life does a given work of art or exemplar express? Here we are entering upon the field of criticism, and fundamental criticism always is rooted in the total realm of value rather than in one department of it.

The study of exemplars affords the opportunity for all four modes of aesthetic experience, and only when the four are combined is there something which deserves to be called aesthetic education.

It should be obvious that if one is to carry on this sort of education in school, the number of exemplars will be small. Even if the performance skills are fairly well developed by Grade 7, it takes considerable time to learn to cherish and appraise an art work that is rich in significance and high in artistic merit.

> We must remember that the worth of any great work of art is not something that can be grasped in a moment. To appreciate and judge an excellent painting, for example, we must do much more than glance at it in a gallery. Ordinarily we must *live* with it until its sensuous qualities, meanings, and forms sink deep into our conscious and subconscious mind. If then, day after day, it works its magic upon us—if its appeal is deep and varied enough to be lasting—we can realize its excellence because our lives are being substantially enriched. The expert critic is one who can sense this amplitude and fineness of value more quickly and surely than the ordinary man.[2]

The choice of a relatively small number of exemplars needs justification, because the current survey type of appreciation course covers a great deal of ground, and performance courses provide a kind of intensive appreciation that is hard to match. The survey course, however, is open to the twin objections of superficiality and irrelevance: superficiality in that it affords

[2] Melvin Rader, ed., *A Modern Book of Esthetics,* 3rd ed. (New York: Holt, Rinehart & Winston, 1960), p. xxxi.

only smatterings and flitting exposures to works that are difficult to appreciate under any circumstances, irrelevance in that they tend to give knowledge about the field primarily and appreciation of it secondarily. If aesthetic education is to be a means toward value education in general, appreciation in terms of direct likings is as necessary as knowledge about works of art and the rules for judging them.

As to relying exclusively on performance courses, the fact remains that for people without talent, such training rapidly reaches the point of diminishing returns, except perhaps on a hobby basis. For it is not at all clear that beyond a certain point technical proficiency promotes appreciation in the other three senses enumerated above.

In short, if the curricular time now given to literature and drawing, art and music can be used for six years of aesthetic education via a study of exemplars, one ought to have a great deal more to show for it than what the secondary school can now produce.

In summary, the area of the curriculum primarily responsible for conveying to the pupil a sense of the style or styles of life found admirable by the connoisseurs of our culture should consist of six years of study devoted to a carefully selected set of paintings, musical compositions, poems, dramas, and novels. In the developmental studies of the culture, knowledge about these exemplars will already have been encountered. The relation of art products and forms to other elements of the culture will have been noted. Perhaps some acquaintance with the names and biographical details of noted artists, writers, and thinkers will have been achieved.

In the exemplar part of the curriculum, the focus of study is a particular work of art. The desired outcome is a change in the quality of the student's perception and feeling about that work. The directions and levels of these desired changes have been indicated. To accomplish this, instruction may have to guide perception by having the student work a while in the medium of the work being studied. Or it may be advisable to discuss styles, periods, and the symbolic conventions illustrated by the work of art. At certain times and on certain levels, a study of the major critical opinions may also be undertaken.

The impact of these diverse modes of instruction is to change the quality of perception, its discernment of details, of form, and, hopefully, of significance. The knowledge *about* the work, while important, is nevertheless a means rather than an end in itself. Until the pupil perceives as the connoisseur perceives, the connoisseur's judgment is not his judgment; his standards are not authentic.

It would be presumptuous of the secondary school to claim that even the most favorable study of exemplars provides the student with a complete interpretive frame. It will be sufficient if a few major guideposts or models in the various arts have been introjected by the student. Indeed, the limitation on the number of exemplars is justified by the opportunities for varied exposure afforded by modern museums, books, and recordings. Much of the power of a work of art comes from the quality and needs of the beholder's experience, and this is not finished and wrapped up by the school. Yet without this frame, we can no more orient ourselves to art than without the basic sciences we can orient ourselves to knowledge. . . .

AESTHETIC EDUCATION AND CURRICULUM

D. K. Wheeler

A major task in every society is the perpetuation of its value systems, structure, and technology in the face of the inevitable mortality of its members. Transmission of the socio-cultural heritage is effected through socialization in the process of social interaction. In view of the fact that educational systems are formal organizations within their society, it seems obvious that formal aims will be derived from this interest in socializing the young, will mirror, more or less well, existing social values, and will be carried out through the use of selected portions of this socio-cultural heritage.

In considering the aims of the educational process, particularly in assessing precisely what parts of the cultural heritage shall be transmitted through the educational process, there is a good deal of semantic confusion, lack of operational definition, use of illicit dichotomies, making of value judgments at the wrong stage, confusion of opinion with data, and of tentative hypotheses with valid conclusions.[1] Above all there is a tendency to consider that there are separate sorts of education —intellectual, moral, physical, social, or aesthetic—because for purposes of analysis it is easier to consider these various aspects of the individual in isolation. Despite Plato's view that the apparent plurality of things, ideas, and sciences reflects an underlying unity, the Aristotelian standpoint seems to have carried most weight in education where much of the tradition is based on the theory that there are three kinds of sciences—the theoretical, the practical, and the productive. Because of historical accidents the emphasis seems to have been placed on the first and the second sort, the discovery of truth or the acquisition of knowledge and the pursuit of the good, especially the human

From the *Journal of Aesthetic Education,* vol. 4, no. 2 (April 1970): 87–108. Reprinted by permission of the *Journal* and the author.
[1] See D. K. Wheeler, *Curriculum Process* (London: University of London Press, 1967), pp. 22–28.

good achieved by action. Yet modern views of science suggest that empirically it does not rest upon absolutes and that it must be regarded, not so much as a body of knowledge, but as a system of hypotheses [2] which must be tested against experience by observation and experiment. Anthropology has shown the vital part played in man's life by the arts; psychology has demonstrated the necessity of considering man as a unitary being rather than as mind, soul, spirit, or body; sociology recognizes the arts as a social institution. Against the long educational tradition of concentration on the theoretical and the practical—the pursuit of the good and the true—one can only suggest the acceptance of an interdisciplinary view, a willingness to recognize the contributions that the perspectives of other disciplines offer to one's own studies, in particular the relevance of the social sciences to education. It is for this reason that we have suggested that insofar as curriculum is the planned experiences offered to the learner under the guidance of the school, its development requires a three-way orientation —toward society, toward the individual, and toward those particular portions of the cultural heritage which it is the job of the school to pass on. In aesthetic education, or rather in those planned experiences directed toward the aesthetic component of man's life, we must avoid the trap, so common in educational literature, of devoting our attention to only one aspect of the total problem or of considering different aims as mutually exclusive. Certainly analysis of particular problems requires delimitation of the general field, but it must be remembered that analysis requires to be followed by synthesis before action is possible. The bio-psychological development of the individual proceeds within a socio-cultural matrix which is the product of man's attempts to solve his problems, that is, of his experiences as an individual or in groups within the total environment. Learning, which changes behavior,[3] proceeds through experi-

---

[2] K. R. Popper, *The Logic of Scientific Discovery* (New York: Basic Books, 1959), p. 17.

[3] I.e., "broadly anything that an organism does, including overt physical action, internal, physiological and emotional processes and implicit activity" (Good's *Dictionary of Education*). Behavior is anything that a human being thinks or feels or does.

encing, directly or vicariously, and through subjecting ideas about that experience to analysis and reflection. The task of education is deliberately to eliminate, consolidate, or change behavior habitually displayed by the individual within his society.

Within the last few years certain schemata have been produced which are of value to the curriculum-maker because they refer to one or more phases of the curriculum process and help in the answering of some of the educational problems associated with its theory and practice. Acquaintance with some of these may be of value to those interested in the development of education in the aesthetic areas.

The concept of *developmental tasks* [4] escapes some of the difficulties inherent in child-centered and socially oriented curriculum directions by considering individuals as responding variably both to their own needs and to social demands. Though the model refers to the total process of socializing the child, it may be used to help clarify educational aims and decisions about the unique role of the school in the educational process. The educator is mainly concerned with the following tasks which offer goals and objectives for consideration:

1. Achieving an appropriate pattern of dependence-independence.
2. Learning to understand and control the physical world.
3. Developing an appropriate system of symbols and conceptual abilities.
4. Developing a conscience, a morality, a scale of values and an ethical system as a guide to behavior.
5. Relating oneself to the cosmos.[5]

The school's major concern with categories 2 and 3 has been seen at the elementary level as the development of literacy and

[4] The concept was developed by Tryon and Lilienthal and elaborated by Havighurst. See Caroline Tryon and J. W. Lilienthal III, "Developmental Tasks: The Concept and Its Importance," in *Fostering Mental Health in Our Schools,* Association for Supervision and Curriculum Development (Washington, D.C.: National Education Association, 1950), and Robert J. Havighurst, *Human Development and Education* (New York: Longmans, Green and Co., 1953). Nine or ten categories of tasks are usually suggested.

[5] Tryon and Lilienthal.

numeracy, but obviously, even in early school years, these tasks are dependent on an extensive exploration of the real world and facilitated by increased understanding and widened concepts of persons, places, and events. Insofar as aesthetic education must be based upon perception, categories 2 and 3 provide justification, if any be required, for this type of education. In addition, 4 and 5 provide materials not only in the aesthetic but in other value domains.

In connection with the major educational tasks indicated in the categories specified, the concept needs to be supplemented by the use of the *Taxonomy of Educational Objectives* [6] to outline intended outcomes and to specify classroom objectives.

So far, Bloom and his colleagues have completed only the first two fields of their projected taxonomy of educational objectives in the cognitive, affective, and psychomotor areas. Though directed toward the classification of educational goals, these works are also pertinent to the selection of experiences and the consideration of content.

The cognitive domain is divided into two areas, *knowledge* and *abilities and skills,* each arranged hierarchically, so that objectives found in any one class are likely to make use of or be built on behavior considered in preceding classes, while within any one class the subclasses are ordered from simple to complex.

Knowledge or information is concerned with phenomena remembered either by recall or recognition, the emphasis being on the psychological processes of memory. Within this class, subclasses progress from simple to complex, concrete to abstract, and from specifics to universals. The first such subclass (1.10) deals with isolated pieces of information, the second (1.20) with ways and means of dealing with them and how they are typically organized, studied, and evaluated. It is concerned with knowledge of characteristic ways of presenting and dealing with phenomena, or trends and sequences, classifications and categories, the criteria employed in judgment, or the methodology (techniques and procedures) used in the field. The most complex level (1.30) is knowledge of universals or

[6] Benjamin S. Bloom, ed., *Taxonomy of Educational Objectives,* Handbook I: Cognitive Domain (New York: David McKay, 1956).

abstractions, the major ways in which phenomena of all kinds are organized.

The other five categories are concerned with *intellectual skills and abilities,* the processes involved in critical thinking and problem-solving. *Comprehension,* or understanding of the literal message transmitted by a communication, involves three types: translation (2.10), interpretation (2.20), and extrapolation (2.20). In the sense that extrapolation requires the receiver to go beyond translation and interpretation to determine corollaries, consequences, and implications, it resembles *Application* (3.00). It differs from it, however, in that thinking is extended to other conditions and situations, whereas in application generalizations and rules of procedure are used and the appropriate abstractions applied to a new and unfamiliar problem.

Analysis (4.00) is concerned with the breakdown of material into its constituent parts, with the relationship of these parts to each other and to the whole, and with organizational schemata. Under it are subsumed analysis of elements (4.10), analysis of relationship (4.20), and analysis of organizational principles (4.30). The fifth class, *Synthesis,* involves the putting together of relevant parts to form a whole. These elements will be derived from numerous sources and must then be combined according to some pattern or schema. The final class, *Evaluation,* may be defined as the making of a judgment for some given purpose, and requires some combination of other classes.

This section of the *Taxonomy* is of great value in that it offers the curriculum-maker a complete classification of educational objectives in the cognitive field. Further, because what is classified is the *intended behavior* of students, it indicates these objectives operationally. Finally, it shows that knowledge of subject matter or information is only part of the cognitive field and that there are abilities and skills to be cultivated. By the "illustrative educational objectives" it helps to bridge the gap between the more general goal and the specific classroom objective, and by its illustrative test items it gives not only evaluative procedures but hints about the kinds of situations or experiences likely to promote the desired behavior.

The first and simplest class of educational objective in the affective domain, classified in the second handbook,[7] is concerned with sensitivity to certain phenomena, with the individual's willingness to receive or attend to them. Thus class 1.00 is *Receiving* or *Attending* with its subclasses 1.1, awareness; 1.2, willingness to receive; and 1.3, selected (or controlled) attention. Class 2.0 *Responding,* with its subclasses, 2.1, acquiescence in responding; 2.2, willingness to respond; and 2.3, satisfaction in response, goes beyond mere attention to phenomena and involves positive emotional responses to stimuli. The third class, *Valuing,* is concerned with the ascription of worth to phenomena. Subclass 3.1, acceptance of a value, deals largely with beliefs; subclass 3.2, preference for a value, with the greater involvement of an individual and the greater investment of his time and energy, and subclass 3.3, commitment, with conviction, loyalty, or faith. Such valuing is enduring over time, involves considerable investment of energy, and issues in overt action.

As values are internalized by the learner, they are gradually built into a system, so that the interrelationships between values and their ordering in a hierarchy become important. Accordingly, the fourth class, *Organization,* is divided into two subclasses, 4.1, conceptualization of a value, and 4.2, organization of a value system. At the highest level, an individual responds consistently to value-laden situations with a philosophy of life, a *Weltanschauung.* The final class describes such behavior as 5.0, *Characterization by a value or value complex,* including 5.1, generalized set, and 5.2, characterization.

In this classification, the terms often used to describe certain response behaviors, such as feelings, attitudes, sensitivities, beliefs, and values may be seen as extending over differing ranges of subclasses.[8] Use of the *Taxonomy* may result in increased specificity and precision in the employment of these terms.

Obviously every classification scheme is an abstraction which divides relevant phenomena into arbitrary categories most useful to the classifier. For purposes of analysis, an arbitrary di-

[7] David R. Krathwohl, Benjamin S. Bloom, and Bertram B. Masia, *Taxonomy of Educational Objectives,* Handbook II: Affective Domain (New York: David McKay, 1964).

[8] *Ibid.,* p. 37.

vision is made between cognitive and affective behavior which has no parallel in the world of reality. If we are prepared to look, we shall find that nearly all cognitive objectives have an affective component, more often implicit than explicit, and usually related to what is called an interest or an attitude. The roughly parallel steps in the two domains overlap.[9] Unfortunately it is usually in the area of aesthetic education that the overlap is most blurred, for a number of reasons. Much of the tradition of schools embodies a cognitive orientation and many teachers feel that their job is to deal only with Knowledge and Intellectual Skills and Abilities. In some objectives in the affective domain, the cognitive component is obscure, as when we ask that a student should respond emotionally to a work of art or be sensitive to "beauty" in general, in nature as well as in art. This latter is complicated by disagreement as to what cognitive behavior should most appropriately accompany the desired affective behavior or what will most usefully promote it.

While some teachers use cognitive objectives as a means to affective goals (cognition being the preferred orientation, as Rosenberg, Rokeach, and Festinger have illustrated),[10] most do this as a matter of intuition rather than as a predetermined policy. In aesthetic education, some teachers see analysis on the cognitive level as necessary to the true appreciation of works of art, while others use cognitive goals in teaching about masterpieces in the field. But goal displacement is always likely to occur and cognitive goals as a means to affective ends may become goals in their own right and the affective goals be neglected. Such cases, as well as cases where results opposite to those desired are obtained, are well documented by Sparshott in his analysis of conflicting objectives.[11] Many of his potential

[9] *Ibid.,* pp. 49–53.

[10] See Leon Festinger, *A Theory of Cognitive Dissonance* (Evanston, Ill.: Row, Peterson, 1957); Milton Rokeach, *The Open and Closed Mind* (New York: Basic Books, 1960); Milton J. Rosenberg, "Cognitive Structure and Attitudinal Affect," *Journal of Abnormal and Social Psychology,* vol. 53 (1956): 637–72.

[11] F. E. Sparshott, "The Unity of Aesthetic Education," *Journal of Aesthetic Education,* vol. 2, no. 1 (January 1968): 15–18.

conflicts may be obviated if we remember that cognitive objectives are usually easier to evaluate, that assumptions must be examined and made explicit, and that the major orientation of the school, in practice, if not in theory, is directed toward the attainment of cognitive objectives. This is not to deny that cognitive behavior does not have an affective component. It simply means that the affective outcome of concentration on cognitive goals may not be the outcome that we have in mind.

In addition to the three-way orientation necessary to curriculum previously mentioned, it is held here that there is a necessary curriculum process which consists of five phases:

1. The selection of aims, goals, and objectives.
2. The selection of learning experiences calculated to help in the attainment of these.
3. The selection of content (subject matter) through which certain types of experience may be offered.
4. The organization and integration of learning experience and content.
5. Evaluation of the effectiveness of phases 2, 3, and 4 in attaining goals detailed in phase 1.

Though these phases may be discussed separately and considered sequentially, they are related and interdependent and combine to form a cyclical process, so that over time, the final phase affects the initial one.[12]

The two schemata so far dealt with are mainly concerned with Phase 1, the selection of aims, and objectives, though the *Taxonomies* by their use of illustrative examples refer to Phase 2 and, by their provision of illustrative test examples, are of use in Phase 5 (Evaluation). The schemata which follow would seem to be directed toward the third of our orientations, the nature of the subject matter to be learned, rather than the nature of the individual or of the society in which he is to be educated.

As one of the main aims of Tykociner's zetetics [13] is the

12 Wheeler.
13 J. T. Tykociner, "Zetetics and Areas of Knowledge," in Stanley Elam, ed., *Education and the Structure of Knowledge* (Chicago: Rand McNally, 1964), Ch. 4.

ordering of recorded knowledge, it can be seen that this schema, a study of the origin of systematized knowledge, of the mental processes involved in research, of the interrelations between various fields of science and of the social conditions facilitating the growth of knowledge,[14] has value in any consideration of the general aims of education and particular value in the selection, ordering, and integration of content.

The five zones or series which include the twelve sectors or areas of knowledge serve different functions, as will be seen.

Zone 1 includes *arts* and *symbolics of information.* The purpose of this sector is to improve communication by developing systems of symbolic representation. The arts are concerned with creative activities, the symbolics of information with formal symbolic systems, including mathematics, linguistics, logic, and information theory. Art criticism and philology serve as connecting links between the sectors.

The arts are the results of creative activity producing unique objects of aesthetic quality and include architecture, choreography, dramatics, graphic arts, landscaping, music, painting, sculpture, literature, and industrial design. Their exponents are concerned with symbolic patterns of light, shade, and color, with sounds, words, and sentences which form perceptual images able to enrich experience by invoking aesthetic emotions and serving communication. The mathematicians, logicians, and other students of Sector 2 are also concerned with patterns, but these patterns have a cognitive character "which nonetheless evokes feelings of elegance and beauty" while the images invoked consist of theorems, inferences, laws, and morals.

Zone 2 contains four areas of science dealing with the world:

1. *Hylenergetics* (a group of sciences dealing with matter and energy) is made up of physics, chemistry, astronomy, geology and mineralogy.
2. *Biological sciences* (botany, zoology, morphology, cytology, genetics, and physiology) are unified by the evolutionary principle.
3. *Psychological sciences.*

[14] *Ibid.,* p. 137.

4. *Sociological sciences* (including human ecology and demography).

The four groups in Zone 2 are linked by biophysics and biochemistry, physiology, and social psychology. The series is associated with Zone 1 by its dependence on the symbolics of information and relates to the next zone through anthropology.

Zone 3, which takes Zone 2 as its foundation, contains four areas of science which deal with the past and which apply this knowledge to regulate the present and provide for the future.

1. *Exeligmology* (or sciences concerned with the past): cosmogeny, evolution, and history.
2. *Pronoetics* (sciences concerned with the future): agriculture, medicine, technology (engineering), and national defense.
3. *Social cybernetics* or *regulative sciences* (systems for the maintenance of cooperation): jurisprudence, political science, economics, and management.
4. *Disseminative sciences:* education, educational psychology, library science, and journalism.

Zone 4 is that of the *zetetic sciences,* which study how knowledge may be increased. Zone 5 is the zone of the *integrative sciences,* which deal with man's attempts to integrate his knowledge in general systems, ideologies, and theories.

It should be noted that exeligmology can itself be further divided into subareas, one of which is concerned with the exeligmology of mankind and his culture and includes the history of the development of art and literature as well as the history of the development of human culture. Because the emphasis is on systematized knowledge, the value of the system is largely in connection with phases 3 and 4 of the curriculum process.

The secondary school curriculum suggested by Broudy, Smith, and Burnett consists primarily of certain content organized into categories of instruction, which, if handled in appropriate ways, bring about student learnings.[15] This content

[15] Harry S. Broudy, B. Othanel Smith, and Joe R. Burnett, *Democracy and Excellence in American Secondary Education* (Chicago: Rand McNally, 1964), p. 79.

is considered as kinds of propositions: facts (singular propositions), concepts (definitions), principles, and norms or rules. The learnings are visualized as changes in dispositions taking place in the student's mental repertory and involve cognitive and evaluative maps, intellectual operations, associative meanings, and skills of manipulatory and executive operations.[16]

The ways in which schooling will be used in modern life give clues to the nature of the curriculum. Typical uses of knowledge are the associative, the replicative, the interpretive, and the applicative. These uses of learning vary in their explicitness, ranging from the least explicit, the associative, to the most explicit, the applicative. For purposes of general education the interpretive use is most fundamental, for the interpretation put on a situation affects what should be further replicated, associated, and applied. Interpretation, however, is primarily for perspective and orientation, and not problem-solving. Categorization according to the uses of knowledge makes it possible, these authors say, to differentiate among subjects in terms of their educational value.[17] The basic elements of knowledge are what should be taught—those facts, concepts, principles, and norms which lead to the most comprehensive interpretation of the world. Insofar as some concepts and principles explain far more than others do, those subjects in the hierarchy of knowledge which provide the most general explanatory concepts and principles are basic to education.

The multiplicity of courses may thus be reduced to five basic strands in general education.

1. *Symbolic studies:* English, foreign languages, and mathematics, as skills and sciences.
2. *Basic sciences:* general science, biology, physics, and chemistry.
3. *Developmental studies* of the evolution of (*a*) the cosmos, (*b*) social institutions, and (*c*) culture.
4. *Aesthetic studies* or exemplars: art, music, drama, and literature.
5. *Molar problems:* studies of typical social problems.

[16] *Ibid.*, pp. 79–80.
[17] *Ibid.*, p. 82.

Situations embodying these basic strands are to be selected primarily in terms of the logical requirements to be made upon the students. In the practical program of aesthetic studies, six units or exemplars are suggested, organized in some historical order by periods or styles with each containing samples of art, literature, music, and architecture. No provision is made for performance training, on the ground that artistic "doing" has been practiced in the elementary school, that there is in the secondary school a rich array of extracurricular activities where it will be provided. Though the aesthetic side of life is recognized as a legitimate mode of self-development and cultivation, these authors say they find it difficult to justify practical activities as essential to general secondary education.

Broudy, Smith, and Burnett see social, recreational, civic, moral, intellectual, aesthetic, and religious value domains,[18] within which are found two loosely related components, the attitudinal, which refers to the objects of liking, and the theoretical, or justifying, component. The two curricular outcomes suggested for these domains are appreciation—an enlightened taste that combines likings and reasons—and a strategy for making choices in situations. The school, however, has to insist on both art for art's sake and art for goodness's sake, that is, for social significance.[19] This means that one looks to the arts, literature, and drama for models or exemplars, which must be great as well as good and must represent the major arts.

Similarly, Phenix offers a "critically examined coherent system of ideas" to identify and order the constituent parts of a curriculum.[20] For him, general education is the process of engendering essential meanings. Analysis of the possible modes of human understanding produces six patterns or realms of meaning, each of which may be described in terms of its typical methods and structures, its basic ideas, and the interrelationships within its constituent subrealms.

1. *Symbolics,* the most fundamental, comprises language, mathematics, and nondiscursive symbolic forms, which

[18] *Ibid.,* p. 215.
[19] *Ibid.,* p. 224.
[20] Philip H. Phenix, *Realms of Meaning* (New York: McGraw-Hill, 1964).

serve as instruments for expressing and communicating meanings.

2. *Aesthetics* embraces the various arts.
3. *Empirics* includes the sciences concerned with man, other living things, and the physical world. These sciences provide descriptions, explanations, generalizations, theories about the world and what can be observed in it. Meanings in this realm are expressed as knowledge gained through systematic analytic abstraction in accordance with logical processes.
4. *Synnoetics* is concerned with personal knowledge of oneself or of others, perhaps even of things, obtained directly or intuitively. It refers to what Martin Buber calls the "I-thou" relationship.
5. *Ethics* deals with moral meanings.
6. *Synoptics* refers to comprehensively integrative meanings, and includes history, religion, and philosophy. Empirical, aesthetic, and synnoetic meanings are here combined into coherent wholes.

At one end of the range are the symbolics, which are the necessary modes of expressing all meanings, while the synoptics, because of their integrative character, mark the other end. Symbolics need early and continuing emphasis; aesthetics and synnoetics are intermediate in degree of experience required for effective learning; ethics needs more prior preparation than descriptive sciences; synoptics are most suited to later stages. These six realms comprise the basic competences to be developed in every person and so indicate the scope of the curriculum. How the content should be ordered depends on principles of integrity, logical order, and human development.

Phenix suggests that the content of education should be exclusively drawn from material produced in disciplined communities of inquiry by men of knowledge who possess authority in their fields.[21] It should be selected and organized to emphasize the seminal ideas and characteristic features of the discipline, should exemplify the methods of inquiry and modes of understanding peculiar to each, stimulate the imagination, and

[21] *Ibid.,* p. 11.

promote creativity. Because these six realms of meaning cover the universally pervasive and perennial forms of distinctively human behavior [22] and are interdependent, the curriculum must provide for learning in all. Though other social institutions may be responsible for some aspects of education, these provisions must be supplemented or corrected by the school. This categorization of man's knowledge does not necessarily imply a particular type of organization (e.g., that of the school subjects as presently taught), but it certainly favors organized realms of inquiry as the source of curricular materials and suggests disciplined understanding as the major goal of education.

These last three schemata exemplify the new interest in the structure of knowledge and the problems of organization, substantive structure, and syntax which confront the curriculum investigator. The relations between them are laid out in Table 1.

Table 1. Relations between three schemata.

Broudy, Smith, and Burnett	Tykociner	Phenix
Exemplars	1. Arts	Aesthetics
Symbolic studies	2. Symbolics of information	Symbolism
	3. Hylenergetics	
Basic sciences		Empirics
	4. Biological sciences	
	5. Psychological sciences	Synnoetics
	6. Sociological sciences	
Developmental studies (drawing on 3, 4, 5, and 7)	7. Exeligmology	
	8. Pronoetics	
	9. Regulative sciences	
(exemplars)	(social ethics)	Ethics
	10. Disseminative sciences	
Molar problems	11. Zetetics	
	12. Integrative sciences	Synoptics

As will be seen from a study of these works, the major orientation is toward content. Each suggests the inclusion of the aesthetic area in general education, but for different reasons.

[22] *Ibid.*, p. 270.

Phenix includes aesthetics because it falls within one of the nine generic classes of meaning obtained by pairing the two logical aspects of quantity and quality. Most of the arts fall within the class of singular form, though one might make a case [23] for the inclusion of certain conventions in nondiscursive symbolism within the class of general form (symbolics) and certain aspects of literature within that of singular fact (synnoetics). The aims of movement, like those of physical education and health and recreational activities, seem to be enrichment of aesthetic meaning, both in individual persons and the life of the society,[24] those of the arts in general to aid in the "fulfillment of human life through the enlargement and deepening of meaning." [25] Musical meanings derive from the cultivation of self-forgetful delight in the direct contemplation of the patterns of musical statement, contrast, accent, progression, repetition, and variation that critical analysis describes.[26]

For Broudy, Smith, and Burnett, the curriculum problem is to find works of art which serve both as invitations to like or admire and as "exemplifications of theories in terms of which they have come to be regarded as deserving of esteem." [27] Art works are to be used for value education with its two outcomes —enlightened taste combining likings and reasons and some strategy for making choices. The school is to present life styles as they appear in the arts (but not in the popular arts) and to use art objects as value exemplars which theoretically afford opportunity for all four modes of aesthetic experience (discriminating appreciation of sensuous, formal, technical, and expressive qualities). Both these authors and Phenix would exclude a large part of common experience and understanding likely to carry aesthetic components.[28]

[23] Philip H. Phenix, "The Architectonics of Knowledge," in Elam, p. 60.

[24] Phenix, *Realms of Meaning*, p. 175.

[25] *Ibid.*, p. 5.

[26] *Ibid.*, p. 151.

[27] Broudy, Smith, and Burnett, *Democracy and Excellence*, p. 216.

[28] E.g., Sparshott suggests that aims of aesthetic education might be to make people "media-conscious" by studying the ways in which information reaches us from our total environment, or to increase responsiveness to the perceptible environment (F. E. Sparshott, "The

Kimball and McClellan [29] refuse to identify the disciplines of thought and action necessary to adolescent education with the academic disciplines of the graduate school, seeing these as "refinements and specialized applications of more fundamental disciplines of thought and action inherent in the very structure of our social order." [30] The first three (logic and mathematics, experimentation, and natural history) are of no concern here, but the discipline of aesthetic form is relevant. Three aspects are recognized. *Confrontation,* or the discipline of isolating the object for contemplation as a unique creation, must be learned. *Construction* may be taken to mean some measure of actual engagement in activity, as against *criticism,* which relates to the possibilities of limitations of materials, functions, and historical traditions. These writers also refer to the question that most classifiers and taxonomists conveniently dismiss, whether one can properly refer to music, the graphic and plastic arts, and the arts of movement as one general area, and, even more pertinently, whether this possibly adventitious unity makes pedagogical sense.

Kimball and McClellan also raise another problem when they say that, though they can see the three aspects of confrontation, construction, and criticism applying to various arts and art products, they cannot see how these can be learned in a general fashion until a certain level of discipline has been achieved in one of them.

Despite the generality of their discussion, these authors do underline two points. One is the contribution that the aesthetic component in education may make to the enhancement and sustenance of individuality. The other is that the discipline of aesthetic form is one of the primordial rules of thought and ac-

Unity of Aesthetic Education," *Journal of Aesthetic Education,* vol. 2, no. 2 [April 1968]: 10). Certainly one objective given in *Art Education for Scientist and Engineer,* Committee for the Study of Visual Arts at Massachusetts Institute of Technology, is "to draw attention to the human control of form and space and color *no matter where it occurs"* (p. 57).

[29] Solon T. Kimball and James E. McClellan, Jr., *Education and the New America* (New York: Random House, 1962).

[30] *Ibid.,* p. 298.

tion that guide our most fundamental interpretations of the world, an "institutionally legitimate mode of social control." [31]

The schemata of Tykociner, Phenix, and Broudy, Smith, and Burnett have to some extent been concerned with what is now generally called "the structure of knowledge." When considering contemporary knowledge from the point of view of Phase 3 of the curriculum process (selection of subject matter content) we are confronted, according to Schwab,[32] with three kinds of problems. First there are those of organization, concerned with the identification of those portions of the sociocultural heritage which it is the work of education to pass on. The interrelations of the scholarly disciplines (or at the school level, the subjects which relate to them) must also be considered in order to determine what may or may not be conjoined and what educational decisions must be made about the sequence of instruction. As far as schools are now concerned aesthetic education, from this point of view, means music and art, and perhaps some dance for girls (and even these subareas are usually taught quite separately). Because one area of the aesthetic domain is based upon musical ideas or tonal and rhythmic patterns, another on dynamic forms using the human body as an instrument, others on the organization of materials in significant spatial patterns, we may well ask: Can these disciplines included in the same broad category be organized together for instructional purposes? Should they be taught separately? Is it feasible to integrate for the purposes of instruction fields that are not integrated at the level of inquiry or practice?

Further, it must be pointed out that some behavior can only be learned through experiences with a particular kind of subject matter, e.g., music, while other behavior can be learned through experiences with any of a number of subjects. So whatever categories in behavior are adopted must include the two

[31] *Ibid.,* p. 303.

[32] Joseph J. Schwab, "Problems, Topics and Issues," in Elam, pp. 4–43. See also G. W. Ford and L. Pugno, eds., *The Structure of Knowledge and the Curriculum* (Chicago: Rand McNally, 1964), and *The Scholars Look at the Schools: A Report of the Disciplines Seminar* (Washington, D.C.: National Education Association, 1962).

broad classes here designated "specifically determined" and "generally determined." Investigation is necessary to determine what behaviors relevant to the aesthetic domain are specifically and what are generally determined.

The second kind of problem is that of substantive structure. Knowledge of structure enables us to isolate the problems inherent in using content from any discipline in the curriculum. In addition, at least at advanced levels, there is probably some obligation to include knowledge about the substantive structure in the content, so that students learn the part played by the structure in making knowledge possible and limiting its validity.[33] The syntactical structure of a discipline is concerned to some extent with methodology, in that it encompasses methods of discovery and proof, criteria against which the quality of data may be judged, and the application of canons of evidence.

If conceptual frameworks are considered as principles or networks of principles which integrate and explain man's observations about particular areas of his environment,[34] three kinds of problems are involved. At the level of a particular discipline, some attempt must be made to identify the major generalizations or principles. Insofar as more than one discipline is included in a category, realm, sector, or zone, there is need to identify common principles and methodologies. Finally, relationships between broad categories of knowledge must be considered. Attempts to set up architectonics of knowledge may help to illuminate these questions as long as they are no more than guide lines or, to use Hanson's happy phrase, "pedagogically heuristic blueprints." [35]

In the field of aesthetic education, these problems are very real ones. Even more than the humanities and the social sciences, the aesthetic domain shows evidence of the concurrent use of different sets of structures. Indeed, there is some doubt whether aesthetic understanding can be gained through the use

[33] Schwab, p. 9.

[34] Presumably Gotshalk would call these "domains." See D. W. Gotshalk, "Aesthetic Education as a Domain," *Journal of Aesthetic Education,* vol. 2, no. 1 (January 1968): 43–50.

[35] N. R. Hanson, "On the Structure of Physical Knowlege," in Elam, p. 162.

of the descriptive propositions that apply in other areas. In general, knowledge is about certain defined aspects of things or relationships; in the arts it is of, rather than about, things in their unique wholeness, and it is obtained by direct experience. Certainly aesthetics and criticism or history in the aesthetic field may be looked at from the point of view of the structure of knowledge, but questions of attitude and appreciation may need a quite different approach. Broudy has suggested where propositional forms are relevant in the arts, but points out that "the sticky points all have to do with the work of art itself and the judgments that are based on it." [36] Whatever works of art may express through images and the inferences based upon them is secondary to the perception they afford. They are primarily objects of contemplation and revelations of reality.

If we conceive the curriculum process correctly, concentration on a particular area or domain as the first step in educational planning is illicit curriculum process. We have already pointed out the dangers in curriculum development of appealing too soon to man's accumulated knowledge, particularly if it is divided up into categories called humanities, sciences, social sciences, arts, and so on. The unexamined assumption will inevitably affect actions with respect to the curriculum.

It is necessary, therefore, to clarify educational ends, aims, goals, and objectives, and elsewhere I have suggested a process whereby ultimate, mediate, and proximate goals and specific objectives may be set out and made operational for the educator. In this system, *goals* refer largely to specific levels in the curricular process and *objectives* to the ends of planned activities in the classroom.[37] One writer [38] on the "objectives controversy" has rejected Tyler's suggestion that objectives should be defined with sufficient clarity for one to recognize the desired behavior when he sees it. Though clear definition may not be necessary for some theorists, it is essential to the classroom teacher, for if education makes no recognizable differences

[36] Harry S. Broudy, "The Structure of Knowledge in the Arts," in Elam, p. 105.

[37] Wheeler, Ch. 5.

[38] Elliot W. Eisner, "Educational Objectives: Help or Hindrance?" *School Review*, vol. 75, no. 3 (Autumn 1967): 250–60, 277–82.

it is pointless. If the teacher cannot recognize the behavioral outcome which is his objective, he has no means of knowing whether his goals, his structured learning experiences, his content, organization, or methodology are of use in the educational process. In plain words, he does not know what he is doing, or else is indulging in activity for its own sake. Confusion about levels of statement of curricular objectives is common enough to explain the undue insistence that subject matter places constraints on educational objectives.[39] Further, it is illicit curriculum process to commence with subject matter, for the school is concerned with change of behavior as previously defined.

Because there are different types of behavioral outcomes, one useful classification is as follows:

Category 1. Recall and comprehension of:
   a) specific facts, events, symbols, and referents;
   b) ways and means of dealing with these;
   c) universals and abstractions in a field.
Category 2. Feelings, sensitivities, beliefs, attitudes, and values.
Category 3. Skills:
   a) intellectual;
   b) social (interpersonal and intergroup);
   c) psychomotor.

Educational outcomes can be identified and assessed much more easily in Category 1, Category 3*a* and Category 3*c* than they can in Category 2, but this is no excuse for talking about modes of curiosity, inventiveness, and insight in metaphoric and poetic terms, instead of attempting to discover some of the parameters which determine them, in order to structure appropriate learning activities. Nor is the semantic confusion endemic in curriculum theory reduced by the addition of "open" and "closed" objectives.[40]

Confusion may be lessened if consideration be given to the difference between *initial behavior,* (before the educational experience), *intended outcomes,* and *actual outcomes,* and between *process* and *product.* Further, it may be said that the

[39] *Ibid.,* p. 254.
[40] *Ibid.,* p. 279.

curriculum process is cyclic in nature, so that there is inter-dependence between Phase 1 (Selection of goals and objectives) and Phase 5 (Evaluation). In translating aims into various sorts of goals in Phase 1, some thought must be given to the means and processes of evaluation. Similarly the various aspects of evaluation may and should affect the derivation of goals, as well as the selection of educational experiences and their organization into sequences. The paradigm is of assessment as continuous feedback.

Some attempt should be made to use a rationale such as the curriculum process to proceed through the various levels of goals and to produce some classroom objectives useful in the educational process. The *Taxonomies* will aid the process of clarification, even if only by making explicit those goals which are implicitly held by the teacher, or by drawing attention to desirable goals which he has neglected. For instance, Gotshalk [41] suggests that aesthetic education should be primarily education in intrinsic perception. The steps necessary to such education would be specification in detail of its differentiating aim structure, the kind of realization required, and the objects best suited to it. These are the first phases of the curriculum process as described. In the behavioral categories given, Category 2 deals with feelings, sensitivities, beliefs, attitudes, and values, and the sensitivities are thought of as sensitivities to objects, relationships, and values. In this sense aesthetic education, as "education directed primarily to the development of sensitivity to aesthetic values," [42] is only a special case of a more general aim of developing sensitivity.

Whether either of these shall be taken as an educational goal is dependent on value judgments determined by a variety of factors, not least among them the bias toward one or another of the three orientations held to be necessary in considering curriculum. While practical school politics may demand emphasis on the need for aesthetic education considered as a separate domain, considerations of man as a unity tend to favor the behavioral approach which is concerned with the total behavior

[41] Gotshalk, p. 44.
[42] *Ibid.*, p. 44.

of organisms in a socio-cultural environment. Behavior is embedded in a cognitive-affective-conative matrix where no true separation is possible. Fears that the aesthetic component in education will be neglected in theory should be obviated by consideration of the criteria against which the general ends of education may be judged, one of which is balance. In practice of course, there are numerous variables which determine what shall be taught where, most of them having nothing to do with curriculum theory. Emphasis on the behavioral approach and on the more adequate treatment of educational goals and objectives arises from the conception that the task of education is to change behavior and that the concern of the schools should be with the sort of persons they turn out.

The determination of what kinds of learning experiences will produce particular sorts of persons is largely an empirical matter, but, where there is little evidence, it is necessary to supplement it by rational considerations and general theory. Some of the difficulties have already been discussed, but others arise from different conceptions of the purpose of education and, in the field of the arts, about the value of various sorts of experiences. There is a considerable gulf between the practicing artist and those who seek rational understanding of the nature of aesthetic form or insight into the processes involved in its creation.[43] Obviously educators must be concerned with the establishment of behavioral patterns in Category 2 (feelings, sensitivities, beliefs, attitudes and values) and this is a category where direct experience is most appropriate. If artistic creativity is a goal, the situation must be structured to provide for experiences in Category 3c, but, if criticism or history or aesthetics be the end of this sort of education, Categories 1 and 3a will be involved.

The extension of sensitivity requires direct experience with objects and people and the opportunity to respond to persons

---

[43] Picasso suggests that the people who occupy themselves with art are for the most part impostors, and D. H. Lawrence tells us of the contradictory and utterly indigestible theories, like nails in an ostrich's gizzard, that painters rammed down his throat. Are artists people who work with images, and aestheticians and critics people who tell other people why they do or do not like those images?

and things. This means a rich environment and opportunities to react to it. One necessity in the cultivation of attitudes is that the environment should have a sympathetic and accepting climate which allows for an appropriate measure of freedom. In addition, attitude development is aided by opportunities to make the kind of intellectual analysis whereby feelings, beliefs, and attitudes can be considered, discussed, and perhaps rethought. The *Taxonomy* of the affective domain gives many examples of appropriate learning activities which may be supplemented by those trained in aesthetic disciplines.

It is impossible to speak in any but the most general terms of Phase 5 (Evaluation) unless one is trained in some aesthetic discipline and in educational measurement in its widest sense. Assessment of art objects is largely a matter of values, though attempts have been made to suggest criteria for judgment.[44] Nevertheless, critics will continue to disagree and artists like Picasso will continue to suggest that academic teaching about beauty is false and that those who try to explain pictures (let alone judge them) are usually on the wrong track.

Again, little more can be said about Phase 4 of the curriculum process. In schools the major areas of concern are music and art, which, in the secondary school at least, are usually taught as separate subjects. Until problems connected with Phases 1 and 3 are satisfactorily solved, they will probably continue in this way, apart from tradition. The principle problem is of organizing learning activities in a field around some center, so that they make sense, provide continuity, and are available for use, and the advantages and disadvantages of various plans for overall organization have been discussed at length in the literature of education. Proposals like Taba's [45] to use the logic of the content may be satisfactory for some aspects of aesthetic education, but are difficult to apply in many crucial areas. Broudy, Smith, and Burnett suggest organization by periods or styles (in historical sequence) while Phenix sug-

[44] Jerome Hausman, "Research on Teaching the Visual Arts," in N. L. Gage, ed., *Handbook of Research on Teaching* (Chicago: Rand McNally, 1963), p. 1113.

[45] Hilda Taba, *Curriculum Development: Theory and Practice* (New York: Harcourt, Brace and World, 1962), pp. 301–4.

gests use of the "seminal ideas and characteristic features of the discipline." Perhaps sensitivities, beliefs, attitudes, and values may be dealt with in terms of central ideas on which it is possible to focus. It is quite clear, however, that there is considerable scope for alternative ways of organization which must be evaluated empirically in terms of their ability to promote the desired behavioral outcomes.

Curriculum development should be based on evidence and research, and this is one of the major problems with respect to educational activities related to the aesthetic component. Compared with other aspects of schooling, research into aesthetic areas has been restricted and not particularly productive. Certainly work in psychophysics has illustrated possibilities in the measurement of values, even in an area where qualitative judgments are of primary concern, and psychoanalysis and depth psychology have some relevance for the investigation of prelogical processes and the relationship between rational and intuitive understandings. The Gestalt psychologists have drawn attention to insight, structure, and field characteristics and the phenomenological psychologists to processes of perception. In the schools, music and art have traditionally been the basic sources of aesthetic experiences and here the research has provided little enough, as it has so far been largely concerned with problems of description and measurement. In the latter it faces particularly difficult problems at the criterion level. Despite developmental studies [46] there is need for inquiry into the factors that characterize growth in awareness and capacity to project visual, aural, and other aesthetic forms. In addition, there is need for extensive research on human expressive behavior and on individual and social symbolic forms and their relationships. What research there is should be noted and used by teachers in the field, despite their prevailing skepticism about research. For example, if reading of musical notation, pitch discrimination, performance, composition, or musical appreciation form part of the organization of a school course, the teacher should at least know what research has been done in these areas.

[46] In art, see Viktor Lowenfeld, *Creative and Mental Growth,* 3rd ed. (New York: Macmillan, 1957). Some work has been done in music, but it is nearly thirty years old.

Attention to curriculum problems will raise certain vital questions for the art teacher and involve him in the attempted resolution of considerable conflict. For the talented, and possibly for all children in some measure, instruction must encourage creativity. But this must be done, at least at first, within the disciplinary tradition of which certain forms and materials have become part. Before these can be discarded they must be learned, as must the bases on which judgments have been made about previous works. Conflict is endemic wherever value judgments are of prime concern.[47]

It would seem that the only way of solving the many questions involved (and this discussion seems to have produced more questions than answers) is by a concerted approach. Until recent years, the practicing artist was the teacher, and it still seems desirable that teachers should at least be practitioners in their field and that there should be greater cooperation between artist and teacher. To them must be added the curriculum theorist and the measurement expert, the philosopher, the aesthetician, and the various research workers in the appropriate fields. The effects of the multidisciplinary approach to curriculum problems are being demonstrated in other fields, so that the same approach should work in the field of aesthetic education.

[47] E.g., Sparshott, pp. 15–18.

A CURRICULUM DEVELOPMENT MODEL FOR AESTHETIC EDUCATION

Stanley S. Madeja and Harry T. Kelly

The intent of this paper is to describe the curriculum development model used by the Aesthetic Education Program of the Central Midwestern Regional Educational Laboratory. No attempt has been made to describe goals, processes, or products. These subjects are reserved for future articles. It is important to note that the model for developing curriculum is not a curriculum model for instruction. Aesthetic education curricula, whether they be complete programs or courses of study, are outcomes of an aesthetic education program; the curriculum development model is the means for obtaining these outcomes.

The general developmental model described in this paper is not original to the program, but was developed by the laboratory for use by its various curriculum development programs.[1] In one sense it is the umbrella that organizes the curriculum development activities, whether these activities be in the field of mathematics or aesthetics. This paper articulates and sometimes modifies the general model and describes the model for constructing aesthetic education materials for use in the public schools of the United States.

The Referents for Curriculum Development

Curriculum theorists have all agreed on three basic referents for building a curriculum: (1) the individual, (2) contemporary society, and (3) subject specialists. They do not, however, agree upon their relative importance to the curriculum. Ralph W.

From the *Journal of Aesthetic Education*, vol. 4, no. 2 (April 1970): 53–63. Reprinted by permission of the *Journal* and the authors.

[1] CEMREL *Program Support and Management*. A basic program plan document of the Central Midwestern Regional Educational Laboratory, Inc. The general model is the work of many people, but especially that of the executive director, Wade M. Robinson, and the deputy director, Tom Johnson.

Tyler, for example, believes that the object for any curriculum must be derived equally from studies of the learner, studies of contemporary society, and subject specialists.[2] Arthur King and John Brownell believe that first priority should be given to subject matter specialists. Society and the learner, they protested, tell only what man is and not what he might be.[3] The disciplines, moreover, are not just accumulations of information but rather ways of knowing and are, therefore, progressive in nature.[4] Equally rational arguments have been made by Franklin Bobbitt for society[5] and by Harold Rugg for the learner.[6] Although each position is supported by powerful arguments, the emphasis on one referent does not exclude the others, but rather the other two become constraints on the first. The only conclusion that can be drawn from the various arguments of the curriculum theorists is that curriculum development should begin with decisions about the referents. The Aesthetic Education Program was, in part, also affected by the nature of an educational laboratory within which the Aesthetic Education Program resides. It is important to reflect upon the nature of the Laboratory before proceeding.

In recent years the responsibility for the development of curriculum materials has begun to shift from the school and its teachers to agencies whose principal responsibility is the construction of curriculum materials. The alphabet soup of federally sponsored curricular programs is a manifestation of this shift. One consequence is that these agencies or programs assume all the responsibilities associated with developing a curriculum that will be nationally distributed. Moreover, the prestige that attaches to these curriculum development organizations as a result of the collection of human and material resources devoted to

[2] Ralph W. Tyler, *Basic Principles of Curriculum and Instruction* (Chicago: University of Chicago Press, 1950), pp. 3–28.

[3] Arthur P. King, Jr., and John A. Brownell, *The Curriculum and the Disciplines of Knowledge: A Theory of Curriculum Practice* (New York: John Wiley & Sons, 1966), p. 27.

[4] *Ibid.*, p. 148.

[5] See Franklin Bobbitt, *How to Make a Curriculum* (New York: Houghton Mifflin, 1924).

[6] See Harold Rugg and Ann Schumaker, *The Child-Centered School: An Approach of the New Education* (New York: World Book Company, 1928), p. 60.

constructing curriculum materials necessitates adoption of organizational values consonant with their assumed responsibilities in education. As a consequence, organizations such as the Regional Educational Laboratory make curriculum decisions not only in light of the arguments posed by the curriculum theorists, but also in light of the social and educational responsibilities as defined by their mission and prestige.

Because the United States is a diversified nation it is difficult to generalize about society or the learner. It would be difficult, if not impossible, to build a curriculum founded on the social or learner referent which would have a national constituency. The referent which appears to have more national application is the disciplines. This is not to say that all agree upon the nature of aesthetic education, but rather that intellectual discourse is relatively unaffected by ethnic background, geographical location, community values, etc. From this kind of argument and those posed by Joseph Schwab,[7] Arthur King, and John Brownell, it seems that the principal referent for the Aesthetic Education Program development should be the disciplines. For aesthetic education this means the arts.[8] With the disciplines chosen as the starting point, the society and the learner become constraints.

There are three principal arguments for societal constraint on the curriculum: (1) education attending to activities of the contemporary society is apt to be more relevant; (2) concepts learned in the context of the contemporary society will result in greater applicability of the learned knowledge to real life situations; (3) a curriculum which incorporates the values of the society to use it will have greater chance of acceptance. The first two arguments can be resolved by using contemporary exemplars and experiences to illustrate concepts and skills of

[7] Joseph J. Schwab, "Structure of the Disciplines, Meanings and Significance," in *The Structure of Knowledge and the Curriculum* (Chicago: Rand McNally, 1964), p. 11.

[8] This does not mean that aesthetic education is limited to the arts, but that the content for aesthetic education is founded in the disciplines of the arts. For further explanation see *Guidelines for Curriculum Development for Aesthetic Education* and "An Operational Definition of Aesthetic Education," Aesthetic Education Program working paper, no. 1, November, 1969.

the disciplines. The third, however, cannot be resolved so easily because it is a problem of value conflicts; the resolution to this problem begins with the exploration of the nature of that conflict.

The value conflict between the teacher or materials with a more cosmopolitan value system and the community with a local value system has been explored at great length in the literature. Willard Waller observed that conflict between the teacher and the community was inevitable because of disparate value systems. Teachers were inclined to view education as cultural advancement, whereas the community was apt to view education as a means for community indoctrination.[9] Alvin W. Gouldner examined this phenomena more generally with regard to occupation but in more depth using role analysis as his research tool. From his investigation he concluded that organizations were composed of "cosmopolitans" and "locals." Cosmopolitans were persons with low loyalty, high professional commitment, and outer reference group orientation. Locals were those with high loyalties to the organization (or the community), low professional commitment, and inner reference group orientation.[10] The cosmopolitan may be typified as the militant teacher who cares a lot about children but nothing about the school or community folkways and mores; the local may be represented by the community businessman who purports to protect the community from external influences that might be deleterious to the community life style. No doubt many teachers often become the protectors of community values, but such teachers are often viewed with suspicion by their more professionally oriented peers. The problem for the curriculum developer in aesthetic education, then, is to create materials that reflect the cosmopolitan values of the disciplines while accommodating to local values.

Besides the societal constraints on education the learner exerts an influence on instruction. John Dewey argued that "fact" education was an attempt to take the internalized ex-

[9] See Willard Waller, *The Sociology of Teaching* (New York: John Wiley & Sons, 1932).

[10] Alvin W. Gouldner, "Cosmopolitans and Locals: Toward an Analysis of Latent Social Rules," *Administrative Sciences Quarterly* Part 1, vol. 2 (1957): 281–306; Part 2, vol. 2 (1958): 444–80.

periences of the scientist and present them externally as facts to the child. According to Dewey, there was no gap in kind between the child's experience and the various forms of subject matter; arithmetic, geography, language, etc., are themselves the experience of the race. The disciplines are not "miscellaneous" heaps of separate bits of experiences but knowledge reflectively formulated in an organized and systematic way. The problem was, according to Dewey, the reinstatement of the discipline's subject matter into the experience of the child. "It needs to be psychologized; turned over, translated into the immediate and individual experience" of its learner.[11] The substance of the content, however, is inviolate; the learner affects only the mode of presentation.

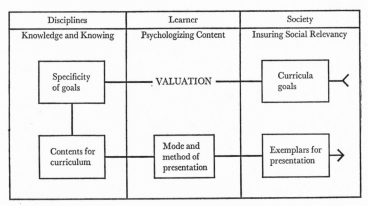

Figure 1. The influence of the disciplines, the learner and society on curriculum construction.

The three referents—disciplines, learners, society—and the elements of a curriculum are depicted to illustrate their relationship to one another in Figure 1.

The diagram shows the Aesthetic Education Program beginning with the definition of goals. Experts were called together and debated the goals for aesthetic education while playing two roles simultaneously; first as the expert in their professional

[11] John Dewey, "The Child and the Curriculum," *John Dewey in Education: Selected Writings* (New York: Modern Library, 1964), p. 351.

field which ranged from the arts to philosophy, and second as intellectuals representing society at large. The need for social change that transcended a discipline was a concern of all. As a result, they developed goals for aesthetic education which would speak to that concern by introducing new ways of knowing and new knowledge into the classroom.

Curriculum content for aesthetic education is knowledge and methods for knowing. In short, content is concepts, skills, and experiences. The learner does not change the nature of the content; he influences only the scheduling or method of presentation according to the level of development of his faculties, mental and physical, and his past experiences. Rational social values determine not knowledge but rather the exemplars that are used to present knowledge to the child. A close examination of most of the curriculum conflicts in the school indicates that a majority of the arguments center on the illustrations or the exemplars which run counter to local values rather than about the truth or falsity of the concept or skills being taught. For example, sex education is taught in all schools whether in biology or in a special sex education class. The community may argue about how sex education should be taught (or the exemplars used), but no community would prevent the school from teaching, somewhere in the curriculum, the fact that biological man is a sexual animal.

Valuation about what should be taught and how it should be taught involves the subject matter specialist, the learner, and that part of the society which has the responsibility for curriculum within the school. Subject matter specialists make judgments about the content and the goals. The ability of the student to perform affects the method of presenting content; and finally the community, including the school, decides whether the curriculum will be permitted in the school. Short of a national or an intense community educational plan there is little that can be done to change unfavorable community attitudes toward aesthetic education. From the curriculum developer's point of view the most feasible way of dealing with the community problem is in providing alternatives rather than arguments for a single way.

From the foregoing discussion two major conclusions can be drawn. First, curriculum content lies in the disciplines. The learner and society may influence the mode of presentation or even the exemplars used to present the content, but the content itself is inviolate. Second, valuations about what should be taught are made at every step in the development of a curriculum. The most difficult valuations to deal with are those made by the school or community. Because of the great diversity of values found in various communities the only feasible way of insuring curriculum implementation without compromising the content is to provide the school or community with planned choices. These conclusions profoundly influenced CEMREL'S curriculum development model for aesthetic education.

The Curriculum Development Model

If the disciplines are accepted as the principal referent and the other two as constraints, the next step is to organize them and the curriculum elements into a rational curriculum development model while keeping in mind the conclusions found in the foregoing discussion. The model begins with surveys which culminate in guidelines for development of materials for aesthetic education, and ends with an aesthetic education curriculum adopted for use in a school. (See Figure 2.)

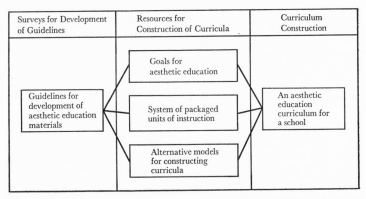

Figure 2. The curriculum development model used by CEMREL's Aesthetic Education Program.

Surveys. The decision to develop a set of guidelines for the Aesthetic Education Program at CEMREL was based on the need for selected ends and means which (1) were addressed to a genuine social need, (2) reflected historical and contemporary thought of the various disciplines relevant to aesthetic education, (3) considered the existing body of research knowledge in the behavioral sciences, and (4) respected the pedagogical requirements of the educational system. From surveys designed to collect such information and from discourse among the scholars came the goals for the program and also the means for selecting and analyzing content for aesthetic education.[12]

Resources for construction of curricula. The resources needed for the development of curriculum consist of three elements: (1) aesthetic education goals which guide the school or community in the construction of its curriculum, (2) a system of instructional packages which have great flexibility of arrangement, and (3) exemplary models which provide the community with alternatives for arranging packages into courses of study or curriculum.

Because it is essential that the general goals for aesthetic education remain constant for all phases of curriculum development and use, school goals for aesthetic education will resemble the goals used by the curriculum developer for construction of materials. This means that goals for aesthetic education can vary according to the school setting and community values, but these variations should be alternative paths which converge on a single set of goals. The principal function of the guidelines, then, will be to define the major goals and outline the means of material development which accommodate an array of school settings and community values.

A system of packaged units of instruction was deliberately chosen to permit as much individualized learning as possible and to provide maximum flexibility for arrangement. The series of packages will be used by a school system as if it were a deck of cards; that is, shuffling order or sequence of units adaptable

[12] Manuel Barkan, Laura Chapman, and Evan S. Kern, *Handbook for Curriculum Development for Aesthetic Education,* The Central Midwestern Regional Educational Laboratory, January, 1970.

to variations in school settings and organizational patterns. Packages, consisting of about ten hours of instruction and composed of such things as slides, film-strips, and puzzles, will be designed for the primary grades, the intermediate grades, the junior high school, and the senior high school. The actual level of use, however, may vary according to student abilities; some packages which are geared to the third level or third grade may be used in the fourth or fifth grade in some school systems or, in other schools, in the second grade. In actual school use an arts specialist may use the package as a minimal base of instruction to extend the concepts and skills beyond their intended outcome, and for the non-arts teacher the package will become, perhaps, the only source of instruction.

According to the previous discussion the package system will contain a balance of instructional content concepts, artistic skills or competencies in production and criticism, and aesthetic experiences that are relevant to aesthetic education. This is not to imply that one package deals with concepts, another with skills, and another with experiences. This would be an artificial and unrealistic distinction which is not found within the structures of the disciplines. On the other hand, to expect all to be emphasized in every package would be equally unrealistic. It is more likely that one of the elements will be emphasized in the package as objectives or ends while the other two will serve as means. Consider the following diagram:

MEANS

	Concepts	Skills	Experiences
Concepts			
ENDS Skills			
Experiences			

If, for example, teaching concepts is the end, then the means of teaching these may be through the use of artistic skills, or aesthetic encounters with objects and events, or perhaps both. The same is true for units with skills and experience objectives. A balance of concepts, skills, and experiences must be maintained. If the system of packages leans too heavily toward concept instruction, then the skills developed are more the manipulation of concepts and it will probably lead more to the development of professional critics; if skill-oriented, then it will more than likely become a program for developing artists; if only experiential, then it would probably be more therapeutic than educational. The problem for the curriculum materials writers is to maintain a balance of packages which employ concepts, skills, or experiences both as means and ends.

The content in a system of packages, however, must not only reflect the nature of the disciplines in what is to be taught, but also the attributes of the student. "Student attributes" refers generally to the level of cognitive development, motor capabilities, and emotional maturity. Cognitive development may limit the range of concepts and conceptual learning skills; motor capabliities may limit the kinds of skills that can be learned and the experiences that a student may engage in; and emotional maturity is most likely to affect the kind of concepts that can be taught and the experiences that the student might engage in. The range of instructional possibilities will increase as the student matures and as he learns. (See Figure 3.)

The problem for the curriculum developer is twofold. He must construct packages that reflect the range of concepts, skills, and experiences that comprise the discipline; and he must develop the packages so that they will accommodate the varying abilities of the student. Figure 3 illustrates the relationship between the disciplines and the student attributes within the system of packages. The individual packages may be conceived as the bricks which make up the inverted pyramid. The bricks may vary (1) in length to include skills, concepts, or experiences, or just skills; (2) in width to utilize objects or events of all the arts and environment, or just an art; (3) in height to accommodate a wide range or a narrow range of student attributes. It should be pointed out that the diagram illustrates only the system of packaged units and not a curriculum for a school.

Exemplary models. Exemplary models for package arrangement are intended to be alternative means for arranging the units or packages of instruction so that the materials can be used in ways compatible to the organization of the school. Some schools, for instance, are organized for more student-centered instruction using individualized or programmed instructional materials, while others are teacher-centered using something like team teaching. But whatever the arrangements, the packages must be flexible enough to fit the variations of school organization and needs.

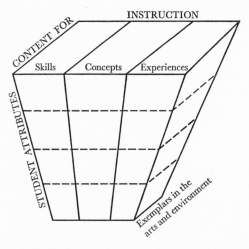

Figure 3. The relationship between instructional content and student attributes within the system of packaged units of instruction.

The long history of public school education in the United States tells us that the successful programs in the school are dependent upon community sanctions. Integrated curricula developed outside the school setting suffer from the fact that there usually exists something that is offensive to the community mores and folkways. In the take-all-or-none curriculum, offensive content may preclude implementation. With regard to the Aesthetic Education Program materials, the community is not forced to sanction all or none. The materials can be selected to meet the particular needs of that school and at the same time conform to the values unique to that community or, perhaps, to that teacher. At first glance, this seems to be a violation of the thing called education, but the alternatives are either impossible or not feasible. Instead of developing accommodating materials, it is possible to conceive of changing the community attitudes to accommodate the materials. For aesthetic education at this period in its history it is not possible to mount a campaign of the size required to change community values; that is, assuming that it is correct to do so. It appears much more feasible to develop materials that can adapt to the needs of the school or community without compromising the content.

Whereas the problem of the curriculum materials writer was to maintain a balance of packages, it becomes the problem of the school system and the community to select and arrange the packages into a unique curriculum which would meet the needs of the students and the instructional objectives of the system. The school using the guidelines and exemplary models and expert advice can make curriculum decisions that are in harmony with the school setting, community values, and school organization of their system. The curriculum model for aesthetic education, then, will be developed at the local level by those who will be using the materials.

This paper has attempted to reveal a part of the rationale for choices that led to the curriculum development model used by CEMREL's Aesthetic Education Program and to describe the model itself. An important distinction was made between the curriculum development model to be used by curriculum developers to construct materials for aesthetic education and a curriculum model which is a system of instruction for a school. The developmental model incorporates a scheme for designing curricula which will meet various needs of the community, the school, the teacher, and the student. By providing for alternative curricula the developer can retain control over the quality of content without intruding on the domain sacred to the community or school which, at least at this point in time, insists upon some control over the exemplars. For aesthetic education, which at most has only a tenuous place in the school, the provision for alternative programs may be the key to its successful implementation.

BUILDING CURRICULA FOR LITERATURE EDUCATION

Alan C. Purves

As a result of the Woods Hole conference and the subsequent writings of Jerome Bruner, curriculum planners and builders took a new look at the sequence and structure of the disciplines. Their impetus came from the following statement in *The Process of Education:* "the curriculum of a subject should be determined by the most fundamental understanding that can be achieved of the underlying principles that give structure to that subject." [1] Among the early results were the curricula in mathematics, biology, and physics, each of which had the appellation "new." English curriculum planners were a bit jealous and rejoiced when Program English (originally Project English) came along with its offer for them to create a "New English." The opportunity has only recently come to the other "humanistic" disciplines— art, music, dance, and the "humanities" as a group.

The "New English" was primarily linguistic in orientation— the projects began at a time when structural grammar, with transformational grammar following close on its heels, was changing teachers' notions of the language and what was important in the teaching of it, so that the structures and sequence were primarily language-learning structures. But the centers paid some attention to literature, and they sought a structure in literature that could form a spiral. I do not intend a review of these curricula, but I should like to examine some of their assumptions so that we can see what structure and sequence might be most appropriate to training in literature and possibly in the humanities as well.

The sequences that were developed derived primarily from the traditional structures of literature courses in the university: history, nationality, genre, myth, and literary structure. Each of

From the *Journal of Aesthetic Education,* vol. 3, no. 2 (April 1969): 103–17. Reprinted by permission of the *Journal* and the author.
[1] New York: Vintage Books, 1963, p. 31.

these, along with certain subsets like the history of ideas and theme, is a viable way for the expert to connect one work with another in order to describe the skein of literature. The questions that must be put to these structures are whether they bear any necessary relationship to the development of the individual reader, whether they can be placed in an inevitable school sequence.

The most popular of these structures, in that it is the one which most frequently circumscribes the spectrum of courses in the university, is based on history and nationality. We have eighteenth-century men, early American men, medieval men, and they teach courses in their specialities. Why they should do so is historically and pragmatically explicable. Early literary study grew out of philological study which demanded that attention be paid to the literature of the early periods, the Anglo-Saxon and Middle English. As the universities broadened the study of the native tongue, other periods were added one at a time. When the concept of literary study moved from the philological to the intellectual and the social, the need to be versed in all the literature and thought of a period became a prerequisite to the study of a particular work because it was deemed necessary to understand the work as it was when it was written. The advent of the "new criticism" did not appreciably change this structure, although it challenged many of its shibboleths.

If, therefore, we are to accept history as the structuring principle for the school as well as for the university, it would seem that students should follow some sort of chronological pattern as they move through their years of study. The best defense of such a sequence remains that put forward by T. S. Eliot in "Tradition and the Individual Talent":

> No poet, no artist of any art, has his complete meaning alone. His significance, his appreciation is the appreciation of his relation to the dead poets and artists. You cannot value him alone: you must set him, for contrast and comparison, among the dead. I mean this as a principle of aesthetic, not merely historical criticism.[2]

Granting Eliot's point, the best solution for the curriculum problem is to have students begin with the Greeks and move

[2] *Selected Essays* (London: Faber and Faber, 1932), p. 15.

slowly to the moderns. Such training would lead students to make the kinds of appreciative statements that would command respect. Were one to think in terms of a twelve-year, or even a six-year curriculum, however, the thought of following out Eliot becomes somewhat appalling. Oedipus and Virgil in grade seven, Shakespeare in grade nine, Yeats and John Barth in grade twelve, seems on the face of it inhumane. The children might read, but their understanding of the dead would probably be a dead understanding. There is a further problem of selection: Eliot implies that "the dead" includes nearly everyone. Since it is true that Shakespeare rests on the Greeks, the Romans, Chaucer, Boccaccio, More, Spenser, Ariosto, Montaigne, and hosts of others, then, if one were to be doggedly programmatic, the student would never make it to Shakespeare by the twelfth grade.

Besides the practical criticism of the historical sequence, there is a criticism which states that the kind of appreciation that Eliot is advancing is a sophisticated one, but it is not the only one—naive appreciations are valid. Another criticism would say that the relation of a work to the reader and his time can be as serious an enterprise as the relation of the work to its author's time and time previous. A third criticism would be that purely formal appreciation can be as meaningful as historical appreciation.

There is merit to Eliot's argument no matter what position one takes about the curriculum, for it is certainly true that literature feeds on itself, and particularly on a substratum of myths, be they Biblical, Graeco-Roman, English, American, or Japanese. The reader must acquire some of this cultural shorthand before he can make sense of much of what has been written; not simply of the depth of the work, but of its surface as well. This being so, a curriculum should insure that the substratum is available to the student. The substratum would consist of nursery rhymes and fairy tales of the order of "Cinderella" and the works of Andersen and the brothers Grimm. It would consist of the Old Testament, particularly of Genesis, Exodus, Judges, Samuel, Kings, Job, and the Psalms; of the stories of the Greek and Norse pantheons and of the legends of Hercules, Jason, Theseus, Perseus, Achilles, Odysseus, and others; of the Matter of Britain and Robin Hood; and of American folk heroes like

Paul Bunyan, Pecos Bill, John Henry, Old Stormalong, and others. From formal literature there might be some works or figures that would be indispensable to mastery: Scrooge, Don Quixote, Sherlock Holmes, Romeo and Juliet, Aeneas, Tom Sawyer, and those others who have become folk figures. Once one has acquired knowledge of these figures and their stories, one is better equipped to read any book because most books make direct or oblique references to them.

From the notion of the substratum could be derived a curricular sequence corollary to the historical: that literature study should move from the folk forms to the sophisticated art forms. The structural assumptions on which this rests are that primitive art underlies sophisticated art and that primitive art is simpler than sophisticated art. The sequential assumption is that ontogeny recapitulates phylogeny. All three of these assumptions are challengeable: much sophisticated art—Shakespearean sonnets, for example—seems to have a tenuous relation to its folk counterparts (and some folk art derives from the sophisticated); the structure of many "folk" stories—Ruth or Job—is more complex than that of many "art" stories—O. Henry; and ontogeny, given the multimedia environment, seems remote from phylogeny. Furthermore, the primitive to sophisticated curriculum like the historical curriculum could, if carried to its logical extreme, deprive a child of any age of much that is relevant, interesting, and potentially useful.

A thematic theory of the curriculum would face the same impasse. It argues that there are certain basic themes or archetypal stories that underlie all literature and serve to connect one piece of literature to another. These themes are best summarized by Northrop Frye in the third essay of *Anatomy of Criticism* [3] as the mythos of Spring or Comedy, related to love and the transformation of society, the mythos of Summer or Romance concentrating on the quest, the mythos of Autumn or Tragedy concentrating on the fall of the hero and sacrifice, and the mythos of Winter or Irony and Satire depicting the world of human bondage. I cannot begin to do justice to Frye's elaboration; I can only comment that although these mythoi do inform litera-

[3] Princeton: Princeton University Press, 1957, pp. 133–69.

ture, they seem not to occur in any order suitable to the development of the child. Common sense would say that the romance, with its tale of the birth of the hero, the quest, and the defense of the city, should precede tragedy with its tales of the fall of the hero, but should comedy precede romance and should tragedy precede irony? Each aspect of this fourfold myth exists less for itself than in relation to the whole. One way of making the total structure available to the student is to take one story that seems to contain all four mythoi, for example, the legend of King Arthur with all its subsidiary stories, and then proceed to present the students with other works that can be related to various parts of the legend and so weave a complex structure for the students. But there is no logical reason—or pedagogical one either—for beginning with Arthur instead of Odin.

When we turn to the other thematic structures—man and God, man and man, man and himself; or love, war, and progress; the search for identity, the search for the good life, and the search for nature; or *homo orans, homo laborans, homo faber, homo ludens*—not only do we find these themes competing with each other as potential images for structuring experience, but also we find their components struggling for priority in the structure. Which of man's relationships does one start with? It would depend on whether one saw theology, anthropology, or psychology as the most important. Sequence is not inevitable, and further, as Frye himself admits, the thematic or mythic structure is only one of a number of structures (central perhaps), and a curriculum founded solely on them would deny a great deal of what makes literature effective in the lives of readers.

If we look at the genres as an informing principle for a sequence of units, we run into similar problems. In some of his writings, James Moffett has argued the primacy of narrative [4] and reasoned that one could structure a curriculum beginning with the story, particularly the first-person narrative. His recent book, *Drama, What Is Happening,*[5] could give one a basis for arguing that drama should be first. I do not think that he has

[4] "I, You, and It," *College Composition and Communications,* vol. 16, no. 5 (December 1965), and *Points of View,* with Kenneth McElheny (New York: New American Library, 1966).

[5] Champaign, Ill.: National Council of Teachers of English, 1967.

changed his mind, but I would suggest that he could equally well argue for the lyric as being the first literary form, since it derives from the natural impulse to song. No one of these three genres seems to underlie any of the others, although they do seem to precede exposition and satire (even of that I am unsure).

It would seem that we cannot find the units of learning upon which to build sequence in the structure of literature, as one might be able to find it in the structure of mathematics or of matter. We cannot do this because of the fact that literary works are as discrete as they are interconnected. Each work is related to every other, but each work is unique.

Further, the curriculum is not founded solely on the structure of a discipline. Rather it should be viewed as one views a simple transitive sentence. Concerning the curriculum, one speaks thus: "Students (or *a student* or *the teacher*) read (or *write* or *respond* or *talk about* or *analyze*) literature(or *a poem* or *a story* or *a film*)." So far we have been analyzing the structure of the object of this sentence in order to derive a sequence, and we have been criticizing the object in terms of the subject (which also has a structure). We must also look at the verb, and particularly the verbs dealing with the perception of a single work, for from that we might derive a structure of the reading of literature and thence move toward a sequence that utilizes all the parts of the sentence.

Let us examine the end of education in literature; that is what a sensitive reader *does* when he reads a work of literature. (One of the curriculum centers, that at Florida State University, does base its sequence on what the reader does and relates these behaviors to the work of Piaget.) [6] I use the term *sensitive reader* rather than *critic* or *scholar,* because some of the activities that these pursue are unrelated to general education. The critic who theorizes about his criticism or the scholar who collates manuscripts and edits letters are not the models for mastery learning.

The sensitive reader, first of all, has read a fair amount, but what he has read seems, as we have shown, incapable of precise

[6] Cf. Herbert Karl, "An Approach to Literature through Cognitive Processes," *English Journal,* vol. 57, no. 2 (February 1968): 181–87.

definition. Let us say, however, that he must recall what he has read. He must also be expected to recall some contextual and critical information, although biographical and historical information seem to me minimally important—partly because such information can, at times, hamper mastery (as knowing about Poe's drinking habits has hampered the understanding of his poetry for many people, leading them to think it is the product of delirium tremens), but mainly because much of it seems irrelevant, and the sorting of relevant and irrelevant information is a highly specialized sort of mastery. The same may be said of historical information; it is useful, but what is necessary is a matter of conjecture. Further, no strong case can be made for presenting this information before a first reading of a text; in fact, it seems that such an action often hampers engagement and limits perception. Despite these arguments, there is a place for contextual information. An understanding of *A Tale of Two Cities* for example, would seem to require a minimal knowledge of French history. Yet knowledge of the French Revolution is not basic to an understanding of many works contemporaneous to it—much of Coleridge and Jane Austen—so that one could argue that the knowledge requisite for a work like that of Dickens is a special case.

As to a knowledge of literary terms and critical systems, there is a stronger argument for saying that the sensitive reader has this knowledge before he reads a literary work, and particularly before he articulates his response to it. The best argument for it is that discourse becomes easier when there is a vocabulary and a rational basis for that discourse. Communication between student and student and between student and teacher improves if all can use words like *plot, character, tone,* and *metaphor* with a shared understanding of what those terms mean and what they refer to. Yet one can contend that the response of the good reader does not depend on a knowledge of these terms, just as the writing of a good writer does not depend on his knowledge of formal grammar. This analogy is somewhat specious, since response is enhanced by its articulation, and the terms are useful for articulation.

Of the importance of knowing critical systems, I can only

say that although the good reader has a method in his reading and responding and that such method should be encouraged, it would be presumptuous for anyone to argue that Aristotle's, or Burke's, or Frye's critical theory is indispensable to good reading of literature—useful, to be sure, but not indispensable.

It would seem that any knowledge is useful to the mastery of literature, but no knowledge is essential save one sort: knowledge of the mother tongue. Reading Yeats to a one-year-old would be useless, as useless as trying to read Proust in French if one knew no French. The child must have acquired the lexicon of the work he is encountering and the basic grammar of his tongue, but he need not, of course, know how to read. He can hear or watch and master. Beyond this area of knowledge, however, and that of the cultural substratum, some of which must be acquired, little can be cited as a necessary unit of learning.

Yet there are certain abilities that the sensitive reader possesses. Some of these are linguistic abilities, some literary, some psychological; all are natural abilities that have been sharpened. To take the linguistic first, one would have to include the ability to distinguish between denotation and connotation, the ability to discriminate among verbal rhythms, the ability to comprehend verbal ambiguities, and the ability to regularize complex syntax. Each of these abilities corresponds to what might be called the linguistic delights of literature: its pool of resonant words, its ability to affect the reader through sound and sound patterns, its potential for multiple meaning, and its intricacy in the arrangement of words. The abilities to discriminate these delights depend on the growth of the lexical, grammatical, and phonetic perceptiveness of the individual so that he can sense the difference between *surprised* and *astonished* (that the latter carries more force to it), so that one can apprehend the two senses of Mercutio's dying lines, "Ask for me tomorrow and you shall find me a grave man," so that he may appreciate the rhythmic difference between "Tell me not in mournful numbers," and "This is the forest primeval, the murmuring pines and the hemlocks," and so that he might untangle and thus comprehend a stanza like Blake's "Where the youth pined away with desire,/ And the pale virgin, shrouded in snow,/Arise from their graves and aspire/Where my sunflower wishes to go."

The psychological abilities refer to powers of inference about human behavior and attitude as described or expressed in language. One must acquire the capacity to hear or read a passage like the first chapter of *Madame Bovary* and derive a sense of the mild, patient, somewhat dull, character of Charles. One must be able to read the opening of *Hamlet* and see that the guards are nervous about the ghost. Similarly, one must infer from "A Modest Proposal" that Swift didn't really want those babies eaten, or that George Orwell does not admire the pigs. These twin abilities are not simply the results of language acquisition, but of the acquisition of a working language dealing with human behavior, much as one acquires a working language of numbers long after one has learned to count. It comes from having observed human behavior and attitude and the words that accompany and describe it and from having acquired a set of norms of behavior.

The literary abilities include those of comprehending metaphor, of discriminating among genres, of making part-whole relationships, and of discriminating between the literary work and one's experience of that work. All of these might be considered kinds of aesthetic perception, but the first is most peculiar to literary art. The person who reads lines like: "That time of year thou may'st in me behold/When yellow leaves or none or few, do hang/Upon those boughs which shake against the cold,/Bare ruin'd choirs, where late the sweet birds sang." must note that the basic comparison is between the age (or mood) of a man and a season, and that a subordinate comparison is between a tree and a church, and that the result of the comparisons is a sense of impending death in that which had been lively and beautiful, and a corresponding sense of melancholy. The reader must, in short, grasp both the vehicle of the metaphor, the actual points of equation, and the tenor, that new sense which is gained from the equation.[7]

In dealing with genres, a reader should, of course, be able to distinguish between drama and the novel, but more than that between the shape of a Petrarchan sonnet and the shape of a Shakespearean sonnet, or between the epistolary novel and the

[7] These terms are drawn from I. A. Richards, *The Philosophy of Rhetoric* (New York: Oxford University Press [Galaxy], 1965).

first-person novel. He must be able to set the work against other works and grasp its individual as well as its generic shape. In addition to having this sense of overall form, the sensitive reader is able to relate parts to wholes. He is able to see how the metaphor of the choirs is related to the metaphor of the seasons, or in a passage like the opening of Donald Davie's "Time Passing Beloved," how the syntax is related to the sense.

> Time passing, and the memories of love
> Coming back to me, carissima, no more mockingly
> Than even before; time passing, unslackening,
> Unhastening, steadily; and no more
> Bitterly, beloved, the memories of love
> Coming into the shore.

In a larger work, he is able to see how one speech or one scene might be related to the whole work.

The final ability, that of distinguishing between the work of art and one's experience of that work, might also be called aesthetic distance. At an early stage it might be defined as the ability to realize that the events that take place in a story or on a television show are not real, that Lassie does not really get hurt. Later it becomes the ability to distinguish between the personal associations of images, words, and events, and the verbal, rhetorical, or structural pattern of events that is presented. It is this ability that enables a reader to tolerate the many resonances that a work has for him at one time and through time, so that he may hold complementary and at times contradictory understandings and responses. A student of mine read a poem by Sylvia Plath called "Mushrooms," a poem which might be said to present the mushrooms' view of reality. They describe themeslves as irresistibly pushing up out of the earth. The student first said that the mushrooms were a symbol of the unborn fetus struggling to come into the world; later she changed her mind and said that it was about the dead, and that the mushrooms were the corpses and their gravestones. Both of these interpretations came in a single paper. When I asked her about them, and why she derived those two and polar interpretations, she replied, "Well, I guess now it was because I wrote that paper the evening after my husband and I had been told we could not have any children." Her example is a dramatic one, I think, of the ability to distinguish between the work and her experience. All of her statements, I might add, are valid, and all are related to her interaction with the work.

These ten abilities, coincident with those phenomena which distinguish literature from writing, comprise the basis of perceptive reading. One other ability, that of formulating a coherent and cohesive response to the work, is the final mark of the sensitive reader, important pedagogically because without this power, one cannot discern whether or not a student is a sensitive reader; our machinery is not yet that sophisticated.

In addition to abilities, we might say that the sensitive reader has certain attitudes toward literature. He likes to read it; he enjoys diverse works; he prefers a more complex work to a simple one (or at least enjoys each of them at its own level); he respects the place of literature in society and the right of the artist to create in accordance with his talent. Whether these attitudes precede or follow from his reading is moot; certainly the decision to read comes early, the diversity of pleasure late. No matter; the attitudes insure that the sensitivity of the reader persists.

Given this picture of the sensitive reader, the curriculum builder could then proceed to arrange the sequence of instruction so as to produce such a picture. The obvious solution would be to arrange the works read so that they form a progression from the simple to the complex. Such were many programs launched under the auspices of "progressive education" and under the auspices of "the new criticism." Each of these, however, chose only a few of the ten abilities for their principles of sequence: the complexity of experience with which the work dealt or the linguistic complexity by which experience was manipulated. A curriculum should strive for a balance between the two positions and deal with all of the abilities, recognizing therefore the facets of an individual's development. The culminating work would therefore be one which had a somewhat abstruse vocabulary, replete with many types of verbal ambiguity, charged with multivalent connotations and networks of connotation, full of literary allusions, complex in its syntax, subtle in its use of rhythms, partaking of a mixture of genres, highly metaphoric, dealing in the most complex of human actions, presented in a variety of authorial attitudes, and dealing with a subject matter that makes it hard for the reader to be detached. That work would probably be Joyce's *Ulysses*. How could one sort out the works that lead from *The Three Little Pigs* to that pinnacle?

Literary works are not consistently difficult in all of their as-pects (the linguistically straightforward might present a complex metaphor; that which deals with subtle human behavior might be told in a nonallusive and nonresonant diction and in a de-tached tone) and thus a sequential curriculum rigidly built on difficulty is doomed to failure. The curriculum builder might see this inconsistency not as an obstacle, but as an opportunity. He can first define the curriculum not as a course in literature, but as a course in reading literature. Knowledge becomes less impor-tant than performance. Structure and sequence become proper-ties of the reader, rather than properties of the read. What deepens is the capacity to perceive and understand more of the ambiguities of language, of human behavior, and of forms. Con-comitantly, the ability to enter into the experience that is pre-sented vicariously and to contemplate that experience and be conscious of the experience as it has operated on and in the individual—that ability will deepen and broaden to include more varieties of experience. From being able to enter into the terrors of *Little Red Riding Hood,* one becomes able to enter into the apathy of Merseult. One is also able to see that both experiences are fictions, but fictions which are related to life and to ourselves.

One could devise a programmatic sequence fostering these abilities through selection of material, but such a sequence poses problems. First the focus of the instruction is one verb only: *read* with its satellites *relate, discriminate, differentiate.* There are other verbs involved: *respond, enjoy, like, ponder, feel, sense,* and a number of words not simply perceptual but con-jointly affective, cognitive, and psychomotor. The purely per-ceptual curriculum sequence might tend to slight these and thus to obviate the prime function of literature, to please and to in-struct. Such a curriculum might create readers who do not want to read. Finally, such a curriculum may enable someone to perceive ambiguities, but not to tolerate them, and it may create aesthetic distance at the expense of commitment to humanistic ideals.

Let us look at those other verbs, particularly the central one, *respond,* and see if that might obviate the dangers of the strictly perceptual curriculum. Response to literature, as it is expressed, will also change, but it will change in quantity, not in quality. Elsewhere, I have categorized the expressed response as being talk about one's engagement, about one's perception, about one's interpretation, and about one's evaluation.[8] My investigations have shown that children, from the first years in school through the university, express their responses in these four categories. They say in a simple or complex manner: "It gets to me," or "It was this way," or "It means," or "It's good." As one progresses through twelve years of education, one does not add one of these categories to his repertoire, nor very many of the subcategories or elements save those which interconnect works or connect works to peripheral information. One's emphases might change, and certainly the subtlety of the statements will increase, and the reader and responder will become more systematic in his discourse, and he will have more to talk about. He will probably, too, make more comparative statements, simply because he has read more and has more works as a frame of reference for the particular work he is discussing.

If the curriculum is to be concerned with the individual's apprehending individual works and responding to one's apprehensions (and apprehension without response would be sterile, like a play without an audience), the sequence will be not a sequence in the normal sense of a movement from arithmetic to geometry to algebra to the calculus, but an accumulation of works read and talked about and thought about. The cycle of apprehension and response is repeated each time a work is read, no matter what work is read, and each cycle feeds on the last in one of a great number of ways. The order in which works are read by

[8] Alan C. Purves, with Victoria Rippere, *Elements of Writing about a Literary Work: A Study of Response to Literature* (Champaign, Ill.: National Council of Teachers of English, 1968).

the student might just as well be random, as long as the talk is incremental, and it will be as long as there are different works and plenty of talk. This nonsequence follows, I think, the way in which perceptive readers read, and is the least inimical to the function of literary works in our world—to present people with unique experiences mediated through language by an artist so that those people may participate in the unique experiences.

Within a gross sequence that is random, there might be small sequences—two or three works that are connected to each other in any one of a number of ways: topically, thematically, structurally, linguistically, chronologically, or the like. These points of connection should be varied just as the connecting points of the network of literary works are various (as Frye has so admirably pointed out in his *Anatomy of Criticism*). One work, that is, might lead to another according to what was said about the work in class. If a class were talking about the Beatles' "Eleanor Rigby" and got interested in the theme of loneliness, perhaps they might turn next to James Joyce's "The Dead." If, on the other hand, the class became interested in the function of the refrain and its effect on them, the next selection might be a ballad by William Morris or Yeats. One problem with such an adaptable curriculum is that it presupposes a teacher with a vast array of works at his fingertips; but most teachers have that array in their anthologies, and they need only break away from the order imposed by the editors and use the anthology creatively. Teachers can, of course, determine these small sequences beforehand and not overly dam the free flow of the classroom talk and the seemingly natural order.

The teacher should insure that the class covers a variety of the reading pleasures or problems (however he chooses to see it) during the course of the year, and that the works are generally appropriate to the experiential level of the students. The subject matter of the literature—not its genesis: its theme or its substructure—might determine the placement of a work at a particular grade level; tales of adventure and of animals are better suited to seventh-graders than are novels dealing with divorce or with the agonies of old age—although not to all seventh-graders. The other constraint on the curriculum builder would be one of complexity. Some animal poems might be so subtle linguistically that they would not be appropriate—the students would have too difficult a time penetrating the surface of the work.

The question of sequence is, as I trust I have demonstrated, a radically different question if one considers the processes of reading, responding to, and talking about literature to be at the heart of education in literature rather than peripheral to the acquisition of a body of lore or the remembering of a number of titles. One should make this shift in his consideration, because through such a shift will he be able to make literature study closer to the function of literature in society—to entertain, inform, and modify that society. Further, such a shift will help students develop more positive attitudes toward literature and the reading of literature; it will, in sum, help us to preserve literature as a part of everyone's life.

Sequence therefore occurs through what happens in the classroom and what happens in the individual, not in the corpus of literature from Homer to Allen Ginsberg. These latter sequences —historical, generic, thematic, mythic—have their use for the student who is going to become a theoretician of literature; they might even have their use for the curriculum builder who would like to give teachers some sense that he knows there is a structure to literature. But they do not have their use for the student who is part of the general audience, who is learning to read poems, plays, stories, and novels so that he may go on to read more. That student will be interested in noting the small connections and possibly in considering the notion of connection, but not in mastering the whole network.

I would suggest that if the humanities are courses in perception and response rather than in a body of lore—aesthetic lore, the lore of intellectual history, the lore of social and cultural history—then the structure and sequence of those courses will deal in the modes of perception and expression relevant to the arts they encompass. The art component of such a curriculum will be concerned with looking at objects; the music component with listening; the theater component with being part of the actor-audience relationship; and the dance component with perceiving, responding, and creating kinesthetically. Surely the literature component will deal with perception of and response to literary works.

In the other arts, perception is intimately connected with creation—at least in the schools; this is particularly so in theater and dance. I have not yet mentioned creation and its place in the cycle of apprehension and response. Certainly its place is important if one includes under creation not only the making of poems and stories and plays but also the re-creation of works through drama, mime, illustration, recitation, and film, and the re-creation of response through talking and writing. The making of works enables people to see for themselves how they mediate experience through language and thus construct their world; from this process they are better able to apprehend the totality of another's creation. The re-creation of the work is a form of response which is immediately expressive of the nexus between work and performer; it is the work reconstructed through the individual or the group. The re-creation of one's response is also creative, and in the same way; be it an essay on form, an argument about meaning, or a testimonial of involvement or even of distaste. These, too, are mediations of experience through language. Creation, re-creation, or response all are facets of the same phenomenon, as Peter Caws has observed in his essay, "What Is Structuralism?"

> "The book is a world," says Roland Barthes. "The critic confronted by the book is subject to the same conditions of utterance as the writer confronted by the world." But the critic can never replace the reader; the individual also confronts the book at a particular time, in a particular context; it becomes part of his experience, presents itself to him with a certain intelligibility as a message (from whom?); it engages him in another episode of the structuring activity which makes him what he is. An old book is not (unless the reader takes pain to make it so) a bit of antiquity, it is a bit of the present; consequently Racine can still be read, and new critical views about Racine, possible only in the light of contemporary events, can find in him without distortion meanings which he and *his* contemporaries could not even have understood.[9]

[9] Peter Caws, "What Is Structuralism?" *Partisan Review,* vol. 35, no. 4 (Winter 1968): 89. See also my "You Can't Teach Hamlet, He's Dead," *English Journal,* vol. 57, no. 6 (September 1968): 832–36.

There should, therefore, be no great distinction in the literature curriculum—or the total English program or the humanities program, for that matter—among "creative" writing (a disgraceful misnomer), oral or dramatic interpretations, and written, spoken, or nonverbal responses. Each is equally important in a curriculum that is designed to allow students to explore their relations with their verbal environment and their verbal and nonverbal transactions with that environment and other environments. Such a curriculum should present people with as many opportunities as they can have to make the explorations, for it is their performance as explorers that will make literature and the imaginative uses of language a vital part of our culture.

BUILDING CURRICULA FOR MUSIC EDUCATION

Bennett Reimer

In the field of music education the junior high school general music class plays a unique and central role. About 85 percent of junior high schools in the United States offer general music, and in most, if not all, the teaching of this course is done by music specialists. After the junior high school, music education involves less than 25 percent of all students, and most of those are reached entirely through performance activities which typically focus on the development of specialized skills rather than broad musical understanding. In the elementary grades only 20 percent of music teaching is done by specialists, the remainder being in the hands of classroom teachers whose level of musical insight tends to be quite limited.

If the aesthetic sensitivity of chidlren is to be improved through music education, the junior high school general music class presently affords the best opportunity. This makes it imperative that serious thought and effort be given to the improvement of this class. Not only will music education have its most immediate effect on most children in junior high school general music, but a much clearer idea can be gained, given a really effective course at this level, of how to improve elementary music education, and also of the best direction to take in high school.

This line of reasoning has guided curriculum research projects in many subjects and seems to have produced some important gains. After good alternatives for secondary level courses had been worked out, attention was turned to the upgrading of elementary teaching, so that children would come to the seventh and eighth grades prepared to deal with the new material. And tangible guidelines existed for elementary teaching because goals had been established at the secondary level. Certainly curricu-

From the *Journal of Aesthetic Education,* vol. 2, no. 2 (April 1968): 97–107. Reprinted by permission of the *Journal* and the author.

lum research at every level is greatly needed in music education. It would seem particularly fruitful, however, to develop effective approaches to musical understanding at the point where most children are reached by specialists.

To date, the only large-scale, subsidized curriculum development project in the area of junior high school general music has been the author's. The decision to do systematic curriculum research in this area was made on the basis of its strategic role in the music program, and also because improvement seemed to be needed. It must be confessed that the extent of needed improvement was not clearly discerned when work began in September, 1964. As more has been learned about this field, the author's position has changed significantly. As the project led first through the study of curriculum reform in American education, then to the study of the present status of general music at the junior high school level and the actual building of a new curriculum and its trial in the schools, the writer began to realize that there is little relation between what is presently being done in junior high school general music and what should be done. It has become clear that the majority of general music courses presently being taught at the secondary level are lacking in precisely those elements which curriculum experts consider most necessary for successful teaching and learning.

This is a strong statement. But dissatisfaction with present practices in this field stems from the conviction that improvement is both necessary and possible. This conviction is held by the many curriculum workers in education who are engaged in the task of rebuilding curricula in the light of new insights and assumptions regarding the process of education. Every one of the curriculum projects in the past fifteen years of the curriculum reform revolution began with the same dissatisfaction which is now being experienced in music education. So there are good and well-established precedents for statements about the weaknesses of junior high school general music.

There are also some good and well-established principles and patterns to follow in attempting to improve this subject. It would be a waste of precious time and effort if educators in the arts ignored the knowledge and experience gained by many people in different subjects—people who have struggled during the past fifteen years to formulate and share new ideas which would make the teaching of their disciplines more effective. No one argues that all or even most of the answers about education are known. But some things have been learned that can help improve the teaching of the art of music.

In what follows, some of the pervasive patterns of curriculum reform will be discussed in the context of their implications for music education. A brief description will then be given of the course developed under the present project.

One of the most striking patterns to emerge from curriculum reform work is the emphasis given to development of new teaching materials. It has been generally agreed that the most strategic way to change the teaching of a subject is to make materials available which embody the new ideas and methods being recommended. Accordingly, several subjects have built teaching "packages"—a collection of material which constitutes the entire course of study in all its aspects.

Now it happened that many curriculum workers had a rather low regard for the average teacher's knowledge and skill. There was a strong feeling, especially toward the beginning of the curriculum reform movement, that the materials being prepared, if they were to do all that they were supposed to do, should be made "teacher-proof." Much of the new material, therefore, is extremely detailed and explicit, leaving little, if anything, to the teacher's imagination. At the same time, however, the materials themselves often embody some of the most imaginative and exciting ideas, methods, and devices ever developed in American education.

As more experience has been gained with the process of change in public education, more and more people have come to realize that no material will ever be teacher-proof. Even the most extreme non-teacher methods, such as computer-based programs, will, in the final analysis, be affected by the personalities of teachers.

Less extreme methods, which depend on the face-to-face confrontation of teacher and student, will doubtless continue to be the most widely used arrangement for teaching and learning in the arts. And whenever face-to-face teaching and learning take place, materials can be no more than aids: they cannot determine the intangible yet essential atmosphere which makes education either dull and ineffective or sparkling and vital. Recognizing this, new and concerted efforts are being made to upgrade teachers through in-service programs, special workshops and institutes, and most important and difficult of all, the overhauling of teacher-education curricula. These efforts are an important part of the so-called second revolution in curriculum reform.

New materials are badly needed for junior high school general music. Certainly some available materials are helpful, but as far as can be determined there is at present no course of study which embodies new ideas about learning or emphasizes the fostering of authentic musical responses to important works of art. Much of the material now available is of poor quality musically and pedagogically, and it is terribly difficult to do a first-rate job of teaching with second-rate or third-rate materials. Thus there is an immediate need for new approaches to junior high general music embodied in material which, hopefully, will give enough guidance to be of help to the teacher, but which will retain the personal element so very important in music education.

The next pattern which must be mentioned in any review of the curriculum reform movement is one which affects the high school somewhat more than the junior high school level but deserves attention, nevertheless. This is the heavy concentration in the new curricula on single subjects. Many attempts were geared to teaching a discipline as it exists *in and of itself*. The point of view most often taken was that the integrity of the discipline must be maintained, and that the relations between disciplines cannot be perceived until a deep understanding is developed of the single discipline. In mathematics, it is only recently that programs are being developed for all of mathematics rather than separate courses for arithmetic, analytic geometry, synthetic geometry, algebra, and so on. Some beginning steps are also being taken to show the relations between mathematics and other sciences. The social studies are also beginning to build integrated curricula in addition to separate courses in the various areas.

It is interesting and revealing that at the same time curriculum workers were trying to determine how to do a good job of teaching single subjects, many of them were suggesting that integrated courses should be developed in the arts. Whatever the plausibility of integrated courses in the arts, there is still no substiute for knowing one's field. Educators in the arts know very well how much there is to be learned about teaching really good courses in music, art, literature, drama, or dance. Anyone who thinks these are easy matters is simply not acquainted with the scope of the problems. So there is little wonder that attempts to develop integrated arts courses have raised so many enormous and extremely difficult problems. This is not the place to discuss these problems in that, for the most part, the seventh- and eighth-grade level continues to teach separate courses in the arts. But it makes the task of improving such courses even more imperative, since it is reasonable to assume that the knowledge gained from curriculum work in separate arts courses can serve as a basis for developing more effective secondary courses in the allied arts or humanities.

The next principle of curriculum reform is perhaps the most important of all. This is the universal agreement that all effort should be focused on teaching what is most fundamental about a discipline. The guideline for choosing fundamental content has been the discipline's structure—i.e., its inner core of interrelated concepts which makes the discipline a coherent, unified field. Understanding the nature of mathematics is more important, in this view, than being able to manipulate numbers or formulas in skillful but mindless fashion. Understanding the nature of physics is more important than memorizing all sorts of unrelated facts, or of being able to carry out experiments which do not give a real sense of how the scientific process is organized. It is more important to know the inner logic of grammar than to parrot rules and regulations which have little meaning except as they are instances of this inner logic.

The concern with structure is a very practical one. It has become impossible to learn all the details of any single discipline. Hence, the most effective, most economical use of the time available for education is to insure that the student has some grasp of what makes a discipline a discipline. This understanding is the very basis of a general education. It is possible, given good materials and good teachers, to foster such understandings about the major disciplines of human thought. Anything less than this scope of insight is inadequate for the complexities of today's and tomorrow's world. Robert Hutchins has suggested that "the best educated man is the most generally educated man." He means by this precisely what curriculum workers mean—that the most effective man is the one who has the widest understanding of the nature of knowledge. It might be added that expertise in a particular field is a necessary requirement for intellectual and practical adequacy. What education is trying to avoid, of course, is the perpetuation of the specialist—whether it be in surgery, sewage disposal, or salesmanship—who is so narrow as to lack a sense of how his effort relates to human endeavor in general.

The arts are the primary source of a particular kind of knowledge about the human condition. This knowledge consists of the insights the arts provide into the nature of human feeling. While the sciences deal with the objective world in which the human being finds himself, the arts deal with the subjective world, in which the human being not only knows, but reacts. We need to know as much about the subjective world in which we exist as about the objective world, and the arts are our means for gaining this kind of knowledge.

This point of view about aesthetic meaning, which may be called "absolute expressionism," is a dominant aesthetic position of our times, receiving its must lucid explanations in the writings of John Dewey, Susanne K. Langer, Leonard B. Meyer, and many others. One might cite as a summary of this position, along with its educational implications, the following excerpt from Susanne K. Langer's "The Cultural Importance of Arts":

> What . . . language . . . does for our awareness of things about us and our own relation to them, the arts do for our awareness of subjective reality, feeling and emotion; they give form to inward experiences and thus make them conceivable. The only way we can really envisage vital movement, the stirring and growth and passage of emotion, and ultimately the whole direct sense of human life, is in artistic terms. . . . A wide neglect of artistic education is a neglect in the education of feeling. Most people are so imbued with the idea that feeling is a formless total organic excitement in men as in ani-

mals, that the idea of educating feeling, developing its scope and quality, seems odd to them, if not absurd. It is really, I think, at the very heart of personal education. . . . Art education is the education of feeling and a society that neglects it gives itself up to formless emotion.[1]

According to this view, the most fundamental thing about the art of music is its ability to give insights into the subjective nature of human reality. Such a statement is far from being of purely academic interest. It tells the curriculum researcher very precisely and concretely what the task of music education—especially of *general* music education— actually is. That task is to make the insights contained in music available to as many people as possible.

How does one go about doing this? Curriculum research consists precisely in the systematic implementation of a consistent, unified view of a subject. It is largely because no synthetic view of the art of music has permeated the teaching of music that so much random, ineffective, unconvincing activity has taken place. Every educator who has tried to reform his subject has had to grapple with the problem of defining the nature of his discipline, and then of developing means for making the nature of his discipline understandable. This is central to curriculum reform. The primary task of curriculum work in the arts is the very difficult but necessary one of developing a consistent view of the nature of art and then translating this view into the context of teaching and learning.

Fortunately, there are some helpful principles available in the building of a course which is intended to teach about the fundamental nature of a subject. The first thing one must do is to translate one's primary objective into terms of behavior. If the objective of a general music course is to make available the aesthetic insights contained in music, what behaviors does one foster which would lead one to hope that aesthetic insights will in fact be gained?

[1] In Michael F. Andrews, ed., *Aesthetic Form and Education* (Syracuse: Syracuse University Press, 1958); reprinted in the *Journal of Aesthetic Education,* vol. 1, no. 1 (Spring 1966). See also Leonard B. Meyer, *Emotion and Meaning in Music* (Chicago: University of Chicago Press, 1956), Ch. 1.

One gets aesthetic insights from a work of art through a particular kind of experience called aesthetic experience. The major purpose of aesthetic education, then, is to develop systematically every person's ability to have aesthetic experiences of works of art. We are now closer to stating our objective in terms of behavior. The behavior to be fostered is a particular kind of experience called aesthetic experience. A further step can be taken to identify actual behaviors which can be influenced. Aesthetic experience itself contains two identifiable behaviors, both of which occur simultaneously. These two behaviors are (1) the perception of what is expressive in a work of art (that is, the perception of that which contains the aesthetic insights in the works), and (2) the reaction to what has been perceived.

The perception part of aesthetic experience is an objective phenomenon. It is concrete, capable of being analyzed, verbalized, organized; it is also measurable by objective means and improvable through practice. In short, it is possible to teach for aesthetic perception.

The reaction part of aesthetic experience is a subjective, creative phenomenon. It is nebulous, unanalyzable; it cannot be verbalized, organized, or objectively measured. In short, it is not possible to teach directly for aesthetic reaction. But since the quality of the *reaction* depends upon the quality of the *perception,* aesthetic reaction can be indirectly influenced by the improvement of aesthetic perception.

We are now back to the everyday world of the teacher, and we bring with us some practical ideas about what to teach. Youngsters should be taught to perceive music more keenly, more subtly, more deeply, so that their reactions to music can be keener and subtler and deeper. It is my opinion that every activity in music education, from kindergarten through college, should contribute to the improvement of musical perception, and therefore of musical reaction, of aesthetic experience, and of the aesthetic insights obtainable from music.

The course being recommended for junior high school general music is systematically organized to improve musical perception in a context which encourages musical reaction. While a detailed rationale cannot be presented here, some of the major principles of curriculum reform which are incorporated in the course can be mentioned.

The organization of the course is based on the structure of the art of music. The course outline itself is an aid to understanding why music is a unified subject. The sequence of topics is as logical, as tight, as necessary as the author knows how to make it. The material is cyclical, or, if one prefers, it is a "spiral" curriculum. The major idea about music—that it is a means for understanding and exploring human feeling through expressive sounds—constantly reappears in different and more subtle contexts.

The content of the course is significant music, and the treatment of this music is entirely musical, never extra-musical. Great care is taken to insure that every student experiences a high degree of success in perceiving music. Since it would ruin the entire effort if expectations were unreasonable, the materials go to extraordinary lengths to provide success experiences as well as individual challenges.

The course is an active one. It includes ideas which are calculated to stimulate young minds. The listenings are organized in such a way as to abolish day-dreaming and fidgeting. This is done through the use of devices which demand concentration and absorption. The children are actually engaged in doing—singing, playing, writing, talking, moving—at every opportunity. But every activity of this sort serves the purpose of heightened perception. The old five-fold curriculum, which music educators will recognize as the basis for the activities in this course, is used to help make concrete the conceptions being taught. In its traditional usage, the five-fold curriculum serves no cohesive, structural purpose. It is a miscellaneous assortment of activities, neither good nor bad in themselves, but helpful or unhelpful depending on how they are used. Unfortunately, the notion that activities by themselves make a curriculum has had the effect of convincing teachers that as long as their children were doing one or another of these activities they were bound to be learning something of importance. In the light of knowledge gained in curriculum research, this assumption is no longer tenable.

What about motivation? Music teachers have traditionally been greatly concerned about motivation, and probably the most concerned of all music teachers have been junior high school general music teachers. This is natural. The junior high school general music teacher deals with an age group that requires the patience of a saint, the energy of an athlete, the mental state of a Pollyanna, the wisdom of an Old Testament judge, and the firmness of a penitentiary guard. Added to this is the long-standing belief that adolescents need the same kinds of experiences with music as elementary children. And they need these experiences, according to this idea, whether they like them or not. In most cases they do not like them at all, because their abilities and needs are quite different from younger children. In technical terms, they have left what Jean Piaget has called the "concrete operations" stage and have entered the "formal operations" stage.

Yet the junior high teacher, armed with outmoded conceptions about what is appropriate for her students, with childish material which embarrasses everyone concerned with the enterprise, and with a bag of tricks she learned in a methods course (the only college course, by the way, specifically geared to her problems) is supposed to capture the hearts and minds of her students. It is no wonder that under these circumstances the junior high school general music teacher must depend so desperately on "motivation."

For teachers in this plight, the curriculum reform movement holds out a simple solution. That is, that motivation *as such* is a waste of everyone's time. One of the most striking outcomes of curriculum reform is the almost total lack of concern about motivation as a separate problem. Instead, the conviction has arisen that all effort must be focused on excellent teaching of significant subject matter. This focus is intended to arouse what curriculum workers have come to regard as the major requirement for successful learning—that is, *interest*. It is interest which leads to learning, and interest is quite different from motivation in its usual sense. One gets interest by dealing with important, respectable, meaningful, and fundamental subject matter, and by teaching this subject matter seriously and skillfully, with an attitude moreover of respect for the subject, one's students, and oneself.

The poorer the student, the more difficult the educational setting, the more demoralized the social and educational background of the children, the more crucial it becomes that the subject matter be significant and the teaching excellent. Such thinking runs counter to the usual conception of motivation, a conception which waters down the subject matter for poorer students and allows the teaching of these students to become essentially entertainment. This, of course, perpetuates the inferiority of their education and insures that they will remain as deprived as they have always been. It is recognized now that such children need better, not worse, education. All children deserve the kind of education which, based on significant material and insightful teaching, will deepen their interest in the realm of knowing.

Having sketched the backgrounds for the approach being taken, the actual course outline and content can be described. The course is comprised of three major topics, each one consisting of a fundamental question about the nature of music. The first question is, "What does music do?" The second is, "How does music do what it does?" And the third is, "How has music done what it does?" These questions sound simple, but the job of condensing all the major aspects of the art of music into a forthright, clear outline was actually one of the most difficult and important problems of the research. In this connection, I was very pleased and quite surprised to read in Jerome Bruner's recent book, *Toward a Theory of Instruction,*[2] his outline for an upper elementary social studies course on the subject of "man." His course is also based on three questions: "What is human about human beings?" "How did they get that way?" "How can they be made more so?" Again, there is an attempt to illuminate the structure of a complex subject by asking basic questions about the nature of the subject.

The three major topics are divided into several units. Under the first topic—"What does music do?"—are three units: (1) the composer, (2) the performer and conductor, and (3) the listener. This section of the course attempts to make clear, at the very outset, what function music serves and what the student

[2] Cambridge: Harvard University Press, 1966.

can do to get from music what it has to offer. As previously mentioned, the position taken is that music is a means for understanding and exploring the realm of human feeling toward the medium of sound.

The second topic—"How does music do what it does?"— helps the student discover ways in which the medium of sound is organized to be expressive, that is, to help us understand and explore feeling. The units are (1) tone color, (2) rhythm, (3) melody, (4) harmony, (5) texture, and (6) form.

The third topic—"How has music done what it does?"—attempts to give the students a flavor of how human feeling was conceived in sound through history. This, of course, involves the notion of "style." The units are (1) baroque style, (2) classical style, (3) romantic style, and (4) our music: the modern styles.

Each unit is divided into many sections, every one of which includes some combination of three things: (1) information and ideas, (2) listening, and (3) activities. The unit on the composer, for example, has thirteen sections, each of which presents material about the composer's function and mode of operation, lists specific listening excerpts which illustrate the ideas, and suggests several activities which help make the ideas concrete.

The listenings are drawn from a basic list of important works. Repeated hearings of many works are provided, so that, for example, the second movement of Brahms's *Second Symphony* is heard at one time for the purpose of comparing conductors' interpretations, at another time to focus on tone color, at another time to explore its melodic content, at another time to discover its form, and at still another time to hear it in the context of romantic music in general. Lest this sound like a graduate course in stylistic analysis, the reader may be assured that it is possible to present such material so that junior high school youngsters can understand it. From a class in the most deprived area of Cleveland's "inner city," to a class in a comfortable but modest suburb, to another class in one of the wealthiest neighborhood in Ohio (or the United States), we have found that children can be taught significant material about significant music.

In the same book in which Jerome Bruner presents his outline for a course on man, he discusses the problem of "the will to learn." It is pertinent here to quote a striking paragraph from that discussion. Bruner says:

> Experienced teachers who work with the newer curricula in science and mathematics report that they are surprised at the eagerness of students to push ahead to next steps in the course. Several of the teachers have suggested that the eagerness comes from increased confidence in one's ability to understand the material. Some of the students were having their first experience of understanding a topic in some depth, of going somewhere in a subject. It is this that is at the heart of competence motives, and surely our schools have not begun to tap this enormous reservoir of zest.[3]

To tap the enormous reservoir of zest for music, which we know exists, is the task of the music education profession. Our success or failure will affect the quality of the lives of our youth. It is my hope that the course described here represents a step toward success.

[3] *Ibid.*, p. 120.

BUILDING CURRICULA FOR ART EDUCATION

Elliot W. Eisner

Art Education today appears to be undergoing a metamorphosis more insistent and radical in nature than any change occurring in the field since Walter Smith was imported from England some 100 years ago to direct the teaching of art in the schools of Boston.[1] What we are seeing, I believe, is a reconceptualization of the means and ends of the field, a reconceptualization based in part upon a changing view of the child and of the contributions of art to his education. In this paper I would like first to identify what I consider to be the salient characteristics of that change, second, to describe a curriculum development project that is based upon the assumptions underlying that change and, finally, to identify some of the problems in curriculum development and curriculum theory that seem to me to deserve the attention of those concerned with research.

The period in art education from which we are emerging is one whose parentage is as ancient as Plato and as modern as Read[2] and Lowenfeld.[3] This is a parentage that conceived of the end of education as the actualization of potentiality and viewed the child as an organism who contains within his being a unique array of latent aptitudes which it was the task of the teacher to educe. This theory of child development saw the task of the teacher as similar to the gentle gardener whose responsibility it is to nurture the young flower by providing the conditions necessary for the complete realization of its unique characteristics.

From *Studies in Art Education*, vol. 9, no. 3 (Spring 1968): 45–56. Reprinted by permission of *Studies in Art Education* and the author.

[1] For an example of Walter Smith's work the reader may wish to review his book *Freehand Drawing* (Boston: James R. Osgood, 1875). For an excerpt from this book, see *Readings in Art Education,* Elliot W. Eisner and David W. Ecker, eds. (Waltham, Mass.: Blaisdell, 1966).

[2] Herbert Read, *Education through Art,* 3rd rev. ed. (New York: Pantheon Books, 1956).

[3] Viktor Lowenfeld, *Creative and Mental Growth* (New York: Macmillan, 1947).

When translated into prescriptions for curriculum and instruction this view tended to emphasize four basic tenets. First, it emphasized the value of the native and naive character of the developing child by honoring the charm and spontaneity of his art. Second, it emphasized the importance of expressive and novel media as vehicles for educing or actualizing latent capacities. New media were, through their novelty, instruments useful for developing the imaginative capacities every child possessed. Third, this conception emphasized the primacy of process over product, of what was happening to the child in the course of his art activities, rather than emphasizing the product of the activity itself. Fourth, this view of the child conceived of art education not as a field concerned with the attainment of ends unique to art but as an instrument useful for the attainment of larger, more general ends, goals which the field shared with most other fields in education when they were properly conceived.[4]

In the area of instruction the teacher was admonished not to interfere with the very personal process of the child's artistic creativity. Since her adult mind was qualitatively different from the child's, she was not to inflict her adult world view on the child's developing conception of reality. This meant not only that the teacher was to encourage spontaneity and creative self-expression but was to discourage if not altogether eliminate copying. And never was she to get her hand in the work of the child. Viktor Lowenfeld, a major spokesman for this view, puts the case succinctly when he says:

> For the child, art is not the same as it is for the adult. Art for the child is merely a means of expression. Since the child's thinking is different from that of the adult's, his expression must also be different. Out of this discrepancy between the adult's "taste" and the way in which a child expresses himself arise most of the difficulties and interferences in art teaching. I have seen and heard educators, intrigued by the beauty of children's drawings and paintings, asking for the "right" proportions and "good" color schemes. The child sees the world differently from the way he draws it. Precisely from our analysis of this discrepancy between the representation and the thing represented do we gain insight into the child's real

[4] Both Read and Lowenfeld endorse this view.

experience. Therefore it is easy to understand that *any* correction by the teacher which refers to reality and not to the child's experience interferes greatly with the child's own expression. This interference starts perhaps when children scribble and eager parents expect to see something that fits their own adult conception. How ridiculous to overpower these little children's souls! [5]

What we see in this conception of the child and of education is one that views child development as a process of maturation occurring primarily from the inside out.

During the past ten-year period a radically different conception of children and of art education has begun to emerge, and during the past three years it has gained force and insistence. This view, too, tends to emphasize certain beliefs about the child's development and the function of art in his education. First, it emphasizes the importance of the environment in shaping artistic aptitudes, including aptitudes in both the production and the appreciation of art. In this newer view the teacher and the curriculum play a critical role in effecting artistic learning.[6] Second, the newer view is concept- rather than media-oriented. This is simply to say that it conceives of media as vehicles for the development of perceptual or productive skills and concepts as well as material out of which something is to be made. Third, this view tends to place greater importance on the product since the quality of the product is a major data source for making inferences about what children have learned or have not learned. Fourth, this newer view conceives of art education as a mode of education that has unique contributions to make to the growing child.[7] This is not to say that art education shares no commonality with the contributions of other subject areas. It is to say that what art education happens to have in common with

[5] Lowenfeld, pp. 1–2.

[6] Elliot Eisner, "Changing Conceptions of Artistic Learning," *Elementary School Journal,* vol. 68, no. 1 (October 1967): 18–25.

[7] For examples of this newer view, see Ralph Smith's Preface in his volume *Aesthetics and Criticism in Art Education* (Chicago: Rand McNally, 1966); Vincent Lanier, "Schizmogenesis in Art Education," *Studies in Art Education,* vol. 5, no. 1 (Fall 1963): 10–19; and Elliot W. Eisner, "Knowledge, Knowing and the Visual Arts," *Harvard Educational Review,* vol. 33, no. 2 (Spring 1963): 208–18.

other fields is less important than what it can provide that is unique. Fifth and finally, the newer view has expanded considerably the scope and character of the field. Unlike the older view which laid almost exclusive emphasis on the idea of the child as an artist, this newer view recognizes a variety of skills and understandings beyond those found in the studio as appropriate, indeed necessary, for providing an adequate education in art.[8]

What has emerged in the field over the past few years is a conception of the child that conceives of development primarily from the outside in, rather than from the inside out. It is a conception which emphasizes environmentalism over nativism, one that is concept- more than media-oriented. The new view concerns itself with what children learn and produce as well as with the process involved in learning and production; it emphasizes the unique contributions of an education in art more than what it shares with other fields. And perhaps most important it has expanded the scope of the field so liberally that it has become imperative to rethink the way in which art educators should be recruited and trained.[9]

In identifying these two orientations I have, of course, placed them in bold juxtaposition. Few of those who have influenced the course of events in art education would make such sharp distinctions. Yet the points of emphasis and difference are not to be denied; hence the starkness of my distinctions I believe to be justified, especially when one considers their implications for both curriculum development and instruction. Indeed the later and newer view of the child and of art education's role in his education makes it possible to formulate concepts and to raise questions about curriculum and instruction that simply were not raised in previous years. What are these concepts and questions, and how can they guide curriculum development?

[8] See Ralph Smith.
[9] It is my view that as the scope of practice and research in art education continue to expand, those concerned with art education in institutions of higher education will need to develop new ways of recruiting and training people for the field. The impact of the new ideas in the field will be minimal if there are few teachers able to put them into action in the classroom.

To identify these concepts and questions I am going to turn to the work that my students and I have undertaken at Stanford University. Through a grant from the Charles F. Kettering Foundation we have embarked on a two-year project aimed at the development of curricula in the visual arts for children in grades one, two, and three. This project . . . is based upon the assumptions that artistic learning is not an automatic consequence of maturation, that it can be facilitated through instruction, and that a curriculum developed with clarity and with instructional support for the elementary school teacher working in the self-contained classroom can be used effectively to enable even the very young child to obtain both competence and satisfaction in the visual arts.

One of the first tasks that needed to be undertaken was that of identifying some of the domains which constitute the visual arts and which were teachable and learnable for children of so tender an age. Although there are a variety of ways of staking out the field, we arbitrarily decided to identify three that seemed to us to be reasonably wide in scope and yet flexible enough so that we could alter our plans if that seemed appropriate. These three domains are the *productive,* that domain dealing with the formulation of objects having expressive and aesthetic quality; the *critical,* that domain dealing with the perception of qualities constituting art; and the *historical,* that domain dealing with the evolution of art in human culture.[10] Within each of these domains we have attempted to identify those concepts and principles that appear both significant and useful for handling the material within the domain. Let me provide some examples.

By a concept we mean the identification of a class. Line, color, composition, impressionism, surrealism, water color, and tempera all are class concepts. Each term refers to a set of particulars that have something in common. We start with the assumption—one supported by a large variety of research—that linguistic labels, vocabulary if you will, can serve as handles or tools for thinking about important phenomena in each of the three domains. Part of the curriculum task, as we see it, is to

[10] Elliot Eisner, "Curriculum Ideas in a Time of Crisis," *Art Education,* vol. 18, no. 7 (October 1965).

identify those concepts that are important and teachable to very young children.

Once having identified the concepts, we have attempted to formulate principles in which those concepts function. A principle is conceived of as a proposition, in this case about artistic phenomena, which contains important information about subject matter in one of the domains. Examples of such principles are, "Line can convey or elicit feeling," "Composition can be active or static," "Artists have frequently criticized the period in which they lived," "The technology of an era affects the form and content of the work of art." Each of these statements is a principle or empirical generalization about art, and each contains one or more concepts considered important by the staff of the Kettering Project. Once having identified those principles that seem to be of most power as conceptual tools, we have ordered the principles in an array according to their presumed degree of complexity. Thus, for a concept like color, we have identified a variety of principles about color that are ordered serially, which are then used for the sequence of learning activities. This sequence of principles, built around a single concept, serves as criteria for the formulation of educational objectives. These objectives are of two types.

In our work we have found it useful to distinguish between instructional objectives and expressive objectives.[11] Instructional objectives are objectives which meet the criteria generally specified as desirable by those who have contributed to curriculum theory.[12] Instructional objectives specify both the content and behavior to be learned; they are couched in terms of student rather than teacher behavior and are stated at a level of specificity that makes it possible to use them as criteria for the formulation of evaluation procedures. An instructional objective identifies the desirable behavior of the student after his having

[11] For an elaboration of this concept, see Elliot W. Eisner, "Instructional and Expressive Educational Objectives: Their Formulation and Use in Curriculum," in W. James Popham et al., *Instructional Objectives,* American Educational Research Association, Monograph Series on Curriculum Evaluation (Chicago: Rand McNally, 1969).

[12] Ralph Tyler, *Basic Principles of Curriculum and Instruction* (Chicago: University of Chicago Press, 1950).

engaged in a series of curriculum activities designed to facilitate his learning. Evaluation of his terminal behavior is made by comparing it to the descriptions found in the instructional objective. An example of an instructional objective is, "To be able to build a pot at least twelve inches in height using a slab method of clay construction," or "To be able to select pointillist painting from an array of paintings which include at least five other styles and periods." In each case the instructional objective describes the competency to be displayed by the student, and evaluation is made in terms of the specifications the instructional objective provides.

Expressive objectives differ from instructional objectives since they do not specify what the student is to learn but rather describe the type of educational encounter he is to have. For example, the statement "To use wire and wood to construct a three-dimensional form" does not specify learning outcomes but indicates what the student is to encounter. The outcome of this encounter is appraised after, and at times during, the course of the student's work. Such an objective places a premium on uniqueness and personalization of learning. While instructional objectives insure the development of necessary technical skills, expressive objectives provide an opportunity to employ them in new and personally expressive ways. The curriculum we are developing has both instructional and expressive objectives related to the concepts and principles identified earlier.

Concepts, principles, and objectives are clearly insufficient to insure learning; somewhere there needs to be an array of activities in which the student is to engage and which are directly related to the concepts, principles, and objectives that have been formulated. The curriculum activity or lesson as we have called it follows in our model. Curriculum activities are not only related to the objectives but must be formulated in a way that will be of interest to the child and appropriate for his level of development. The formulation of such activities is done more through the pooled experience and education of those on the Project than it is by consulting developmental psychological theory. We have found that theories of child development and learning in art are at best general and do not provide as much direction for formulating curriculum activities as the experience of good teachers and doctoral students in the field. Whether our hunches turn out to be useful remains to be seen, but at present we are appealing more to experience than to rigorous theory for guiding the construction of these curriculum activities.

In order to provide the teacher with curriculum options two or three activities are formulated for each objective or principle. This is done to allow her to select that activity that seems most appropriate for her own capabilities or for those of the class. Some teachers will probably use all of the optional activities in an effort to individualize programs for students of different abilities or interests.

Partial Curriculum Model for the Kettering Project

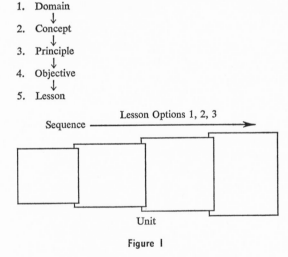

1. Domain
   ↓
2. Concept
   ↓
3. Principle
   ↓
4. Objective
   ↓
5. Lesson

Lesson Options 1, 2, 3

Sequence

Unit

Figure I

Figure I presents schematically the components of the model I have described thus far.

To summarize up to this point, we have identified three domains in which curriculum is being developed. These are the productive, the critical, and the historical. In each of these domains we have identified concepts that are non-trivial and which will serve as conceptual handles for illuminating subject matter in one of three domains. Each of the concepts is used to formulate principles expressing important empirical generalizations, and each of these principles is ordered with respect to its supposed degree of complexity.

From these principles two types of educational objectives have been formulated: instructional objectives and expressive objectives. Instructional objectives specify terminal student behavior, while expressive objectives designate the type of encounter the student is to have. These objectives are then used to formulate an ordered sequence of curriculum activities or lessons related directly to the objectives. This sequence then constitutes a curriculum unit.

Four other characteristics are a part of the curriculum model that we are using. One of these is a rationale for teachers; a second is a suggested motivation activity; a third is an array of supportive instructional devices; and the fourth is suggested evaluation instruments and procedures.

It seems important to us that teachers understand not only the concepts, principles, objectives, and activities they are to use but the reason the concept and principle is of importance. To facilitate such understanding, each lesson carries with it a brief rationale of perhaps two or three paragraphs which attempts to explain as lucidly and simply as possible why the concept and principle selected are considered important. We fully realize that our effort to explain in a brief form what is complex and often subtle cannot be complete or final, but we hope it will make a start at rationalizing the import of the curriculum content we are using.

A second characteristic of our curriculum model is a suggested warm-up or motivating activity. This is not different from other such activities used to generate interest, to induce a conceptual set, or to provide focus for the students' attention. These suggested activities are simply cues for the teacher for initiating curriculum activities.

A third characteristic is the formulation and design of supportive instructional materials. When one thinks of media in art education, one generally thinks of paint, paper, clay, and other types of materials found in elementary and secondary classrooms. Instructional media in art education are almost synonymous with art supplies. Yet, since art media are essentially instruments used to facilitate artistic learning, it seemed reasonable to us to expand the usual conception and to design instructional materials that would assist the teacher and the student in learning the concepts, skills, and principles with which we are concerned. Thus every unit that is formulated contains an array of instructional materials designed specifically to enhance and facilitate a specific type of learning. Let's say we want children to become aware of the fact that some paintings are characterized by a pervasive mood and that the mood is influenced by the painting's dominant color. We can show the child the same painting executed in a radically different color scheme and discuss with him how he thinks the change in color affected the mood or expressive content of the work. Here is another example. Suppose we want to help the child recognize that in a painting everything counts and that a change in one part means a change in the whole. We can demonstrate this phenomenon by providing reproductions of paintings whose parts can be altered. What happens to a Rembrandt portrait when the color of the man's frock is changed from a dark blue to a light green? How is the structure of a Mondrian changed when one or more of its lines are removed? Devices such as these and others that await construction can provide the type of instructional support that teachers and students need to grasp the meaning of the concepts and principles we wish to help them understand. Yet such instructional materials have been absent from the classroom in part because the conception of art education that has been most pervasive historically made no provision for their employment. The Kettering Staff is attempting to develop these tools and to test them in the classroom.

Finally, accompanying each unit or lesson within a unit there are one or more suggested evaluation procedures. These evaluation materials are intended to provide the teacher with feedback regarding the effectiveness of the activities and materials that have been employed. In this area, too, there are a host of untapped possibilities.

The literature of art education is a virtual desert when it

comes to the area of evaluation. *Tests in Print,*[13] for example, the most extensive catalogue of tests published in the world, lists approximately 2,100 tests published in a variety of areas, but only 1.4 percent deal with the fine arts, and of these ten are in the visual arts; of the ten in the visual arts, five are art aptitude tests. Since adequate evaluation instruments are unavailable, we are attempting to construct some that will be useful for assessing the outcomes with which we are concerned. These evaluation tools accompany each unit in each of the three domains; thus there will be instruments designed to assess productive skills, instruments dealing with critical skills, and instruments assessing knowledge and understanding of art history. While some of the instruments will be of a verbal nature, by no means will all or even most of them be verbal. The recognition of style, period, expressive content, and the use of graphic and plastic skills do not require verbal responses. We hope that it will be possible to make a contribution to the field of educational measurement through the procedures and instruments we design in the course of our work in curriculum development.

When these four characteristics of our curriculum model— concepts, principles, objectives, and activities—are combined with the four characteristics identified earlier, the schema in Figure II emerges.

The schema in Figure II is far neater on paper than in practice. One problem we have encountered is that of determining more rigorously the optimal sequence of learning activities. How can we more rationally determine what should precede what? A second problem is that of finding ways to insure maximum transfer since we are not simply concerned with facilitating learning within the confines of our own materials. A third problem is one of developing materials that meet at least three criteria for classroom use: 1) it must be clear enough to be used by a teacher relatively untrained in art, 2) it must teach nontrivial content, and 3) it must be interesting and appropriate for the range of children for whom it is intended. These problems and a host of others both conceptual and administrative have

[13] Oscar Buros, ed., *Tests in Print* (New Jersey: Gryphon Press, 1961).

accompanied our efforts. Some of these problems can, I believe, yield to the impact of insightful research, and it is this third and final area to which I will now turn.

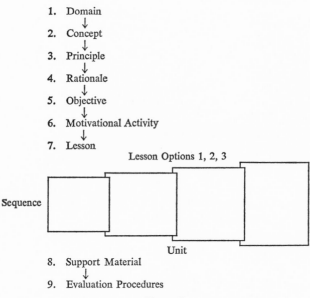

Curriculum Model for the Kettering Project

1. Domain
2. Concept
3. Principle
4. Rationale
5. Objective
6. Motivational Activity
7. Lesson

Lesson Options 1, 2, 3

Sequence

Unit

8. Support Material
9. Evaluation Procedures

Figure II

I think it is fair to say that educational research has not been a major factor in altering curricula in American schools. Changes in school programs have been influenced more by changes in political climate than by conclusions developed from systematic empirical inquiry. One of the reasons for this is due to the fact that education in America is a political creature and subject to winds of politics. But beyond this the questions that have been asked by researchers and the methods and controls they have employed have not, in the main, been of great use in guiding curriculum development or teaching. One of the most fruitful outcomes of the Kettering Project so far has been the fact that it has forced us to come to grips with the problems of curriculum construction, thereby highlighting theoretical needs in the field and the research that it demands.

For example, it has become clear that if we are going to be able to solve the problem of how to determine optimal curriculum sequence, we will need a taxonomy of learning in the visual arts. We will need to know if there is some sort of learning hierarchy involved in learning to respond aesthetically to two- and three-dimensional art. Should certain qualities, say the primary surface of the work, be attended to first, or should one begin with the secondary surface and discuss the work's expressive content? When should evaluation of the work enter into the picture, and what type of art should be selected for the initial instructional encounter? The development of a taxonomy would provide a format for the organization of the curriculum and would identify the competencies to be developed.

Work on the Project has also highlighted the need for the development of a technical language for the field of art education. We simply do not have in our professional discourse the degree of specificity that we need in order to communicate with precision. And we cannot get this precision simply by borrowing concepts from psychology. The concepts that will be of greatest use in art education are those that have been tailor-made to suit our particular concerns. We need a language that will illuminate and define operationally those key qualities that we are interested in studying. To develop such a language will require much more than filling a lexicon with new terms; it requires the exercise of insight and perceptivity so that the concepts formed have as their referents qualities and ideas of significance.

The Project has also underscored the need for new and better evaluation tools. Ideally these tools would be both diagnostic and evaluative. That is, we need instruments that would enable us to identify the salient features in a context of children, teachers, and community, and a set of instruments that would allow us to assess the effectiveness of a program designed to affect individuals in that context. To do this requires, of course, a theory of artistic learning useful for moving from diagnosis to prescription. We are a long way from such theory both in education generally and art education specifically.

Research dealing with the effects of alternative modes of curriculum organization is also greatly needed. The depth versus breadth study at Penn State [14] was an effort in that direction, but we need other studies in this area dealing with other variables. For example, what are the consequences of developing and employing a curriculum which moves gradually from a restricted range of qualities—say, white and black—to an unlimited range compared to a curriculum which introduces students to a full range of qualitative options initially?

What role does vocabulary play in sharpening the perception of aesthetic qualities? What is the cost of attending to visual elements in isolation from one another, and what are the assets? If you recall, the curriculum we are building is developed around single concepts that call the students' attention to particular qualities in the work of art. In one sense this does violence to a work that depends upon organic relationships in order to function. We recognize the risk we are taking but are gambling that the simplification of attention will pay off in the long run. As the student proceeds in the program he will encounter activities designed to facilitate the perception of multiple qualities in the work. If the relevant research studies were available, we would have more to go on than hunch.

We need research that will provide principles useful for determining the type and amount of guidance teachers need in order to be able to use curriculum materials effectively. One of the most frightening aspects of our work is the recognition that between the cup and the lip there is a chance of slip. Although we are attempting to make the materials we develop as lucid and as easy to use as possible, we are not sure how teachers will receive and use them. The teachers on the Project are not typical either in interest in art or in competency as professionals. And their closeness to the Project affords them insights that the elementary school teacher in the field will not have. We have precious little data to help us predict the type and quality of information teachers need to have for the curriculum to be used effectively.

[14] Kenneth R. Beittel, Edward Mattil et al., "The Effect of a 'Depth' vs. a 'Breadth' Method of Art Instruction at the Ninth Grade Level," *Studies in Art Education,* vol. 3, no. 1 (Fall 1961): 75–87.

Yet despite these problems, one gets the sense when building curriculum that one is working at the heart of the educational enterprise, for it is in the construction of the program that theory and practice meet most forcefully. Coping with the practical concerns of building an educational program for young children reveals strengths and weaknesses in theory more clearly than any form of educational task I know. And theorizing about artistic learning in the context of curriculum construction provides direction for its development.

I began this paper by comparing an older view of art education to one that has emerged with insistence and force during the past decade. While the persuasiveness and plausibility of these two views make them attractive, the field needs evidence dramatic enough to convince even the visually naive of the power and value of art in education. . . .

THE AESTHETIC AS A CONTEXT FOR GENERAL EDUCATION

Donald Arnstine

The term "aesthetic education" will be used very broadly here to indicate whatever conditions might increase sensitivity to the artistic features of the world and to the aesthetic qualities of experience and whatever might increase the understanding, appreciation, and enjoyment of those features and qualities. Aesthetic education (in the visual arts) is currently promoted in schools by setting aside a specific time of day for the study of works of art and for practice in a variety of art media and techniques. This arrangement makes it clear to the student that what is pursued in the art course is a quite different sort of affair from what is pursued in other school courses. I will try to show that art courses so organized are not likely to contribute very much to aesthetic education. The reasons why this is so stem from certain untenable assumptions about art and the aesthetic which are usually implicit in art courses. I will first make these assumptions explicit, then expose some of the difficulties one encounters in trying to maintain them, and finally, by suggesting some alternative conceptions about art and the aesthetic, show what the results might be for instruction throughout the school curriculum.

I

The curriculum is usually made up of a number of courses, one of which focuses on the practice and study of art. The very existence of an art course is predicated on certain beliefs assumed to be true. First, it is assumed that works of art have a special significance not possessed by other sorts of things. This significance is often called aesthetic quality, and it is thought to be valuable for students to become sensitive to it. Second, since it is assumed that aesthetic quality is to be found in works of art,

From *Studies in Art Education,* vol. 8, no. 1 (Autumn 1966): 13–22. Reprinted by permission of *Studies in Art Education* and the author.

it is also assumed that the other subjects of school study—e.g., science and history, language and mathematics—do not possess this quality. And third, since aesthetic quality is not a feature of what is studied elsewhere in school, it is assumed that an understanding and appreciation of such quality can be developed by exposing students to works of art and by affording them some practice in creating works of art.

Taken together, these assumptions provide a sort of justification for courses in the arts. In the visual arts they are variously called art, survey of art, art history, and art appreciation. What has been the result of sending students to these courses? It is not easy to tell, but one might suppose that when it rains on Sundays, well-intentioned parents take their children to the art museum instead of to the zoo. But if the arts of the mass media or of public architecture are indicators of the sensitivity of the public to aesthetic qualities, then great success could not be claimed for art education in schools. If art courses have not been very effective in fostering aesthetic education, the mischief can probably be traced to the assumptions on which those courses are based. How well do they stand up under investigation? We will examine each of them in turn.

1. The first assumption is that works of art have a special significance, usually called aesthetic quality, which is not possessed by other sorts of things. Experts disagree about what aesthetic quality might be,[1] but whatever it is, difficulties appear when we try to conceive it as uniquely the property of works of art. If it were such a property, we would be at a loss to tell how it came to reside in works of art alone. Art is created by men, but no one who watched an artist at work ever saw him put the aesthetic quality into his painting. How did it get there, then? Claims about the intervention of divine inspiration guiding the hand of the creator [2] only offer a mystery to explain a riddle.

[1] A broad sampling of such opinions may be found in *A Modern Book of Esthetics,* Melvin Rader, ed. (New York: Holt, 1952). Analyses of many of these opinions may be found in *Aesthetics and Language,* William Elton, ed. (Oxford: Blackwell, 1959).

[2] An analysis of this particular range of opinions may be found in Milton C. Nahm, *The Artist as Creator* (Baltimore: Johns Hopkins Press, 1956).

On the other hand, the notion that it is the viewer who *finds* aesthetic quality in art simply gives the viewer license to find aesthetic quality in anything at all he chooses.

The problems that appear whenever aesthetic qualities are treated as properties of particular things only recall earlier failures in assigning properties to objects. Whether a body possesses aesthetic quality is a far less determinable question than whether it possesses color or weight. Yet the fact that a body may under certain conditions appear to be any color at all or even weightless suggests that, far from being properties possessed by objects, color and weight are functions of the manner in which observers situated in a certain way relate to certain events. If color and weight are not permanent properties of objects, it is even less likely that something so diffuse as aesthetic quality is a property possessed by objects.

Before scales and spectroscopes are brought into the picture, let us admit that weight and color are most assuredly experienced by people. That a thing is heavy or of a certain color is immediately felt by someone who tries to lift it or distinguish it from other things. Weight and color, we might say, are qualities of the experience of people when they come into contact with certain features of the world. Only the need to be specific about weight and color and the consequent need to check our experience against the experience of others called forth the use of measuring instruments. The common use of those instruments probably gave rise to the usually harmless error of thinking that somehow the instruments "found" certain properties "within" the things being measured.[3]

The point is that if weight and color are qualities of experience, it makes at least as much sense to say that the aesthetic is a quality of experience, too. It is not, then, something possessed by objects—much less by certain objects called works of

[3] To assign a weight of five pounds to a package for the purpose of mailing it is harmless enough. But to assign a certain numerical score to a person for the purpose of teaching him has many dangers. For the person is then labeled as "having" just so much "creativity" or "intelligence." The expectations and teaching procedures respecting that person are then adjusted to his score, and attention is unduly drawn away from considering and adjusting the conditions under which the individual's performance resulted in that score.

art. But while experience is attended by the quality of weight when we try to lift something, it is not so easy to specify the conditions under which experience is marked by aesthetic quality. Since aesthetic education must remain a will-o'-the-wisp unless we have some understanding of the conditions for the appearance of aesthetic quality, I will make a rather sketchy attempt to indicate those conditions.

If the way people typically describe their reactions to art and to other things is any indication, we might hypothesize that aesthetic quality pervades experience when people find some intrinsic interest in the way in which perceptible elements of the world are related to one another. The term "perceptible elements" refers to what can be felt or heard or seen. To speak of the relations of perceptible elements to one another is to refer to what artists and critics sometimes call form. And to speak of intrinsic interest in this regard is to refer to the way in which the perception of form can call forth and hold attention on its own account. All this amounts to saying is that when one's attention or interest is attracted and held by his having perceived the relations of, for example, colored shapes to one another, then his experience is aesthetic in quality. This is not all that may occur when experience is aesthetic in quality, but it is minimally what must occur.

We are, of course, surrounded by sights and sounds, but we are not lovers of them all. Why is aesthetic quality relatively uncommon in our experience? An answer to this will further clarify some instructional implications for aesthetic education.

Our most common orientation to the world is a practical or an intellectual one. We are concerned about what it will do to us, or what we can do to it, or about what it really is, or how it got to be that way. Thus what we see or hear or feel is most usually related not to other perceptible things, but rather to these interests and concerns. Practical and intellectual concerns, then, often render us insensitive to form and block the appearance of aesthetic quality in experience.[4]

[4] The intrusion of these practical and intellectual concerns is what Edward Bullough called a loss of psychical distance. See "Psychical Distance as a Factor in Art and an Aesthetic Principle," *British Journal of Psychology,* vol. 5 (1912–13): 87–118.

Yet experience is not always aesthetic in quality, even when we deliberately attend to the formal relations of perceptible elements. This is simply because we do not always find those elements interesting in their own right. What may account for this is the fact that what is seen or heard may be perceived as regular or, on the other hand, as complex and disorganized. Perceived regularity is felt as monotony or boredom; perceived disorganization is felt as confusion. And what is boring and confusing seldom holds interest for very long. The appearance of aesthetic quality in experience, then, depends both on the posture taken by the perceiver and on the perceived features of what is before him.

With this in mind, we may consider again works of art. Without making any claim about their "possessing" aesthetic quality, we may grant their special significance. For they are usually made in such a way that the relations among their perceptible elements are neither oppressively regular nor confusingly chaotic. That is, works are art are organized in such a way as to facilitate the perception of form for a viewer who is willing to attend to the relations among the things he perceives. While this sort of facilitation is intended by artists, it is also true that a great many other man-made things are also intended by their makers to facilitate the perception of form. And it is equally true that a multitude of natural objects and events may be such as to make possible the perception of form. Aesthetic quality, then, may characterize virtually any sort of experience at all and is in no reasonable sense limited to confrontations with what are traditionally called works of art. The special significance that works of art do have lies in their capacity to emphasize and heighten the qualities of experience that we meet only accidentally when confronting other things and events in the world.[5] Aesthetic education which ignored works of art would thus lose a valuable resource. But aesthetic education which ignored examining the rest of the world in its artistic dimensions could only result in a sharp distortion of both art and the world.

[5] A systematic exposition of these views is to be found in John Dewey's *Art as Experience* (New York: Minton, Balch, 1934), esp. Chs. 1 and 5.

I shall return to this point later, but it is now time to examine the second assumption underlying art courses.

2. The existence of art courses is also predicated on the assumption that aesthetic qualities cannot be felt and enjoyed in connection with the other offerings in the curriculum. Put more concretely, it is assumed that science is science, and history is history, and neither one is art. But on the basis of what has been said, this is an oversimplification so gross that it distorts the truth of what is relevant. The world is full of many things and happenings, but none of these things is in itself "science" or "history." So far from denoting things *found* in the world, science and history rather connote particular *ways of dealing* with those things. A flower or the topic of yesterday's headlines are not *in themselves* science or history. They *are* just what they are. We may, of course, attend to them in different ways. Thus our experience of them may be dominantly practical or cognitive or aesthetic in quality. And depending on how we attend to flowers or to yesterday's events, we may treat them as agriculture or politics, as botany or history, or as art or drama.

Thus it makes no sense to say that the matters treated in the so-called academic courses are themselves *without* aesthetic quality. It is simply that aesthetic quality may not always characterize experience when things become matters of cognitive concern. And it is equally true that the things and events which are examined scientifically and historically may also figure in experience that is aesthetic in quality. It would never occur to scientists and historians to treat cognitively their respective subject matters *unless* they were found to be, at least initially, of interest on their own account.[6] And this is simply to say that the experience from which inquiry grows is itself not without some minimal aesthetic quality.

One could not attach too much importance to the implica-

---

[6] What is initially found as attractive or interesting may be pursued in respect to its artistic features; wherein the quality of experience is dominantly aesthetic. Or it may be pursued cognitively; in which case, the initial attraction stimulates curiosity that may eventuate in scientific or historical investigation. See Donald Arnstine, "Curiosity," *The Record—Teachers College,* vol. 67 (1966): 595–602.

tions of this for instruction in science and history. Some people find certain events in the world interesting and fascinating. When they become curious about the spatial and temporal connections of those events with other events, they may conduct inquiries that result in what is called science and history. Scientists and historians have good reasons for being interested in their disciplines, but do children in schools? Boredom and confusion are not uncommon reactions for students of science and history, but this should only be expected to result when students are required to pursue cognitively events that are neither interesting nor fascinating *to them*. To present the materials of scientific and historical study in ways that afford aesthetic quality to students' experience is simply to act on the obvious truth that people are likely to attend to matters that they find interesting. There are, of course, many ways to initiate learning. But to assume on a priori grounds that the materials of scientific and historical study are somehow *without* aesthetic quality or artistic worth is prematurely to abandon an effective resource for learning.

3. The third assumption underlying most art courses is that an understanding and appreciation of aesthetic qualities is to be developed by exposing students to works of art and by affording them some practice in creating works of art. As far as it goes, this assumption is justifiable, for we have seen that works of art can heighten and make more explicit the artistic features that are easily overlooked elsewhere in the world. But this assumption does not go far enough, for its exclusive emphasis on works of art may be as inimical to aesthetic education as it would be to ignore art works altogether.

Art, like science and history, is made by men. Like science and history, art is the result of treating things and events in the world in a certain way. And, as in the case of a scientific explanation and an historical generalization, it is a long way from the world, just as we perceive it, to a work of art. To cover this distance and thereby to find meaning in art (or in science or history) requires much time and effort at learning. It follows, then, that school children—who may respond with interest and enjoyment to much of what they find in the world—are as far removed from meaning in art as they are from meaning in science.

The instructional consequences of the need for deliberate education in order to understand art parallel those that follow from the need to educate people to understand science and history. We may present to students a table of atomic weights or a chronology of English kings. But if the tables and the chronologies have no immediate appeal, and if students have neither familiarity with nor an interest in the events of which the tables and the chronologies are the cognitive formulations, then they have no recourse but to memorize them. In a similar manner, we may confront students with a still life or a reproduction of the Parthenon. And if students neither find them immediately appealing nor have much familiarity with or interest in the things or events of which the still life and the Parthenon are artistic expressions, then they can be treated only as things to be recognized. This is, of course, the outcome of much art teaching, but recognition is no more closely related to the appearance of aesthetic quality in experience than memorization is related to understanding or inquiry.

The upshot of all this is that works of art can forward the aims of aesthetic education only insofar as they facilitate the appearance of aesthetic quality in the experience of students. Such works are more likely to do this the more they are artistic expressions of what school children already, and on other grounds, find interesting or personally significant. The same conclusion follows in the case of the creative activity assigned to students. The aims of aesthetic education are more likely to be forwarded the more possible it is for students to make things that embody what they think and feel about what is of interest and concern to them. The other side of this coin is equally important for aesthetic education. There are things in the world in which students are interested, but which themselves could not be called works of art. Yet those things, whether they be cars or clothing, can both become invested with greater meaning and serve as vehicles for the development of aesthetic sensitivity if they become the focus, in schools, of aesthetic analysis.

II

I have tried to show how a critical examination of some of the assumptions which underlie art teaching can result in the adoption of a quite different approach to aesthetic education. In light of this approach, we might briefly consider some of the directions aesthetic education might take.

As already indicated, formal instruction in art must be so organized as to make possible the appearance of aesthetic quality in students' experience. If students do not experience such qualities, they cannot have the slightest idea why they are enjoined to "take" art. In a utilitarian culture like ours, it is hard enough to arouse interest and support for art which is allegedly nonutilitarian. And, if the art presented to students and the art activities they pursue fail even to be interesting or enjoyable on their own account, students can only draw the conclusion that art is wholly without value.

The chances of making an aesthetic impact on students through the presentation of works of art will be greatly increased if those works render into artistic terms that in which students have an interest. In many cases this will reduce the emphasis put on classic exemplars of art and focus attention on more contemporary and even popular arts. These latter arts treat an enormously wide range of topics, many of which are within the range of students' experience. Little damage is risked by having a class consider a work which is not, and may never be, universally acclaimed as great. But to be drawn into the analysis of a work which throws a highlight on what already concerns students may not only broaden that concern but may increase sensitivity to aesthetic qualities as well. If the art of the connoisseurs is ever to be appreciated and enjoyed, this may be the only way to bring it about.[7]

[7] Expressing his distrust of the "classics" and the traditional liberal arts as means of developing taste and sensitivity in students, Bernard Mehl writes, ". . . it may well be that high culture á la Swinburne is not the saviour of taste but, rather like *Kitsch,* the sure way to make taste meaningless and phony." See "Come Back to High School, Huck, Sir." *The Record—Teachers College,* vol. 67 (1966): 449.

For the same reasons, works of art need not be the sole focus of the art course. The common objects of daily experience—from bathtubs to cooking pots to apartment houses—can serve as a focus of aesthetic analysis and creative activity. In considering such things, both artistic qualities and practical meanings come under investigation when the question is asked, "Does the thing *look* like the way it is intended to be *used?*" [8] Such a question put to a student who is, for example, designing a garment focuses critical attention both on artistic qualities and on social conventions which may be elaborated by those qualities. A question about the relation of form to function in the consideration of an apartment house may eventually reveal the intimate connection of aesthetic with political, sociological, and economic considerations.

The same considerations that hold for the kinds of art to which students are exposed also hold for the creative experiences in which students might engage. The isolated practice of skills may be appropriate for professionals, but public school students are not yet professionals, and most of them never will be. Greater sensitivity to the problems and satisfactions of creative artwork can result only from the opportunity to try putting into artistic terms what one feels about what is important to him. This is to suggest that having students dutifully and interminably render in pen and ink the teacher's still-life set-up may be just the wrong way to develop aesthetic sensitivity or enjoyment of art. If it be noted that Van Dyck may not have been very interested in his portrait subjects, it should also be remembered that Van Dyck, unlike public school students, was already a professional.

Aside from considerations about instruction in art courses, this conception of aesthetic education bears important implications for instruction throughout the school curriculum. The aesthetic is a quality of experience and may be cued by any sort of thing or event, and it is for this quality that experience is prized on its own account. It follows, then, that an artistically

[8] The import of this question is pursued with great insight in Rudolf Arnheim's "From Function to Expression," *Journal of Aesthetics and Art Criticism,* vol. 23 (1964): 29–41.

organized presentation of any subject matter in school becomes one important way of helping students find an interest in subjects of study and become sensitized to the reasons for the cognitive examination of those subjects. A thing or event presented in a dramatic or in an aesthetically problematic context is directly perceived as a topic of thought and inquiry. Seen the other way around, the cognitive development of what first appears in artistic form makes more meaningful subsequent confrontations with those forms and with other forms of art. A consideration of the paintings of Orozco, for example, may give point and meaning to a study of certain social and political problems. But at the same time, the study of those problems affords greater meaning to the paintings of Orozco.

Finally, this conception of aesthetic education suggests a transformation of the role of the art teacher (and, indeed, of teachers of all the arts). From his role (as perceived by many of his students and some of his colleagues) as a specialist in the teaching of esoteric skills and leisure-time enjoyments, the art teacher may become an aesthetic consultant for the entire school. Such a broadening of responsibilities is indicated by the notion that aesthetic quality may pervade the experience of any kind of thing or event.

Thus, in addition to teaching courses in art, the art teacher can function as an advisor on educational method. His experience and training have made him especially sensitive to perceptible qualities that attract and hold interest and to the perceptible features of things that are likely to cue boredom and confusion. The same things that make paintings and novels interesting or dull also make lectures, demonstrations, and textbooks interesting or dull. The art teacher is thus able to play a part in making more effective the teaching of all school studies.

At the same time, the art teacher, his room, and his materials may become resources available to all students in schools, whether or not they are enrolled in art. For it is to these resources that students might come who wish to explore artistically the things and events that are explored in other ways elsewhere, in or out of school. As an aesthetic consultant, the art teacher can both help increase the meaning and import of other school studies and at the same time increase sensitivity to aesthetic qualities and to art itself.

Objections have frequently been made to the integration of art with the rest of the school curriculum. It is said that art will be swallowed up and made a mere handmaiden of science and history.[9] But the objection either underestimates the impact of art or presupposes a poor choice of artistic materials. If the creation of an aesthetic context assists in the pursuit of cognitive studies, much has been gained. If that initial context was one of genuine artistic merit and one which was experienced aesthetically by students, then they can be depended upon to return to it again. If they do not, and the interest of students in the aesthetic disappears, it might be suspected that what initially aroused that interest did not merit further attention. Art presented as mere decoration and plastered incidentally onto a subject matter deserves all the contempt it has won.

So long as art and the sciences are competitors with each other, neither will compete very successfully with the arts of the juke box and the box office or the sciences of public relations, war, and space shots. These latter arts and sciences, however shallow or destructive they may often be, at least have appeal. But art studied in school that is disconnected from the natural and social events which are its chief source of meaning and significance is at best an esoteric amusement and at worst a bore. And history and sciences that are presented in isolation from the aspects of immediate aesthetic appeal which constitute the very motivation for their cognitive study are at best mere rituals to perform and at worst a form of persecution. What I am proposing is a conception of aesthetic education in which all studies are initiated and carried forward by what is of immediate appeal and in which sensitivity to artistic presentations themselves is maintained and developed, because what is presented is perceptibly significant to the world in which students live.

[9] See, for example, Thomas Munro's "Modern Art and Social Problems," *Art Education Today* (New York: Bureau of Publications, Teachers College, Columbia University, 1938), pp. 49–64.

FURTHER READING

Barkan, Manuel, Laura Chapman, and Evan Kern. *Guidelines: Curriculum Development for Aesthetic Education.* St. Ann, Mo.: Central Midwestern Regional Educational Laboratory, Inc. (CEMREL), 1970. The first publication of the major government-supported curriculum project in aesthetic education.

Bantock, G. H. "Education and the Literary Intelligence," in *Education and Values.* London: Faber and Faber, 1965, pp. 33–52.

Clark, Walter, Jr. "On the Role of Choice in Aesthetic Education," *Journal of Aesthetic Education,* vol. 2, no. 3 (July 1968): 79–92; reprinted in Jane R. Martin, ed., *Readings in the Philosophy of Education: A Study of Curriculum.* Boston: Allyn and Bacon, 1970, pp. 252–63.

Journal of Aesthetic Education, vol. 4, no. 2 (April 1970). A special issue devoted to "Curriculum and Aesthetic Education."

Karel, Leon C. "Allied Arts: An Approach to Aesthetic Education," *Journal of Aesthetic Education,* vol. 1, no. 2 (Autumn 1966): 109–19.

Katz, John S. "An Integrated Approach to the Teaching of Film and Literature," *The English Quarterly* (Winter 1969).

Leavis, F. R. *Education and the University.* London: Chatto & Windus, 1943. Also *Sewanee Review* (Autumn 1947): 586–609.

Marvel, Robert. "Constancy and Continuity in Music Education," in Robert W. Heller and Alice M. Rosenthal, eds., *The Child and the Articulated Curriculum.* Danville, Ill.: Interstate Press, 1968, pp. 59–67.

Schwadron, Abraham A. "Some Thoughts on Aesthetic Education," *Music Educators Journal,* vol. 56, no. 2 (October 1969): 35–36, 79–88.

Shoemaker, Francis. "Communication Arts in the Curriculum: Some Educational Implications of the Philosophy of Susanne Langer," *The Record—Teachers College,* vol. 51, no. 2 (November 1955): 111–19.

Wolff, R. J. "Visual Intelligence in General Education," in G. Kepes, ed., *The Education of Vision.* New York: Braziller, 1965, pp. 212–30.

TEACHING-LEARNING IN AESTHETIC EDUCATION

INTRODUCTION

The articles in this section are divided into those which deal with the problems of teaching-learning in the arts—literature, art, music, and film—and those which explore the aesthetic dimension of teaching-learning in general.

A. Teaching-Learning in the Arts

Writers in this section once again reflect the interest of educationists and aestheticians in the nature of value judgments and criticism. This renewed interest in valuing is not surprising. An era in doubt about substantive values will stimulate speculation about procedural matters. And when attention is centered on procedure it is soon discovered that the classification of canons of criticism in different domains goes to the heart of educational epistemology. As Mary Jane Aschner correctly points out, "Criticism is always carried on within a context. The context includes both the purposes and the relationships of the people involved as well as the subject matter under discussion. The context determines to a great extent what standards of judgment are appropriate to an actual discussion." This is part of Aschner's conclusion to a discussion that relates the manner in which secondary students in an English class were helped to an understanding of the ways ratings, reasons, and rules function in critical discourse.

Monroe C. Beardsley's essay explains the kinds of reasons that are relevant in assessing objects as works of art. After pointing out the difference between reasons which explain why an object is good (or bad) and reasons for merely supposing it to be good (or bad), Beardsley distinguishes one class of critical reasons—aesthetic objective reasons—the content of which features such qualities as a work's unity (or disunity), complexity (or simplicity), or human regional intensity (e.g., its "vitality" or "restlessness"). That is, practically all critical statements that are aesthetically relevant to evaluating works of art,

Beardsley believes, can be subsumed under statements about unity, complexity, and intensity. A work need not have all three qualities in high degree in order to deserve our praise. A work may be highly unified and intense yet not very complex; or a complex design may yield rich regional quality while apparently lacking a high degree of unity; etc. Beardsley's schema imposes order in an area where confusion has been notorious, and teachers and students might profit by testing his schema in the pedagogical manner of Aschner.

The essay "Appreciation as Percipience" by Harold Osborne contains perhaps the best explanation of the concept of appreciation available in current aesthetic writings. Osborne points out that the meaning of appreciation today is closely linked to the concept of aesthetic experience, and his characterization of this experience should do much to clarify both the components of this distinctive mode of attention and the problems of cultivating it.

The next selection, cognizant of the problems peculiar to the aesthetic domain, is an attempt to delineate a concept of criticism that is applicable to all of the arts. Perhaps the feature most worth singling out in Smith's approach is a realization of the need to ground a concept of aesthetic criticism not only in a special theory of aesthetic value but also in a curriculum theory believed pertinent to meeting the demands of value education. It has not been uncommon that the framing of prescriptions for aesthetic education has bypassed both aesthetic and educational theory. After setting forth the nature of the curriculum theory that serves as a context for the discussion of aesthetic education (not reprinted here), Smith explains aesthetic criticism as consisting of four analytically distinct yet overlapping phases: description, analysis, interpretation, and evaluation. He emphasizes, however, that the practicing of critical procedures is no guarantee that students will inevitably be brought to see all that is aesthetically relevant in a work of art. Aesthetic criticism is not an exact science and therefore its critical skills and procedures cannot be equated with a method which, when followed conscientiously, ensures success, i.e., a perfect judgment or appraisal.

The next four selections exemplify the work of criticism in the readings of literary texts, the analysis of musical meaning, the description of paintings, and the understanding of films.

James J. Zigerell proposes a method of explicating poems that moves from the explicit to the implicit, or from the part to the whole. It is not so much highly disciplined literary criticism that he propounds for literature education as "a method of close reading that opens the door on the aesthetic experience," which for Zigerell implies an art of contemplation that results in a distinctive type of pleasure. It might be noted that his "close reader" resembles Alan Purves's "sensitive reader" (see Section Two) while the emphasis on aesthetic experience seems to imply the type of value Beardsley says we properly take an interest in while criticizing objects as works of art. The moving from the explicit to the implicit suggests the spectrum of Smith's critical statements ranging from the cognitively secure (description) to the more indefinite (characterization and interpretation).

Asserting a close interconnection between analysis and intuition in the development of sensitive performance and appreciative listening, Jan LaRue presents an account of musical analysis that avoids the vices of overcompleteness and incompleteness. His discussion emphasizes that good analysis requires examination of stylistic elements (sound, harmony, rhythm, melody, formation) in not only the small but also in the middle and large dimensions of musical structure.

Virgil C. Aldrich provides an analysis of aesthetic perception and the possibility of teaching it in the context of visual art education. Extrapolating from Wittgenstein's notions of "seeing as" and "aspects," Aldrich suggests that any material thing can be perceptually realized either as a physical or as an aesthetic object. In perceptually realizing a thing as a physical object, we "observe" its physical space qualities which can be measured and quantified in the manner of science. In realizing an aesthetic object we "prehend" emergent aesthetic qualities. The point is that each way of seeing—either as physical object or as aesthetic object—is an educated way of looking, the development of which requires special modes of teaching and learning.

Aldrich's brief description of André Derain's *Still Life with a Jug* illustrates the nature of prehension, or the aesthetic way of seeing. The task becomes proportionately difficult as more complex works are the object of the critic's expressive portrayal.

How shall film be taught? And toward what end? William Arrowsmith's answers are to be understood not only in light of film's hypnotic power, but also in view of the professionalization of humanistic scholarship to such a degree that many humanists in universities no longer teach their subjects humanely. Arrowsmith challenges filmmakers and teachers to rescue general education, for only film and the other mass media, he believes, can perform "the great task of education in our times—the creation of a humane culture. . . ." It is suggested, however, that traditional and classic literature be set alongside film and engage it in a form of crucial cultural rivalry. In brief, film can do today what tragedy did for fifth-century Athens; it can combine art and entertainment in the higher effort of education.

B. The Aesthetic Dimension of Education

The essays in this section treat the aesthetic in education from perspectives that encompass the abstract disciplines or the generic processes of teaching-learning in general.

This latter approach is characteristic of Max Black's essay which shows that there is an important parallel in the relation of the artist to his material and in the learner's to his, whatever the subject. The aspect of the relationship stressed is the disciplinary value of experiencing the tension between materials (organized fields of knowledge that have to be organized anew by students) and a certain mastery and appreciation of materials. Although, Black emphasizes, the conditions for experiencing this tension do not satisfy the conditions for full aesthetic experience, there can nonetheless be a sense of conflict, resistance, and excitement similar to the artist's engagement. The "good learner," moreover, enjoys such tension.

Kenneth R. Conklin's provocative essay ranges further afield than Black's and attempts to show that the aesthetic is far more pervasive in epistemology and education than is commonly thought. Conklin's arguments, relying heavily on the writings of mathematicians themselves, appear to make a convincing case for his claims. Noteworthy, however, is the admission early in the essay that no attempt will be made to present a definitive characterization of aesthetic experience, an omission that does not preclude such later assertions as "the role of intuition in mathematical discovery is closely similar to the role of aesthetic sensitivity in artistic creation and appreciation," "There can be no doubt that mathematical discovery is an aesthetic experience of the most profound kind," and that "Following a single proof or studying a whole branch of mathematics provides an aesthetic experience closely similar to reading a novel or seeing a dramatic performance. . . ." Many aestheticians and aesthetic educators would not go this far, but at least it can be said that Conklin has stated his ideas clearly enough to be defended or criticized.

Countering the tendency to draw misleading parallels between the arts and teaching, the last two essays by Maxine Greene and R. A. Smith stress some of the important differences between art and teaching.

A. TEACHING-LEARNING IN THE ARTS

TEACHING THE ANATOMY OF CRITICISM

Mary Jane Aschner

The responsibility for teaching criticism—the art of intelligent appraisal—seems to be one willingly assumed by a growing number of teachers. At adolescence, students may be presumed to have reached that point of maturation at which certain intellectual skills, among them the capacity to exercise sound critical judgment, are ready for more direct cultivation.

High school students, and their teachers with them, are daily engaged in criticism. "Does *Moby Dick* present a better character study than *Stella Dallas?*" is a question calling for criticism in the English class. At the jukebox in the student lounge we hear, "I like Lena Horne's record of 'Love Me or Leave Me' better than Doris Day's." "Your swing is too choppy, Joe," says the gymnasium teacher. In a student council session someone proposes, "I move we begin an honor study hall." In a social studies class someone asks, "Was Dulles wise in taking sides with Portugal at Geneva?" Back and forth fly the questions and the judgments—in the classroom and out of it, in school and out of school. Such is the domain of criticism.

A Definition of Criticism

Criticism, as it will be discussed here, is a verbally expressed act of evaluation. A person expresses an opinion or a preference, an acceptance or a rejection of something. He will usually, if called upon, give reasons for his opinion. If these reasons are then brought into question, he may be called upon to state the criteria or standards of judgment upon which he has based his appraisal.

Criticism also involves a general procedure followed by an individual whenever he states and supports an opinion or conclusion. Whether he judges the merits of a novel, appraises the

From *The School Review,* vol. 64, no. 7 (October 1956): 317–22. Reprinted by permission of *The School Review* and the author.

soundness of a political argument, or merely tells why he likes raw rutabagas, the individual is engaged in criticism. As the term is used here, criticism carries no derogatory weight as in, "Jones criticizes his wife in public." A criticism can express praise as well as blame, for it is an act or process of assessment and evaluation. Thus literary criticism presupposes merely evaluation, and not necessarily the favorable or the unfavorable judgment of the cri

It is suggested here that high school students can learn certain general principles of criticism and can learn to apply them in any field of discourse where evaluations are expressed and explained. At the present stage of research such a proposition is necessarily viewed as a hypothesis subject to test and not as a stated claim. However, recent exploratory work with a junior English class at the University High School of the University of Illinois suggests that rigorous testing of the hypothesis in the classroom may provide its most convincing support.

A Recent Exploration in the Teaching of Criticism

The following is a brief account of what took place during the exploratory work mentioned above. The activities to be described were purely exploratory and were not conducted under experimental conditions. The writer made merely a first attempt to put into practice an idea that looked promising.

To launch the class upon a critical discussion, it was thought important to select a topic which would arouse active interest, stimulate general participation among boys and girls alike, and provide a common ground for conversation among students and between students and teacher. The range of abilities among students in the class would be found comparable to that in any public school. For our purposes a discussion of current jukebox stars and hit records proved to be "a natural."

We began by recording on the blackboard a number of opinions expressed by students as the discussion got under way. One such opinion was, "Rosemary Clooney is a good singer of commercial-type popular ballads." Next, under each statement of an opinion we listed the "reasons why" offered by the individual in support of his views. Under the statement about Rosemary Clooney three reasons were listed: (1) "She has a warm, womanly voice." (2) "Her songs are put across with novel techniques of accompaniment." (3) "Her voice is well suited to commercial ballad-type songs." The discussion was then pursued further by asking why these reasons were offered in support of the opinion about Rosemary Clooney. This resulted in the following series of statements: (1) "A singer's voice must appeal to most people's feelings." (2) "The piece must have some element of novelty in it." (3) "The voice and the song must be well matched."

Up to this point the discussion had been purely evaluative. We had gone through three distinct steps in expressing our evaluations. In the first step we had expressed and recorded statements of opinion, such as, "Rosemary Clooney is a good singer of commercial-type popular ballads." Then we had recorded statements expressing reasons for these opinions, for example, "She has a warm, womanly voice." Finally, we had listed statements made in support of the reasons. "A singer's voice must appeal to most people's feelings" is an example of the latter.

Now the discussion moved into a second phase, one of analysis. The teacher asked the students to examine the three kinds of statements on the board and to tell what "jobs" they had been given to do. After some discussion it was decided that each kind of statement had its own job to do, although they all "went together" somehow. Statements expressing opinions and preferences we decided to call "ratings"; for they were used to tell how the speaker rated something—whether he rated a song as a good one or a bad one, and so on. It was understood that rating statements are made, not to describe something, but to express how somebody is judging some matter. Next, the students decided that the "reasons" did the job of telling why this or that particular song or singer was assigned the rating expressed in the rating statement. They were then asked to see if there was any difference between the reasons and the "reasons for the reasons," as the latter were first called. After some speculation two distinctions were drawn: (1) the "reasons for the reasons" seemed to be working as rules by which ratings were assigned to particular singers or records; (2) the reasons themselves did the job of showing how someone fitted the rule to the particular case.

At this stage someone suggested that "rules are for measuring things." So the teacher then asked whether the same rule could be used to make a rating of some other singer than Rosemary Clooney. "What about Georgia Gibbs? Can she sing commercial ballads?"

"No!" came the emphatic answer. "She's a belter—she sings the rock-and-roll stuff!"

"Well, then, what about this rule that 'a voice must appeal to most people's feelings'?" the teacher asked.

It wasn't long before someone made the observation, "You can use the same rule to show why Georgia Gibbs can't sing commercial ballads. She doesn't have the right kind of voice. She doesn't make you feel all emotional the way Rosemary Clooney does." Further discussion produced agreement that the same rule could be used to rate one singer favorably and another singer unfavorably with respect to some common characteristic —in this case, the matter of emotional appeal in voice quality. It was a simple thing to go on to the observation that the same rule could be applied to any number of cases and thus be used to rate some singers favorably and other singers unfavorably as interpreters of the commercial ballad.

Before closing the discussion, we went back over the ground we had covered, making clear the distinctions we had drawn among ratings, reasons, and rules. The teacher emphasized the general character of the "rules," their wide applicability to all sorts of cases, and their function as measuring rods or standards for giving ratings. The "tailoring" function of reasons was also emphasized, to bring home their peculiar role in critical discussions: that cf fitting the rule to the case at hand. Finally, we observed that we had done two kinds of things. First, we had expressed and recorded our appraisals of certain singers and pieces of music in the field of "pops" music. Second, we had then turned around and analyzed the jobs that our statements had been given to do and how these statements worked together.

Thus ended the first discussion and the first adventure of the class into the domain of criticism.

It is to be noted that at no time in this initial discussion did the teacher introduce any strange or unfamiliar terminology. Toward the end of the conversation we began to use the word *standards* as a familiar synonym for what we had been calling "rules." It is also to be noted that, although the students were fully aware that the second phase of the discussion represented a different activity from the one in which they were first engaged, they seemed to have no difficulty in carrying on this analysis of their own statements and of the relations holding among them.

The discussion just reported proved a useful means for engaging students in criticism and in the analysis of the critical process. It was perhaps even more useful as a common point of reference when we moved into areas of study where the critical judgments of people other than ourselves would be examined.

Work in junior English soon brought us to a study of that most revered document of American letters, the Declaration of Independence. First we examined it for the grace and elegance of its language, for its clarity and precision of statement. Then we decided to trace the line of argument used in the Declaration of Independence to see what made it such a powerful and convincing document. Here we referred back to the earlier discussion about ratings, reasons, and rules. Were there any ratings expressed in the Declaration of Independence? Were there any reasons given for them? Were there any rules or standards upon which ratings and reasons might be based? The students, in a questing frame of mind, began a thoughtful analysis of this great American document. Space limits prohibit the reproduction of students' written and oral work in which they recorded their analysis of the argument of the Declaration of Independence. However, student responses were judged to be more than satisfactory as a whole, and because of these first "results" the writer was encouraged to carry the exploration further.

It may be asked whether students were at any point permitted merely to accept some rules or standards of judgment uncritically or whether their attention was turned to the critical evaluation of the rules themselves. The answer is that, in the beginning, the students' attention was centered upon the *function* of rules and their *relations* to other phases of evaluation rather than upon the substance or content of the rules. It was felt that, once students gained some notion of how rules are used in making judgments, they would be in a better position to evaluate rules themselves.

At this stage the class was prepared to move for the first time into a direct study of criticism in practice. They would be asked to study a variety of book reviews by literary critics; their task would be to discern the ratings, reasons, and rules used by these critics in appraising the books they reviewed. In preparation for this step, two points left untouched in earlier discussions were brought out. The first point involved giving a name to what we had been doing. We referred back to the "jukebox discussion" and gave the name of *criticism* to the activity of expressing and explaining ratings assigned to various matters.

The second point brought out was that rules are not something fixed and final, to be followed or rejected blindly. Most rules, it was said, can be seen as the product of agreement among people. The more people who are found to agree, for example, that honesty is the best policy, the more strongly will this notion act as a rule to govern their behavior in matters of telling the truth. It was also pointed out that sometimes persons have their own rules, especially in matters of personal tastes and preferences. However, these "private" rules were seen to be those most often challenged and unfavorably criticized, especially if individuals use them without considering the tastes and feelings of others.

Finally, the students heard a brief description of the profession of criticism as it is practiced in the arts today. The fact was restated that criticism is a process or an activity which people carry on by oral or written discussion. It was stressed also that criticism is an act of judging or rating. Thus a critic might either praise or condemn a book, but in either case he would be acting as a critic.

The students were then sent to the Sunday book-review sections of the *New York Times*. Each was instructed to select a

major review from a recent issue. He was then to write a report
of the way the writer of the review made a criticism of his subject. The admonition was given more than once, "Remember,
your task is to tell about the ratings, reasons, and rules that
you think the critic used in his review. You are not asked to
tell about the book he is reviewing except to show *how* he
criticized it in his review." This was not an easy assignment; it
required the student to examine the critical elements of a book
review without getting involved in a description of its substance.

Results were again encouraging, indicating in most cases that
the students had grasped the idea that criticisms involve ratings,
reasons, and rules. They were able to point out these features
in the reviews they had studied. But two fairly common shortcomings cropped up, neither of which would be a surprise to
teachers. In the first place, in cases where the critic failed to
state explicitly some standard or rule of judgment that he was
using (and this is most often the case), students did not venture
their own inferences as to what standards seemed to be suggested in the ratings and reasons given in the review. The other
weakness revealed in the papers was the tendency to get involved with the critic in his review—to applaud his opinions
and to predict that the book was probably a good book if the
critic had praised it highly. This tendency to agree with the
critics indicated where, in future work along these lines, teaching would be necessary if students were to see criticism as a
process which can be applied, upon appropriate occasions, to
criticism itself.

The Process of Teaching Criticism

The first step in teaching students how to make sound evaluations involves acquainting them with the threefold process by
which judgments are expressed and explained. Once students
understand the distinction between ratings, reasons, and rules,
and their relations to one another in the evaluative process, then
it is time to examine more directly the bases of evaluation, the
standards of judgment; for an understanding of what criticism
is and how it is carried on by no means guarantees that an

individual will use appropriate and sound criteria in his evaluations.

The next step in training students in the judgmental skills involves two ways of studying the rules or standards. First, the standards should be studied for the way they govern preferences. The standards that a person holds will cause him to judge a matter in a certain way. Actions taken or opinions expressed upon the basis of certain standards often have serious consequences. The causal relation holding between a person's principles of evaluation and the actions he may take or the opinions he is likely to express is one that students should be led early to understand. Once they sense the weight of consequences that can follow from basing an action or an opinion upon a given criterion of judgment, students are likely to recognize more readily the crucial importance of grounding judgments upon appropriate, well-founded standards.

In the second way to study rules or standards, students should confront questions of what are "good" and "poor" standards for judging different matters. Students should not be permitted to adopt the absurd notion that, since anything can be criticized, there is no way of establishing one standard of judgment as better than another. It is true that anything can be criticized. It is equally true that rules and standards themselves are man-made to serve man's purposes and are therefore fallible. Students have a right to understand that such is the case. But then to deny, or even to fail to insist, that there are good standards as well as poor ones is to deny all that man has struggled for in his search for knowledge and the good life. Even worse, it is to foster sophomoric cynicism and intellectual irresponsibility— both harbingers of social and moral chaos.

Students should be brought to a thoughtful examination of standards always within a particular *context* of judgment. Here "context" means more than just the subject matter or domain of discussion in which criticism is carried on. The context of discussion includes not only the subject discussed but also the purposes for which evaluation is being made. A consideration of the purposes must necessarily involve the roles and relationships among the individuals participating in the discussion.

These considerations are important because they determine what criteria of judgment will be appropriate to a given criticism. For example, in critical discussions of literature, it may at one time be the purpose to rate a work for its status as great literature. At another time a book may be appraised as an expression of the culture or era in which it was written. Upon another occasion someone may be recommending a book for vacation reading or as a sure-fire soporific. Clearly, the criteria by which a book is judged to be of great or miserable literary quality are of a different order from the criteria by which a book is rated a good or a poor document of the era whence it sprang.

In social studies, science, and English classes, the purposes for which a critical discussion is conducted will determine what criteria are appropriate to the situation. Are students formulating their own principles of procedure for a given task? Are they learning through critical discussion what principles of scientific experimentation have been found most reliable? Or are they learning criteria for assessing the qualities of statesmanship? The purposes of both students and teachers always enter into determinations of what criteria are to be used in making criticisms. But, by virtue of the teacher's role, his purposes must often determine what criteria are to be used as the basis of criticism in a class discussion; for the teacher is, or should be, the arbiter of what educational values are to be realized through the conduct of any critical discussion in his classroom.

Concluding Remarks

Some of the following points have been mentioned or are implied in the foregoing discussion. However, in conclusion it may be helpful to state them as related groups of explicit understandings toward which students should be guided in their study of criticism.

1. Criticism is an act of evaluation verbally expressed. It presupposes neither unfavorable nor favorable judgment. It is carried on by the use of three types of statements, each repre-

senting a distinct phase of the critical process. In discourse, standards are usually left implicit or unexpressed unless they are called for. Ratings and reasons should be examined for standards which seem to be implicit in them.

2. Criticism is an instrument for clarification and understanding as well as one of appraisal. Persons who are familiar with the critical process and are aware of the role that standards play in expressions of opinion possess the means by which to discover whether differences of opinion are "merely verbal" or whether they arise because disputants are using different standards of judgment.

3. Criticism is a general process, one that can be carried on profitably in a great variety of situations. Standards are also general. The same standard can be used to reject, as well as to accept, given items under appraisal. With respect to some questions, a single standard can be applied to great numbers and varieties of cases.

4. Criticism is always carried on within a context. The context includes both the purposes and the relationships of the people involved as well as the subject matter under discussion. The context determines to a great extent what standards of judgment are appropriate to a critical discussion.

5. Criticism itself can, and often should, be criticized. This does not mean that any one set of standards is as good as any other set. There are both good and poor standards of judgment; there are means for establishing their reliability. The importance of basing opinions and actions upon appropriate and well-founded standards is seen in the consequences of their use.

THE CLASSIFICATION OF CRITICAL REASONS

Monroe C. Beardsley

When a critic makes a value judgment about a work of art, he is generally expected to give reasons for it—not necessarily a conclusive argument, but at least an indication of the main grounds on which his judgment rests. Without the reasons, the judgment is dogmatic, and also uninformative: it is hard to tell how much is being asserted in "This painting is quite good," unless we understand why it is being asserted.

These reasons offered by critics (or "critical reasons") are, of course, extremely varied. Here is a small sampling:

> [On Haydn's *Creation*] "The work can be praised uncondi-
> tionally for its boldness, originality, and unified conception.
> But what remains so remarkable in this day and age is its
> over-all spirit of joy, to which a serene religious faith, a love
> of this world and a sense of drama contribute" (Raymond
> Ericson).
> [On the finale of Bruckner's Fifth Symphony] "Perhaps this
> movement is the greatest of all symphonic finales" because "It
> is a vision of apocalyptic splendor such as no other composer,
> in my experience, has ever painted" (Winthrop Sargeant).
> [On a novel by Max Frisch] "Rarely has a provocative idea
> been spoiled more efficiently by excessive detail and over-deco-
> ration" (Richard Plant).
> [On a motion picture of Pasolini's] "The sleeper of the year
> is a bone bare, simple, and convincingly honest treatment of
> the life of Jesus, *The Gospel According to St. Matthew*"
> (Ernest Schier).
> [On Edvard Munch's lithograph and oil painting *The Cry*]
> "This cry of terror lives in most of Munch's pictures. But I
> have seen faces like this in life—in the concentration camp
> of Dachau. . . . With "The Cry," the Age of Anxiety found
> its first and perhaps to this very day, its unmatched expres-
> sion" (Alfred Werner).

Probably the first question that will occur to a philosopher who looks over such a list of reasons is this: Which of them are

From the *Journal of Aesthetic Education*, vol. 2, no. 3 (July 1968): 55–63. Reprinted by permission of the *Journal* and the author.

relevant? That is, which of them really are grounds on which the judgment can legitimately and defensibly be based? Just because *The Cry* is an "unmatched expression" of the Age of Anxiety, does that make it a good painting (or lithograph)? What reasons are there for supposing that this reason counts in favor of the painting?

Many large and difficult issues in aesthetics will loom ahead whenever this line of inquiry is pursued very far—too many to cope with here. The task can be somewhat simplified and clarified, however, if we sort these issues into two main categories with the help of an important distinction having to do with reasons. There are *reasons why* something is a good work of art (or a poor one), and *reasons for supposing that* something is a good work of art (or a poor one); in other words, there are reasons that serve to explain why the work of art is good or poor, and reasons that constitute logical support for a belief that the work of art is good or poor. That these are not the same can easily be shown. If Haydn's *Creation* has a "unified conception," that would help to explain why it is a good musical composition. On the other hand, if we know that a large-scale musical work was composed by Haydn in his mature years, this fact is in itself a reason to believe that the work is probably very good, even though we have not yet heard it; but this fact does not provide any explanation of its goodness—being composed by Haydn is not one of the things that is good about the work.

One way of setting aside some of the reasons offered by critics as irrelevant to the value judgment they accompany would then be to insist that relevant critical reasons (or critical reasons in a strict sense) be those that are reasons in both of the senses just distinguished. A relevant reason is one that provides support to the value judgment for which it is a reason and also helps to explain why the judgment is true. If the critic judges that a novel is poor, or at least less good than some other novel with which he compares it, and gives as one reason that there is a great deal of "detail" and "decoration," then this reason not only helps to lower our estimate of the work's value but also points out part of what is wrong with it.

If we insist that a relevant critical reason must have both of these functions, it follows that in order to be relevant, reasons must be statements about the work itself, either descriptive statements about its parts or internal relations (including its form and regional qualities) or interpretive statements about its "meaning" (taking this term loosely enough to include such things as what it represents, symbolizes, signifies, expresses, says, etc.). For statements about external matters, although they may serve as indications of probable goodness or poorness, do not explain that goodness or poorness by telling us what in the work itself makes it good or poor.

The class of relevant critical reasons in the strict sense—those that are both explanations and grounds—itself contains an enormous variety, the range of which is only barely hinted at in the examples above, though it will be familiar to those who have thought seriously about any of the arts. A miscellaneous collection like this is a challenge to the philosophical aesthetician, who is bound to inquire whether the items cannot be arranged in certain basic and illuminating categories, and whether there is not a small set of principles at work here. Some aestheticians are very dubious about this suggestion: they say that by its very nature, art criticism is too complicated and too loose for any such attempt at classification to be feasible. But why not see how far we can go, if we are careful not to force reasons into categories where they don't fit? If it should in fact turn out to be the case (astonishingly, perhaps) that all relevant critical reasons in the strict sense fall into a few basic categories, that would not be without interest, and it might suggest further lines of inquiry of considerable philosophic importance.

One such classification I have proposed in Chapter 11 of my book *Aesthetics: Problems in the Philosophy of Criticism*.[1] My procedure for constructing it is based on the observation that critical reasons are not all on the same level—that some are subordinate to others. We ask the critic, for example, "What makes the Max Frisch novel so poor?" He replies, "Among other things, excessive detail." We ask again, "What is so bad

[1] New York: Harcourt, Brace, and World, 1958.

about the detail? Why is it excessive? How does it help to make the work poor?" If he is cooperative, the critic may reply once more: "The detail is excessive because it distracts the reader from those elements in the work (elements of plot, perhaps) that would otherwise give it a fairly high degree of unity," or perhaps, "The detail is excessive because it dissipates what would otherwise be strong dramatic and emotional qualities of the work." So it seems that the objectionableness of the detail is itself explained by an appeal to a more fundamental and general principle: that unity is desirable in the work, or that intensity of regional quality is desirable in the work.

If we press further, however, and ask the critic why greater unity would help to make the work a better one, this question, too, deserves an answer, but it would have to be of a quite different sort. In explaining why excessive detail and over-decoration are objectionable, the critic appeals to other features of the work itself, which these features either increase or diminish. But what makes unity desirable is not what it does to other features of the work; thus, as far as the work itself is concerned, unity is a basic criterion. The fine arts critic could reasonably say that a particular group of shapes and colors in a painting is good because it creates a very subtle balance, and he could also say that balance is good because it is one way of unifying the painting; but he could not say that unity in a painting is a good thing because it makes the painting contain these particular shapes and colors.

In my view, there are exactly three basic criteria that are appealed to in relevant critical reasons, and all of the other features of works of art that are appealed to in such reasons are subordinate to these, or can be subsumed under them. There is unity, which is specifically mentioned in connection with Haydn's *Creation* and presupposed in the criticism of the Max Frisch novel. There is complexity, which I think is part of what Winthrop Sargeant admires in Bruckner's Fifth. (Insofar as the simplicity of Pasolini's film is regarded as a positive merit, I take it not as a low degree of complexity but as absence of "excessive detail and overdecoration.") And there is intensity of regional quality: the "over-all spirit of joy" in Haydn, the "cry of terror" in Edvard Munch.

Any such simplifying scheme as this ought to arouse immediate skepticism and protest. It is obviously too neat to be correct. It is tempting, no doubt, because it really does embrace and tidy up a very large number of critical reasons, and it enables us to distinguish the relevant ones from the irrelevant ones on a fairly clear principle. But certainly it needs to be examined and tested severely before it can be accepted.

Some searching questions can be asked about the three proposed criteria of judgment. First, are they sufficiently clear? Some aestheticians who have considered unity, for example, have expressed doubt (1) that it has a sufficiently well-defined meaning to be used in this highly general way, and (2) that it has the same meaning across the arts (the same, that is, for painting as for poetry or music). I do not know how to prove that I am right in rejecting both of these doubts. We can surely find examples of pairs of paintings or prints where it is perfectly evident that one is more unified than the other. And even though what tends to unify a painting is, of course, not identical to what tends to unify a poem or a musical composition, as far as I can tell I mean the same thing when I say that one poem is more unified than another or when I say that one painting is more unified than another.

I do not mean to imply, of course, that we can estimate infallibly the degree to which a basic aesthetic property (such as unity) is present in a particular painting. When we look at a painting and it fails to hang together, that may be because we are tired, or our perceptions are dulled by an adverse mood, or we are not attending closely enough, or we have had too little acquaintance with works of that sort. A negative conclusion must usually be somewhat tentative and rebuttable; for it may well be that if later we come to the painting again, in a more serene mood, with sharper faculties, and with greater willingness to give in to whatever the painting wishes to do to us, we may find that in fact it has a tight though subtle unity that is perfectly apparent to the prepared eye. But if we return again and again, under what we take to be the most favorable conditions, and it still looks incoherent, we have reasonable grounds for concluding that probably the painting cannot be seen as unified.

Even a positive conclusion may not be final. The painting may on one occasion fleetingly appear to us as unified. But suppose that unity turns out not to be a stable property—that it is hard to capture and to hold. Then we may decide that we were the victims of an illusion. The judgment of unity ultimately has to be based on a gestalt perception—on taking in the regional qualities and dominant patterns of the whole. But such perceptions can always be checked by analysis—by which I mean simply the minute examination of the parts of the work and their relationships with one another. A prima facie description of the work as having unity or disunity to some degree does have this kind of check: that it should hold up under analysis. For the perception that occurs after analysis may correct the earlier one: it may turn out that we have overlooked some parts or some internal relationships that, when taken into account in perception, make the work more unified—or less unified—than it at first appeared.

Second, are the three basic criteria really basic? One of the marks of being basic (as I have said) is that the question "Why is X good (or poor) in the work?" seems to come to a turning-point in them, for at this point it takes one outside the work itself. Another mark is that the subordinate reasons are contextually limited. That is, the features they allude to may be desirable in some works but not necessarily in all. A particular cluster of shapes and colors may work well in one setting but badly in another; balance is not necessarily always a good thing; and details that would be excessive in one novel might not be excessive in another. But the basic criteria, I would claim, are all one-way. Unity, complexity, and intensity of regional quality never count against a work of art (we cannot say the painting is good because its regional quality is so insipid, or because it is so elementary a design, or because it falls apart into messiness), but always count in favor of it, to the extent to which they are present. The example of simplicity, which I mentioned earlier, might seem to refute at least part of this claim; but it seems to me that whenever simplicity is held up as a desirable feature, either it is not strictly simplicity (the opposite of complexity) that is referred to, but some sort of unity, or it is not the simplicity that is admired, but the intensity of some regional quality that happens to be obtainable in this case only by accepting simplicity.

Third, are the three proposed criteria really adequate to cover the entire range of relevant critical reasons? Consider "boldness" or "originality," for example, which are cited in the praise of Haydn's *Creation.* "Boldness" could no doubt benefit from further clarification: it could refer to a regional quality of the work, or it could refer in a somewhat roundabout way to originality (perhaps Haydn was bold to try out certain hitherto unheard of, or at least unfamiliar, ideas in it). But originality does not seem to fit under the three basic criteria. Or consider the description of Pasolini's film as "convincingly honest." Honesty, again, might be a certain quality of the work —absence of sentimentality and melodrama, etc. But it might be a correspondence between the film itself and the actual feelings of the filmmaker (even though he is a communist, he could still have certain feelings about this story, which he sincerely puts into his work); and honesty in that sense, like sincerity, does not seem relevant to unity or complexity or intensity of regional quality.

Criteria like originality and sincerity I have already ruled out of the class of relevant critical reasons by making the rule that a relevant critical reason must not only support the critical judgment but also (at least partially) explain why the judgment is true. But here, of course, is a serious aesthetic issue, since many critics regard originality and sincerity as highly relevant reasons. They would consider me wholly arbitrary in ruling them out.

This challenge leads into the fourth question I intend to raise here: What good (philosophical) reason is there for holding that any particular (critical) reason is relevant or irrelevant to the judgment of a particular work? If someone says that the Bruckner Fifth is great because it presents a "vision of apocalyptic splendor," there are always two questions we can ask. First, is it true that the work presents such a vision? (Granted that the music is splendid, and therefore splendor can be heard in it, how do we know that it is "apocalyptic?")

Second, if the statement is true, why is it a ground for saying that the work is great? (How does apocalypticity make the music good?) To ask a question of the second sort is to plunge us into some of the hardest questions about the arts and art criticism. Without pretending to dispose of them, I want at least to face up to them.

Anything so complex as a work of art can usually be regarded from more than one point of view. It is (let us say) a visual design, an example of skilled workmanship, a source of income for the painter and (even more) for the art dealer, a political document, an excellent example of a certain historical style, and so forth. And one very broad way of sorting out all the various remarks that people might want to make about the painting is to say that they are made from different points of view: economic, or art-historical, or political, or other. Then how are we to distinguish between one point of view and another? According to some philosophers, one point of view can be distinguished from another only in terms of the sort of reason given: thus if one says that the painting is costly, we can classify his point of view as economic; and if another says that the painting is a good example of mannerism, we can classify his point of view as that of the art historian. But in that case, we could not use points of view to help us sort out the reasons, or we would be going in a circle. I would prefer to distinguish between one point of view and another in terms of a kind of value that one might take an interest in: market value or art-historical value (that is, usefulness in illuminating some phase of art history).

Speaking very broadly (and for some purposes too sweepingly), the various kinds of value that may be found in works of art can be classified under three headings. There is cognitive value (of which art-historical value would be a species). We often speak well of works of art if they contribute in some way to our knowledge. Perhaps Winthrop Sargeant is suggesting that Bruckner gives us a kind of insight into the nature of apocalypses, and perhaps Alfred Werner is suggesting that Munch gives us a better understanding of our Age of Anxiety. In any case, claims like these are frequently made, and if they are valid claims, then they certainly do show that the work is worth creating and preserving. But I do not think they are relevant reasons for saying that the work is good music or good painting—only that it is good as religious intuition or a social document.

Next there is what might be called moral and social value. Someone might follow Winthrop Sargeant's suggestion (and his remarks elsewhere) by saying that Bruckner's music is religiously significant, and under suitable circumstances can strengthen religious faith (assuming that this is desirable). Someone else might praise Pasolini's film because it can produce moral uplift or strengthen character. And, quite apart from whether or not "The Cry" is a good painting, it may be of great social worth as an "unmatched expression," a minatory reminder, of the ills of our age. But again, even if all these claims are admitted, they would not properly lead us to say that these works are good works of art.

Finally, there is aesthetic value. This is the kind of value that we look for most especially and suitably in works of art, and the kind of value whose presence and degree we report when we say that the work is good or poor. If we set aside all those reasons that clearly depend upon a cognitive or a moral/social point of view, we may consider those that remain to be peculiarly aesthetic. They are, however, not all equally relevant. Relevance depends on our theory of aesthetic value. If we hold, as I do, that the aesthetic value of an object is that value which it possesses in virtue of its capacity to provide aesthetic experience, then certain consequences follow. For the only way to support such a judgment relevantly and cogently would be to point out features of the work that enable it to provide an experience having an aesthetic character. And thus the relevant reasons, as I assumed above, will be those that both support and explain.

There is one more set of distinctions that I have found useful in dealing with critical reasons. Any statement that a critic may make about a work of art must be one of three kinds. (1) It may be a statement about the relation of the work to its antecedent conditions—about the intentions of the artist, or his sincerity, or his originality, or the social conditions of the work, and so forth. If such a statement is given as a reason for a critical judgment, it is a genetic reason. It may help explain why the work has a particular feature that in turn helps explain why the work is good (as one might say that something in Munch's childhood experience explains the "cry of terror" in so much of his work, while the presence of that "cry of terror," as an intense regional quality, helps explain why the works are good). But the genetic reason itself does not explain directly why the work is good, and it is therefore not a relevant reason: we cannot say that a work is good because it is sincere, or original, or fulfills the intention of the artist. (2) The critic's statement may be a statement about the effects of the work on individuals or groups: that it is morally uplifting, or shocking, or popular at the box office. If such a statement is given as a reason, it is an affective reason. And since it does not say what in the work makes it good, but itself has to be explained by what is in the work (which is shocking because of the nudity or the sadism or whatever), it is not a relevant critical reason. (3) When the genetic and affective reasons are set aside, what remain are descriptions and interpretations of the work itself, as has already been said. When given as reasons, such statements may be called objective reasons, since they draw our attention to the object itself and its own merits and defects. These are the reasons, I would argue, that are properly the province of the critic.

APPRECIATION AS PERCIPIENCE

Harold Osborne

It is only in the course of the present century that the word "appreciation" has gradually been adopted as a key term into aesthetic discourse. As it is now current, "appreciation" is one of those utility locutions, so common in every language, which has made its way in response to a felt need until it now seems so essential that no synonym or substitute comes easily to mind. Indeed when some years ago a paper of mine was to be translated into Polish it came as a surprise to me to realize that that language has no equivalent term, and the difficulties which we experienced in rendering it satisfactorily brought to light ambiguities inherent in the English word. In a practical way we all know what "appreciation" means—or everyone seems to know until the question is put. Yet the concept is difficult to pin down and there is no authoritative definition of it. When educational courses in art appreciation are announced it is not unusual for some people to query whether appreciation can be taught; yet few ever pause to ask what appreciation is.

It is clear that in the context of artistic discourse "appreciation" is not—or is not primarily—an evaluative term in accordance with its dictionary definition: "to estimate a thing at its true worth." We may make a valuation of a work of art as a result of appreciation, and indeed it has often been said that the only genuine aesthetic valuation is that which arises from an act of appreciation. But appreciation is understood rather as a basis for achieving possible valuation than as itself an act of evaluation. The current aesthetic usage of "appreciation" is closer to an older meaning which the *Oxford English Dictionary* gives as: "perception, especially of delicate impressions or distinctions." In the 1920's Clive Bell used it to mean sensi-

From *The Art of Appreciation* by Harold Osborne, published by Oxford University Press (New York, 1970), pp. 16–37. Reprinted by permission of the author and the publisher.

tive and emotionally tinged percipience, as for example in the paragraph from his essay "The Aesthetic Hypothesis" in which he amplifies his often-quoted sentence: "To appreciate a work of art we need bring with us nothing but a sense of form and colour and a knowledge of three-dimensional space." [1] In the 1930's John Dewey in the United States brought the word in as an occasional synonym of "aesthetic perception." [2] Since then the word has established for itself a far more central position and Dr. Munro is fully in line with contemporary practice when, in his book *Evolution in the Arts,* he equates it with "to understand and enjoy," and writes: "We are now beginning to teach children how to see pictures, hear music, and read poetry so as to grasp the form, style, and subtle nuances of individual expression. Experts differ on the best ways of doing so." [3]

In a rather similar fashion during the nineteenth century the word "aesthetic" established itself without formal definition in philosophical and general artistic discourse after it had been introduced as a neologism by the German philosopher Alexander Baumgarten (1714–62). Both words are now so ubiquitous that it is difficult to realize how the English writers on "aesthetics" from the third Earl of Shaftesbury to Archibald Alison and Dugald Stewart managed without either of them. The very vagueness of the word "aesthetic" contributed to its usefulness as a signpost marking out in the most general way our characteristic manner of commerce with natural beauty and the fine arts, while the psychology and phenomenology of so-called "aesthetic" experience have remained a primary preoccupation of the branch of philosophy which has also been named "aesthetics." The newer concept of appreciation is linked closely with that of aesthetic experience and is therefore central to any inquiry into appropriate ways of cultivating a skill for the enjoyment of the arts. In its application it is narrower than "aesthetic," which covers both the production

---

[1] Clive Bell, *Art* (1915), p. 27. Reprinted in *Aesthetics and the Philosophy of Criticism* (1963), ed. Marvin Levich.

[2] John Dewey, *Art as Experience* (1934

[3] Thomas Munro, *Evolution in the Arts* (1964), p. 400.

and the enjoyment of whatever is beautiful. In current usage "appreciation" is complementary to "creation": the former term covers the appropriate activities of the consumer and the latter the activities of the producer. The artist creates; his public appreciates what he has created. But built into the notion of appreciation, as the term is used, there is an implication of a sort of consumption which is appropriate and peculiar to things of beauty and particularly characteristic of works of art. The term "appreciation" is linked to a kind of consumption to which the term "aesthetic" can properly be applied. It does not make nonsense to say that such and such a business magnate paid vast sums of money for an artistic masterpiece which he was unable to appreciate. Nor do we commit a logical solecism if we say of some art historians that they have a very extensive knowledge *about* certain works of art—knowledge of their iconography, techniques, the social conditions in which they were produced, etc.—but that they are without a capacity to appreciate these works. Appreciation is wedded to the concept of "aesthetic" apprehension. Through a successful act of appreciation we make aesthetic contact with an object, achieve a more adequate awareness of its aesthetic properties, enjoy the aesthetic impact which it makes upon us. It is through the qualifications implicit in the word "aesthetic" that we distinguish appreciation of the arts from economic or other forms of non-appreciative contact.

Therefore in order to study appreciation, and to reach a clearer understanding of its varieties and methods, it is necessary first to know in a general way what is meant by calling any experience "aesthetic" and the characteristics in virtue of which we call any contact with the world around us an "aesthetic" contact.

In quite general terms, when we take up an aesthetic attitude toward something, one may say that we are engaged in appreciation of it insofar as without abandoning or disrupting that attitude we achieve an experience which is full and satisfying, free from frustration. Frustration may occur either because the object is not suitable to sustain aesthetic interest or because we are not adequately equipped to apprehend that particular object aesthetically. It may well be misleading to speak, as is often done, of *the* aesthetic attitude. We are obviously doing very different things, very differently occupied, when we are engaged in aesthetic appreciation of say Durham Cathedral, an oratorio by Handel, a miniature by Hilliard, *Anna Karenina, King Lear,* the sculptures of the Parthenon, and so on. Our aesthetic commerce with the environment is as multifarious as our practical, intellectual, or emotional commerce. Yet despite arguments to the contrary, as we can differentiate practical from theoretical attitudes, scientific analysis from attitudes of will or emotional response, so we can sensibly differentiate aesthetic attitudes as a class from the other modes of behavior in which we indulge.[4]

4 For some decades past it has been argued by some philosophers that the concept of art cannot be defined in terms of any feature or set of features which all works of art have in common and without which no artifact can properly be called a work of art. It is maintained that "art" is what has come to be known as a "family resemblance term," that it refers not to one single kind but to a number of different classes of things, which may indeed display various and intricate strands of similarities but which there is no reason to believe will turn out to have properties common to all of them. Or, it has come to be believed by many such philosophers, any features which are common to all things which are traditionally and currently accepted as works of art will prove to be trivial and not worth pursuing. More recently a similar argument has been put forward in regard to aesthetic experience. A typical formulation of it will be found in a paper contributed by Marshall Cohen under the title "Aesthetic Essence" to the collection *Philosophy in America* (1965) edited by Max Black. Cohen attacks the idea that "if there is no property common to all works of art there may yet be some property or properties common to our proper experience of these works of art, or to the preconditions of that experience or to the criteria of our aesthetic judgements." His method is to adduce not always quite convincing counter-instances to any description of aesthetic experience, and by this method he repudiates the hedonistic theory as recently revived by J. O. Urmson in his paper "What Makes a Situation Aesthetic?" (reprinted in Joseph Margolis, ed., *Philosophy Looks at the Arts,* 1962), Edward Bullough's theory of "aesthetic distance," and the widely accepted theory of aesthetic contemplation. He concludes: "There is no way of determining the preconditions of all aesthetic experience, just as there is no way of knowing what qualities such experience must bear."

In favor of this way of thinking we may admit that it would be silly to belittle the important differences that exist between the activities in which we engage when we enter into aesthetic commerce with such

Appreciation is a complicated and many-sided activity; nevertheless we are saying something to the point when we say that it is to be described in terms of taking up an aesthetic attitude to something rather than thinking analytically about it or responding to it emotionally or assessing its utility value or failing to notice it at all. Perhaps most basically of all to be aesthetically preoccupied with a thing is to apprehend it, to enter into growing awareness of it, in a special kind of way which will here be described as "percipience." It involves the

diverse works of art as, for example, the Taj Mahal, a miniature by Hilliard, a Tiepolo ceiling, a Mahler symphony, a play by Ionesco, and a Shakespeare sonnet. Even when we attend an exhibition of paintings by a single artist it may well be important to know that one picture is to be looked at in a different way from another because it is doing different things; that different modes of attention are called for and different sorts of things require notice. But it would be equally irresponsible to deny prematurely that there can be any common features of appreciation in virtue of which my words have meaning when I say that I am attending to something aesthetically and not in some other way. A person says that he is reading Homer as literature and not for purposes of textual criticism or in furtherance of archaeological research into the social customs of the ancient Hellenes; that he is drinking in the beauty of the landscape and not assessing its suitability as the site of an aerodrome; that he is enjoying the beauty of a Degas and not assessing its market value. We do in fact understand such statements even if we cannot articulate our understanding in theoretical terms. There is tacit knowledge of what sort of thing appreciation is and what it is not. When in such circumstances we say that a person is having appreciative contact with an object or attending to it aesthetically, we are not talking idly and we expect our interlocutors to comprehend us. And they do indeed comprehend. For in order to understand one another it is not necessary to be able to render tacit knowledge **articulate by laying down** a set of precisely defined common features. In order to clarify and extend understanding the method is rather to hold out typical instances of appreciation in various modes, paradigm cases from which we can both construct a central core of meaning and gradually, by radiating examples, illuminate the penumbra of similar but not quite identical cases.

Cohen speaks of the practical as well as the theoretical importance of a correct understanding of aesthetic experience. "For [he says] in so far as conditions that are not necessary are taken to be so, inappropriate training is proposed, and false instructions are offered, to those who wish to quicken their aesthetic responses. Quickening one's aesthetic responses is not a general problem, but a series of specific problems. In addition, in so far as insufficient conditions are taken to be sufficient, inadequate training and preparation are suggested." This reveals an intel-

cultivation of awareness for its own sake and without practical motivation. It is from this point of view that aesthetic activity is discussed in the present chapter.

We no longer look to the arts, as was normal a century ago, for a moral or a didactic message. Instead it is nowadays commonly claimed that appreciation of the arts affords a counterpoise to the rationalistic bias of contemporary technological culture and offers many people a field in which to exercise faculties which might otherwise remain stunted and impoverished. A typical example of such claims may be quoted from Sir Herbert Read, who in *The Form of Things Unknown* said:

> So long as civilisation was based on handcrafts, there always existed, in the actual mode of living, some counterpoise to abstract conceptual thought. But during the course of the last two centuries millions of people have become divorced from all perceptual effort. Of course, people still have to use their eyes (automatically, with the same kind of reactions we might expect from a calculating machine, but with less reliability); but there is little need for any positive co-ordination of hand and eye, for any visual exploration of the world, for any constructive use of perceptual experience. [He goes on to allege that through cultivation of the arts men] will correct the bias of an exclusively linguistic mode of thought, and, what is equally important, correct the bias of a mechanised mode of life.[5]

lectualist misapprehension. One must indeed have a correct notion of appreciation in order to be able to guide others and anyone whose notion is a false one will be a misleading guide. But having a correct notion of something does not necessarily involve being able to define it in terms of necessary and sufficient conditions. As has been said, art appreciation is a form of skill, an activity which is conducted according to rules not all of which are completely specifiable. It is itself an art. Some people are more proficient at it and some less so. Like other skills, it must be mastered by trial and error and perfected by guided practice; it is taught by demonstration and example, by general indications of method and by illustration through typical instances. If at some future time the tacit know-how which is latent in a skill to appreciate can be made articulate in clearly formulable rules, then it would be possible to evolve a technology of appreciation such as Munro desiderates. As will appear in the sequel, there may be reasons which make this impossible. But guidance and instruction in the art of appreciating are not for that reason impossible.

5 Herbert Read, *The Form of Things Unknown* (1960), p. 46.

Underlying such generalizations we might point to the empirical facts that many people whose habits are preponderantly intellectual and verbal—those for example who teach and write in the universities, work for banks or insurance companies—and some people who move primarily in the fields of technology and applied science, frequently experience difficulty in throwing off analytical and practical habits of mind which impede appreciative commerce with the arts. And, if we may cap generalization with generalization, it is perhaps not too far-fetched to suggest that the recent massive expansion of interest among people who are neither patrons nor professionals of the arts may stem in part from an unrecognized impulse to find some compensation for an imbalance in contemporary life and education whose tendency is to cramp and confine the faculties of perception. Be that as it may, there is certainly prevalent a belief that through the visual even more than the literary arts can be found occasion and inducement to exercise faculties of perceptiveness which otherwise are in danger of becoming blunted through neglect.

Nevertheless, the heritage of romanticism continues so strongly to color the presuppositions of our thinking that a proposal to discuss appreciation from the point of view of a perceptual skill to be cultivated and trained does at first blush seem to many people too cool and unemotional an approach to what is still primarily conceived to be a matter of feeling and emotional rapport. The ever more voluminous ephemeral literature of the arts—concert programs, exhibition catalogs, reviews, popular criticism, and history—is permeated with a tacit if unargued alternative: that in coming to terms with a work of art we must seek either to understand it theoretically or to achieve a correct emotional response to it. The same assumption is reflected in popular discourse. When the subject of the arts crops up in any tea-table conversation you may hear one man remark: "I don't understand modern art," while another will say: "I have read it up but it still leaves me cold." Both statements conceal the same fundamental error, namely the assumption that to perceive a work of art, to grasp it fully in awareness, is an automatic thing and easy of accomplishment, something equally within the competence of any man, while the difficulties of appreciation begin later with the "understanding" of what has been perceived or with the emotional response to it. Almost the complete opposite is the case. The difficulty and the skill are not of the understanding but of apprehending in perception, and we may confidently assume that neither of the participants in our tea-table conversation has successfully perceived the art works about which he speaks. The manner of perceiving works of art will therefore be our first topic.

We pass our lives, strenuously or languorously, in a never-ending give and take with a partly malleable, partly resistant environment, material and human, adapting it to our ends when we can and accommodating ourselves to it when we must. Occasionally the busy flow of life's intricate involvements is interrupted as there occur sudden pauses in our practical and theoretical preoccupations, moments of calm amidst the turmoil like clear patches of blue behind the clouds scurrying in a wind-blown sky, as our attention is caught by the rainbow sheen ruffing a pigeon's neck, the rhythmic rise and fall of susurration on a summer's day, the smoky calligraphies of wheeling birds painted on a transparent grey sky in winter, the grotesque contorted menace of an olive tree's branches, the lissom slenderness of a birch, or the sad sloppiness of a rain-crushed dandelion. Sometimes, if more rarely, we catch a glimpse of familiar things in an unfamiliar light. Commonplace objects suddenly shed their murk and enter the focus of attention. Perhaps for the first time in our memory we *see* a familiar sight. The trite fenestration of the house across the way reveals itself in a flash of insight as a limping, rather pathetic four-square pattern against the tangential folds of the curtains behind. A pillar box is seen not merely as a receptacle but as a shape. Our eyes are opened to the squat lugubrious block of the desk telephone whose primly rounded lines can't make up their minds whether to be rectilinear or curved or to fake a streamlined sophistication. The clumsily pretentious cornice appears as irritating as a crookedly hanging picture and a disproportionately small doorknob looks so ludicrous that discomfort battles with the impulse to laugh.

In ordinary life we are accustomed to use our perceptions as clues to practical situations, signposts to action, and the raw material of conceptualizing thought. We do not notice the perceptual qualities of the things we see beyond what is necessary to enable us to recognize, classify, and place them. We are aware of generalized and indeterminate perceptual qualities. Exceptions occur most frequently when we look at things which have (in the context in which we see them) no practical significance—such as flowers, scenery, sunsets, shells, objects of art—or objects of personal adornment when our interest is precisely in their decorative qualities. On such occasions, and whenever our practical concerns are in abeyance and we look at things for their own sake, there is a tendency—which may indeed be fleeting and slight but which can always be detected —for attention to be deflected from other things and focused upon the object which moves towards the center of our awareness. There is also a tendency for perceptual activity to be enhanced and to predominate over analytical and classificatory thinking as we become engrossed, however momentarily, in the perceptual object which holds our attention. Our interest "terminates" in the object and our concern with it goes no further than perceiving, bringing it more fully and more completely into perceptual awareness. When attention is set into this posture and we look at things for their own sake, the vague and indeterminate qualities which we habitually see become more precise and determinate: the perceptual object— the object of which we are aware—changes as its qualities are transformed, although the physical thing at which we are looking is not changed. As the intensity and the manner of attention changes so the object of each man's perception is transformed and it may be that, except when looking at the world conventionally and practically, no two men's perceptual experience of the same physical thing is the same. In the words of Merleau-Ponty, "attention is . . . the active constitution of a new object which makes explicit and articulate what was until then presented as no more than an indeterminate horizon." [6] This is

[6] M. Merleau-Ponty, *Phenomenology of Perception* (Eng. trans., 1962), p. 30.

why when we do sometimes see a familiar object in this way, for itself and shorn of its practical implications, the impact is as a revelation of something new and strange. The principle is fundamental also when we compare and discuss the "aesthetic objects" which we have actualized in perception on the basis of physical works of art. . . .

To some people these moments of heightened perception are exciting and important, even to the extent of experimenting with hallucinatory drugs in order to induce them artificially.[7] For others they are frivolities which besmirch the solemnities of work and entertainment. In yet others the capacity for them has been submerged, and these are the people who in sober truth have lost the power of vision. Some artists—not all—have been exceptionally alert to such ways of perceiving and one of the things which they have done is to crystallize and make concrete such perceptions, helping others in their turn to render the commonplace once more visible and, because visible, unfamiliar. When this happens in a painting we experience a feeling of illumination—so *that* is what it really looks like! To bring back visibility to the ordinary and present familiar things in an unfamiliar significance which nevertheless strikes us as a revelation of their true nature is one of the things which the artist can do, and Schopenhauer is not the only philosopher who has drawn attention to this.

The sort of perceptual experiences which I have been trying to describe are the raw material of aesthetic experience and their cultivation is useful for the training of appreciation. They do not take us all the way, perhaps not even very far. But they,

---

[7] In his essay "The Doors of Perception" (1954) Julian Huxley described how after taking mescalin his ordinary perceptions attained a heightened vividness and became fraught with metaphysical significance. "Mescalin," he said, "raises all colours to a higher power and makes the percipient aware of innumerable fine shades of difference, to which, at ordinary times, he is completely blind." He developed a theory that: "What the rest of us see only under the influence of mescalin, the artist is congenitally equipped to see all the time. His perception is not limited to what is biologically or socially useful. A little of the knowledge belonging to Mind at Large oozes past the reducing valve of brain and ego into his consciousness. It is a knowledge of the intrinsic significance of every existent."

and still more the attitude of mind and attention which favors their arousal, are the prototype from which can be developed the habit of aesthetic contact with works of art and other objects capable of supporting more sustained acts of appreciation. By accustoming himself to them a man does predispose himself to the sort of perceptual attitude which is most favorable to successful contact with the arts.

The engrossment with the object which lies at the heart of aesthetic appreciation has been traditionally known by the term "disinterested enjoyment"—a turn of phrase at first sight singularly inappropriate to describe a posture of attention where interest falls wholly upon the object. The term may be explained historically. The notion of "disinterestedness" came to prominence in opposition to the "intelligent egoism" of Thomas Hobbes, who had argued that all the precepts of morality and religion can in the last resort be reduced to enlightened self-interest. Against this view Lord Shaftesbury, and with him Cudworth and other of the Cambridge Platonists, maintained that virtue and goodness must of necessity be "disinterested": that is, they must be free from self-interest, pursued for their own sake and not from motives of self-interest, however enlightened. Also in the religious sphere the concept of "disinterested" love of God—that is the love of God for His own sake and not from hope of heaven or fear of hell—arose out of a controversy between the Jansenists and the Jesuits about the same time. This idea of disinterested interest—interest in something for its own sake alone—was applied in the field of aesthetics when Shaftesbury contrasted the disinterested attention which is essential to what is now called an aesthetic attitude with any desire to possess, use, or otherwise manipulate an object. Shaftesbury gave as a paradigm of this attitude of disinterested attention our enjoyment of mathematics, where our perception does not relate to any "private interest of the creature, nor has for its object any self-good or advantage," but, as he said, "the admiration, joy or love turns wholly upon what is exterior and foreign to ourselves." This line of thought was summed up by Archibald Alison, who excluded from the sphere of the aesthetic "the useful, the agreeable, the fitting, or the convenient." [8] The word "contemplation" has been used to express this kind of disinterested engrossment which is central to aesthetic commerce with the environment. Edmund Burke, for example, defined beauty as "that quality . . . in bodies by which they cause love" and defined the love which is "symptomatic" of beauty as the satisfaction which "arises to the mind on the contemplation of anything beautiful." Two centuries later Professor C. W. Valentine, wanting to describe the concept of "aesthetic attitude" assumed by him for the purposes of experimental aesthetics, said in *The Experimental Psychology of Beauty* (1962): "We may say roughly that an aesthetic attitude, in the wider sense of the term, is being adopted whenever an object is apprehended or judged without reference to its utility or value or moral rightness; or when it is merely being contemplated." This is the attitude of perception, the activity of the spectator pure and simple, the mental stance and the posture of attention which are habitual in those who have developed a trained skill to appreciate.

The concept of disinterested contemplation was renewed in the present century under the name of "psychical distance" by Edward Bullough, who gives one of the most vivid descriptions on record of what is meant by seeing the ordinary and commonplace in an aesthetic light. He takes as his example a fog at sea:

> Imagine a fog at sea: for most people it is an experience of acute unpleasantness. Apart from the physical annoyance and remoter forms of discomfort such as delays, it is apt to produce feelings of peculiar anxiety, fears of invisible dangers, strains of watching and listening for distant and unlocalised signals. The listless movement of the ship and her warning calls soon tell upon the nerves of the passengers; and that special, expectant, tacit anxiety and nervousness, always associated with this experience, make a fog the dreaded terror of the sea (all the more terrifying because of its very silence and gentleness) for the expert seafarer no less than for the ignorant landsman.
>
> Nevertheless, a fog at sea can be a source of intense relish and enjoyment. Abstract from the experience of the sea fog,

[8] Archibald Alison, *Essays on the Nature and Principle of Taste* (1790).

for the moment, its danger and practical unpleasantness, just as everyone in the enjoyment of a mountain-climb disregards its physical labour and its danger (though, it is not denied, that these may incidentally enter into the enjoyment and enhance it); direct the attention to the features 'objectively' constituting the phenomenon—the veil surrounding you with an opaqueness as of transparent milk, blurring the outline of things and distorting their shapes into weird grotesqueness; observe the carrying-power of the air, producing the impression as if you could touch some far-off siren by merely putting out your hand and letting it lose itself behind that white wall; note that curious creamy smoothness of the water, hypocritically denying as it were any suggestion of danger; and, above all, the strange solitude and remoteness from the world, as it can be found only on the highest mountain tops: and the experience may acquire, in its uncanny mingling of repose and terror, a flavour of such concentrated poignancy and delight as to contrast sharply with the blind and distempered anxiety of its other aspects. This contrast, often emerging with startling suddenness, is like a momentary switching on of some new current, or the passing ray of a brighter light, illuminating the outlook upon perhaps the most ordinary and familiar objects—an impression which we experience sometimes in instants of direst extremity, when our practical interest snaps like a wire from sheer over-tension, and we watch the consummation of some impending catastrophe with the marvelling unconcern of a mere spectator.[9]

The change of attitude—which Bullough calls "distance"—is produced, he explains, in the first instance

by putting the phenomenon, so to speak, out of gear with our practical, actual self; by allowing it to stand outside the context of our personal needs and ends—in short, by looking at it 'objectively,' as it has often been called, by permitting only such reactions on our part as emphasize the 'objective' features of the experience, and by interpreting even our 'subjective' affections not as modes of *our* being but rather as characteristics of the phenomenon.

The attitude of disinterested attention, which we may henceforward call the attitude of *contemplation,* has been admirably described also by Pepita Haezrahi, taking as her example the sight of a falling leaf in the autumn.

[9] Edward Bullough, " 'Psychical Distance' as a Factor in Art and Aesthetic Principle."

Our leaf falls. It detaches itself with a little plopping sound from its place high up in the tree. It is red and golden. It plunges straight down through the tree and then hesitates and hovers for a while just below the lowest branches. The sun catches it and it glitters with mist and dew. It now descends in a leisurely arc and lingers for another moment before it finally settles on the ground.

You witness the whole occurrence. Something about it makes you catch your breath. The town, the village, the garden around you sink into oblivion. There is a pause in time. The chain of your thoughts is severed. The red and golden tints of the leaf, the graceful form of the arc described by its descent fill the whole of your consciousness, fill your soul to the brim. It is as though you existed in order to gaze at this leaf falling, and if you had other preoccupations and other purposes you have forgotten them. You do not know how long this lasts, it may be only an instant, but there is a quality of timelessness, a quality of eternity about it. You have had an aesthetic experience.

The attitude of mind and attention which is involved in this experience and which makes it possible she then characterizes as follows:

A farmer on seeing the leaf fall might mark the arc it describes in its descent, deduce from this the direction of the wind, the imminence of rain, and hurrry off to do whatever farmers do when the rain is imminent. A botanist may observe the leaf, think that it is falling rather earlier in the year than usual, pick it up and examine its capillaries, look for signs of disease or other causes for the weakening of the tissues and so on. A sensitive soul, on seeing the leaf fall may be induced to reflect on the transience of worldly glory, the uncertainty of human existence, the fickleness of human nature and generally indulge in sad musings. A poet on seeing the leaf fall, may or may not experience this experience aesthetically, but may be led to think of a metre or a rhythm he could use in his next poem, or of a striking metaphor. We, here, would think of how to analyse the aesthetic experience of seeing a leaf fall, if someone could be induced to undergo one.

Only the spectator who had that experience, and was content to stop at the experience, without trying to draw any conclusions from it, or make any further use of it, without trying to go behind the given appearance of the falling leaf to what it may purport (like the weakening of vegetable tissues) or symbolise (like the shortness of human life), has remained within the aesthetic domain.

You will have observed that, apart from the spectator's, all those various ways of looking at the falling leaf had two features in common. They all amounted to attempts, first, to relate this occurrence to things outside itself, to find a place for it in some system or other of well-defined causal connections. And secondly, to relate this occurrence to various preoccupations in life, to make use of it for some ulterior purpose . . . .

The spectator alone made no attempt to relate the falling leaf to anything beyond itself, made no attempt to use it for any purpose whatever. He treated it as a thing complete, absolute and valuable in itself, which need be neither explained, nor utilised in order to justify the amount of attention paid to it. We have therefore described the attitude of the spectator as a non-utilitarian, non-volitional, non-emotional, non-analytical attitude. We have described it as an attitude of pure attention, an act of unselfish almost impersonal concentration, an incorporeal 'gazing.' In fact we have described an act of contemplation, the expression of a contemplative attitude.[10]

The foregoing descriptions by Bullough and Haezrahi will pinpoint a mode of experience which, although naturally sporadic, can be cultivated and will be familiar to many people. It is this which I take to be paradigmatic for aesthetic experience generally and it is basic to an understanding of appreciation in its more advanced forms.

From the time when men awoke to aesthetic self-consciousness and began deliberately to think and philosophize about the appreciation and enjoyment of beauty, aesthetic experience has been presented in terms of an attitude of mind, sometimes called the contemplative attitude, which involves a particular posture of attention, a special way of being interested in things, differing in certain respects from the usual habits of interest and attention we display in the conduct of practical affairs and in our scientific and theoretical preoccupations.[11] I now

[10] Pepita Haezrahi, *The Contemplative Activity* (1954), pp. 25, 35–36.

[11] Appreciation can hardly be characterized otherwise than in terms of attention, and readers may find it useful here to refer to Appendix I, in which my use of the concept of 'attention' is particularized.

propose to examine more systematically some of the features which have been regarded as characteristic of this attitude and I will list eight features in virtue of which in the main experiences have been classed as aesthetic. Some of these features are closely linked, others less so. I do not wish to claim that all of them are necessarily present in any experience properly called aesthetic—that, after all, is a matter of linguistic usage and dictionary definition. Our actual aesthetic commerce with the environment is as many-sided and diverse as the sort of experiences which are called practical or scientific or sentimental or moral, and it will not be regimented or stereotyped. Just as moments of aesthetic experience interpenetrate in the practical affairs of life (as, for instance, when we recognize a person by gracefulness of posture, clumsiness of gait, serenity of demeanor, etc.), so our mature appreciation of complex aesthetic objects such as works of art is usually interwoven with theoretical and analytical procedures as we bring ourselves to greater familiarity with them. I do wish to claim that the eight features listed are important, individually and collectively, in determining us to regard any experience as aesthetic rather than practical or theoretical, and I would be prepared to insist that trained facility in all these ways of apprehending the environment is an important step in the cultivation of skill in the art of appreciation. Understanding of these characteristic slants of attention and interest will help to bridge the gap from the archetypal manifestations of aesthetic apprehension already described to the mature and more exacting appreciation of accomplished works of art.

1. When we perceive anything aesthetically there is a tendency for attention to be deflected from other things and centered upon it. It is therefore abstracted in attention from the environmental system of which it forms a part. As is sometimes said, it is "framed apart" for attention. Attention is "arrested" upon it and we do not apprehend it as a unit in a system of things held in awareness.

It is notorious that some of the arts employ deliberate devices to favor this concentration of attention and to facilitate the isolation of the object from its environment. Pictures are enclosed in frames, which isolate them from the surrounding wall, contract the field of vision, and help us to fix attention within the area marked out by the frame. So important is this that many amateurs are unable to "see" an unframed picture. It takes considerable practice to do this and many people who can do it succeed only by setting an imaginary frame round the picture. Conversely an unsuitable frame can "kill" a picture by taking attention from it, by suggesting deep recession when the point of the picture is flat pattern in the picture plane, or for other such reasons. When we see a play or a film we look out from a darkened auditorium on to a lighted scene or screen, and our awareness of our immediate surroundings falls temporarily into abeyance. Music is a structure built up of artificial sounds which do not occur in nature and concentration within the world of structure which they create is ordinarily so intense that the listener is no longer fully aware of his surroundings and the intrusion of an alien sound impinging willy-nilly on the attention—such as the blare of a motor horn—causes disproportionate shock. Even our more elementary moments of aesthetic vision involve some isolation of the object and it is this which causes, in part at any rate, the sense of a pause and an interruption to the tenor of our practical concerns.

2. Implicit to the isolation of the object for attention is the fact that we do not conceptualize or think discursively about it. We do not classify it as an instance of a kind with such and such common class features and such and such distinguishing characteristics. We do not ponder its causes or deliberate about its uses or effects. Our interest and attention are arrested by it and do not go outside it. We are not concerned to signpost it or "place" it in a wider environment. It is this, chiefly, which distinguishes the attitude of appreciation from that of the art historian. The historian's concern is with fixing the individual work as a unit in a systematic context, establishing its origins, its sociological implications, drawing stylistic and other comparisons and contrasts, tracing all the various vicissitudes it has undergone. The information he provides, or some of it, may well be of use to the connoisseur, helping him to apprehend the work more completely, to perceive aspects and fea-

tures of it which might otherwise have passed him by or only imperfectly come to his awareness. But it will be as background information only, predisposing him to notice things germane to appreciation. The intellectual interest in knowing all that can be known *about* a work of art may be ancillary to, but is not identical with, the aesthetic interest. The two interests are related but distinct. A historian can get by passably with small powers of appreciation and a connoisseur need have little historical knowledge, though he would be rash to belittle the help that can accrue from historical orientation in some cases.

3. When something is apprehended aesthetically we do not analyze it into an assemblage of constituent parts standing in such and such relations to each other. We do indeed *perceive* it as a complex structure of interrelated parts, but this is a different thing from theoretical analysis. . . . Here it is sufficient to say that when a thing is analyzed in discursive thought it is broken up into a set of constituent parts each of which can be fully articulated and described in isolation, the whole being composed of these determinate parts standing to each other in the relations in which they do stand; but when a thing is perceived as a complex structure, the perceived parts do not as it were pre-date or stand independently of the structure in which they are perceived but are articulate to perception only as parts of that structure. An art critic may analyze the component parts of a picture—the images contained in Picasso's *Guernica,* for example. He may point out: "This is a lamp; this is the head of a horse in agony; this is a screaming woman." In each case he mentions a class of things to which the particular image belongs and describes it conceptually. He may go on to analyze and explain the symbolism of these images and trace their significance in the personal history and the *oeuvre* of the artist.[12] All this may be of the utmost importance in helping the viewer to achieve full aesthetic awareness of the picture and to direct his attention upon its significant features. But it is not itself an aesthetic mode of attention; it does not take the place of seeing the picture as a picture.

[12] An exemplary instance of this sort of criticism may be seen in Anthony Blunt, *Picasso's* "Guernica" (1969).

4. "An aesthetic experience," said Paul Weiss, "is all surface, and here and now." [13] The "here and now" character of the experience has been analyzed particularly by the Polish aesthetician Stanislaw Ossowski.[14] The greater part of our waking life, he says, is lived in such a way that present experience is colored by expectations for the future and associations from the past. This happens not only when we envisage some far-reaching aims, when we are planning ahead or exercising forethought. The future and the past are implicit in our most ordinary and everyday perceptions; we attend to them primarily for their practical significance and in the very act of perceiving we interpret them for the implications of what is to come. Whenever we are expectant, whenever we are anxious or apprehensive, hopeful, confident, or exultant, whenever we become aware of something as suspect, dangerous, or innocuous—in all such situations as these we are molding the present experience in the light of its implication for the future. So too, when we are surprised, disappointed, moved by regret or self-congratulation, soothed by a comfortable feeling of familiarity, or disturbed by a sense of the unfamiliar, we are experiencing the present in the context and coloring of a selected past. All such attitudes and emotions are foreign to aesthetic contemplation—although they may, of course, enter into the content of the art work which is the object of our contemplation.

It is because, or partly because, when we attend to anything aesthetically, these practical attitudes are arrested and put into abeyance that the aesthetic experience has its own characteristic emotional color. Too many writers from too many points of view have testified to the serenity and detachment of aesthetic contemplation for this to be an accidental feature: it is noticed even when the object of contemplation has dynamic or dramatically emotional characteristics, and it seems to be a distinguishing feature of the aesthetic mood. A very similar emotional state has been claimed by Henri Michaux to result from the taking of psilocybine.

It eliminates [he says] in a surprising and practically total fashion the preparation for the next act, the state of mobilisa-

[13] Paul Weiss, *The World of Art* (1961).
[14] Stanislaw Ossowski, *U Podstaw Esteyki* (3rd ed., 1958), pp. 271ff.

tion in which the adult finds himself with a view to the day to be filled, the acts to be accomplished, the things to be done, to be avoided. Every minute is pregnant with a programme for the future. To be alive is to be *ready*. Ready for what may happen, in the jungle of the city and of the day. One must possess an incessantly and subconsciously adjusted foresight. The normal state, far from being one of repose, is a *placing under tension,* with a view to efforts to be exerted (should occasion arise, or presently). A placing under tension which is so habitual that one does not know how to reduce it. The normal state is a state of preparation, of disposal towards. Of pre-organization.

By psilocybine (and, we may say, during aesthetic contemplation) "you are put into a state of calm, of arrest." [15]

These things will be discussed at greater length in their appropriate place. Here two consequences may be noted for future elaboration. (i) Our emotional dispositions, our unconscious expectations, our manner of putting out tentacles for the appropriate associations from the reservoir of our past experience: these are the things which determine what features and what aspects of anything we are predisposed to notice, attend to, and bring more fully to awareness. When we are engaged in the appreciation of fine art it is necessary not only that the ordinary practical predispositions are put in abeyance but also that a proper and appropriate alternative set of predispositions takes over in each case. (ii) Aesthetic interest leads to outward-turning forms of activity and inclines us typically to absorption in an object presented for perception, not to an inward dwelling upon our own moods and emotions. During aesthetic contemplation we are less rather than more conscious of our own feelings than usual.

5. If, as our analysis has indicated, aesthetic contemplation is a fixing of the attention upon a presented object and a process of bringing ourselves to increasing awareness of that object in perception, then it follows that those meditative musings and plays of the imagination in which poetic sensibility delights to indulge are also foreign to an aesthetic engrossment. And this, startling as it may seem, is in fact the case; for such

[15] Henri Michaux, *Light through Darkness* (1964).

imaginative play necessarily deflects attention for the object and weakens our absorption in it. He who sees a falling leaf and muses on it as a symbol of transience, meditating on the impermanence of all earthly things, the brevity of human existence, etc., is not contemplating the falling leaf aesthetically. Such musings and meditations are not alien to an artistic temperament; they may themselves become the raw material of poetry. But they are not germane to an aesthetic experience of the leaf. As a symbol the leaf loses its individuality and particularity; *any* falling leaf is a symbol of transience, not just this one. Insofar, then, as we muse upon presented things as symbols of ideas or allow them to spark off trains of imaginative imagery or thought, to that extent our preoccupation with them has ceased to be aesthetic percipience.

In saying this we are going counter to one of the most popular trends of art criticism from the earliest times until the present day. In antiquity, from Homer to Philostratus, it was usual and expected for a critic to describe the narrative features of a picture and to extrapolate imaginatively from them, suggesting incidents and events which were not, and often could not be, depicted in the picture itself. Even a century ago it was a general practice of critics to offer similar imaginative extrapolations concerning the moral message or philosophical implications of pictorial art. . . . At the end of the eighteenth century Archibald Alison maintained at length that such play of imagination is central to aesthetic appreciation, consisting in the indulgence of a stream of ideas and images activated by and emotionally related to the object of appreciation.[16]

> Thus [he says] when we feel either the beauty or the sublimity of natural scenery—the gay lustre of a morning in spring, or the mild radiance of a summer evening—the savage majesty of a wintry storm, or the wild magnificence of a tempestuous ocean—we are conscious of a variety of images in our minds, very different from those which the objects themselves can present to the eye. Trains of pleasing or solemn thought arise spontaneously within our minds; our hearts swell with emotions, of which the objects before us seem to afford no adequate cause; and we are never so much satiated with

[16] Archibald Alison, *Essays on the Nature and Principles of Taste.*

delight, as when, in recalling our attention, we are unable to trace either the progress or the connection of those thoughts which have passed with so much rapidity through our imagination.

He instances the tendency of scenery in spring to "infuse into our minds somewhat of that fearful tenderness with which infancy is usually beheld." And he says:

With such a sentiment, how innumerable are the ideas which present themselves to our imagination! Ideas, it is apparent, by no means confined to the scene before our eyes, or to the possible desolation which may yet await its infant beauty, but which almost involuntarily extend themselves to analogies with the life of man, and bring before us all those images of hope and fear, which according to our peculiar situations have the dominion of our heart!

He asserts a similar principle for the appreciation of the arts.

The landscapes of Claude Lorraine, the music of Handel, the poetry of Milton, excite feeble emotions in our minds when attention is confined to the qualities they present to our senses, or when it is to such qualities of their composition that we turn our regard. It is then, only, we feel the sublimity or beauty of their productions, when our imaginations are kindled by their power, when we lose ourselves amid the number of images that pass before our minds, and when we waken at last from this play of fancy as from the charm of a romantic dream.

Alison's account was not idiosyncratic. In believing that he had shown it to be "consonant with experience" that the indulgence of these trains of thought and imagery, the musings and emotionally colored meditations, are an essential feature of aesthetic commerce with the world around us Alison was in keeping with the outlook of his day. Kant seems to say much the same sort of thing in his doctrine of aesthetical ideas. It is a view which runs directly counter to the more rigorous aesthetic understanding of today. Nowadays every competent instructor would recommend his students to concentrate attention firmly on the object and avoid like the plague those temptations to daydreaming and the emotionally colored divagations of fancy which for earlier critics and theorists were the essence of appreciation. Not that they are to be condemned in themselves. But appreciation, we now think, is something else again.

6. In illustration of what he meant by the "disinterested" interest which is characteristic of aesthetic commerce with anything Kant said: "One must not be in the least prepossessed in favor of the real existence of the thing, but must preserve complete indifference in this respect, in order to play the part of judge in matters of taste." [17] This repudiation of interest in the *existence* of asthetic objects, which Kant took over from English eighteenth-century writers, has often been misunderstood. As practical men and lovers of beauty we are interested in the continued existence of beautiful things. If the palace which we now contemplate with enjoyment were a mirage with no real existence, we should not be able to see it and enjoy its beauty next time we passed that way. As Leibniz said earlier, the man who suffers pain from the destruction of a beautiful picture even though it belongs to another man, loves it with a disinterested love. We certainly have a practical interest in the real existence of beautiful things since the possibility of continuing in the future to enter into aesthetic commerce with them and enjoy their beauty depends upon their existence. But within the process of appreciation itself, while we are aesthetically intent on the object, considerations of its real existence are irrelevant. Aesthetic contemplation is concerned with the object as presented, with the appearance.

Another problem arises in connection with aesthetic attitudes

[17] Kant, *The Critique of Judgement,* Pt. 1, sec. 2. Kant himself conduces to the misunderstanding of which we take notice when he says (sec. 42): "In this connection, however, it is of note that were we to play a trick on our lover of the beautiful, and plant in the ground artificial flowers (which can be made so as to look just like natural ones), and perch artfully carved birds on the branches of trees, and he were to find out how he had been taken in, the immediate interest which these things previously had for him would at once vanish. . . ." Again: "But it is the indispensable requisite of the interest which we here take in beauty, that the beauty should be that of nature, and it vanishes completely as soon as we are conscious of having been deceived, and that it is only the work of art—so completely that even taste can then no longer find in it anything beautiful nor sight anything attractive." There appears to be here an intrusion of metaphysical dogma into what purports to be a phenomenological analysis.

to properties of appearance which turn out to be deceptive. Let us say I have given aesthetic admiration to the appearance of strength and hardness displayed by a tall tree trunk. When I approach it I find that the appearance was deceptive: the tree was in fact rotten and crumbles at a touch. In these circumstances, it has been argued, I can no longer enjoy aesthetically the appearance of sturdiness and soundness in the tree. "If I know that the tree is rotten, I shall not be able again to savor its seeming-strength. I could, no doubt, savor its 'deceptively strong appearance'; but that would be quite a different experience from the first." [18] There is, I think, some inadequacy of analysis here. When I first see the tree and attend aesthetically to what I see, I accord aesthetic admiration to an appearance which I describe as an appearance of strength and hardness. I describe the appearance in these terms because trees which look like this usually do prove to be strong and hard. But I do not in fact make inferences from the appearance to a belief that the tree really has many years of life before it and that if cut down, it would yield good hard timber—or if I do make such inferences, they are irrelevant and an interruption to the mood of aesthetic attention, an intrusion of practical assessments. If later I acquire knowledge that the tree is rotten and therefore these inferences, if I drew them, would be false, this is a contingent fact which may in the particular instance of this tree act as a psychological impediment, making it difficult or impossible for me again to attend aesthetically to the appearance of this tree. I may never again be able to bring myself into the mood of contemplating aesthetically an appearance whose description, and the factual implications implicit in the description, conflict with what I now know to be the case. In just such a way for many centuries European people were unable aesthetically to appreciate the wild grandeur of mountain scenery because they were inhibited by a latent sense of insecurity, a knowledge of likely danger, from according unmixed aesthetic attention to them. But the impediment which now makes aesthetic con-

[18] R. W. Hepburn, "Aesthetic Appreciation of Nature," *British Journal of Aesthetics,* vol. 3, no. 3. Reprinted in *Aesthetics and the Modern World* (1968), ed. H. Osborne.

templation of the tree impossible does not alter the nature of the earlier experience I had before this impediment existed.

Considerations of this sort seem niggling. Nevertheless they do attain some importance in principle when we come to consider the aesthetic bearing of truth, genuineness, and verisimilitude in connection with works of art.

7. Aesthetic contemplation has been described as a form of absorption. It is not the only form. We may be absorbed in a puzzle, a piece of research, or a football match; children are absorbed in a fairy story. Whenever anything interests us we tend to become absorbed in it while the interest lasts, and the degree of our absorption depends on the strength of the interest in relation to whatever else is occupying us at the time. In aesthetic contemplation, however, the field of attention is narrowed, our usual practical concerns are put into abeyance, and our mode of awareness is confined to direct percipience. For these reasons, it would appear, as has been frequently noticed, that aesthetic contemplation is one of the activities which especially tends to invite absorption. For the time being at any rate we tend to become engrossed with the aesthetic object which has attracted attention to itself. As a correlate of this, an aesthetic object upon which attention has been turned is apt to stand out and strike us with the impact of a heightened and enhanced reality. There is a peculiar vividness about aesthetic experience which favors mental alertness and stimulates the faculties.

Certainly absorption is not always successful and may be frustrated. When there come to us moments of aesthetic vision amidst the turmoil of practical concerns, we do not always accord them more than a modicum of attention: other, more urgent demands may hold us back from answering the call. Even when we set ourselves to the express purpose of enjoying aesthetic experience, when we attend a concert or visit a gallery, we may not be in the mood, the encroachment of other interests or the dominance of practical anxieties may make too great claims on the attention and frustrate our intention. Or we may just be unable at that moment to call up the necessary alertness and acuity of percipience. But when aesthetic contemplation is successful and absorption is achieved there is a loss of subjective time sense, a loss of the sense of place, and a loss of bodily consciousness. We are no longer fully conscious of ourselves as persons sitting in a concert hall or standing before a canvas in a picture gallery. We are no longer conscious of the passing of time (interesting problems arise concerning the relations between the artificial time-intervals set up within a musical structure, the subjective time sense of the absorbed listener and objective time lapse). In a sense to be examined later, we become identified with the aesthetic object by which our attention is gripped and held.

Nevertheless absorption is never complete to the point where ego-consciousness disappears. That this is so may be proved from our behavior with the representational arts. We retain always a residual awareness of ourselves as spectators at a play or a cinema; we never quite lose sight of the fact that we are looking at a picture or reading a novel. And this seems to be not merely a contingent fact but a logical requirement of the aesthetic mode of awareness. For if we were to become absorbed to the point of undergoing illusion and behaved as if we were in the presence of the realities represented, our condition would no longer be called "aesthetic." [19]

8. Moments of aesthetic vision may be courted deliberately or they may flash upon us unsolicited and unexpectedly. Anything at all may be made the object of aesthetic attention. But not all things are capable of sustaining attention in the aesthetic mode. Attention can be prolonged only so long as awareness is being expanded or diversified thereby. The artificial fixing and prolongation of attention under any other conditions leads inevitably to reverie, somnolence, or self-hypnosis. If we try to force ourselves to hold an aesthetic object actively in attention beyond what it can support, our mode of attention changes from aesthetic to discursive or analytical. This is why moments of aesthetic vision in daily life are for the most part sporadic and fleeting. The objects which engage them are not in general sufficiently complex for percipience; after a relatively short period

[19] See my article "Artistic Illusion," *British Journal of Aesthetics* (April 1969).

we cannot bring them more fully into perceptual awareness, and attention must either pass from them or must be changed to some other mode. We smell a flower repeatedly in order to enjoy the pleasure which this gives. But putting aside the subjective pleasantness of the experience, we cannot for long periods, or even repeatedly, concentrate upon perceiving the specific *quale,* the olfactory character in perception, of that particular odor. And it is the latter, not the former, which we call "aesthetic."

Works of art are aesthetic objects specifically designed or particularly adapted to favor prolonged and repeated activity of aesthetic percipience. If successful, they are above all other things capable of sustaining aesthetic attention and they afford to percipience more ample scope. Indeed it has sometimes been alleged that great works of art have no exhaustion point for appreciation.[20] Works of art can, at their best, extend the perceptive faculties to the full without satiation and as it were demand ever increased mental vivacity and grasp to contain them. This, it may be thought, is at any rate a major part of what has been meant when philosophers and critics have spoken of the "life-enhancing" quality of art appreciation. Years of study and experience, half a lifetime of growing familiarity, may contribute to the full appreciation of a great work of art: the experience itself is always accompanied by a feeling of heightened vitality; we are more awake, more alert than usual, the faculties are working at greater pressure, more effectively, and with greater freedom than at other times, and the discovery of new insights is their constant guerdon. When a work no longer holds anything new for us, aesthetic boredom inevitably sets in and for the time being at any rate we have "outgrown" that particular work or artist.

I have written at some length about aesthetic percipience because it is paradigmatic for the appreciation of fine art and a basic element in the cultivation of that skill. There is probably a minority of people totally immune to the experience, although in many the capacity for it has been suppressed and submerged. It may occur as a sudden gleam of beauty seen momentarily

[20] For example, by Richard Wollheim in *Art and Its Objects* (1968).

amidst the more pressing predicaments of practical affairs or in moments of leisure it may stamp more precise and prolonged hiatuses in the stream of practical concerns. An aesthetic attitude, with its characteristic marks of heightened percipience and a temporary alienation or sloughing of practical and theoretical interests, can be taken up toward anything at all. But only works of art, or perhaps their equivalents in nature, can extend to full capacity the faculties of perception exercised within this mode of attention. Some people find it easy to assume this attitude toward works of art and can assume it more or less at will. Others find it difficult or are completely at sea, occupying themselves with art works, if at all, in irrelevant and unprofitable ways. But to engage successfully in prolonged and intense "disinterested" attention—or in repeated acts of "disinterested" contemplation over an extended period—as is necessary in order to bring any masterpiece of art fully into awareness, needs cultivation and directed practice. It is the first and necessary step toward mature appreciation.

AESTHETIC CRITICISM: THE METHOD OF AESTHETIC EDUCATION

R. A. Smith

. . . A survey of successful critical statements, i.e., those which have released a work's value potential previously inaccessible to untrained sensibilities, discloses little unity. The statements of critics range from crisp, schematic analyses to eloquent literary essays. The description of the phases and techniques of critical activity that follows is therefore neither exhaustive nor definitive, but it does seem to hold potential for formulating and planning defensible educational objectives and experiences.

Critical activity may be described first of all in terms of overlapping phases which contain statements ranging from the cognitively certain to the cognitively less certain, beginning with description and phasing into analysis, interpretation, and evaluation. Again, this division is open to challenge since the terms are used ambiguously and the boundaries between phases are not always precise.[20]

1. *Description.* By and large description involves naming, identifying, and classifying, a kind of taking stock which inventories cognitively established aspects of a work of art, e.g., knowledge concerning the type of thing an object is (triptych, symphony, or work of prose fiction), information about the materials and techniques used, and knowledge of the extra-aes-

From *Studies in Art Education,* vol. 9, no. 3 (Spring 1968): 20–32. Reprinted with minor changes by permission of *Studies in Art Education* and the author.

[20] For a similar classification of critical phases, see Edmund B. Feldman, *Art as Image and Idea* (Englewood Cliffs, N.J.: Prentice-Hall, 1967), Ch. 15. It might also be noted that the usual trinity is description, interpretation, and evaluation. Because of the pedagogical importance of formal analysis, however, this phase is isolated. Especially relevant in understanding the nature of critical activity is Morris Weitz's *Hamlet and the Philosophy of Literary Criticism* (Chicago: University of Chicago Press, 1964). Weitz takes the criticism of *Hamlet* as a paradigm of what criticism is and isolates the following modes: description, explanation, evaluation, and poetics (aesthetics).

thetic function of the work when this is relevant. This category would further comprise art-historical data, and in the case of representational works, knowledge of mythology, cultural history, or whatever is required to identify the subject depicted.

Descriptive knowledge of the foregoing types is often depreciated because so-called art appreciation courses frequently degenerate to this level, or so it is said. Assuredly, memorization of dates and names and drills in the identification of period styles and artists fall short of the principle objectives for aesthetic education. Yet descriptive information of the right sort is obviously important and relevant to aesthetic response. Relevant descriptive knowledge interrelates with the other, more properly aesthetic phases of criticism and thus enriches the total critique. Further, since aesthetic education as an epistemological or knowledge enterprise often seems to falter with the recognition that, on the whole, secure empirical knowledge might not be present in the arts, those areas in which knowledge is possible should be indicated. Lastly, it is conceivable that ability to talk with cognitive assurance about the descriptive elements of works of art, even though they are not necessarily the most aesthetically relevant, may give teacher and student greater confidence to venture into more ambiguous and uncharted territories.

2. *Analysis.* This involves a close look at the components, elements, or details that make up a work, the larger groups or complexes into which they are composed, and the relationships they sustain. Analysis in art is not a mere enumeration or cataloging of components; it cannot be done in a meaningful way, it seems, without at the same time describing and often characterizing what is singled out for inspection. The distinction between "description" and "characterization" introduces different ways in which parts, complexes, and regional properties can be talked about.[21] Such considerations further introduce the

[21] The distinction between "description" and "characterization" is for convenience. I use "characterization" whenever aesthetic qualities are pointed out; whereas description is restricted to indicating the more literal properties of objects. The characterization of elements, however, may be regarded as a kind of description.

complex notion of aesthetic qualities, concepts, or predicates—
a topic that invites analysis of the terms, particularly adjectives,
often used in critical talk.

a. There is a first group of predicates so matter-of-fact and
uncontroversial that it probably is not proper to consider them
as aesthetic. A color may have a certain degree of saturation,
a musical note a given pitch, a shape a geometric configuration,
a word a definite meaning, and so on. These characteristics,
which anyone whose sensory and mental apparatus is not im-
paired should be able to perceive, are literally in the work.
Ascription of such characteristics is normally accompanied with
the certitude distinctive of propositions cited in support of
fundamental knowledge claims. That an element is crimson,
circular, cylindrical, or a high C is not usually subject to further
confirmation.

b. The next class of predicates typically finds employment in
aesthetic contexts but may also be used in other situations, e.g.,
words such as "harmonious," "delicate," "graceful," and many
others. Here agreement among critics is still substantial but by
no means unanimous. Some persons may detect subtle rhythms
where others utterly fail to do so. Similarly, a feature appearing
"graceful" to one critic may appear "flaccid" to another. Indeed, one cannot always decide whether terms like "delicate,"
"garish," or "harmonious" are used to describe or characterize,
or even to evaluate, whether they are closer to the cognitively
certain or to the cognitively uncertain end of the critical spectrum. Once more, it is sometimes impossible to maintain sharp
and clear distinctions. Nor is it always necessary to do so.

c. There is another, more properly aesthetic, group of characterizing predicates which cannot be certified through simple
inspection. They have one thing in common: their normal application lies in a different modality of experience; hence to ascribe
them to works of art is to use them metaphorically. Thus critics
speak of "strident" colors, "luminous" tones, "lugubrious"
movements, "taut" story lines, or "stern" passages, to take
only a very few simple examples. While often construed as a
source of perplexity, it should not be concluded that this kind

of talk is imprecise and is to be corrected by recourse to a more accurate and purely descriptive language of criticism. Of matters metaphorical some reasonably certain things can be said.

(1) In the first place it is clear that the metaphorical use of terms is predicated on identifiable features in the work of art; aesthetic judgments containing such terms do not (or need not) report gross or idiosyncratic impressions. Although it may be thought that "violent" does not properly characterize a certain component or pervasive regional property, people generally know what is being talked about. Nor is it impossible to develop some understanding of what led an individual to make such an ascription.

(2) Furthermore, divergent judgments are usually not poles apart but seem to lie along a qualitative range. For instance an arrangement of elements may be called "restful" by some and "monotonous" by others, but it is highly unlikely that such elements would be characterized as being "turbulent." And a concept of aesthetic knowing requires only that we can speak intelligently about matters of relevance and appropriateness.

(3) It is also pointed out that the use of metaphorical language is neither unnatural nor esoteric. The shift from literal to metaphorical, or quasi-metaphorical, uses of words is due to "certain abilities and tendencies to link experiences, to regard certain things as similar, and to see, explore, and be interested in these similarities. It is a feature of human intelligence and sensitivity that we do spontaneously do these things and that the tendency can be encouraged and developed. It is no more baffling that we should employ aesthetic terms of this sort than that we should make metaphors at all." [22] Moreover, the propensity for metaphor, or what is sometimes called figurative language, is cultivated at an early age by emulating the actions of parents and peers, a fact perhaps fraught with unexplored educational consequences.

Some additional remarks about the analytical phase are in order. In the first place, it should be clear that the characterization of elements and relationships in a work of art already shades over into the next, the interpretive, phase. Furthermore, descriptive and characterizing terms are in many cases normative as well, thus anticipating the evaluative phase. In most contexts words like "harmonious," "unified," and "graceful" tend to have positive connotations, while "shrill," "harsh," "unbalanced," "disjointed," etc., seem to be not only descriptive characterizations but negative judgments as well, though perhaps not always. In a great deal of modern art criticism the judgments "harsh" and "shrill," for example, seem to have positive connotations, owing no doubt to that peculiar tendency of contemporary sensibility to assert intensity of expression as a norm.

3. *Interpretation.* The proper concern of this phase is to say something about the meaning of a work of art as a whole, as distinct from an interpretation of its parts. Judgments of this sort are frequently the first ones made about works of art, which is to say they tend not to be preceded by descriptive and formal analysis. But to justify or support interpretations a critic will often resort to description and analysis. Such activity may have the effect of amplifying, modifying, or even radically altering a viewer's, listener's, or reader's own interpretation—or as David Hume said, such activity can correct "a false relish."

Since interpretation is often taken as the most meaningful and enriching phase of a transaction between a percipient and a work of art, just what and what not to expect from it should be indicated. Interpretation, it is suggested, should not be attempted where human significance is obviously irrelevant, e.g., in the case of works primarily concerned with pattern and decoration. Further, the impression should be avoided that interpretation is merely a summing up of what is found in analysis. The interpretation of a work of art as "an image of lonely despair" seems to follow logically from the characterization of its components as "somber," "drooping," "mournful," "dark-hued," "slow-paced," etc. But not necessarily. Transvaluation may also occur.

For instance, normative connotations of interpretative ascriptions may be altered when elements characterized negatively as "unbalanced," "top-heavy," or "murky" are perceived as necessary to a forceful expression, say, of "menace" or "impending disaster." Original characterizations may also take on ironic or disturbing twists when, e.g., details which one would normally call "gay" and "sprightly" are seen as essential to a "sinister" or "anxiety-ridden" mood. This is often the mark of significant transitional works. Mannerist works from the sixteenth century come to mind in which traditional forms were used to create powerful new imagery. The delicate color of Hieronymus Bosch is another example, whose *Garden of Earthly Delights* incidentally is anything but delightful. Indeed, the modern movement of surrealism in painting, literature, and now film trades on such devices to create queasy and unsettling qualities. The work of the expressionist composer Schönberg is also said to have used nineteenth-century values of unreality and modish display in the service of an ultimate seriousness. All of this is merely to indicate that while the citing of analytical findings in support of interpretations is required by responsible criticism, the manner in which interpretive judgments emerge from analytical ones is complex and not productive of general agreement. Perhaps this is one reason why certain works of art continue to have universal appeal: their infinitely rich forms continually give rise to new interpretations when seen from a different angle of vision.

If the connection between interpretation and analysis is often ambiguous, the relationship between the subject matter of a representational work and its message or content is even more so. It is probably a good rule to say that a critical response is inadequate if it offers as an interpretation merely a description of subject matter. Content, on the other hand, is a kind of distillation, abstraction, or compaction of whatever is depicted or portrayed. And often it is in more significant works that striking discrepancies are found between what the work ostensibly represents and what it is interpreted to be, or what it is said to be a metaphor or image of. A clear-cut case is Masaccio's mural *The Tribute Money* which is impressive not because it depicts a particular biblical episode, in itself not high in the hierarchy of biblical events; rather it is impressive because it shows the dignity of the individual. An aesthetic interpretation of the *The Tribute Money*, then, delivers the judgment that the picture's significance resides in its image of human nobility, such image being the essential import of what is depicted, i.e., its content in contrast to its subject matter.

4. *Evaluation*. The term as used here implies some kind of summation or assessment of the merit of the work of art in question. The simplest kind of verdict is one saying that the work is good or bad, based on an examination of its aesthetic qualities, say, its degree of unity, complexity, intensity, or some combination of these.

As for import or significance, the only acceptable aesthetic evaluation is one of sufficiency or deficiency. A work may be judged sufficiently expressive to reward contemplation, or, as in the case of certain elaborate and technically brilliant productions, it may be dismissed as shallow, insignificant, not worth the percipient's time. To praise or condemn on the basis of *what* a work says, however, is to make a moral, cognitive, or extra-aesthetic, and not a distinctively aesthetic evaluation. To condemn or praise a work *because* it depicts, say, moral decadence would be a case in point. But an aesthetic evaluation would arise from an assessment of the work's parts, complexes, relations, and regional aspects, the overall interpretation of which might give rise to the kinds of content statements previously referred to. However, since extra-aesthetic judgments will be made by teachers and learners anyway, it is no use ruling them out of aesthetic education. Indeed, it may be necessary to know how to handle them in order to understand better what is involved in aesthetic judgments. The only stipulation would seem to be that teachers and learners understand that different sorts of judgments can be made of works of art.[23]

There are at least two ways in which even a work that rates high in expressiveness and is solid and respectable on every

[23] For a discussion of cognitive, moral, and aesthetic judgments, see Monroe C. Beardsley, *Aesthetics: Problems in the Philosophy of Criticism* (New York: Harcourt Brace, 1958), Ch. 10. Also "The Classification of Critical Reasons," *Journal of Aesthetic Education*, vol. 2, no. 3 (1968): 55–63.

other count may yet draw a negative critical assessment. One is to find it derivative and unoriginal; there simply are too many things of this kind around. Second, an aesthetically good work may be rejected as poor when it fails to serve what extra-aesthetic functions it may have. Paul Rudolph's Art and Architecture Building at Yale may be a case in point; it is purportedly interesting to perception, yet students are said to complain about working in it.

Another pair of evaluative terms are "successful" and "unsuccessful." Now "successful" and "good" are almost equivalent. But to ascribe lack of success to a work appears to mean that certain expectations were not fulfilled. This could refer to the artist's intentions: he did not achieve what he set out to do. Speculations about what the artist had in mind, however, are sometimes difficult, if not impossible, to verify, and for purposes of aesthetic evaluation it would seem that the work itself provides most of the necessary information. If "unsuccessful" indicates that a work is not quite what it might have been, then some description of what would have constituted success should be expected.

Last, critics will frequently sum up their reaction, the nature of their experience with the work, with such terms as "interesting," "impressive," "challenging," "stimulating," "dull," "preposterous," etc.[24] In other words, an assessment of the value possibilities of a work may be rounded off by a statement about the nature or intensity of the liking or valuing, and the latter is not always predictable in light of the former. It is perhaps the mark of the highly educated aesthetic observer that he can recognize a work's value potential, endorse it, and even recommend it wholeheartedly to others, yet say that it is not his cup of tea. This recognition of the irreducible differences in temperament and personality which have no effect on, nor are affected by, the aesthetic evaluation of a work of art is perhaps the highest degree of objectivity one can hope for in art or in aesthetic education. But there are still problems.

[24] See the distinction between "emotional-arousal" and "recognition of emotional quality" words made by R. W. Hepburn in "Emotions and Emotional Qualities: Some Attempts at Analysis," *British Journal of Aesthetics*, vol. 1, no. 4 (1961); 267.

Even if the foregoing constitutes a reasonable and acceptable description of critical activity, it does not explicitly prescribe content or procedures for doing criticism. Needed is a comprehensive set of concepts and critical *techniques* as distinct from critical *phases*.

Very briefly, some content that might be used to help develop critical capacities are the concepts (or topics) of medium, form, content, and style. These are some of the more inclusive notions. Regarding *form* we may mention the principles of harmony, balance, centrality, and development, aspects which can be displayed by the devices of recurrence, similarity, gradation, variation, modulation, symmetry, contrast, opposition, equilibrium, rhythm, measure, dominance, climax, hierarchy, progression, etc.[25] In addition, somewhere in instruction such topics as symbol, meaning, truth, intention, and metaphor should be dealt with.[26] The generality of content from one art to another should not, however, be taken for granted lest a spurious unity be imposed on materials. Content as transfigured subject matter, i.e., the subject as presented in the medium of the materials, is an important and accepted idea in the visual arts, but more problematic in music. And it is an open question how one should talk about the significance of some examples of nonobjective and abstract painting. Does a Mondrian or a Kandinsky, or a work of "op" art, have either content or subject matter? It depends on how the terms "content" and "subject matter" are used and on how the properties of such works may be construed. Clearly content or expressiveness is minimal in some objects, and the question of the medium presents difficulties in poetry. How important, e.g., is the sound of poetry, the timbre of the spoken word? Should some novels be read aloud? And how, after all, is the term "form" to be used? Does "form" simply mean structure, or design, i.e., the elements in

[25] See the discussion of content in H. S. Broudy, "The Structure of Knowledge in the Arts," in Smith, *Aesthetics and Criticism* . . . , pp. 37–40.

[26] Any standard anthology of aesthetics will reveal a sense of the topics currently structuring the discipline. In this connection, see the collection of articles from the *Journal of Aesthetics and Art Criticism* in *Aesthetic Inquiry,* ed. Monroe C. Beardsley and Herbert M. Schueller (Belmont, Calif.: Dickerson Publishing Co., 1967).

relation? Or is form a normative concept implying something achieved and valuable, as it is in several theories? Awareness of some of these important differences among the arts has prompted one philosopher to organize his discussion such that painting and music are examined together with respect to their descriptive aspects, separately with respect to problems of interpretation, whereas literature is a separate topic altogether, except in dealing with critical evaluation where most judgments, it is claimed, can be supported by making appeal to a fundamental set of canons.[27]

Regarding critical procedures or techniques, again as distinct from critical phases, recent studies of the critic's activities suggest methods and procedures for teaching. These techniques have been described as involving approximately seven tactics.[28] There is (1) the pointing out of nonaesthetic features. Examples would be: "Notice these flecks of color." "Did you see the figure of Icarus in the Breughel? Notice how he has made use of the central figure." The idea, of course, in mentioning or pointing out nonaesthetic features is that by indicating one thing the learner is encouraged to see something else, presumably more aesthetically relevant. Then there is (2) the pointing out of aesthetic features and qualities. In doing this the critic simply mentions aesthetic qualities. "See how nervous and delicate." "Observe the tension." "Feel the vitality!" Simply mentioning the quality may do the trick, achieve the perception in the learner. There may also be (3) a linking of remarks about aesthetic and nonaesthetic aspects. This, of course, is quite common. "Do you notice how the horizontals give a feeling of tranquility?" "See how the red adds to the intensity of expression." I have already said something about the metaphorical use of terms in criticism, but the (4) use of genuine metaphors and similes may be noted. "The light shimmers, the lines dance, everything is air, lightness, and gaiety." The critic may also (5) make use of contrasts, comparisons, and reminiscenses, e.g., "It has the quality of a Rembrandt." "In the Botticelli the edges of forms are stressed as lines, whereas in the Rubens there is a

[27] Beardsley, *Aesthetics: Problems* . . . , pp. 469–70.
[28] Sibley, "Aesthetic Concepts," pp. 336–39.

tendency toward fusion and interplay." The (6) use of repetition and reiteration is another tactic, as is (7) making use of expressive gestures. This latter is merely to say that nonverbal behavior may help: a sweep of the arm, a dip of the body, a certain facial expression.

It is important to note that there can be no guarantee that such techniques will be successful in bringing others to see, hear, or feel what is to be experienced, for critical skills and procedures cannot be equated with a method which, when followed conscientiously, ensures success, i.e., a perfect judgment or appraisal: there is no such thing. The teaching of categories, concepts, criteria, and procedures, though seeming to hold out the only hope for making sense of what can be known in a work of art, constitutes no more than elements of heuristic devices, or sets of questions to ask without expectation that each of them will necessarily be revealingly answered.

But, it may be asked, how can it be determined whether a student is genuinely developing as an aesthetic knower? It is suggested that initial evidence of growth in this direction is found in written and oral responses to works of art. With respect to the problem of authenticity two things may be said. First of all, excessive parroting, or what may be called the "replicative" use of learning, can be avoided by selecting works for test responses which are sufficiently different from the ones used in trial demonstration, yet similar enough to allow learnings to be used "interpretively." [29] To deal with the discrepancies that are bound to occur in student responses, clues may be sought in the appropriateness of the reasons given in support of various types of judgments and evaluations. A sense of what is reasonable and appropriate, however, can come only with experience; hence critical dispositions must be fashioned over a relatively long period of time. Actually, what differentiates the very good from the inferior in student responses is not difficult to discern. Once again, one thing to

[29] For a discussion of four different kinds of learning—associative, replicative, interpretive, and applicative—see Harry S. Broudy, B. Othanel Smith and Joe R. Burnett, *Democracy and Excellence in American Secondary Education* (Chicago: Rand McNally, 1964), Ch. 3.

look for is the organization of critical statements, the ways in which descriptive, analytical, interpretive, and evaluative remarks are interrelated. Neither would one want to overlook matters of style and persuasiveness. Thus criteria for assessing student responses are relevance, appropriateness, cohesiveness, and persuasiveness.

ON THE METHOD OF EXPLICATION

James J. Zigerell

Much of what passes for a reading of literary texts—especially poems—in our universities is little more than a gathering in of vague impressions. Both teachers and students are satisfied once they have attached a label to whatever effect a poem has upon them: "thoughtful," "pensive," "run through with overtones of meaning." How often does the student, undergraduate or graduate, sample the distinctive aesthetic pleasure that derives from contemplation of the poem as a work of art? How often are students encouraged to read poems in a way that will lead to this act of contemplation?

In French schools, the kind of reading to be discussed in this paper is called *explication de texte*. Reading a passage of prose or poetry, according to this method, means explaining both its *explicit* and *implicit* meanings. Thus explication is not mere paraphrase or restatement. Nor is it summary. Nor does it involve one in an investigation of an author's life, in a search for parallels, or in a quest of sources or borrowings. Paraphrase or summary are, however, necessary preliminaries to explication. Searches for parallels and sources lead to literary scholarship, however, rather than to close and critical reading of texts, although such searches are at times necessary to a full reading—especially of older texts.

Explication is derived from a Latin term which means "to unfold." When a reader explicates a passage, he "unfolds" or "unravels" its meanings. He explains syntax, lexical meaning, figures of speech, allusions. The tools used are reading skills (skills never really developed to their fullest measure) and certain indispensable tools of reference—e.g., the *Oxford English Dictionary,* standard unabridged dictionaries, historical, biographical, and mythological dictionaries, concordances, books

From the *Journal of Aesthetic Education,* vol. 3, no. 4 (October 1969): 81–96. Reprinted by permission of the *Journal* and the author.

of quotations. The latter tools are helpful particularly in explaining what is explicit in the text.

But in reading a literary work—that is, a work that gives aesthetic pleasure—the student cannot stop with the explicit. Instead he proceeds from the explicit to the implicit. Putting it another way, he moves from the *part* to the *whole*. If, for example, the reader is acquainted with the conventions of the epic (an instance of the explicit), he knows that the opening lines of Alexander Pope's *The Rape of the Lock* with their epic statement of theme:

> What dire offence from am'rous causes springs,
> What mighty contests rise from trivial things
> I sing—

suggests a disproportion of disparity between the subject matter —a silly lovers' quarrel and its "serious" consequences in high society—and the treatment (*Arma virumque cano*). Still other epic devices are used throughout: for example, a game of cards becomes a deadly contest between epic heroes; the contents of the heroine's dressing table are listed grandiloquently as an epic catalogue. The reader who recognizes these *explicit* signs —conventions of the classical epics deriving from Homer and Virgil—is led to an understanding of *implicit* meanings. That is, he recognizes that the poet is poking fun at idle people of the *haut monde* who magnify their own trifling affairs out of all proportion. He achieves effects, caustic and aesthetically pleasurable at once, by casting his material in mock-heroic terms.

Explication can become literary criticism. As a matter of fact, in recent years the method has become both the means and the end in the influential critical writings of the New Critics, a group whose members like to regard every literary text as a self-contained linguistic unit. Terms such as "texture" (to refer to the quality that makes the language of poetry different in kind from the language of ordinary discourse), "ambiguity," "paradox," "irony," stand for key critical concepts in their commentary. Every student of modern literature is acquainted with outstanding products of this critical school. Prominent examples are William Empson's *Seven Types of*

Ambiguity and Cleanth Brooks's *The Well-Wrought Urn,* both widely-read books concerned with revealing what is implicit in the text itself. There is also a journal entitled *The Explicator,* the editors of which publish only papers bearing directly on explication of short texts. (It should be noted that book-length explications of a writer's complete works or of a lengthy work inevitably include consideration of sources and parallels. A classic example of this kind of thorough analysis is J. L. Lowes's brilliant *The Road to Xanadu,* a study of the workings of Coleridge's imagination.)

The serious student, however, is not interested so much in writing literary criticism as he is in mastering a method of close reading that opens the door on the aesthetic experience. Perhaps the following discussion and examples of the method of explication will be helpful. We will begin by showing how paraphrase, summary, and restatement—processes with which every student is familiar—are preliminary to explication. Let us work with a familiar poem.

Here is the justly renowned Sonnet 73 by William Shakespeare:

> That time of year thou mayst in me behold
> When yellow leaves, or none, or few, do hang
> Upon those boughs which shake against the cold,
> Bare ruin'd choirs, where late the sweet bird sang.
> In me thou see'st the twilight of such day
> As after sunset fadth in the west;
> Which by and by black night doth take away.
> Death's second self, that seals up all in rest.
> In me thou seest the glowing of such fire,
> That on the ashes of his youth doth lie,
> As the death-bed whereon it must expire
> Consum'd with that which it was nourish'd by.
> This thou perceiv'st, which makes thy love more strong,
> To love that well which thou must leave ere long.

Concentrate for a moment on the opening four lines (quatrain). Plainly the "speaker" is stating that he has reached the fullness of his physical maturity. But how much have we said when we say this? Any explication of these lines—and ones of extreme subtlety have been published (see Empson's *Seven Types of Ambiguity*)—not only must consider the overtones of meaning imparted by locutions like "yellow leaves," "bough," "cold," "bare ruin'd choirs," "birds," but also must consider the dominant metaphor, or analogy, contributing to the total argument clinched in the last two lines (couplet). The analogy can be formulated as follows: late summer is to the year as a whole as my time of life is to the life of man as a whole. Thus, in this instance, explication begins with simple lexical analysis (i.e., analysis of the words themselves) and simple grammatical sorting out (What is the subject? What verb is tied to the subject? What is the object? What is a phrase in apposition to?) moves on to close examination of the richly suggestive images (e.g., "bare ruin'd choirs where late the sweet birds sang"), and finally arrives at an awareness of the functioning of a suggestive analogy as part of the sonnet's total argument. To repeat: explication moves from the explicit to the implicit.

II

Explication is simple or complex as the work to be explicated yields its meaning immediately, without elaborate grammatical analysis and exegesis of image and idea, or only after elaborate analysis or unraveling of allusions and the like. This should not be taken to mean that simplicity of statement marks a poem or passage of prose as artistically inferior—although some modern critics who see language itself as the irreducible poetic element tend to discredit poetry of direct statement. Note how the following poem ("Song") by Christina Rossetti combines a limpid flow of language with an almost sardonic complication of thought:

> When I am dead, my dearest,
>   Sing no sad songs for me;
> Plant thou no roses at my head,
>   Nor shady cypress tree:
> Be the green grass above me
>   With showers and dewdrops wet;
> And if thou wilt, remember,
>   And if thou wilt, forget.
> I shall not see the shadows,
>   I shall not feel the rain;
> I shall not hear the nightingale
>   Sing on as if in pain:

> And dreaming through the twilight
> That doth not rise nor set,
> Haply I may remember,
> And haply may forget.

But since so many "poetic" effects stem from compression—and since effective compression is often achieved by means of syntactic distortion, subtle use of figures of speech, deliberate use of ambiguity, a bold employment of paradox and irony—when we read poetry we must face up to tricky problems of interpretation. Note how an almost outrageous paradox and a striking compression enable the following poem by Emily Dickinson—a mere forty-four words in length—to speak volumes. We need only write out an explication of these stanzas to see how much she says in so narrow a compass:

> My life closed twice before its close
> It yet remains to see
> If immortality unveil
> A third event to me.
> So huge, so hopeless to conceive,
> As these that twice befell.
> Parting is all we know of heaven,
> And all we need of hell.

The key terms of the poem are equivocal. That is, words like "life," "closing," "event," "parting," "heaven," "hell" are not confined to their ordinarily accepted meanings, but are intended to suggest climactic moments within the poet's allotted span of years.

Patient, painstaking preliminary work is extremely important in explication. Even a poem as formidable looking as the following by E. E. Cummings (a modern poet who, like some seventeenth-century poets, was so intrigued by the look of verse on a page that he at times made the arrangement of his lines emblematic—i.e., graphically suggestive of his theme) yields its meaning as soon as an attentive reader perceives that the poem is a dialogue: whatever is inside parentheses represents the heart, or the intuiting faculty, speaking, and whatever is outside parentheses represents the mind, or intellect, or "abstracter," speaking:

IF EVERYTHING HAPPENS THAT CAN'T BE DONE

if everything happens that can't be done
(and anything's righter
than books
could plan)
the stupidest teacher will almost guess
(with a run
skip
around we go yes)
there's nothing as something as one

one hasn't a why or because or although
(and buds know better
than books
don't grow)
one's anything old being everything new
(with a what
which
around we come who)
one's everything so

so world is a leaf so tree is a bough
(and birds sing sweeter
than books
tell how)
so here is away and so your is a my
(with a down
up
around again fly)
forever was never till now

now i love you and you love me
(and books are shuter
than books can be)
and deep in the high that does nothing but fall
(with a shout
each
around we go all)
there's somebody calling who's we

we're anything brighter than even the sun
(we're everything greater
than books
might mean)
we're everyanything more than believe
(with a spin
leap

    alive we're alive)
    we're wonderful one times one

       (From *Collected Poems,* Harcourt, Brace and World,
       1963)

We have seen why the poet encloses part of his poem in parentheses. Is it relevant to ask too—aside from consideration of rhythmic groupings of words—why the lines spoken by the mind (outside the parentheses) are more discursive and longer than those spoken by the heart? Is it that the heart is less dependent on the verbal, the discursive, the elements that obscure what it knows immediately and fully? Isn't it significant, too, that the second statement within parentheses in each stanza is a childlike, joyous whoop?

We have seen how examination of the punctuation and the "look" of lines can lead to understanding. Perhaps now is the time to see how important grammatical and lexical analysis can be. Poets, because of the demands of their medium—especially English poets of the early seventeenth century and contemporary poets in England and America—resort to grammatical distortion to achieve a cryptic compression of meaning or allusion, as well as to achieve unusual rhythmic or sound effects. Let us look at the following well-known poem by G. M. Hopkins, a man whose work when published in 1918, about twenty years after his death, stimulated radical departures in poetic technique on both sides of the Atlantic:

THE WINDHOVER
To Christ our Lord

I caught this morning morning's minion, king-
    dom of daylight's dauphin, dapple-dawn-drawn Falcon in his
      riding
  Of the rolling level underneath him steady air, and striding
High there, how he rung upon the rein of a wimpling wing
In his ecstasy! then off, off forth on swing,
    As a skate's heel sweeps smooth on a bow-bend: the hurl and
      gliding
  Rebuffed the big wind. My heart in hiding
Stirred for a bird,—the achieve of, the mastery of the thing!

Brute, beauty and valour and act, oh, air, pride, plume, here
  Buckle! AND the fire that breaks from thee then, a billion
Times told lovelier, more dangerous, O my chevalier!

No wonder of it: sheer plod makes plough down sillion
Shine, and blue-bleak embers, ah my dear,
Fall, gall themselves, and gash gold-vermillion.

T. S. Eliot once remarked that lines from Dante's *The Divine
Comedy* when read aloud in their original language can be
impressive and beautiful, even if the listener knows no Italian.
The above poem read aloud by a skillful reader might very well
please the ear of the listener who knows no English. The
rhythmic rush, the grouped stresses intensified by the patterns
of alliteration, the musical patterns of assonance and consonance—all these overwhelm a sensitive listener without regard
to meaning. But the "performer," or reader, of the poem must
have some understanding of its meaning. (Critics, as we all
know, are in sharp disagreement as to the meaning of certain lines and images.) This understanding, or explication,
must start with several humble tasks: first, a rearrangement or
restatement of the lines in the syntactic patterns of ordinary discourse; second, a careful search in the dictionary for the meanings of the words like "dauphin," "dapple," "rung," "wimpling." (Since an ordinary dictionary does not completely solve
problems like that posed by the compound epithet "dapple-
dawn-drawn," we must summon to our aid some little ingenuity.
Hopkins, a keen student of Anglo-Saxon alliterative verse, was
fond of compounding alliterating, assonantal words for special
rhythmic effects.) Or, perhaps, we must seek out a term like
"rung," which is derived from the ancient art of falconry, in a
special dictionary. Once all this has been done in the course of
line-by-line analysis, we can begin to see broader meanings
implicit in "Falcon," "dauphin." The terms will take on symbolic dimensions, and the dedication which follows the title
will seem more than the conventionally pious gesture of the
priest.

III

The mention of "rung" and the sport of falconry has introduced another important step involved in the explication of
texts: the problem of allusions. Every teacher tells students who

are at all serious about the study of literature that they must have at hand certain indispensable reference tools, among which is a handbook or dictionary of mythology. Poets—particularly poets of earlier times—often allude to classical myths as they have come down to us from the Greek and Roman antiquity through Hesiod, Homer, and Ovid. Indeed, Christian poets of all ages make frequent reference to the Bible. How can one study John Milton without ready access to a concordance to the Bible, since he refers so often to Scripture?

Allusions serve several purposes. At times, as they are used by inferior writers, they are merely decorative. At other times, they serve only to remind us of our common heritage. But when used by the genuine poet, they become a symbolic shorthand, enabling him to compress as well as ornament his meaning. On occasion a rich allusion will serve as a hinge on which the total meaning of a work swings.

Read these closing lines from a poem by George Peele, a contemporary of Shakespeare:

> Love is a great and mighty lord;
> And when he list to mount so high,
> With Venus he in heaven doth lie,
> And evermore hath been a god
> Since Mars and she played even and odd.

Just a few moments spent with a dictionary or handbook of mythology (Edith Hamilton's *Mythology* is easily available in an inexpensive paper reprint) will solve the problem of the allusion: a decorative reference to classical myth. A careful reader, however, would also want to consult the appropriate volume of the *Oxford English Dictionary* on "even and odd." The allusion is a pretty one indeed.

But the following stanzas composed by Thomas Nashe, another of Shakespeare's contemporaries, show how allusions can act as a symbolic shorthand useful in calling up a host of associations—provided, of course, that we recognize the allusions to the *Iliad*.

> Beauty is but a flower
> Which wrinkles will devour:
> Brightness falls from the air,

> Queens have died young and fair,
> Dust has closed Helen's eye.
> I am sick, I must die.
>   Lord have mercy on us!
> Strength stoops unto the grave,
> Worms feed on Hector brave,
> Sword may not fight with fate . . .

For a magnificent example of a modern reflective poem in which reference to a myth serves as an organizing principle we need only return to Yeats's "Leda and the Swan." (Since the poem is in most anthologies, it need not be reprinted here.) Everyone remembers how the poet establishes as his context a myth well known to poets, painters, and students of the classics: Zeus visits Leda in the form of a swan and fathers Helen, who is later stolen by Paris to become the poetic "cause" of the Trojan War. Relying on a reader's familiarity with the story, Yeats can omit details and achieve a striking tautness and terseness of expression. The following lines alluding to the mythological union of god and mortal possess a mysterious, understated intensity which reinforces the reader's feeling that the speaker of the poem is being teased out of thought as he reflects on the godlike and the bestial elements combined in human nature:

> A shudder in the loins engenders there
> The broken wall, the burning roof and tower
> And Agamemnon dead

To explicate these lines we must use many more words than the poet did. Yeats could assume that his readers were well acquainted with events leading up to the war described by Homer in the *Iliad*. Thus, he left much unsaid, relying on the myth as the symbolic shorthand mentioned several times earlier: humankind manifests the divine and the mortal, the bestial and the beautiful. . . .

When a work is organized around an allusion, as is the case in "Leda and the Swan," great care must be taken in explicating it. Look at the following sonnet by John Keats:

> Keen, fitful gusts are whisp'ring here and
>   there

Among the bushes half leafless, and dry;
The stars look very cold about the sky,
And I have many miles on foot to fare.
Yet feel I little of the cool bleak air,
Or of the dead leaves rustling drearily,
Or of those silver lamps that burn on
high,
Or of the distance from home's pleasant
lair:
For I am brimful of the friendliness
That in a little cottage I have found;
Of fair-hair'd Milton's eloquent distress,
And all his love for gentle Lycid
drown'd;
Of lovely Laura in her light green dress,
And faithful Petrarch gloriously
crown'd.

The allusions in this poem are by no means so suggestive as those of "Leda and the Swan." But note how the allusions to Petrarch and Milton in the last six lines present a sharp contrast to the rather bleak scene presented in the first eight lines. This contrast suggests the pleasures of literature: Milton's elegy on the death of Lycidas and Petrarch's delicately wrought lines on his beloved Laura raise the poet above the dreariness of everyday life.

IV

What has just been said about allusions can also be said about imagery and figures of speech—e.g., simile, metaphor, personification, etc. They are merely decorative—as is often the case in sentimental verse—or they function to organize a work and become vehicles of meaning. As for imagery: any word or combination of words appealing to our senses, visual or other, can be regarded as an image. The first eight lines of Keats's sonnet just quoted are rich in images, and besides appealing to almost all the senses, are delightful in themselves—e.g., ". . . fitful gusts are whisp'ring here and there." In addition, insofar as the development of thought is concerned, they help organize the contrast between the first eight lines (the octave) and the last six (the sestet). They have one important element in common: they suggest the bleakness of nature in early winter. Always when reading a poem, we look for qualities the images have in common. Images impart additional dimensions of meaning.

As for figures of speech, note how a personification is the organizing principle of the following poem by Shelley:

A DIRGE

Rough wind, that moanest loud
　Grief too sad for song;
Wild wind, when sullen cloud
　Knells all the night long;
Sad storm, whose tears are vain,
Bare woods, whose branches strain
Deep caves and dreary main,
　Wail, for the world's wrong!

To explicate this poem adequately, we explain how aspects of nature are personified so as to suggest someone given over to uncontrollable grief at the spectacle of the evil and injustice in the world.

Or, a poet may expand a metaphor to carry the burden of a poem. Keats's magnificent sonnet "On First Looking into Chapman's Homer" supplies an instance of this expansion. The entire poem is an extended metaphor in which the speaker's discovery of Homer in an Elizabethan translation is likened to a voyage of exploration and discovery.

v

Just a few concluding words about explication. Once we as patient, methodical readers have straightened out grammar and syntax, investigated the denotative (dictionary) and connotative meanings of words, explained allusions and figures of speech, we must still recognize and comment on a poem's total effect. This is part of the task of explaining what is implicit. That is, a lyric may be a brief meditation delivered by a speaker (not necessarily the poet himself), or an argument presupposing the actual or imagined presence of a listener. For example, in the following poem by William Blake, the speaker muses on the human lot (note the function of the sunflower):

AH! SUN-FLOWER

Ah! Sun-flower! weary of time.
Who countest the stops of the sun;
Seeking after that sweet golden clime,
Where the traveller's journey is done;

Where the Youth pined away with desire,
And the pale Virgin shrouded in snow,
Arise from their graves, and aspire
Where my Sun-flower wishes to go.

The following lyric by Emily Brontë ("Sympathy") contains the germ of an argument:

There should be no despair for you
While nightly stars are burning,
While evening pours its silent dew,
    And sunshine gilds the morning.
There should be no despair—though tears
    May flow down like a river.
And not the best beloved of years
    Around your heart for ever?

They weep, you weep—it must be so;
Winds sigh as you are sighing.
And Winter sheds its grief in snow
    Where Autumn's leaves are lying:
Yet, these revive, and from their fate
    Your fate cannot be parted:
Then, journey on, if not elate,
    Still never broken-hearted!

Finally, after all this discussion, some of which has been distressingly obvious, we should examine a complete explication. Below are two: the first of a frequently anthologized sonnet by Sir Philip Sidney, the second of a poem by a contemporary poet, Conrad Aiken. These explications, it will be noted, become critical pieces:

Loving in truth, and fain in verse my love to show,
    That she, dear she, might take some pleasure of
    my pain,
    Pleasure might cause her read, reading might
    make her know,
    Knowledge mighty pity win, and pity grace ob-
    tain—
    I sought fit words to paint the blackest face of woe;

Studying inventions fine, her wits to entertain,
Oft turning others' leaves to see if thence would
   flow
Some fresh and fruitful showers upon my sun-
   burned brain.
But words came halting forth, wanting invention's
   stay;
   Invention, nature's child, fled step-dame Study's
      blows,
   And others' feet still seemed but strangers in my
      way.
Thus, great with child to speak, and helpless in my
   throes,
   Biting my truant pen, beating myself for spite,
   Fool, said my nurse to me, look in thy heart and
      write.

This sonnet, at first reading, seems little more than a conventional effort in the mannered Petrarchan tradition. The poet
describes an attempt to express cogently his love for a woman
who, according to the rules of the love game, looks upon him
and his suit with indifference, if not disdain. His fervent hope
is that she will be moved by his words—the kind of humble
hope expressed by unnumbered sixteenth- and seventeenth-
century sonneteers.

The total rhetorical strategy is also in the accepted Petrarchan
manner. The octave poses the problem—how to win the ear
of an icy mistress. The sestet, after showing how ordinary
means will not do (an ironic touch), is skillfully pointed toward
the climax of the final line, in which a somewhat dramatic solution is presented—a daring and ironic solution in view of the
artificiality of the convention.

The first four lines explain why the poet is consumed with
desire to find poetic expression for his love: not because he
hopes he can move her to return his love, but because he hopes
that, from the godlike pedestal on which she stands, she will
deign—cruel mistress that the convention demands she be—
to take pleasure in his pain. This pleasure, the despairing poet
argues, will perhaps soften her thoughts of him and encourage
her to read through his poem. If she does read on, continues
the argument, the knowledge of his plight obtained thereby will

move her to pity, and pity, in turn, will move her, in her character of goddess, to single him out for favor ("grace").

Once he has given his reasons for writing, the poet describes his frenzied quest for the right words to express his despair. He poured over the lines of others ("inventions fine"), hoping to bring on the showers that will make his parched imagination ("sunburned brain") fertile. But borrowed words, lacking the firm guidance of an organizing principle or support ("invention's stay"), will not flow. (A search of the OED shows "support" to be the best general meaning for "stay." The word in Sidney's time also was used to refer to a frame, or support, on which plants were trained to grow.) In desperation, the poet concludes that invention, which is only a reflection of nature, is not to be aroused or prodded by books ("step-dame Study's blows"), which are still further removed from nature. Thus, verse containing the grief of other disappointed lovers ("others' feet") proved alien to his grief and served only to block the flow of inspiration. Helpless, agonized, and distraught like the woman despairing of ever delivering the child with which she is about to burst, he bites the pen which strays from its obstetrical task. He berates himself in his frustration—until suddenly he hears a voice speaking within himself. It is his muse who speaks: Fool, stop speaking in phrases borrowed from others and let your heart (like the woman in labor) deliver itself of its burden.

The thought pattern of the sonnet, as the above paraphrase makes apparent, falls into two main divisions. The opening quatrain, as is quite in keeping with the Petrarchan ritual prescribing the attitude of the lover toward his beloved, outlines the steps the sincere Christian follows in achieving salvation. (The love convention is often clothed in religious terms and imagery.) Once the lover avails himself of the almost sacramental act of confessing his love, his beloved may be moved to pity his state and shower grace upon him. (The poet, of course, puns on the word "grace," employing it in both the ordinary and the theological senses.)

The second and third quatrains, after listing the places to which the poet mistakenly repairs for assistance, give the answer—again with more than faint religious overtones. The Christian who despairs of salvation need only listen for the voice within him for guidance. So too, the despairing lover will find the answer in his heart.

The solution to the problem posed—although the problem is a conventional one—raises the sonnet much above the limitations of the artificial Petrarchan tradition. An attentive reading gives the reader the feeling that he has heard a sincere cry of the heart.

Now for the modern poem. This time little attention need be given to lexical or syntactic matters, or to allusions or figures of speech. Explication is focused on what is significant and crucial: the association of ideas central to the poem.

DEAD LEAF IN MAY [1]

One skeleton-leaf, white-ribbed, a last year's leaf,
Skipped in a paltry gust, whizzed from the dust,
Leapt the small dusty puddle; and sailing then
Merrily in the sunlight, lodged itself
Between two blossoms in a hawthorn tree.
That was the moment: and the world was changed.
With that insane gay skeleton of a leaf
A world of dead worlds flew to hawthorn trees,
Lodged in the green forks, rattled, rattled their ribs
(As loudly as a dead leaf's ribs can rattle)
Blithely, among bees and blossoms. I cursed,
I shook my stick, dislodged it. To what end?
Its ribs, and all the ribs of all dead worlds,
Would house them now forever as death should:
Cheek by jowl with May.

That was the moment: and my brain flew open
Like a ripe bursting pod. The seed sprang out,
And I was withered, and had given all.
Ripeness at top means rottenness beneath:
The brain divulging seed, the heart is empty:
The little blood goes through it like quicksilver:
The hand is leather, and the world is lost.
Human, who trudge the road from Here to There:
Lock the dry oak-leaf's flimsy skeleton
In auricle or ventricle; sail it

[1] From *Selected Poems* by Conrad Aiken (Oxford: Oxford University Press, 1961). Reprinted by permission of the publisher.

Like a gay ship down red Aorta's flood.
Be the paired blossoms with dead ribs between.
Thirst in the There, that you may drink the Here.

Conrad Aiken

In this poem we can observe the data of direct observation being transmuted in the alembic of the poet's imagination. A trained sensibility finds illumination in simple event, seeks out the analogues figured in the events, and fits an impressive insight into a narrow compass. Yet the transmutation is not entirely successful. Attentive reading leaves one persuaded that the shift from the quiet introspection of the first one-and-a-half stanzas to the solemn exhortation of the ending is maladroit. Further, the poem displays the virtues and the risks of employing association of ideas as an organizing principle.

The first stanza centers on a burst of illumination experienced by the "I" of the poem. Last fall's shriveled leaf, lifted by an errant gust—its workings as fortuitous as those of the force of evil in the universe—is lodged between two blossoms of a hawthorn the speaker has been admiring. Suddenly "the world was changed"; that is, the "world" of the hawthorn in May (and here we see association at work as an organizing principle) merges with a wider "world of dead worlds." This untimely reminder of death (referred to as "rottenness" in the second stanza) so annoys the speaker that he shakes the dead leaf loose. Nonetheless, the world of the blossoming hawthorn, which only a moment before had seemed an emblem of youth and life unalloyed, is now seen as part of a world in which death (the "ribs" of the leaf) must always "house" the vigor of spring ("bees and blossoms").

The recognition occasioned by the leaf's crazy flight is succeeded by the "moment" of stanza 2, when the speaker's thoughts are turned inward and the blossoms and leaf appear an analogue of the creative act of the imagination. A poem, like a blossom, is a "seed" springing out of a brain that is only productive when it shares the ripeness of a pod—the ripeness hiding the "rottenness," the waste of past experience that lies beneath. All that lives (blossom, seed, poem) must feed on dead and dying substances. And, ironically, each seed or poem produced, marking progress toward life's end, leaves the pod or brain which gave it life closer to death—the state of the "skeleton-leaf."

Thus far the poet has effectively employed an unforced association of ideas to impose form on the reflections of a day in May. But he strains to associate the blossoms of the opening stanza with the two-chambered heart of his ending. The anatomical details ("auricle," "ventricle," "Aorta's flood") do not lead the reader easily to thoughts of the heart as the center of the imagination or the softer emotions. Furthermore, is not the message wrested from the paired blossoms and the two-chambered heart ineptly imperative and blurred? Does the concluding pompous reminder of the naturalness of death and the necessity of living the moment to the fullest teeter on the edge of bathos? Why expatiate upon the eloquent and mute message of the blossoms and the leaf? [2]

[2] The commentary on the poem "Dead Leaf in May" is reprinted from *The Explicator,* vol. 25, no. 1 (September 1966): 8–9. Reprinted by permission.

THE ANALYSIS OF MUSIC

Jan LaRue

. . . Many musicians are convinced that sensitive performance and appreciative listening require analytical as well as intuitive response. The proportion of emphasis placed on these two approaches to music is entirely personal, but both avenues are needed, for they reinforce and diversify each other. A sound knowledge of the way in which musical elements create a musical structure places intuitive responses on a higher level, wherein more refined perceptions become possible. Conversely, the final insights of analysis depend on value judgments that emerge more convincingly from one's deepest intuitions than from his highest logic.

This close interconnection of analysis and intuition presents an important opportunity to musical scholars. Analysis, if properly communicated, can act as a channel for many of the conclusions based on intuition. It is difficult to talk about emotional responses, such as one's reactions to musical events. Mere everyday vocabulary communicates rather inefficiently, since emotion-conveying words mean such different things to writer and reader or to talker and listener. A clear analysis, however, checked constantly against the judgments and conclusions of intuition, can project and reinforce in a concrete way many values originating in one's most fundamental underlying responses. Notice the intuitive values implicit in questions such as these: Which melody stimulates the performer to use more crescendo? Which rhythm is more exciting? Which harmony is more expressive? Though subjective and emotional, the distinctions that result from these and similar questions can be logically arranged to show many aspects of objective order that underlie musical expression.

Two malfunctions can be noticed in many analytical writ-

From the *Music Educators Journal,* vol. 55, no. 2 (October 1968): 35–37. Copyright © *Music Educators Journal,* October 1968. Reprinted with permission of the *Journal* and the author.

ings: over-completeness and incompleteness, sometimes both within a single discussion. The commonest form of over-completeness is bar-by-bar analysis, which floods us with a mass of undigested detail, like the breathless, blow-by-blow descriptions of a prizefight reporter. Unless we are especially interested in the smallest subtleties of a given composer, bar-by-bar analysis helps us hardly at all; it merely presents the music all over again in words, taking up more space with symbols that are less precise than the original musical notation. What the reader-listener would find more helpful are not these chips from the workshop but rather the insights and overviews that the analyst gleans from his studies of the piece at various degrees of magnification. Here and there he will certainly need to quote specific bars to illustrate particular effects—but these examples merely support his broader conclusions, conclusions that actually communicate more depth of understanding than the seeming deepness of the massively but merely detailed approach. Music depends partly on details, of course, but it also stretches broadly through time. If composers intended us to examine only details, they would write tiny miniatures packed with infinitely significant subtleties. Webern took exactly this approach, but most music requires a wide-angle lens, and telescopes as well as microscopes. We must suit our analysis to the dimensions in which it moves, both large and small.

This brings us to the second common malfunction of analytical discussions: incompleteness. As we have seen, any analysis that concentrates exclusively on details cannot succeed completely—it malfunctions by sheer neglect of large dimensions. But even if we have studied a piece "in the large" as well as "in the small," the job is still incomplete—what of middle dimensions? Considering just the element *harmony,* for example, in small dimensions we could study chord forms and progressions, whereas in large dimensions we might concentrate on key relationships between movements. Yet, equally important are middle-dimension considerations, such as methods and direction of modulation to secondary key areas beyond the tonic and dominant emphases. All three dimensions, therefore, furnish valuable paths to further understanding; the omission of any appropriate dimensional measure or magnification will render our appreciation incomplete.

Within each dimension, true completeness demands a full examination of all stylistic elements, which for convenience can be summarized under the somewhat over-simplified headings of sound, harmony, rhythm, melody, and formation.[1] Discussions of these elements in analytical articles commonly deal quite effectively with small-dimension aspects of *melody,* such as thematic structure. The themes of symphonic masterpieces, the mutations in Wagnerian motives, and similar questions have been quite thoroughly investigated. Too few analysts, however, have gone on from these small- and middle-dimension considerations to study large-dimension controls, such as the overall contour of movements. Where, for example, can we read about Haydn's treatment of melodic climax, of his skill in arranging a gradual progression of successively higher peaks in the formation of a movement? The approach to melodic analysis, despite much good work, remains incomplete.

Next to melody, *harmony* has received the most attention from analysts, and there are even textbooks on the subject (for example, Walter Piston's *Principles of Harmonic Analysis,* Boston, 1933). We can count on any title that includes expressions such as "A Harmonic Analysis of . . ." to contain informative material on chord progressions, modulations, and the like, but most historical discussions of music make no concrete observations on harmony. And if any harmonic comments by chance occur, the discussion typically concentrates on small dimensions, venturing only slightly into middle dimensions when taking up the subject of modulation, but all too rarely extending to large-dimensional approaches, such as complete timeline mapping of the tonalities involved in the structure of the piece.

Two other elements, *sound* and *rhythm,* fall so far behind *melody* and *harmony* in actual amount of analytical treatment —or even brief mention—in the literature that one can hardly comment on questions of completeness or incompleteness in

[1] See "On Style Analysis," *Source Book III* (Washington, D.C.: Music Educators National Conference, 1966), pp. 139–51.

these areas. To make a beginning, we simply need more discussion of any sort! Apart from superficial observations of instrumentation and orchestration, discussions of *sound* can seldom be found. A rare exception is the illuminating differentiation of Baroque textures used in William S. Newman's *The Sonata in the Baroque Era* (Chapel Hill, 1959). Fortunately, the present preoccupation of contemporary composers with textures and fabrics of sound and with programmed dynamics and subtle (and unsubtle) extensions of the color spectrum will gradually advance our analytical knowledge simply as a by-product of new compositional directions. *Rhythm,* however, seems in danger of continued severe neglect, perhaps because it has fallen between the two extremes of generality and specificity in the few studies that exist. On the one hand, we find a broad historical approach, as in Curt Sach's *Rhythm and Tempo* (New York, 1953), which too rarely comes to grips with functional points that one can use to increase analytical understanding. On the other hand we struggle with an almost overwhelmingly detailed analysis, such as Cooper and Meyer's *The Rhythmic Structure of Music* (Chicago, 1960). Unlike Sachs, the authors of the latter book make valiant and valuable efforts to apply their theory (describing musical rhythm in Greek poetic terms) at several "hierarchic levels," that is, in more than small dimensions; at times, however, these hierarchies present a picture more complex than the music itself.

Formation, the last of the style categories, results mainly from the motion-producing forces of the other elements. (For purposes of style analysis, the somewhat unusual term "formation" replaces the more familiar "form" in order to emphasize the emergence of this final category as a combination of the other elements, as well as to avoid the overly specific conventional connotations of form, as in rondo form, sonata form, and so on.) The formation of a piece of music is partly a rhythmic phenomenon, since it takes place in time; but it also creates shapes in our memories, just as the motion of a figure skater leaves a tracing of visible arabesques on the ice when the movement has passed far away. The shifting relationships between movement and shape impart a frequent and highly intriguing ambiguity to musical form.

The critical problem in discussions of formation, just as in other style elements, is dimensional completeness. In books on music we usually read either superbly saturated motivic analyses or breezy historical generalities. Naturally, the determination of relevant and illuminating dimensions varies greatly from piece to piece. But as a point of departure we can apply the usual dimensions to musical formation according to the following general diagram:

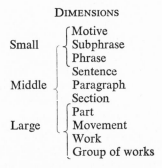

DIMENSIONS

Small
- Motive
- Subphrase
- Phrase

Middle
- Sentence
- Paragraph
- Section

Large
- Part
- Movement
- Work
- Group of works

Each of the style elements contributes to formation, notably in such functions as articulation of the larger parts, building of climax, and thematic relationship (particularly if we remember that a theme need not be a melody: it can be an arresting rhythm, a striking chord, or an evocative combination of instruments).

All the studies mentioned above constitute together mainly a preparatory phase of stylistic observation. The second phase, interpretation of our observational evidence, is less strenuous and more interesting; any analyst would rather interpret time-lines than draw them! The main axiom of interpretation admonishes us to judge a piece in its proper frame of reference. For example, considering medium as a frame of reference, we gain little insight if we judge a small piano piece by symphonic standards. Stokowski's transcriptions of Bach keyboard preludes thus grossly violate and even explode the frame of reference of these little pieces by applying vast dimensions of sound to the modest material of the originals. The frame of reference must also be properly adjusted chronologically. For example, despite some similarities in dramatic outlook among Monteverdi, Gluck, and Wagner, one cannot greatly increase his understanding of musical style in the earlier composers by placing them in the orbit of the nineteenth-century titan. Once the frame of reference is properly adjusted, however, one is ready to identify the controlling sources of movement and shape, the conflicts, coordinations, and concinnities between the style elements.

Evaluation, the final phase of style analysis, requires the greatest wisdom and modesty on the part of the analyst. In some areas of judgment, for example, one can only speak for himself. Once more, the most useful guard against the dangers of subjectivity is completeness of analytical presentation. The analyst should certainly express his personal opinion; in fact, other musicians count upon him to do so, to profit by the judgment of one who has actually passed through the tortuous trials of complete stylistic observation. The charge of subjectivity can be neutralized by presenting the *relevant* evidence (not all the sawdust from the observational workshop!) fully rather than selectively, leaving the reader to judge for himself, if he cannot accept the analyst's determinations.

The relentless harping on the theme of completeness in this brief discussion points up an apparently crippling paradox in the foregoing arguments. In many areas definitive monographs cannot be written until smaller specific studies lay the foundations, yet how can these partial studies achieve an acceptable completeness? This paradox can be resolved with remedial action in three directions: (a) proper definition of the area under investigation: if we survey our boundaries clearly, the scope and intent of our studies cannot be misunderstood; (b) genuinely comprehensive procedures: within whatever limits we predetermine, we must follow up with observations, interpretations, and evaluations as complete as possible; and (c) deflation of pretentious, imprecise titles: if we intend to discuss two or three shocking progressions in the madrigals of Gesualdo, we have no right to use a title such as "Gesualdo's Harmonic Style." Analysis must come down to earth—and down to notes. We must promise less and deliver more.

EDUCATION FOR AESTHETIC VISION

Virgil C. Aldrich

By "vision" I do not mean anything visionary; I mean visual perception. The remarks I make about this apply also in principle, *mutatis mutandis,* to the nonvisual arts, though literature presents special complications; but I bypass this larger question in this essay.

My main question here is (a) whether there is a way of perceiving or experiencing things that can be distinguished as aesthetic perception, and (b) whether it can be taught. Along with the latter goes, of course, the question of how to teach it. I raise the first part of the question not so much for the sake of getting at its answer alone, but for the direction that this can give the second part.

For the general readers who are unaware of current Anglo-American philosophical treatments of the notion of aesthetic experience, it will seem a waste of time to ask if there is any such thing, since the answer seems to them to be too obviously affirmative for words. It was also obvious, in the affirmative, for previous philosophers of art more in the swim of the great tradition of philosophy. In those old days, aestheticians did not wonder whether there was aesthetic perception, as distinguished, say, from scientific observation. They directed their efforts to finding out what it was, assuming its occurrence. But what they finally said about it, in terms of "psychic distance" or "disinterestedness" or "organizing into unity-in-diversity," was too vague or general to be very helpful either to critics-in-practice or to the new more analytical theorists who need to spell out the issues and the answers in greater detail. Moreover, the tendency in many quarters was to rest the case on empirical findings of psychology and that tended to an underestimation of what conceptual analysis can do in clearing matters up in aesthetics which is, after all, in good part a philosophical discipline.

From the *Journal of Aesthetic Education,* vol. 2, no. 4 (October 1968): 100–7. Reprinted by permission of the *Journal* and the author.

A quite recent essay called "Structure in Art Education" [1] exhibits nicely the old and, to these new analysts, the wrong way of doing aesthetics, including education for the experience of art.

My own view places me in the crossfire between these mighty opposites. [2] As I see it, the linguistic or conceptual-analytic approach has purged some of the smog from aesthetic theory, while phenomenological description and explanation of the phenomena of aesthetic experience substantiates or provides underpinning for some of the results of these conceptual analyses. Without some such noticing and talk about the phenomena of aesthetic perception, one especially serious flaw is left in both the old and new treatments of issues in aesthetics. This concerns the notion of illusion in art. I think first of Gombrich [3] on the side of the psychologists who either make aesthetic experience look more illusory (subjective) than it is, or (like Gombrich) take no clear stand about the issue. The conceptual analysts also bypass the question by leaning only on the notion of two ways of talking about things, [4] the physicalist way (objective?) and the aesthetic way (subjective?). They leave unexplained why there should be this duality of descriptions. The question that this naturally raises, "Isn't the duality grounded in and prompted by something in the nature of things?" is left unanswered.

A simple, short, yet adequate answer to this question is at this point a consummation devoutly to be wished. Brevity and adequacy do not usually go together, but let me try. I shall attempt to illuminate and justify the impression that most of us have, in the full innocence of aesthetic experience itself, that we are looking at "things" in the world about us and noticing their

[1] Harold J. McWhinnie, *The British Journal of Aesthetics*, vol. 6, no. 3 (July 1966).

[2] See my "Back to Aesthetic Experience," *Journal of Aesthetics and Art Criticism*, vol. 24, no. 3 (Spring 1966). Also *Philosophy of Art* (Englewood Cliffs, N.J.: Prentice-Hall, 1963).

[3] *Art and Illusion*, Bollingen Series, vol. 35, no. 5 (New York: Pantheon Books, 1960).

[4] E.g., Margaret McDonald, "The Work of Art as Physical," in M. Rader, ed., *A Modern Book of Esthetics*, 3rd rev. ed. (New York: Holt, Rinehart & Winston, 1960), esp. p. 219.

characteristics, not enjoying the "subjective effects" they are producing in us in a kind of illusion of out-thereness. Moreover, if this impression of something objective is done justice, another impression, namely, that one does not have the experience of things such as "aesthetic objects" unless he looks at the things in the right or relevant way, will also get the recognition it deserves.

A good first pedagogical maneuver for this purpose, especially if people are being educated on the high school or college level for aesthetic perception and theory, is to present them with one of those trick drawings that can be seen as this or as that. Perhaps the most famous of these is the duck-rabbit picture, but for my purpose here I prefer the diagram below.[5]

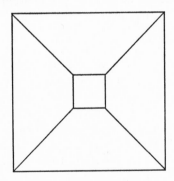

Let it be drawn on a fairly ample square cardboard—say, two feet—and held up to the view of the class, and called simply a "thing." The diagonal lines are to extend to the very corners of this thing (cardboard), making its edges the square outline of the diagram.

Now, the point to be driven home is that, if questions are asked about the space characteristics of this thing, the answers will be ambiguous unless suggestions are antecedently given as to how to perceive it. As simply encountered and noticed, it is pregnant only with potentials for this or that actual space determination. This point can be made as follows.

Ask the class if it is flat. Someone in the back of the room

[5] Taken from my *Philosophy of Art* p. 20.

may complain that he cannot tell from that distance. You hold it edgewise to his line of sight. He nods affirmatively. It is flat. Then you remind him that he was not thus simply seeing the flatness in question with the thing held edgewise but that his edgewise looking was an elementary visual test of flatness in the "physical" sense of the term. Another such test would involve getting closer for a better look at the surface of the thing, the surface being seen in this sense when its texture is visible (granularity, smoothness, etc.). But even this is not simply seeing that it is flat; it is testing it for flatness, physically speaking. You then ask how a still more "objective" observational test of physical flatness might be made with, say, a string. Someone says to stretch it taut and hold it across the surface. If the string touches the surface all the way across in various horizontal and vertical applications, the thing is flat. "Physically speaking," you add.

Now, you tell them, this thing is appearing as a physical object. Looked at this way, it is seen as a physical object. Its being a physical object is partly and basically defined by how it appears under such measuring looks or observations and correlating procedures. Moreover, this way of looking is called "observation"—for what this means in the language of science—a specially controlled way of looking that can become highly educated and exclusive by measuring techniques. The important thing to notice in this connection is that the space properties ("magnitudes") thus determined are not "simply" perceived. Indeed, they turn out in the end to be imperceptible characteristics of things as physical objects—that is, as scientific observation and thought become sophisticated. Thus it is that, in the end, things as physical objects are conceived to consist essentially of "primary qualities," meaning metrical or geometrical ones, all out of sight in the finished analysis. Space-characteristics, thus experienced and refined in thought, become the defining characteristics of anything as a physical object.

You conclude, "Let us call this general metrical way of appearing, determined by incipient comparison with external standards of straightness, flatness, etc., a 'categorial aspect' that things have as physical objects. This defines the category 'physical.' "

The point of this discourse is going to be, of course, that there is another categorially different way that the same thing may appear, another sort of categorial "aspect" or transformation it may undergo. The notion to be introduced is that of things appearing as aesthetic objects.

Someone else in the class has said that the thing he sees is not flat, that it has depth, like a tunnel. Another says no; it protrudes towards the point of view, as does a lampshade looked down on from above.

The spokesman for physical flatness remarks that these are illusions. "Only under a certain way of looking called observation," you remind him. The thing simpliciter or in itself does not initially or necessarily appear that way. It is not intrinsically a physical object. One must take an educated and exclusive sort of look at it to perceive it in that physicalistic way—a look that excludes what he is calling illusory appearances and which in effect defines them as merely subjective impressions. Initially, the thing you are holding up is what might be called a "material thing," with "thing" (not "object") underscored and "material" meaning "potential for various determinations," as has been remarked. An object presupposes a subject experiencing it in a certain way, which correlation determines both the object and the mode of perception as being of a certain sort. "Thing" is more neutral and has no such correlations.

Now your job is to define the category of the aesthetic as you have that of the physical. Some of your pupils are already looking, with unpremeditated artfulness, in the aesthetically relevant way at the thing in question, so some of the stage-setting has already been done. If you accomplish your mission, you will have shown that the thing as an aesthetic object and the correlated mode of perception have their own characteristic objectivity or out-thereness, which is the aim of the classroom demonstration. Of course, one may go wrong or have "illusions" even in aesthetic experience, but the term will no longer mean what it does in the physicalistic language of observation. (Drive home to the class that restriction on "observe.")

So somebody says the thing is not flat—the square within the square is in back or out front. But, you say, what if one sees the thing as a square suspended within a square frame? "Flat again," they say. But "again" is wrong here since they do not mean this time what the first fellow meant by "flat" who was for using a taut string to test for flatness. This is your occasion to introduce and define the notion of "plane of the picture." The suspended square is in this plane, so we say that the thing, viewed with this title in mind (square suspended in a frame), is flat. Now you get to the really important point.

What would a test of flatness in this sense be like? Or is the notion of testing nonsensical in such cases? The test by comparison with another thing functioning as an external standard is, to be sure, out of order. Only physical flatness is ascertained that way. Still, a check of some sort is feasible. One looks at the thing (now functioning as a picture) with the title in mind, and sees whether it is flat or not, in the relevant sense of "in the plane of the picture."

Whether it is to be flat or not, viewed thus, depends in the aesthetic case on the relationships of elements all internal to the thing as aesthetic object. There is no reference to an external standard or to any other thing for comparison. This explains the old notion of the "autonomy" of what is under aesthetic consideration. The space characteristics are determined by contours and—in most cases—colors. What these "do to one another" in their relationships is what fixes picture space,[6] such that any check on the resultant space characteristics will consist in an educated view of them as "aspects" of the composition of colors and contours.

Now that you are talking about colors as determinants of aesthetic space, put some colors (pastels for convenience) into the figure, showing how a darker area bordering a brighter one tends to make the boundary between protrude like the corner of a solid by virtue of the relationship of the colors alone, without yet seeing the composition of them as any recognizable thing in particular.

It is this basic perception of related-linear-and-color-elements-as-space-structure that defines things as aesthetic objects. It helps to define the general category of the "aesthetic," con-

[6] See my "Picture Space," *Philosophical Review,* vol. 67, no. 3 (July 1958).

trasting it with that of the "physical." Purists or formalists in art, you will point out to the class, tend to compose with a view primarily to this space feature. A modern artist has said that painting is the art of hollowing out a surface, and even Whistler's portrait of his mother was done, as the first title he gave it shows, for the sake of structuring by colors (especially grays) and their interanimation, not for the likeness to anything outside the composition. Call this "first-order form."

Consideration of likenesses, as in representational art, brings into focus the second principle of space formation of things as aesthetic objects and a second sense of both "aspect" and "seeing as." Briefly, this principle locates the elements of the composition in accordance with what they are seen as—parts of a landscape, limbs of a woman. Depth, solidarity, etc., may be achieved this way as well. Call this "second-order form." The artist generally composes under both the first and the second principles, in order to achieve a greater and richer formulation. Thus does he get beyond the excessive ambiguity of form of so meager a figure as the one used in class for pedagogical purposes. Exciting tensions are revealed in the space of the composition by, say, a yellow that is seen as close to the plane of the picture by its intrinsic brightness (first-order form) but is also seen as a strip of sunlit sand in the background (second-order form).

All the while, you will have had the class looking, wide-eyed, at something. Drive home to them, at the end, that their aesthetic vision is an objective experience of things in which they become aware of aspects—call such perceiving "prehending" to distinguish it from "observing"—and that these aspects are formations that things reveal in the aesthetic view of them. Add that a work of art is such a thing, one that is especially designed to tempt the prehensive way of looking.

For example, consider how André Derain's *Still Life with a Jug* tempts the prehensive (aesthetic) way of looking. It plainly shows and celebrates the materials (oil paints), especially in the parallel brush strokes typical of Cézanne, at the lower left and in the skillful overlaying of pigment on pigment. This work on the material shows up as sculptural or solid volumes, shot through, however, and softened with luminous color expanses, despite the suggestion of cubism. In this view of the painting, the light-brown triangular area left of the dark turquoise of the jug protrudes toward the plane of the picture. But the painting may also be seen as a still life with a jug, and this view tends to recess that color element into becoming a part of the table, back of the jug. In this way Derain weaves a web of images and dynamic tensions, a set of factors that expressively portrays not only the subject matter but also an elemental affection for the staples of human life.

A concluding brief remark—beyond the boundary of this essay's concern—that brings a nonvisual art into this framework. There is such a thing as "hearing as," and space-oriented descriptions of the experience. Sound may be loud, high, flat, far, close, low. Such formations are featured in a musical composition, whose elements are to be "heard as" determining its form ("space"). Such form is primarily of the first order in, say, a Bach fugue or a Hindemith quartet. Beethoven's *Pastoral Symphony* is the favorite example of a piece that exhibits second-order form as well (representational). But, in music, the "spacing" (intervals) is also in time. It is in space-time. But there is a sense in which the content of a painting is also in space-time. Thus, music may be characterized as fluid painting, and painting as frozen music.

FILM AS EDUCATOR

William Arrowsmith

In humanistic education the future lies with film. Of this I am firmly convinced. I do not mean by this either "audio-visualism" or educational filmstrips. I mean that film will be not only the future medium of instruction, but that film also will challenge and eventually claim the place and prestige accorded to literature and the arts in the traditional curriculum. In short, film not merely as medium but as curriculum, too. This conviction rests upon a faith that human society cannot do without the humanities, cannot forsake its faith in the project of making men more fully human, helping men to "become the thing they are." If real education—and not merely the transmission of knowledge—is to take place, a curriculum is required which corroborates and exemplifies moral discovery, the making of a fate, the hunger for identity. Literature and the arts have always been at the heart of the humanities because they provided just such corroboration; our most enduring use for art has been precisely in education—and it is an end worthy of art, this "expansion of love beyond ourselves," which Nietzsche called education.

But I recognize, with distress and sadness, that this literature which is for me so crucial a curriculum that I cannot imagine my life without it, is for others, especially many young people, no longer at the center of things. It has come to seem to them artificial, even faintly anachronistic; its conventions suddenly seem conventional, labored, and unreal. Its crucial illusion crippled, participation becomes constrained or even impossible. This constraint comes not only from the comparative spaciousness and realism of the new media, the superior complexity and power of their conventions, but also from the way in which literature is too often taught; that is, as technical or professional virtuosity or as a decorative cultural "accomplishment." We have become very adept, as Edgar Friedenberg points out, "at

From the *Journal of Aesthetic Education,* vol. 3, no. 3 (July 1969): 75–83. Reprinted by permission of the *Journal* and the author.

driving cadmium rods into the seething mass of our cultural heritage and rendering it inactive." [1] The schools do it by castrating art, by disguising its true subversiveness, or by forcing it to yield a crop of acceptable clichés. The universities do it by treating literature as though it were written not for our enjoyment and instruction, but as part of a curriculum, for analysis and instruction.

The constraint students feel with literature has noticeably increased as scholarly attitudes have moved from the graduate schools to the undergraduate and even the secondary curricula. Constraint now becomes the rule; the student begins to suspect, resent, and reject a literary culture and education that flourish apparently for their own sakes or for their professors', without pertinence to his life. And so the conventions that support the art of the spoken word—the artificialities that used not to trouble us, that *we* took in our stride once—begin to seem dubious and then to dissolve. One no longer feels the *necessity* of the style, or its necessities are no longer ours. Constraint is not easily unlearned; and poetry and drama seem now no longer second nature, but come to us increasingly touched by the self-consciousness of all high culture that has been educationally formalized. I have heard Jesuits say that they could not teach in clerical garb, because the authority of their robes tainted the subjects they taught, troubling education with the problems of resented or refused authority. It is the same with the spoken arts in education; what is bad and merely authoritative or professional in education has corrupted them and weakened their enabling conventions. They no longer speak to us naturally, and our responses are becoming fatally self-conscious. Or so it seems to me.

Film itself may be highly self-conscious, but it is surely unique in possessing audiences who take it naturally, who attend to it without fuss or pretense or shame; who for the most part trust its makers and feel unmistakably at ease with its conventions. People go to movies as they go to take a bath or a stroll. You cannot assume that one student in ten has read a given book;

[1] *The Humanities in the Schools,* ed. Harold Taylor (New York: Citation Press, 1968), p. 145.

chances are high that half the students will have seen—and seen well, or at least intensely—any film you care to mention. What is more, students see films with a natural confidence, a confidence unembarrassed by the grosser kinds of self-consciousness. By comparison, audiences for poetry, drama, or music are notoriously unsure, inclined either to dogmatic arrogance or deferential ignorance. The fear of the expert—the academic expert above all—hovers over them. But in film the climate is freer, more tolerant. The experts have not yet invaded the film and claimed it "No Trespassing—For Experts Only. Everybody Else Get Out!" as scholars have done with the Renaissance and musicologists with baroque music; or in literature where one sees the sad spectacle of writers and periods that were once of enormous seminal significance to the general reader and that, thanks to the claims of scholars, and the reluctance of the non-expert to take on the expert, have been rendered almost wholly useless and inaccessible.

In this openness and exemption from the self-consciousness of "high" culture lies the enormous promise of film. Its technical possibilities are, of course, staggering, but they would have almost no significance unless the audience could accept them easily and naturally within the context of conventions that audiences feel at home with. Indeed, one of my fears in the wave of technical experiment in film now is that the experiments may succeed in making the audience as killingly conscious of the camera and mere technical artifice as they are now mostly unconscious of it, content to accept a tale or a visual sequence as though it possessed its own internal necessity and could no more be questioned than wind on water. In saying this, I run the risk of offending those who are eager to see film accorded an equal place—i.e., a *technical* place—alongside the other arts. But the unique situation of film is surely that it comes to us, not as a part of our educationally acquired "high" culture, but as part of the common culture itself.

It may be that films are still a part of common culture because film began not as an art but as an industry, and for a long time refused to be taken, or to take itself, seriously. But whatever the reason, the film-maker enjoys in this respect a precious advantage over all his peers in the other arts. Only he has a real hope of creating on this basis an art which is not only great but also popular. What the novel was to the nineteenth century, the film might be to the twentieth: *the* genre, the only genre wholly congenial to the majority of a culture. In ancient Greece tragedy was just such a genre—popular, democratic, of enormous appeal to all classes; anything but the tiresome Mandarin nonsense it has become in modern production. Even in Italy as late as thirty years ago Italian opera was an unmistakably popular art form; you heard it as a matter of course on bar radios and in piazzas, interspersed with vivid comment. Now the same music brings dismay and anger and cries of *Abbassa la radio!* This *currency,* this conventional acceptability and viability belong, as I say, uniquely to film. And they suggest just how enormous an influence film might come to exert throughout the culture.

I said earlier that film would come to prevail in the educational curriculum of schools and universities, and that it would do so not only as a medium but also as a curriculum. It will be able to do this, I suggest, precisely because it is itself still a part of common culture and therefore can be meaningfully utilized in programs of general education. At present, general education is in disrepair and disesteem throughout the learned world. But general education was not defeated by its own inadequacy but by the professionalization of universities. Specialists cannot, for obvious reasons, confer a general education any more than plumbers can design a landscape. And general education in this country withered because specialists could not be persuaded to educate themselves or their students except as specialists. Yet our need for a valid form of general education is urgent, and grows more urgent all the time. We have learned recently how terrible is the cost to culture of its rejection by those who, because they have no stake in it, cannot use it. How, for instance, can you meaningfully teach Greek tragedy—with its conviction of each man's freedom to find his own fate and his responsibility for it—to those who have never experienced such freedom, who lack precisely the power to alter their fates or even to find them? You cannot. And what the ghetto child violently refuses, the middle-class child accepts because it is sugared with the promise of later material success. What we desperately need is a general education, a general curriculum, which could focus the realities of our present existence, present them as fact or hypothesis in a telling way—which could deal with our obsessions and tell the truth about our lives. Such a curriculum clearly must be designed and taught in such a way that it does not elicit irrelevant refusal or suspicion—that is, a curriculum whose style and conventions would seem, because shared by both teacher and student, to carry their own necessities, to require neither apology nor defense. That curriculum is film, a medium which is instantly acceptable, which provides, as reading does not, an immediate and shared experience of unparalleled intensity, which is still largely unencumbered by a scholarly literature, and whose vitality and future seem undeniable.

But it is not merely a matter of intensity and community. Here, after all, we have an art that is wholly available to the whole world, a truly ecumenical art. Given only subtitles, it is accessible to anyone, anywhere. And precisely because it *can* go anywhere, it tends to have, at least among the great directors, precisely the kind of ecumenical ambitions—the hope of reaching all mankind—that great writers, to some degree always imprisoned in the parish of their language, have hungered for. Even if the culture is formidably remote—Korean, say, or even Indian—the director can quickly and vividly familiarize it as no writer conceivably can. Yet the only purpose of familiarizing it must be to transcend what he has familiarized—to speak to *any man* in *any* place. Ecumenical ambitions may produce pretentious failures—but at least they will not produce a precious art. If there is little comfort in living in an age of violent change, of feeling only transitional, always uncertain of where one is or might be going, it is in such conditions, especially when they are universal, that we can hope for something like a Homeric vision, for a generous image of humanity. And the hope is measurably augmented when artists of great talent—I think of Kurosawa and Antonioni—apply themselves to portraying the human psyche—its powers and weaknesses—as it strives to adapt to nearly unbearable change, to the destruction of the very ecology by which it was once—and may still be—fatally defined. This is, admittedly, a theme particularly suited to film, which can show with compelling beauty and detail the relation between psyche and ecology, which can re-create the old poetry of earth and the nightmarish new world in stunning proximity. But it is also one of the great universal themes—perhaps *the* great theme of the age—and it is, *I* think, no accident that it should be film—that ecumenical art—that is now attempting to treat it.

I know of no art with such potential for stating our problems, complexities, anxieties, and powers more naturally or comprehensively than film. And this is why film seems to me a *natural* curriculum—a curriculum-in-process, a creative project—with which to replace much of what we now do in literature and philosophy and humanities. At least film is where we might most intelligently begin, taking advantage of an existing motivation, of a living art form—in order to deepen and widen common culture. There is always the chance—doubtless high—that we shall stultify film in the process, but I cannot see how serious educators can fail to make use of the most powerful art form that has ever existed, above all when that art has an unmistakable popular life. One would have to be *mad* not to use it. There is no way of guaranteeing that we shall not abuse it too. But, unlike the other arts, film is intrinsically *interdisciplinary;* it *fuses* all the existing arts in a new mode whose marvellous complexity will defeat all but the ablest academic critics. It is a medium congenial to ideas, and to *present* ideas above all, and its hunger for an ecumenical audience should, at least for now, keep it relatively honest. Ideally, I think such a film curriculum should be complemented by literature—literature which criticizes the film, or which is criticized or amplified by the film. For I assume that the past still matters enormously and still has things to teach us, and also that the past can be bettered by present achievement—and that this rivalry between dead and living, this effort by the present to outdo the past— *imitare superando*—is supremely educational. In a time when the old are despised by the young, and the young feared by the old, it stands to reason that the past will seem irrelevant to the present. But surely it is not; certainly all education in the

humanities is based on the premise of the relevance of the past
to the present—that present which is, as Whitehead said, "holy
ground."

The present is, like our culture, an *oecumene.* We are all
ecumenical men and good Europeans these days. But the human
oecumene runs backward too; it includes the dead, no less than
Australian bushmen and the Hairy Ainu. And the dead are the
vast majority. "Now that you're in Hell, Timon," the poet asks
the famous misanthrope, "which do you prefer, the darkness or
the light?" "The light, man. There are more of you here in
Hell." The living are not diminished by honor done the dead.
These, I suppose, are the pieties one expects of classicists, but
I enter them as a protest against the jaunty McLuhanite moder-
nity and the perky technical *hybris* of too many cineasts. Any
valid general education should strive to keep past and present in
constant creative and critical connection. Resnais's *Hiroshima
mon Amour,* for instance, should be set against the poem it
unknowingly, I suspect, imitates—the *Iliad.* And the point of
the contrast should not be to batter the modern work with the
ancient masterpiece, but to show why, in this case, in strategy
and taste and power, the ancient work does so much more
compellingly what the modern tries to do. Here, I would want
to say, is a case of crucial cultural rivalry. Renais attempted
an honorable task; he attempted—probably unknowingly—the
greatest theme of the greatest poet; a theme we badly need for
our own time, and whose power and viability can be glimpsed
in the passionate enthusiasm this rather poor film aroused
among the young.

Or one might perhaps show how Antonioni, allusively and
powerfully, attempts to create for film a visual vocabulary
capable of taking what is still alive in the art of the past and
renewing it in a fresh context. Thus in *Blow-Up,* when the
photographer returns to find the corpse in the park, we see him
look at the bare grass, the body gone, while the leaves scatter
in a fresh dawn wind around him; and he turns suddenly and
looks upward, and the camera holds momentarily on the leafy
branch overhead; nothing but the leaves and the wind sound.
And then at the close of the film, as the camera holds on the

photographer, his eyes fill with tears as he turns, in the grip of a starker reality now, unable to participate any longer in the illusion of the mummers' tennis—turns and looks at the green grass. And then he too is gone, and there is only the grass left, under and behind the closing legend. Ephemerality, anonymity, the vision of man's days like the grass and the leaves, and the great Homeric figure: "As is the generation of leaves, so is that of men. One generation is born, and another dies. . . ." All these are in the aura of Antonioni's work. An aura of visual association, utterly without educated snobbery or pretense, a re-creation in cinematic terms of the oldest metaphors of human anonymity and impermanence in a world of change. In *La Notte* the same theme: the millionaire Milanese Trimalchio who seeks to leave a permanent monument; in the grass a battered marble Roman head, all permanence, gazed at by a fascinated cat, all animal transience. In *L'Eclisse,* as Ricardo leaves Vittoria's apartment, one sees above the gate, perfectly squared in iron, an Umbrian landscape of the fourteenth century—the old poetry of earth framed by the imprisoning enclosures of the new megalopolis. In *The Red Desert,* the Sardinian beach fantasy, the girl, a brown and gawky adolescent, runs to hide, peering out from the green shrubbery; and she brings irresistibly to mind one of Gauguin's Tahitian girls—the cultural suggestion supporting the psychological purpose of the fantasy—the wonder and fear that accompany the arrival of "the other"; the waking out of oneself. None of these echoes, I stress, function for cultural show; they are rather Antonioni's way of using the past, transmuting it, and making it newly available, for contrast or for direct statement. In this respect, this attempt to affiliate himself in a cinematic—but not a literary—way to a great literary and artistic tradition, Antonioni is unique.

This, of course, is merely a suggestion of the sort of connection that can legitimately be found when past and present, literature and film, are meaningfully juxtaposed. The result of such juxtapositions would be, it seems to me, to demonstrate one of the ideal relations of past and present and to show unmistakably the pertinence of the past, whether achievement or challenge. A legitimate form of general education could be created on the basis of the available film resources, and the effect of such education would be both to rescue literature and to enrich film. Let me say bluntly that I think the education of film-makers could be remarkably improved if they could be brought into a reasonably respectful and lively relation to past literature and the arts. I have the distinct impression that film-makers are all too often lamentably ignorant or even contemptuous of the literary tradition whose rightful inheritors they are. If they were not, they would not make many of the films they now make, and many of their dreadful adaptations of literary material would show either more respect for the original or more imaginative and radical adaptation than one now sees. And they would be bolder in appropriating material which is conducive to their ends. We need, in short, educated film-makers if we are to entrust the curriculum of education to them. I personally fail to see how one can legitimately expect to improve the training of film-makers except by educating them well in the great tradition of Homer, Sophocles, Plato, Shakespeare, and Racine. The achievements of film are already impressive, but they are not so impressive that we can lightly condone mere technical virtuosity combined with a radical illiteracy. The film-maker is as much the heir of literature as the American is the heir of Europe. But he lacks the humility to seize his inheritance, perhaps because, like most Americans, he cannot rid himself of his obsession with money and his populist assumption that literature and the past are either boring or bunk.

Let me close by saying that I think the mission of the film-maker goes far beyond mere artistic prowess or achievement. The film-maker alone has the opportunity, in conjunction with the other mass media, to reshape and reinvigorate the culture. The novelist has lost his chance; the poets and dramatists no longer have one. The educators have for the most part renounced education. And that means that the great task of education in our times—the creation of a humane culture in its apparent absence or defeat—rests with the maker of films. Art is not enough. Or rather we need an art that can perform the task of education—the task that literature and the other arts once performed until they somehow lost the consent on which their power was based. The legacy of literature, however, is immense. What is required is the kind of sensibility that can seize it and transmute it to another medium, with equal power and simplicity and complexity, much as Montaigne and Shakespeare seized and transmuted the classical world they found in Plutarch, or as the Greek dramatists deliberately democratized the aristocratic ethos of *arete* they found in Homer and the poets. It is an art of translation that I am speaking of here—translation so accurate that it controls the matter and power of the original, and so radical that it utterly reshapes, transmogrifies, the values it discovers. You can transform great talent into genius only by energizing it in a task that requires exceptional powers, that makes talent transcend itself. Neither entertainment nor what we conventionally call art are likely to do it; we need a vision—and Virgilian powers in both artist and educator —that will transcend both art and entertainment. I suggest education, by which I mean both art and entertainment, be subsumed in a higher effort.

B. THE AESTHETIC DIMENSION IN EDUCATION

EDUCATION AS ART AND DISCIPLINE

Max Black

Prolonged exposure to the addresses and writings of educational theorists may generate some excusable impatience with the elastic generalities and resounding platitudes which constitute so large a part of current educational philosophy. But too much must not be expected of the first principles of education, as of those of any other study. If they promote a preliminary organization of intentions (as the creation of an electric field facilitates motion along the established lines of forces), they will have done all that can reasonably be expected of principles of the highest generality.

Now it will be found that many of the most influential educational theorists of the past have achieved this preliminary organization by the use of some single persuasive analogy. Thus Rousseau, Pestalozzi, Froebel, and a multitude of later advocates of "negative education" have been inspired by the partially valid analogy between a child and a "natural" biological organism. Emphasis upon noninterference with "natural" growth was once the fitting expression of revolt against a repressive authoritarianism; but today it is all too often a symptom of the abdication of the teacher's responsibility. It may well be that the overworked analogy of the biological organism has served its purpose and that the time has come to experiment with alternative "root metaphors."

If we need to be sustained in our educational planning, as no doubt we do, by some principle of high generality, we might do well, accordingly, to turn to the relatively neglected field of *aesthetic* experience. In speaking of "the creative nature of learning" or "the art of getting an education," we often assume, in a casual way, the existence of some parallel between the activity of a learner and that of an artist. Taken sufficiently seri-

From *Ethics*, vol. 54, no. 4 (July 1944): 290–94. Reprinted by permission of The University of Chicago Press, copyright 1944 by The University of Chicago Press and the author.

ously, the experience of the artist might be expected to provide some valuable clues to the purposes of higher education. Let us begin, then, by reflecting upon the circumstances attending genuine artistic creativity. We shall, of course, not be so romantic or simple-minded as to conceive of the artist as impressing upon his chosen material a vision which forms and completes itself in the seclusion of his imagination. The relation between the artist and his material is a great deal more complex and more interesting; no work of art springs fully formed from its creator, and the process of externalizing a design in the sensuous medium is an essential aid to self-criticism and self-correction. But the material is not merely a medium for the tentative embodiment of the artist's design—a mode of expression and nothing more. There is, rather, in all artistic creation a characteristic *tension* between the man and the material in which he works. The artist will not gladly think of his material as wholly passive; it has for him "a kind of life of its own."

Thus the relation between artist and material, far from being that of active agent to passive substance, tends rather to resemble human contest. As in all social interaction (but in combat most conspicuously), the tentative purpose and actions of the participant are constantly modified and determined by awareness of and adaptations to the protagonist, so also in the practice of the arts, the artist literally *wrestles* with his material, while it both resists and nourishes his intention.[1]

It is not hard to see why this should be so. To create a work of art having a determinate form is to reveal a potentiality of the material used. Now the form is not a kind of rubber stamp

[1] ". . . En art comme en tout chose on ne bâtit que sur un fonds résistant; ce qui s'oppose à l'appui s'oppose aussi au mouvement. Ma liberté consiste donc à me mouvoir dans le cadre étroit que je me suis à moi-même assigné pour chacune de mes entreprises. Je dirai plus: ma liberté sera d'autant plus grande et plus profonde que je limiterai plus étroitement mon champ d'action et que je m'entourerai de plus d'obstacles. Se qui m'ôte une gêne m'ôte une force. Plus on s'impose de contraintes et plus on se libère de ces chaines qui entravent l'esprit. A la voix qui me commande de créer, je réponds d'abord avec effroi, je me rassure ensuite en prenant pour armes les choses participent de la création mais qui lui sont encore extérieures; et l'arbitraire de la contrainte n'est là que pour obtenir la rigueur de l'exécution" (I. Stravinsky, *Poétique musicale* [Harvard University Press, 1942], p. 45).

pressed upon the material; the artist must *learn,* by repeated and
endless experiment, what the material can do and how far it can
satisfy his creative intention. Such knowledge does not lie on
the surface; the creation of a work of art is likely to proceed,
not by some smooth manipulative adaptation, but far more often
by a process of stubborn interaction, for which the term "conflict" is not too strong a description. The incidental difficulty of
the process (and it may be considerable) is unimportant: there
is a kind of difficulty, often experienced by the ungifted, which
arises from a sheer failure to understand or master the medium.
But the gifted artist meets with a different and educative resistance, which is one of the sources of that energy of artistic
creation so striking to the onlooker. He finds himself constantly
excited by the qualities objectively present in the material which
it is his aim progressively to discover. All art is, in an important
sense, a process of education of the artist in the possibilities of
the medium.

So important is this "resistance" of the material, as a necessary condition for aesthetic tension, that the artist will resent
any attempt, by the use of mechanical aids, to blur or muffle
those objective and resistant qualities by whose mastery his own
intention becomes evident to himself and visibly manifest in the
final work of art. Artistic creation demands respect for the
materials of creation. At its best, such respect merges into a
love for the intrinsic nature of the material upon which all
artistic integrity is founded.

The sacrifices and renunciations, the schooling in self-criticism
which such a love demands, make it proper to speak of the
practice of an art as a "discipline." But the discipline of art
must not be confused with that of a drill sergeant or taskmaster.
Inasmuch as mastery of the material means for an artist the
molding of it into an expression of himself, there can be no
question of subjection to alien authority, and the tension of all
creation comes increasingly to be felt as an *internal* struggle,
joyfully accepted, for self-realization.[2]

[2] Much of what I have been trying to say here is well expressed in
S. Alexander's *Art and the Material* (New York: Longmans, Green &
Co., 1925), as when he urges that "the artist's work proceeds not from

How far do these considerations apply to the process of learning? There are some obvious differences, to be sure. The student is not expected to make original contributions to knowledge; and, if his situation were to be regarded as essentially parallel to that of the interpreter or recipient of art, we could expect to find the excitement and tension of which I have spoken occurring only insofar as "the hearer or spectator is thrown by the work into what may be conjectured to have been the condition of the artist in which it was produced." [3] An important part of education does consist of growth in the experience and understanding of literature and the fine arts; and to such aesthetic education our analysis will apply directly, when due allowance has been made for the different roles of artist and appreciator. But this paper does not advocate education of predominantly literary and artistic content; and it is in fields of instruction in which the subject matter does not consist of deliberate works of art that the relevance of the basic aesthetic metaphor is at once less obvious and more important.

The study of a natural science (to consider a test case) may, indeed, seem remote from the artist's struggle for expression: the young physicist is not expected to create new physical

---

a finished imaginative experience to which the work of art corresponds, but from passionate excitement about the subject matter; that the poet sings as the bird sings, because he must; that his poem is wrung from him by the subject that excites him, and that he possesses the imaginative experience embodied in his words just insofar as he has spoken them. . . . The imaginative experience supposed to be in his mind does not exist there. *What does exist is the subject matter which detains him and fixes his thought and feeds his interest,* giving a colour to his excitement which would be different with a different subject matter. Excitement caused and detained by this subject, and at once enlarged, enlightened and inflamed by insights into it, bubbles over into words or the movements of brush or burin or chisel" (pp. 11–12).

The whole lecture is relevant to the thesis of this paper. I would not wish to deny (nor perhaps would Alexander) that attention to the objective qualities of the material may be less important than I have suggested in *some* forms of art. Some artists may create as spontaneously as the birds sing. But I am inclined to think that this happens most often in primitive arts and that the importance of the constraint exercised by the material is particularly evident in arts in which well-established traditions are to be found.

[3] *Ibid.,* p. 14.

knowledge, nor are the physical data and laws to which he is exposed themselves works of art. Nevertheless, the experience of the good learner, in science as elsewhere, includes, besides assimilation and retention, the selection and, above all, the organization of knowledge. For the learner, the data of a science are, or ought to be, by no means inert; they are to be seen as connected with other data which, as they are recalled to consciousness, reveal incomplete patterns of relationship and impel toward the examination of further elements of knowledge. Every new item of knowledge comments upon, disagrees with, tries to enter into relationship with, what is already known.

Education so conceived is very far from being a performance in which the learner is a mere passive spectator. If the subject is to detain him, fix his thought, and feed his interest, "giving a colour to his excitement which would be different with a different subject matter," his attitude toward the subject must resemble very closely that of an artist toward his material. He, too, must respect his subject matter in a manner which depends essentially upon his belief in the independent existence of its potentiality for value; he, too, must be prepared to enter into that complex relation of submission and mastery from which the *discipline* of the art emerges.

It is easy to allow reflection upon education to be too strongly dominated by the conception of the subject matter as some objectively determinate material or stuff. And it ought never to be forgotten that at its best the excitement "caused and detained" by an intellectual subject and "enlightened and inflamed by insight" into it, falls short, in some important respects, of supplying *all* the conditions necessary for full aesthetic experience. The inevitable absence of sensuous embodiment of the aroused excitement makes an essential difference. Certain branches of mathematics are capable of arousing aesthetic enjoyment in those who can understand them; but we can suspect that such experiences appear emotionally "thin" when compared with those accompanying the hearing of even minor musical works.[4]

---

[4] Thus I am not prepared to accept G. H. Hardy's account of mathematical beauty without some reservations. He says: "The mathemati-

But, after all, chemistry is not studied for the sake of enjoying beautiful experiences; and the same is true even of history. The argument of this paper depends upon no such supposition; for, with all due reservations and qualifications, it remains true that there is, in the experience of all who are genuinely devoted to learning, something very similar to the tension which is present in aesthetic creation. The fascination even of a sport or game is closely connected with the attempt to express individuality within the limits set by unyielding and independently determined rules; and there would be no pleasure in a game in which one could tamper indefinitely with the rules of play. In studies capable of evoking a larger loyalty, something analogous is present; so that the mathematician and the archaeologist and the physicist alike are constantly inspired by the conception that the object of their pursuit has independent existence, a nature of its own not arbitrarily to be changed by the first crude desires of those who wish to know it.

Certainly, the nature of what constitutes objectivity varies from one subject to another; and, if it is hard to understand the nature and value of the objectivity in question except through direct experience, it is still harder to describe to the uninitiated how such objectivity, as it is progressively revealed to the student, can be made to minister to his own developing individuality. But what is here being evoked in general terms is familiar in the experience of ordinary men and women no less than of scholars. Respect for a material, recognition of objectivity, submission to the conditions limiting and forming creative activity, self-discipline in the service of an ideal, are admirable qualities displayed by most people at some times and in some occupations—in household skills, sports, and personal relations. The problem of any university is to arouse and foster such qualities in the more remote fields of intellectual and aesthetic activity—

---

cian's patterns, like the painter's or the poet's, must be beautiful; the ideas, like the colours or the words, must fit together in a harmonious way. Beauty is the first test: there is no permanent place in the world for ugly mathematics" (*A Mathematician's Apology* [Cambridge University Press, 1940], p. 25). But perhaps "beauty" is too strong a word for such uses as this.

to provide the conditions in which the student will be inspired by a passion for truth and beauty which will shrink from no extremes of self-discipline to achieve its ends.[5]

The general method of approach here advocated might have important implication for the practice of higher education. The word "discipline" has been used in referring to that central and dynamic interrelationship between artist and material which is here taken as a clue to educational reform. And it may be feared that in practice such a program would encourage reversion to an outmoded psychology of "mental discipline" and a vicious encouragement of formalism in higher education—of learning for learning's sake, irrespective of the utility, or even of the intrinsic value, of the subjects studied.

If the point of view here developed were to have such consequences for practice, it would stand condemned. There is nothing to be said for a return to the good old days when the drudgery of labor was piously thought to be its own reward—and ineffectual attempts to imitate Horace or cross the *Pons Asinorum* believed to induce, by some hidden alchemy of the mind, concentration and intellectual growth.

A cautious man will not advocate today the intensive study, for educational purposes, of chess or Middle English, symbolic logic or diplomatics—subjects which, for all their charm and specialist importance, are too remote from the intellectual interests of most undergraduates to serve as adequate educational instruments. The choice of materials of instruction ought cer-

[5] I am inclined to believe that the aesthetic aspects of the learning process have in general been too much underrated and neglected by educational theorists. It may be that the fascination exercised upon immature minds by Marxist dialectic or the pretentious classifications of our contemporary pseudo-Thomists arises from some groping desire for simplicity and harmony. There is an aesthetic satisfaction in finding data marshaling themselves into order—provided one can forget that the order has been predetermined and the facts selected to fit. The patterns and the orders which reveal themselves in the more objective pursuit of truth are inevitably more complex and so, for the uncultivated taste, less agreeable. It should be a prime object of higher education, insofar as it is committed to the cultivation of the intellectual virtues, to encourage and develop a taste for the more austere but, in the end, more satisfying aesthetic progressively to be discovered in the realms of objective facts and values.

tainly to be determined by considerations of utility in a very wide sense of the term; but judgment of the value of the *content* of a field of study should also be balanced by an opinion of the disciplinary value of the relation which is likely to subsist between the learner and the instructional materials he is offered. If the earlier emphasis of this paper has been justified, evidences of the manifestation of objectivity of value, to which earlier reference was made, will be of crucial importance; and, since such objectivity is more easily attained in some subjects than in others, there may well be an initial partiality (without prejudice to balancing considerations of intrinsic value) for mathematics and certain branches of elementary science and literature in which direct contact with the material is relatively easy to achieve.

In claiming for such subjects—and, indeed, for all subjects in some degree—a *disciplinary* value, we shall not be impressed by the authoritative reproof of contemporary psychology; for there is very little resemblance between the relatively perfunctory instruction in a small area whose effects have been experimentally studied and the large-scale, massive initiation toward which the proposals of this paper aim. Pending the time when the followers of Thorndike are able to discover and to measure the mental growth of those students in whom university teaching at its best inspired a lifelong devotion to mathematics or poetry or philosophy, we may rest with some assurance upon the commonsense belief of the high potential disciplinary character of the humanities and the sciences.

To suppose that the disciplinary value of university studies is achieved spontaneously by mere exposure to facts, specimens, generalizations or techniques would be a gross fallacy whose prevalence is responsible, perhaps more than any other single factor, for the present disrepute of the liberal studies.

But there can be no simple or compendious answer to the search for adequate instruments of higher education. If the argument of this paper is sound, there is no more likelihood of finding a recipe for education than there is of finding an infallible method for making painters or poets.

THE AESTHETIC DIMENSION OF EDUCATION IN THE ABSTRACT DISCIPLINES

Kenneth R. Conklin

There are two senses in which education can be said to have an aesthetic dimension: the processes of teaching, learning, and knowing may have aesthetic aspects, as may the subject matter itself. The present article seeks to show that all education has an aesthetic dimension in both senses and that, indeed, the aesthetic dimension is so essential that no education is possible without it.

It is fairly obvious that teaching and learning have aesthetic aspects, although the aesthetic aspect of knowing is quite interesting and highly controversial. These topics are discussed in section one. Section two explores the aesthetic aspect of subject matter—especially subject matter composed of abstract concepts. Section three discusses concomitant learnings as aesthetic by-products of content and method. Finally, section four relates these ideas to certain problems in curriculum development, teaching methods, school administration, and teacher education.

1. The Aesthetics of Teaching, Learning, and Knowing

Regardless of the subject matter involved, teaching is a performance. Teachers, of course, should not be judged according to the standards applied to actors, opera singers, ballet dancers, or artists; yet, it is clear that teachers do convey moods, use their voices, gesture and move about, and make drawings on the blackboard and, therefore, aesthetic criticisms are possible. There may well be disagreement concerning the importance of aesthetic criteria in evaluating teacher performance, and certainly, it is impossible to specify criteria as either necessary or sufficient for effective teaching. But there is general agreement that good teaching requires considerably more than knowledge

From the *Journal of Aesthetic Education,* vol. 4, no. 3 (July 1970): 21–36. Reprinted by permission of the *Journal* and the author.

of subject matter. Subject matter must be presented effectively, and this effectiveness is primarily determined according to aesthetic considerations.

An effective teacher may have a voice which soothes his students but on occasion may employ a harsh, rasping voice with equal effectiveness. But in either case, qualities of voice are significant. Sometimes teacher enthusiasm will stimulate the productivity of students, while at other times teacher apathy (perhaps deliberately portrayed) will disturb students and thereby encourage their productive thought or action. An effective teacher, like an effective actor, controls his performance, adjusting it to the requirements of changing circumstances in order to produce intended results. A teacher must appreciate the moods of his students, but he must also maintain an appropriate psychological distance in order to provide an intelligently manipulated organization of his conduct. For best results in handling "the discipline problem," a teacher must achieve an appropriate balance between empathy and distance.

While the learner's primary task may be to attend to the content of a lesson, it is also true that he undergoes an aesthetic experience as a spectator of the teacher's performance. Indeed, as we shall later see, some of the most important learnings occur as concomitant results of this aesthetic spectatorship. A behaviorist might well argue that teaching and learning are entirely analyzable as sequences of empirical stimuli and responses, but the behaviorist would also analyze art, poetry, music, and drama in the same way. In short, however one might analyze the fine arts, the same mode of analysis and criticism will yield significant observations about the processes of teaching and learning.

In examining teaching and learning as aesthetic processes, we tend to ignore that these processes serve the purpose of conveying subject matter and that the conveyance of subject matter may also be subordinated to the still larger purpose of putting the subject matter to use after the teaching-learning process has ended. But this argument does not destroy the validity of regarding teaching and learning as aesthetic performances: many works of art (including all that are "representational") portray subject matter in the same sense and sometimes have the purpose of providing social or religious commentary. Whether there is recognizable subject matter and whether there are propositional lessons to be learned have nothing to do with the fact that criticism of a performance may be made on aesthetic grounds. Indeed, it has been asserted that a primary purpose of education is the sheer enjoyment of undergoing it.

Those who most strongly defend education for self-realization usually draw a distinction between learning and knowing. Learning enables one to cope with sensory phenomena, while knowing transcends the senses and has no purpose beyond itself. To use Plato's way of speaking: learning can provide right (or wrong) opinion about the world of appearances, while knowing provides certainty and wisdom pertaining to the world of forms. Knowing is considered infinitely more valuable than learning; knowing is both a cause and a result of intense personal involvement and commitment; knowing is the highest kind of aesthetic experience.

The personal involvement and commitment to be found in the act of knowing have been explored at length by Michael Polanyi. He shows that knowing requires the creative integration of whatever evidence or propositions are available. Knowing always goes beyond the data. No proof ever *forces* the acceptance of its conclusion; rather, a successful proof expresses a truth in such a *convincing* way that whoever wrestles with the proof *comes to agree* with its conclusion. Knowing is a personal commitment to that which is known, as indicated by the tenacity and fervor with which knowledge is held and proclaimed.[1] The aesthetics of mystery are involved in a problematic situation; a drama unfolds as evidence is organized and partially understood; tension resolution, emotional release, and psychological closure occur as knowledge is finally discovered.

An excellent review of the history of the claim that knowing is an aesthetic activity is given by Frederic Will in his book *Intelligible Beauty in Aesthetic Thought*.[2] Will notes that Plotinus supplied a monistic, mystical completion to Plato's

[1] Michael Polanyi, *Personal Knowledge* (London: Routledge and Kegan Paul, 1958).

[2] Frederic Will, *Intelligible Beauty in Aesthetic Thought* (Tübingen: Max Niemeyer Verlag, 1958).

doctrine of ideas, and subsequent aestheticians have used this tradition as a basis for the notion of intelligible beauty. According to Will, the notion of intelligible beauty is "the belief that man's higher cognitive faculties are deeply and appropriately engaged in aesthetic experience." [3] Will shows how the notion of intelligible beauty functions in the philosophies of a number of thinkers. He claims, "The most general agreement of Plotinus with Hegel, and with the post-Kantians in general, is on the tenet that reality is essentially thought, or intelligibility, and that the end toward which reality strives is total intelligibility." [4]

Plato's sun, cave, and divided-line allegories in the *Repubilc* provide metaphysical explanations of what is being asserted in the claim that knowing is essentially an aesthetic activity. It will be recalled that as a potential philosopher-king acquires greater knowledge at higher levels of reality, he approaches knowledge of the supreme form of the good. When he finally does achieve this highest kind of knowledge, he undergoes a mystical conversion experience which alters his personality characteristics. There is thus profound personal involvement in the struggle for wisdom. Furthermore, goodness, truth, and beauty are regarded as three aspects of the unified form of the good, so that knowing and aesthetic experience are identical at the highest level.

In speaking about the rise of the soul into the world of the Absolute, Plato says in the *Phaedrus,*

> It is there that Reality lives, without shape or color, intangible, visible only to reason, the soul's pilot; and all true knowledge is knowledge of her . . . when the soul has at long last beheld Reality, it rejoices, finding sustenance in its direct contemplation of the truth and in the immediate experience of it. . . .[5]

In the *Symposium* Plato is even more explicit:

> This is the right way of approaching or being initiated into the mysteries of love, to begin with examples of beauty in this

[3] *Ibid.,* p. 16.
[4] *Ibid.,* p. 205.
[5] Plato, *Phaedrus,* trans. W. C. Helmbold and W. G. Rabinowitz (New York: Liberal Arts Press, 1956), p. 30.

world, and using them as steps to ascend continually with that
absolute beauty as one's aim, from one instance of physical
beauty to two and from two to all, then from physical beauty
to moral beauty, and from moral beauty to the beauty of
knowledge, until from knowledge of various kinds one arrives
at the supreme knowledge whose sole object is that absolute
beauty, and knows at last what absolute beauty is.[6]

The following points made by Plato deserve special emphasis
here: particular phenomenal instances of beauty are inferior to
and derive their beauty from more general, abstract kinds of
beauty; both physical and moral beauty are particular embodiments of the beauty of knowledge; ultimate reality (and hence
ultimate beauty and ultimate knowledge) is "without shape or
color, intangible, visible only to reason."

One of the most controversial points here is the claim that
pure cognition, without any immediately antecedent sense perception, can be an aesthetic experience. It is customary to
speak of aesthetic experience in connection with the perceptions
of the five physical senses; yet, as Hospers points out,[7] aesthetic
experience is actually concerned with meanings, associations,
and emotions, whether these come to us through the senses or
otherwise. This assertion is especially true of literature, where
the actual sound (if any) is not important. Of course it may be
claimed that reading produces mental images, so that some kind
of sensory-like basis exists for the aesthetic experience in
literature. But Hospers refutes this claim:

> . . . many readers can read appreciatively and intelligently
> without having any visual or other images evoked in their
> minds. . . . The inclusion of literature in the category of the
> perceptual by means of some image evocation theory consti-
> tutes a desperate attempt to make the facts fit a theory. How-
> ever, the dismissal of literature as not being the object of
> aesthetic attention because of its nonperceptual character
> would seem to be a prime case of throwing the baby out with
> the bathwater.[8]

[6] Plato, *Symposium*, trans. W. Hamilton (Baltimore: Penguin Books,
1956), p. 94.

[7] John Hospers, "Problems of Aesthetics" in *The Encyclopedia of
Philosophy*, ed. Paul Edwards (New York: Macmillan, 1967), vol. 1,
pp. 38–39.

[8] *Ibid.*, p. 39.

We shall see in the next section of this paper that abstract mathematics has important aesthetic aspects, although it is completely nonperceptual. As Hospers says,

> When we enjoy or appreciate the elegance of a mathematical proof, it would surely seem that our enjoyment is aesthetic, although the object of that enjoyment is not perceptual at all: it is the complex relation among abstract ideas or propositions, not the marks on paper or the blackboard, that we are apprehending aesthetically. It would seem that the appreciation of neatness, elegance, or economy of means is aesthetic whether it occurs in a perceptual object (such as a sonata) or in an abstract entity (such as a logical proof), and if this is so, the range of the aesthetic cannot be limited to the perceptual.[9]

Indeed, according to Plato the best aesthetic experiences are the most abstract and least perceptual.

Any attempt to provide a definitive characterization of what is meant by "aesthetic" or "aesthetic experience" is beyond the scope of this paper. Our purpose in the present section has been to indicate important similarities between activities generally acknowledged to be aesthetic and the activities of teaching, learning, and knowing. The significance for education of those similarities will be explored in section four. We have emphasized the aesthetics of abstract knowing in preparation for the remainder of this paper. The author has elsewhere provided a more extensive analysis of what is meant by "aesthetic" and how the aesthetic aspects of teaching, learning, and knowing are interrelated.[10]

2. The Aesthetics of Abstract Subject Matter (Especially Mathematics)

Let us imagine that the subjects in a school curriculum have been arranged according to the relative "aestheticness" of their subject matter as normally conceived. Surely the arts would be close to one end of the continuum, while the abstract, logical

[9] *Ibid.,* p. 38.
[10] Kenneth Robert Conklin, "The Aesthetics of Knowing and Teaching," *The Record—Teachers College,* vol. 72, no. 2 (December 1970): 257–65.

disciplines such as mathematics and theoretical physics would be at the opposite end. Yet we shall see that the arts have a mathematics-like aspect, and that the subject matter of mathematics has an essential aesthetic aspect. The continuum suggested above is therefore really a continuum rather than a multichotomy. But what is most significant for our purposes here is that abstract subject matter has an aesthetic aspect and that, therefore, teaching mathematics and other abstract subjects for appreciation is as reasonable and, indeed, as necessary as teaching art for appreciation.

In claiming that mathematics possesses an essential aesthetic aspect, we must distinguish between mathematics as it is written and mathematics as it is held in the mind. Mathematicians may have poor handwriting, small in size and hard to read. Mathematical symbols might be considered ugly. Although it is true that configurations of symbols are manipulated by the mathematician in the process of proving theorems, and that seeing the configurations is usually helpful and sometimes apparently necessary in making discoveries. Manipulating symbols on paper strongly resembles moving furniture in a room or assembling a jigsaw puzzle: we often must try out a configuration before deciding whether it fits together and is pleasing. But the way the symbols appear on paper is obviously not crucial to the mathematician, who can adopt alternative systems of notation with no effect on his mathematical results. What really matters is the fittingness and pleasingness of the configurations of abstract concepts in the mind of the mathematician.

Mathematical discovery is a species of knowing, and as such has already been discussed in section one. Plato, for example, regarded mathematical objects as "shadows" of the forms in his divided-line allegory. He recommended a ten-year program of abstract mathematics in the curriculum of prospective philosopher-kings to accustom their minds to the abstract beauty of the forms and to develop the power of intuitive, aesthetic appreciation of nonsensuous entities in order to prepare them for their "vision" of the form of the good.

The role of intuition in mathematics has been widely discussed. On the one hand, proofs must be based on strictly logical reasoning and must avoid overt dependence on intuitive or heuristic appeal. On the other hand, mathematical discovery seems to draw heavily upon intuition, and the most profound discoveries were often the products of the most profound intuitions. While it is true that intuition sometimes leads mathematicians to false conclusions, it is also true that mathematicians accept numerous theorems as intuitively obvious even though all efforts at proving them have failed.

Kurt Gödel, who has been among the most successful mathematicians in using rigorous techniques of logic, is also one of the strongest defenders of the role of intuition. He argues that mathematical intuition is very much like sense perception, and that the question of the objective existence of the objects of mathematical intuition "is an exact replica of the question of the objective existence of the outer world." [11]

> I don't see any reason why we should have less confidence in this kind of perception, i.e., in mathematical intuition, than in sense perception, which induces us to build up physical theories and to expect that future sense perceptions will agree with them and, moreover, to believe that a question not decidable now has meaning and may be decided in the future. The set-theoretical paradoxes are hardly any more troublesome for mathematicians than deceptions of the senses are for physics.[12]

> What, however, perhaps more than anything else, justifies the acceptance of this criterion of truth in set theory [clarity of intuition] is the fact that continued appeals to mathematical intuition are necessary not only for obtaining unambiguous answers to the questions of transfinite set theory, but also for the solution of the problems of finitary number theory (of the type of Goldbach's conjecture), where the meaningfulness and unambiguity of the concepts entering into them can hardly be doubted. This follows from the fact that for every axiomatic system there are infinitely many undecidable propositions of this type.[13]

Intuition in cognitive discovery functions much like sensation in artistic appreciation. Perhaps Plato (doctrine of reminis-

[11] Kurt Gödel, "What Is Cantor's Continuum Problem?" in *Philosophy of Mathematics*, ed. Paul Benacerraf and Hilary Putnam (Englewood Cliffs, N.J.: Prentice-Hall, 1964), p. 272.
[12] *Ibid.*, p. 271.
[13] *Ibid.*, p. 272.

cence) and Jung (racial memories) would argue that intuition in cognitive discovery is more like memory than sensation, but they would also say that the "aestheticness" of sense experience comes from memory as well. In any case, the role of intuition in mathematical discovery is closely similar to the role of aesthetic sensitivity in artistic creation or appreciation. Henri Poincaré uses vivid language to describe the drama, beauty, and joy of mathematical discovery in his own experience,[14] and Jacques Hadamard has made a major study of the psychology of mathematical discovery.[15] There can be no doubt that mathematical discovery is an aesthetic experience of the most profound kind.

We distinguished earlier between mathematics as it is written and mathematics as it is held in the mind, and we noted that only the latter kind of mathematics has a genuine aesthetic aspect. What should be compared with the arrangement of pigments on canvas is not the arrangement of symbols on paper but the arrangement of concepts in the mind as suggested by the written symbols, a kind of perception not far removed from the artistic appreciation of our perception of the colored shapes rather than an appreciation of the colored shapes themselves.

Thus far we have viewed the aesthetics of mathematics from the perspective of someone who discovers important mathematical truths, and the discussion to this point may seem relevant only to creative mathematicians engaged in original research. But this is not the case at all. The aesthetics of mathematical discovery is valid whether the discovery adds something new to the stock of mathematical knowledge or whether it is merely a rediscovery by a child of a truth commonly known to all who are not mathematically illiterate. Each discovery is original for the person who makes it.

But there is clearly a distinction between making a discovery independently and following a given argument, just as there is a distinction between creating a symphony and listening to one

---

[14] Henri Poincaré, "Mathematical Creation," in *The World of Mathematics,* ed. James R. Newman (New York: Simon and Schuster, 1956), vol. 4, pp. 2041–50.

[15] Jacques Hadamard, *The Psychology of Invention in the Mathematical Field* (New York: Dover Publications, 1954).

created by someone else. Yet, some of the aesthetic experience of discovery is surely present even for the person who only appreciates the work of another. Following a single proof or studying a whole branch of mathematics provides an aesthetic experience closely similar to that of reading a novel or seeing a play: there is a plot with sometimes unexpected twists and turns, there is a buildup of suspense, and in the end things either get resolved or stimulate us to look for a sequel. Even though a mathematician may have read a particular proof several times, if it is a significant or beautiful proof he enjoys reading it again. Mathematicians enjoy creating or reading many different proofs for the same theorem, just as music and drama lovers enjoy variations on a common theme. Just as there are standards of aesthetic judgment for works of art, music, and drama, so we should expect there to be standards of aesthetic judgment for mathematical products—and indeed there are such standards.

Poincaré talks in general terms about the feeling of mathematical beauty, the harmony of numbers and forms, and elegance.

> Now, what are the mathematic entities to which we attribute the character of beauty and elegance, and which are capable of developing in us a sort of esthetic emotion? They are those whose elements are harmoniously disposed so that the mind without effort can embrace their totality while realizing the details. This harmony is at once a satisfaction of our esthetic needs and an aid to the mind, sustaining and guiding. At the same time, in putting under our eyes a well-ordered whole, it makes us foresee a mathematical law. . . . The useful combinations are precisely the most beautiful, I mean those best able to charm this special sensibility that all mathematicians know, but of which the profane are so ignorant as often to be tempted to smile at it.[16]

G. H. Hardy, a professional mathematician, wrote a book celebrating the aesthetic aspect of mathematics as a justification for devoting his life to the subject. He provided a lengthy and precise description of standards for the aesthetic criticism of mathematics. Hardy notes that the mathematician is a maker

[16] Henri Poincaré, pp. 2047–48.

of patterns with ideas. Creating or reading mathematics has aesthetic qualities like those found in playing or watching a chess game, except that mathematics is superior to chess in many ways.[17]

According to Hardy, the beauty of a mathematical theorem depends greatly on its seriousness, and the seriousness of a theorem is determined according to the theoretical significance of the mathematical ideas which the theorem connects.[18] Significant mathematical ideas are those having generality and depth.[19] A theorem is general if it summarizes a host of concrete facts or lower-level generalities,[20] and it is deep if it is somehow essential to a number of important truths.[21] In addition to seriousness, a beautiful theorem or proof also has unexpectedness (either in its conclusion or its development) combined with inevitability and economy.[22] Mathematics has a crude utility, but the "real" mathematics of the "real" mathematicians is almost completely abstract and "useless" [23] and "must be justified as art if it can be justified at all." [24]

Another author, John W. N. Sullivan, agrees that mathematics, like chess, is a beautiful art pursued for its own sake but claims that some of the beauty of mathematics comes from its applicability to the phenomenal world. Sullivan's main point, however, is that both abstract and applied mathematics make explicit the Kantian categories of knowing and perceiving and thus serve the same function as all the arts in telling us about ourselves! [25] "Mathematics" he concludes, "is of profound significance in the universe, not because it exhibits principles that we obey, but because it exhibits principles that we impose." [26]

[17] G. H. Hardy, *A Mathematician's Apology* (Cambridge: University Press, 1967), pp. 84–85.
[18] *Ibid.*, pp. 89–98. Hardy gives two examples of theorems with proofs which he considers beautiful.
[19] *Ibid.*, p. 103.
[20] *Ibid.*, pp. 104–9.
[21] *Ibid.*, pp. 109–12.
[22] *Ibid.*, pp. 112–15.
[23] *Ibid.*, pp. 115–21, 131–43.
[24] *Ibid.*, p. 139.
[25] John W. N. Sullivan, "Mathematics as an Art," in *The World of Mathematics*, vol. 3, pp. 2015–21.
[26] *Ibid.*, p. 2021.

Other authors have noted that mathematics, like art, is a cultural product and presumably gives us important insights into the culture that produced it.[27] The culture determines what kind of mathematics is studied and what counts as mathematics.[28]

Von Neumann agrees that mathematics is a cultural product and points out that changing cultural standards have changed the concept of mathematical rigor and the style in which proofs are written.[29]

> I think that it is correct to say that [the mathematician's] criteria of selection, and also those of success, are mainly aesthetical . . . one expects a mathematical theorem or a mathematical theory not only to describe and to classify in a simple and elegant way numerous and a priori disparate special cases. One also expects "elegance" in its "architectural," structural makeup. Ease in stating the problem, great difficulty in getting hold of it and in all attempts at approaching it, then again some very surprising twist by which the approach, or some part of the approach, becomes easy, etc. . . . These criteria are clearly those of any creative art.[30]

Von Neumann tells us that the criteria of excellence in these aesthetic factors change with changes in general cultural patterns, so that mathematics is subject to cultural influences just like any art.

Mathematicians, like artists, manifest their creativity at an early age. Hardy points out that most of the great discoveries in mathematics were made by men of age forty or less and that virtually nothing really new was done by people over fifty. Not only is mathematical discovery a "young man's game," it is also a field with many prodigies. Galois, the discoverer of vast and valuable territory in abstract algebra, died in a duel at age 21. Abel died at 27. Newton made his greatest discoveries in mathematical physics by age 24.[31]

[27] See "Mathematics as a Culture Clue," in *The World of Mathematics*, vol. 4, pp. 2312–64.

[28] Raymond L. Wilder, *The Foundations of Mathematics* (New York: John Wiley and Sons, 1965), pp. 281–99.

[29] John Von Neumann, "The Mathematician," in *The World of Mathematics*, vol. 4, pp. 2053–57.

[30] *Ibid.*, p. 2062.

[31] G. H. Hardy, pp. 70–73.

Perhaps youthful prodigies are possible only in endeavors which, like mathematics and logic, meet the following two conditions: (1) the knowledge required is independent of the breadth of the knower's life experiences; (2) internal consistency is the primary standard for measuring the success of a product. The more nearly a field meets these conditions, the more frequently we would expect to find child prodigies making significant contributions to it. Thus, we would expect chess to have its prodigies—witness the case of Bobby Fischer, who has dominated U.S. chess for a decade since first becoming U.S. champion at age fourteen—but not personnel management, medicine, or psychology. The two requisite conditions seem to describe areas which philosophers would call analytic and a priori.

Among the arts, music would seem to satisfy the criteria best, while art and sculpture satisfy them to a lesser extent, and epic-novel-writing or opera or playwriting satisfy them least. Common knowledge of these fields confirms the predicted relative frequencies of child prodigies in them. To the extent musical compositions include elements of common folk music or expressions of sentiments about life activities, as many classical pieces do, they depend upon broad cultural experience and prodigies would be unlikely. But the performance of music as a soloist requires no cultural experience, and it is here that we find many prodigies. We might recall that music in ancient times was studied as mathematical harmonics and was included in the quadrivium of mathematical subjects (with arithmetic, astronomy, and geometry) among the seven liberal arts. Many of the qualities which determine the aesthetic characteristics of music are essentially mathematical: internal consistency, temporal progression, "logical" inevitability or predictability, etc. Indeed, such mathematical qualities enable us to appreciate a finished product in any of the arts. Regardless of how much cultural experience may be necessary to create a work of art or to appreciate fully the associations it alludes to, any work of art can be appreciated to greater or lesser degree for its internal qualities of balance, form, rhythm, etc.

We have seen in detail how mathematics has an essential aesthetic aspect and how the arts have an important mathematics-like aspect. It should also be clear that any subject, when organized for formal study, has a mathematics-like aspect. Whenever general principles are used to explain particular phenomena, we have a species of mathematical, deductive logic. The beauty of a concept in an organized body of subject matter can be analyzed precisely as Hardy analyzed the beauty of a mathematical theorem: according to the significance of the ideas it connects, according to its generality and depth, and whether it possesses unexpectedness combined with inevitability and economy. Any subject can be made more inspiring and aesthetically enjoyable for students if teachers and curriculum planners organize the subject matter to maximize its logical beauty.

3. The Aesthetics of Concomitant Learnings

Imagine that the professor of an education course of 500 students recommends in his lecture that large group instruction and the lecture format are not suitable pedagogical devices. We might well suspect his sincerity or integrity, but the humor and cognitive dissonance we experience occur because what is taught overtly in the lecture is the opposite of what is taught concomitantly by the example of the lecture.[32]

A method teaches itself concomitantly whenever it is used for the overt teaching of subject matter. Methods may be applied beyond the subject being taught, so that the concomitant lesson learned from a method may be more significant to the student in the long run than the subject matter that was overtly taught. Likewise, the teacher's attitudes toward the subject matter, toward teaching, and toward life in general are taught concomitantly. The teacher is a value exemplar with whom students identify, and thus the aesthetics of knowing, teaching, and learning has a more general, long-range impact upon the student than the aesthetics of subject matter.

Indeed, subjects also teach methods. A subject teaches con-

---

[32] Kilpatrick pioneered in the study of concomitant learnings. For a summary and interpretation of his work on this subject, see David W. Ecker, " 'Concomitant Learning' in Tomorrow's Schools," *Studies in Philosophy and Education*, vol. 1 (November 1961): 190–202.

comitantly whatever disciplined methods of study and organization are found in its subject matter, and in this way the aesthetics of subject matter may have an influence beyond the field to which the subject matter belongs. A person who has studied and enjoyed mathematics at least moderately may well apply rigorous methods of proof to other subjects and will probably try to organize concepts in other fields into hierarchically constructed deductive systems.

Participation in, or concerned spectatorship with, a method and content alters our character toward closer conformity with that method and content. Plato recognized this fact and insisted that drama, art, and music be severely censored to ensure a morally sound upbringing for the young. Likewise, there are those who currently argue that people, especially the immature and impressionable, who are exposed to violence on television tend to become violent and to tolerate violence in real life. Similarly, role-playing is effective in helping someone to understand an opponent's ideas and feelings precisely because of the tendency to identify with what is done or observed.

The appreciation of a work of art may be enhanced through empathy, both cognitive and emotional. The argument presented in this section may be regarded as an explanation of what is meant by saying that a learner empathizes with the learning situation to whatever extent he is successful in learning. Empathy automatically involves both cognitive and emotional aspects, and whichever aspect is attended to carries the other aspect with it concomitantly. Likewise, both method and subject matter are involved in a learning situation, so that the overt learning of one results in the concomitant learning of the other. The interactions between cognition and emotion and between content and method are obviously within the realm of general aesthetic analysis.

We may also note that actions and value commitments are concomitants of each other. When we assert a value commitment at a high level of generality, we are concomitantly asserting a host of lower level value commitments applicable to whatever situation is at hand. Conversely, when we take action in a particular situation, our action concomitantly teaches a commitment to the general values which justify the action. Some people might argue that "actions speak louder than words," but what is claimed here is simply that actions and words interact concomitantly. There is an aesthetic relation between actions and words, so that each signifies the other and a given combination of actions and words constitutes either a consonance or a dissonance.

4. Some Applications to Education

We have seen that teaching, learning, and knowing, as well as subject matter, have essential aesthetic aspects. We have also seen that there are concomitant learnings accompanying all teaching-learning situations, and the concomitant learnings may be more profound and far-reaching than the overt ones. In the present section we shall explore some important applications of these observations to curriculum planning, educational methodology, school administration, and teacher education.

One obvious conclusion from all that has been discussed is that a much larger portion of the curriculum than simply the arts can be used to enhance a student's appreciative sensitivity. We have seen that the appreciation of mathematics is just as possible as art appreciation or music appreciation.[33] Indeed, the importance of mathematics and the other abstract symbolic disciplines in modern life suggests that learning the appreciation of them is indispensable in a well-rounded education. Traditionally, mathematics was taught for applicative use in adding up grocery bills or computing income taxes, and grammar was taught as a way of getting students to improve their speaking and writing habits, and both subjects were taught as though students were to become professional mathematicians or grammarians. But within the last decade there has been an upsurge in "new" math, "new" grammar, and other "new" subjects which emphasize the study of subject matter for appreciation rather than merely for application in professional or ordinary

[33] For a brief comparison of the appreciation of mathematics with music appreciation, see Hans Rademacher and Otto Toeplitz, *The Enjoyment of Mathematics,* trans. Herbert Zuckerman (Princeton, N.J.: Princeton University Press, 1957), pp. 5–7.

life. The aesthetic dimension of general education has thereby been greatly expanded, and further expansion can be hoped for. Only a few years ago observers were amazed that grade school children could understand some of the most significant mathematical discoveries in set theory, abstract algebra, and topology. Yet, as was pointed out in the discussion of prodigies, a child is most capable of performing creatively in a subject which is independent of breadth of life experiences and in which internal consistency is the primary measure of successful products—and mathematics is clearly such a subject.

Curriculum planners must also pay more attention to concomitant learnings than they have in the past. Usually only the methodologists have studied concomitant learnings; yet, these learnings are as much a part of the content of a curriculum as what was overtly put there. While it is true that some concomitant learnings may be unforeseeable, it is also true that they can usually be foreseen if we take the trouble to think more carefully about content and method. In some cases we have seen that what is learned concomitantly is far more important than what is learned overtly. Furthermore, important concomitant learnings may be unteachable as overt curriculum content because of their delicacy, profundity, or the psychological resistance students might have to them. For example, good study habits, respect for the authority of the teacher, and sportsmanship are probably best taught concomitantly rather than overtly. In general, values are best instilled concomitantly. Since concomitant learning, as was explained in section three, is analyzable as an aesthetic process, the aesthetician can be of great help in curriculum planning.

Teaching methods can obviously be improved by taking account of the aesthetics of teaching, learning, and knowing as discussed in section one. The aesthetician's analyses of methods can help improve teacher effectiveness in transmuting curriculum content. Furthermore, the aesthetic dimension of education can be expanded at no cost, and often at considerable gain, to the brute content by organizing the subject matter so as to enhance its structural beauty. By understanding the aesthetics of teaching, learning, and knowing we can enhance the enjoyment of the educational process and help make the mastery of subject matter intrinsically rewarding. Discipline problems might be decreased, potential dropouts might be averted, and everyone might enjoy school more.

Both the internal disciplinary system and the external relations between school and community concomitantly teach values and modes of interpersonal conduct, which must be consonant with curriculum content if a credibility gap and cognitive dissonance are to be avoided. The effectiveness of a school administrator is, therefore, affected by his ability to foresee the aesthetic concomitants of his administrative decisions. As Dewey, Kilpatrick, and the progressivists point out, school is a place where life itself goes on. A student's character will be shaped more powerfully by what he lives through than by what he merely hears, reads, and writes.

Everything that has been said about curriculum, teaching methods, and school administration can be applied not only to elementary and secondary education but also to teacher education at the university level and in particular to the education courses they take. The teacher-education curriculum could be improved by emphasizing the appreciation dimension of theory courses. Prospective teachers who learn to appreciate philosophical and psychological theory will be more likely to master and carry out the practical concomitants of that theory and to assume a more professional attitude toward their work. A professor should strive to make his class aesthetically enjoyable and pedagogically exemplary, since the methods he uses teach themselves as they convey the subject matter to the prospective teachers who are his students.

ART, TECHNIQUE, AND THE
INDIFFERENT GODS

Plagued by a sense of ineffectuality, conscious of protest on all sides, certain educators are turning to art as a means of resisting "technique." More and more frequently, we hear talk of an "aesthetics of teaching" to which the "technology of teaching" is to give way. Some compare the teacher with the creative artist; others perceive the knowledge taught as analogous to the art object. There is a suggestion that aesthetic values (expressiveness, harmony, wholeness, order) can be transmuted into educational aims, and that—if they are—the cause of personal autonomy will be served.

The technique such educators are resisting is what Jacques Ellul describes as the fundamental characteristic of "the technological society." [1] It is technique that has become autonomous and self-perpetuating, that gradually absorbs human beings to such an extent that they are no longer aware of its influence on their thinking and their lives. For Ellul, it follows that education becomes progressively oriented "toward the specialized end of producing technicians . . . as a consequence, towards the creation of individuals useful only as members of a technical group, on the basis of the current criteria of utility. . . ." Whether they read Ellul or not, great numbers of people are beginning to picture society in this fashion. Minority groups express their resentment of the single standard ("the current criteria of utility") which tends to make a mockery of "equal opportunity." Students act out their outrage at the "processing" they feel they are experiencing in colleges and universities. Junior high school children "rap" furiously against what adults tell them is required for success—which means becoming "useful only as members of a technical group." It is not surprising that concerned and committed teachers should want to do something to combat mechanization, dehumanization, and "product orientation." What is surprising—and to us somewhat questionable—is the desire to read "aesthetic" as the antithesis of "technological" and to seek, in the domain of art, models for humane teaching in this difficult age. We cannot but recall Stephen Daedalus's metaphor for the creative artist (in James Joyce's *Portrait of the Artist as a Young Man*). The artist, says Stephen, is like the indifferent God of creation, remaining "within or behind or beyond or above his handiwork, invisible, refined out of existence, paring his fingernails."

We strongly believe in the importance of cultivating personal autonomy and authenticity in the classroom. . . . We are deeply troubled by the ambiguities in the approach to "achievement standards." . . . We believe that a good education ought to make possible "authentic personal existence," the choice of an "image of man." We also happen to believe in the importance of liberating increasing numbers of people for significant encounters with works of art. It does not, however, seem likely to us that the cause of authenticity will be served if teachers turn to the aesthetic for their models or criteria. A person who can engage sensitively and perceptively with a novel, a painting, or a concerto is, we grant, less likely to be absorbed by technique than the one impervious to aesthetic delights; but this is not what the "aesthetic" educators seem to have in mind.

They are not concerned about experiences with particular works of art. They want to see teachers behave like artists. They want to subsume the language and interactions of the classroom under the rubric of "art." Some propose to conceive teachers as "artists in human relations," [2] with all the awareness, the impatience with the humdrum, and the "immediately felt joy" presumably characteristic of the practicing artist. Others propose that the knowledge communicated by a teacher be aesthetically valued and conceived as if it were "an aesthetic form." [3] It seems to us that those who see the teaching act as

[2] See Clyde E. Curran, "Artistry in Teaching," in Ronald T. Hyman, ed., *Teaching: Vantage Points for Study* (Philadelphia and New York: J. B. Lippincott Co., 1968).

[3] See Dwayne Huebner, "Curricular Language and Classroom Meanings," *ibid.*

analogous to artistic "making" somehow assume that artists are peculiarly moral and joyful people, exerting a primarily beneficent influence upon the world and their fellow men. Those who treat the knowledge presented in the classroom as analogous to an art object are, we think, assuming that it is possible to define "art" successfully and absolutely, or that it must be understood once and for all as "the form of feeling" and used to counterbalance the discursive communications given such prominence in the contemporary school. Both assumptions—respecting the artist and the work of art—strike us as unwarranted. To build a conceptual structure upon them, and to act in terms of them might well increase the danger the "aesthetic" educator wishes to combat. Impersonality, manipulativeness, and preoccupation with technique (albeit not in Ellul's sense) are as much a part of artistic creation as are expressiveness, feeling, and forming. An artist works with neutral raw materials (paint and canvas, stone, tonal elements, words) which he calls his "medium." He shapes and structures those materials —perhaps in an effort to give his own feelings or perceptions or intuitions objective embodiment, perhaps in response to the internal qualitative demands of the work as it advances, perhaps in order to "imitate" or represent something beyond—in the visible world or in a world behind the visible. Is this an appropriate model for what happens in a classroom?

George Steiner,[4] Hannah Arendt,[5] and others have made it painfully clear that (using Steiner's words) "When barbarism came to 20th century Europe, the arts faculties in more than one university offered very little moral resistance, and this is not a trivial or local accident." Not only is there little evidence that the reading of great literature or the ability to appreciate the arts in general makes a man humane; there is even less evidence that the writing of great literature (or the composition of great pictures or great music) makes a human being more sensitive, joyful, or concerned than any other human being. There have been artists who conceived themselves as seers and poet-priests, who—like Emerson and Whitman—created in "wonder" and joy. But there have also been artists

[4] *Language and Silence* (New York: Atheneum, 1967).
[5] *The Human Condition* (New York: Doubleday Anchor, 1959).

—like Baudelaire, Dostoevsky, Wagner, Nietzsche—who were tortured individuals, given to melancholia, deadly fits of boredom, contempt for the middle class and the masses, various sorts of depravity. Steiner has recently written about the French novelist, Céline, a great artist who was a vicious, murderous anti-Semite. The career of the miraculous poet named Ezra Pound is universally known. "Artists are as different as men are," writes the novelist and critic William Gass.[6] "It would be wrong to romanticize about them. In our society indeed they may live in narrower and more frightening corners than most of us do. We should not imitate their ways; they're not exemplary, and set no worthy fashions." He concludes his warning by saying that poets are almost certainly "liars": "They lie quite roundly, unashamedly, with glee and gusto, since lies and fancies, figments and inventions, outrageous falsehoods are frequently more real, more emotionally pure, more continuously satisfying to them than the truth, which is likely to wear a vest . . . take technicolor movies, and long snoozes through Sunday."

There is clearly no objection to educators discovering certain aspects of an artist's craft to be worthy of study and emulation. The point here is that to posit a good gray poet or a woodsy fellow piping wild or a gentle spinster performing verses like sacraments—and then to speak hopefully of the teacher as artist—is to romanticize shamelessly. "Teachers as artists," writes Clyde Curran,[7] "strive for harmonious human relations." What paint is to the painter and language is to the poet, human relations are presumed to be for the teacher. Just as the artist manipulates and controls his medium to achieve a certain fullness and harmony, so (says Curran) does the artist-teacher manipulate and control "the motivating force of emotions" until he achieves *his* finished product, i.e., harmonious relations. Like the painter, then, the artist-teacher becomes "a part of the finished product." Would he talk this way if he did not imagine that anyone deeply involved in artistic activity must somehow be concerned for individual integrity, personal sensi-

[6] *The New Republic,* July 27, 1968.
[7] "Artistry in Teaching."

tivity, and growth? This troubles us, as does the notion of manipulation, which is quite appropriate in the domain of art when the artist speaks of arranging and rearranging his raw materials to the end of creating a significant form, but which seems highly questionable when the raw materials concerned are "the motivating force" of human emotions.

Those who find their analogy in the artist, and those who find one in the art object often lay particular emphasis upon the presentative, formal, objective character of the work of art. This would be acceptable if they were functioning as art critics; but it is something else again when they propose to develop a model of teaching after objectivist approaches to art. If his overriding concern were to become "aesthetic"—shaping component parts, perhaps, to achieve an aesthetic end—a teacher might well be inclined to place order and harmony first in his priority scale. Harmony in human relations certainly has value, but it is not the highest of all possible values. If a teacher's intent is to treat emotions as his medium in his effort to attain harmony, he might find himself being dominated (as the artist frequently is) by a need to discover an interrelated value texture and, with this in mind, pay heed only to those values which appeared relevant to *his* end-in-view. He might begin subordinating all the component parts of the classroom situation to *his* dominating aesthetic concern. Only someone who believed that the aesthetic preoccupation per se ennobles and humanizes the individual involved would, it seems to us, be inclined to use an aesthetic model of this sort for a conceptualization of the teaching act.

Nor does it help to revise the view of art being applied, to conceive it as primarily expressive, sensuous, and emotive in nature. This, unfortunately, is often done, especially by those much afflicted by the technological, the "cognitive," the formalist approaches to curriculum. They want, understandably, to find ways of humanizing the educational process, to "educate the emotions," to overcome the means-ends orientation in the ordinary curriculum. They become convinced that the aesthetic is somehow polar to the technological, that they will find a palliative concern for the spontaneous and the authentic in the realm of art. Committed as we are to self-expression and self-creation, disturbed as we are by the cold detachment which often accompanies statistical thinking and abstraction, we object to an "aesthetic of teaching" built upon expressivist theories as much as we object to one built on formalist approaches.

There are some illuminating expressivist theories of art, of course, although an expressivist theory serves no better than any other theory to account for *all* the phenomena categorized as art—from the *Iliad* to Burroughs's *Naked Lunch,* from the Lascaux cave paintings to Picasso's *Guernica,* from *Oedipus Rex* to *Bonnie and Clyde.* Most such theories explain art as the expression of emotion—often, as Wordsworth put it, "emotion recollected in tranquillity." Many talk of art as an "overflow" of images, feelings, even ideas transmuted by imagination. All, at some point, talk of a union of the inner and the outer with respect to art forms; they use words like "sincerity," "authenticity," "subjectivity," "sentiency." But they also emphasize (and this is too often neglected by those seeking models for teaching in what they say) that the emotions which overflow or are recollected, and which seek expression by means of art, are given objective embodiment in formed presentations, works which —once created—exist as autonomously and independently as any other. They distinguish sharply between artistic expression and "mere" self-expression. Coleridge's "Ode to Dejection" is quite different from an expression of unhappiness by the living Coleridge. Yeats's "Second Coming" is quite different from an outcry by the living Yeats regarding the disorder of his time and loss of the "ceremony of innocence." Picasso's *Guernica* is not the same thing as an expression of Picasso's outrage at the moment of the bombing.

The teacher who proposes to conceive the teaching act as an art-like act of self-expression usually hopes that his own spontaneity and emotionality will reach his students and arouse them to feeling and awareness. He forgets, however, that an artist is not and can rarely be spontaneous in the same way. The original stimulus for the poet, let us say, arouses a response that is anything but deliberately contrived. It must be acknowledged that if, at the moment of the stimulus, the poet comes up

with two or three lines, even eloquent ones, they probably will
not be poetry. Many things must occur before the response can
be transmuted into art. The poet must move into himself. The
particular event or color or sound which moved him and
evoked a response must somehow be made part of him, must
be submerged for a time in the well of his memories, in the
depth of his consciousness. Consider Emily Dickinson:

> There's a certain slant of light,
> Winter afternoons,
> That oppresses like the heft
> Of cathedral tunes.

Obviously, this was not produced one long, dull winter afternoon in the parlor. Something made the slant of light noticeable on that particular day—something in the past perhaps,
below the level of consciousness. For it to take on symbolic
significance, for it to become a poem, the poet had to brood,
to nurture, to permit whatever it was that made the stimulus
meaningful somehow rise to the surface. There had to be time
for the imagination to work, time to play with the medium of
language, as Emily Dickinson so marvelously did. Eventually
(and who can say precisely when?) the poem became the complex enactment of experience one goes through when one perceives one's own mortality, when something happens that
makes a tremendous "internal difference where the meanings
are." It all happens by means of language, imagery, intricate
interactions between words, meanings, feelings on more levels
than anyone can count.

Is the teacher's work like this? Surely, a teacher who wants
to engage in immediate encounters with his students cannot
remove himself for the time it takes to create a formed presentation. He cannot spend hours or days playing and working
with his medium. He cannot brood, consider, dream before he
arrives with his communication. Encounters of the sort he has
in mind, we believe, are quite, quite different from what the
poet has in mind when he is moved to write.

Some of the interest in this aesthetic model may be due to a
return of the romantic spirit, which meant—in the case of
writers like Wordsworth and Emerson—a rebellion against tra-

ditional artifices and rules. Part of the appeal of the romantic point of view may be attributed to the romantic feeling for childhood, for wonder, for innocence and spontaneity. It is not surprising that educators become troubled by the restraints our technological society imposes upon individuals and by the narrowness of the channels down which human energies are forced. Like the romantic poets, they see urban life, crowds, materialism, and the rest setting barriers between the aims of life and what Wordsworth (like some of the young radicals today) called "joy."

This may be why they turn to the poets, not so much to reread their works, but to discover them as exemplars. This may be why so many of them think of spontaneity in connection with "artistic," think of being childlike, even—literally speaking—"wonder-full." Our point here simply is that it is neither necessary nor helpful to attempt to realize such values by patterning teaching after art. The arts, hopefully, will play an increasingly central role in education; and more and more attention will be paid to cultivating the kinds of aesthetic perceptiveness required if works of art are to be enjoyed. But the arts will never play the role they might play unless teachers become somewhat clearer about the way they conceptualize the arts. An identification of teaching with the aesthetic process or the aesthetic object too often springs from an oversimplification of the nature and function of the arts; and this may lead to dehumanization or to a trivialization of what happens in schools.

Mechanization, manipulation, dehumanization—these are certainly the great bads where teaching is concerned. Teachers need to become self-aware, intensely conscious of what they are doing as they engage in teaching, free and open enough to experience encounters with the diverse human beings in their classes, courageous enough to tolerate and even to promote tension and discord, strong enough to avoid sentimentality. Teaching can be conceived as a process of opening gates, a mode of introducing young people to ways of doing a variety of interesting things, enabling them to participate and make independent moves on their own initiative. It is unlikely that an intentional process of this sort can be carried on spontaneously, even though good teaching (like engagement with the arts) may create situations in which spontaneous activity can occur.

A good teacher is one who is continually trying out ideas, thinking critically himself, giving honest reasons, welcoming honest and even radical questions. Hopefully he is one who has chosen himself as a teacher—the kind of a person whose "fundamental project," whose mode of self-creation is the action which is teaching. If so, he is quite different from the person who has chosen himself to be a poet, a painter, a composer. The artist's object is not to inspire, not to liberate, not to teach. He is consciously devoted to the possibilities within the act of writing, or painting, or composing; and what he creates may indeed inspire, liberate, teach. But the possibilities offered to the reader or listener or spectator by the finished work of art should not be confused with the enterprise of "making" works of art.

Of course it is necessary to combat "technique" and indifference. Of course it is necessary to cultivate authenticity. It remains possible to work for face-to-face encounters in the classroom in an inharmonious world. This cannot be done by the teacher modeling himself on the artist. It can be done by the teacher willing to act so that others can make sense—and, in the making sense, form themselves as they live.

IS TEACHING AN ART?

R. A. Smith

The notion that there are important similarities between the activity of the artist and the enterprise of teaching-learning is encountered with increasing frequency in educational discourse. Here is a sampling:

> [A distinguished teacher of the classics] "I believe that teaching is an art, not a science. . . . Teaching is not like inducing a chemical reaction: it is much more like painting a picture or making a piece of music, or on a lower level like planting a garden or writing a friendly letter."

> [A professor of philosophy on the nature of learning] "Education . . . is very far from being a performance in which the learner is a mere passive spectator. If the subject is to detain him, fix his thought, and feed his interest . . . his attitude toward the subject must resemble very closely that of an artist toward his material. . . . [He] must be prepared to enter into that complex relation of submission and mastery from which the *discipline* of the art emerges."

> [A philosopher of art] "Teaching itself may be considered an art, and not in the merely technical sense of the word. A teacher manages a complex of qualities. What he does at any given moment must depend upon what he sees developing between the students and himself. His aim is always increased communication, i.e., participation in the social process."

> [The president of a major teachers college] ". . . the treatment of teaching as a form of art. Here the field of teacher education has splendid opportunities for new development. If we can find the intelligence and the imagination to examine and study the art of teaching as we have other performing and interpretive arts, we may be able to add an element of immeasurable importance to teacher education."

> [An educational researcher] "The artist is . . . the prototype of the teacher. . . . The art of teaching lies . . . in communication and projection of an essentially private experience.

From the *Journal of Aesthetic Education,* vol. 2, no. 4 (October 1968): 5–9. Reprinted by permission of the *Journal* and the author.

. . . The art of teaching is as valid a subject for artistic criticism . . . as is the painter's canvas."

[A philosopher of education] ". . . the effective lecturer who is capable of promoting learning in his students has rendered his performance into a work of art. . . . It arouses emotion; it is carefully and formally organized with a view to the emotions enhancing the content . . . and its direct and immediate effect on an audience is aesthetic in quality."

[An art education specialist] ". . . the classroom considered as theater would prompt the researcher to focus his attention on the pervasive quality of teaching-learning situations in the classroom as well as on the qualitative elements of voice, gesture, action of the participants as *dramatis personae*."

These remarks strongly suggest that aesthetics can contribute to our understanding of generic educational concepts and procedures. If this is the case, strong support would be given to the study of aesthetic foundations in teacher preparation, for it could then be argued that teachers need aesthetic theory not only because of the light it sheds on one of the important forms of knowing—aesthetic understanding in the arts—but also because it can help them become more effective as teachers of anything. Art in other words may be capable of providing a model for learning or the educational experience in general. This is what the writers quoted above seem to intend in holding that, in contrast to inducing a chemical response, teaching is more like painting a picture or composing a piece of music; that, like the artist, the teacher manages a complex of qualities, the direction or outcome of which cannot always be determined in advance; that the act of teaching is as fit an object for artistic criticism as the painter's canvas; that the direct and immediate effect of a good lecture on its audience is aesthetic in quality; that teaching closely resembles acting; and that the study of teaching as an art provides splendid opportunities for new developments in teacher education.

Insofar as such remarks impute a significant analogy between art and teaching, the question is whether the analogy is a good one, that is, whether it is one in which the parallels are significant and the comparisons are between elements of roughly equal importance in either domain. If on the other hand expressions such as "teaching is an art" do not propose a serious analogy but are slogans, they can be understood as performing a persuasive or ceremonial function. Still, as others have said, assert them long enough and slogans tend to be taken literally and thus eventually need to be evaluated as straightforward assertions.

To say that the teacher is an artist can mean first of all that he is either a performing or creative artist. Initially it appears that teachers are best cast in the role of performers. During a class period they perform in front of an audience, their students, and try to elicit reactions. Yet it might be asked if the relationship of the teacher to the student is not rather different from that of the performer to his audience. What counts as a *successful* performance differs in each case. An actor, for example, may give a thoroughly competent and sensitive dramatic performance but fail to elicit reaction from his audience. The audience may be put off or bewildered by the strangeness or controversial nature of the content. A teacher too may be said to be teaching his students (according to one accepted meaning of "to teach") even though there is no recognizable effect on pupils. However, it cannot be said that such a teacher is teaching *successfully* without making a travesty of the educational enterprise. And this points to at least one major flaw in the analogy that teaching is like performing. Teaching is expected to have specifiable and measurable results of *some* kind. But the same expectation does not hold for acting or performing. It would be odd to say that a play cannot be a success unless members of the audience are enlightened in specific, testable ways.

With the emphasis now shifted from procedures to outcomes, the image of the teacher as a creative artist is perhaps more apt. But difficulties still obtain. In general an artist is someone who transforms antecedently existing materials into a work of art, the result of his having composed with the special characteristics (or timbres) of his materials. But what is the medium of the teacher? The qualities of the students as persons? If so, individually or collectively? Is it their states of readiness? Prior learnings? Or are the primary materials of the teacher concepts, principles, topics, and the various demands these make on learning? Furthermore, what would be analogous to the work of art in teaching? The learnings of the students, doubtless. But there is a different kind of causal relationship between the artist and his finished product and the teacher and his "product." Were this not so, educational research would be a closed chapter. In brief, the teacher is not a causal agent in the same sense as the artist. What happens to a canvas or piece of stone can be observed to be the direct outcome of the artist's actions. What happens to a student does not depend on the teacher alone. Live persons in other words are more intractable than artistic materials—and perhaps fortunately so, considering how many "teacher-artists" and others attempt to shape or manipulate them.

There are other differences. One is the degree of freedom enjoyed by artists and teachers. It is unethical for teachers to give free rein to their creative impulses, to compose with the special characteristics of their pupils in the way that a painter composes with the qualities of his pigments and canvas. Artistic creation, it may be argued, is also less goal-directed than teaching. Teachers often have fairly clear notions of course objectives. Quite frequently, however—and accounts of artistic creation bear this out—artists know only vaguely what they seek or want to come up with. Often the final product bears little resemblance to the original vision.

But most telling of all are the types of judgments made by artists and teachers. The serious artist proceeds by making judgments of aesthetic fittingness: how well or interesting things look, sound, and feel, or whether new elements contribute to or detract from what already exists. The art critic proceeds along similar lines; aesthetic standards are preeminent and what a work of art says doesn't count if it isn't aesthetically well presented. In teaching, on the other hand, aesthetic judgments, criteria, and experiences are of secondary importance. Appraisal of learning is a cognitive matter. Even the judgment that a student is beginning to master the aesthetic form of understanding is basically cognitive, not aesthetic. And again, no matter how much dramatic interest, suspense, and intensity a teacher exhibits in the performance of teaching, if students fail to master specified skills or to develop relevant dispositions, the educational enterprise will be judged ineffective. In short, it is misleading to construe teaching as preeminently aesthetic. Thus the teaching-is-an-art analogy does not appear to be justified.

Why, it might be asked, would a teacher want to think of himself as an artist? Or why do others propose that he be so characterized? The value that the public rhetoric of our culture attaches to novelty, originality, and creativity—a legacy from the romantic period of the nineteenth century—has perhaps resulted in an affinity for the artist and artistic creation as a paradigm for all human activity. Further, as perennial criticism testifies, the status of the teacher as a professional is not beyond question; thus there is all the more reason for wanting to elevate his status by any means possible. It is also apparent that dramatics in the classroom is thought by some to be the solution to meeting student demands for relevance. But relevance is more than dramatics.

The recommendation that teaching be concerned with aesthetic quality is of course not entirely without merit. Aesthetic techniques and devices are properly part of a teacher's repertory of skills that can be used to make learning more inviting and interesting. That beauty of surroundings and environment is a desideratum is too obvious to merit discussion. But the instrumental use of aesthetic quality to promote learning is a case of one kind of activity making use of the elements of another, and this is not the same as an identity. It is an added decorative dimension and thus not a very significant application of aesthetics to teaching and learning. In brief, if it is really art and drama that one wants, the classroom is the last place to look for it. Script-writers and directors know this, and in films or television shows dealing with teaching the camera never lingers long in the classroom.

There is a moral in the teaching-is-an-art literature. Aesthetics is relevant to general educational theory not only in showing what teaching might be like when examined under the aspect of art and the aesthetic. It is also useful in revealing the points at which analogies with art and the aesthetic break down. The writings of enthusiasts of the aesthetic sometimes suggest that a term, "aesthetics," has been discovered, but not its substantive literature.

FURTHER READING

Berleant, Arnold. "Education as Aesthetic Process," *Journal of Aesthetic Education,* vol. 5, no. 3 (July 1971).

Boas, George. "Art, Morals, and the Teaching of Art," *Journal of Aesthetic Education,* vol. 2, no. 3 (July 1968): 93–104. From a special issue devoted to "Art, Morals, and Aesthetic Education."

Broudy, Harry S. "The Preparation of Teachers of Aesthetic Education," *Art Education,* vol. 20, no. 3 (March 1967): 29–32. From a special issue devoted to "Aesthetic Education."

Champlin, Nathaniel L. "Education and Aesthetic Method," *Journal of Aesthetic Education,* vol. 4, no. 2 (April 1970): 65–85. From a special issue devoted to "Curriculum and Aesthetic Education."

Ecker, David W., Thomas J. Johnson, and Eugene F. Kaelin. "Aesthetic Inquiry," *Review of Educational Research,* vol. 39, no. 5 (December 1969): 577–92. A review of methodological assumptions of current work in psychological and philosophical aesthetics and aesthetic education.

Feldman, Edmund B. "The Critical Act," *Journal of Aesthetic Education,* vol. 2, no. 2 (April 1968): 23–35. Also *Art as Image and Idea.* Englewood Cliffs, N.J.: Prentice-Hall, 1967, Ch. 15.

Fowler, Charles B. "Perspectivism: An Approach to Aesthetic Education," *Journal of Aesthetic Education,* vol. 2, no. 1 (January 1968): 87–99.

Friedman, Norman. "Three Views of Poetic Form," *College English,* vol. 26, no. 7 (April 1965): 493–500.

Hansen, Forest. "A Broadway View of Aristotle's Poetics," *Journal of Aesthetic Education,* vol. 3, no. 1 (January 1969): 85–91.

Hartshorn, W. C. "The Study of Music as an Academic Discipline," *Music Educators Journal,* vol. 49, no. 3 (January 1963): 25–28.

Hyman, Ronald T., ed. *Teaching: Vantage Points for Study.* New York: J. B. Lippincott, 1968. Sec. 6, "Aesthetics."

Journal of Aesthetic Education, vol. 5, no. 2 (April 1971). A special issue entitled "Film II: The Teaching of Film." See also vol. 3, no. 3 (July 1969), devoted to "Film, New Media, and Education."

Kaelin, E. F. "Method and Methodology in Literary Criticism," *The School Review,* vol. 72, no. 3 (Autumn 1964): 289–308; reprinted in Bertram Bandman and Robert S. Guttchen, eds., *Philosophical Essays on Curriculum.* New York: J. B. Lippincott, 1969, pp. 317–32.

Katz, John, ed. *Perspectives on the Study of Film.* New York: Little, Brown and Co., 1971.

Knapton, James, and Bertrand Evans. *Teaching a Literature-Centered English Program.* New York: Random House, 1967, Chs. 6, 7, passim.

Leavis, F. R., and D. Thompson. *Culture and Environment: The Training of Critical Awareness.* London: Chatto & Windus, 1933.

Pappas, George, ed. *Concepts and Art Education.* New York: Macmillan, 1970.

Peters, J. M. L. *Teaching about the Film.* New York: Columbia University Press, 1961.

Rosenthal, M. L. "On Teaching Difficult Literary Texts," *College English,* vol. 20, no. 4 (January 1959): 155–63.

Schwadron, Abraham A. "Structural Meaning and Music Education," *Journal of Aesthetic Education,* vol. 3, no. 4 (October 1969): 109–22.

Schwartz, Sheila, ed. *Teaching the Humanities.* New York: Macmillan, 1970.

Smith, B. O. "The Logic of Teaching in the Arts," *The Record—Teachers College,* vol. 63, no. 3 (1961): 176–83.

Smith, R. A. "Teaching Film as Significant Art," in John Katz, ed., *Perspectives on the Study of Film.*

Steiner, George. "Humane Literacy," in *Language and Silence.* New York: Atheneum, 1967, pp. 3–11.

Stolnitz, Jerome. "The Educative Function of Criticism," in *Aesthetics and Philosophy of Art Criticism.* New York: Houghton Mifflin Co., 1960, pp. 493–501; reprinted in R. A. Smith, ed., *Aesthetics and Art Criticism in Art Education,* pp. 364–72.

Walton, Charles W. "Analyzing Analysis," *Music Educators Journal,* vol. 55, no. 6 (February 1969): 57–59, 139.

INDEX